Robert Brown, Leo Africanus

The History and Description of Africa and of the Notable Things therein Contained

Vol II

Robert Brown, Leo Africanus

The History and Description of Africa and of the Notable Things therein Contained
Vol II

ISBN/EAN: 9783743384613

Manufactured in Europe, USA, Canada, Australia, Japa

Cover: Foto ©ninafisch / pixelio.de

Manufactured and distributed by brebook publishing software (www.brebook.com)

Robert Brown, Leo Africanus

The History and Description of Africa and of the Notable Things therein Contained

WORKS ISSUED BY

The Hakluyt Society.

THE

HISTORY AND DESCRIPTION OF AFRICA

OF

LEO AFRICANUS.

VOL. II.

AND

DESCRIPTION OF AFRICA

AND

OF THE NOTABLE THINGS THEREIN CONTAINED,

WRITTEN BY

AL-HASSAN IBN-MOHAMMED AL-WEZAZ AL-FASI,

A MOOR, BAPTISED AS GIOVANNI LEONE, BUT BETTER KNOWN AS

LEO AFRICANUS.

DONE INTO ENGLISH IN THE YEAR 1600,

BY

JOHN PORY,

And now Edited, with an Introduction and Notes,

BY

Dr. ROBERT BROWN.

IN THREE VOLUMES.—VOL. II.

LONDON:
PRINTED FOR THE HAKLUYT SOCIETY,
4, LINCOLN'S INN FIELDS, W.C.

M.DCCC.XCVI.

COUNCIL

OF

THE HAKLUYT SOCIETY.

SIR CLEMENTS R. MARKHAM, K.C.B., F.R.S., *Pres. R.G.S.*, PRESIDENT.
THE RIGHT HON. THE LORD STANLEY OF ALDERLEY, VICE-PRESIDENT.
SIR A. WOLLASTON FRANKS, K.C.B., F.R.S., VICE-PRESIDENT.
C. RAYMOND BEAZLEY, ESQ., M.A.
MILLER CHRISTY, ESQ.
COLONEL G. EARL CHURCH.
THE RIGHT HON. GEORGE N. CURZON, M.P.
ALBERT GRAY, ESQ.
THE RIGHT HON. LORD HAWKESBURY.
EDWARD HEAWOOD, ESQ., M.A.
ADMIRAL SIR ANTHONY H. HOSKINS, K.C.B.
REAR-ADMIRAL ALBERT H. MARKHAM.
A. P. MAUDSLAY, ESQ.
E. DELMAR MORGAN, ESQ.
CAPTAIN NATHAN, R.E.
ADMIRAL SIR E. OMMANNEY, C.B., F.R.S.
CUTHBERT E. PEEK, ESQ.
E. G. RAVENSTEIN, ESQ.
COUTTS TROTTER, ESQ.
REAR-ADMIRAL W. J. L. WHARTON, C.B., R.N.

WILLIAM FOSTER, ESQ., *Honorary Secretary.*

CONTENTS.

VOLUME II.

	PAGE
THE SECOND BOOK	225
Notes to Book II	325
THE THIRD BOOK	393
Notes to Book III	561
THE FOURTH BOOK	659
Notes to Book IV	690

IOHN LEO HIS
SECOND BOOKE OF
the Historie of Africa, and
of the memorable things
contained therein.

Auing in my first booke made mention of the cities, bounds, diuisions, and some other notable and memorable things contained in Africa; we will in this second part more fully, particularly, largely, and distinctly describe sundrie prouinces, townes, mountaines, situations of places, lawes, rites, and customes, of people. Insomuch that we will leaue nothing vntouched, which may any way serue to the illustrating and perfecting of this our present discourse. Beginning therefore at the west part of Africa, we will in this our geographicall historie proceede eastward, till we come to the borders of Aegypt. And all this our narration following we will diuide into seuen bookes; whereunto (God willing) we purpose to annexe the eighth, which shall intreat of riuers, of liuing creatures, of trees, of plants, of fruits, of shrubs, and of such other most delightfull matters.

Of the region of Hea lying vpon the west part of Africa.

HEa[1] being one of the prouinces of Maroco is bounded westward and northwarde with the maine Ocean, southwarde with the mountaines of Atlas, and eastward with the riuer which they call Esfiualo.² This riuer springeth out of the foresaide mountaine, discharging it selfe at length into the riuer of Tensift, and diuiding Hea from the prouince next adiacent.

Of the situation and description of Hea.

THis region of Hea is an vneeuen and rough soile, full of rockie mountaines, shadie woods, and chrystall-streames in all places; being woonderfully rich, and wel stored with inhabitants. They haue in the said region great abundance of goates and asses, but not such plentie of sheepe, oxen and horses. All kinde of fruites are very scarce among them, not that the ground is vncapable of fruit, but because the people are so rude and ignorant in this behalfe, that very few of them are skilfull in planting, graffing, or pruning of trees. Whereof I was easily perswaded: for I remember that I founde among some gardiners of Hea great abundance of fruits. Of graine they haue not much plentie, except it be of barlie, mill, and panick. They haue great abundance of honie, which they vse in stead of ordinarie foode, but the waxe they cast away little regarding it, because they know not the value thereof. Likewise there are found in this region certaine thornie trees bearing a grosse kinde of fruit, not vnlike vnto those oliues which are brought vnto vs from Spaine: the said fruit they call in their language *Arga*. Of this fruit they make a kinde of oile, being of a fulsome and strong savour, which they vse notwithstanding for sauce and for lampes.³

The fruit called Arga.

The manner of liuing, and the foode of the people of Hea.

THis people for the most part eateth barlie-bread vnleuened, which is like rather vnto a cake, then to a loafe: this bread is baked in a kinde of earthen baking-pan, somewhat like vnto that wherewith in Italie they vse to couer iuncats⁴ and daintie dishes: neither shall you finde many in Hea which eate ouen-bread. They vse also a certaine vnsauourie and base kinde of meate, which in their language is called *Elhafid*,⁵ and is made in manner follow- *Elhafid*. ing: they cast barlie-meale into boiling water, continually tempering and stirring the same about with a sticke, till they perceiue it be sufficiently sodden. Then setting this pap or hastie-pudding vpon the table, and powring in some of their countrie-oile, all the whole familie stand round about the platter, and eate the said pap not with spoones, but with their hands and fingers. Howbeit in the spring and summer season they temper the said meale with milke, and cast in butter instead of oile: and this kinde of meate is not vsuall among them, but only at supper. For in winter time they breake their fast with bread and honie; and in summer with milke, butter, and bread. Moreouer sometimes they vse to eate sodden flesh, whereunto some adde onions, other beanes, and some other, a kinde of seasoning or sauce called by them *Cuscusu*.⁶ With them tables and table-cloathes are quite out of vse, in stead whereof they spread a certaine round mat vpon the ground, which serueth among this rude people both for table, cloth, and all.

The apparell and customes of the foresaid people of Hea.

THE greatest part of them are clad in a kinde of cloath-garment made of wooll after the manner of a couerlet, called in their language, *Elchise*, and not vnlike vnto those couerlets or blankets which the Italians lay vpon their beds. In these kinde of mantles they wrap themselues; and then are they girt with a woollen girdle, not about their waste, but about their hippes. They haue also a certaine piece of cloath of ten handfuls in length and two in bredth, wherewith they vse to adorne their heads: these kinde of ornaments or head-tires they dye with the iuice of walnut-tree-rootes, being so put vpon their heads, that their crownes are alwaies bare.⁷ None of them weare any cap, except it be an olde man, or a man of learning; albeit learned men are verie rare among them: which caps of theirs are double and round, not much vnlike to the caps of certaine Phisitians in Italy. You shall seldome finde any linnen shirts or smockes among this people; and that (as I suppose) either because their soile will yeeld no flaxe nor hemp, or else for that they haue none skilfull in the arte of weauing. Their seats whereon they sit, are nought else but certaine mats made of hayre and rushes.⁸ For beds they vse a certaine kinde of hairie flockbed or mattresse;⁹ some of which beds are ten elles in length, some more, and some lesse, yea some you shall finde of twenty elles long, but none longer: one part of these mattresses they lye vpon insteed of a couch, and with the residue they couer their bodies as it were with blankets and couerlets. In the Spring-time alwaies they lay the hairie side next vnto their bodies, because it is somewhat warmer; but in Sommer-time not regarding that side, they turne the smooth side vpwarde, and thereon they rest themselues. Likewise of such base and harsh stuffe they make their cushions:¹⁰ being much like vnto the stuffe which is brought hither out of Albania and Turkie, to serue for horse-cloathes: The women of Hea goe commonly with their faces vncouered, vsing for their huswifery turned vessels and cups of wood: their platters, dishes, and other their kitchin-vessels be for the most part of earth. You may easily discerne which of them is married, and who is not: for an vnmarried man must alwaies keepe his beard shauen, which, after hee be once married, hee suffereth to grow at length. The saide region bringeth foorth no great plentie of horses, but those that it doth bring foorth, are so nimble and full of mettall, that they will climbe like cats¹¹ ouer the steepe and craggie mountaines. These horses are alwaies vnshod: and the people of this region vse to till their ground with no other cattell, but onely with horses and asses.¹² You shall here finde great store of deere, of wilde goats,¹³ and of hares: Howbeit the people are no whit delighted in hunting. Which is the cause (as I thinke) why the said beasts do so multiply. And it is somwhat strange, that so many riuers running through the countrey, they should haue such scarcitie of water-mils: but the reason is, because euerie houshold almost haue a woodden mill of their owne,¹⁴ whereat their women vsually grinde with their hands. No good learning nor liberall artes are heere to be found; except it bee a little skill in the lawes, which some few chalenge vnto themselues; otherwise you shall finde not so much as any shadow of vertue among them. They haue neither Phisition nor Surgeon of any learning or account. But if a disease or infirmitie befall any of them, they presently seare or cauterize the sicke partie with red hot *Cauterizing.* yrons, euen as the Italians vse their horses. Howbeit some chirurgians there are among them, whose duty and occupation consisteth onely in circumcising of their male children. They make no sope in all the countrey, but instead thereof they vse to wash with lee made of ashes.¹⁵ They are at continuall warre, but it is ciuill and among themselues, insomuch that they haue no leisure to fight against other nations. Whosoeuer will trauell into a forren countrey must take either a harlot, or a wife, or a religious man of the contrarie part, to beare him companie.¹⁶ They haue no regard at all of iustice, especially in those mountaines which are destitute of gouernours or princes: yea euen the principall men of this verie region of Hea, which dwell within townes and cities, dare scarce prescribe any law or good order vnto the people, so great is their insolencie in all places. The cities of Hea are few in number, but they haue great store of villages, townes, and most strong castles:¹⁷ whereof (God willing) we will hereafter speake more at large.

Of Tednest one of the cities of Hea.

THE auncient citie of Tednest[s] was built by the Africans vpon a most beautiful and large plaine, which they inuironed with a loftie wall built of bricke and lime. Likewise a certaine riuer running foorth of the citie serueth to fill vp the wall ditch. In this citie are certaine merchants that sell cloath, wherein the people of the same place are clad. Here is likewise vttered a kinde of cloth which is brought thither out of Portugall: howbeit they will admit no artificers, but taylors, botchers, carpenters, and a few gold-smithes which are Iewes. In this citie there are no innes, stoues, nor wine-tauerns: so that whatsoeuer merchant goes thither, must seeke out some of his acquaintance to remaine withall: but if he hath no friends nor acquaintance in the town, then the principall *Their manner of entertaining strangers at Tednest.* inhabitants there cast lots who should entertaine the strange merchant: insomuch that no stranger, be he neuer so meane, shall want friendly entertainment, but is alwaies sumptuously and honourably accepted of. But whosoeuer is receiued as a guest, must at his departure bestow some gift vpon his host in token of thankfulnes, to the ende he may be more welcome at his next returne. Howbeit if the saide stranger bee no merchant, he may chuse what great mans house he will to lodge in, beeing bound at his departure to no recompence nor gift. To be short, if any begger or poore pilgrim passe the same way, he hath some sustenance prouided for him in a certaine hospitall, which was founded onely for the reliefe of poore people, and is maintained at the common charge of the citie. In the middest of the citie stands an auncient temple, beeing most sumptuously built and of an huge bignes, which was thought to bee founded at the verie same time when as the King of Maroco bare rule in those places. This temple hath a great cestern standing in the midst thereof, and it hath many priests and such kinde of people which giue attendance thereunto, and store it with things necessarie. In this citie likewise are diuers other temples, which, albeit they are but little, yet be they most cleanly and decently kept. There are in this citie about an hundred families of Iewes, who pay no yeerely tribute at all, but only bestow each of them some gratuitie vpon this or that nobleman, whom they thinke to fauour them most, to the ende they may enioy their fauour still : and the greatest part of the said citie is inhabited with Iewes. These Iewes haue certaine minting-houses wherein they stampe siluer coine, of which 170. Aspers (as they call them) doe weigh one ounce, beeing like vnto the common coine of Hungarie, sauing that this Asper is square, and the Hungarian coine is round. The inhabitants of Tednest are free from al tributes & yeerely taxations : howbeit if any summe of money be wanting for the erection of a publique building, or for any other common vse, the people is foorthwith assembled, and each man must giue according to his abilitie. This citie was left desolate in the yeere 918. of the Hegeira. *Tednest left desolate.* At what time all the citizens thereof fled vnto the mountaines, and from thence to Maroco. The reason they say was, because the inhabitants were informed that their next neighbours the Arabians ioyned in league with the Portugall Captaines (who as then held the towne of Azaphi) and promised to deliuer Tednest into the hands of the Christians, which thing so danted the citizens, that they presently sought to saue themselues by flight. My selfe (I remember) sawe this citie vtterly ruined and defaced, the walles thereof beeing laide euen with the ground, the houses beeing destitute of inhabitants, and nothing at that time to be there seene, but onely the nests of rauens and of other birds. All this I saw in the 920. yeere of the Hegeira.

Of Teculeth a towne of Hea.

Pon the foote of an hill eighteene miles Eastwarde from Tednest stands a towne called by the Africans Teculeth, and containing about one thousand housholdes. Hard by this towne runneth a certaine riuer, on both sides whereof are most pleasant gardens, and all kindes of trees. Within the walles of the saide towne are many pits or wels, whereout they draw most cleere and pleasant water. Here also is to be seene a most stately and beautifull temple; as likewise fower hospitals and a monasterie of religious persons. The inhabitants of this towne are farre wealthier then they of Tednest; for they haue a most famous port vpon the Ocean sea, commonly called by merchants, Goz. They haue likewise great abundance of corne and pulse, which grow in the fruitfull fields adiacent. These also of Teculeth send waxe into Portugall to be solde: and they are verie curious in their apparell and about the furniture of their horses. When I my selfe was at Teculeth, I found there a certaine nobleman, who was the president or chiefe of their senate: this noblemans duety was both to procure tribute which was yeerely to be payed vnto the Arabians, and also to make attonement and reconciliation betweene them, when they were at ods. This man had gathered great riches vnto himselfe, which he imployed rather to purchase friends, then to fill his coffers: most liberal he was vnto the poore, most bountifull and fauourable vnto all his citizens; insomuch that all men did reuerence and honour vnto him, as vnto their father and best protectour. Of whose curtesie I my selfe also made triall: and being not meanely but verie sumptuously entertained by him, I remained with him for a certaine time, and read in his

house diuers histories of African matters. This good man togither with his sonne was slaine in a skirmish against the Portugals: which was done, according to our computation, in the yeere of the Hegeira 923. that is to say, in the yeere of our Lord 1514. After which misfortune we heard, that the citie was razed, that the people were part of them put to flight, part lead captiue, and the residue slaine by the enimy: all of which particulars we haue declared more at large in that Booke, which is now lately printed and published concerning African affaires.[20]

Teculeth destroyed by the Portugals. 1514.

Of Hadecchis a towne of Hea.

THE citie of Hadecchis[21] being situate vpon a plaine, standeth eight miles Southward of Teculeth: it containeth seauen hundred families: and the wals, churches, and houses throughout this whole citie are all built of free stone. Through the midst of the towne runneth a large and faire streame, hauing many vines & galleries on both sides thereof. There be many Iewes artificers in this citie. The citizens here go somewhat decently apparelled: their horses are good: most of them exercise merchandize: also they stampe a kinde of coine; and they haue certaine yeerely faires or martes, whereunto the nations adioining do vsually resort. Here is to be sold great store of cattell, of butter, oyle, yron,[22] and cloath, and their said mart lasteth fifteene dayes. Their women are very beautifull, white of colour, fat, comely, and trim. But the men beare a most sauage minde, being so extremely possessed with ielousie, that whomsoeuer they finde but talking with their wiues, they presently goe about to murther them. They haue no iudges nor learned men among them, nor any which can assigne vnto the citizens any functions and magistracies according to their worthines: so that hee rules like a king that excelleth the residue in wealth. For matters of religion, they haue certaine Mahumetan priests to administer them. Who neither pay tribute nor yeerely custome, euen as they whom we last before mentioned. Heere I was entertained by a certaine curteous and liberall minded priest, who was exceedingly delighted with Arabian Poetrie. Wherefore being so louingly entertained, I read vnto him a certaine briefe treatise as touching the same argument: which he accepted so kindly at my hands, that he would not suffer mee to depart without great and bountifull rewards. From hence I trauelled vnto Maroco. And afterward I heard that this towne also, in the yeere of the Hegeira 922. was sacked by the Portugals, and that the inhabitants were all fled into the next mountaines, and the verie same yeere I returned home to visit my natiue countrey, which was in the yeere of our Lord 1513.[23]

Hadecchis sacked by the Portugals. 1513.

Of Ileusugaghen a towne of Hea.

THis towne[24] is situate upon the top of a certaine high mountaine which is distant eight miles to the South of Hadecchis: it consisteth of about two hundred families: and by the foote of the hill runneth a small riuer. Heere are no gardens at all, nor yet any trees which beare fruit: the reason whereof is (as I suppose) because the inhabitants are such slothfull and grosse people, that they regard nothing but their barley and their oyle. They are at continuall warre with their next neighbours, which is performed with such monstrous bloodshed and manslaughter, that they deserve rather the name of beasts than of men. They have neither iudges, priests, nor lawyers, to prescribe any forme of liuing among them, or to gouerne their common-wealth: wherefore iustice and honestie is quite banished out of their habitations. Those mountaines are altogither destitute of fruits: howbeit they abound greatly with honie, which serueth the inhabitants both for food, and for merchandize to sell in the neighbour-countries. And because they know not what seruice to put their waxe vnto, they cast it foorth, togither with the other excrements of honie. The saide towne of Ileusugaghen hath a verie small and narrow chappell, which will scarce containe a hundred persons, whither notwithstanding the people doe so slowly resort, that they need not to haue any greater; so much do they neglect religion and pietie. Whensoeuer they goe abroad, they carrie a dagger or a iauelin about with them: and you shall often heare of the slaughter of some one or other of their citizens. No people vnder heauen can be more wicked, trecherous, or lewdly addicted, then this people is.

I remember that I my selfe went once thither with a Scriffo or Mahumetan priest, (who made challenge vnto the gouernment of Hea,[25]) to the ende that we might arbitrate certaine strifes and contentions: for it were incredible to report, what cruel warres, partly for murthers, and partly for robberies, were practised among them. But because the Scriffo had brought no lawyers with him, nor any iudges to decide controuersies, he would needes, that I should take that office vpon me. Immediately the townsmen come flocking about vs: one complaines that his neighbour hath slaine eight of his kinred and family; his neighbour on the contrarie alleageth, that the former had slaine ten of his familie; wherefore, according to the auncient custome, he demaundeth to haue a summe of money giuen him. For (saith he) there is some recompence due vnto me, sithens ten of my people haue beene slaine, and but eight of this my neighbours. Whereunto the other replied that the saide ten persons were iustly slaine, because they went about by violence to dispossesse him of a certaine piece of ground which his father had left him by inheritance; but, that his eight were murthered onely for vniust reuenge, against all equitie and lawe. With these and such like friuolous allegations we spent that whole day,

neither could we decide any one controuersie. About
midnight we sawe a great throng of people meet in the
market-place, who made there such a bloodie and horrible
conflict, that the fight thereof would haue affrighted any
man, were he neuer so hard harted. Wherefore the saide
Scriffo fearing least those lewd varlets would make some
trecherous conspiracie against him, and thinking it better
to depart thence immediately, then to expect the conclusion
of that fraye, wee tooke our iourney from that place to a
towne called Aghilinghighil.

Of the towne of Teijeut in Hea.

MOreouer, the tower of Teijeut[26] standing vpon a plaine
ten miles Westward of Heusugaghen, containeth
about three hundred housholdes. The houses and wall of
this towne are built of bricke. The townesmen exercise
husbandrie; for their ground is most fertile for barley;
albeit it will scarcely yeeld any other graine. They haue
pleasant and large gardens, stored with vines, fig-trees, and
peach-trees: also they haue great abundance of goates.
About this towne are many lyons, whereby the townesmen
are not a little endamaged: for they pray continually vpon
their goats and vpon other of their cattell. Certaine of vs
vpon time comming into these parts for want of a lodging
were cŏstrained to repayre vnto a little cottage which we
escried, being so olde, that it was in danger of falling:
hauing prouided our horses of prouender, we stopped vp all
the doores and passages of the said cottage with thornes
and wood, as circumspectly as possibly we could: these
things happened in the moneth of Aprill, at what time they
haue extreme heat in the same countrey. Wherefore we
our selues got vp to the top of the house, to the end that in
our sleep we might be neere vnto the open ayer. About
midnight we espied two monstrous lyons, who were drawen
thither by the sent of our horses, and endeuored to breake

downe that fence of thornes which we had made. Whereupon the horses being put in feare, kept such a neighing, and such a stirre, that we misdoubted least the rotten cottage would haue fallen, and least our selues should haue become a pray vnto the lyons. But so soone as we perceiued the day begin to breake, we foorthwith sadled our horses, and hyed vs vnto that place, where we knew the Prince and his armie lay. Not long after followed the destruction of this towne. For the greater part of the townesmen being slaine, the rest were taken by the Portugals, and were carried as captiues into Portugall. This was done in the yeere of the Hegeira 920. and in the yeere of our Lord 1513.

Teijeut destroyed by the Portugals.

Of Tesegdelt a towne of Hea.

THe towne of Tesegdelt being situate vpon the top of a certaine high mountaine, and naturally enuironed with an high rocke in steade of a wall, containeth more than eight hundreth families. It is distant from Teijeut southward about twelue miles, and it hath a riuer running by it, the name whereof I haue forgotten. About this towne of Tesegdelt are most pleasant gardens and orchards, replenished with all kinde of trees, and especially with walnut-trees. The inhabitants are wealthie, hauing great abundance of horses, neither are they constrained to pay any tribute vnto the Arabians. There are continuall warres betweene the Arabians and them, and that with great bloudshed and manslaughter on both parts. The villages lying neere vnto Tesegdelt do vsually carry all their graine thither, least they shoulde be depriued thereof by the enimie, who maketh daily inrodes and inuasions vpon them. The inhabitants of the foresaid towne are much addicted vnto curtesie and ciuilitie; and for liberalitie and bountie vnto strangers, they will suffer themselues to be inferiour to none other. At euery gate of Tesegdelt stande

The curtesie of the citizens of Tesegdelt towards strangers.

certaine watchmen or warders, which do most louingly
receiue all incommers, enquiring of them, whether they
haue any friends and acquaintaine in the towne, or no?
If they haue none, then are they conducted to one of the
best Innes of the towne, and hauing had entertainment
there, according to their degree and place, they are friendly
dismissed: and whatsoeuer his expences come to, the
stranger paies nought at all, but his charges are defraied
out of the common purse. This people of Tesegdelt are
subiect also vnto iealousie; howbeit they are most faithfull
keepers of their promise. In the very middest of the towne
standes a most beautifull and stately temple, whereunto
belong a certaine number of Mahumetan priests. And to
the ende that iustice may be most duly administred among
them, they haue a very learned iudge, who decideth all
matters in the common wealth, except criminall causes
onely. Their fieldes where they vse to sowe their corne,
are, for the greater part vpon the mountaines. Vnto this
verie towne I trauelled with the foresaide Scriffo in the
yeere of the Hegeira 919. that is to say, in the yeere of our
Lord 1510.

A description of the citie of Tagtess.

THE most ancient citie of Tagtess[28] is built rounde,
and standeth vpon the toppe of an hill: on the
sides whereof are certaine winding steps hewen out of the
hard rocke. It is about fourteene miles distant from
Tesegdelt. By the foote of the saide hill runnes a riuer,
whereout the women of Tagtess draw their water, neither
haue the citizens any other drinke: and although this
riuer be almost sixe miles from Tagtess, yet a man would
thinke, looking downe from the citie vpon it, that it were
but halfe a mile distant. The way leading vnto the said
riuer being cut out of the rocke, in forme of a payre
of stayres, is verie narrow. The citizens of Tagtess are

addicted vnto theft and robberie, and are at continuall
warre with their neighbours. They haue no corne-fields,
nor any cattell, but onely vpon the said mountaine: they
haue great store of bores; but such scarcitie of horses,
that there is not one almost to bee found in the whole
citie. The way through their region is so difficult, that
they will suffer none to passe by without a publique
testimoniall.[29] While I was in that countrey, there came
such a swarme of Locusts, that they deuoured the greatest *Locusts.*
part of their cornes which were as then ripe: insomuch
that all the vpper part of the ground was couered with
Locusts. Which was in the yeere of the Hegeira 919.
that is, in the yeere of our Lord 1510.

The towne of Eitdeuet.

Fifteene miles Southward from Tagtess stands another
towne called Eitdeuet,[30] being built vpon a plaine, and
yet vpon the higher ground thereof. It containeth to the
number of seuen hundred families; and hath in the midst
thereof most cleere and coole fountaines. This towne is
enuironed on all sides with rockes and mightie woods. In
the said towne are Iewes of all occupations: and some
there are which affirme, that the first inhabitants of this
towne came by naturall descent from King *Dauid:* but so
soone as the Mahumetan religion had infected that place,
their owne lawe and religion ceased. Heere are great
store of most cunning lawyers, which are perfectly well
seene in the lawes and constitutions of that nation: for I
remember that I my selfe sawe a very aged man, who
could most readily repeate a whole volume written in their
language, called by them *Elmudevuana*, that is to say, the
body of the whole lawe. The said volume is diuided into
three tomes, wherein all difficult questions are dissolued:
together with certaine counsels or commentaries of a
famous author, which they call *Melic*. They haue a kinde

of tribunall or iudgement-hall, wherein all contentions happening betweene the citizens of this place, and their neighbour-cities, are presently decided and set through. Neither doe the said lawyers deale onely in commonwealth matters, but also in cases pertaining to religion: albeit in criminall cases the people doe not so greatly credit them, for indeede their learning little serueth them for that purpose. Being amongst them, it was my hap to soiourne in the house of a certaine great lawyer, who was a man of great learning. This lawyer, to the end he might giue me more solemne entertainmẽt, would needs inuite diuers learned men of his owne profession to beare vs companie at supper. After supper, we had many questions propounded: and amongst the residue this was one; namely, Whether any man might iustly sell that person for a bondslaue, who is nourished by any commoditie of the people. There was in companie at the same time a certaine aged Sire, hauing a graue beard and a reuerend countenance, vnto whom each one of them ascribed much honour; him they called in their owne language *Hegazzare*. Which name, when I had heard thrice or fower times repeated, I demanded of some that were in presence, what was the true signification thereof. They told me that it signified a butcher: for (say they) as a butcher knoweth right well the true anatomy of euery part of a beast; euen so can this aged Sire most learnedly dissolue all difficult questions & doubts of lawe. This people leadeth a most miserable and distressed life: their foode is barlie bread, oile arganicke, and goates-flesh. They know no vse of any other graine but barlie.[31] Their women are very beautifull and of a louely hue: their men be strong and lustie, hauing haire growing vpon their brestes, and being very liberall and exceeding iealous.

*Of Culcihat Elmuridin, that is to say, The rocke of
disciples ; a castle of Hea.*

THis Culcihat Elmuridin[32] is a castle built vpon the top
of a certaine high mountaine, hauing round about it
diuers other mountaines of a like heighth, which are
enuironed with craggie rocks and huge woods. There is
no passage vnto this castle, but onely a certaine narrow
path vpon one side of the mountaine. By the one side
thereof stands a rocke, and vpon the other side the
mountaine of Tesegdelt is within halfe a mile ; and it is
distant from Eitdeuet almost eighteene miles. This castle
was built euen in our time by a certaine apostata or
renouncer of the Mahumetan religion, called by them
Homar Seyef ; who being first a Mahumetan preacher *A pestiferous
vnto the people, propounded vnto a great number of Mahumetan
preacher.*
disciples and sectaries, whom he had drawen to be of his
opinion, certaine new points of religion. This fellow
seeing that he preuailed so with his disciples, that they
esteemed him for some petie-god, became of a false preacher
a most cruell tyrant, and his gouernment lasted for twelue
yeeres. He was the chiefe cause of the destruction and
ruine of the whole prouince. At length he was slaine
by his owne wife, because he had vnlawfully lien with her
daughter which she had by her former husband. And
then was his peruerse and lewd dealing laide open vnto all
men ; for he is reported to haue beene vtterly ignorant of
the lawes, and of all good knowledge. Wherefore not
long after his decease all the inhabitants of the region
gathering their forces togither, slew euerie one of his
disciples and false sectaries. Howbeit the nephew of the
said apostata was left aliue : who afterward in the same
castle endured a whole yeeres siege of his aduersaries, and
repelled them, insomuch that they were constrained to
depart. Yea euen vntil this day he molesteth the people

of Hea, and those which inhabitie neere vnto him, with
continuall warre, liuing vpon robberie and spoile ; for which
purpose he hath certaine horsemen, which are appointed to
watch and to pursue trauellers, sometimes taking cattel,
and sometimes men captiues. He hath likewise certaine
gunners, who, although trauellers be a good distance off
(for the common high way standeth almost a mile from
the castle) will put them in great feare. Howbeit all
people doe so deadly hate him, that they will not suffer
him to till one foote of ground, or to beare any dominion
without the said mountaine. This man hath caused his
grandfathers[33] body to be honorably buried in his castle,
suffering him to be adored of his people, as if he were a
god. Passing by that way vpon a certain time, I escaped
their bullets very narrowly. The life, religion & manners
of the foresaid *Homar Seyef* I perfectly learned by a disciple of his, hauing at large declared the same in a certaine
briefe treatise, which I haue written concerning the
Mahumetan religion.

A treatise written by Iohn Leo concerning the Mahumetan religion.

Of *Igilingigil* a towne of Hea.

Oreouer the Africans in olde time
built a certaine towne vpon an hill,
called by the inhabitants Igilingigil ;[34]
being distant from Eitdeuet about
six miles southward, and containing
almost fower hundred families. In
this towne are sundry artificers,
employing themselues onely about things necessarie, to the
ende they may make their best gaine & aduantage thereby.
Their ground is most fertile for barlie ; as likewise they
haue great abundance of honie and of oile Arganicke.
The passage or way vnto this citie is very narrow, lying
onely vpon one side of the hill. And it is so hard and
difficult, that horses cannot without great labour and perill

goe vpon it. The inhabitants are most valiant people and
wel exercised in armes, maintaining continuall warre
against the Arabians, and that for the most part with
very prosperous successe, by reason of the naturall and
strong situation of the towne. A more liberall people then
this, you shall hardly find. They generally exercise
themselues in making of earthen pots and vessels, which
(I thinke) none of their neighbours thereabout can doe.

Of Tefethne a port and most famous mart-
towne of Hea.

NEere vnto the Ocean sea standeth a citie, most strong
both for situation and building, commonly called
Tefethne, being westward of Ingilingigil about fortie miles.
They say that this towne was built by certaine Africans,
and that it containeth more than sixe hundred housholds.
Here ships of meane burthen may safely harbour themselues; and hither the Portugall merchants resort to buy
goats-skins and waxe. Corne-fields they haue none, but
onely certaine hils, which yeeld great increase of barlie.
Neere vnto this towne runs a certaine riuer, whereinto the
ships put themselues in tempestuous weather. The towne-
wall is built of white hewen stone and of bricke. They gather
their yeerely customes and subsidies; all the whole summe
whereof is equally distributed among such citizens as are
meete for the warres. In this towne are great plentie of
Mahumetan priests and of iudges; howbeit, for the inquirie
of murther and such like crimes these iudges haue no
authoritie. For if any kinsman of the slaine or wounded *A punishment*
partie meeteth with him that did the fact, he is presently *of murther.*
without any iudgement to haue *Legem talionis*, that is, like
for like, inflicted vpon him: but if he escape that, he is
banished seuen yeeres out of the citie: at the end of which
seuen yeeres the malefactor hauing paid a certaine summe
of money to the friends of the wounded or slaine partie, is

afterward receiued into fauour, and accounted among the
number of citizens. All the inhabitants of Tefethne are of
a most white colour, being so addicted vnto friendship and
hospitalitie, that they fauour strangers more than their
owne citizens. They haue a most stately and rich hospitall;
howbeit those which are there placed may for the most
part remaine in citizens houses. My selfe being in companie with the Seriffo or Mahumetan prelate, continued
for the space of three daies among this people; which three
daies seemed three yeeres vnto me, both for the incredible
number of fleas, and also for the most loathsome and
intolerable stench of pisse, and of goates dung. For each
citizen hath a flocke of goates, which they driue in the day-
time to pasture, and at night they house them at home in
their owne habitations, yea euen before their chamber-
doores.[35]

*Of the people called Ideuacal who inhabite the beginning
of mount Atlas.*

HAuing hitherto made report of al the cities of Hea,
which are worthie of memorie, I thought good in
this place (to the end that nothing should be wanting in
this our discourse, which might delight the reader) to
describe the inhabited mountaines also. Wherefore the
greatest part of the people of Hea dwelleth vpon mountaines, some whereof being called Ideuacal (for so are they
named) inhabitie vpon that part of Atlas, which stretcheth
it selfe from the Ocean sea eastward, as farre as Igilingigil;
and this ridge of mountaines diuideth Hea from Sus. The
bredth of this mountaine is three daies iourney. For
Tefethne, whereat this mountaine beginneth from the
north, is distant from the towne of Messa, where it endeth
southward, as farre as I coulde conueniently ride in three
daies. Whosoeuer knoweth this region as well as my selfe,
can sufficiently beare me witnes, howe it is replenished

with inhabitants and countrey-villages. Their ordinary
food is barly, goates-flesh, and hony. Shirts they weare
none at all, nor yet any other garments which are sowen
togither ; for there is no man among them which knoweth
how to vse the needle : but such apparell as they haue,
hangeth by a knot vpon their shoulders. Their women
weare siluer rings vpon their eares, some three, and some
more. They haue siluer buttons of so great a scantling,
that each one weigheth an ounce, wherewith they fasten
their apparell vpon their shoulders, to the end it may not
fall off. The nobler and richer sort of people among them
weare siluer rings vpon their fingers and legs, but such as
are poore weare ringes onely of iron or of copper. There
are likewise certaine horses in this region, being so small of
stature and so swift, as it is woonderfull. Heere may you
finde great plentie of wilde goats, hares, and deere, and yet
none of the people are delighted in hunting. Many fountaines are heere to be founde, and great abundance of trees,
but especially of walnut-trees. The greater part of this
people liueth after the Arabians manner, often changing
their places of habitation. A kinde of daggers they vse
which are broad and crooked like a wood-knife ; and their
swords are as thicke as sithes, wherewith they mowe haie.
When they go to the warres they carrie three or fower
hunting toiles with them. In al the said mountaine are
neither iudges, priestes, nor temples to be founde. So
ignorant they are of learning, that not one among them
either loueth or embraceth the same. They are all most
lewd and wicked people, and applie their mindes vnto all
kinde of villanie. It was tolde the Seriffo in my presence,
that the foresaide mountaine was able to affoord twentie
thousand soldiers for a neede.[36]

Of the mountaine called Demenfera.

THis mountaine also is a part of Atlas, beginning from the mountaine last before mentioned, and extending it selfe eastward for the space of about fiftie miles, as farre as the mountaine of Nifif in the territorie of Maroco. And it diuideth a good part of Hea from the region of Sus before named. It aboundeth with inhabitants, which are of a most barbarous and sauage disposition. Horses they haue great plenty : they go to warre oftentimes with the Arabians which border vpon them : neither will they permit any of the saide Arabians to come within their dominions. There are no townes nor castles vpon all this mountaine : howbeit they haue certaine villages and cottages, wherein the better sort do hide their heads. Great store of noble men or gouernors they haue in all places, vnto whom the residue are very obedient. Their grounde yeeldeth barly and mill in abundance. They haue euery where many fountaines, which being dispersed ouer the whole prouince, do at length issue into that riuer, which is called in their language Siffaia. Their apparel is *Plentie of yron.* somewhat decent : also they possesse great quantitie of iron, which is from thence transported into other places ; and these people are well giuen to thrift and good husbandry. Great numbers of Iewes remaine in this region, which liue as stipendarie soldiers vnder diuers princes, & are continually in armes ; and they are reputed and called by other Iewes in Africa Carraum, that is to say, heretiques. They haue store of boxe, of mastick, and of high walnut trees. Vnto their Argans (for so they call a kinde of oliues which they haue) they put nuts ; out of which two simples they expresse very bitter oile, vsing it for a sauce to some of their meates, and powring it into their lampes. I heard diuers of their principall men auouch, that they were able to bring into the field fiue and twentie thousand most expert soldiers. In my returne from Sus they did me exceeding honour, in regard of certaine letters, which I deliuered vnto them from my Lord the Scriffo : and to manifest their good will towardes the said Scriffo, they dismissed me with most ample gifts and gratuities. This was done in the 920. yeere of the Hegeira, that is to say, in the yeere of our Lord, 1520.[37]

Of the mountaine of Iron, commonly called Gebelelhadih.

THis mountaine is not to be accounted any part of Atlas : for it beginneth northward from the Ocean ; and southward it extendeth to the riuer of Tensift ; and diuideth Hea from Duccala and Maroco. The inhabitants are called Regraga. Vpon this hill are waste deserts, cleere fountaines, and abundance of hony, and of oyle Arganick, but of corne and pulse great scarcitie, vnlesse they make prouision thereof out of Duccala. Few rich men are heere to be founde, but they are all most deuout and religious after their manner. Vpon the toppe of this mountaine are many Hermites, which liue onely vpon the fruits of certaine trees, and drinke water. They are a most faithfull and peaceable nation. Whosoeuer among them is apprehended for theft or any other crime, is foorthwith banished the countrey for certaine yeeres. So great is their simplicitie, that whatsoeuer they see the Hermites do, they esteeme it as a miracle. They are much oppressed with the often inuasions of their neighbours the Arabians ; wherefore this quiet nation choose rather to pay yeerely tribute, then to maintaine warre. Against the saide Arabians Mahumet the King of Fez directed his troupes : insomuch that they were constrained to leaue their owne countrey and to flee into the mountaines. But the people of the mountaines being aided with Mahumet his forces, vanquished the Arabians ; so that three thousand of them were slaine, and fower-score of their horses were brought vnto K. Mahumet. After which prosperous battaile, the said mountainers remained free from all tribute. I my selfe, while these things were a dooing, serued the king. It was in the yeere of the Hegeira 921. that is to say, in the yeere of our Lord 1512. When this people vndertake any warre, they bring commonly into the fielde an armie of twelue thousand men.[38]

Of the region of Sus.

NOw comes the region of Sus to be considered of, being situate beyond Atlas, ouer against the territorie of Hea, that is to say, in the extreme part of Africa. Westward it beginneth from the Ocean sea, and southward from the sandie deserts: on the north it is bounded with the vtmost towne of Hea; and on the east with that mightie riuer whereof the whole region is named. Wherefore beginning from the west, wee will describe all those cities and places which shall seeme to be woorthy of memorie.

Of the towne of Messa.

THree small townes were built by the ancient Africans vpon the sea shoare (each being a mile distant from other) in that very place where Atlas takes his beginning: all which three are called by one onely name, to wit, Messa, and are enuironed with a wall builte of white stones. Through these three runneth a certaine great riuer called Sus in their language: this riuer in sommer is so destitute of water, that a man may easilie without perill passe ouer it on foote; but it is not so in the winter time. They haue then certaine small barkes, which are not meete to saile vpon this riuer. The place where the foresaide three townes are situate, aboundeth greatly with palme trees, neither haue they in a manner any other wealth; and yet their dates are but of small woorth, *Dates which will last but one yeere.* because they will not last aboue one yeere. All the inhabitants exercise husbandry, especially in the moneths of September and Aprill; what time their riuer encreaseth. And in May their corne groweth to ripenes. But if in the two foresaide moneths the riuer encreaseth not according to the woonted manner, their haruest is then nothing woorth. Cattell are very scarce among them. Not farre from the sea side they haue a temple, which they greatly esteeme and honour. Out of which, Historiographers say, that the same prophet, of whom their great Mahumet foretold, shoulde proceed. Yea, some there are which sticke not to affirme, that the prophet *Ionas* was cast foorth by the whale vpon the shoare of Messa, when as he was sent to preach vnto the Niniuites. The rafters and beames of the *Great store of whales.* saide temple are of whales bone. And it is a vsuall thing amongst them, to see whales of an huge and monstrous bignes cast vp dead vpon their shore, which by reason of their hugenes and strange deformitie, may terrifie and astonish the beholders. The common people imagine, that, by reason of a certaine secret power and vertue infused from heauen by God vpon the saide temple, each whale which woulde swim past it can by no meanes escape death. Which opinion had almost perswaded me; especially when at my being there, I my selfe sawe a mightie whale cast vp: vnless a certaine Iewe had told me, that it was no such strange matter: for (quoth he) there lie certaine rockes two miles into the sea on either side; and as the sea mooues, so the whales mooue also; and if they chaunce to light vpon a rock, they are easily wounded to death, and so are cast vpon the next shore. This reason more preuailed with me then the opinion of the people. My selfe (I remember), being in this region at the same time when my Lord the Seriffo bare rule ouer it, was inuited by a certaine gentleman, and was by him conducted

A whales rib of incredible greatnes.

into a garden: where he shewed me a whales rib of so great a size, that lying vpon the grounde with the conuexe or bowing side vpwarde in manner of an arche, it resembled a gate, the hollow or inwarde part whereof aloft we could not touch with our heads, as we rode vpon our camels backs: this rib (he said) had lien there aboue an hundred yeeres, and was kept as a miracle. Here may you finde vpon the sea-shore great store of amber, which the Portugal, & Fessan merchãts fetch from there for a very meane price: for they scarcely pay a duckat for a whole

Amber.

ounce of most choise and excellent amber. Amber (as some thinke) is made of whales dung, and (as others suppose) of the Sperma or seede, which being consolidate and hardened by the sea, is cast vpon the next shore.[39]

Of Teÿcut an ancient towne of Sus.

TEijcut being (as the report goeth) built by the ancient Africans in a most pleasant place, is diuided into three partes, whereof each one is almost a mile distant from another, and they all make a triangle or three-square. This Teÿcut containeth fower thousand families, and standeth not farre from the riuer of Sus. The soile adiacent is most fruitfull for graine, for barlie, and for all

Store of sugar.

kinde of pulse. They haue here likewise a good quantitie of sugar growing; howbeit, because they know not how to presse, boyle, and trim it, they cannot haue it but blacke and vnsauorie: wherefore so much as they can spare, they sell vnto the merchants of Maroco, of Fez, and of the land of Negros. Of dates likewise they haue plentie; neither vse they any money besides the gold which is digged out of their owne natiue soile. The women weare vpon their heads a peece of cloth woorth a duckat. Siluer they haue none, but such as their women adorne themselues with. The least iron-coine vsed amongst them, weigheth almost an ounce. No fruites take plentifully vpon their soile, but onely figs, grapes, peaches, and dates. Neither oile nor oliues are here to be found, except such as are brought from certaine mountaines of Maroco. A measure of oile is sold at Sus for fifteene duckats; which measure containeth an hundred and fiftie pounds Italian waight. Their peeces of golde (because they haue no certaine nor proportionable money) doe weigh, seuen of them & one third part, one ounce. Their ounce was all one with the Italian ounce: but their pound containeth eighteene ounces, and is called in their language *Rethl*; and an hundred *Rethl* make one such measure of oile as is aforesaid. For carrying of merchandize from place to place, their custome is to pay for a camels load, that is, for 700. pounds of Italiã waight, 3. peeces of gold, especially in the spring time: for in sõmer they pay somtimes 5. & somtimes 6. pieces of gold, as the time requireth. Here is that excellent leather dressed, which is called leather of Maroco; twelue hides whereof are here sold for sixe duckats, and at Fez for eight. That part of this region which lieth toward Atlas hath many villages, townes, and hamlets: but the south part thereof is vtterly destitute of inhabitants, and subiect to the Arabians which border vpon it. In the midst of this citie standeth a faire and stately temple, which they call The greatest, and the chiefest, through the very midst whereof they haue caused a part of the foresaid riuer to runne. The inhabitants are sterne and vnciuill, being so continually exercised in warres, that they haue not one day of quiet. Each part of the citie hath a seuerall captaine and gouernour, who all of them together doe rule the common-wealth: but their authoritie continueth neuer aboue three moneths, which being expired, three other are chosen in their roume. Their apparell is somewhat like vnto that of the people of Hea: sauing that some of them make their shirtes, and other of their garments of a certaine kinde of white stuffe.

Cordouan leather of Maroco.

A Canna (which is a measure proper to this region, containing two elles) of course cloth is solde for halfe a peece of gold: but fower and twentie elles of Portugall or Neatherlandish cloth, if it be any thing fine, is vsually sold there for fower peeces of their gold. Likewise in this towne are many iudges and priests, which are conuersant onely in matters of religion: but in ciuill matters, he that hath most friends, obtaineth greatest fauour. Whensoeuer any one is slaine, all the friends of the slaine partie doo foorthwith conspire to kill the murtherer. Which if they cannot bring to passe, then is the malefactor by open proclamation banished out of the citie for seuen yeeres, vnlesse he will in despight of all men continually defend himselfe by maine force. They which returne from exile before the time prefixed, are punished in such manner as we will hereafter declare in place conuenient. But he that returnes after the seuen yeeres are once expired, maketh a feast vnto the Burghmasters, and so is restored againe to his former libertie. In this citie dwell many Iewes, and many notable artificers, who are not compelled to pay any yeerely tribute or taxation at all: except it be some small gratuitie vnto the principall citizens.[40]

Of Tarodant a towne of Sus.

THE towne of Tarodant built by the ancient Africans, containeth about three thousand housholds. It is distant from Atlas Southward about fower miles, and fiue and thirtie miles Eastward of Teyeut. For the fruitfulnes of the soyle and manners of the people, it is all one with Teyeut; sauing that the towne is somewhat lesser, and the people somewhat more ciuill. For when the family of *Marin* gouerned at Fez, part of them also inhabited Sus, and in those daies Sus was the seat of the King of Fez his Vice-roy. There is to be seene euen at this present a certaine rocke lying vpon the ground, which was there placed by the foresaid king. But the said family of *Marin* decaying, the inhabitants recoucred their former estate. Their garments are made partly of linnen, and partly of woollen ; and they haue manie artificers of all sorts. All authoritie is committed vnto their noble or principall men ; who gouerne fower by fower, sixe moneths onely. They are wholy giuen to peace : neither doe I read, that euer they endamaged any of their neighbours. Betweene this towne and Atlas are many villages and hamlets : but to the south of this towne lye the Arabians desert. The townesmen pay large yeerely tribute, to the ende that merchants may haue safe and secure passage to and fro. This towne in our time waged warre against the Arabians : which, that they might the more prosperously bring to passe, they yeelded themselues vnto my Lord the Seriffo ; in the yeere of the Hegeira 920. which was in the yeere of our Lord 1511.[41]

Of the castle Gartguessem.

THE castle of Gartguessem[42] is built vpon the top of Atlas in a most impregnable place, ouer against that part of the Ocean whereinto the riuer of Sus dischargeth his streames : the soyle is most profitable and fruitfull. This place about twentie yeeres sithens the Portugals surprised ; which caused the inhabitants of Hea and Sus foorthwith to arme themselues, to the end they might recouer the castle by maine force, which was by force taken from them. Wherfore leuying a mightie army as wel of home-bornes, as of strangers ; they chose for their Captaine a certaine Mahumetan Seriffo, being a man descended of the family of *Mahumet* ; and so besieged the castle. But they had vnhappie successe in this their enterprise ; for they which came to the siege, seeing that they could not preuaile, and that so many of their companie were slaine, left the castle, and returned home.

Gartguessem surprised by the Portugals

Except some few which remained with the Seriffo, to the end they might maintaine warre against the Christians, euen till the last hower. The inhabitants of Sus not being desirous to liue in warfare, allowed the Seriffo money for the maintenance of fiue hundred horses. Who hauing with his money hyred a great number of souldiers, and growing famous ouer all the region, at last vsurped the gouernment thereof. This I know for a certaintie, that the Seriffo, when I came from his court, had aboue three thousand horsemen; and such numbers of footemen and summes of money, as were almost innumerable.[43]

Of Tedsi a towne of Sus.

TEdsi being a very great towne, and built many yeeres agoe in a most pleasant and fertile place by the Africans, containeth moe then fower thousand families; it is distant from Tarodant Eastward thirtie miles, from the Ocean sea sixtie miles, and from Atlas twentie. Heere groweth great abundance of corne, of sugar, and of wilde woad. You shall finde in this citie many merchants, which come out of the lande of Negros for trafiques sake. The citizens are great louers of peace & of all ciuilitie: and they haue a flourishing common-wealth. The whole citie is gouerned by sixe Magistrates which are chosen by lots: howbeit their gouernment lasteth for sixteene moneths onely. The riuer of Sus is distant three miles from hence. Here dwell many Iewes, which are most cunning goldsmiths, carpenters, and such like artificers. They haue a verie stately temple and many priests and doctors of the lawe, which are maintained at the publike charge. Euery munday great numbers of Arabians both of the plaines and of the mountaines come hither to market. In the yeere of the Hegeira 920. this citie of their owne accord yeelded themselues into the hands of

Store of sugar and of woad.

the Seriffo: and here the common councell of the whole
region was established.[44]

Of the citie of Tagauost.

IN all Sus there is no citie comparable vnto that which is
commonly called Tagauost: for it containeth aboue
eight thousand housholdes: the wall thereof is builte of
rough stones. From the Ocean it is distant about threescore miles, and about fiftie miles southward of Atlas: and
the report is, that the Africans built this citie. About
ten miles from this place lieth the riuer of Sus: here are
great store of artificers and of shops: and the people of
Tagauost are diuided into three parts. They haue continuall ciuill wars among themselues, and one part haue
the Arabians alwaies on their side; who for better pay
will take parte sometime with one side, and sometime with
the contrarie. Of corne and cattell heere is great abundance; but their wooll is exceeding course. In this citie
are made certaine kindes of apparell, which are vsually
carried for merchandise once a yeere to Tombuto, to
Gualata, and to other places in the lande of Negros.
Their market is twise euery weeke: their attire is somewhat decent and comely: their women are beautifull; but
their men are of a tawnie and swart colour, by reason they
are descended of blacke fathers and white mothers. In
this citie such carrie the greatest authoritie and credit, as
are accounted the richest and the mightiest. I my
selfe remained heere thirteene daies with the Seriffo
his principall chancellour, who went thither of purpose
to buie certaine slaues for his Lord, in the yeere of
the Hegeira 919. which was in the yeere of our Lord,
1510.[45]

Of the mountaine of Hanchisa.

THis mountaine beginneth westward from Atlas, and from thence stretcheth almost fortie miles eastward. At the foote of this mountaine standeth Messa, with the residue of the region of Sus. The inhabitants of this mountaine are such valiant footmen, that one of them will encounter two horsemen. The soile will yeeld no corne at all but barly; howbeit hony there is in great abundance. With snowe they are almost at all times troubled: but how patiently and strongly they can endure the colde, a man may easily gesse, for that the whole yeere throughout they weare one single garment onely. This people my Lord the Scriffo attempted often to bring vnder his subiection: howbeit he hath not as yet preuailed against them.[46]

Of the mountaine of Ilalem.

THis mountaine beginneth westward from the mountaine aforesaid; on the east it abutteth vpon the region of Guzula, and southward vpon the plaines of Sus. The inhabitants are valiant, hauing great store of horses. They are at continuall warre among themselues, for certaine siluer mines: so that those which haue the better hande digge as much siluer as they can, and distribute to euery man his portion, vntil such time as they be restrained from digging by others.[47]

Mines of siluer.

The situation and estate of the region of Maroco.

THis region beginneth westward from the mountaine of Nefisa, stretching eastward to the mountaine of Hadimei, and northward euen to that place where the most famous riuers of Tensift and Asfinual meete togither, that is to say, vpon the east border of Hea. This region is in a manner three square, being a most pleasant countrey, and abounding with many droues and flockes of cattell: it is greene euery where, and most fertile of all things, which serue for foode, or which delight the senses of smelling or seeing. It is altogither a plaine countrey, not much vnlike to Lombardie. The mountaines in this region are most colde and barren, insomuch that they will bring foorth nought but barly. Wherefore (according to our former order) beginning at the west part of this region, we will proceed in our description eastward.

Of Elgihumuha a towne of Maroco.

VPon that plaine which is about seuen miles distant from Atlas, and not farre from the riuer of Sesseua, standeth a towne called by the inhabitants Elgihumuha, which was built, as they suppose, by the Africans. A while after it was brought vnder the subiection of certaine Arabians, about that verie time when the family of Muachidin aforesaid began to reuolt from the kingdome. And at this day the ruines and reliques of this towne can scarce be seene. The Arabians which now dwel thereabout do sow so much ground onely, as to supply their owne necessities; and the residue they let lye vntilled and fruitles. Howbeit when the countrey thereabout was in flourishing estate, the inhabitants payed yeerely vnto the Prince for tribute 100000. ducates: and then this towne contained aboue sixe thousand families. Trauelling that way I was most friendly entertained by a certaine Arabian, and had good experience of the peoples liberality: sauing that I heard of some, that they were most trecherous and deceitfull.[48]

Of the castle of Imegiagen.

THe castle of Imegiagen is built vpon the top of a certaine hil of Atlas, being so fortified by naturall situation, that it neither hath nor needeth any wall. It standeth southward of Elgihumuha (as I take it) 25. miles. This castle was in times past vnder the iurisdiction of the noble men of that region, vntill such times as it was taken by one *Homar Essuef* an apostata from the Mahumetan religion, as we will afterward declare. The said *Homar* vsed such monstrous tyrannie in that place, that neither children, nor women big with childe could escape his crueltie ; insomuch that he caused the vnborne infants to bee ripped out of their mothers wombes, and to be murthered. This was done in the yeere of the Hegeira 900, and so that place remained destitute of inhabitants. In the yeere 920. of the Hegeira the said region began to be inhabited anew : howbeit now there can but one side of the mountaine onely be tilled, for the plaine vnderneath is so dangerous, both by reason of the daily incursions of the Arabians, and also of the Portugals, that no man dare trauell that way.[49]

The crueltie of Homar Essuef.

Of the towne of Tenessa.

Vpon a certaine hill of Atlas named Ghedmin standeth a towne, which was built (as some report) by the ancient Africans, and called by the name of Tenessa, being a most strong and defensible place, and being distant about eight miles eastward from the riuer of Asifinuall. At the foote of the said hill lieth a most excellent plaine, which, were it not for the lewd theeuish Arabians, would yeeld an incomparable crop. And because the inhabitants of Tenessa are depriued of this notable commoditie, they till onely that ground which is vpon the side of the mountaine, and which lieth betweene the towne and the riuer. Neither doe they enioy that gratis ; for they yeerely pay vnto the Arabians for tribute the third part of their corne.[50]

Of the new towne of Delgumuha.

VPon the top of a certaine high mountaine was built in our time a most large and impregnable forte, being enuironed on all sides with diuers other mountaines, and called by the inhabitants New Delgumuha. Beneath the said mountaine springeth Asifinuall, which word signifieth in the African toong, the riuer of rumor, because that breaking foorth by the side of the hill with a monstrous noise, it maketh a most deepe gulfe, much like vnto that, which the Italians call *Inferno di Tivoli*. The said forte containeth almost a thousand families. It was sometime gouerned by a certaine tyrant, which came thither out of the king of Maroco his court. Here may you finde great store of soldiers both for horsemen and footemen. They gather yeerely tribute of the people bordering vpon Atlas, to the summe of a thousand crownes. They haue alwaies had great league and familiaritie with the Arabians, each of whom haue accustomed to salute and gratifie the other with mutuall gifts: for which cause they haue oftentimes much prouoked the kings of Maroco against them. They haue alwaies beene great louers of ciuilitie, and haue worne neat and decent apparell; neither shall you find any corner in the whole towne which is not well peopled. In this towne are plenty of artificers, for it is but fiftie miles from the citie of Maroco. Vpon the said mountaine there are great store of gardens and orchards; which yeeld the inhabitants abundance of fruit yeerely. They reape likewise barlie, hempe, and cotton; and their goates are almost innumerable. Likewise they haue many priests and iudges: but as touching their mindes, they are ignorant, froward, and exceedingly addicted to ielousie. In this towne I aboad certaine daies with a kinsman of mine, who while he dwelt at Fez being impouerished with extreme studie of Alchimie, was constrained to flee vnto this towne, where in processe of time he became Secretarie vnto the gouernour.[51]

Of the citie of Imizmizi.

Vpon a certaine part of Atlas standeth a citie called Imizmizi.[52] Westward it is distant from new Delgumuha about fourteene miles: and this citie the Arabians are reported to haue built. Neere vnto this citie lieth the common high way to Guzula ouer the mountaines of Atlas, being commonly called Burris, that is, A way strowed with feathers: because snow falles often thereupon, which a man would thinke rather to be feathers then snow. Not far from this towne likewise there is a very faire and large plaine, which extendeth for the space of thirtie miles, euen to the territorie of Maroco. This most fertile plaine yeeldeth such excellent corne, as (to my remembrance) I neuer saw the like. Sauing that the Arabians and soldiers of Maroco doe so much molest the said plaine countrie, that the greater part thereof is destitute of inhabitants: yea, I haue heard of many citizens that haue forsaken the citie it selfe; thinking it better to depart, then to be daily oppressed with so many inconueniences. They haue very little money, but the scarcitie thereof is recompenced by their abundance of good ground, and their plentie of corne. In the time of my aboad with them I went vnto a certaine Hermite, which they called *Sidi Canon: which famous and woorthie man gaue me such friendly entertainment, as I cannot easily expresse.

* Sidi signifieth a Saint in the Arabian toung.

Of the three townes of Tumelgast.

These three townes called by the name of Tumelgast[53] are situate vpon a plaine, about thirtie miles from Maroco, and fourteene miles northward of Atlas, being replenished with palme-trees, vines, and all other trees that beare fruit. Their fields are very large and fertill, were they not continually wasted by the lewd Arabians. So few are the inhabitants of these three townes, that I thinke there are not in all aboue fifteene families, all which are ioined in affinitie and kinred vnto the foresaid hermite : for which cause they are permitted to till some part of the plaine, without paying of any tribute vnto the Arabians. Saue onely, that they entertaine the Arabians when they trauell that way. Their lowly and base habitations a man would take rather to be hogs-cotes, then dwelling places for men : hence it is, that they are so continually vexed with fleas, gnats, and other such vermine. Their water is exceedingly salt. This prouince also I perused in the companie of my deere friend *Sidi Iehie*, who went thither to gather vp the tribute of the countrie on the behalfe of the king of Portugall. This *Sidi* was appointed gouernor ouer all that circuit which is called by them Azafi.[54]

Of the towne of Tesrast.

THis towne is situate vpon the banke of the riuer Asifelmel. It standeth westward of Maroco fourteene miles, & about twētie miles from Atlas. Round about this towne they haue diuers gardens & enclosures abounding with dates and corne ; and the chiefe part of the inhabitants earne their liuing with gardening. Howbeit sometimes the increase of their riuer is so great, that it drowneth all their gardens and corne-fields. And they are by so much the more miserable, in regard that the Arabians all summertime doe possesse the whole region, deuouring all things which the poore husbandmen by their great care and industrie had prouided. With these people I made no longer tarrying but onely till I could haue well baited my horse : howbeit in that short time I hardly escaped with life and goods, from certain Arabian theeues.[55]

A most exact description of the great and famous citie of Maroco.

The first founder of Maroco.

His noble citie of Maroco in Africa is accounted to be one of the greatest cities in the whole world. It is built vpon a most large field, being about fourteene miles distant from Atlas. One *Ioseph* the sonne of *Tesfin*, and king of the tribe or people called Luntuna, is reported to haue beene the founder of this citie, at that very time when he conducted his troupes into the region of Maroco, and setled himselfe not farre from the common high way, which stretcheth from Agmet ouer the mountaines of Atlas, to those deserts where the foresaid tribe or people doe vsually inhabite. Here may you behold most stately and woonderfull werkmanship : for all their buildings are so cunningly and artificially contriued, that a man cannot easily describe the same.⁵⁶ This huge and mightie citie, at such time as it was gouerned by *Hali*

Maroco in times past contained aboue 100000. families.

the sonne of king *Ioseph*, contained moe then 100000. families. It had fower and twenty gates belonging thereto, and a wall of great strength and thicknes, which was built of white stone and lime. From this citie the riuer of Tensift lieth about sixe miles distant. Here may you behold great abundance of temples, of colleges, of bath-stoues, and of innes, all framed after the fashion and custome of that region. Some were built by the king of the tribe of Luntuna, and others by *Elmuachidin* his successor : but the most curious and magnificent temple of all, is that in the midst of the citie which was built by *Hali* the first king of Maroco, and the son of *Ioseph* aforesaid, being commonly called the temple of *Hali ben Ioseph*. Howbeit one *Abdul-Mumen* which succeeded him, to the ende he might vtterly abolish the name of *Hali*, and might

make himselfe onely famous with posteritie, caused this
stately temple of Maroco to be razed, and to bee reedified
somewhat more sumptuously than before. Howbeit he
lost not onely his expences, but failed of his purpose also :
for the common people euen till this day doe call the said
Temple by the first and auncientest name.⁵ Likewise in
this citie not farre from a certaine rocke was built a Temple
by him that was the seconde vsurper ouer the kingdome of
Maroco : after whose death his nephew *Mansor* enlarged *Mansor the king of*
the saide Temple fiftie cubites on all sides, and adorned *Maroco.*
the same with manye pillars, which he commanded to be
brought out of Spain for that purpose. Vnder this temple
he made a cesterne or vault as bigge as the temple it selfe :
the roofe of the saide temple he couered with lead : and at
euery corner he made leaden pipes to conueigh raine
water into the cesterne vnderneath the temple. The
turret or steeple is built of most hard and well framed
stone, like vnto *Vespasian* his Amphitheatrum at Rome,
containing in compasse moe then an hundreth elles,
and in height exceeding the steeple of Bononia. The
staires of the said turret or steeple are each of them nine
handfuls in bredth, the vtmost side of the wall is ten ; and
*the thicknes of the turret is fiue. The saide turret hath * *Obscurum.*
seauen lofts, vnto which the staires ascending are very
lightsome : for there are great store of windowes, which to
the ende they may giue more light, are made broader
within then without. Vpon the top of this turret is built
a certaine spire or pinnacle rising sharpe in forme of a
sugar-loafe, and containing fiue and twentie elles in compasse, but in height being not much more then two speares
length : the saide spire hath three lofts one aboue another,
vnto euery of which they ascend with woodden ladders.
Likewise on the top of this spire standeth a golden halfe
moone, vpon a barre of iron, with three spheares of golde
vnder it ; which golden spheares are so fastened vnto the

saide iron barre, that the greatest is lowest, and the least highest. It woulde make a man giddie to looke downe from the top of the turret; for men walking on the grounde, be they neuer so tall, seeme no bigger then a childe of one yeere old. From hence likewise may you plainly escrie the promontorie of Azaphi, which notwithstanding is an hundreth and thirtie miles distant. But mountaines (you will say) by reason of their huge bignes may easily be seene a farre off: howbeit from this turret a man may in cleere weather most easily see fiftie miles into the plaine countries. The inner part of the saide temple, is not very beautifull. But the roofe is most cunningly and artificially vaulted, the timbers being framed and set togither with singular workmanship, so that I haue not seene many fairer temples in all Italy. And albeit you shall hardly finde any temple in the whole worlde greater then this, yet is it very meanly frequented; for the people do neuer assemble there but onely vpon fridaies. Yea a great part of this citie, especially about the foresaid temple lieth so desolate and void of inhabitants, that a man cannot without great difficultie passe, by reason of the ruines of many houses lying in the way. Vnder the porch of this temple it is reported that in old time there were almost an hundreth shops of sale-bookes, and as many on the other side ouer against them: but at this time I thinke there is not one booke-seller in all the whole citie to be founde.[58] And scarcely is the third part of this citie inhabited.[59] Within the wals of Maroco are vines, palme-trees, great gardens, and most fruitefull corne-fields: for without their wals they can till no ground, by reason of the Arabians often inrodes. Know yee this for a certaintie, that the saide citie is growen to vntimely decay and old age: for scarcely fiue hundreth & sixe yeeres are past, since the first building thereof, forasmuch as the foundations thereof were laide in the time of *Ioseph* the son of

Great store of bookes in olde time to be sold in Maroco.

Tesfin, that is to say, in the 424. yeere of the Hegeira. Which decay I can impute to none other cause, but to the iniurie of continuall warres, and to the often alterations of magistrates and of the common wealth. After king *Ioseph* succeeded his sonne *Hali*, and the sonne of *Hali* was ordained gouernour after his fathers decease.⁶⁰ In whose time sprung vp a factious crue, by the meanes of a certaine Mahumetan preacher named *Elmaheli*, being a man both borne & brought vp in the mountaines. The saide *Elmaheli* hauing leuied a great army, waged warre against *Abraham* his soueraigne Lord. Whereupon king *Abraham* conducting another armie against him, had maruelious ill successe: and after the battaile ended, his passage into the citie of Maroco was so stopped and restrained, that he was forced with a fewe soldiers, which remained yet aliue, to flee eastward to the mountains of Atlas. But *Elmaheli* not being satisfied with expelling his true soueraigne out of his owne kingdome, commanded one of his captaines called *Abdul Mumen*, with the one halfe of his armie to pursue the distressed king, while himselfe with the other halfe laide siege to Maroco. The king with his followers came at length vnto Oran, hoping there to haue renewed his forces. But *Abdul Mumen* and his great armie pursued the saide king so narrowly, that the citizens of Oran told him in plaine termes, that they would not hazard themselues for him. Wherefore this vnhappie king beeing vtterly driuen to dispayre, set his Queene on horsebacke behinde him, and so in the night time road foorth of the citie. But perceiuing that he was descried and knowen by his enimies, he fled foorthwith vnto a certaine rocke standing vpon the sea-shore: where, setting spurs to his horse-side, he cast himselfe, his most deere spouse, and his horse downe headlong, and was within a while after found slaine among the rockes and stones, by certaine which dwelt neere vnto the place. Wherefore

The miserable death of Abraham king of Maroco and of his Queene.

Abdul Mumen hauing gotten the victorie, returned in triumphant manner toward Maroco, where the foresaide *Elmaheli* was deceased before his comming, in whose place *Abdul* was chosen King and Mahumetan prelate ouer the fortie disciples, and tooke tenne persons to be of his priuie councell, which was a new inuention in the law of Mahumet. This *Abdul Mumen* hauing besieged the citie of Maroco for the space of an whole yeere, at last ouercame it : and killing *Isaac* the onely sonne of King *Abraham* with his owne hand, he commanded all the soldiers, and a good part of the citizens to be slaine.[61] This mans posteritie raigned from the fiue hundred sixteenth, to the sixe hundred sixtie eight yeere of the Hegeira, and at length they were dispossessed of the kingdome by a certaine king of the Tribe called *Marin*. Now, attend (I beseech you) and marke, what changes and alterations of estates befell afterwards. The family of *Marin* after the said kings decease bare rule till the yeere of the Hegeira 785. At length the kingdome of Maroco decreasing dayly more and more, was gouerned by kings which came out of the next mountaine. Howbeit, neuer had Maroco any gouernours which did so tyrannize ouer it, as they of the family called *Marin*.[62] The principall court of this family was holden for the most part at Fez ; but ouer Maroco were appointed Vice-royes and deputies : insomuch that Fez was continually the head and Metropolitan citie of all Mauritania, and of all the Western dominion : euen as (God willing) we will declare more at large in our briefe treatise concerning the law and religion of Mahumet.[63] But now hauing made a sufficient digression, let vs resume the matter subiect where we left. In the said citie of Maroco is a most impregnable castle, which, if you consider the bignes, the walles, the towers, and the gates built all of perfect marble, you may well thinke to be a citie rather then a castle. Within this castle there is a stately temple,

hauing a most loftie and high steeple, on the top whereof
standeth an halfe moone, and vnder the halfe moone are
three golden spheares one bigger then another, which all
of them togither weigh 130000 ducates. Some kings there *Three golden spheares.*
were, who being allured with the value, went about to take
downe the saide golden sphears : but they had alwaies
some great misfortune or other, which hindered their
attempt: insomuch that the common people thinke it
verie dangerous, if a man doth but offer to touch the said
sphears with his hand. Some affirme that they are there
placed by so forcible an influence of the planets, that they
cannot be remooued from thence by any cunning or deuice.
Some others report that a certaine spirite is adiured by
Arte-magique, to defend those sphears from al assaults
and iniuries whatsoeuer. In our time, the king of Maroco
neglecting the vulgar opinion, would haue taken down
the said sphears, to vse them for treasure against the
Portugals, who as then prepared themselues to battell
against him. Howbeit his counsellours would not suffer
him so to doe, for that they esteemed them as the principall
monuments of all Maroco. I remember that I read in a
certaine historiographer, that the wife of King *Mansor*, to
the ende she might be famous in time to come, caused
those three sphears to be made of the princely and pretious
iewels which her husband *Mansor* bestowed vpon her, and
to be placed vpon the temple which he built.[64] Likewise
the said castle containeth a most noble college, which hath *A great college.*
thirtie hals belonging thereunto. In the midst whereof is
one hall of a maruellous greatnes, wherein publique lectures
were most solemnely read, while the studie of learning
flourished among them. Such as were admitted into this
college had their victuals and apparell freely giuen them.
Of their professours some were yeerely allowed an hundred,
and some two hundred ducates, according to the qualitie of
their profession : neither would they admit any to heare

them read, but such as perfectly vnderstood what belonged to those Arts which they professed. The walles of this beautifull hall are most stately adorned with painting and caruing, especially of that hall where lectures were woont publiquely to be read. All their porches and vaulted roofes are made of painted and glittering stones, called in their language *Ezzulleia*,[65] such as are yet vsed in Spaine. In the midst of the said building is a most pleasant and cleare fountaine, the wall whereof is of white and polished marble, albeit low-built, as in Africa for the most part such wals are. I haue heard that in old time here was great abundance of students, but at my beeing there I found but fiue in all; and they haue now a most senceless professour, and one that is quite voide of all humanitie.[66]

In the time of mine abode at Maroco I grew into familiar acquaintance with a certaine Iewe, who albeit his skill in the law was but meane, was notwithstanding exceeding rich and well seene in histories. This Iewe in regard of many singular duties which he performed to his prince, found the kings bountie and liberalitie extended vnto him. All others which beare any publike office are (in mine opinion) men of no high reach.[67] Moreouer the foresaide castell (as I remember) hath twelue courts most curiously and artificially built by one *Mansor*. In the first lodged about fiue hundreth Christians, which carried crosse-bowes before the king whither soeuer he went. Not farre from thence is the lodging of the Lord Chancellour and of the kings priuie counsell,[68] which house is called by them, The house of affaires. The third is called The court of victorie; wherein all the armour and munition of the citie is laid up. The fourth belongeth to the great Master of the kings horse. Vpon this court three stables adioine, each one of which stables will containe two hundreth horses. Likewise there are two other ostleries, wherof one is for mules, and

the other for an hundreth of the kings horses onley. Next
vnto the stables were two barnes or garners adioining, in
two seuerall places, in the lower of which barnes was laide
straw, and barly in the other. There is also another most
large place to laye vp corne in, euerie roume whereof will
containe moe then three hundreth bushels. The couer of
the saide roume hath a certaine hole whereunto they ascend
by staires made of stone. Whither the beasts laden with
corne being come, they powre the saide corne into the hole.
And so when they woulde take any corne from thence,
they doe but open certaine holes below, suffring so much
corne to come foorth as may serue their turnes, and that
without any labour at all. There is likewise a certaine other
hall, where the kings sonne, and the sonnes of noble men
are instructed in learning. Then may you beholde a
certaine fower-square building, containing diuers galleries
with faire glasse windowes, in which galleries are many
histories most curiously painted: heere likewise the
glittering and gilt armour is to be seene. Next vnto this
building is another, wherein certaine of the kings guard
are lodged: then follows that wherein state-matters are
discussed: whereunto adioineth also another, which is
appointed for ambassadours to conferre with the kings
priuie counsell in. Likewise the kings concubines and
other ladies of honour haue a most conuenient place
assigned them: next vnto which standeth the lodging of
the kings sonnes. Not farre from the castel wall, on that
side which is next vnto the fields, may you behold a most
pleasant and large garden, containing almost all kinde of
trees that can be named. Moreouer, there is a sumptuous
and stately porch built of most excellent square marble:
in the midst whereof standeth a piller with a lion very
artificially made of marble, out of the mouth of which lion
issueth most cleere and christall water, falling into a
cesterne within the porch: at each corner of the saide porch

Excellent spotted marble. standeth the image of a leopard framed of white marble, which is naturally adorned with certaine black spots : this kind of particoloured marble is no where to be founde but onely in a certaine place of Atlas, which is about an hundreth & fiftie miles distant from Maroco. Not farre from the garden stands a certaine woode or parke walled round about : And here I thinke no kinde of wilde beasts are wanting : for heere you may behold elephants, lions, stagges, roes, and such like : howbeit the lions are separated in a certaine place from other beasts, which place euen to this day is called The lions den.[69] Wherefore such monuments of antiquity as are yet extant in Maroco, albeit they are but few, do notwithstanding sufficiently argue, what a *This king called Mansor was he vnto whom Rasis that famous phisitian dedicated his Booke.* noble citie it was in the time of *Mansor*. At this present al the courts and lodgings before described lie vtterly voide and desolate : except perhaps some of the kings ostlery which tend his mules and horses do lie in that court, which we saide euen now was to lodge archers and crossebowemen : all the residue are left for the fowles of the aire to nestle in. That garden which you might haue named a paradise in olde time, is now become a place where the filth and dung of the whole citie is cast foorth. Where the faire and stately librarie was of old, at this present there is nothing else to be founde, but hens, dooues,[70] and other such like foules, which builde their nests there. Certaine it is, that the foresaid *Mansor*, whom we haue so often mentioned, was a most puissant and mightie prince : for it is well knowen that his dominion stretched from the towne of Messa to the kingdome of Tripolis in Barbary, which is the most excellent region of Africa, and so large, that a man *The huge dominions of king Mansor.* can hardly trauell the length therof in fourescore & ten daies, or the bredth in fifteene. This *Mansor* likewise was in times past Lord of all the kingdome of Granada in Spaine. Yea, his dominion in Spaine extended from Tariffa to Aragon, & ouer a great part of Castilia and of

Portugall. Neither did this *Iacob* surnamed *Mansor* only possesse the foresaid dominiõs, but also his grandfather *Abdul Mumen*, his father *Ioseph*, & his sonne *Mahumet Enafir*,[71] who being vanquished in the kingdome of Valençia, lost 60000. soldiers, horsemen & footemen: howbeit himselfe escaped and returned to Maroco. The Christians being encouraged with this victorie, refrained not from warre, till, within 30. yeeres space, they had woon all the townes following, to wit, Valençia, Denia, Alcauro, Murcia, Cartagena, Cordoua, Siuillia, Iaen, and Vbeda. After which vnhappie warre succeeded the decay of Maroco.[72] The said Mahumet deceasing, left behinde him ten sonnes of a full and perfect age, who contended much about the kingdome. Hereupon it came to passe, while the brethren were at discord, and assailed each other with mutuall warres, that the people of Fez called Marini, and the inhabitants of other regions adiacent began to vsurpe the gouernment. The people called Habdulvad enioyed Tremizen, expelling the king of Tunis, and ordaining some other, whom they pleased, in his stead.[73] Now haue you heard the end of *Mansor* his progenie and successors. The kingdome therefore was translated vnto one *Iacob* the sonne of *Habdulach*, who was the first king of the familie called Marin.[74] And at length the famous citie of Maroco it selfe, by reason of the Arabians continuall outrages, fell into most extreme calamitie: so great is the inconstancie of all earthly things. That which we haue here reported as touching Maroco, partly we saw with our owne eies, partly we read in the historie of one *Ibnu Abdul Malich*, a most exact chronicler of the affaires of Maroco, and partly we borrowed out of that treatise, which our selues haue written concerning the law of Mahumet.[95]

The Christians happie successe against the Moores.

Ibnu Abdul Malich.

Of the towne of Agmet.

THE towne of Agmet built of old by the Africans vpon the top of a certaine hill which beginneth almost from Atlas, is distant from Maroco about fower and twentie miles. In times past, when *Muschidin* was prince thereof, it contained moe then sixe thousand families: at what time the people were very ciuill, and had such plentie and magnificence of all things, that many would not sticke to compare this towne with the citie of Maroco. It had on all sides most pleasant gardens, and great store of vines, whereof some grew vpon the mountaine it selfe, and others on the valley. By the foote of this hill runneth a faire riuer, which springing foorth of Atlas, falleth at length into Tensift. The field which lieth neere vnto this riuer is said to be so fruitfull, that it yeeldeth euery yeere fiftie fold encrease. The water of this riuer looketh alwaies white; albeit if a man stedfastly behold the said riuer, it may seeme vnto him in colour to resemble the soile of Narnia, or the riuer Niger of Vmbria in Italie. And some there are which affirme, that the very same riuer runneth vnder ground to Maroco, and not to breake foorth of the earth, till it come to a certaine place very neere vnto the said citie. Many princes in times past, being desirous to know the hidden and intricate passages of the said riuer, sent certaine persons into the hollow caue, who the better to discerne the same, carried candles and torches with them. But hauing proceeded a little way vnder ground, there met them such a flaw of winde, that blew out their lights, and perforce draue them backe to the great hazard of their liues, so that they said they neuer felt the like. They affirme likewise, that, the riuer being full of rocks, which the water driueth to and fro, and by reason of the manifold chanels and streames, their passage was altogether hindred. Wherefore that secret remaineth vnknowne euen till this

A riuer running vnder the ground to Maroco.

day, neither is there any man so hardie as to attempt the same enterprise againe. I remember that I read in some histories, that king *Ioseph* which built Maroco, being forewarned by the coniecture of a certaine astrologer, that the whole region should perpetually be vexed with warre, prouided by arte-magique, that the passage of this riuer should alwaies bee vnknowen: least, if any enimie should afterward practice mischiefe, he might cut off the course thereof from the saide citie. Neere vnto this riuer lies the common high way, which crosseth ouer mount Atlas to Guzula a region of Maroco. Howbeit the citie of Agmet, which I haue now described vnto you, hath at this day no other inhabitants but woolues, foxes, deere, and such other wilde beasts. Except onely at my being there I found a certaine Hermite, who was attended vpon by an hundred persons of his owne sect: all of them were well-horsed, and did their best endeuour to become gouernours and commanders, but their forces were insufficient.[76] With this Hermite I staide (as I remember) for the space of tenne daies, and founde one amongst his followers, with whom I had old acquaintance, and familiaritie: for we were certaine yeeres fellow-students together at Fez, where being of one standing and seniority, we heard that booke of the Mahumetan religion expounded, which is commonly called the epistle of *Nensefi*.[77]

The desolation of Agmet.

Iohn Leo student at Fez.

Of the towne of Hannimei.

VPon that side of Atlas which lieth towards the plaine countrey, standeth a certaine towne called by the inhabitants Hannimei, being about 40. miles eastward of Maroco: by which towne, on the same side of Atlas, lieth the direct way to Fez. From the said towne the riuer of Agmet is almost fifteene miles distant: and the fielde lying betweene the saide riuer and towne is a most fruitefull soile, like vnto the fielde adioining vpon the citie of Agmet before mentioned. All the region betweene Maroco and the foresaid riuer is in subiection vnto the gouernour of Maroco, but from the riuer vnto Hannimei the townes-men of Hannimei beare rule. This towne had a famous yoong captaine, who maintained continuall warre against the gouernor of Maroco, and somtimes against the Arabians also. He had likewise a most ample dominion vpon the mountaines of Atlas: by naturall disposition he was right liberal & valiant, and hauing scarce attained to sixeteene yeeres of age, he slue his owne vncle, and vsurped his gouernment. Whereof so soone as the Arabians had intelligence, ioining three hundreth Christian horsemen, which came out of Portugale, vnto their great forces, they marched on the sodaine euen to the very gates of the towne. And the forsaide captaine with his armie containing scarce an hundreth horsemen, with a very fewe footemen met the Arabians, and gaue them such a valiant onset, that the greater part of them was slaine, and the Christians were so discomfited, that (as I suppose) not one of them returned home into Portugale: which (they say) came to passe, both by reason that the Christians were ignorant of the place, and vnskilfull of the Africans manner of warfare. These things were done in the 920. yeere of the Hegeira, and in the yeere of our Lorde 1511. Afterward being wearied by the king of Fez his warres (which king demaunded tribute of the townes-men of Hannimei) he was slaine with a bullet: whereupon the towne remained tributarie to the king of Fez. Yea, the deceased captaines wife deliuered as prisoners certaine burgesses of the towne vnto the king himselfe. And the king so soone as he had placed a lieutenant ouer Hannimei, departed from the same towne in the 921. yeere of the Hegeira, and in the yeere of our Lord 1512.[78]

Of the mountaine of Nififa.

Auing before described all the cities and townes of Maroco, it now remaineth that we briefly declare the situation and qualitie of the mountaines there· Wherefore we will begin with the mountaine of Nififa, from whence the region of Maroco it selfe beginneth westward, and is thereby diuided from the prouince of Hea. The said mountaine hath great store of inhabitants : and albeit the tops thereof are continually couered with snowe ; yet doth it yeerely affoorde maruilous increase and abundance of barley. The rude people there are so destitute of all humanitie and ciuill behauiour, that they do admire not onely all strangers, but also do euen gaze and woonder at their apparell. I my selfe remained two daies among them, in which space all the people of the towne came flocking about me, greatly woondring at the white garment which I wore (being such as the learned men of our countrey are vsually clad in) so that euery one being desirous to handle and view this garment of mine, in two daies it was turned from white to blacke, and became all greasie and filthie. Here one of the townes-men being allured with the strangenes and noueltie of my sworde, which I bought at Fez for halfe a ducate, woulde neuer leaue intreating of me, till I had exchanged it with him for an horse, which cost (as himselfe affirmed) aboue ten ducates. The reason of which fonde and childish behauiour I thinke to be, because they neuer trauaile vnto Fez nor to any other cities. And were they neuer so desirous to trauaile, yet dare they not aduenture vpon the common high waies, in regard of the great number of robbers and theeues. Of honie, goates, and oile Arganick they haue woonderfull store :

for in this mountaine beginneth the saide oile to be put in vse.⁷⁰

Of the mountaine called Semede.

AT the bounds of Nififa a certaine other mountaine called by the inhabitants Semede taketh his originall: and these two mountaines are separated by the riuer of Sefsaua. Semede extendeth eastward almost 20. miles, the inhabitants whereof are most base & witlesse people. Great store of springs & fountaines are here to be found; the snowe is perpetuall; all good lawes, ciuilitie, and honestie are quite banished from hence, except perhaps the people be mooued thereunto by the aduise of some stranger, whom they finde to be of a modest and sober disposition. Here being entertained by a certaine religious man of the same place (who was had in great reputation by the people) I was constrained to eate of such grosse meats as the saide people are accustomed vnto, to wit, of barlie meale mingled with water, and of goats-flesh, which was extremely tough and hard by reason of the stalenes and long continuance. After supper we had no other bed but the bare ground to lie vpon. The next morning being ready to take horse, and desirous to depart, fiftie of the people came about me, laying open each man their causes and suites vnto me, as our people vse to doe before a iudge. Vnto whom I answered, that I had neuer in all my life either knowen or heard of the manners and customes of that region. Foorthwith comes one of the chiefe men amongst them, affirming that it was their custome neuer to dismisse any stranger, till he had both heard and throughly decided all the quarrels and controuersies of the inhabitants. *Iohn Leo constrained to play the iudge.* Which words he had no sooner vttered, but immediately my horse was taken from me. Wherefore I was constrained for nine daies, and so many nights, longer to abide the penurie and miserie of that region. Moreouer my

trouble was the greater, for that, in such abundance of
suites and affaires, there was not one man present, which
could set downe so much as a word in writing: wherefore
I my selfe was faine to play both the iudge and the notarie.
Vpon the eight day they all of them promised to bestowe
some great rewarde vpon me. Wherefore the night following seemed vnto me a yeere long: for I was in good hope
the next morrow to haue receiued a masse of golde from
my clients. So soone as the next day began to dawne,
they placed me in a certaine church-porch : whither, after
an vsuall and short praier ended, each man full reuerently
presented his gift vnto me. Here some offered me a cocke,
others brought me nuts and onions, and some others
bestowed a handfull of garlicke vpon me. The principall
and head-men amongst them presented me with a goat;
and so by reason that there was no money in all the said
mountaine, they proffered me not one farthing for my
paines : wherefore all the said gifts I bequeathed vnto
mine oste for his woorthie entertaining of me. And this
was all the notable reward which I reaped in regarde of so
great and intolerable paines. All things being thus dispatched, they sent fiftie horsemen to accompanie and guard
me from theeues in that dangerous way.[80]

Of the mountaine called Seusaua.

THis mountaine of Seusaua taketh his beginning where
Semede endeth, out of which springeth a certaine
riuer, hauing one name with the said mountaine from
whence it proceedeth. Neuer were the tops of this mountaine seene destitute of snowe. The inhabitants leade a
brutish and sauage life, waging continuall warre with their
next neighours : for which purpose they vse neither swords,
iauelins, nor any other warlike instruments, but onely
certaine slings, out of which they discharge stones after a
strange and woonderfull manner. Their victuals consist of

barlic, honie, and goates-flesh. In the same mountaine
great multitudes of Iewes exercising handy-craftes, doe
inhabite: likewise they make sope, yron-hookes, and
horse-shooes. Diuers masons are here to be found also.
They build their walles of no other matter but onely of
rough stone and lime, and the roofes of their houses they
vse to couer with thatch: neither haue they any other
kind of lime or bricks. They haue among them also
abundance of learned men & of skilful lawyers, whose
counsell they vse at all times. Among whom I found
some, who had heretofore beene my fellow-students at
Fez, and for our old acquaintance sake, gaue me most
courteous entertainment: and, to the end I might escape
the danger of theeues, they conducted me a good part of
my way.[81]

Of the mountaine called Sesiua.

VPon this most lofty and cold mountaine there is nothing
almost to be found, but continuall snowe and woods.
The inhabitants weare white caps: and the region in all
places is full of springs and fountaines. Out of the said
mountaine springeth a riuer, which in the discourse before-
going we called Asifinuall. All ouer this mountaine are
most deepe and hollow caues, wherein euerie yeere, for the
three cold moneths of Nouember, Ianuarie, and Februarie
they vsually winter their cattell, laying vp so much fodder,
namely hay, and the leaues of certaine trees, as they thinke
will suffice them. Most of their victuals are brought vnto
them from the next mountaines, because their owne soyle
yeeldeth no corne at all: onely in the spring time and in
sommer, they haue good plentie of new cheese and butter.
Their old age they beare most lustily and stoutly, sometime at ninetie, and sometime at an hundred yeeres. They
giue attendance to their cattell all their life long, neither
doe they at any time, or seldome, see any strangers. They

weare no shooes at all, but certaine sandals only, to defend the soles of their feete: and their legs they wrap in a certaine piece of cloath or list insteed of an hose, to keepe themselues from the iniurie of the snow.[82]

Of the mountaine called Temnella.

THis high and cold mountaine hath verie many inhabitants: vpon the top whereof standeth a towne which is called by the name of the mountaine it selfe. In this towne are great store of dwellers, and a most stately and beautifull temple. It hath likewise a most pleasant and cleere riuer. This towne is adorned with the monuments of *Elmahdi* (who was in times past a most learned Mahumetan priest) and of *Abdul Mumen* his disciple. And albeit the inhabitants are accounted heretiques by all other Mahumetans, yet is there no kinde of learning which they will not arrogate vnto themselues: because perhaps they are well read in the workes of *Elmahdi*, who was notwithstanding the ringleader of all the saide heretiques: so that if any stranger come among them, they presently chalenge him to dispute in matters of learning. In their apparell they goe verie ragged and beggerly, by reason that they haue no taylors in the whole towne. Their common-wealth is gouerned after a wilde and sauage manner, albeit they haue a certaine priest, which vseth all the policie and meanes he can to bring it into good order. Their victuals are barley-bread and oyle of oliues: likewise they haue great store of nuts, and of pine-trees.[83]

*Or Elmaheli.

Of the mountaine called Gedmeua.

GEdmeua beginneth at the West frontier of the foresaide mountaine of Semede, and stretcheth Eastward almost fiue and twentie miles, extending vnto the border of Mizmizi. All the inhabitants are rude, miserable, and hunger-starued people, being subiect to the Arabians, for that they border vpon those fields which adioine vpon the mountaine of Teinnella. This hill of Gedmeua aboundeth with oliues, barley, wood, and fountaines.[84]

Of the mountaine called Hanteta.

NEuer did I see (to my remembrance) an higher mountaine, then that which the Africans call Hanteta. Westward it beginneth from Gedmeua, and stretcheth fiue and fortie miles Eastward, to the mountaine of Adimmei beforenamed. The inhabitants are valiant and rich, hauing great store of horses. Heere likewise standeth a most strong and impregnable castle subiect vnto a certaine nobleman, which is reported to be of alliance vnto the prince of Maroco: howbeit they are at continuall warre for certaine landes situate within their dominions. Many Iewes exercising diuers handie-crafts doe here inhabite, and do yeerely pay vnto the gouernour of this mountaine great summes of money. As concerning religion, they follow them especially which are called Carrain. The top of this mountaine is continually couered with snow. When I first beheld this mountaine, I thought it had bin clouds; so great is the height thereof. The sides of this mountaine being altogether destitute of herbes and trees, are in many places stored with excellent white marble, which the people might dig, and make a good commoditie thereof, were they not so sluggish and so ignorant in hewing and polishing of the same. In this place are many pillars and arches which were most artificially and sumptuously built by those mightie princes whom we have often before made mention of: which pillers they would haue vsed for the building of water-conduits, had they not beene hindred by the violence of warres. To be briefe, in the said mountaine I saw many

notable things, whereof I will here make no discourse at
all, partly because they are out of my remembrance, and
partly for auoiding tediousnes to the reader; because I
haue determined to passe ouer these small matters, and to
proceede vnto greater.⁸⁵

Of the mountaine called Adimmei.

FRom Hanteta beginneth another huge and high
mountaine called by the inhabitants Adimmei,
extending eastward to the riuer of Tescut. Vpon this
mountaine standeth that citie, the prince whereof (as we
said before) was slaine in battell against the king of Fez.
This mountaine is well stored with inhabitants and
aboundeth with woods which bring foorth acornes, oliues,
and quinces. The people heere inhabiting are most
valiant, possessing beasts and cattell of all sorts, their
ayre being verie temperate, and their soile exceeding
fruitfull. Springs they haue great plentie, and also two
riuers issuing foorth of the said mountaine, whereof in
due place we will discourse more at large. Wherefore
hauing described all the cities and mountaines of Maroco
bordering southward vpon Atlas, let vs now passe ouer
the said mountaine of Atlas, and take a view of the region
beyond it commonly called Guzzula.⁸⁶

*Of the region of Guzzula.*⁸⁷

THis region is exceeding populous: westward it
abutteth vpon Ilda a mountaine of Sus; northward
it ioineth vnto Atlas, and eastward it stretcheth vnto the
region of Hea.⁸⁸ It is inhabited with sauage and fierce
people, beeing most needie of money, and yet abounding
greatly in cattell.⁸⁹ Great store of copper and yron is here *Yron and co-*
digged out of mines, and here are brazen vessels made *per mines.*
which are carried into other countries to be solde: and these

vessels they exchange for linnen and woollen cloth, for horses, and for other wares necessarie for the said region. In all this whole region there is neither towne nor castle enuironed with walles. Great villages they haue, which contain, many of them, more then a thousand families a peece. They haue neither king nor gouernour to prescribe any lawes vnto them: but euerie one is his owne captaine and commander; whereupon they are at continuall warres among themselues, neither haue they any truce at all, but three daies onely euery weeke; during which time euery man may safely and freely bargaine with his enemie, and may trauell whither he listeth. But these daies of truce being past, the wretched people of this region do continually commit most horrible slaughters. The foresaide daies of truce a certaine Hermite appointed vnto them, whom they honoured and reuerenced like a god. This Hermite with one eie I my selfe saw, and found him to be a trustie, sincere, courteous, and most liberall person. The common attire of the people of Guzzula is a woollen iacket streight to their bodies & without sleeues. They weare crooked, broad, and two-edged daggers: and their swords are like vnto the swords of Hea. Once euery yeere they haue a faire of two moneths long: all which time (though the number of merchants be neuer so great) they giue free entertainment vnto all such as either bring wares with them, or come thither to fetch away their wares. When the time of their faire approcheth, they foorthwith make truce, and each faction appointeth a captaine ouer an hundred soldiers, to the end they may keepe themselues in safetie, and may defend their said faire from the inuasion and iniurie of all lewd persons. If any offence be committed, the captaines immediately giue sentence vpon the guiltie person: and whosoeuer bee conuicted of theft, is foorthwith slaine like a brute beast, and his theeues carcase is throwne out to be deuoured of dogs, wilde beastes, and

Continuall wars in Guzcula.

Free entertainment for merchants.

rauenous foules. The saide faire is kept in a certaine plaine or valley betweene two hils. All the wares are contained in tents and in certaine cottages made of boughes, so that each particular kind of merchandize hath a seuerall place to lie in by it selfe. They which sell droues of cattell are remooued farre from the tents. And euery tent hath a cottage made of boughes belonging thereunto, for their principal and head men to repose themselues in. And in the said cottages or bowers are merchant strangers (as we noted before) freely entertained and bourded. Also they haue certaine Caters & puruciers among them, which make prouision of victuals, and take vpon them the friendly and well entertaining of strangers. And albeit an huge deale of money is spent for this behalfe, yet make they a good gaine thereof: for thither doe resort all the merchants of that region for traffiques sake, yea and a great number out of the land of Negros, who bring with them maruellous plentie of all kindes of wares. And although they are men of a dull and grosse capacitie, yet are they very industrious in gouerning and maintaining the said faire: the beginning whereof is vpon the birth-day of that great deceiuer Mahumet,[90] that is, vpon the twelfth day of their moneth called Rabih, which is the third *Haraba* of the yeere, according to their account. I my selfe was present at this faire in the companie of my Lord the Scriffo for the space of fifteene daies, in the yeere of the Hegeira 920. which was in the yeere of our Lord 1511.[91]

A briefe description of the region of Duccala.

THis region beginneth westward from the riuer of Tensift; northward it is bounded with the Ocean sea; the south part thereof lieth vpon the riuer of Habid; and the east part abutteth vpon the riuer Ommirabih. It is three daies iourney long, and about two daies iourney broad. Very populous it is; the inhabitants being a rude people, and most ignorant of all ciuilitie and humanitie. Walled cities it hath but a few, of all which we will in their due places particularly discourse, neither wil we (by Gods helpe) omit any thing which may seeme woorthie of memorie.[92]

Of the towne of Azaphi.[93]

IT was built by the Africans, and standeth vpon the shore of the Ocean sea, containing fower thousand families: inhabitants there are great store, being for the most part very vnciuill and barbarous. In times past there dwelt many Iewes in this towne, which exercised diuers handy-crafts. Their soile is exceeding fertill; but so grosse is their owne vnskilfulnes and negligence, that they know neither how to till their ground, to sow their corne, or to plant vineyards: except perhaps some few of them (who would seeme to be more prouident then the residue) sow a quantitie of pot-herbes in their smal gardens. After the kings of Maroco gaue ouer the gouerment of the saide region, the citie of Azafi was vsurped by certaine which were said to fetch their originall from Farchon.[94] Howbeit in our daies the said citie was gouerned by a certaine prince called Hebdurrahmam: this man for a greedy and ambitious desire of raigning murthered his owne vncle: after whose death he gouerned the towne for certaine yeeres.[95] He had a daughter of most excellent beauty, who falling in loue with a certaine courtier (whose name was *Hali*, being sonne vnto one *Goesimen*)[96] by the helpe of her mother and her wayting maide enioyed oftentimes the companie of her paramour. Which when her father had intelligence of, hee rebuked his wife, threatening death vnto her, if shee reformed not the manners of her daughter: howbeit afterwarde hee dissembled his furie. But the mother thoroughly knowing her husbandes intent, tolde her daughters paramour that the prince was not to bee trusted, and therefore aduised him to take heede vnto himselfe. Whereupon *Hali* fearing least some mischiefe might light vpon him, began to determine with himselfe the princes death, and for his associate in this conspiracie he tooke a trusty friend of his who had been most familiar with him from his childhoode, and was captaine ouer a certaine band of footemen.⁹⁷ Wherefore both of them being alike mischieuously bent against their prince, expected nothing else but a fit place and oportunitie to put their bloudie determination in practise. Contrariwise the king seeking by all meanes an occasion to effect his purpose, sent word vnto *Hali* vpon a certaine festiuall day, that after their Mahumetan deuotions were finished he shoulde come and walke with him; appointing a place, where he had laide a troupe of men in ambush to kill *Hali* at his comming: which being done, he went to church. *Hali* suspecting no harme at all, told his associate, that now was the time wherein they might bring their purpose to effect. And this intent of theirs they foorthwith declared vnto ten other of their adherents: and to the end that the whole matter might go securely and certainly forward, they presently assembled a great multitude of footemen (which they fained that they woulde sende the next day vnto Azamor) that, if they were constrained to flie, they might haue aide and succour in a readines. All their complices being armed, they came to church at the very same time when as the king with all his traine was entring thereinto, and had placed himselfe next vnto the Mahumetan preacher. The church was full of auditors, and the king had his guard attending vpon him, who bicause they knew the two foresaid yoong gentlemen to be very familiar with the king, suspected none euill, but suffered them to draw neere vnto his person. Wherefore one of the saide yoong courtiers, as though he would haue done obeizance vnto the king, came before him, but *Hali* got in at his backe and stabd

The occasion of the prince of Azafi his death.

The prince of Azafi slaine, as he was hearing of a Mahumetan sermon. him through with a dagger: and at the verie same instant the other thrust him in with his sworde, and so this vnhappy king, imbrued in his owne bloud, gaue vp the ghost. The kings guarde went about to apprehend the authors of this fact; but being ouermatched by the contrarie part, and suspecting, least the people were authors of this conspiracie, they sought to saue themselues by flight. And after them followed all the rest of the assemblie, till the authors of the saide murther were left alone. They also immediately came foorth, and perswaded the people with many words, that they had slaine the king for none other cause, but onely in regard that he had attempted the vtter ouerthrow both of themselues and of the whole people. The citizens beeing to too credulous, aduaunced the two foresaid conspiratours to the gouernment of the kingdome; howbeit they agreed not long thereabout, but the common-wealth was diuersly tossed hither and thither, sometime inclining to one, & sometime to another. Wherefore the Portugall merchants which vsually frequented that citie in great numbers, wrote vnto their king to sende foorthwith an armie of soldiers thither: for they were in good hope, that he shoulde most easily and with small disaduantage winne the saide citie. Howbeit the king being nothing mooued with this message of theirs, would not send any forces at al, til he was more certainly informed by his said merchants touching the death of the king of Azaphi, & the dissension betweene the two new gouernours. As also, that they had made such a compact with a certaine captaine of the contrary faction, that it was the easiest matter in the world for him to cõquer the towne. For they had built them a verie strong castell vpon the sea-shore, wherein their merchandize might safely be bestowed. For the Portugals had perswaded the townes-men, that during the great tumult about the kings death, they were all of them in danger to lose both their liues and goods. Wherefore into this castell, among their vessels of oile and other wares, they cunningly conueied gunnes and all other kind of warlike instruments: but the townes-men being ignorant heereof, exacted nothing of the Portugals saue onely custome due for their wares. Now after the Portugales had sufficiently prouided themselues of all other kinde of armour and warlike munitions, they sought by all meanes an occasion to fight with the citizens. At length it came to passe that a certaine Portugals seruant buying meat in the citie, did so prouoke a butcher, that after much quarrelling they fell to blowes, whereupon the seruant feeling himselfe hurt, thrust the butcher with his sworde, and laide him along vpon the colde earth, and then fledde speedily to the castell, wherein he knewe the merchants to be. The people immediately rose vp in armes, and ranne all of them with one consent vnto the castell, to the end they might vtterly destroy it, & cut the throats of all them which were therein. But the guns and crossebowes which were there in a readines made such hauock among the townes men, that it cannot be, but they were greatly daunted. At this first encounter there were an hūdreth and fiftie citizens slaine outright; howbeit the residue woulde not therefore giue ouer, but gaue the castle daily assaults. At length the king of Portugall sent aide vnto his subiects, to wit fiue thousand footemen, two hundreth horsemen, with a great number of gunnes. Which forces when the citizens sawe to approch, they presently betooke themselues to their feete, and fled vnto the mountaine Benimegher: neither durst any man staie in the towne but onely he that was the author of building the castle. And so it came to passe that the Portugall forces woon the towne without any perill or labour. Soone after the generall of the whole armie sent the builder of the castle vnto the king of Portugall. But the king sent him with a

Azafi woon by the Portugals.

certaine number of attendants backe againe to Azafi, and appointed him gouernour of all the region adiacent. For the Portugall king was not acquainted with their customes, nether did he sufficiently know how they gouerned their common-wealth.[98] Soone after ensued the miserable desolation and ruine, not onely of the citie but of the whole region thereabouts. In this discourse we haue beene somewhat tedious, to the end we might shew of how great euill a woman may be the instrument, and what intollerable mischiefes are bred by dissension. These things were a dooing (as I remember) when my selfe was but ten yeeres olde :[99] and being fowerteene yeeres of age, I had some conference with the Portugall captaine aforesaide. This captaine with an armie of fiue hundreth Portugals, and more then twelue thousand Arabian horsemen giuing battaile to the king of Maroco, conquered all the foresaid prouince on the behalfe of his master the Portugall king, in the yeere of the Hegeira 920. as in our briefe treatise concerning the Mahumetan religion we will declare more at large.

John Leo ten yeeres old at the winning of Azafi.

Of Conta a towne in Duccala.

This towne is situate from Azafi about 20. miles, & is said to haue bin built by the Gothes at the verie same time when they possessed the whole region of Duccala: but now it is vtterly layde waste: howbeit the field belonging thereto is in subiection vnto certaine Arabians which dwell in the said prouince of Duccala.[100]

Of Tit a citie in Duccala.

This ancient citie of Tit built of olde by the Africans vpon the Ocean sea-shoare, is about twentie miles distant from Azamur. It hath most large and fruitfull fields belonging vnto it. The inhabitants are men of a grosse conceit, who regard neither husbandrie nor ciuilitie.

Their apparell indeed is somewhat decent, by reason that they continually haue so great traffique with the Portugals. At the same time when Azamur was subdued, this citie also yeelded it selfe vnto the kings captaine, and for certaine yeeres paied tribute vnto the king. *The citie of Tit tributarie vnto the King of Portugall.* In our time the king of Fez attempted to set Duccala at libertie : howbeit not speeding of his purpose, he caused a certaine Christian (which was his owne treasurer) and a Iewe, to be hanged. And that companie which remained with him, he brought vnto Fez, giuing them a certaine portion of grounde to dwell vpon, which was destitute of inhabitants being distant about twelue miles from Fez.[101]

Of the famous citie of Elmedina in Duccala.

ELmedina being in a manner the chiefe citie of the whole region, is (according to the manner there) enuironed with wals of no great force. The inhabitants are homely as well in witte and behauiour, as in apparell : wearing such cloth as is wouen in their owne countrie. Their women weare certaine siluer ornaments : the men are valiant, and haue great store of horses. They were all of them banished by the king of Fez out of his dominions, for that he suspected them to be friends to the Portugals. For he had heard that a certaine gouernour of that region had counselled his subjects to pay tribute vnto the Portugall king. This gouernour I sawe barfoote led so miserablie captiue that I could scarce refraine from teares ; because he did not ought vpon trecherie, but being constrained. For, good man, he thought it much better to pay a little tribute vnto the Portugals, then sodainly to lose both his life and his goods. For the restoring of whom vnto his former libertie, diuers noblemen greatly laboured : and so at length for a great summe of money he was released. But afterward the citie remained voide of inhabitants, about the yeere of the Hegeira 921.[102] *Elmedina left desolate.*

Of the towne of Duccala called Centum putei.

Corne preserued 100. yeers.

THis towne is built vpon a rocke of excellent marble: in the suburbes whereof are certaine caues, wherein the inhabitants vse to lay vp their corne: which is there so woonderfully preserued, that it will continue an hundreth yeeres without any ill fauour or corruption. Of the number of which caues resembling pits or wels, the towne it selfe is called Centum putei. The inhabitants are of small reckoning or account, hauing no artificers dwelling among them but certaine Iewes. When the king of Fez had forced the inhabitants of Elmadin to come into his dominions, he attempted also to bring thither the inhabitants of this towne: but they refusing to go into a strange place, chose rather to inhabite neere vnto the towne of Azafi, then to forsake their owne natiue soile. Which when the king vnderstoode, he presently caused the towne to be sacked; wherein nothing was found but corne, hony, and other things of small value.[103]

Of the towne of Subeit in the same region.

SVbeit is a small towne built vpon the south side of the riuer of Ommirabih. It is distant from Elmadin about fortie miles, and is said to be subiect vnto certaine Arabians dwelling in Duccala. Honie and corne they haue great abundance: but such is their vnskilfulnes and ignorance, that they haue neither gardens nor vineyardes. At the same time when Bulahuan was woon, the king of Fez brought all the people of Subeit into his dominion, and allotted vnto them a certaine peece of grounde neere vnto Fez which was neuer before inhabited: so that Subeit remained waste and void of inhabitants euen vntill this day.[104]

Of the towne of Temeracost.

ALso in Duccala neere vnto the riuer Ommirabih standeth a certaine small towne, which was built by the founder of Maroco, from whom the name thereof is thought to be deriued. Inhabitants it hath great store, and containeth more than fower hundreth families. It was subiect in times past vnto the people of Azamur; but Azamur being spoiled by the Portugales, this towne also came to nought, and the people heerof went to Elmadin.[105]

Of the towne called Terga.

THis towne being distant about thirtie miles from Azamur, is situate neere vnto the riuer Ommirabih: it is well peopled, and containeth about three hundreth families. In times past it was subiect vnto the inhabitants of Duccala; but after the sacking of Azafi, *Hali* which fought against the Portugals, for certaine daies lay with his armie in this towne. But afterward being repelled thence by the king of Fez, the towne became so waste and desolate, that from thenceefoorth it was an habitation for owles & bats.[106]

Of the towne of Bulahuan.

THis towne likewise standeth vpon the banke of Ommirabih, & containeth about fiue hundreth families: in times past it had most noble and woorthie inhabitants, especially in that streete which lieth next vnto the riuer, upon the high way to Maroco. In this towne was a famous hospitall built, which had manie roomes and mansions: wherein all strangers trauailing that way, were sumptuously and freely entertained at the common charge of the towne. The inhabitants are most rich both in cattell & corne. Euery citizen almost hath an 100. yoke of oxen, and some of them yeerly reape two thousand, some three thousand measures of corne: so that the Arabians do carrie graine from thence sufficient to serue them all the yeere following. In the 919. yeere of the Hegeira, the king of Fez sent his brother to gouerne and defende the region of Duccala, who comming vnto this towne, was informed that the captaine of Azemur approched thither with a great armie, of purpose to destroy the towne and to lead the people captiue. Whereupon the king of Fez his brother sent immediately vnto the saide towne two captaines with two thousand horsemen, and eight hundreth archers. But at the very same time when they entred the towne, they met there the Portugall soldiers accompanied with two thousand Arabians : by whom, being fewer in number, they were so miserablie slaine, that scarcely twelue archers of all the eight hundreth could escape with the horsemen vnto the next mountaines. Howbeit afterward the Arabians renewed the skirmish, & 150. of the Portugall horsemen being slaine, they put the enimie to flight. Whereupon the king of Fez his brother passed on to Duccala, requiring tribute of the people, and promising that as long as he liued he would stand betweene them and their enemies. Afterward being vanquished, he returned home to Fez vnto the king his brother. But the inhabitants seeing that the kings brother had receiued tribute of them and had stood them in no stead, they presently forsooke the towne, and fled vnto the mountaine of Tedles : for they feared least the Portugals armie would come vpon them, and exacting a greater summe, would lead them presently captiue which could not disburse it. At all these accidents I my selfe was present, and saw the foresaid slaughter of the archers: for I stood about a mile distant from them, and was mounted vpon a swift courser. At the same time I was trauelling to Maroco, being sent by the king of Fez, to declare vnto the king of Maroco, and vnto the Seriffo, that the king of Fez his brother was presently to depart vnto

Duccala : for which cause they were requested to prouide soldiers for the better resistance of the Portugals armie.[107]

Of the citie of Azamur.

Zamur, a towne of Duccala, was built by the Africans vpon that part of the Oceā sea shore where the riuer of *Ommirabih disemboqueth ; being distant from Elmadina southward about thirtie miles.[108] Very large it is, and well inhabited, and containeth to the number of fiue thousand families.[109] Here doe the Portugall merchants continually reside. The inhabitants are very ciuill, and decently apparelled. And albeit they are diuided into two parts, yet haue they continuall peace among themselues. Pulse and corne they haue great plentie; though their gardens and orchards bring foorth nought else but figs. They haue such plentie of fishes, that they receiue yeerely for them sometime sixe thousand, and sometime seuen thousand duckats. And their time of fishing dureth from October to the end of Aprill. They vse to frie fishes in a certaine pan with oile, whereby they gather an incredible quantitie of trane: neither vse they any other oile to put into their lampes. Once a yeere the Portugals make a voiage hither, and doe carrie away so great abundance of fish, that they onely doe disburse the summe of duckats aforesaid. Hence it is, that the king of Portugal, being allured for gaine, hath often sent most warlike fleetes to surprise this towne : the first whereof, in regarde of the Generals indiscretion, was the greatest part dispersed and sunke vpon the sea.[110] Afterward the king sent another nauie of two hundred saile well furnished, at the very sight whereof the citizens were so discomfited, that they all betooke themselues to flight ; and the throng was so great at their entrance of the gates, that moe then fower-

* *Or Marbea.*

score citizens were slaine therein. Yea a certaine prince which came to aide them, was, for his safetie constrained to let himselfe downe by a rope on the farther side of the citie. The inhabitants were presently dispersed hither and thither; some fleeing on horse-backe, and others on foote. Neither could you (I know) haue refrained from teares, had you seene the weake women, the silly old men, and the tender children run away bare-footed and forlorne.[111] But before the Christians gaue any assault, the Iewes (which shortly after compounded with the king of Portugall, to yeeld the citie to him, on condition that they shoulde sustaine no iniurie) with a generall consent, opened the gates vnto them:[112] and so the Christians obtained the citie, and the people went to dwell part of them to Sala, and part to Fez. Neither doe I thinke that God for any other cause brought this calamitie vpon them, but onely for the horrible vice of Sodomie, whereunto the greatest part of the citizens were so notoriously addicted, that they could scarce see any young stripling, who escaped their lust.

Azamur woon by the Portugals.

Of the towne called Meramei.

THis towne was built by the Gothes vpon a plaine, almost fourteene miles distant from Azafi, and it containeth to the number of fower hundred families: the soile thereabout aboundeth greatly with oliues and corne. It was gouerned in times past by the prince of Azafi; but afterward being surprised by the Portugals, and the inhabitants being all put to flight, it remained well nigh one whole yeere destitute of people. Howbeit soone after making a league with the Portugals, each man retired vnto his owne home. And now I thinke it not amisse to report as concerning the mountaines of Duccala those things which may seeme woorthie of memorie.[113]

Of the mountaine called Benimegher.

BEnimegher is distant from Azafi about twelue miles, containing diuers artizans of all sortes, euery one of which hath an house at Azafi. This mountaine is so exceeding fruitful for oile and corne, that a man would scarce beleeue it. It was once in subiection vnto the prince of Azafi, but the inhabitants of Azafi being put to flight, as hath beene aforesaid, had no other place for their refuge, but onely this mountaine of Benimegher. Afterward they paid tribute for certaine yeeres vnto the Portugals; but when the king of Fez came thither with his army, he caried with him part of them vnto Fez, and the residue returned to Azafi : for they were determined rather to indure any iniurie, then to submit themselues to the Christians gouernment.[114]

Of the greene mountaine.

THis mountaine is of an exceeding height, beginning eastward from the riuer of Ommirabih, and extending westward to the hils called in their language Hafara, and it diuideth Duccala from some part of Tedles.[115] Likewise this mountaine is very rough and full of woods, affoording great store of acornes and pine-apples, and a certaine kinde of red fruit which the Italians commonly call Africano. Many Hermites also doe inhabite vpon this mountaine, liuing with no other kind of victuals, but such as the woods yeeld vnto them. For they are aboue fiue and twenty miles distant from all townes and cities. Here are great store of fountaines and of altars built after the Mahumetan fashion, and many auncient houses also erected by the Africans. At the foot of this mountaine there is a notable lake, very like vnto the lake of Bolsena in the Roman territorie. In which lake are found infinite numbers of fishes, as namely eeles, pickrels, and of diuers

The fruit called by the Italians Frutto Africano.

other sorts, which, to my remembrance, I neuer saw in Italie: but there is no man that goeth about to take any fish in this lake, no maruell therefore though the number be so great. Vpon a certaine time when Mahumet the king of Fez trauelled that way towards the kingdome of Maroco, he encamped his armie eight days vpon the side of this lake. Some of his companie he licenced to fish the same, amongst whom I saw certaine that tooke of their shirts and coats, sowing vp their sleeues and collars, and putting certaine hoops within them to keepe them from closing together, and so vsed them in stead of nets, wherewith notwithstanding they caught many thousand fishes: but others which had nets indeed, got more then they. And all by reason that the fishes (as we will now declare) were perforce driuen into the nets. For king Mahumet being there accompanied with fourteene thousand Arabian horsemen, which brought a great many more camels with them; and hauing fiue thousand horsemen vnder the conduct of his brother, with an huge armie of footemen, caused them all at once to enter the lake, insomuch that there was scarce water ynough to satisfie the camels thirst: wherefore it was no maruell though the fishes came so fast into the nets. Vpon the banks of this lake are many trees bearing leaues like vnto pine-leaues, among the boughes whereof, such abundance of turtles doe nestle, that the inhabitants reape woonderfull commoditie by them. Mahumet hauing refreshed himselfe eight daies by the foresaid lake, was then desirous to view The greene mountaine aforesaid: my selfe with a great number of courtiers and learned men attending vpon him. So often as he saw any altar, he would command his armie there to make a stand, and lowly kneeling on his knees, would say these words following: " Thou knowest (oh Lord my God) that "I came hither for none other cause, but to release the " people of Duccala from the Arabians and cruell Christians:

Great plentie of fish.

"which attempt of mine if thou thinkest to be vniust, let
"me onely feele the punishment of this offence: for these
"my followers are guiltlesse." And thus we ranged vp and
downe the greene hill one whole day: but at night we
returned vnto our tents.[116] The next day it was king
Mahumets pleasure to go on hunting and hauking, whereupon his hounds and haukes (which he had in great
abundance) were brought foorth: howbeit that sport
yeelded nought but wilde geese, duckes, turtle-doues, and
other fowles. But the day following the king called for his
hounds, faulcons, and eagles: their game were hares, deere,
porcupikes, roe-deere, woolues, quailes and starlings: and
by reason that none had hunted or hawked there an
hundred yeeres before, they had very good pastime. And
after we had here staied certaine daies, the king with his
armie marching vnto the said Elmadin a towne of Duccala,
willed all his learned men and priestes which hee had
brought with him, to returne vnto Fez. But my selfe (as *John Leo sent ambassadour from the King of Fez vnto Maroco.*)
ambassadour) and a certaine number of soldiers he sent
vnto Maroco: this was done in the 922. yeere of the
Hegeira, and in the yeere of our Lord 1512.[117]

A description of the region of Hascora.

THis region is bounded northward with certaine mountaines which adioine vpon Duccala; westward with
a riuer running by the foote of mount Hadimmei, which
we called before Tensift; and eastward by the riuer
Quadelhabid, that is, the riuer of seruants, which riuer
diuideth Hascora from Tedles. And so likewise the hils of
Duccala doe separate Hascora from the Ocean sea.[118] The
inhabitants of this region are far more ciuil, then the people
of Duccala. This prouince yeeldeth great abundance of
oyle, of Marockin skinnes, and of goates, of whose haire
they make cloath and sadles. And hither do all the
bordering regions bring their goat-skins, whereof the

foresaid Marockin or Cordouan leather is made. This
people hath great traffique with the Portugals, with whom
they exchange the foresaid leather and sadles, for cloath.
Their coine is all one with the coine of Duccala. Also the
Arabians vsually buy oyle and other necessaries out of this
region. Now let vs in order describe all the townes and
cities of the said region.

Of Elmadin a towne in Hascora.

THis towne of Hascora being called by the inhabitants
Elmadin,[110] is built vpon the side of mount Atlas,
and containeth moe than two thousand families. It
standeth almost fourescore and ten miles eastward of
Maroco, and about 60. miles from Duccala. Heere may
you finde many leather-dressers, and all other kinde of
artizans, with a great multitude of Iewish merchants.
This towne is enuironed with a certaine wood, which is full
of oliue, and walnut-trees. The inhabitants are continually,
in a manner, oppressed with warres among themselues, and
against a certaine little towne beeing fower miles distant
from thence. Neither dare any come vpon the plaine
lying betweene these two townes, (saue women onely and
slaues) except he be well and strongly guarded. So that
euerie man is faine to maintaine an harquebusier or archer
for his defence, whom he monethly alloweth ten or twelue
pieces of gold, which are woorth sixteene ducates Italian.
Likewise in Elmadin there are certaine men of great and
profound learning, which are appointed to be iudges and
notaries. Whatsoeuer tribute or custome strangers doe
pay, is deliuered vnto certaine treasurers and customers of
the towne; which imploy it afterward for the publike
benefite. They are likewise constrained to pay certaine
tribute vnto the Arabians, for sundrie possessions which
they enioy in the foresaide valley; but that money gaineth
them at the Arabians hand ten times so much, or more.

In my returne from Maroco I thought good to trauell by
this towne, where I was right sumptuously entertained by
one of Granada my countrey-man, who was exceeding rich,
hauing serued as an archer in this region for fifteene yeeres.
And albeit the towne of Elmadin had a stately hospitall,
wherein all merchants trauelling that way, were entertained
at the common charge : yet my countrey-man would not
suffer vs there to lodge, but for three daies together most
curteously welcommed my selfe, nine courtiers, and all the
seruants and retinue which we brought with vs : vnto which
companie of ours the townesmen presented, some of them
calues, some lambes, and some other brought hens. Seeing
vpon a time so many goates in the towne, I merily
demaunded of my countrey-man, why he gaue vs no kids-
flesh to eate : hee answered that that was accounted among
them of all others the most base and homely meate. Their
faire and beautifull women are so fonde of strangers that
if secret occasion be offered they will not refuse their
dishonest companie.

Of the citie of Alemdin.

NEere vnto the foresaide towne standeth another
commonly called Alemdin,[120] being situate fower
miles to the west thereof in a valley, amidst fower most high
hils, whereupon the place is exceeding cold. The inhabitants are merchants, artizans, and gentlemen, & families it
containeth to the number of one thousand. This towne
hath been at continuall war with the towne last before
mentioned : but in our time both of them were by the
meanes of a certaine merchant brought in subiection vnto
the King of Fez, as we will now declare. There was a *By what means*
merchant of Fez which had a paramour in this towne, *the townes of Elmadin and*
whom he determined foorthwith to marrie ; but when the *Alemdin be-came subiect*
marriage day was come, this merchant was beguiled of his *vnto the King of Fez.*
loue by the gouernour of the towne himselfe, which

disappointment grieued him full sore, albeit he dissembled the matter as well as he could. Returning home to the King of Fez, the said merchant presented vnto him most rich and costly gifts, making humble suite vnto his maiestie that hee would allow him an hundred principall archers, three hundred horsemen, and fower hundred footemen; saying, that himselfe would maintaine them all at his owne costs and charges, and would winne the said towne of Alemdin for the Kings behalfe, and would assure the King seuen thousand ducates for yeerely tribute. This offer pleased the King right well, and that he might declare his princely liberalitie, he would not suffer the merchant to giue wages vnto any, but onely to the archers. And so with all expedition he commanded his gouernour of Tedles to prouide the saide merchant so many horsemen and so many footmen, and two captaines ouer the armie. At length comming before Alemdin they besieged it sixe daies: which being expired, the townesmen told their gouernour in plaine terms, that they would not for his cause incur the king of Fez his displeasure, nor suffer any inconuenience. Whereupon he putting himselfe in a beggers weede, attempted to escape away : but being knowen and apprehended, he was brought before the merchant, who committed him to prison. And so the townesmen presently opening their gates receiued the merchant with all his troops, & yeelded themselues to him & to the king of Fez. The parents of the foresaid maid protested vnto the merchant, that the gouernour by maine force had depriued them of his paramour. Howbeit she herselfe was big with childe by the gouernour ; but after the merchant knew that she was deliuered of her childe, he bore her affection againe, and at length married her. And the wretched gouernour was the same day by the iudges pronounced guiltie of fornication, and was stoned to death. Well, the merchant remained gouernour and Lord of both townes, establishing most firme peace betweeen them, & duely paying vnto the king of Fez all the yeerly tribute which he had promised. I my selfe afterward comming to the foresaide towne grew familiarly acquainted with this famous merchant. The same yeere departing from Fez I tooke my iourney towards Constantinople.

Of Tagodast a towne in Hascora.

THis towne is built vpon the top of a certaine high mountaine, hauing fower other high mountaines round about it. Betweene which fower mountaines and the said towne are diuers most large and beautifull gardens replenished with all kinde of fruits: quinces here are of an incredible bignes. Their vines dispersing themselues vpon the boughes of trees doe make most pleasant bowers and walkes: the grapes whereof being red, are for their bignes, called in the language of that people, hennes egs. *Grapes of maruellous bignes.* They haue here great abundance of oile and most excellent honie; some of their honie being white, and some *White honey.* yellow. This towne hath many fountaines about it, which ioyning into one streame, do serue for many water-mils thereabouts. Here are likewise great store of artizans, who exercise themselues onely about things necessarie. The inhabitants are somewhat ciuill, their women are most beautifull, being most gorgeously decked with siluer iewels. Their oile they carrie vnto the next cities southward of them on this side Atlas : but they send their leather vnto Fez and Mecnasa. Their plaine is almost sixe miles long : the soile being most fruitfull for corne : in regard whereof the townes-men pay certaine yeerely tribute vnto the Arabians. This towne hath iudges, priests, and a great number of gentlemen. Vpon a time as I trauelled this way, it was my hap to meete with a certaine ancient gouernour of the same place, who was growne blinde with extreme age. This aged sire (as by some I understood) was in his youth a most valiant and stout person, insomuch that after many other noble exploits, he slew with his owne hand fower captaines which were most deadly enemies vnto the people of Tagodast. And afterward he handled the matter so wisely, that he ioyned those in perfect league which before time had waged continual warre. Here no commonwealth-matter is concluded by the magistrates of the towne without his speciall aduice and authoritie. By this worthie Senatour my selfe with fower-score horsemen were honorably entertained, and had dainty meates euery day set before vs, of game which was newly hunted. He recounted most familiarly vnto vs all his labours which he had bestowed in concluding of the foresaid league: neither had this good man any so entire and hidden secrets, which he reuealed not vnto vs, as to his louing friends. At my departure I offered him money for my selfe and my companie: but he, like a liberall man, would by no meanes accept of it; saying, that albeit he ought the king of Fez much dutie and good will, yet did he not bestowe that liberaltie for his sake: but that whatsoeuer wealth he enioied, his parents bequeathed vnto him vpon this condition, that he should shew himselfe kinde and bountifull vnto all his kinred, acquaintance, and strangers trauelling that way: and although he were free from that condition, yet his loue towards God, and the liberaltie which God had planted in him, could require no less at his hands. Yea, he said, that by Gods good blessing and prouidence he had reaped the same yeere seuen thousand bushels of corne; insomuch, that himselfe and all his neighbours were prouided for in abundance. Moreouer, that he possessed of sheepe and goates moe then an hundred thousand, the wooll whereof only, and some small portion of butter, he reserued for himself, but as for the cheese and milke, he gaue it all frankly vnto his shepherds. In this towne there is none that selleth either cheese, butter, milk, or any other such commoditie, though each one hath great abundance of cattell. Howbeit their hides, oile, and wooll they vtter in the prouinces thereabout. The reuerend sire added this moreouer : If it shall please (saith he) the king of Fez to returne home from Duccala through this my region, I will come foorth to meete him, and will submit my selfe wholly vnto him, as vnto my most liege soueraigne prince. Thus my selfe a meere stranger being so honorably dismissed by this woorthie Senatour, could not sufficiently commend his courtesie and bounteous dealing towards strangers.[121]

Of the citie of Elgiumuha.

NEere vnto the foresaid towne, within fiue miles, standeth Elgiumuha.[122] It was in our time built vpon the top of an high mountaine, and containeth to the number of fiue hundred families, besides so many families comprised in the villages of that mountaine. Here are innumerable springs and fountaines, and most pleasant and fruitfull gardens in all places. Here are likewise walnut-trees huge and tall. The little hils enuironing this mountaine doe yeeld barlie and oliues in great abundance. In the said towne are great numbers of artizans, as smithes, leather-dressers, and such like. And because they haue here notable yron-mines, they make plentie of horseshooes. And whatsoeuer commoditie proceedeth of their labour, they carrie it to forren regions where they thinke it is wanting : from whence they bring home slaues, woad, and the skins of certaine beastes, whereof they make most defensiue and warlike shields : these shields they transport vnto Fez, exchanging them there for weapons, cloth, and other such things as they stand in neede of. This towne standeth so neere vnto the high way, that the boyes will stand gazing and woondering at merchants as they come by, especially if they weare any strange attire. The residue of inhabitants vpon this mountaine are all commanded and gouerned by them of the towne. They say that the people of Tagodast aforesaid were the first founders of this towne: for so vpon a time it befell, that whereas the principall men of Tagodast grew to dissension among themselues, the common sort fauouring neither faction, built Elgiumuha, and left Tagodast to be inhabited by their gouernours: hence it is, that euen at this day they are here onely ignoble and base people, whereas there they are all gentlemen.

Of Bzo a towne in Hascora.

THE ancient towne of Bzo is built vpon an high hill about twenty miles westward from the towne last mentioned. Within three miles of Bzo runneth the foresaid riuer of Guadelhabid. The townesmen are honest people, exercising merchandize, and going decently apparelled: To them which inhabite the deserts they carie cloth, oile, and leather. Their mountaines abound with oliues, corne, and all kinde of fruits: and of their grapes they make euery yeere most excellent and sweete raisins. Figs they haue great plentie: and their walnut-trees are so high, that a puttocke may securely builde his nest vpon the tops: for it is impossible for any man to climbe vp. On each side of the way which leadeth from hence to the riuer Guadelhabid there are most pleasant and beautifull gardens. My selfe (I remember) was here present when their oranges, figs, and other fruits were growen to ripenes; and was entertained by a certaine priest, who dwelt not farre from a stately Mahumetan temple, standing by that riuer which runneth through the market-place of the towne.[123]

Of the mountaine called Tenuenes.

THis mountaine is situate ouer against Hascora vpon that part of Atlas which trendeth southward.[124] It hath many most valiant and warlike inhabitants both horsemen and footemen; and a great number of horses of small stature. It yeeldeth abundance of woad and barlie: but other graine they haue none at all, so that they haue no other but barlie bread to eate. At all times of the yeere you shal here see plenty of snow. Here are likewise sundry noblemē & gentlemen, all which are subiect vnto one prince. To this prince they pay great yeerely tribute for the maintenance of his soldiers, for he wageth continuall war with the inhabitants of mount Tensita. The said prince hath welnigh 1000. most valiant horsemen alwaies in a readines: & so many likewise do the noblemen of this mountaine continually keepe at their owne costs and charges. Moreouer the prince hath an hundreth soldiers part of them bowmen, and part harquebusiers, to guard and attend vpon his person in all places. Comming my selfe to see this mountaine, it was my chaunce to finde out the saide prince, who was desirous exceedingly to be praised of all men: but for liberalitie, curtesie, and ciuilitie, his like I thinke was not to be founde. Vnto the Arabian toong (albeit he were ignorant thereof) he bore a maruelious affection: and was greatly delighted to heare any man expound a sentence or verse, which was penned to his own commendation. At the very same time when mine vncle was sent ambassadour from the king of Fez to the king of Tombuto, I my selfe also trauailed in his company: we were no sooner entred the region of Dara (which is an hundreth miles distant from the saide princes dominions) but he hearing of my vncles fame (who was an excellent Oratour, and a most wittie Poet) sent letters vnto the prince of Dara, requesting him that he woulde perswade

The vncle of Iohn Leo sent ambassadour to the king of Tombuto.

mine vncle to trauaile vnto Tombuto by mount Tenueues: for he had a great desire to see him, & to speake with him. Howbeit my vncle answered, that it beseemed not a kings ambassadour to visite any princes farre out of his way, and so to deferre his masters waightie affaires. But, to the end that he might in some sort satisfie the saide prince, he promised to sende me his nephew vnto him, which might in his name salute him and do him due honour. Afterward he deliuered me certaine costlie gifts to present the prince withall: as namely a curious paire of stirrups double gilt and finely wrought in the Morisco fashion, which cost (as I remember) fiue and twentie ducates; and a rich paire of spurs of fifteene ducates price. Moreouer he sent two bands of silke artificially entwined with gold, one whereof was tawnie, and the other blew. He sent also a most excellent booke, containing the liues of certaine famous and deuout men of Africa, togither with certaine verses in the commendation of the prince himselfe. Thus being furnished with the things aforesaid, I set foorth on my iourney, taking two horsemen to accompanie me vnto the foresaid mountaine: and so as I road, I inuented verses in the princes praise. At our first arriuall there, the prince with a great traine of his nobilitie was ridden foorth on hunting. Who being enformed of my comming, caused me foorthwith to be sent for, and after salutations had, he asked me how my vncle did: I answered that he was in good health, and at his highnes disposition. Then he commanded me to be carried vnto a stately lodging, where, after my tedious journey, I might repose my selfe, till he were returned from hunting. And so within night returning from his game, he sent for me immediately to come into his chamber of presence: where, hauing first performed due obeisance vnto him, I presented him with mine vncles gifts: which (as I suppose) were most acceptable vnto him. At length I gaue him the

verses which mine vncle had indited: which he presently
commanded one of his secretaries to read. And as he was
expounding each sentence and worde vnto the prince, it was
a woonder to see, what exceeding alacritie and ioy appeered
in his countenaunce. The verses being read, he sate downe
to supper, willing me not onely to be his guest, but also to
sit next vnto his person. His table was furnished with
mutton, veale rosted and sodden, and with bread baked
like a cake. Diuers other dishes likewise were serued in,
but I remember not all the particulars. Supper being
ended, I greeted the prince in this wise: Your highnes (my
lord) hath receiued all those gifts, which your humble
seruant mine vncle (in token of his loiall disposition, and
that he might be had of your highnes in remembrance)
hath sent you: Now I being both his sisters sonne and his
scholler, haue nought else but a fewe wordes to present
your princelines withall: may it please you therefore to
accept of such homely stuffe as my witte could sodainly *The excellent*
affoord in the time of my iourney. These words ended, I *wit & toward-*
began to read my verses vnto him: and being as then but *linesse of Iohn*
sixteene yeeres of age, the prince gaue right ioyfull and *Leo at 16. yeers*
diligent care vnto me; and whatsoeuer he vnderstood not *of age.*
sufficiently, he would cause it to be interpreted. Now
being wearie with his hunting, and perceiuing the night to
be farre spent, he wished all of vs to goe to bed. Early
the next morning I was sent for, to a stately breakefast,
after the conclusion whereof, he caused an hundreth ducates
to be deliuered me for a present vnto my vncle, togither
with three slaues, which should attend vpon him in his
iourney. But on me he bestoowed fiftie ducates and a
good horse; and to each of my two seruants he gaue
ten ducates: giuing mine vncle to vnderstand, that his
meane gift which he bestowed, was sent not in regard
of his woorthy presents, but for a recompence of his
excellent verses. For as touching mine vncles gifts,

he saide he would deferre the requitall thereof till his returne from Tombuto, what time he would more fully manifest his good will towards him. Then commanding one of his secretaries to direct vs on our way, & most courteously bidding vs farewell; he told vs that the same day he was going to make an assault vpon his enimies. And so departing from him, I returned to mine vncle. Thus much I thought good to set downe, for to shewe, that euen Africa is not vtterly destitute of courteous and bountifull persons.

Of the mountaine called Tensita.

TEnsita is a part of Atlas, beginning westward from the mountaine last before mentioned, eastward extending to mount Dedes, and southward bordering vpon the desert of Dara.[125] This mountaine is well stored with inhabitants, hauing moe then fiftie castles about it, the wals whereof are built of lime and rough stone: and by reason of the southerly situation it is euer almost destitute of raine. All the said castles stand not far from the riuer of Dara, some being three, and some fower miles distant there from. The greatest prince in all this region hath vnder his command well nigh fifteene hundreth horsemen, and about so many footemen as the prince of Tenucues before named. And albeit these two princes are most neerely conioined in bloud, yet can neither of them refraine from most cruel wars against the other. It is a woonder to see, what plentie of dates this mountaine affoordeth: the inhabitants giue themselues partly to husbandry, and partly to traffike. Barly they haue in great abundance: but of other graine and of flesh their scarcitie is incredible: for that region hath no flockes nor droues at all. The prince of this mountaine commonly receiueth for yeerly tribute twentie thousand peeces of golde: euery of which peeces containeth not so much by one third part, as an Italian ducate. There hath alwaies beene so great amitie betweene the king of Fez and this prince, that either often sendeth rich gifts vnto other. My selfe (I remember) once saw a most magnificent gift *A most stately and rich present.* presented to the saide king in the name of this prince, to wit, fiftie men slaues, and fiftie women slaues brought out of the land of Negros, tenne eunuches, twelue camels, one Giraffa, sixteene ciuet-cats, one pound of ciuet, a pound of amber, and almost sixe hundreth skins of a certaine beast called by them Elamt, whereof they make their shieldes,[126] euerie skin being woorth at Fez, eight ducates; twentie of the men slaues cost twentie ducates a peece, and so did fifteene of the women slaues; euery eunuch was valued at fortie, euery camell at fiftie, and euery ciuet-cat at two hundreth ducates: and a pound of ciuet and amber is solde at Fez for threescore ducates. Besides these were sent diuers other particulars, which for breuities sake I omit. I my selfe was in presence when these gifts were offred to the king: the princes ambassadour was a Negro borne, being grosse and of a low stature, and for his speech and behauiour most barbarous: this fellow deliuered a letter vnto the king, which was most absurdly and rudely penned: but the Oration which he made in the behalfe of his prince was well woorse: so that at the pronouncing thereof the king and all that were in presence could hardly refraine from laughter, but were faine to hold their hands and garments before their faces, least they should haue seemed too vnciuile. Howbeit his oration being ended, the king caused him to be most honorablie entertained by the priest of the chiefe temple; with whom himselfe and all his company hauing remained fourteene daies, were at length by the kings liberalitie frankely and freely dismissed.

Of the mountaine called Gogideme.

NEere vnto the foresaid mountaine standeth another called Gogideme.[127] This mountaine is inhabited only vpon the north part thereof: but the south side is vtterly destitute of inhabitāts: the reason whereof they affirme to be, because that when *Abraham king of Maroco was vanquished and expelled out of his kingdome by his disciple *Elmaheli*, he fled vnto this mountaine. The inhabitants mooued with the kings distresse endeuoured (though to small purpose) all that they could, to succour him: whereof his disciple *Elmaheli* was no sooner enformed, but comming with an huge armie and with great furie vpon them, he destroyed all their mansions and villages, and the inhabitants he partly put to flight, and partly to the sword.[128] And those which now remaine there are most base, beggerly and slauish people: Howbeit they sell some quantitie of oyle and barley: neither indeed will their soyle affoorde any other commodities. They haue plentie of goates and mules; but their mules and horses are but of meane stature. The situation and qualitie of this mountaine will not suffer the inhabitants to be liberall.

Read of this Abraham before in the description of the citie of Maroco.

Of the two mountaines called Tescuon.

TEscuon consisteth of two mountaines standing together, beginning westward from Gogideme, & ending at the mountaine of Tagodast. The inhabitants are oppressed with extreme pouerty: for their ground will yeelde nothing but barley and mill. Forth of this mountaine springeth a certaine riuer, which runneth through most pleasant fields. But because the mountainers neuer descend into the same fields, hence it is that the Arabians onely enioy that riuer.[129] To haue said thus much of these may suffice: now let vs come vnto the description of Tedles.

A description of the region of Tedles.

THE small region of Tedles beginneth westward at the riuer of Guadelhabid, and stretcheth to that part of the great riuer Ommirabih where Guadelhabid taketh his beginning; southward it bordereth vpon Atlas, and northward it extendeth vnto that place where Guadelhabid falleth into Ommirabih. This region is in a manner three square: for the said two riuers springing out of Atlas run northward, till approching by little and little, they meet all in one.[130]

Of Tefza the principall towne in Tedles.

TEfza the chiefe towne of all Tedles, was built by the Africans vpon the side of mount Atlas, some fiue miles from the plaine. The towne wals are built of most excellent marble, which is called in their language Tefza,[131] and hereupon the towne was so called likewise. Heere doe reside most rich merchants of all sorts: of Iewes here are two hundred families, who exercise merchandise and diuers other trades. And here you shall finde many outlandish merchants which buy from hence certaine blacke mantles with hoods, commonly called *Ilbernus*:[132] of these there are great numbers both in Italy and Spaine. Neither are there in Fez any kinde of wares, which are not heere to be bought: if any merchant will exchange his wares for other, hee may the sooner be dispatched: for the townesmen are furnished with diuers kindes of merchandise, as namely with slaues, horses, woad, leather, and such like: whereas if the forreiners were desirous to sell their wares for ready money, they should neuer attaine to the value of them. They haue golden coine without any image or superscription: their apparell is decent: and their women are beautifull and of good behauiour. In this towne are diuers Mahumetan temples, and many priests and iudges.

Ilbernus.

Their commonwealth was woont alwaies to be most prosperous and well-gouerned; but degenerating from better to woorse, they were afterward so turmoyled with dissensions and wars, that certaine being expelled hence, came vnto the king of Fez, humbly beseeching him that by force he would restore them to their natiue countrey, conditionally that all matters wel succeeding on their side, they should deliuer the towne vnto the king. This condition was accepted, and the king hauing a thousand braue horsemen readie to doe the feat, ioyned fiue hundred horse, and two hundred gunners on horsebacke vnto them. Moreouer he wrote vnto certaine Arabians (which are commonly called *Zuair*,[133] and haue almost fower thousand horsemen at commaund) that, if need so required, they would come in, and ayde his troupes. Ouer the saide armie the king appointed as captaine one *Ezzeranghi*, a most valiant and redoubted warriour. Who hauing pitched his tents neere vnto the towne, began presently to give the townesmen an assault. But when he had done his best, the warlike citizens easily gaue him the repulse. Moreouer the Arabians called Benigeber[134] were comming with fiue thousand horsemen to succour the towne. Which so soone as Captaine *Ezzeranghi* was aduertised of, he raised his siege, and went suddenly to meete with the foresaid Arabians; whom after he had discomfited in three daies, he then safely returned to lay new siege. The citizens seeing themselues cut off from all hope of the Arabians ayde, began seriously to treat of peace with the enemie; which the easier to obtaine, they promised to defray all the kings charges layde out in this expedition, and to pay him for yeerly tribute, more then ten thousand ducates: howbeit with this prouiso, that they for whose cause the king had sent the said armie, if they entred the towne, should bee secluded from all Magistracie and gouernment. But they hearing of these conditions, spake vnto the

Captaine in manner following: Sir, if it shall please you to restore vs vnto our former dignitie and state, we will procure you aboue an hundreth thousand ducates. Neither is there cause why any man should feare any iniurie or violence; for we protest vnto you that no man shall be a farthing endamaged by vs: onely we will exact at our aduersaries handes the reuenues of our possessions which they haue these three yeeres vniustly detained from vs. The summe whereof will amount vnto thirtie thousand ducates, all which we are most willing to bestow vpon you, in regard of those labours which you haue vndergone for our sakes. Moreouer the reuenues of the whole region shall bee yours, which will come to twentie thousand ducates. And the Iewes tribute shall yeeld you ten thousand more. Vpon these speeches the Captaine returned answere vnto the citizens, that his master the king of Fez had most faithfully promised those which mooued him vnto this warre, that he would neuer forsake them till they had attained their harts desire: for which cause he was more willing to haue them gouerne, then the townesmen which were now in possession, and that for many reasons: wherefore (saith he) if you be determined to yeelde vnto the king, assure your selues, that no inconuenience shall light vpon you: but if you will to the ende remaine peruerse and obstinate, be yee assured also, that the king will deale most extremely with you. This message was no sooner knowen vnto the people, but foorthwith they began to be distracted into diuers factions: some there were which stood for the king, and others chose rather manfully to fight it out, then that the king should be admitted: insomuch that the whole citie resounded with brawlings, quarels, and contentions. This tumult came at length by spies vnto the Captaines eare, who presently caused halfe his forces to take armes; and by their meanes in three howers space he wan the citie with little slaughter on his part. For those townesmen that fauoured the king, did what they could on the inside, to set open the gates, and so did the assailants on the outside, neither did any resist their attempts, by reason of the foresaid ciuill dissensions. Whereupon Captaine *Ezzeranghi* entring the citie, caused the kings colours to be aduanced in the market-place, and vpon the wals, charging his horsemen to range about the citie, that no citizens might escape by flight ; and last of all made a proclamation vnto all his souldiers, that they should not vpon paine of death offer any iuiurie vnto the townesmen. Then he caused all the chieftaines of the contrarie faction to be brought prisoners vnto him : to whom he threatned captiuitie and thraldome, till they should disburse so much as the king had spent in that expedition : the totall summe was twelue thousand ducates, which the wiues and kinsfolkes of the captiues presently payde. Neither could they yet obtaine their libertie : for the exiles, for whose cause the king had sent that armie, demaunded restitution of all their goods, which the other had for certaine yeeres detained from them. The captiues therfore were committed that night, & the next morning lawyers & atturnies came to plead on both sides before a iudge & the captaine. Howbeit after a great deale of tedious fending and proouing, hauing concluded nothing at all, the captaine was so weary, that he left them, and went to supper. Afterward he caused the captiues to be brought foorth, wishing them to pay the sums demaunded ; for (saith he) If you come before the king of Fez he wil make you to disburse more than twice the value. At which words being terrified, they wrote vnto their wiues, if they woulde euer see them aliue, to procure them money by some meanes. Eight daies after, the women brought as many golde rings, bracelets, and other such iewels, as were valued at eight and twenty thousand ducates : for they had rather bestowe these for the ransome of their husbandes, than to reueale their great wealth; bringing foorth all their costly ornaments, as if their money had beene quite exhaust. When therefore the king and the exiles were fully satisfied, insomuch that nothing seemed nowe to let the said captiues from libertie, the captaine spake vnto them in this wise: Sirs, I haue signified (though vnwillingly) vnto my master the king all matters which haue here passed betweene vs: for I dare by no meanes release you, till the kings letters authorize me so to do: Howbeit, I wish you to be of good cheere; for sithens you haue honestly restored to euery man his owne, there is no doubt but your selues shall shortly be set at libertie. The same night the captaine called a friend of his, whose counsell he founde oftentimes to take good effect, and asked him by what meanes he might without suspicion of guile or trechery, wring any more sums of money from them. Whereunto his friend replied: make them beleeue (quoth he) that you are willed by the kings letters to put them all to death: howbeit, that you will not, for pitties sake, deale so extremely with innocent persons: but that you will send them to Fez to receiue punishment or pardon at the kings pleasure. Heereupon the kings letters were counterfeited, which the day following the captaine with a lamētable voice published vnto his two & forty prisoners. My friends (quoth he) so it is, that the king hauing receiued some sinister and wrong information, that you should go about to make a conspiracie: most firmely enioineth me by these his letters, to put each one of you to death: which, though it be ful sore against my wil, yet needs I must obey my prince, if I wil not wittingly runne vpon mine owne destruction. And then shedding some fained teares: sithens (quoth he) we can vpon the sodaine deuise no better course, I thinke it most conuenient to send you with a troupe of horsemen vnto the king, whose wrath (perhaps) you may by some meanes pacific. Whereupon the captiues growing farre

A notable and effectuall practise to wring more money out of the townesmens purses.

more pensiue than before, recommended themselues vnto God, and the captaines clemencie, requesting his good will with many teares. And foorthwith there comes one in among them, who aduised them to make vp some round summe of money, & therewithall to trie if they could appease the king: and seemed likewise to intreat the captaine, that he woulde by his letters stande their friend to the king. Heereunto the captiues agreeing with one voice, promised that they would giue the king a great summe of golde, and woulde most liberally reward the captaine. The captaine, as though forsooth this condition much disliked him, asked at length how much golde they ment to send the king: one saide that he woulde disburse a thousand ducates, another, that he would giue fiue hundreth, and the third, eight hundreth. But the captaine making shew, that this was too little, saide that he was loth to make signification of so small a summe vnto the king: howbeit, better it were for you (quoth the captaine) to goe your selues vnto the king, with whom perhaps you shall make a more reasonable end than you are aware of. But they fearing hard measure, if they should be caried vnto the king, were far more importunate with the captaine then before, that he would (to his power) be good vnto them. Wherefore the captaine (as though at length he had been mooued with their vehement petitions) spake unto them in this wise: heere are of you (my masters) two and fortie noble & rich persons; if you wil promise two thousand ducates a man, I will signifie on your behalfe so much vnto the king, and so I hope to perswade him: but if this condition will not please him, then must I needs send you to make answere for your selues. This condition they al of them yeelded vnto; howbeit with this prouizo, that euery man should giue proportionablie to his wealth, and that they might haue for the paiment fifteene daies of farther respite. The twelfth day following the captaine fained, that he had receiued letters from his king, signifying that the king, for his sake, woulde shewe the captiues more fauour. The fifteenth day he had paied vnto him eightie fowre thousand ducates: neither coulde he sufficiently woonder, how in so small a towne, among two and fortie inhabitants onely, such huge sums of money could so readily be found. Then wrote he vnto his king how all matters had passed, demaunding what should be done with the gold. And so the king foorthwith sent two of his secretaries with an hundreth horsemen to fetch home the saide golde vnto Fez. The captiues being restored to their libertie, presented the saide captaine with horses, slaues, ciuet, and such like gifts, to the value of two thousand ducates: giuing him exceeding thankes for their libertie; and requesting him to take their presents in good woorth: for, had not their treasure beene quite consumed, they saide, they woulde haue bestowed farre greater vpon him. Wherefore, from thence forward, that region was subject vnto the king of Fez, and to the forsaide captaine *Ezzeranghi*, till he was trecherously slaine by certaine Arabians. Moreouer the king receiueth from that citie, euen at this present twentie thousand ducats for yeerely tribute. I haue in this narration beene indeede somewhat more large then neede required;[135] howbeit perhaps I did it, bicause I my selfe was present in al the expedition, and was an earnest mediatour for the citizens release: neither saw I euer (to my remembrance) a greater masse of golde, than was by subtiltie drawne from them. Yea the king himselfe neuer had so much golde in his coffers at one time: for albeit he receiueth yeerely thirtie thousand ducates, yet neuer could he store himselfe with so much at once, nor his father before him. These things were done in the yeere of the Hegeira 915. and in the yeere of our Lord 1506.[136] And here I would haue the reader to consider, what mans industrie and wit may doe in getting of money. The King maruelled much at this summe of gold ; but afterward he had greater cause to woonder at the wealth of a certaine Iewe, who payed more out of his owne purse, than all the forenamed captiues. And his riches were the cause, why the King of Fez exacted fiftie thousand ducates from the Iewes, for that they were said to fauour his enimies. I my selfe bare him companie, that went in the Kings name to receiue the sayd summe of the Iewes.

Of Efza a towne of Tedles.

THis towne standeth two miles from Tefza, and containeth almost sixe hundred families, being built vpon a little hill at the foote of mount Atlas. In this towne are many Moores and Iewes which make *Bernussi. The naturall inhabitants are either artificers or husbandmen, being in subiection to the gouernours of Tefza. Their women are excellent spinsters, whereby they are saide to gaine more then the men of the towne. Betweene this towne and Tefza runneth a certaine riuer called by the inhabitants Derne, which springeth foorth of Atlas, runneth through the plaines of that region, till at length it falleth into Ommirabih. On both sides of this riuer are most beautifull and large gardens replenished with all kindes of fruits. The townesmen here are most liberall and curteous people, and will permit merchants trauelling that way freely to come into their gardens, and to take thence as much fruit as they will. No people are slower then they for paying of debts: for albeit the merchants lay downe readie money to receiue Bernussi within three monethes, yet are they sometime faine to stay an whole yeere. Myselfe was in this towne when the kings armie lay in Tedles, and then they yeelded themselues to the king. The second time that the kings generall of his armie came vnto them, they presented him with fifteen horses, and as many slaues. Afterward they

* Or Ilbernus, being a kinde of garment.

gaue him fifteene kine, in token that they were the kings loyall subjects.[137]

Of Cithiteb.

THis towne was built by the Africans vpon an high hill, almost tenne miles westward of Efza. Well peopled it is with rich and noble inhabitants: and because Bernussi be here made, it is alwaies frequented *Ibernus.* with store of merchants. The top of the said high mountaine is continually couered with snow. The fields adioyning to the towne are full of vineyards and gardens, which bring foorth fruits in such abundance, that they are nought woorth to be sold in the markets. Their women are beautifull, fat, and comely, being adorned with much siluer: their eies and haire are of a browne colour. The inhabitants are so stout and sullen, that when the other cities of Tedles yeelded to the king, they alone stood out: yea they assembled vnder a certaine captaine an armie of a thousand horsemen, wherewith they so vexed the kings forces, that he was often in danger to haue lost al that which he had got. Afterward the king sent his brother with a new supply of men to aide his lieutenant; but he also had hard successe. At length hauing maintained warre for three whole yeeres, the king commanded a Iew to poyson their captaine. And so at last the king wan this citie also, in the yeere of the Hegeira 921.[138]

Of the towne of Eithiad.

THis towne being built by the Africans vpon a certaine hillocke of Atlas, containeth to the number of three hundred families. It is walled onely towards the mountaine; for that side which respecteth the plaine, is so fortified naturally with rocks, that it seemeth not to need any wall. From Cithiteb it is about twelue miles distant. The temple of this towne is little, but most

beautiful, round about which runneth a mote, in manner of
a riuer. The inhabitants are wealthie and noble: they
haue great store of merchants, as well townesmen as
forreiners. The Iewes here inhabiting are partly artificers
and partly merchants. About this towne are abundance of
springs, which breaking through the rocks of the mountaine, doe fall into a certaine riuer vnder the towne. On
both sides of this riuer are diuers gardens woonderfully
replenished with grapes, figs, and walnuts. Likewise the
sides of the mountaine it selfe abound greatly with oliues.
Their women are no lesse beautifull then ciuil, being adorned
with much siluer, and wearing fine rings vpon their fingers
and armes. Their vallie is fruitfull for all kinde of graine,
but their hill is meete onely for barly, and for goates-
pasture. In my time one *Raoman Benguihazzan* vsurped
this towne, and enioied it to his dying day. My selfe was
once entertained by a priest of this place, in the yeere of
Hegeira 921.[139]

Of *Seggheme a mountaine of Tedles.*

ALbeit this mountaine standeth much southerly, yet
is it to be accounted one of the mountaines of
Tedles. Westward it beginneth from the mountaine of
Tesauon, extending it selfe eastward to mount Magran,
from whence the famous riuer of Ommirabih is said to
take his beginning. The south part bordreth vpon mount
Dedes. The inhabitants are said originally to bee
descended from the people of Zanaga: they are personable,
cheerefull, valiant, and warlike people. Their weapons
are dartes, Turkish swords, and daggers. They fling
stones likewise with great dexteritie and force. They are
at continuall war with the inhabitants of Tedles, insomuch
that no merchants can passe that way without publike
safe-conduct, and without great expense of mony. Their
houses are so homely built, that somtime three or fower

roomes are contained in one. Of goates they haue great abundance, as likewise of mules scarcely so big as asses, which range so farre into the forrest to seeke their foode, that they are often deuoured of lions. They would neuer submit themselues to any prince ; for their mountaine is so rough and steepe, that it seemeth almost impregnable. In my time the same captaine which had woon the townes of Tedles went about to assaile them in like manner. Which when the mountainers vnderstood, assembling a great armie, they shrowded themselues in a certaine part of the mountaine, neere which they knew their enemies would passe. And so soone was as they saw all the enemies horsemen ascended vp the hill, suddenly rushing foorth, they gaue them the onset. The skirmish was not so long as bloodie : for the captaines armie being too weake for the mountainers, could neither march on, nor retire : wherefore they were constrained to fight it out by hand-blowes : many of them with their horses being throwen headlong downe the rocks, were miserably crushed in peeces : the residue were either taken or slaine, so that I thinke scarce one man of them escaped. But of all others the captiues were most miserable : for the mountainers themselues would not slay them, but deliuered them ouer to their wiues to be tormented, who, as if they had beene she-tigres or lionesses, put them to a most horrible and vile death. From thencefoorth they had no traffique nor familiaritie with the people of Tedles, neither seemed they greatly to stand in need of their friendship (for they haue great store of barlie, of cattell, and of sweet fountaines) vnlesse it bee for that they are excluded from all trade of merchandize.[140]

Of the mountaine called Magran.

SOmwhat beyond the foresaid mountaine of Seggheme standeth mount Magran. Southward it bordereth vpon the region of Farcala, neere vnto the Lybian desert: westward it beginneth at Seggheme, and extendeth eastward to the foote of mount Dedes. It is continually couered with snow. The inhabitants haue such abundance of small and great cattell that they cannot long remaine in one place together. They build their houses of the barke of certaine trees, the rooffe whereof dependeth on slender sparres, fashioned like vnto the hoops enuironing the lids of such chests or trunks, as the women of Italie, when they trauell, carrie vpon their mules. So likewise these people transport their whole houses vp and downe by the strength of mules, till they haue found a fit place of aboad ; where, so soone as they arriue, they plant their said houses, remaining there with their whole families, so long as they haue grasse sufficient to feed their cattell. Howbeit all the spring time they settle themselues in one place, making certaine low stable or cottages, & couering thē with the boughs of trees, which serue for their cattel to lie in a nights: and to the end that the cold may not pinch them ouermuch, they kindle certaine huge fires neere vnto their said stables, wherupon sometimes the winde so violently driueth the fire, that vnles the cattell escape by flight, they are in great danger to be consumed : and as their houses are destitute of walles, so are their stables. They are continually molested and haunted with lions and woolues. In their apparell and customes they wholy agree with the foresaid people of Seggheme, sauing that these haue houses of bark and wood, and the other of stone. I my selfe, in the 917. yeere of the Hegeira, was in this mountaine as I trauelled from Dara to Fez.[141]

These people liue like the Tartars.

A description of mount Dedes.

THis high and cold mountaine greatly aboundeth with fountaines and woods. Westward it beginneth at mount Magran, extending thence almost as far as the mountaine of Adesan; and southward it bordereth vpon the plaines of Todga. The length thereof is almost fowerscore miles. Vpon the very top of this mountaine there was a citie built in ancient time, whereof a few ruinous monuments are to be seene at this present; namely certaine walles of white stone, wherein are diuers letters and wordes grauen, which the inhabitants themselues doe not vnderstand. Many are of opinion, that this citie was built long agoe by the Romans: howbeit I my selfe could neuer finde so much affirmed by any African writer, nor yet the citie it selfe mentioned. Sauing that *Seriffo Essacalli* in a certaine storie of his maketh mention of Tedsi, which he saith is neere vnto Segelmesse and Dara: but he declareth not whether it bee built vpon mount Dedes or no. Howbeit for mine owne part I thinke it to be the very same: for there is no other citie in the whole region. The inhabitants of Dedes are in very deede most base people; of whom the greater part dwell in caues vnder the ground: their foode is barly and Elhasid, that is to say, barly meale sodden with water, and salt, which we mentioned before in our description of Hea: For heere is nothing but barly to be had. Goates and asses they haue in great abundance. The caues wherein their cattell lodge are exceedingly full of *Nitre: so that I verily thinke if this mountaine were neere vnto Italy, the saide Nitre woulde yeerely be woorth fiue and twentie thousand ducates. But such is their negligence and vnskilfulnes, that they are vtterly ignorant to what purposes Nitre serueth. Their garments are so rude, that they scarce couer halfe their nakednes. Their houses are very loathsome, being annoied with the stinking smell of their goates. In all this mountaine you shall finde neither castle nor walled towne: when they builde an house, they pile one stone vpon another without any morter at all, the roofe whereof they make of certaine rubbish, like as they doe in some places of Sisa and Fabbriano: the residue (as we haue saide) do inhabite in caues, neither sawe I euer, to my remembrance, greater swarmes of fleas then among these people. Moreouer they are trecherous and strong theeues, so giuen to stealing and quarrelling, that for one vnkinde worde they wil not onely contend, but seeke also the destruction one of another. They haue neither iudge, priest, nor any honest gouernour among them. No merchants resort vnto them: for being giuen to continuall idlenes, and not exercising any trades or handie-crafts, they haue nothing meet for merchants to buy. If any merchant bring any wares into their region, vnlesse he be safe conducted by their captaine, he is in danger to be robbed of altogither. And if the wares serue not for their owne necessarie vses, they will exact one fourth part of them for custome. Their women are most forlorne and sluttish, going more beggerly apparalled then the men. So continual and slavish are the toiles of these women, that for miserie, the life of asses is not comparable to theirs. And, to be briefe, neuer was I so wearie of any place in all Africa, as I was of this: howbeit in the yeere of the Hegeira 918. being commanded by one, to whom I was in dutie bound, to trauell vnto Segelmesse, I could not choose but come this way.[142]

NOTES TO BOOK II.

(1) Hea, modern province of Haha.

(2) Esifnual, in the original: Asif el Mel, Azif en Mul, or Acifelmal, as the Arabic is variously transliterated, the lower part of which is sometimes known as the Wad Bu el Gheras.

(3) Arga, the Argan tree (*Argania Sideroxylon*), one of the most interesting products of Morocco, being peculiar to it, and almost confined to the province of Haha, where most of the oil extracted from its fruit is made. This is the first mention of the tree.—Hooker and Ball, *Tour in Morocco*, pp. 395-404. The mountains of Haha are also notable for the forests of the famous Arar (*Callitris quadrivalvis*), the wood of which is prohibited from being exported. Its "gum sandrac" is better known. Haha, also, in spite of what Leo says, yields fine crops of almonds, grapes, citrons, pomegranates, oranges, lemons, limes, pears, apricots, and other fruits, including monster water melons.

(4) Torte.

(5) Elasid, El ásid. This porridge is still much esteemed. After being slightly salted it is boiled for about fifteen minutes, and is allowed to set before adding the butter, which in summer is substituted for oil.

(6) More correctly "Kes Ku", though, possibly owing to the influence of Leo's orthography, usually pronounced "Kus Kus", or, more frequently, "Kus Kussu", by Europeans. It is the one great national dish of the Moors.

(7) El K'sá. This dye (Es-suak) is still a favourite one, though the head covering described is not now common. Instead of this, a strip of European cotton is more frequently used. Turbans are white even in the plains of Morocco, being of imported cotton stuff. Green turbans denoting descendants of the Prophet are not very often seen.

(8) Hasaira. (9) Tilis.

(10) Libda. "This bolster and pillow is a sort of woollen bag, coarse and rough."

(11) A common expression among these people, especially when wishing to sell you a horse.—Meakin.

(12) Horses are nowadays more often shod with continuous iron plates in stony districts, though not invariably. On the plains, immediately after the first rains, when the ground gets soft enough for ploughing, oxen, mules, asses—any domestic animal—are pressed into the farmer's service, and cases are known in which a woman and a donkey have been yoked into the one stilted plough of prehistoric form.

(13) The "Audad", or wild sheep of the Atlas (*Ovis tragelaphus*), is what is meant by "wild goat". The hare is really the rabbit (*Lepus cuniculus*), which has become considerably modified in the African climate, though I am not aware whether, like those which have devoured the herbage of Porto Santo, they refuse to breed with their European kindred.

(14) "Ogni casa a dentro gli istromenti di macinare"—every household being supplied with the implement for grinding. But the "mill" is not "wooden" but stone, and is identical with the Celtic "quern".

(15) Cauterization is still universally used, and one of the most familiar personages in the markets and fairs of Morocco is the Doctor selling charms, written on dirty scraps of paper, for the cure of internal diseases, and with the "actual cautery" in the fire before him, ready to apply it with equal readiness to man and beast. His pharmacopœia, where he pretends to higher skill than the ordinary cauterizer, might have been selected from the stock-in-trade of Macbeth's witches.

They also use certain herbs in some places (such as "Ghassul", a species of *Mesembryanthemum*), though with poor results. In towns, the Jews make soft soap of olive oil and wood ashes, etc., greatly to the profit of these monopolists.—Meakin, *Times of Morocco*, August 8th, 1891.

(16) "Ese ad alcun del popolo fa dibisogno di passar da un luoco all' altro, conviene che egli prenda la scorta di qualche, o religioso o donna, della parte avversa." That is, if anyone finds it necessary to pass from one place to another, it is incumbent on him to go under the escort (*Anaia*) of some saint or woman of the part traversed. Pory is perhaps too severe on the character of the female escort, for though a woman acting in this capacity to a solitary traveller in a Moslem country is, inferentially, not of the highest reputation, the word "Donna" does not necessarily imply the meaning given to it. "Wife" is an addition, and naturally so, considering the intense jealousy of

the Arabs or Berbers (Shluhs) with whom this account of the Haha people is mainly concerned. At one time the traveller received one of the Chief's spears, which, being recognised, acted as a passport.

(17) Compared with the country north of it, Haha is remarkable for the number of little walled stone-built towns, picturesquely situated in strategic positions, each house with a tower on some place of vantage.

(18) For corrections of this account of Tednest, cf. Introduction. During three centuries it was the capital of Haha, a province which in Leo's and Marmol's day comprehended the present government of Shiedma also. Leo seems to have visited it after the place had been utterly ruined by the Portuguese. According to Marmol (t. ii, pp. 8-9, 103-104), copying Leo, this happened in March 1514 (A.H. 920), the same year in which the latter saw it, "abitate dalle cornacchie e da si fatti uccelli". But Diego de Torres (pp. 46-49), a better authority in this respect, fixes 1516 as the date, which I am inclined to accept as the correct one. The reason why Nuño Fernandes d'Ataide (Governor of Saffi or Zafin), aided by the renegade Yahia ben Tafuf, destroyed Tednest, was that, as the residence of the Sheriff Mohammed ebn Ahmed and his two sons, it had become a menace to Azamor and Saffi. But from the pillage obtained, and the number of people slain, Leo would seem scarcely accurate in saying that it was deserted two years before he visited it. Moreover, if his visit was in 1515, this could not have been the case, since the Portuguese attack was not made until 1516. Accordingly, one of the two original authorities is in error. At all events, the place seems to have been, if not large, of some importance. Marmol, indeed, mentions that the Sheriff Mohammed ebn Ahmed erected a sumptuous palace, so that at all events, when the place was sacked and practically destroyed by the Portuguese and their "Mezonars"—or renegade Moorish allies—it must in any case have had a large garrison, with the usual following of a Moorish military adventurer.

Less than four centuries ago none of the minor Moroccan cities was better known. According to Marmol it was 22 leagues, or close on 76 English statute miles, from Saffi, while Leo places it at 18 miles east of Taculet, or from 20 to 25 miles to the east or south-east of the mouth of the Tensift River. Possibly Marmol made it too far from Saffi, though the existence of a town of its consequence could scarcely be a question for dispute. De Faria y Sousa (*Africa Portuguesa*, p. 115) refers to it as "una de las más antiguas en la Prouincia de Hea". Yet Tednest had vanished soon after the event mentioned; and the place drops out of history. Indeed, had it not been rebuilt after its destruction by the Portuguese in 1516, it could scarcely have contained 3,000 inhabitants in Marmol's day. Höst inserts it on his map (1779) as "Todenst", on the route from Mogador (or Mogadul, as he calls it) to Merakish, without however mentioning it in the text. Nor is there any such place in that part of Morocco. Of late it has disappeared from the maps. Renou inserts it solely on Leo's and Marmol's authority, and though Gräberg gives it a prominent place, his description is simply an uncritical condensation of Leo's. The last notice of it is a curious but not very intelligible one. It is in Lord's *Algiers, with Notices of the Neighbouring States of Barbary* (1835), vol. ii, p. 142 (a compilation of little authority), in the shape of a letter "from Dr. Naudi to the Rev. C. S. Hawtrey", dated Malta, Oct. 15th, 1816, though whence derived by Lord is not mentioned. "A Jew from Tedvest, an ancient town in the province of Hea, in the Morocco Empire, and with whom I am often here, and to whom I gave some of the Gospels printed by your [Bible] Society," the writer remarks, "assures me that . . . . . Tedvest contains about five hundred dwellings, and is the capital of the Province [which it was not in 1816]. It was entirely destroyed about the beginning of last century [?], and built again by the Jews, and now (which is very particular) is inhabited only by this people. The Tedvestine here with us" . . . etc. There cannot be any doubt about Tedvest being the same as Tednest, which Diego Torres calls "Tendeste", on the Sheshawa, a tributary of the Tensift. There are many ruins near this river, but none easily fixed upon as those of Tedvest. Tchaset has been suggested as the place. But other reasons apart, this little place is too far from Sheshawa, though Gräberg, while placing Tednest, "Sul fiume Scuisciava", in his text (p. 59), on his map gives a locality far from that river. The latest mapmaker who has ventured to "locate" it is Mr. Weller in the map affixed to Rohlf's *Adventures in Morocco* (1874), but he places it still nearer the coast, and not on a tributary of the Tensift, as does Petermann, in the one which accompanies the German original. One of the latest and best maps of Morocco, Paul Schnell's in Petermann's *Geographische Mitteilungen*, No. 103 (1890), does not insert the name of this vanished town. Nor is it on that by the R. G. S. (*Supp. Papers*, vol. iii, Part III, 1893).—Höst, *Efterretninger om Marókos og Fes, samlede der Landene fra Ao. 1760 til 1768* (1779).

(19) Teculet also is a vanished town. Marmol is perhaps right in saying that it was built by the Musamadi Berbers, and was destroyed by A'bd-el Mumen, the Almohade (1130-1162 A.D.), after which it lay for a long time in ruins without any inhabitants. In 1514 (A.H. 920, not 923) Nuño Fernandes d'Ataide found the place again so flourishing that it was considered worth sacking, with

such ruthlessness, that numbers of the inhabitants of both sexes were despatched as slaves to Portugal. The Sheriffs, however, once more revived and re-peopled the town, only for it again to be destroyed, so that at present it is impossible to fix its site exactly among the nameless ruins that litter the province of Haha, which for twelve centuries has been one of the principal "cock-pits" of Morocco.

"Goz", mentioned by Leo, is a place which has likewise disappeared. It is noted by El Bekri under the name of Rabat Kuz, or Guz—the "sanctuary of Guz"—and in its time was the port of "Armat-Urika", an unidentified Atlas town, 120 miles inland, and about half way to Sheshawa (Chafchaun) situated on a river which bears that name. The first point south of Saffi (Asfi) on the Catalan Chart, and other maps of the earliest date, is Guz, Gus, or Gur, though the Tensift is not marked, and a little later Guz is displaced by Gus. In Marmol's day the town of Guz, or Aguz, as he indifferently writes it, defended by an adjoining fort, was almost in ruins, and paying tribute to the Portuguese rulers of Saffi. Since Leo's day, when, owing to the patronage of the Sheriffs, it was a flourishing place, Goz must have ceased to possess its old importance probably owing to the destruction of Teculet, and the persistent hostility of the Portuguese. Leo does not mention whether Goz is on a river or directly on the coast; but Marmol notes that it is at the mouth of a river of the same name in the position assigned by Ptolemy "to the enbouchure of the Diure". Ptolemy's "Diur" ($\Delta\iota o \acute{u} \rho$ $\pi o \tau a \mu o \tilde{u}$ $\grave{\epsilon} \varkappa \beta o \lambda a \acute{\iota}$) is, however, not very clearly, we venture to think, assigned by M. Tinot to Daïa de Walidya, the former port of Aïyer, the Vior of Pliny, which is only another form of the same name given to a place in exactly the same position. Phthuth (or Fut)—$\phi \theta o \tilde{\upsilon} \theta$ ($\mathring{\eta}$ $\Theta o \tilde{\upsilon} \theta$) $\pi o \tau a \mu o \tilde{u}$ $\grave{\epsilon} \varkappa \beta o \lambda a \acute{\iota}$—must, therefore, if we are to apportion the Ptolemaic names to modern representatives—be attached to the Tensift or Thasift (the Berber word *asif*, signifying river), and the $M \upsilon \sigma o \varkappa \acute{\alpha} \rho \alpha \varsigma$ $\lambda \iota \mu \acute{\eta} \nu$ to Saffi. But as Marmol distinctly says that during the 1514 [16] expedition against Teculet the Portuguese were detained for three days on their march by the river of Aguz swollen by the rain, and, as the Tensift runs directly across this route, this is clearly the river meant. Marmol, as is still common, calls a river by the principal town on its banks. In Sanson's maps (1656) "Gozota" is placed far to the south of the Tensift, which is made to flow under the walls of Saffi, showing, notwithstanding the Portuguese occupation of the coast during the preceding century, how little geography had gained by their military escapades. The maps attached to the narratives of Mouette (1682), and Braithwaite (1729), the latter being largely copied from its predecessor, call the Tensift the "Goudit", which may perhaps be an echo of Guz, and bring it into the Atlantic close to Saffi. Dapper (1686) entirely ignores the name Tensift in favour of Rio Dagas (Da Guz, that is

"River of Goz", the old name), and places Goza a little to the north of the continuation of that river.

Then Goz begins to disappear from charts until Gräberg, with characteristic inaccuracy, shifts the "Porto di Goz" some forty-six statute miles south of Mogador, and, to make all in unison, puts Teculet near its shore. Quatremère even places Goz at the mouth of the Vad Sus. The ruins of Goz were thought to have been identified by Lieutenant Arlett on the seashore at a little distance from the right bank of the Tensift. There are ruins there and in many other places; but I cannot learn that they have any claim to be those of Goz or that any ancient legends cling to them. Even the name has been lost. These ruins seem to be the same which Jackson considered to be those of "the *Asama* of Ptolemy". But the Asama—the *Anates* of Polybius—was not a town but a river ('Ασάμα ποταμοῦ ἐκβολαὶ), which was not the Tensift, but the Um-er-R'bia. More likely the abandoned Kasbah or Castle of Ben Ami Dush on the left bank of the river, where there are still great cemented Silos (*Matamoras*) for storing grain, battlements, and rooms, is either built on its site or was the fort which defended the river. Gerhard Rohlfs mentions that he failed to find Rabat El Kus or Guz, but saw the romantic ruin of an old castle called Kasbah Hanmedah. Pellow, early in the last century, refers to it as the "Castle of Allaber-Hanmedush", or "Eleben Hamedush", and in Gräberg's map it is indicated as "Ben Hamuda". The ruined Portuguese castle, which is situated close to the sea to the north of the Tensift mouth, and called by the natives "Soueira Kedima", is little known, as it lies on the route along the coast. M. Humot, who is an old resident in Morocco, tells me that "Gurzee" is applied to the fording-place on the Tensift —Renou, *Exp. scientifique de l'Algérie*, vol. viii, pp. 198-201, 203; Marmol, *L'Afrique* (Perrot d'Ablancourt ed. is always quoted), vol. ii, pp. 14-15, 84, 86, 104, 110; Vivien de St. Martin, *L'Afrique dans l'antiquité*, pp. 362-3; Tenot, *Recherches sur la géographie Comparée de la Maurétanie Tingitane*, pp. 102-5, 115, 117; Sanson, *L'Afrique en plusieurs cartes*, p. 9; Gräberg di Hemsö, *Specchio geografico et statestico dell' impero di Marocco* (1834), p. 61; Rohlfs, *Adventures in Morocco*, pp. 309-10; Pellow, *Adventures*, etc., edited by Robert Brown, pp. 279, 290, 366; De Campou, *Un Empire qui croule*, p. 205; De Faria y Sousa, *Africa Portuguesa* (1681), pp. 136-137; Quatremère, *Notice d'un manuscrit Arabe de la Bibliothèque du Roi* [Geography of El Bekri] (Notices et Extraits des manuscrits de la Bib. du Roi, t. xiii, 1831); Arlett, *Survey of some of the Canary Islands and part of Western Coast of Africa in 1835* (*Journ. R. G. S.*, vol. vi), and *Admiralty Charts*.

"Nobleman", in Pory's translation, is "genteluomo" in the Italian. There are no nobility in Morocco or (beneath the Royal family) any differences of rank except what office gives ; and it is too precarious for any man to claim social superiority by the mere holding of it. A subject of His Shereffian Majesty may be a slave to-day and governing a province to-morrow ; a wealthy Kaid when the sun rises, and a beggar in prison before it sets.

"Senate" = consiglio, council.

"The yeere of the Hegira 923" is not A.D. 1514, but 1517.

(20) The passage is mistranslated, in so far that it intimates that Leo published a book on African affairs. He might have written such a volume, but there is nothing to show that he had, according to Pory's gratuitous amplification. Leo's words are : "Sicome noi habbiamo scritto nell."—*Historie Moderne di Africa* (Ramusio, vol. i, p. 13).

The passage about the Jews of Teculet and Hadeechis coining money is no doubt quite accurate ; for, until recently, before the very debased Moorish coinage was struck in Paris by contract, the Hebrews were the regular moneyers in the Fez and Merakish mints. But we do not find the names of either of these two towns marked on any of the Morocco coins in the British Museum. Possibly the coins in question may be among the pieces without any indication of where they were struck, or the capitals were substituted as the locality of the mints, if Teculet and Haddechis are, as it seems likely, the names by which these vanished towns were officially known.—Lane Poole, *The Coins of the Moors of Africa and Spain : and of the Kings and Imáns of the Yemen : in the British Museum, Classes* xiv B. xxvii (1880).

(21) Hadeques of Marmol.

(22) "Gran multitudine d'animali, lana, butirro, olio di argan e similmente ferri, e panni del paese"—a great many animals, wool, butter, argan oil, also iron and country cloth. Marmol adds wax among the articles sold at the annual fair of Haddechis, though, as a rule, the Berbers made little use of the wild bees' wax, as Leo, indeed, notes in his description of Heusugaghen.

(23) Beyond mentioning that the place was captured by the Portuguese and renegade Arabs under Nuño Fernandes d'Ataide and Yahia ben Tafut in 1514, and the number of beautiful slaves sent to Portugal, Marmol adds little to Leo's account. The Sheriffs, he tells us, re-peopled the place, and at the time when he wrote the inhabitants were "very rich", mainly owing to their not inconveniencing the Portuguese, since the latter had evacuated Saffi in 1641 ; A.H. 922 is not A.D. 1513, but 1516.

(24) Il (or El) Eusugaghen, Eusaguen of Marmol, "situated three leagues from the town of Hadequis", though it is evident he knew nothing about it except what he plagiarised from Leo.

(25) "Serif, il quale si fa principe di Hea e vi veñe per paceficare insieme il popolo", "or Mahumetan priest", is an interpellation: a Sheriff is a descendant of Mahommed.

(26) "Piccola terriciuola nel piano". It is the Téchevit of Marmol. The Portuguese captured it by order of Dóm Joao de Meneses, Governor of Azamor, in 1514, in the same campaign which was undertaken to harry the strongholds of Tednest, Teculet, and Haddechis. It was afterwards repeopled, and, Saffi having been abandoned, it was permitted to remain undisturbed. It does not, however, appear again in history, and must at present, if it exists at all, be a place of very small importance. In 1846, M. Delaporte, French Consul at Mogador, informed M. Renou that "Tihout est un lieu dont le nom est connu". But that is all, and possibly M. Delaporte mistook for it "Tileut, a considerable place in the Atlas". "Takat" is a district in the region Leo is describing to the south of the Tensift. There is another Tejiut in Sus (*q. v.*) : A.H. 920 is 1514.

(27) Tesegdelt is found in Edrisi under the name of Tarkdelt, the name of a Berber tribe which occupied this strong hill town. Marmol tells us that the place was notable for its little horses, surefooted as goats among the rocks. The position of the place giving the inhabitants an advantage in the assaults to which they were subjected by the Arabs and Portuguese, they prospered by the sale of fruit, argan oil, and barley. A place of such consequence could scarcely disappear. Accordingly we find it under the old name, Tasgedlt, in the Mezgita district of the Wad Dra Basin, with the Wad Tidili (the stream the name of which Leo forgot) flowing at the base of the hill on which it stands. De Foucauld visited it in 1883, and has sketched the castle ruins, evidently unaware—as seems to be the case very generally throughout his valuable itineraries—of its having any history. The *enceinte* is nearly square, and furnished with towers at regular distances. The walls are thick, of masonry at the base and of clay (talia) higher up, but they are rapidly crumbling away. On the south side they are better preserved, though inside the *enceinte* little remains except heaps of stones and rubbish, evidently the work of the treasure seekers. There are many caverns below the castle, concerning which a thousand legends are told in the neighbouring country. Among them is a story about "three princesses", daughters of a Christian king, one of whom, Dula bent Wad, lived in Tasgedlt. Another, Zelfa bent Wad, on the Asif Marren, "near Teççaiout" (Teijeut?), and a third, Stouka bent

Wad, at Taskukt, on the Wad Imini, similar ruins being said to be found in all three places. According to these legends—which were affirmed to be written down in books—the princesses were continually at war with the Moslems until the ladies were driven away. In the *Wad Nun* there is also a tale about a Christian princess. De Foucauld imagines that the three castles were built by the same Sultan who also erected the bridge over the Wad Rdat. But this can only be a pious belief. It is a pity that the French traveller—now a Trappist monk—had not been better acquainted with Leo, otherwise he might easily have ascertained the condition of Culcihat Elmuridin, which must be close at hand, and other sites, though, no doubt, Tasgedlt being known, the others may be allocated. Mr. Joseph Thomson was also not very far from the spots mentioned, though not nearer Tasgedlt than Teleut. Tasgedlt is now deserted, its ruin possibly dating from the enmity of some Sultan. Yet the place seems to have been rebuilt not very long before Leo visited it, no doubt on the way from Marekest to Sus, or *vice versâ*. For in 1296, Abu Yakub, acting on behalf of Othman I, the Hasside, ruined a place of that name "on Mount Guedara", in revenge for the inhabitants having helped his enemies, the Merimidis.—Ibn Khaldun, *Hist. de Berbers*, t. iii, pp. 374, *et seq.; Roudh el Kartas* (Beaumier's Ed.), pp. 540, *et seq.;* Mercier, *Hist. de Afrique Sept.*, t. ii, p. 239; De Foucauld, *Reconnaissance au Maroc*, pp. 93-94 (Atlas Map No. 8): A.H. 919 is not A.D. 1510, but 1513.

(28) Tagteza in the original, Tegteza of Marmol. It is said to have been built by the Musamudi Berbers.

(29) A safe-conduct—"espressa licentica e salvacōdotto".

(30) Eit Devet is evidently the name of the Aït Diouit, or Ait Dasud, a Berber tribe still existing in the basin of the Wad Um-er-R'bia, though no such important town now exists on any plateau known to geographers or to the European residents in the neighbouring town of Mogador. There is also a Kubba, or domed tomb of Sidi Daoud, outside a village on the Wad Dra (De Foucauld, *Reconnaissance au Maroc*, pp. 262, 263, 280). The fact of certain tribes in Morocco being composed of converted Jews has been already referred to: the late Grand Vizier, whose features were distinctly Jewish, was always affirmed by the Moors to belong to an Atlas sept of this origin. In every Berber village, and in many families, it is still quite common to see Jews living under the protection of some influential individual, who finds his interest in seeing that his *protégé* is not wronged. By "Melic", who wrote the "Elmudevuana", which "the aged man" could repeat by heart, Malek ben Amas, who compiled the collection of traditions called *Mowatta*, or Beaten Path, is meant.

(31) This is a loose translation. In the original the passage is :—
"Di formento non si fa mentione tra loro"—that is, of wheat they have
no knowledge whatever ; or, as "formento" is an antiquated form of
"fermento", and "frumento" both, it may mean either wheat or leaven.
Temporal choses the former. Florianus at once gives the Latin
equivalent of formento as *frumentum* = corn ; any kind of grain,
"Nullum nouerunt *frumenti* vsum", an inaccuracy which Pory follows.

(32) Culeyhat Elmuhaydin of Marmol, who declares that it means
"the city of the prophets", though Leo is perhaps more correct in
translating it "the rock of the disciples" (la rocca di discepoli).
Its position on the other side of the mountain (Guarden ?), on which
Heusugaghen is built, has never been determined. The "piccola
fortezza" mentioned by Leo, is certainly destroyed as might be predicted
from the habits of the people, and the hatred with which they were
regarded. "Homar Seyef" seems to be the same person who is referred
to by Mohammed Essegher ben Elhadj ben Abdallah Eloufrani as Omar
Elmeghîti Ecchiâdhmi, "known under the name of Esseyyaf" (the
executioner, villain, or butcher), though I am not favoured with any
particulars regarding the traits which gave him that uncomplimentary
title (Houdas, *Nozhet-Elhâdi*, pp. 35, 36). According to Marmol,
Omar was a native of Tesegdelt (*q. v.*). Renou, who equally with the
present commentator failed to identify Calcihat Elmuridin, thinks that
the name easily resolves itself into "K'lia'tel-Mouah'h'edin, the
"fortress of Almohades". From Omar's nephew being ruler when
Leo passed, it is probable that the castle was not more than fifty years
old in 1512, which must have been about the period of Leo's visit. It
may be added that either from actual knowledge or geographical
inference, "Culcihat" is marked on the summit of a hill, close to the
coast, about 28 miles south of Mogador, on "*A new Chart of the
Coast of Africa, laid down chiefly from the observations of Monsr. de
Borda, who was sent in 1777 by the French Government to explore that
Coast*", etc. (London : Laurie and Whittle, 12th May 1794). On the
same chart, "Tesegdelt" is marked as a village in a creek. But it
cannot be Leo's Tesegdelt, as suggested by his description, as it is
nearly nine miles from Culcihat.

(33) There is a contradiction here ; for while the ruler is (*ut supra*)
called the nephew (*nipoto*) of Omar, he is here his grandson.

(34) This Berber village—or "towne"'—the Egue Leguingil of
Marmol, means, according to M. Delaporte, if Irél-m-Guiguil is to be
accepted as the exact orthography, "the orphan's hill", a not inappro-
priate name for a locality the inhabitants of which, in spite of the
friendship with which the Sheriffs treated them, were continually at war

with the Arabs in the low country, who were vassals of the Portuguese King. Their wax and honey they sold to Christian merchants.

It must not be inferred, from the failure of geographers to identify these places mentioned by Leo, that they were absolutely non-existent. They may still survive in a decayed or ruined condition, or be known under different names from those which he gives to them. Allowance must also be made for Leo's treacherous memory—for which he more than once apologises—and for the mistakes made by his editor, Ramusio, in deciphering his handwriting, as well as for the errors of Leo himself in translating from the Arabic into Italian. It must also be held in recollection that the region of Haha is still only partially explored, and, except near the coast, or on one or two beaten lines of travel, has never been examined with even moderate care by any intelligent visitor. On the other hand, it is extremely likely that the conclusion most readily arrived at is well founded, for it is far from probable that important towns such as those of Tednest, Teculeth, Hadecchis, Ileusugaghen, Teijeut, Tagten, Eitdeuet, Culcihat Elmuriden, Igilingigil, &c.—even admitting that Leo made the most of them—can exist without the Europeans on the coast hearing of them, or doing business with them, directly or by agents. All over the region of Morocco, described in the preceding pages, are scattered ruins of what seem to have been large towns or villages, the desertion or destruction of which is attributed to famines and epidemics, or to the vengeance of Sultans, powerful chiefs, and the "Rume" or Christians. Indeed, so impressed have the people been by the masterful ways of the European masters of the coast, that any ruin which they do not know the history of—and their traditions are few and inaccurate—are immediately attributed to the Portuguese. The charts of less than a century ago were dotted with notes of ruined towns all the way up from Tangiers to Agadir. Old Marmora, Anfi, El Iunes, Tit, Waladia, and Air or Eder, are among those which appear on the maps of 1795, and, with one exception, their ruin is now so complete that they have generally ceased to claim attention from the most conscientious cartographer. But we know of other places of which no remains—or remains of the most disputable description—attest the fact of their having been, before and after Leo's day, busy hives of traders and fanatics, and fighters, and robbers. They do not rest upon a note in the chronicles of one or even two men, but are familiar in the history of the sixteenth and seventeenth centuries. Yet where are Tul, and Targa, and Guz, and where is Tefethne, which appears in Leo's Chronicle a little later? If they have vanished in from two to four centuries, need we be surprised at the others, the exact positions of which were not defined, having so disappeared that their very names have ceased to linger in popular tradition? Nearly all the "lost cities" are Berber strongholds, and to this hour the

Berber hill tribes seldom pay their taxes until remonstrated with by the Sultan's guns. Every summer the Sultan travels about with an army for no other purpose, and not a year passes without a revolt of the "hill men". Their hand is against every man in the places which their little fortresses overlook, and, as a consequence, the owners of the harried herds in villages and douars (tent villages) have a hereditary feud with the races which twelve centuries of Islam have not reconciled to owning the Prince of True Believers master in things temporal, however they may admit his sanctity as the Prophet's heir.

After the introduction of artillery such easily attacked places as those near the coast, on hills, in the plains, or on spurs of the lower Atlas, could not long hold out against the Sultan, or his Kaïds either, during the long civil wars—when, as Leo tells us, so many places were desolated—or in the course of asserting his authority against these rebellious owners. And to any one acquainted with the ruthless manner in which an African victor treats the vanquished, it is scarcely necessary to explain the speed with which not only a captured Berber town but its inhabitants also disappear. The latter are mercilessly slaughtered, and their heads taken by the camel-load to decorate the gates of the capital, or of some other town suspected to stand in need of such a gruesome hint of the fate of rebels. In former days, in spite of what the Koran says against the practice, they were enslaved, and we have seen that the Portuguese exported many of the Moorish captives. The remnant who escaped joined some friendly tribe, or took refuge in some other stronghold of their sept, so that all over Morocco we find broken fragments of what seem to have been at one time powerful tribes. Then, on the principle of destroying the nest of the eagles so that they should not return, the sacked town is set on fire, after everything destructible or unportable has been smashed, pulled down, or blown up with gunpowder. And in a few years the weather finishes what man has not been able to accomplish. If the buildings are of "talia" or some flimsier material, the sun and rain will soon crumble them into clay and sand. Every nomad will help the work by overturning what has been left standing in search of buried treasure, the chief's house being the first to be subjected to this process, as the walls and the floors formed his usual bank. On the other hand, should the buildings have been of stone, the survivors will in time carry them away to rear other dwellings, until the palmetto scrub covers the few crumbling walls; and as caravans have no temptation to pass that way, the very name of the "Djin" haunted spot may be forgotten. Perhaps, if a few wanderers are tempted to make their homes there, the place gets a new name. But the chances are that the tales of evil spirits, who have their abode among its graves, effectually deter any one from such a venture, should the place have been long uninhabited. Possibly even, it is said to have been one of the "Rumes" works, and that the Nazarene, who is measuring it with a tape covered with cabalistic marks, and recording all so gravely on paper, after again and again consulting a map, is in possession of the very words which will enable him to recover the ancient people's hidden wealth. But the only wealth he is in search of—namely, the position where the towns of four centuries or more ago were built—has hitherto eluded him. The Romans built little, and though little remains of their cities, their architects have left more solid monuments of their skill.

(35) Tefethne "città di porto in Hea", Tafetana, Teftana or Tefetne, according to Marmol, is one of those "most famous mart-townes" which no longer exists. Even the map makers, who cling with amazing fidelity to a name, have ceased to engrave its position on the coast south of Cape Tefetneh. One of the latest recognitions of it is in Gräberg de Hemsö's *Carta del Moghrib-el-Acsa* (1834), where "Tafelane" is duly placed on the northern side of the "Iguzul", or Tidsi River mouth, about thirty miles south of Mogador. But as Culeihat appears on the same map as a town on the coast a little north of it, and Tesegdelt a place a few miles inland from Ras Tegrivelt or Cape Ossin, the authority for this curiosity in cartography is of the smallest.

However, the African charts of a century ago never hesitate about its position. Yet long before that date the port of Tefetne must have ceased to have any existence, so far as shipping traders, and even houses, were concerned. In the Catalan map of 1375, a town is mentioned under the name of Teftana, a name that under various disguises appears on all the older maps subsequent to that date. Tefelneh is the erroneous form it takes on the map of Arlett and Washington (*Journal R. G. S.*, vol. i, p. 123). Tefelane is that of De Borda (1780), a variation in nomenclature which Gräberg de Hemsö compromises by giving the first name to the cape, and the second to the town. The etymology of the word is, according to Delaporte, from the Berber term signifying a cauldron, a simile suggested by the hollow which the little port occupies.

The Catalan chart places between Tefetna and Cape Irir (Agadir-Igir) a port named Zebedech, evidently the Zebadet of Levaneur's map of 1610, in which it is placed at the embouchure of a river. In 1625 Jean Dupont indicates the river as the Zebedet, and after a variety of shapes Zabedecha appears on the Sanson map as half-way between Tefetna and Cape Irir. On the map of De Testu, Zebedet is given to Tafetenne, so that most probably it was at the mouth of the Wad Tedsi, or possibly at that of the Wad Tamer. On Andrea Bianco's map of 1456 we find a point called Gayulu at the embouchure of a river a little south of "Obdec", which may reasonably enough be accepted as Zebedech. After Bianco's day the cartographers indulged in that wide variety of opinion which makes their handiwork so extremely puzzling, most of them placing Gayulu north of the point last named, and altering the name almost beyond recognition. Thus Benincasa has it Gaççola, and Sanson Gazola, which he places between Tefetna and Zebedech. Gazola is perhaps only one of the many derivations of the Berber word Guezzula—which in Arabic authors takes the shape of Gzula, Gdala, Tedala, Tezula, etc., and was of old applied to the entire Berber population of Sus and Dra, Mersa-Guezzula, and, of course, the " port of the Guezzulas".

But though it is now difficult without a special expedition, which as the long official search of the old Spanish port of Santa Cruz di Mar Pequeña on the same coast amply proves, might have little result ; to fix the exact position of "Tefethne", there cannot be any doubt that it existed on the banks of a river near the Cape of the same name. But no ships of even "meane burthen" come there now, so that there is every likelihood that the river and port have been silted up, and the town wall of hewn stone and brick (*di pietre lavorate e di mattoni*) which protected the filthy houses of 3,000 people is now buried under mounds of the sand which covered so much of the coast for miles inland. The "stately hospital" (*un grande spedale*), under which pompous designation the "foudak" or caravan serai for sheltering strangers is meant, was very requisite in a place visited by traders, if indeed the hospitality of the citizens might not have been embarrassing owing to their peculiar sanitary notions. Curiously enough neither Leo nor Marmol has a word to say of Mogador. For though the present town was begun by Sidi Mohammed about 1760, a native village existed near the site long before that date. Possibly it was Ptolemy's Tamusega, a name which lingers in Sufega or Surega on various seventeenth-century maps. The Arab name for Mogador or Mogadul—derived from the tomb of Sidi Mogdul—is S'oueira, "the picture" ; but the Berbers knew it as Tasurt. Yet even in Leo's day the place must have been well known, from the pilgrims resorting to this shrine.

Domegador, which appears on Hondius' map of 1608 as the name of Mogador Island, appears to have been familiar at that period. Indeed, as early as 1604 John Smith, of Virginia, made a voyage to "Santa Cruze (*Agadir*), Cape Goa (*Ghir*), and Magadore", and in documents of 1660 "Mogator" is repeatedly referred to as a place of trade. In 1644 the Touraine Capuchin Fathers mention that there was a port on Mogador Island, and that sixteen years before that date Abdel Malik II had intended employing the Christian slaves to erect fortifications around the bay. Charant (*Lettre ecritte*, etc., p. 202) calls it "Mongador", which in the English translation (1671) becomes

"Mogatoz". This so-called "Portuguese Fort" was, some local scepticism notwithstanding, actually erected by the Portuguese, not to hold the place, but to protect their traders who called in here, or to keep up the communication between Saffi and Agadir. De Faria y Sousa expressly mentions that the fort was erected by Diego de Azambujo in 1505 : "Este propio año con que vamos prosiguiendo, mandó el Rey levantar en frente de la Isla de Mogador el Castillo que se llamó Real. Executólo Diego de Azambujo á pesar de mucha resistencia de Moros que concurrieron para estorvar la prosecucion desta fabrica." This passage has been strangely overlooked. At all events the omission of any reference to Mogador in Leo's account is curious, even though there was no European settlement there at the time he wrote.—Renou, *Exp. scientifique de l'Algérie*, t. viii, pp. 47-51 ; Brown, Appendix to *Pellow's Adventures*, pp. 366-368 ; *Hist. de la Mission des frères capucins de la province de Touraine, au royaume de Maroc en Afrique* (1644), pp. 222, 270 ; De Faria y Sousa, *Africa Portugesa* (1681), p. 76.

(36) Idevacal, in the original : the mountainous district of Berber people called Idau Bakil, the Ida-ou-Baagil of Foucauld's *Reconnaissance au Maroc*, p. 342. This great tribe of the Idau Bakil, at one time almost independent, was forced to submit to the Sultan Mulai el Hasan, during his punitive expedition in 1882, and was placed with several others under the Kaidate of Hadj Tahar, son of Sidi el Hosein, the "Saint" of Tazerualt. They are rich in horses, and from the number of picturesque little castles scattered over these mountains, are still powerful for evil. They lead a sedentary life, and speak the "Tamazul" dialect of the Shelluh division of Berbers. In manners, dress, etc., Leo's description applies almost precisely to the present day. The "Keshshaba" of "Khent", or blue cotton (imported from England mostly, in imitation of a much better and dearer stuff from the Sahara), supplies the place of a shirt. It is not stitched, the sheet being knotted at the corners, and the sides remaining open. By wild goats (*capriuoli*) the wild sheep or aoudad is meant : hares (*lepri*) are rabbits, and deer (*cervi*) Barbary stags, no longer common. The walnut grows to great perfection, and is carefully protected by the Berbers on the Atlas and its spurs.

(37) The Tenzera of Marmol. The only other mention of the mountain by this name is in De Mairault's *Relation de ce qui s'est passé dans le Royaume de Maroc depuis l'année 1727 jusqu'en 1730* (1742), pp. 178, 183, in which it is told how the Sheriff 'Abd-Allah, in the month of August 1730, defeated the revolted natives in the province of Haha, five leagues from the "Mountain of Tenzera". Even in Leo's day it seems to have been an unimportant locality

having no "Kasbahs" or fortified places. Still, in 1730, 'Abd Allah and his black troops had no easy task in their attack upon what De Mairault loosely terms "les Alarbes", and the wealth of the latter is shown by the booty of 6,000 horses, 800 camels, 12,000 oxen, and a great number of sheep, which the victors carried off or destroyed. Indeed, from the manner in which Haha was at that date laid waste it is not remarkable that so many places have now been effaced.

The statement that the streams from this mountain flow into the Sheshawa (Siffaia), a tributary of the Tensift, at once shows that they are in the basin of that Haha river, and flow from the western spur of the Atlas which divides Sus from Haha, and reaches the sea at Agadir.

It is, however, almost certain that people of that neighbourhood do not nowadays know any mountain by that name near the Bibauan pass, in the vicinity of which it must have been often crossed. The statement that many Karaite Jews live among the people of the mountain as mercenary soldiers is remarkable. In the Sus country and in many parts of the Atlas (Teleut for example) and other portions of the "Blad es siba" which does not recognise the authority of the Sultan (as distinguished from "Blad el makhsen" the region under his control), the Jews are permitted to ride horses and to bear arms under the supervision of their Berber or Arab "owners" or protectors. But in the list of localities inhabited by the Morocco Jews drawn up by De Foucauld, there is no place in the Tensift Basin at all like Demensera or Tenzera. However, the spot where the Wad Tefnut arises in the Great Atlas is called Tenzer (the Nostrils), and it is not unlikely that the two places are, if not identical, of the same name, though Leo evidently takes Demensera to express a large area.

"Nell' anno nove cento venti", the year of the Hegira being understood. But the "yeere of our Lord 1520" is, as usual, an interpolation of Florianus translated by Pory, and, as usual, is erroneous, A.D. 1514 being the probable equivalent of A.H. 920, according to the month in which it began. In some of the Italian editions these equivalents are given, but they are all omitted in the 1837 reprint. In 1520 Leo was captured by the pirates of Djerba.

(38) "Gebeleadi", in the original Italian, Gebelethadih, a clump of hills, still known as "the iron mountain", though really a range, the few people who inhabit it being the Regraga or Rekrek Berbers, of the Musnudi stock. It is in the Takat district, and is about 2,470 feet in height, rising abruptly from the plain of Akkermut. There are still plentiful traces of the hydrous oxide of iron from which the mountain derives its name ; having been rudely mined by races who lived possibly before the Arab invasion, though at present it pays

better to buy metal from the European merchants. Even in Leo's day the mines do not seem to have been worked. The summit is crowned by a Kubba, or domed tomb, of Sidi Yakub, probably the same which Arlett calls that of "Sidi-Wasman", and Renou, "retablie, d'apres M. Delaporte en Sidi-'Otmân". But the "Hermites" (*romiti*), like the population generally, are no longer in evidence. The people, indeed, seem to have been driven away, killed in raids, or absorbed into the races surrounding them. Mohammed Ebn-Said's campaign of which Leo speaks was in 1516, not in 1512, which is an erroneous addition to the text by Florianus and Pory.—Thomson, *Travels*, etc., pp. 99-106; Hooker and Ball, *Tour*, etc., p. 313.

(39) Massa, or Messa, one of the oldest settlements in Morocco, is still in existence in a condition between dormancy and death; though in reality consisting of nine contiguous villages, instead of three as in Leo's day. The principal of these is Arbalu, or Aghbalu; but the river, near the mouth of which these villages are situated, is now almost drifted up with sand, so that for ages no ships have visited the place, and the fields and gardens, which under irrigation yield good crops, are only kept from a similar fate by the thick thorn fences and walls around them.

Leo, however, blundered in describing Messa as on the River Sus, instead of between Agadir and Aglu, nearly twenty-five miles further south on the north side of a smaller river, the Wad Ulrass, or more correctly, Wad el-Ghas. This mistake of Leo's has, until very recently, been perpetuated on a number of maps, with a variety of forms of the river's name, for which the earlier copyists are responsible. Thus in the Pizzigani map of 1367, the embouchure of the river is indicated as the Alvet-Sus, a corruption, most probably, of the real name, and on other maps it appears as Albetsus, Alberful, etc., until altered beyond recognition, it began, after Leo's day, a fresh lease of life as the Sus, though Sanson, while accepting Leo as his authority for the course of the Sus, places it a little further north at a point which he calls Albetsusa, a Latinisation of the Albetsus or Alvetsus of the ancient maps. In 1781 the River "Suz" is placed in its true position and under its right name on Borda's Chart, and Davidson traced it for some distance through the district of "Stouka" (the name of a tribe) described by Marmol as "Estuque", and in more recent times by Venture and Riley, and Foucauld, as Chtouka. Jackson (who visited "Shtuka"), was, however, the first to point out (1811) Leo's mistake, though he continues to call the river the Messa, a practice followed, so far as the lower portion of it is concerned, by Paul Schnell in his excellent though sometimes, so far as discriminating between authorities is concerned, rather compromising map. Davidson obtained, in 1835, its true name, which he spells "wholgrass", thus correcting Bordas' further mistake of putting "Macas" on the "River Ana". Yet as late as 1860 Beaudon's map shows "Massé" on the south side of the Anaka—the Anaka being further south. Renou, on Delaporte's information, speaks of the "Ouad Ouelras" (the "Oulghav" of Venture) as one of the principal tributaries of the Messa. However, Edrisi refers to the Wad Messa, and to the port of Meset, and Marmol mentions that the place was sometimes known by its Berber name of Temest. The same historian calls the "temple" (mosque) of Massa "Rabita", diminutive of Rabat, a sanctuary or place of refuge. One of the latest blunders is on the map of Gråberg de Hemsö, where "Guertessen", a corruption of Garguenem, which is Santa Cruz, or Agadir, is placed at the mouth of the Messa, though, in his text, the author shows himself perfectly acquainted with the various names applied to the town in question. When Jackson visited Messa nearly a century ago, he found, as at the present day, the cultivators irrigating their fields by canals from the river. But the river was no longer navigable as in the period when the Portuguese had a settlement here, a sand bar separating it at low tide entirely from the ocean, though at high water it was not navigable. The river valley, inhabited by the Massa or Mast tribe, a branch of the Ait Ulrass, is very fruitful, though to this day, as Leo notes, their dates are held in little esteem.

The belief that the Mosaic and Moslem Prophet Jonah (Yunas) was vomited out of the whale near Messa, or, at all events, on the Sus Coast, was current at the time of Jackson's visit, and is still repeated. The Persians, however, declare that this event took place at Yunsi, in the Desert of Khurasan, at that time covered with the sea. The Koran has many passages on the miracle of Yunas (Goldsmid, *Proc. Roy. Geog. Soc.*, October 1890, p. 589). Until lately a pair of gigantic lower jaw bones of a whale were erected at Messa in the form of an arch, and pointed out as those of the identical "fish thrown on shore with the man called Jonah in its belly". Spermaceti whales are frequently stranded along this sandy coast, or cast up on it dead, and large lumps of ambergris are picked up by the natives, and sold in Mogador to the wealthy Moors, who are fond of flavouring their green tea with it. It is called El Amber, and is held in esteem as an aphrodisiac.—Cf., *The Voyage of François Leguat* (Hakluyt Society), vol. i, pp. 87-152.

The gold and silver mines which Jackson hints at as being in the vicinity of Messa are doubtful. His etymology of Segelmessa as being Sijn-Messa, "the prison of Messa", because the State prisoners of Morocco were anciently sent to Segelmessa, is ingenious, as they are still banished to Tafilet, which replaced it. But it is a trifle unintelligible so far as Messa is concerned; or it could never have been so important a place as to have prisoners enough to send into the interior, unless, indeed, the State prisoners were taken by sea to Messa, and thence sent by a safer and shorter road to their destination. The history of the Portuguese, indeed of any European connection with Messa, is very obscure. The people still have traditions of "the Christians leaving"; but as to what were their relations to the place, or when they ceased to frequent or live in the place, the Portuguese records afford little if any information.—Jackson, *An Account of Timbuctoo and Housa*, etc., pp. 145-146; *An Account of Morocco*, pp. 9, 125; Renou, *Expl. Scientifique de l'Algérie*, vol. viii, pp. 58-60; Erckmann, *Le Maroc Moderne*, p. 55.

Mr. R. L. Johnston, H.M. Vice-Consul in Mogador, visited Messa in 1892, but does not seem to have been aware that it had in former days been a port frequented by Europeans. He refers to a once "populous settlement still partially inhabited" on the right of the entrance into the river, and to many extensive villages now more or less deserted.—*Moorish Lotus Leaves*, pp. 212-215.

(40) This place Renou imagines to be the same as that mentioned as Tescut or Techeut by Marmol. Finding that a village on the Sus River was reported to be called Tichout, he jumps to the conclusion that the latter was identical with the former. He even speculates whether it might not be the Tergunt of Marmol or the Tuet of Diego de Torres. This is, however, impossible. For Tiguiut, of which in De Atarde's time a Genoese renegade was Governor (Marmol, *L'Afrique*, vol. i, p. 446), is in Haha, so that it is more probably the Haha Teijut already discussed, while the Tuit of Diego de Torres is even more problematical. But we now know the course of the Sus tolerably minutely, and can say for certain that if there is any "Tehout" near that river, it is a mere village of no consequence. What Leo describes is Sus Teijut, then a considerable commercial centre. Renou's identification must therefore be dismissed. Vivien de St. Martin is more ingenious. Finding that Ptolemy names six towns (Antolala, Tagœna, Thuilath, Magura, Ubrir, Tarzitha), he is inclined to believe that *Thuilath* may be Leo's Teculet, *Magura* Amager, a former centre of the Masmudi, which Marmol describes as existing between Mogador and Agadir (vol. ii, p. 22), that *Tarzitha* is Tezekht, and that Tezekht is near the left bank of the Sus, and that Atlahe is unquestionably the Teijut of Leo (Ibn Khaldun, *Hist. des Berbers*, t. ii, pp. 256-277, etc., and t. i, p. cxii; *Mémoires de la Soc. de Géog. de Paris*, t. vii, p. 221). Finally, he offers the hypothesis whether *Antolala* has not some connection with the old Antolales (*Le Nord de l'Afrique dans l'antiquité*, p. 373).

I know of no place called "Tezekht" near the Sus River, or anywhere else. But there is Tizuit south-east of Aglu, the furthest point reached in Mulai El Hassan's hunting expedition in 1882. The identification of it with the Sus Teijut is not very satisfactory. For it is a comparatively small place in itself, and not in the position assigned to it by Leo, though one of several large villages, thus agreeing with Leo's description. But the place was formerly fortified, and the Sultan built a castle (Kasbah) to overawe the turbulent inhabitants, whose character will readily enough bear out the reputation of the old Teijutees.

Leo, it will be noticed, does not say that his Teijut is "on", but "not far from" the Sus, and it must be remembered that he considered the Wad Ulass, or Messa River, from which Tizuit is not far, as a branch of the Sus. Still it is not anything like so important a town as Temdant, though all these places have, in the course of four centuries, been greatly altered. But unless Tizuit is accepted, I do not see any other claimant for the representation of Teijut which has more in its support. In any case, Leo has either transliterated the actual word wrongly, or his editor has made some mistake in deciphering his cheirography, since the place in Haha and the one in Sus cannot, for reasons already mentioned, have been spelt exactly the same, and yet have borne different names.

By "Sus", where a measure of oil is sold for "quindici ducati il cantaro", Leo must mean in the towns on the Sus river; for Sus is a province in which Teijut is situated.

"Morocco" leather is still made in great quantities from goat skins, chiefly for slippers, and dyed pink, yellow, and other colours. But though it is excellent in its softness, little is exported, the Morocco of Europe being preferable for the purposes to which it is applied.

"Burghmasters"—*gentiluomini* in the original Italian.

The valley of the Sus River is one of the great Jewish countries in Morocco, but there are not many in the "Sahel", where Tizuit is situated, though some seventy or eighty families still find a profit out of the trade of Tizuit, Tazeruall, and the vicinity.

It is doubtful whether the *Tebuiern*, or perhaps *Teiutuin* or *Teiutin* of Edrisi, a place situated in Sus al Aksa, is Leo's Teijeut (Hartmann, *Edrisi Africa*, pp. 140-42). But there is nothing inherently against the suggestion.

(41) Tarudant is a well-known town, and one of the most ancient in Morocco, though now so fanatical that it is perilous for an unprotected European to visit it. But it enjoys little of its old prosperity, the closing of Agadir, two days' journey distant, having almost put an end to its commerce and industry. The walls, about $3\frac{3}{4}$ statute miles in circuit, are now in a very dilapidated condition, and many of the houses inside them are uninhabited. Altogether, according to Captain

Erckmann, the chief of the French Military Commission, who visited it in 1882 with the Sus Expedition of Mulai el Hassan, it may have a stationary population of six or seven thousand. Most of these are Shillah Berbers, who swagger through the dirty lanes armed to the teeth, staring at every stranger with a ferocious glare. Black barley cakes is almost the only bread used, and the food supplies, if plentiful, are not luxurious. The town is, however, environed with groves of olives, oranges, dates, almonds, palms, and other fruits, and in some of the little shops Morocco goods are for sale. In the small " Mellah", or Jews' quarter there, most of the houses are falling into decay; some petty trade is done with the greatest care not to suggest wealth on the part of the oppressed traders, and even the Kasbah palace is fast falling into ruins. The Sultan is represented by a Kaid; but so slight is his power, or desire to exercise it, that assassinations in full daylight in the open street, are quite common, and are seldom, if the murderer has friends or money, visited with any more immediate punishment than the vengeance of the victim's relatives. From that there is no escape, unless the murdered man happens to be an unprotected Jew, or, it may be, a wandering Christian, whose king has not an arm long enough to reach the feeble Lord of Maghreb al-Aksa. The Sus river flows near the town, and it is said that rings can still be seen to which, previous to the fourteenth century, ships which had navigated the river for forty miles from the sea were moored. If so, this is no longer possible : indeed, in summer, it is almost dry. Apart from the fact of the water in it being drained off for irrigating purposes, the country seems to be getting more arid, and the streams more choked up by shallower silt. Near the town is the country of the Uled-el-halluf (Children of the Wild Boar), so called from their untameable savagery. Sugar cane (Lukseb), which in the sixteenth century brought such wealth to Tarudant, is not now cultivated, but it grows in places spontaneously. Rich copper ores, gold and antimony, have been brought from the vicinity of the town. Nickel, also, is said to be plentiful in the neighbouring Atlas, and at Gondolfi (Gondafy?), not far from the source of the Sus, is a rich vein of silver. The late Abdul Kerim Grant (a Scotch renegade, and perhaps the last Briton who was) succeeded in reaching it in 1877, and bringing back rich specimens. His companion, Captain Robertson, was imprisoned, and died soon after his return from the effects of poison. The mine is in the territory of the Shaikh Hassan Amr, who is independent of the Sultan.— Erckmann, *Le Maroc*, pp. 52-54 ; De Campon, *Un Empire qui croule*, p. 250.

(42) Gartguessem seems to have been one of the names applied in Leo's day to Agadir-Igir, which again received from the Portuguese the title of Santa Cruz, a designation now almost forgotten. Agadir

is from a Berber word signifying the wall; and is a common name in Morocco. The original Agadir was, however, the miserable fishing village of Fonte, on the sea-shore, the nucleus of the picturesque town on the hill above being the wooden shelter which the Portuguese merchant or "senhor" built towards the end of the fifteenth century for the protection of the fishermen and traders. This building, named Santa Cruz by the founders, was called Tiguimmi-Roummi (or the Christian house) by the Berbers, and Dar-Roumiya by the Arabs, which means exactly the same. Sometime later Manoel, the Fortunate, King of Portugal, built a little port here, which kept the name of Santa Cruz, or Santa Cruz de Barbaria. This is what Leo refers to when he says that "about twentie yeeres sithens" (that is, from the time he was there—say 1500) "the Portuguese surprised" the place.

Fonti, or Fonté, is a Portuguese word, but the Berber name is Aguram, Fonte being evidently derived from the spray or fountain, still protected by a domed building, on which are the Portuguese arms.

The etymology of Garguessem is not clear. It was probably the original name of the native village, and may be connected with the Berber *Gar*, a place, or some derivation of Aguram. Most localities in Morocco have more than one name: many half-a-dozen. Agadir-n-Igir is the wall or strong place of "the elbow", that is, of the cape —the cape in question being the Gher, Ghar, Guer, or Aguer, of charts. But the Arab name is Ras-Afourni, which has got corrupted into Aferni, Fernit, Ferne, Ras-Aferne, Afarnie, etc., on different maps (cf. Renou, *Expl. Scient. de l'Algérie*, vol. viii, pp. 36-38).

This variety of names for Agadir has puzzled map makers, Santa Cruz being put at one place and Garguessem (in endless variations) in another. After acquiring possession of Santa Cruz, the King fortified it so that the place was able to resist all attacks upon it until 1536. But in that year the Sheriff Mulai Mohammed el Arrani, aided by a Genoese renegade, named Numen, besieged it with an army of—it is recorded— 50,000 men, and, after a stout defence by the garrison, captured it by mining the walls with gunpowder. Among the prisoners taken, and either massacred or enslaved, was the Commandant, Gutierre de Monroi, of whose beautiful daughter Mencia, the Sheriff became so enamoured that, without, so it is said, requiring her to adjure Christianity, he married her. The lady and her child died about a year later, being supposed, as Diego de Torres tells us, to have been poisoned by some of the other jealous inmates of Mulai Mohammed's harem. But so affectionately did her lord remember his Portuguese wife, that he never permitted a day to pass without laying fresh flowers on the tomb of the hapless Mencia de Monroi.—Diego de Torres, *Istoria de los Xarifes*, pp. 109, 112, 142, 467.

After this the place, under the name of Agadir, remained in the

Sultan's hands, and for many years was the entrepot of an extensive trade with Timbuctoo and the Sudan, the port being the best in Morocco, and the natural outlet for the rich province of Sus. This fact, however, aroused the jealousy of the Sultan. The people were too wealthy, and obtained arms and ammunition too easily. Accordingly Sidi Mohammed in 1773 resolved to close the port to foreign trade—which meant all shipping—and after some trouble with a refractory Governor (who declined to surrender the fortress) ordered the European merchants to take up their quarters in the new town of Mogador. This was done, and since then, with the exception of a short time when the port was specially opened to the Dutch, Agadir has sunk deeper and deeper into decay until at present there are only a few hundred people in the place, who eke out a poor livelihood by carrying freight to or from Mogador and Tarudant, by catching the fish with which the bay swarms, or in smuggling. Over the doorways may be seen inscriptions in Dutch and other languages, indicating the European mercantile houses, and on two old Portuguese guns, which lumber the ramparts, may be read, "Maria et Petrus III reges", with the Royal escutcheon and the date, 1782, showing that they had been imported after the place passed into Moorish hands. Above the entrance-gate of the town is cut the emblem of the Sacred Heart, surmounted by a cross and the letters "S. C.". There is a good view of the place in Hüst's *Efterretninger* (1779), tab. ii ; but the author is wrong in dating the close of the Portuguese rule in 1580.

(43) Here a clause is omitted—" siccome nelle abbreviazione nostre habbiamo detto" (as we have given in our Abbreviation), the "Abbreviation" meaning, no doubt, not that history of Mohammedan affairs to which Leo so frequently refers, but to a summary which, if ever written, has been lost.

(44) Tedsi has long been a snare to the map makers. Jackson, finding a small river reaching the sea a few miles south of Tegrevelt and Cape Ossim under the name of Tidsi, hastily concluded that this was " where the ancient city of Tidsi formerly stood ", an impossibility in so far that Leo expressly says it is 60 miles from the Atlantic. Possibly, some vague recollection of Tafelane was running in Jackson's mind. Gråberg, indeed, places the vanished town on the north side of the " Iguzal or Tidsi", though in his text (p. 63) he puts it near " un ramo grosso del fiume Sus", in deliberate contradiction of what Leo says about its distance from that river, and not being on any river at all. In reality, the place is found exactly where Leo indicated it, in the shape of three large villages, which are often the "cities" of Leo. Tidsi, which gives the name to this district of the Sus Sahel, can

furnish 300 markets, and El Korba 200, while Umsediklit is 700 strong. The three villages lie close together, and might originally have been quarters of one town. Tidsi is governed by a single Sheikh, who, at the time of De Foucauld's visit, was a Marabout or "Saint" named Sidi el Hanafi, though in a way it recognises the Sultan by the hereditary Sheikh sending every year some tribute to Tarudant. There are not now many Jews in this district, a sure test of the decadence of this once flourishing centre. Nor is sugar any longer a crop, a fact which may account for its desertion by the Israelites, the extraction and refining of sugar being, in the palmy days of that source of wealth, largely in their hands. But a market of great importance, the Khemis Tidsi, is still held in Tidsi, which is sometimes called Ez Zauïa, because it is the Zauïa, or sanctuary, which is the Sheikh's residence. The land is, however, fertile, wheat, barley, maize, lentils, and olives being grown. There is no river in the district, the soil being irrigated from the numerous springs which arise from the foot-hills of the Atlas; but the village lies on a plain, and is inhabited almost entirely by Shillah Berbers, who speak the Tamazirt dialect. In the sixteenth century it had for one of its rulers the renegade Genoese Yahia, or Mohammed-el-Euldj. In a letter of Mulai Mohammed, son of Mulai Zeidan (*cir.* 1620), Tidsi is referred to as "one of the Ksors of the Wad Dra", so that before this period it must have dropped out of notice. For in A.H. 918 (A.D. 1512-13) the Sheriff had his abode there, and obtained the allegiance of the place for his eldest son, Abd-el-Kebir (*Nozhet Elhâdi*, pp. 15, 32, 33).

(45) Tagavost is the Tagoast of Marmol, who calls it "the greatest town of the province of Sus", from the termination of which it is eight days' travel. M. Renou believed that he had re-discovered the place in "Tarabust". But beyond M. Delaporte's notes, I am not aware of any other mention of it. There is, however, a village on the Sus basin called Tagoast, which may have been the remnants of what was, in Leo's day, a large Berber town, though it is quite certain that no place of the size described by Leo exists in the Sus valley nowadays. Marmol's position and Leo's differ much. The continual civil wars of the population no doubt account for the place being now broken up into several villages. For 1510 A.D. read 1513, and the equivalent of A.H. 919.

(46) This, if not a mistake of Leo or his editor, cannot now be identified. For though the position is minutely given, I cannot ascertain that, on the numerous spurs of the Atlas, there is any name which corresponds to Hanchisa or Anchisa. Diego de Torres does not mention it in his narrative of the Sheriff's exploits. Evidently it must be looked for in the Tizen-Ibergagen, and the neighbouring

hills, inhabited by Uled Iahia and other fierce tribes whom the Sheriffs found it impossible to subdue.

(47) This refers to one of the strongholds of the Halem people, the most numerous of all the Tamazirt-speaking Berbers, and who, under various forms, have already been noticed. The reference to silver mines is interesting. Jackson mentions silver in the vicinity of Messa, though rather unintelligibly, and says that at Msegina, near Agadir, there is a mine which was probably worked by the Portuguese. At "Elala", and Shtuka in Sus, he also notes the existence of a rich silver mine. "But being situated between two clans, they are continually fighting about it, and by this means both parties are deprived of the benefits it offers. I have purchased lumps of the silver, which has been refined by the natives, and it was more pure than the silver of Spanish dollars." The "Elela" is evidently the same as Leo's "Halem".

(48) Renou is convinced that "Elgiumuha città della sopradetta regione", on the River "Sesseua", Sheshawa, Sevsava, Cheuchava, Schouchâoua, Seinsciaua, or Chouchaoua, to give it a few of its various orthographies, is only El Djama, the Mosque, though he does not explain why he thinks so. "Muachidin" is Muahhedin, "believer in the Unity of God", corrupted into Almohades. But it is quite different from Elgihumuha, the Gemaa-el-Carvar, *i.e.*, in more literary Arabic, Jâmi (Djâmi)—K'aruach, the Berber village of 'Ain-Garuâch (Marmol, *L'Afrique*, vol. ii, p. 205). It lay on the caravan route from Fez to Larach, and was destroyed in the wars of the Said. Leo's "Elgihumuaha" on the Sheshawa, "a towne of Maroco", which in his day was almost effaced, is, if El Guima, very problematical. Possibly Sok Djama may be the site.

(49) Or Umegiaque. Perhaps Imagheren.

(50) This little Berber mountain town has not been identified. The "river of Afifnuall" is the Wad-Arif-el-Mel. Is it not Tenin ez Za?

(51) According to Leo, this town is called "New Delgumuha", having perhaps been built to take the place of the other Gihumuha (Elgihumuha). If the name is put into Arabic, it is Gemaa-Jided (Djâmi' Djedid), the new mosque. Delgumuha appears simply as a corruption of this—possibly a misprint of the abbreviation — "Djo' gemaa". There are, however, so many little places in Morocco named from this mosque, that "Djama", as a name, has really little significance. Thus there are Djama Amerri, Djama Amzou, Djama Tinzut, Djami Tizeigat, Djama Huara, etc., all mere tribal hamlets or castellated "Ksors"; they are like "church towns" in Cornwall. But from the

Asif-el-mel ("boiling river") arising below the town, we are able to determine Delgumuha approximately, if not actually, as the modern Marossa, where, at a height of more than 3,000 feet, the river boils along in a deep gorge or cañon.—Thomson, *Travels*, p. 323.

(52) This is Amsmes or Amsmez (variously spelt Imzmizi, Amizimizi, Imesimis, or Almishmish), a large village of about 2,000 people, a considerable proportion of which are Jews, lying on the northern slope of the Great Atlas at a height of more than 3,000 feet above the sea, and at some elevation above the place which Leo mentions. The Wad Amsmes issues from the mountains, in the shape of a torrent, just below the town. Thomson (*Travels*, p. 282) has given a photograph of Amsmes. Marmol calls the mountain on the eastern extremity of which "Imesimis" is built, Guidimiva (Gedmeva). *Cf.* note 50.

Burris of Leo, *Barrix* of Marmol, is, perhaps, *Bu-Rich*, the "Father of Feathers" (Renou, *Expl. Scientifique de l'Algérie*, t. viii, p. 193).

(53) The Tamdegort of Marmol (*L'Afrique*, t. ii, p. 50). The name exists in Tamesloht, near the Wad Basha, between Agadir ben Selam and Marakesh, though the actual remains of the three villages ought to be sought near Fouga. In Leo's day the "townes", as he calls the wretched villages not containing over 60 or 70 people, seem to have paid tribute to Portugal, and, in spite of what Leo affirms, we have the authority of Marmol for saying that at times they were so bled by the Arabs and the "King of Fez", that they deserted their villages until, under the protection of the Sheriffs, they returned.

(54) "My deer friend Sidi Iehie" was a native chief who had the Arabs and Berbers of the coast-lying country so completely at his service that, it is said, he could bring 5,000 horsemen and 100,000 foot into the field. He was a vassal of Portugal, a bitter enemy of the Sheriffs, and a warm friend of Nuño Fernandez d'Ataide, the governor of Saffi, for whom, and the Portuguese, Yahia performed splendid services, penetrating with the expedition to Marakesh and sticking his lance in its principal gate. Considering what Leo tells us of the extent of the Portuguese power in that region, this audacity is not remarkable. Ataide and Yahia failed, however, in their design on Marakesh, being unable to force its defences, and were pursued by the Sheriffs for a long distance from the walls.

Yahia, in spite of his services, was scurvily treated by Portugal. After the death of Nuño Fernandez d'Ataide, his successor, Nuño de Mascareñas, became jealous of Yahia in his new dignity of Captain-General, and probably secured his assassination, in 1517, by two Arabs of the Ulâd-'Omrân. The Sheriffs, being the chief gainers by the dastardly act, were suspected of employing the murderers.

(55) Tesrast or Tazarot, on the Asif-el-Mel, cannot be satisfactorily identified with any modern place. In Leo's day it was so badly placed by reason of floods and Arab marauders that most likely the harassed Berbers deserted it soon after.

(56) "La gran città di Marocco"—in the 1613 edition misprinted "Marocoo": Marakesh, or Maraksh (spelt in various ways) is the native name, and the one almost universally used by European residents in Morocco. Most likely the French Maroc, the German Marokko, the Spanish Marruecos, the Danish Marokos, and so forth are all corruptions of Marakesh, which Leo does not mention as the native name, but calls the city by the Italian Marocco; though, according to Burton (*Arabian Nights*, Supp., vol. ii, p. 252), the earliest form of it is "Marakiyah", mentioned in Al-Mas'udi (vol. iii, p. 241), as applied to a district whither the Berbers emigrated. Some recent authors insist that the English corruption of Morocco should be displaced by M*a*rocco. But the latter is not less a corruption than the former. Morocco city was founded (A.H. 454, A.D. 1062-3) by the Almoravide, Yusuf Ibn Tashfin, whose capital previous to this was Aghmat. This date is sometimes given as 1072 A.D. His son, Ali Ibn Yusuf, continued the building which his father had begun by laying the foundation of a mosque, and a castle in which to keep his treasures. Ali surrounded it with a stone wall, and it was increased by his successors, but not completed until the reign of Abu Yusuf Yakub (El Mansur), grandson of Abdu-l-Mumenu, in the year A.H. 585 (A.D. 1189-90), when it became the capital.

In a MS. history of Morocco, quoted by Gayangos, and erroneously ascribed to Ibn Batuta (the work being dated at a period when Ibn Batuta was 92), the foundation is ascribed to Abú Bekr Ibn Omar, the first of the Almoravides, and the father of Yusuf Ibn Tashfin, who reigned from A.D. 1061 (A.H. 453) to A.D. 1106 (A.H. 500). This city he called "Morekosh" (a form also used in the *Karbas*, and by Ibn Khaldun), and says that the site of it was known from time immemorial as the "Plain of Morekosh", and was in the hands of the Berber tribe of Masmuda, from whom the ground was purchased.

Ptolemy knew the Plain of Morocco as Πυρρὰ Πεδίον, which Mannest thinks means "the plain in flames", from the inhabitants being all charcoal burners. In reality, the name in Arabic (Bahret el-Hamra) means exactly what it does in Greek, viz., the grand, dry, reddish plain, which stretches to the west of Morekesh, between the Atlas and the Tensift. But there are no grounds for looking for a Roman city anywhere in this quarter, far less for the Bocanum Hemerum as the predecessors of the city of Yusuf Ibn Tashfin. The "very ancient city named Ta Maroc", which Keating speaks of as on the Um-er-Rbia, is not known to me, nor do I know his sources of information.—

Gayangos, *History of the Mohammedan Dynasties of Spain* (trans. from Al-Makkari), vol. i, pp. 349 and App. L and III ; Conde, *Hist. de la Dominacion de los Arabes en España*, etc., vol. ii, pp. 384-409, *et passim;* Tissot ; Keating's *Travels in Europe and Africa*, vol. i, pp. 239-280 ; *Roudh el Kartas* (Beaumier's ed., pp. 194-5).

(57) "Hali, son of Joseph", is Ali Ibn Yusuf (A.D. 1106-1142-3, A.H. 500-537). "The King of the Tribe of Lumtana" (Lemtuna) must mean Yusuf Ibn Tashfin. "Elbnuachedin" is Abd-el-Mumenin, commonly called El-Movahhidi ; but he was not Yusuf's immediate successor, but a sovereign of another (Almohade) dynasty (A.D. 1130).

The "temple of Hali ben Joseph" is still called the "Djâmi Sidi Yusuf". "The second usurper over the kingdome of Moroco" was 'Abd-el-Mumen, as El-Mahdi is not usually counted, but Abu-Yusuf-Yakub-el-Mansur was not his nephew (nipote), but his grandson. De Slane (and Godard following him), make out El Mansur to be the son of Abd-el-Mumen. But the *Roudh el Kartas* (Beaumier's Ed., pp. 303-4) is positive that he was the grandson, "The Emir of the Musulmen, servant of Allah. Yakub ben Yusuf ben 'Abd-el-Mumen, surnamed El Mansur bi Fadhl Allah (the victorious by the grace of God), was the son of a negress who had been given to his father, and he was born in the house of his grandfather, 'Abd-el-Mumen, at Morocco, in the year 555. He was also surnamed Abu Yusuf".

(58) The mosque which he enlarged and decorated is El Kutubia, with a tower built like the one near Rabat, after the style of the Giralda in Seville, now so utterly ruined by the "restorer". Indeed, all three were begun and finished by Yakub-el-Mansur, and tradition has it, from the designs of the same architect. This artist's name is said by Antonio Pans to have been Guever, "a Christian", though the style of the buildings, almost identical, does not favour the supposition. From the summit of the Lantern Tower (Samâ el Fanar), Leo tells us that Cape Cantin ("the promontone of Azaphi"), 130 miles distant, can be seen, a statement copied by Chenier and Jackson, though it is doubtful if either was ever within or at the top of the tower. It is about 270 feet in height, and the only mosque tower in the city which is built of stone, and, like the entire building, is substantially and even tastefully constructed.

"Vespascan his Amphitheatrum" (Vespascani amphitheatrum" of Florianus) is "il coliseo di Roma" in the original.

"An hundred elles"—"cento braccia di Toscano" in the original.

"The steeple of Bomonea" ("turrim ipsam Bomonicrsem" of Florianus) is in the original "torre degli Asenelli di Bologna"—the reference being to the leaning tower of the Asinella (274 feet high) in Bologna, the ancient Bomonea.

The passage to which Pory has added the note "obscurum", is in the original:—" La scala per cui s'ascende, è piana, e larga nove palme : la grossezza del muro di fuori dieci ; e il masso della torre è grosso cinque." Actually the walls of this square tower are four feet thick, and the ascent is not by stairs, but by a gradually winding terrace, composed of lime and small stones, so firmly cemented together as to be nearly as hard as iron.—Jackson, *Morocco*, p. 61. Jackson intends it to be inferred that he saw the interior, though his description, like that of Chenier, has a strong likeness to that of Leo. Christians and Jews are not permitted to enter any mosque in Morocco. Most probably his descriptions are from hearsay, or are as old as Leo. The three "golden" balls on the tower are sometimes described as the "spheares of gold", around which so many romantic legends have gathered.

The illiterate character of Marakesh three hundred years ago is even more true nowadays. There is not only not a book shop in the city, but, perhaps, not even a scholar.

(59) It is difficult to believe that the population of Marakesh has not been grossly exaggerated, notwithstanding the decrease in the population of the empire. Chenier doubted if it had more than 30,000 permanent citizens. But Jackson, less than half-a-century later, rated them as 270,000, while Gråberg, on even less data, put the people at 50,000, including 4,000 Shillahs and 5,000 Jews. Erckmann estimates the fixed population at less than that of Fez, and puts it at 55,000. But he was there only when the Sultan was in residence. Most likely 30,000 is nearest the mark, though when the Sultan is there the mouths to feed will run up to double that number. Even now half the city is in ruins, and from what we know of it in the seventeenth century, it is utterly impossible that it could then have contained five or six hundred thousand people (*Relation du royaume de Maroc et des villes qui en dépendent*, a MS., No. 778 of the French MSS. in the "Bibliothèque de roi" cited by Hoefer, *Empire du Maroc*, p. 307).

(60) The date given by Leo (A.H. 424) for the foundation of Marakesh seems erroneous. The *Roudh el Kartas* give A.H. 454 as the year after Yusuf Ibn Tashfin began to reign.

Ali Ibn Yusuf began to reign in A.D. 1106 (A.H. 500) and his son Tashfin Ibn Ali in A.D. 1146-7 (A.H. 541).

(61) "This certain Mahumetan preacher" was Mohammed Ibn Tumart El Mahdi, founder of the Almohade dynasty in A.H. 522 (A.D. 1128), already referred to.

Tashfin Ibn Ali was slain at Oran in the struggle against the

Almohades (A.D. 1146-47, A.H. 541). His brother Ibrahim succeeded, but was deposed for his incapacity. Ishak, son of Ali Ibn Yusuf, was then called to power: but in return for opening the gates of Marakesh to Abd-el-Mumen, was, with his followers, massacred by that ferocious chief who succeeded his master, the Mahdi, Mohammed Ibn Tumart (A.D. 1174, A.H. 541). Versions, however, differ considerably, one making Ishak the sovereign who committed suicide in so romantic a manner—Solvet's ed. of *Abulfeda*, p. 149; *Roudh el Kartas*, pp. 242-288, as well as Ibn Khaldun and others, tell the tale of Tashfin Ibn Ali. The *rebat* in which he took asylum from the Almohades stood near where Saint Clotide, on the route from Oran to Mess-el-Kebir, is built, and the place where tradition declares the tragic act to have occurred is still called *Salto di Cavallo*.

(62) The Beni Merini, or El-Merini, who removed the seat of government to Fez, ruled from the death of Idris IV, in A.D. 1269 (A.H. 668), to A.D. 1470 (A.H. 875), when the El-Wated branch of the Merinides (as they are usually called) succeeded, and reigned till A.D. 1550 (A.H. 957). The authorities for the dates of these dynasties are rather contradictory. Leo, for instance, gives the Almohades rule from A.H. 516 till A.H. 668; Novairi, A.H. 514 till A.H. 668; the author of *Nighearistan*, A.H. 524 till A.H. 686, which date some put at A.H. 672 (A.D. 1273). Leo gives too short a period for the Beni-Merini dynasty.—Solvet's *Abulfeda*, p. 150; De Slane, *Catalogue des Manuscrits Arabes de la Bibliothèque Nationale, Paris* (1883-1889), No. 1575-77; *Encyc. d'Al-Nowari* ("Hist. des Almohades d'Espagne et d'Afrique et de la conquête de la ville de Maroc"), etc.

(63) This again refers to his "meno Abbreviamento da noi fatto nelle croniche maumettane".

(64) For the history of these golden or, more likely, gilt balls, see my notes to *The Adventures of Thomas Pellow* (1891, pp. 340-342). There is little probability that they were of gold, or that if they were even superstition would have permitted them to remain so long. Several other mosques have gilded balls, but the Kutubia is generally regarded as the one with "the golden spheares", though that of Sidi Yusuf puts in a claim. The doors of one of the mosques—of which there are many—are covered with overlapping plates of brass. According to a not very trustworthy tradition, these doors are the gates of Seville.

(65) "Ezzulcia", or glazed tiles, a very tasteful and common mode of decoration in Morocco.

(66) Leo's sarcasms on the Professors of Marakesh University are those of a graduate of the rival seminary at Fez. Yet at one time the

learned men of the southern capital could very well compare with those of the north.

The Palace is like all Moorish residences, in no way beautiful without, but it has many fine rooms with Arabesque painting and plaster work, and differently coloured marbles. The gardens are also pretty, with an artificial lake and pavilion. But the entire city is decaying, and could not bear an hour's cannonade with the lightest piece of artillery. The best plans of Marakesh are to be found in Marcet, *Le Maroc, voyage d'une mission française à la Cour du Sultan* (1885), p. 100; Thomson, *Travels*, etc., p. 351; Erckmann, *Le Maroc Moderne*, p. 38.

(67) This reference to Jews holding office must seem strange to those who know the contempt with which they are now regarded. Yet at one time this race monopolised certain lucrative offices, for which their business capacity rendered them better suited than the Emperor's Moslem subjects. Thus a Jew was, for many years, the trusted agent of Mulai Abderrahman, in Gibraltar, and to this day there are Tangier Jews who are enjoying certain financial privileges conferred by former Sultans on their ancestors. Under Mulai Mohammed, Mulai Suleman, and other Sultans, they were the Custom House officers and the invariable intermediaries between the Government of Morocco and the European Powers. No embassy thought of proceeding to Fez or Morocco without a Jewish interpreter, who did not fail to profit by his position by asking something for himself without always acquainting the Envoy with the manner in which he had used his name. Indeed, until very recently, nearly all the European Consuls were Jews—and a few of the Vice-Consuls and Consular Agents are still. Jews coined the money, and generally acted as "the Sultan's merchants", as his business representatives at the ports were called not inappropriately, as many of the Sultans— the late Mulai el Hassan among the number—were not above doing a lucrative piece of trade in grain or other commodity. In still earlier days Jew scholars and physicians enjoyed much favour, though by a succession of the illiterate Sultans, beginning with the Sheriffs of the Fileli dynasty, learning was neglected. Shrewd Mulai Ismail employed them as tax-gatherers in the coast-lying regions. What between recognised perquisites, peculation, and usury, when a victim was squeezed almost dry, and nothing but a gaol or beggary faced him, they must have found these offices extremely lucrative. Every year, as a bribe towards the continuance of his goodwill, they presented the Sultan with a saddle, the trees of which were covered with gold plates, and the buckles, stirrups, and bridle furniture were of the same metal—the whole costing upwards of twelve hundred pounds. In those days the Jews were more numerous than at any subsequent

period, and money also seems to have been more plentiful. As tribute they paid a hen and twelve chickens in gold, the whole skilfully wrought with the feathers in flakes and shaded in coloured marble. It is questionable if in those times so much gold could be collected in the "Mellahs" ("places of salting", the Jewish Quarter, so called because the Jews had to salt the heads of criminals before they were fixed over the town gates), and it is certain that the art capable of fashioning such a gift is lost. It will be curious to know if any specimen exists in the Imperial Treasury? The intricacies of the palace are beyond penetrating. But inquiries which I was enabled to make on this and other subjects did not encourage the belief that art in so precious a metal long escaped the Sheriffian necessities—or avarice.—Chenier, *Recherches historiques sur les Maures et historie de l'empire du Maroc*, vol. iii, p. 248.

Jews have, indeed, been virtual, if not actual, Viziers to the more enlightened, or less fanatical, Sultans. Even yet, what between European protection and Moorish stupidity, the astute Hebrew manages to prosper a great deal better than might be imagined, from the not always undeserved contumely with which he is treated.

(68) "The Chancellors [Viziers] and Secretaries" is the less fantastic rendering of this passage. The "five hundred Christians" in Said El-Uatas' service is only in keeping with a period when military adventurers—soldiers of fortune and broken men generally—hired themselves to do anybody's fighting. Long after this period, Captain John Smith of Virginia came to Marakesh in 1604, Dugald Dalgetty-like, to seek "a turn" of mercenary employment with Abd el Aziz, "understanding of the warres in Barbarie" (*True Travels and Adventures*, etc., p. 34). At that time several free Englishmen were living in the city, well treated by the Sultan. The Almoravides had large numbers of "Christian" soldiers in their employment. Many of them were, no doubt, Mozarabes, or Christianized Spanish Arabs, but a large portion may have been masterless men of all nationalities. Ali Ibn Yusuf always had a Christian guard, just as European sovereigns had Moors and other foreigners in their employment, and not improbably for the same reason. He could trust them better than natives. His mother, Romaica, was of a Christian family, and perhaps, for her sake, the Emir put her co-religionists into various high places about the Court. "Hali delixit eos (Christianos) super omnes homines orientales gentes suæ. Nam quosdam fecit cubicularios secreti sui, quosdam vero millenareos et quingentareos et centareos, qui præerant militæ regni sui" (*Chron. Adelfonsi Imp.*, p. 360).

When Mocquet visited Merakesh in 1606, he found there Del 'Isle, agent for Henry IV, acting as physician to the Sultan, and in the

Mellah, where he lived, there were some Christians, and numbers engaged in the Custom Houses (*Voyages en Afrique, Asia*, etc., p. 140). Nowadays, I know of only one European — who is a native of Gibraltar—in Marakesh.

(69) The Sultan has a menagerie at Fez. But the only elephant seen in Morocco, within living memory, was the Indian one presented to the late Mulai el Hassan by the Queen of England. The sculptures spoken of do not seem to be now in existence.

In the year A.H. 1001 (A.D. 1592-93) an elephant was sent from the Sudan to Ahmed II. The day when it was brought to Marakesh was quite an event in the annals of the city. The entire population of the city, men, women, and children, young and old, turned out to meet it. Seven years later it was brought to Fez. "Some authors", writes Eloufrani, "pretend that there came into Maghrib with this animal the smoking plant called *tobacco*, the negroes accompanying the elephant having brought the tobacco with them, and affected to see very great advantage in using it. This habit of smoking spread from the Dra into Morocco, and thence all over the west. The Doctors of the law (*tholba*) pronounced at that period very contradictory opinions on the subject of tobacco. Some declared its use unlawful; others decided that it was sinful, while the third party refrained from offering any views on the question. God only knows what it is necessary to think in this respect." The advice of Mulai el Hassan seemed to have been more decided, for a few years before his death he forbade smoking and the sale or growth of tobacco in Morocco, only modifying this decree as regards foreigners in the coast towns. The order, though still unrepealed, is a dead letter. Tobacco is, however, less used in Morocco than " Kef" or Indian hemp.

(70) "Colombi, cornacchie, civette, gufi "—pigeons, ravens, horned owls, screech owls (hawks, perhaps, which nest in all old buildings in Morocco).

Abd el Mumen, though he rebuilt much of what he destroyed, was so incensed at the Almoravides that he declared he would sift the dust of their palaces through a sieve. Even yet the city has not quite recovered from the wars of the last few centuries. The city walls are about thirty miles in circuit, the foundations of stone; but the upper part of tabia in many places, are dilapidated. That around the outer Agadl, or park, is in a ruinous condition, and the whole space nearly waste; the rusty sugar-making machinery, put up by an English engineer more than thirty years ago, and never used, being, with some unhoused and unattended machinery for cartridge-making, about the only occupants of this open ground. The red soil through which the Tensift runs slightly tinges its waters, but the city is supplied from the mountains twenty miles distant. The date palms near the city are not indigenous, but were introduced from Tafilet, which produces famous dates.

Sidi ben Abbas is the patron saint of the city. But it is really under the tutelage of seven : hence it is often called Saban Rijàl, *i.e.*, [the city of] seven [holy] men. Like its sister capital of Fez, Marakesh has a great reputation for sanctity, and a pious Moor will always cast a stone on the large cairn, which has accumulated alongside the caravan roads. At the Murstan is a kind of prison for lunatics, where they are chained up, and in addition to the two regular prisons—one for murderers and state prisoners, in the Kasbah, the other, in the Medina, or town proper, for minor offenders—there is a lock-up for women. The Murstan just mentioned is attached to the mosque of Sidi ben Abbas. It is a charitable institution, where, in Ali Bey's day (1800) some 1800 people were supported by endowments and subscriptions. Finally, to close these notes on Marakesh, there is a tradition that one of the gates of the Sultan's palace was brought from Spain in pieces.—*Times of Morocco*, December 15th, 1888.

(71) Here Leo gives El Mansur his correct relationship to Abd el Mumen, and to Mohammed III en Nasir, who died in A.D. 1213 (not 1199, according to De Slane, as the date of the battle of Navas de Tolosa prevents this).

(72) This battle was that of the Navas de Tolosa, to the north of Jaen, fought 16th July 1212 (14 Safar, A.H. 609). It is computed that on the Moor's side there were ranged 500,000 men, in four lines, the Berbers, Moors (Arabs), Andalus (Spanish Moors), Almohade regulars —negroes and volunteers from all parts of the empire amounted to 160,000 horsemen. En Nasir died the year following (11 Shaban, A.H. 610) of a debauch, or, as the Moorish historian hints, of poison, leaving the throne to his young son, Yusuf el Muntaser.— *Roudh-el-Kartas*, p. 343. It was in the reign of En Nasir that King John of England is said to have offered to hold his crown as a vassal of the Moslem Khalif in return for help against the Pope and the King of France—a monkish tale which rests on mere legend.

(73) In the civil war following El Muntaser's death, Abu Zekeria declared himself independent, and founded the Hafside dynasty at Tunis, Yahia raised a rebellion in Dra, Tafilet, and the Idraren-Dran Atlas, and Abu Mussa, brother of the Emir El Mamum (son of El Mansur), declared his independence at Ceuta.

(74) Abd el-Hak (A.D. 1195, A.H. 591) was the first Beni-Merin King. But before and after his reign Marakesh was so frequently sacked that it fell into ruins, and never recovered its former prosperity.

(75) This was Ibn Abdu-'l-Malik, who wrote a biographical dictionary which Leo admits that he made affluent use of.—Dozy, *Recherches*, etc., t. ii, App. No. V. Leo Africanus, *De Viris quibusdam*, etc.

(76) This is Aghmat, to the south of Marakesh, and near Miltsin, the capital of the Almoravides before Yusuf-ben-Tasfin laid the foundation of Marakesh. There were two towns of that name, Aghmat-Urika and Aghmat-Ailan, six miles east from it, "at the point of Mount Daran", to quote Abulfeda, who again cites the work entitled, *Nozhat-el-Moschak*. He describes it on the authority of Ibn Said, as surrounded by gardens and running streams, with a healthy climate, and the air fragrant with the odour of sweet-scented herbs. Edrisi is equally enthusiastic, adding that sometimes during winter the river is covered with ice thick enough to bear children. This is the Aghmet, called Urika. In the *Kitab elbayân el moarib an akhbar el Maghrib* of the Sheikh Abu Abdallah ben Adhari l'Andalus, their pleasant waters are mentioned as supplying verdure to the gardens of Essâliha. The same writer mentions El Mansur visiting the saints formerly here. In Charant's day (prior to 1660) there was, at a place called "Gomet", a monument which the people affirmed to cover the grave of St. Augustine, whom they call "St. Belabech". This is a common trick of the Arabs. Witness, for example, Sidi Bu-Said, near the site of Carthage, which is affirmed to be the burial-place of St. Louis, who on his death-bed became a convert to Al-Islam; and the story told in Egypt, of St. George having embraced the faith. The Coptic monks of Dar-al-abiad, in Girgel, have, however, adopted the opposite plan to protect their patron saints' belongings from Mohammedan outrage, for they have converted them into a Moslem Sheikh, who commands the respect of the Faithful under the name of Abu Shenudah. Godard, on what authority he does not mention, states that in 1860, Aghmat had not more than 6,000 inhabitants. There is probably not a tenth of that number. From what I have learned, it is now little more than a squalid village, the few inhabitants living mainly by the pilgrims who visit the saints' "Zouas" here. Even the Jews point out the graves of two Rabbis, who escaped from the second destruction of Jerusalem. As late as A.H. 1178 (1764-65), the Sultan Mulai Abdallah is reported by Ezziani to have made a "pilgrimage to Aghmat which he had given in fief to the sons of Enneksis. He remained there some time, visiting the fields about the town, in company with jurisconsults and secretaries, and at this time he received from the Kadi of Aghmat "the celebrated ram"—an animal of which the fame has not descended to our times. There is no foundation for the belief that Aghmat, or its people, are of "Roman origin", as stated by Lenz without giving his authority, for he did not visit the place.—*Timbuktu*, vol. i, p. 254.

Yet to-day the reputation of Aghmat is all but gone. I do not know a single European who has visited the Almohade capital, though no doubt the fanaticism of this holy town, which lives by pilgrims, is not very favourable to the reception of infidels. It has even disappeared from maps, though it appears as Aghmat-Urika in the itineraries of El Bekri given by D'Avezac, which may be the Ureka of Washington and De Foucauld ; Edrisi (Hartnam's Ed.), pp. 140, 141 ; Charant, *Lettre ecritte en réponse de diverses Questions curieuses sur les parties de l'Affrique où regne aujourd'huy Muley Arxid, Roy de Tafilete, par M. . . . . qui a demuré 25 ans dans la Mauritanie* (1670); Godard, *Le Maroc*, p. 35 ; D'Avezac, *Geog. critique de l'Affrique Sept.*, p. 179 ; Washington, *Journ. R. G. S.*, vol. i, p. 139. The underground river is curious, but in a region with so many caves, not remarkable. The "soil of Narnia" is "citta di Narne", and the 'River Niger of Vmbria" "Negra fiume in Umbria". In Marmol's day, the aqueduct supplying Marakesh tapped the Wad Agmet, which formed a lake below the town. The Kasbah was then inhabited by holy men of the Masmudic tribe. These inhabitants, all of whom were Berbers of that stock, were mostly potters, gardeners, or farmers. But he is merely guessing when he suggests that Agmet might be Ptolemy's Emere. Renou, from finding "Armat" in El Bekris itinerary (though D'Avezac gives it Aghmat), invariably spells the word thus. Bab Ghmat, one of the seven gates of Marakesh, may refer to Aghmat, while the Bab-Ailan may possibly point to the existence of Aghmat-Ailan in the shape of some village even more wretched than Aghmat-Urika, the ancient capital of an Empire, which has only preserved the second part of the name, and, if John Davidson's information is correct, contained in 1835 only sixty heads of families.—Davidson, *African Journal*, p. 61. The Urika Valley and the Wad Urika are well known. But Urika itself has not been visited.—Thomson, *Travels*, etc., pp. 137, 445-455.

(77) I do not find this is a list of book now read in the "University of Fez".

(78) This seems to be Demnat, or Demenet, a tabia-built, fairly prosperous Berber town, with a picturesque castle, in which resides a Kaid representing the Sultan. Among the inhabitants are many Jews, of whose oppression Europe has of late years been hearing a great deal. Yet they seem more prosperous than their Moslem neighbours, and are not even obliged to live in a Mellah, though their quarters are, if possible, filthier than those of the Berbers, and most of them, as in many Moroccan towns, are afflicted with ophthalmia. Everything is cheap—a family being able to live, and have meat twice a day, on about 3s. a week. There are some

remarkable caves in the limestone; and the Wad Demnat, after an underground passage like that described by the Wad Aghmat, emerges from under what is really a natural bridge, the roof which is hung with stalactites. Of course, the natives believe that there is great store of hidden gold and silver here abouts, which the wise men of Sus and the Dra—a people who can handle snakes with impunity—get by pronouncing certain incantations written in old books. In the neighbouring Atlas region there are great caves on the banks of the Wad Dadi. A few are still inhabited by a portion of the tribe known as "the sons of the Caves". Some of the caverns are looked upon with particular reverence, and in one the Jews are said to expose their dead for a night before burial (Harris, *Geog. Journal*, vol. v, p. 327). Near Demnat there are ruins which the natives ascribe to the "Rumi"—*e.g.* Romans—or Christians. But Mr. Thomson, who examined them, pronounces them to be simply the remains of some mountain stronghold, of which many in decay are scattered all about the Atlas, or are perched like sentries on almost inaccessible precipices without the people around having any tradition regarding their origin and history. They are simply the work of "the Rumi". Jackson seems to have heard of these remains; for on his map he marks at this place, "Ruins of a Roman or Portuguese Temple", and a little way further south, "Copper Mines", while "Saltpetre" is the legend inscribed on it nearer Marakesh, and about the same distance from "Dimenit". On Chenier's map (English Ed., in two vols., 1787) it is marked "Hanimed". But the town does not seem to be of great antiquity, and it is not mentioned by any of the older Arab historians. The earliest notice of it is that piece of history for which Leo is the sole authority. Ezziána tells us that when Mulai Sheriff died in 1652, his son, Mulai Er-Rashid (afterwards Sultan), quitted Tafilet for Demnat, and that Mulai Abdallah (1746) received the submission of the rebels of "Demnat, Sanaga, and other Berbers of the mountains in the vicinity of Demnat". This submission was of short duration. For his son, Sidi Mohammed, had to march with a powerful army against Demnat, and by a bold stratagem succeeded in surprising the revolted mountaineers and burning their houses. In those days the Demnatees were accounted so incorrigible, that the then Sheikh had always to reside at Court as a hostage for their good behaviour. They are more cowed now-a-days, but their former conduct may account for the many nameless ruins scattered round this and neighbouring provinces. There are photographs of Demnat in Thomson's *Travels*, etc., pp. 158, 161; and sketches in Foucauld, *Reconnaissance*, pp. 77-78. For "yeere of our Lord" 1511, read 1514, the equivalent of A.H. 920; and for 1512, read 1515, the equivalent of A.H. 921. Both are additions of Florianus.

The Ait H'aïmmi have now their home in Sus. It is quite possible that the tribe may have been the one from which "Hanimmei" took its name, these Berber septs having shifted out very much in the last four centuries. For instance, the Zanaga who, in Leo's day, inhabited the valley of the Ziz, or Siss, have since then migrated across the Sahara, and, under the old name, are not the best of neighbours to the Senegal valley.

(79) Nisifa, or Nisipha, is Marmol's Nefrisa. Renou is, perhaps, correct in considering it the Jebel-Nefis of Edrisi, and the Nefes-el-Jebel of Ben-Aiâs. It is also the name of one of the principal tributaries of the Tensift, which Marmol expressly declares to rise in the mountains of Nefrisa. This Wad Nefis, or Nefisa, is a well-known stream. It may be the Jebel Tiza, near the head-waters of the Nefis, and certainly not so far west as Renou indicates it to be. There is, in Tripoli, a Nefussa tribe which formerly inhabited a Jebel-Nfus between Gabes and Tripoli city. But they do not appear to have any direct connection with Nefrisa.

(80) The position of Semede, or Cemmede, is precise, the Shesawa River lying between it and Nisifa. But this does not agree with the Nefis rising on the Nesifa mountain, and though that part of the Atlas is not minutely known, there are at present no two mountains under that name, or in that position laid down on our maps. The natives acquainted with that region, whom I caused to be questioned on this and other geographical difficulties, did not recognise the names. Leo and Marmol are the only authors who have mentioned them, and De Foucauld did not identify them. The only two—following Leo's description and ignoring Marmol's addition, which may be a mere guess—at all corresponding to his position are the Jebel Ida Mohammed, over 13,000 feet in height, and the Jebel Drigis, on the other side of the Sheshawa to the north-east : but neither has been examined.

(81) "Seusaua", Sesava, or Chauchava, is clearly the source of the Shesawa River, and is the part of the Atlas bearing that name (Seksaua on Schnell's Map). In the *Nozhet-Elhadi* (p. 150) it is mentioned that Abu Suliman Daud ben Abd-El-Mumen ben El-Mahdi (*i.e.*, Hosein ben Mahommed, founder of the dynasty of the El-Hoseini Sheriffs), a nephew of Ahmed II (sometimes also known by the lofty title of El Mansur), rebelled against his uncle, and declared himself sovereign "in the mountain of Seksaua, where he took refuge, and some Berber" bands rallied to him. The Seksaua people were routed, and Daud again sought asylum among the mountain folk of Huzala, who were in the habit of harassing the Dra tribes. The latter, therefore,

joined the Sultan's troops in taking vengeance on their enemies, and compelling Daud once more to become a wanderer, until his death in A.H. 998 (A.D. 1588-90), among the Udaïas Arabs.

(82) Sesiua, Secsiva cannot be identified under that name, unless the Jebel-Ogdimt, between twelve and thirteen thousand feet, is the mountain, it being near, or at, the source of the Asif-el-Mal. The Berbers who inhabit its valleys are described as very fierce. Thomson ascended it.—*Travels*, etc., pp. 328-345.

Secsiva seems so like the previous name as to suggest confusion. The description is that of the Atlas Berbers.

(83) Tenmelle, Tinmal, Tynmal (the proper pronunciation), Tinmelet, Tenmalt, or Tenmalet, is to the south of Aghmat, and though not now a place of any consequence, was at one time famous as the cradle and the burying-place of the Almohades.

When Mohammed ben Tumert, "El Mahdi", arrived in Tinmal, he was received well, and made converts of the population to his doctrines. After preaching in the Mosque, attended by his ten companions (the names of whom are preserved in the *Roudh al-Kartas*), all armed with sabres, the people proclaimed the new Imam, and helped to secure the allegiance of the neighbouring mountaineers. It was for them that he wrote the *Tawahhud* which the Masmuda regarded as of equal authority with the Koran: they invoked his name on all occasions, and even prayed in the name of the Mahdi, "the Infallible Imam". And to Tinmal, an eagle's nest among the snows, the Mahdi returned, after capturing all the castles of the Atlas, and receiving succour from the Hentata, Jenfysa, Hargha, and other tribes, to prepare for his attack on Marakesh. Then, after capturing that city, the conqueror came to rest in his well-beloved Tinmal, and to this faithful town his body was brought to be interred in its Mosque. Abd-el-Mumen (or Mumenin) was equally attached to Tinmal. He was a Zeneta tribesman, and the son of a potter, a trade which, according to a current tale, furnished two other Barbary conquerors, in the persons of Barbarossa and his brother. He also was proclaimed at Tinmal as Emir of the Mussulmen (Emer-al-Mumen—Prince of Believers—often disguised by old historians as Miramomolin, or Yiramulmin), and, according to the *Roudh al Kartas*, he sent the head of the last Almoravide Emir—Mohammed Ibn-Tashfin-Ishak—to be hung on a poplar tree (*Safsaf*) in Tinmal. In 1153, after crucifying, on the chief gate of Marakesh, a relation of the Mahdi who had played false at Ceuta, Abd el-Mumen visited the Mahdi's tomb at Tinmal, which he enlarged and beautified, and distributed large sums to the loyal citizens. And in this mosque, after a reign of thirty-three years, four months, and twenty-three days, his body was laid by the side of the Mahdi; but there are wide differences regarding the duration of his reign. I have followed the *Roudh al Kartas*, written in 1326, at Fez, most probably by Abu 'l-Hassan ben Abd-el-Halim of Grenada, though, according to some copies, the writer was Abu'l-Hassan ben Abd Allah ben Abi Zara' al-Fasi (see Gayangos' Ed. of *Al Makkari*, vol. ii, pp. 515-16; Playfair and Brown, *Bib. of Morocco*, No. 871.

It is the mosque which Leo refers to, though he is unable to conceal his sectarian hatred of "Elmadi predicatore e il suo descepolo Abdul Mumen". Even after more than three centuries the Tinmalees appear to have preserved the old "heresy", and to have been extremely arrogant on account of their connection with the two first Almohades, and their knowledge of the "teologia e dottrina del detto predicatore" (*Elmahdi* in the translation). Yet they were in Leo's day by no means flourishing. Besides the two Almohades mentioned, Yusuf El-Mansur, and, it is probable, some of his successors, were interred here. The early Almohades fortified it strongly, but if it was one of the sixteen castles of the Deren (Adrar-n-Dren), of which Edrisi, Ibnu-l-Wardi, and other historians speak under the names of Tanimal, Tamilat, or Tanmalat, it must always have been a place of arms. To-day it is forgotten: it is not even accorded the distinction of a word on maps which preserve the names of spots which have disappeared.— See also El Kairouani, in *Expl. scientifique de l'Algérie*, vol. iii, pp. 184, *et seq.*

(84) Gedmeva, or Guidneva, is, perhaps, in better transliterated Arabic, Djedmiua or Guidmua, though no mention of that name is known in the position assigned to it. It is evidently one of the fort hills of the Adrar-n-Deren (Idraren Drann, etc.), but like most of Leo's mountain names cannot be identified. Minmizi (Imirmizi in the original) is of course Asmis.

(85) Hantera is one of the few mountain peaks in the Atlas which can be identified by Leo's description, though no longer, if at any time, bearing the name he gives to it. The name has been altered a good deal in the course of passing through the printer's hands. Some of the earlier editions of Ramusio have the word *Hantera*, and *Anteta* at the beginning of the article. The Latin edition (taken from the first issue of Ramusio) and the translation therefrom have invariably Hantata. The French of Temporal follows suit in Hantera, and the last Italian issue (1837), with its usual practice of dropping the aspirate, has *Anteta*, while the beautiful, but entirely unedited, reprint of Temporal's version (1830), copies his blunder of *Hantera*. Marmol, however, has Henteta (Henteté) in his plagiarism of Leo's description.—Marmol, *L'Afrique*, t. ii, p. 75 (Spanish ed.),

vol. ii, p. 39); Moura, *Historia dos sobranos Mahometanos*, etc., p. 195; D'Avezac, *Géog. critique sur l Afrique Sept.*, pp. 167-68.

It is evidently the modern Jebil Mlitsin, or Miltsin, of the Asif Sig, which Washington believed to be the highest Atlas peak visible from Marakesh. But though Ball estimated it considerably over 13,300 feet (nearly 2,000 feet higher than Washington did), it is probable that several peaks reach that or an even loftier elevation,—the Tizi-Nzaewti for example, which might possibly be accepted as Gedmeva, only Leo describes it of smaller height than Hanteta.

The name he gave seems to have been derived from the Hentela, a Berber tribe of the Masmuda, frequently mentioned by Arab historians, as a troublesome people of a district comprised in this mountain. Leo possibly named it simply from these people, the Berbers knowing the various valleys and ridges by different names. This is common among rude races. They have seldom any general name for a mountain range or river or island. Allwana must also be made from the "personal error". He might have picked it up erroneously, and further altered it in transliterating from the Arabic into Italian. Ramusio, who may again have mistaken his handwriting, and the printer, without any one to correct their errors who had acquaintance with Africa, might have made still further puzzles for geographers. This applies to the whole of Leo's work. Yet it is remarkable how few of his mountain names, even in well known districts, we can now recognise. If correct originally, they must have changed in four hundred years; and as Leo almost invariably gives them the name of tribes inhabiting them, that is not improbable. It is not often that the Berber races have been permitted to remain where they were in 1500. In many instances they seem to have been exterminated, to have been forced to migrate, or to have lost a tribal existence. And the remembrance of their old wrongs keeps those who remain from encouraging too great curiosity on the part of stray travellers. "El-Hentete"—the Hentatian—is the name of several personages with whom we meet in the history of Morocco. In addition to a large part played by them in founding the Almohade dynasty, they gave to Tunis the Beni-Hafy dynasty, which ruled there for three centuries. For the distribution of the Morocco Berbers, *see* Quedenfeldt, *Eintheilung und Verbreitung der Berber-bevölkerung in Marokko* (Zeitschrift für Ethnologie, Berlin, 1885; Bd. xx, s. 98-130, 146-160, 184-210; Bd. xxi, 3, 81-108), papers written with Teutonic completeness, but with little discrimination as regards authorities.

(86) Adimmei is the mountain on which Hannemei, identified as Dennat, is built, and extending from Militsen (Hateta) to the Tessant River, a tributary of the Um-er-Rbia, its possible position is therefore circumscribed by that portion of the main range and its spurs, in

which the Jebel Taurvit, Tizi Amsug, Tizi-Tarkeddit, and Jebel Taseragh are the chief peaks. By "monte" Leo does not always mean summit, but clump, "massif", or range.

(87) By Guzzula, Guzula, or Gezula, Leo means the mountainous region south of the Atlas, or between the Great Atlas (Adrar-n-Dren) and the so-called Anti-Atlas (Adrar-n-Bani), but separated by Sus from the sea, while the Arab writers generally mean by this, one of the great divisions of the Berber race. It is not improbable that Leo was the first to apply—after his custom—the name of the people to the region they inhabit, for I cannot find any previous writer using the name. In a letter addressed by Pierre Treillault to the Constable de Montmorency, quoted by Renou, the word "Gouzula" is employed. But that was in 1597. There exists a mountain, the Dar Kezul, in Oran Province, Algeria, which might mark a colony of these people, and the suggestion has been frequently been made that Guzula is a memory of the ancient Gætulians, or the country of Getulia, which was in nearly the same part of Africa. Possibly, however, the Gætulians (Γαιτούλοι) may be derived from the Berber tribe Godala, who, according to Ibn Sayd (Abul-Hassan Nur-eddin Ali, A.D. 1214), lived in the Mandron mountain of Ptolemy, whence descend the rivers Saladus, Chusareus (Wad Messa), Ophiodes (Wad Nun), Nugies (Wad Sabi), and Massa (Albach). Ibn Khaldun, at the close of the fourteenth century, refers to the wars of the Sus people with the Guzzula races. But the "Djodalah" are mentioned much earlier by El Bekri (A.H. 392, A.D. 1001-2). To this day the inhabitants of the country between the Wad Sus, the Wad Dra, and the "Sahel" (or region bordering the ocean south of the Wad Sus) is divided into great families, the Seketana and the Gezula. Yet in all material points Leo's description of the people is still applicable. The Gezula—or Kezula—played some part in history, having, in the thirteenth century, occupied Jaen and Xeres in Spain, until, in 1255, they were driven out of the latter. They claim, as one of their race, Abd-Allah Ibn Yasin, who began the movement which culminated in the rise of the Almoravide dynasty.

The geographical name applied by Leo has, however, long been lost, if, indeed, it was ever once recognised by the Arabs, except in the sense already suggested. It is now the Bled-Filleli, and further south the Bled el-Jerrid, and none of the seven provinces in which the Bled-Filleli, or Tafilet, is officially divided off has received a designation even remotely like Gezula. The Atlas mountains, according to Jackson, a writer of less authority than a cursory reader might imagine, are, in Arabic, Jebel Attils, *i.e.*, the Mountains of Snow, which might be excellent etymology for Atlas. There are, however, two difficulties, first, that this is not the Arabic name, and secondly, that the Atlas was a familiar name long before the Arabs came to Barbary.

Mannert, *Géog. ancienne des États Barbaresques* (Marcus and Duesberg's Ed.) pp. 257, 482, 723; Vivien de Saint-Martin, *Le Nord de l'Afrique dans l'antiquité Grecque et Romaine*, pp. 124, 128, 437; Abulfeda, *Géographie* (Reinaud's Ed.) vol. ii, p. 216.

(88) Ilda is not known under that name to geographers. It is, apparently, a spur from the Atlas, and may be Idekel. The statement that Guzula stretched into Haha may be understood from Leo's statement that in his day the Sus River separated the provinces of Haha and Sus. At one time Cape Gir (Igir Ufrani) was the boundary line. Jackson was the first to point out that Leo, in describing the Sus to fall into the Atlantic at Agadirt blundered by six miles—Agadir being that distance north of the mouth of the river.

(89) Here add "with great quantities of barley" (e molta copia di orzo).

(90) This pious abuse is an intercalation of Pory's.

Mohammed, according to Abulfeda, was born on "Monday, the 12th of Rabia I [the third lunar month] in the year of the Elephant". "Now the coming of the elephant happened in the middle of the month Moharram, that year being the forty-second of the reign of Kosri Anusherwan, which was the year eight hundred and eighty-one of Alexander [the Great], and one thousand three hundred and sixteenth of Bukht-Masser" (Nebuchadnezzar), that is, about A.D. 570.—*Ismaïl Abulfeda, De Vita, et Rebus gestis Mohammedis*, etc. (Ed. Gagnier), p. 2.

(91) For A.D. 1511, read 1514. I cannot learn that this great fair is held nowadays. The scattering or extermination of the tribe has, no doubt, broken it up among a variety of places.

(92) Dukala is still a well-known province. "Habid", is the Wad el-Abid, the Slave's River, and "Ommirabih", the Wad Um-er-Rbia, which falls into the Atlantic at Azamor. "Diis sauentibus" is an addition of Florianus, though, as an Arab, such a pious phrase would be continually in Leo's mouth.

(93) Saffi, Asafi, Asafa, Asafie, Sefi, Saffee, Saffy, Safi, Zafin (Portuguese, corrupted from Azaafi, according to De Faria y Sousa), Azafo (old Italian), Saffin (old French in trans. of Diego de Torres), Czafi (Spanish), is a very old town. Abn-l-feda mentions it under the name of Asfi, and describes it from the information of Ibn Said (A.D. 1214), and still earlier Edrisi has a reference to it as Asafi.

M. Berbrugger found Moula-Ahmed using Asfi-Azar, Asif-Azar, or Asfi-Azâra. "Asif", in the Shelluh dialect means, he thinks, the same as "Uâdi" in Arabic, viz., a pilgrimage station, though other authorities insist that it may be translated "river" (*Expl. scientifique de l'Algérie*, vol. ix, p. 172). The Moors generally known as Asfi, and the Europeans as Saffi. It may have been the Μυσοκάρας λιμήν of Ptolemy, but must yield to Mazagan its claim to be the Portus Rutubis of Polybius.

But it first rose into European fame when the Portuguese captured it in 1508, under the circumstances mentioned, and abandoned it in 1541 (see *Introd.*). Chenier, and his copyists, put the date in 1641, and Thomassy (*Relation de la France avec Le Maroc*, p. 156) still further widens the blunder to 1661. But though the data regarding the Portuguese proceedings in Africa, if any exist, lie for the most part in the inaccessible Lisbon archives, there is a certainty (from facts to be presently mentioned) that they evacuated Saffi in 1541, while there is nothing to support the belief that they re-occupied it. After the unsuccessful siege (Diego de Torres, *Istoria de los Xarifes*, pp. 120-124) in 1539, by the two Sheriffs (Shorfa, if we were not writing in English), sons of the original Sheriff, the Portuguese did not care to be harassed any further. Their attention was beginning to be more engrossed in the Indies, and less in Africa. Accordingly, Saffi and Azimor were both abandoned after being fired, and the garrison and merchants transferred to Mazagan.

There is no ground for holding that Saffi was at any time a Phœnician or a Visigothic town, or that its name was originally Sophia, though most likely it was always a Berber village. But, probably, it grew to the extent it covered before the Portuguese occupation round the sanctuary or mosque of Sidi Bu Mohammed Salah, a famous saint, whose fame as Mohammad el-Wari(?) has extended as far as Alexandria, where, on a Mecca pilgrimage, he is credited with some wonderful feats. A "Rabat" (camp), the quarter in which it is situated, is a well-known asylum for criminals of any degree of heinousness. In 1874, all the prisoners escaped from the town and took refuge there. Yet, in spite of the 2,000 inhabitants being mostly of bad or dubious reputation, this cliff-town, within a stone's throw of the main gate of Saffi, is very orderly, and is the place in which the European merchants have their stores. Before the Portuguese, however, there is evidence of Saffi covering a much larger space than at present. But the continual attacks upon it led its new masters to raze the ancient walls, which then encircled the suburb of Rabat, so as to have a less extensive front to defend. They also erected a fort upon the cliff overhanging the water port, which was connected with a strong wall with a castle overlooking the slope on which the town is built. This castle was afterwards converted into a palace by Sid Mohammed ben

Abd Allah (1757-1790), the founder of Mogador and Fedala, which, after a short flicker of trade, was abandoned by the Europeans, and is now in ruins. The palace is still a picturesque object from the sea, but has long been dismantled, though there are several beautiful courts or halls in a fair state of preservation.

During the Portuguese *régime*, Saffi enjoyed great prosperity in spite of the harassment it suffered from the Moors. If we are to believe De Faria y Sousa, it had at one time 3,500 houses. Except that the Portuguese ceased to be welcome, the place, nevertheless, continued to do a considerable foreign trade, and to have foreign "factories". Thus, when Sir Anthony Sherley went as Ambassador to the King of Morocco from the Emperor [of Germany] in 1605, sixty-three years after the Portuguese left, he stayed in Saffi ("Saphia"), or "Saphie", four months, kept open house, and invited all Christian merchants—English, Flemish, French, and Spanish—"both to dinner and supper daily" [Ro. C.], *A True Historicall Discourse of Muley Hamet's rising to the three Kingdoms of Moruecos, Fes, and Sus*, etc., 1609, cap. xi. This is the black-letter pamphlet, from which there are extracts in Purchas (Bk. VI, c. i, s. 3). Sherley's visit also shows, in common with the fact of Louis XIII of France and Mulai El Valed signing a treaty in 1631, "à la Rade de Saffi", that the Portuguese were not there at that period, and that the 1641 and 1661 dates of some writers, for the evacuation of Saffi, must be erroneous. Sherley bought a ship of "an English merchant factor", and "got credit of Jewes to take up money and pay them in Moruccos". Eight years earlier—in 1577—Edward Hogan [Huggins?], Queen Elizabeth's Ambassador to Morocco, landed at "Azafi". At that time there were eight merchants in the place, and the Moors were in possession. There were also in Marakesh English and French traders, who came out to meet the Ambassador several miles from the city. The "Jewes", likewise, had dealings with Master Hogan and his suit, in those notable days of English enterprise (*Hakluyt*, vol. ii, Part II, pp. 64-67).

It is thus clear, notwithstanding the general impression, that Saffi was not deserted by Christians after the Portuguese left. On the contrary, the "Portugalls" having ceased to exercise their illiberal monopoly—all nations had an opportunity of doing business here. Yet the town under the Moors never recovered from the condition in which it had been left. In 1753, a Danish company obtained the exclusive right of the trade of Saffi and Sallee. But it was unable to compete with Larache and Mogador, to which the merchants removed, and Saffi like Agadir was closed to foreign trade.

It then ceased to be visited. This place is very hot in summer, and in winter the floods from the neighbouring plains accumulate in the valley and inundate the chief thoroughfares to the depth of several feet, occasionally destroying the contents of low-lying houses and rendering the place damp and unhealthy. Add to this a heavy surf which often renders landing difficult, the presence of a fanatical clan in the town, and a savage set of tribesmen outside it, and the neglect of Saffi may be understood. At one time, it was the point from which embassies and other travellers disembarked for the land journey to Marakesh; but after 1760 Mogador and then Mazagan—on the evacuation by the Portuguese—had that distinction. It was not until 1817 that the place began to revive, on Lenda ben 'Adi Shriki, an influential Jew, obtaining the Sultan's permission to export some wool through the port. Finding that he could do a very profitable business here, he settled in the town and waxed rich on the shipment of skins, wool, wheat, and barley to London and Marseilles, and the importation of cotton, tea, sugar, and iron. The exchange was, in those days, ideal. The dollar was taken for 12½ okiat, and the peseta passed for 2½, instead of 120 and 24 respectively, with six large copper "filus" to each okia. In the Rabba, or grain market, wheat and barley were so cheap that the country-folk bringing either for sale were compelled to give security at the town gate for removing any not sold, instead of leaving it to litter the place. Now-a-days, the place is moderately busy, though the anchorage is a dangerous one when the south-west wind blows. Then the chances are that a vessel unable to run to sea will, in a few hours, be driven on the sandy beach.

The town, in spite of its sacks and sieges and burnings, still presents an old-world appearance, and many of the houses are fine specimens of heavy cool Portuguese mansions, though in filth it surpasses any of the Morocco coast towns. In the vicinity are many substantially-built tombs, or "Saints' houses" as the Europeans call them, which attract pilgrims, by whom the holy men inside—Sidi Bu Zid, Sidi Bu Zikri, and so forth—are sincerely venerated, and their real or apocryphal history related in interminable tales; while at the village of Sidi Wastel, nestling among the hills to the south, the number of white domed "Kubbas" give the place a picturesque appearance. In the Rabat are the remains of a palace, with painted ceilings, frescoes, richly carved door frames, and marble columns, which was built by 'Abd er-Rahman ben Nasir, a son of Mulai Yezid, the "red Sultan", himself a native of Saffi, and the son of a reputed Irish (more likely Hessian) woman. During the reign of Mulai Suliman (1795-1822) 'Abd er-Rahman was so powerful along the coast from Sallu to Messa, that he was popularly known as the "Sultan es-Seghir"—the little Sultan. Being like so many of the Imperial line not above business, he trafficked with Spaniards, who supplied him with cannon and gunpowder, and built mosques and houses, bought land, and greatly improved the town of Saffi. But all these favours from royalty in the shape of princes and palaces, and from Heaven in the guise of that rank product of Morocco, its holy men, have made the Mesfiwi—as the inhabitants are called—most arrogant, if not very fanatical. They have no desire to see Europeans, and prohibit any Jew—of whom there are many in the town—from entering the quarter in which Sidi Bu Mohammed Salah's sanctuary is situated. Even Europeans consider it prudent not to put themselves too much in evidence during the procession of the Aisawa and Hamadsha sects, and on the occasion of certain forms and holidays when religious rancour is apt to get the better of discretion. Up to 1767 no Christian was permitted to ride into Saffi, or a Jew to enter it, as in Fez and other cities, except barefooted. But in that year Chenier, the French representative, who had removed the Consulate for a time from Mogador, refused to obey this humiliating mandate, and ever after it was not enforced in the case of Europeans (though more than a century later a French Envoy tried to curry favour with Fasces by dismounting while passing a saint's tomb which the English minister had ridden past !). Yet even the Portuguese when masters of the place, so far humoured the Moslems as to adopt this habit out of respect for the saints who reposed within the walls. After the Portuguese seized the place they tried to prevent treachery by expelling all the disloyal Mussulman citizens. These settled in a Gentile district, one day's journey to the south-east of Marakesh, which they named "Mesfiua", and where they have become a prosperous Kabila in the Wad Imspini country, among whom many Jewish families live.

Portuguese heraldic devices are still discernible over the chief gateway of the crumbling and untenanted, but still beautiful palace; and a church, of which the vaults are intact, with similar arms, etc., has been detected amid the rubbish heaped up to the cornice.

All south of the town the sea is undermining the cliffs, so that 'Abd-er-Rahman's house (p. 370) had to be abandoned, and it is no longer possible to walk along the shore to the Tensift—18 miles to the south —as old men are reported to have done in their youth. The "Jew's Rock" (Jerf el Yudi), a limestone cliff, upwards of 400 feet, about four miles south, is dangerous from its repeated crumbling of masses from the edge. Yet it is doubtful whether the coast is not actually undergoing a slow secular rise, and that the lakes between the Sebu and El Kus (Lakos) are not old lagoons, which have, by the rising of the coast, been shut off from the Atlantic.—*Times of Morocco*, Nos. 137, 138 (June 23rd and 30th, 1888); De Faria y Sousa, *Africa Portuguesa* (1681), pp. 76-114; Berago (Avogadro), *Historia Africana della divisione dell'imperio degli Arabi*, etc. (1650), pp. 94-99; Castellanos, *Marruscos*, pp. 96-110.

(94) Most of Leo's allusions are explained in the *Introduction*. He visited the place immediately after the Portuguese had obtained

possession of it, so that his account is, therefore, a first-rate, if not a unique, historical authority.

"Their originall from Farchon" (La famiglia di Faron), or Beni Farhon, are the "usurpers", who raised Saffi into a species of republic on the decline of Merinides.

(95) 'Abd er-Rahman ("Abdear-Rahman, hombre de Valor", according to De Faria y Sousa) was a member of the Beni-Farhon family. He murdered his uncle, Ameduy, then head of the State, and usurped sovereign power, though, as the sovereignty seems to have been hereditary in the Beni-Farhon family, the republic was, probably, one something like that of Holland under the House of Orange—only about as free as a South American Commonwealth under a military dictator.

(96) Ali ebn-Goesimen—Sidi-Ali, "Cide Alcadux mancebo noble" —as he is variously called.

(97) This "trusty friend" was the afterwards celebrated Sidi Yahia ben Tafut.

(98) Under Diego Arambuja, governor of Mazagan, and Garcia de Melo, Captain of the Carvals, the Portuguese intrigued as described. Ali showed himself less tractable than Yahia ben Tafut, and had to seek asylum in Targa, a town now all but vanished. But Yahia, after explaining his conduct at Lisbon, was appointed Captain-General. He was the "builder of the castle".

Leo actually says so:—"detto capo, nominato Ichia", though the words are omitted in the translation, and he was not sent "back again to Azafi", but to "Africa".

(99) *Introduction*. The subsequent history of Saffi is given in note 93. Marmol (*L'Afrique*, t. ii, p. 2) follows Leo, but has expanded his account from other sources of information not mentioned, and, unless original, for the most part now either lost or difficult to trace.

(100) Conta. Marmol confounds this with Cotes—(Κώτης κόλπος, or rather, Κώτης ἄκρον) of Ptolemy, the Ampelusia Promontorium of Mela, the Ras Achakar of the Arabs—under the name of Cape Comte, and declared it was ruined under the government of Tarek. Chenier fancies it to have occupied the site of Waladia. The town was probably founded by Mulai el Waled about 1645, near a lagoon which could be made the best harbour in North Morocco; but, after a brief trial, was abandoned, and is now almost deserted, no Europeans having resided there for many years, and, as there are no ships, the caravans pass it by. During the usurpation of Krom el Haj (1645-52) the place was used as a basis of operations against Saffi. When Mouette was captured in 1670, one of the pirate ships ran from Waladia, and in Pellow's day (1715-38) the harbour seems to have been regularly frequented Tissot makes it out to be the "very safe

port" of El Ghant mentioned by Edrisi (*Bull. Soc. Géog. Paris*, 6me ser., t. x, pp. 67-71, with plan).

But neither El Ghant nor Aïyir can be Leo's Comte. It is just as little likely to be the "ancient town called by the Africans Cantin", the recess of which Jackson notes on Cape Cantin. The promontory —the Promontorium Solis, Σόλεις ἄκρα, Ἥλιου ὄρος— of the ancient geographers—the Ras Kantin of the Arabs (if Tissot's identifications are accepted), was the headland on which Hanno erected a temple, or fane, or sanctuary to Neptune (Poseidon). There is a Moslem sanctuary here. But the spot seems to have been a sacred one long before Islam appeared in Africa. In this respect the history of the cape is, therefore, continuous from Carthaginian times. The word Soleis, in the Punic language, meant probably the same thing as Ras Kantin in Berber. "Kant", its singular, being, it is suggested, applied to a steep cliff in the Riff country—the Ras Kant-ez-Zit. But Cape Kantin is spelt with a *kef*, whereas Kant-ez-Zit begins with a *qáf*. M. Tissot, however, goes further. In a rounded eminence which dominates the cape, he recognises the ἀκρωτήριον of Scylax, and on the summit of this tumulus is one of the rude Cromlech structures, in the shape of a stone circle, which the natives call "heuch", plural, "heuchet". Not improbably more lies concealed by the mound; but the superstitious awe with which this ancient structure, like so many of its kind in Morocco, is regarded, must prevent excavation. It is the "Medjma'a es-Salihin"—the Reunion of Immaculate—and is one of the most venerated sanctuaries of a region which to-day, as in the time of Scylax, is one of the holiest in that part of Africa. Numbers of Kubbas (dome) sanctuaries, "heuchets" (those open to the sky), and "sid" (any not circular), with the usual swarm of sanctimonious, but not always moral, attendants dot the country around. The tradition of its being the χώρα ἱερωτάτη is a legend uninterrupted from the days of the Periplus (Tissot, *Recherches sur la Géog. Comp. de la Tingitane*, pp. 105-111).

It would, perhaps, be rash to say that the original of the "heuch" was Hanno's fane to the Carthaginian Neptune. But it is very probable that as Leo and Jackson do not mention it in any other significance, it is their ruins of Conte, or Conta, as Pory has it.

(101) Tit still stands, in a ruinous condition, with the walls in the last stage of dilapidation, and, so far as people and business are concerned, might be removed from the map. It is probably the "Teturit" of the Catalan map and its copyists, and the Teturia of Sanson (1656) between Canthenum Caput (Cape Cantin) and Carvoccum Caput (Cape Blanc?), in a bay beyond which in this fanciful map of the best French geography of the day the altogether apocryphal "Duccalæ Insulæ" are placed (note 108). Some of the inhabitants of Mazagan have ancient burying-places here, with tomb-

stones on which inscriptions can still be read.—*Discurso da Jornada de D. Gonçalo Coutinho*, p. 54 ; Castillanos, *Marruecos*, p. 94.

Jackson, whose etymologies, like his acquaintance with ancient geography, were primitive, tells us that "Tett signifies in Arabic Titus, and is, therefore, supposed to be the ruins of the ancient city of Titus, founded by the Carthagineans" (*Morocco*, p. 43). In reality, the word enters into the composition of various Berber names — Tit-n-Ali, Tituga, Titutla Fukia, Titutla Tahtia, Tittal, etc. Tétuan (Titauen), for instance, is the plural of Tit, *a* in the Berber language meaning much the same as the Arabic *aïn, aïun*, spring. Marmol's notion that the name was formerly Tut, according to Josephus, named from Tut, the grandson of Noah, who led the Tuteians into Mauretanea Tingitana, is, of course, only amusing.

When the Duke of Braganza took Azamor (1513), then under the command of Sidi Mansur, "Tite" with "Almedina" were abandoned by the citizens, the inhabitants going elsewhere until the Portuguese took possession of them. Then most of the people returned, and became vassals of the King of Portugal, under the command of Sidi Yahia ben Tafut (Diego de Torres, *Istoria de los Xarifes*, pp. 23, 24). Mulai en Nasir, brother of the Sultan Mohammed El Oate (1527), failing to raise a holy war in the province of Dukala, after capturing the Christian Treasurer of the King of Portugal and a Jew, his commissary, removed the people of the province to a place about twelve miles from Fez. There is nothing in the original to warrant the rendering of the passage as Florianus and Pory have it. The "certain Christian" and "a Jew" were not "hanged", though, of course, there would have been nothing extraordinary in this drastic retribution, except that they were more valuable as slaves than as dead men. Nor is there a word to justify the intercalation about the Christian being "the King of Fez . . . his owne Treasurer". The pair were most likely a tax-gatherer and his assistant, who were caught while going about their unpopular, though, in Morocco, lucrative business.

Tit does not appear to have fully recovered after this proceeding, though some of the inhabitants no doubt returned on the evacuation of Azamor. But the presence of the Portuguese in Mazagan must have checked the re-peopling of the deserted little towns in Dukala. After this it almost disappeared from history—the latest plunder of it being in A.H. 1211 (1796-99), when the Sultan, Mulai Suliman, visited it at the head of an army, and received the submission of El Hakemi bel Arusi and the recently rebellious people of Dukala (Ezziani, *Nozhet Elhâdi*, p. 179), which shows that Tit was not completely deserted so early as is generally supposed.

(102) Elmedina means "the city", and is a common name all over the Arabic-speaking world, and seems at that time to have been the chief town of Dukala. It was depopulated in the same expedition of

Mulai en Naser as Tit and other places were (p. 374). It was situated on a plain about eight or nine miles from the sea, and may be the large ruined town called "Medinat (or M'dina) el-Gharbia", according to the note kindly sent me by Mr. Vice-Consul Hunot of Saffi.

The Portuguese expedition in which it suffered is described by Marmol (t. ii, pp. 64-66), Birago (pp. 96, etc.), though not at first hand, and Diego de Torres (pp. 18-20). Mulai en Naser's expedition, in which it was sacked the year previously (1514), is noticed in Marmol, t. ii, p. 107.

(103) Centum putei (Cento pozzi is the original) is a case in which Leo translated the name of a place into Italian. But as he could not have done this without knowing the Arabic or Berber, we must assume either that he omitted the native one, or that the editor could not decipher it. The place described is Miat-Bir-u-Bir, literally, "the hundred and one wells", a village situated on the right bank of the Tensift, at some distance from the mouth of that river. It is mentioned by Ezziani (p. 181) as the place where, in A.H. 212 (A.D. 1797-98), 'Abd er-Rahman ben Naser, a rebellious chief of Dukala, did homage to Mulai Suliman. Marmol describes " Miatbir" in his day as a scattered village on the slope of a hill, with some rude fortifications erected by the Berber inhabitants. The place gets its name from the "matamoras", or underground cellars, excavated in the rocks for storing grain, after the custom of the country. Corn, it is said, has remained good after lying for many years in these "matamoras". The tradition that these were originally rocks, may perhaps be supported by an ancient inscription which Marmol saw on a piece of alabaster, as big as a man, which marked the sepulchre—now vanished—which three centuries ago stood near the " Bibeltobul " (Báb-et-Tobul), a gate not now in existence or known by that name. These were the words :—" Here lies Ali, son of Atia, who was Kaïd over a hundred thousand men. He had ten thousand horses, and in one day dug a hundred and one wells for them to drink. He married three hundred girls, and was faithful, victorious, and one of the twenty-four generals of Yakub el Mansur. I ended my days at forty years. Whoever reads this epitaph, pray God to pardon me."—*L'Afrique*, t. ii, p. 51 ; *Francisco de San Juan Mission historial de Marruecos* (1708), p. 77.

Höst mentions that he often hunted francolins near Miat-Abrar-u-Bir.

(104) Subeït was one of the places which met the same fate as Tit, etc. It was waste in Leo's day ; but it still exists as a little walled town on the left bank of the Um-er-Rbia ; it must have been again partially re-peopled.—*Godard, Maroc*, p. 40. Renou suggests that the

name might possibly have been derived from the Sbeit or Sbeita, a tribe of Northern Morocco.

(105) Tamaroch, or Temeracost, is another of the little places to which the same remarks apply as to Subeit, etc. They were all early deserted, and may now, if the name has survived, be sought among the ruined villages scattered in Shécdona, Abda, and Dukala—the last two provinces being in Leo's description considered as one. Renou was inclined to regard the name as the same as Temarkest, the diminution form of the Berber name for Marakesh.

(106) Terga. This a Berber name, which occurs frequently, signifying "a glen", perhaps the glen through which a rivulet flows. The Um-er-Rbia town in which Ali-ben-Goesin fought against the Portuguese, and the chief of which came to the help of Azamor (note 111, p. 379), was, in Leo's day, in ruins, must not be confounded with Targa, or Terga, on the Mediterranean in quite as woeful a plight. In fact, though we know its exact position, it is now difficult to trace any remains of this once important place. There is another Terga in the Wad Azgemerzi, in the Wad Dra Basin.

(107) Bulauan, or Bu el-Auan, is still existing in Tabulawan, on the south side of the Um-er-Rbia, not far from the Meshra Bu el Auan, and the little Bene Meskin desert. It is at a place where the river narrows between high banks before spreading out into the plain through which it runs for the rest of its course. At one time, there was a bridge across the Um-er-Rbia, built by Mulai bel Hassan, one of the Ben Marini family, not far from Bulawan. Before this work was completed, and after it disappeared, travellers had to be ferried across the river on rafts of inflated goat skins (Madia el gerb), or on bundles of rushes and reeds, a primitive contrivance on which I crossed the Sebu in 1884. Being on the route from Sallee to Marakesh, Bulawan—to use the common spelling which Renou describes as "the English"—was frequently visited last century. Chenier saw it in 1781, and describes the strong castle which guards the passage of the river here. It stands on a wild and barren spot near the bank, on a pyramidal eminence more than 200 feet high, below which flows the swift, deep river. In May, 1785, when Keatinge halted at "Bulaughuan", mud houses occupied part of the internal area of the castle, the flanks of which extended down to the water's edge. Castle, soil, buildings, beings, and river were all of one tint of colouring, except where the verdure of the gardens by the river's edge broke the dreary monotony. Lempriere visited "Buluane" in 1790, but though he was not struck, any more than was Höst (who called it "miserable"), with the place, from an architectural point of view, the strength of the walls amazed him. It was then inhabited by some negroes, banished there when Sidi Mohammed thought it proper to disband the black troops, who were

beginning to play the parts of Prætorian guards, Janizaries, or Mamelukes. These unruly "Bok hari", who still speak a dialect called "Guenani" (that is, "Guinea"), were also in charge at the time of Chenier's visit. The bridge, however, seems to have long ago broken down, the people of Tabulawan village, on the other side of the river, and another near the castle—built of rough-hewn stones, without mortar—being exempt from taxes on the condition of helping travellers across the ferry. The goat-skin raft is very ancient. It is common all over barbarous Africa, and is mentioned by Livy as used by Hannibal in passing his army over the Rhone, Ticinus, and Po. But the Sultan usually crossed the river by a kind of temporary suspension bridge.

The town of Um-er-bia (Ommrbia), mentioned by Edrisi, is probably Bulawan. But the castle was not begun before the time of Abd-el-Mumim, who began to reign in 1130; and, according to an inscription over the gateway, it was built, enlarged, or repaired, by Sid Ben Elcheat, who was in the service of Mulai Ismail, in 1709.

In Marmol's day the people of "Bulaguen", a "good place" of 500 houses, were rich, owing to the favourable position of the village on the way to the southern capital, and Saffi, and Sallee ; and, in spite of the melancholy waste around them, they cultivated the soil in a laborious manner.

The battle in which Leo took part, in 1514, between the Azamor Portuguese, probably under Juan de Meneses, and Mulai en-Nasir, brother of Mohammed VI. It was one of the many skirmishes in which nearly all of Dukala came under the short-lived power of Portugal. Now-a-days, the place is seldom heard of.—Chenier, *Recherches historiques sur les Maures*, vol. i, pp. 75, 77, 273 ; Lemprière, *Tour to Morocco*, p. 419 ; Höst, *Efterretninger om Marokos og Fes*, p. 76 ; Jackson, *Morocco*, p. 6 ; Renou, *Expl. scientifique de l'Algérie*, vol. viii, p. 217 ; Edrisi (Hartman ed.), pp. 160-61 ; Marmol, *L'Afrique*, vol. ii, p. 614 ; Keatinge, *Travels in Africa*, vol. ii, p. 22 ; De Faria y Sousa, *Africa Portuguesa* (1681), p. 117.

(108) Azamur, or Azamor, as it is spelt in the earliest Portuguese documents. Azamoor, as it is usually pronounced by Europeans, the Azamor-es-Sidi-Schaib of the natives. Azamor meaning, in Berber, olives, and Sidi-Schaib being one of the many saints whose tombs give a pseudo piety to the place. Not improbably the town grew rapidly around the Kubba of that holy man. But a place so well situated for fishing shebbel (a shad, *clupea alosa*), the only good fresh-water fish in Morocco, must have always attracted some inhabitants to the mouth of the Um-er-Rbia—"the river of forty springs", on the south side of which it stands. The Um-er-Rbia—corrupted into Morbeya—was probably the Anatis flumen of Polybius, the Asana flumen of Pliny, and the Ἀσάμα ποταμοῦ ἐκβολαί of Ptolemy, but the

permanent settlement nearest was at Portus Rutubis, Ρουβίς λιμήν, or the modern Mazagan.

About the earliest notice of Azamor is by Abu-l-feda, who describes it as one of "the towns of Berr-el Udvah. "Azamor is written with an *elif hamza*, surmounted by a *fatha*, a *za*, a *mem* with a *teschdid*, a *wa*, and a *ra*", which ought to fix the spelling. It was then a place of 2,000 inhabitants, partly "Sanhadjites" of the Zanaja or Sanhaja tribe. But Azamor first came into European history when it was attacked without success by the Portuguese in 1508, and then was taken by them on the 2nd of September 1513, after an assault in which Magellan was wounded, and evacuated after thirty-two years of troubled possession.

In 1546, the Sherif Mohammed proposed to raze the city, "a form of vengeance which explains the disappearance of more than one place, but, at the solicitation of three Marabouts, permitted it to stand as a check to the Portuguese incursions from Magazan, and as a base for raids upon them. These three holy men were Sidi 'Abd-allah-ben-Sasi, Sidi Mohammed de Caque (?), and Sidi Canon, whom Leo refers to in his account of Armez. The second of these is known by being mentioned in Diego de Torres, while the first, the most venerated of the three, is buried on the banks of the Tensift, fourteen miles east of Marakesh. It was near the sanctuary of the holy personage, and at his mediation, that the Sherif Ahmed was persuaded to definitely abandon the Empire to his brother Mohammed, and retire to Tafilet. But Captain Major Luiz de Loureyro, Governor of Magazan, had less esteem for the three saints. For, as an inscription over the chief gateway of Mazagan in part indicates, when he learned through his spies that they were plotting mischief against the Portuguese, he immediately marched the eight miles from Mazagan, seized the three, and held seven of their children as security for the payment of a fine of 22,000 ducats.

Since then Azamor has played almost no part in history. A bar across the river mouth prevents the entrance of ships, and no European lives in the town. Weaving and fishing shebbel is the chief employment of the eight or nine thousand (if so many) people, many of whom are Jews. The walls are falling into decay, like the place generally, but some of the houses bear traces of the Portuguese occupation.

Shebbel has always been one of its sources of wealth, 10,000 dried fish being part of the tribute exacted by the Portuguese after the double treachery of Mulai Sidan-n-Zejam, in 1508, by which Azamor was not captured in that year.

The large number of storks, which build their nests in every mosque-tower and ruined fortification in this sleepy city of the past, add to its sanctity, the stork being a sacred bird. On the charts from the fourteenth to the seventeenth century, the cape near Azamor is called Scossor, Fcossor, Zozor, etc., which Sanson finally Latinises into Cacorum Caput (note 101).

(109) This was, perhaps, an exaggeration, considering that Leo wrote so soon after the siege and sack. De Faria y Sousa, in 1680, after the place had recovered from the disaster and was again under the Moors, reckoned it to have 5,000 Moslems and 400 Jews.

(110) The indiscreet general was Juan de Meneses, Governor of Arzilla, who depended on the treachery of Sidan-n-Zejam, a relation of Mohammed the Beni Mereni King of Fez, who had offered his services to deliver the city into the King of Portugal's hands. But Sidan proved false, and the citizens bidding fair to set the Portuguese fleet on fire, Meneses withdrew. The Christian merchants in the city also acted as spies, advising the Portuguese of the weakness of the garrison and defences.

(111) The Duke of Braganza's fleet consisted in reality of 400 ships —mostly, however, very small—carrying 8,000 infantry and 2,500 cavalry. The "certaine prince", who had to escape in so undignified a manner, appears to have been "Alchengue Cim"—the spelling is Diego de Torres'—the Chief Terga, who had come to help Sidi Mansur against the Infidels.

(112) Leo is quite correct in accusing the Jews of treachery. After Sidi Mansur, the Governor, was killed, a Jew, named Jacob Adibe, managed to communicate with the enemy.

Mazagan (Mazagaõ)—or Castello-Real—a town built by the Portuguese in 1506 under Diniz Gregorio de Mello Castro e Mendonça, and abandoned in 1769, is not mentioned by Leo, though he must have been acquainted with it. The place existed originally as a Berber town, called Maziren, by Edrisi. This name was forgotten by the natives, who applied to the fortress which the Portuguese built the title of El Brídja (Boreycha of Marmol, El Breza of Venture, the Bureejá of Jackson, the Berigia of Gråberg de Hemsö, etc.). Even that name is ceasing to be used. This place, with its crumbling walls and antiquated guns, some with "G. R. III" on them, often dismounted and always rusty, is no longer a fortress (Bridja). After the Portuguese left it was called "Meheduma" (the Ruined), a name changed in 1770 by the Sultan, Sidi Mohammed, into El-Jedida (the New). It bears many traces of the Portuguese : a jetty of stone, a large cistern with pillars, and bearing marks of having been struck by a bomb, a building said to have been the Inquisition, great galleried houses, etc. It is about the only place in Morocco where ducks are kept. Jews and Europeans are nearly as numerous as Arabs and Berbers ; but Rohlfs shows entire ignorance of the conditions of commerce in supposing that the trade of Mazagor could be carried on in Azamor were it not for the fanaticism of the latter. The Um-er-Rbia

River bar alone is an almost insuperable difficulty. Yet after the Portuguese left the town was for a time uninhabited. Sidi Mohammed (who to obtain means to defray the cost, for a time permitted the export of cereals) had, indeed, laid siege to it with 30,000 men, 36 guns and mortars, after the order of Dom José to evacuate the place had been received. But at the date when Chenier wrote (1786) Mazagan was "entirely ruined and almost uninhabited. The Moors have taken away the timber and left the walls standing. . . A little to the south-west of Mazagan is an old tower, called Borisha, whence the name of Bridja, which the Moors confound with that of Mazagar". This is mainly copied from Marmol, who adds, that this tower (Boreycha) marked the ancient port of Almedina, where there was a ruined village. But El Bordj is Arabic for any tower. So fanatical was the hatred felt towards the Christians, that the Moors, who were unable to make the Mecca pilgrimage, were instructed by their religious teachers that to come and discharge their markets at Mazagan was compensation enough for the neglect of their religious duty. The garrison on a certain occasion having fired at a group of these fanatics, one was killed by a cannon ball. His comrades gave him a saint's burial, but they took care not to risk the same glorious fate, by in future keeping out of range while indulging in the harmless marketing mentioned. The Moors were also prohibited from buying or selling in the hated town; but as they did a clandestine trade through the tributary natives, the departure of the Portuguese from the last place they held in Morocco was much regretted, until more Europeans came, and greater freedom of commerce began. Yet it was not until 1777 that Portugal had Consuls in Morocco. The inscription in stone over the main gateway, under the arms of Luiz de Loureyro, gives a succinct history of the early days of the city. In 1502, a Portuguese ship having been wrecked on this part of the coast, the crew erected a stockade. In 1509 this grew into a small quadrangular fortress, to protect the builders of the town, which began in 1513, and was completed on the 1st of August 1541, the year that Saffi was evacuated, evidently with the intention of concentrating here, as the garrison of Azamor also was soon withdrawn. From 1510 to 1541, Luiz di Azambugá was commandant; in the latter year he was succeeded by Luiz de Loureyro, who died in 1547.

The town must have cost an enormous sum, the huge blocks of stone having been brought from Lisbon ready hewn and all numbered for the workmen and Moorish slaves to fit into position. So strong was the place that, after trying to take it by treason, the siege by the Moors in 1562 had no effect upon it. Mulai Abd-Allah had resolved on this enterprise, at the instigation of one of the many renegades in his army. He brought 80,000 men into the field, but the Governor, Rodreguez de Sousa, conducted the defence with a skill and courage worthy of the heroic era of Portugal. The Villa Nova de Mazgam, in the Brazilian Province of Grão, in Pará, was built by the exiled Portuguese in memory of their old home in Mazagan.—Luiz Maria do Conto de Albuquerque Da Cunha, *Memorias para a historia da praça de Mazagão*, etc. (1864) ; Galvão, *Vida do famoso heroe Luiz de Loureiro ;* De Sousa, *Documentos Arabicos para a Historia de Portugal :* Castellanos, *Marruecos,* pp. 77-93 ; *Sommario dell' assedio di Mazzagano nel regno di Marocco per i Portughesi 1562 nell' aprile,* Trad., N. C. Amaroglio (1563) ; References in Playfair and Brown's *Bibliography of Morocco* (R. G. S.), under " Mazagan", *Times of Morocco,* No. 48, Oct. 9th, 1886 ; De Faria y Sousa, *Africa Portuguesa* (1681), pp. 107, 207 ; Diego de Torres, *Istoria de los Xarifes,* pp. 17, 171, 199, etc. One of the rarest pieces of early literature on Morocco is the letter of Emanuel the Fortunate, King of Portugal, to Pope Leo X, describing the capture of Azamor and the subjugation of the surrounding country (*Bib. of Morocco,* No. 39).

(113) Meramer in the original. In Cochelet's narrative Meramer is mentioned as two days from Marakesh, and is probably the place of the same name found in El Bekri. It is not now a place of any consequence, and was certainly not " built by the Goths", a people who seem to dominate Leo's imagination. The Beni-Merer are a tribe of the Sheadma Berbers, though using the Arabic " Beni " instead of the Berber " Aït".—Renou, *Expl. scientifique de l'Algérie,* vol. viii, p. 215.

(114) The Jebel Beni Megher. Rohlfs refers to them as the " Dja Megher mountains, which begin or end in Cape Cantin, and which pass round the town [Saffi] sending out little spurs close up to it, relieve the monotony of the coast line, and charm the eye with their lovely tree-clad slopes".—*Mein Erster Aufenthalt in Marokko,* etc. (2nd Ed., 1885), pp. 340-399. In the English translation (1874), " Di-Megher mountains " do not help the reader's understanding. The " Dj. Megher " also appear on Petermann's map attached to some of the German editions.

(115) Monte verde is simply a translation of Jebel el-Akder, a range, the more southerly continuation of which is known as Jebel Falhnassa. Westward, according to Leo's description, they extend to the Hasara hills (Colli di Hasara), a range not mentioned by any other writer. No such mountains exist in this region, or under that name. The Jebel Hessaia are too far north to fall into Leo's description, so that unless Hasara is a misprint for Hescura (Escura), an old province bordering Tedla (Tedles), on the frontier of which the mountains in question lie, it means simply the extension of the Jebel Falhnassa through Ahmar country almost to the Tensift.

This is rendered all the more probable from Leo describing a lake at the foot of the " monte "—that is, mountain range. The only lake in that part of the country is the brackish Sebka-Sima, on the route from Saffi to Marakesh, close to the Sok el Khamis and the village of Sima.

Leo says that the camels drink of the water, which, with all a camel's catholicity for quenching its thirst, it may be questioned whether a camel would do now. But its saltness may be of later date. All Morocco shows strong signs of dessication in recent times, which might, by equalling evaporation and supply, render the lake saline. It seems also decreasing in size, if Leo is correct in likening it to the Italian Bolsena, a water lake 45 miles in area. At all events, no other sheet with which the lake can be identified exists in that region.

M. de Breugnon, French Envoy Extraordinary to the Moorish Court, passed the sebka in May 1767. His geographical nomenclature is quite that of a period when "men of quality did not spell". But though it is placed too near Saffi, and Azac-Haim *Zima* is mentioned at one day from Saffi, "Gutna-Rasselin, saline mineral", must be the sebka, which again is described in the itinerary of a Portuguese embassy in 1773.—Thomassy, *lib. cit.*, p. 159 ; *O Panorama, jornal de litterario*, etc., 1839, cited by Renou, *lib. cit.*, p. 212.

"Pine apples" (e anche delle pine) ; "pine apples" is wrongly rendered. They are neither cultivated nor wild in Morocco. The word may mean the seeds or nuts of the *Pinus halpensis*, which are sometimes eaten, or the fleshy seeds of the *Pistachio*. This also may be the tree "bearing leaues like vnto the pine-leaues". "Frutto rosso che è detto affricano" is dubious.

"Great store of fountaines" shield the saints (molti santi), or rather, saints' tombs, and "altar", "Kubbas", "heuchet", or "sidi", at which every good Moor behaves as Mohammed did on his expedition to drive the Portuguese and their Arab allies out of Dukala.

(116) Hawking and, to a less degree, hunting with hounds, are still favourite pastimes with the Moors. The game Mulai Mohammed got in the "bosco, nel circuito del detto lago" (omitted in the translation) were "oche salvatiche, anitre, e altera sorte d'uccelli d'acqua, e tortorelle"—wild geese, snipe, and other kinds of water birds and pigeons. "Aquile" eagles would appear to mean hawks, for eagles have not been trained to hawk.

"Hares, deere, porcupines, roe deere, woolues, quailes, and starlings" are, in the original, "lepri, cervi, porchespini, capriuoli, lupi coturneci, e di starne". Though often called "hare" by the Europeans, the rabbit (*Lepus Caniculus*) is the animal meant, that being the only member of the Leposidæ family in Barbary, with the exception of the dubious *L. ægyptius* (Desm.). M. Lataste, after examining a number of skulls of the Barbary rabbit, came to the conclusion that it does not differ essentially from that of Europe

NOTES TO BOOK II. 383

(*Actes de la Soc. Linnéenne de Bordeaux*, vol. xxxix, pp. 129-289, and *Etudes sur la Faune des vertébrés de Barbarie—Cat. provisiore des Mammifères apelagiques sauvages* (1885), p. 157. The "cervi" may be the now rare, if not extinct, *Cervus Corsicanus*, the Barbary stag (*C. barbarus*) of some zoologists; the "porchespine" is the common porcupine (*Hystrix cristata*) still occasionally met with, even on the hills near Tangier, where I have seen it. "Capriuoli", admitting that Leo did not mistake some antelope for it, may refer to *Dama dama*. The wolf is not a Morocco mammal, but the jackal (*Canis aureus*) and the fennec (*C. cerdo*) are, not to mention the hyena.

(117) For A.H. 922, read 921, and for A.D. 1512, A.D. 1516, as its equivalent, the first date being a blunder of the translator, the second of Leo himself, as it is in the original, though not in the 1837 reprint.

(118) Hascora, Heskoura, Ecura, Escura.

Though put on maps well into this century, and described as such by Chenier and his copyists, is not now recognised as a province. With Rhumna it formerly composed one government, but was separated from the more western province so as to keep the mountain tribes more firmly under subjection. The "Heuz" of Marakesh and the modern province of Chragna now occupy much the same area in the old kingdom of Morocco.

(119) Elmadina in the original, literally, El Medina, "the city".

(120) Almedin in the original. Here we have two towns in "Hascora", and a third in Dukala, all three with practically the same name, and that meaning simply "the city", or town. The Dukala one (p. 288) figures more than once in Portuguese history, so that as neither of the two, as "Hascora", appear to have had, in Leo's time at all events, any participation in the troubles of which he speaks so frequently, the Dukala "Elmedina" may be considered entirely different from the two now under consideration. Each of these was, no doubt, "commonly called Almedin"; for, at this moment, just as an Englishman will speak of "going to the town", or a cockney of "coming to town", or "going into the city" (meaning London), so a country Moor, talks of visiting "El M'd'nah", instead of referring to the particular one by name, if indeed it has any other of which he knows. Every large town in Morocco has a "Medinah" section, just it has a "Mellah", or Jewry, and a "Kosbah", or Government quarter. Whether the names Leo gives were actually those of the places described, or simply those which he heard the people apply to them in familiar discourse, can never be known. And his data are too vague to enable us, at this time, to affix them to any particular spot, even if they now exist, or have not fallen victims to time, or the rage of some vengeful tyrant who had vowed to "sift" the rebellious towns "through a sieve", as Abd-el-Mumen promises to treat Mara-

kesh, and Mulai Abd' Allah the rebellious city of Fez. All that we can determine is that El Medinah was the more easterly of the two. Renou, who equally failed to identify either, suggests that Leo made some *lapsus penna* in the manuscript, such as a writer does not notice until his words appear in print (and not always then), and that probably the one place might have been M'dinet-ech-Chergui, the eastern, and M'dinet-el-R'arbi, the western town. But we have seen that there is a M'dinet-el-Gharbia (R'arbi) in Dukala. The position of the other two is, therefore, as puzzling as their names, which afford almost no clue to their identity. Possibly "Haskoura", which occurs in two itineraries from Marakesh to Tafilet, and from Akka to Dades, may be the same.—Renou, *Expl. scientifique de l' Algérie*, vol. viii, pp. 162, 163. 225.

There is an El Medinah on the Wad Dmini in the Dra basin, which, with the villages of Ifelt, Iril, Tagnet, Afella Isli, Tauirt, and Amerzeggan, form the place known by the general name of Imini. There is another "Almedina", in ruins at the time Chenier wrote, but as it was near Tit, must undoubtedly have been the Dukala town of that name already noticed (pp. 288, 373), and which frequently figures in *De Faria y Sousa* (pp. 100, 101, etc.), and other writers on the Portuguese struggle in Morocco.

(121) Tagodast, or Isadgaz (Marmol), has not been fully identified, like many places in the Atlas, or its spurs which intersected "Hascora". There is a Tagaust, near the headwater of the Sus. But "Tag", a Berber word, occurs in the composition of many place-names—Tagadert, Tagliet, Tagdurt, Tagemt, Tagendut, Tagenduzt, Tagentat, Tagentaft, Tagenza, Tagenzalt, Tagergent, Tagergust, Tagerra, Tagersift, Tagerhot, Tagjdet, Taglaut, Tagmadart, Tagmut, Tagnit, Taguiämt, Tagulemt, Tagummast, Tagunza, Tagust, Tagressalt, Tagrvit, Tagzart, Tagzvit, etc., all mentioned by De Foucauld. But Leo's description does not permit us to identify his Tagodost with any one of them. Marmol seems to have had some personal acquaintance with "Isadagaz". For he notes that though independent during the decline of the Beni-Marinis, the people submitted to the Sheriffs, and were, in his day, governed by a Berber of the "Hascora" branch of the Musamuda Berbers. But the place was not strong, either by nature or art, and did not contain over a thousand people, including some Jews, mostly traders and artizans (vol. ii, pp. 122-24).

(122) This "El Jama" may, perhaps, not mean "Jemâa" (in the Berber tongue "Anfaliz"), or tribal assembly, but really mosque (pp. 384), though in neither case the etymology will help us in the difficulty of identification. It was on the top of a hill, four miles from Tagodost, of which it was an off-shoot, when the dissensions of the aristocracy of that place became (about 1500?) too hot for the

humbler folk. There is a Jama (Djemoua) Tisergat in the Tezuata District, near the source of the Dra, though I am more inclined to seek Leo's place in the country of the Jemua (Djemoua), one of the many fractions of the Chauïa Berbers of the upper part of the Um-er-Rbia basin—perhaps Jema (Djemaa) Entifa, a place of about 1,500 people, including 200 Jews. In any case it can be only a little hill, "Ksor", of the kind very plentiful all over this region.

(123) Bzo, or Bizu—in all likelihood the "Bezzou" marked on Beaudouin's map as lying on the route from Marakesh to Tedla, about the distance mentioned from the Wad el-Abid. The inhabitants, like those of the preceding places, are Musmuda Berbers.

(124) Teneves, or Tenendez, is, like all of Leo's mountains, too loosely described to be now identified. No known summit bears that name, though it appears to have been the site of a considerable Berber town, if the magnificence of the chief may be accepted as any criterion of his people's wealth. There are many places beginning with "Ten", such as the "Tenin" of the Ida on Mohammed, etc. (De Foucauld, *Reconnaissance au Maroc*, p. 489—Index). Probably it was the home of a Berber tribe, whose name has been corrupted from the Tenaï-ou-Dez, or some such form which has now disappeared. They made continual war on the Ten-sita people. But what it all ended in we may suspect, but cannot say for certain, these wild mountaineers not keeping any annals. "Woad" is, in the Italian, "guado".

(125) Tensita, or Tensit, though called "a mountain", is avowedly "a part of Atlas". *Monte*, meaning in Leo's descriptions almost invariably a spur or range, and which receives from him the name of the tribe inhabiting it, is of some large "Ksor" in the neighbourhood. Marmol knew a place called Tinzeda, which he describes, rather vaguely, as on the River Dra. In reality there is such a large Ksor in the Dra Basin, still called Tanzida, which quite corresponds to Leo's description, though much reduced in power since his day, when it seems to have been the capital of a powerful confederation, extending, most probably, over the Tisint District. De Foucauld visited it, and found it "un grand qçar [Ksor] peuplé de Haratin", a Berber tribe. But it is governed quite apart from any other district, though it recognises the sovereignty of the Ida u Blal. The valley, "ou plutôt l'encaissment au bood duquel il s'élève", is about 3,000 feet wide. On the south it is bordered by the Bani, and on the north by the "Feïja", or hilly desert, whence the Wad Tanzida, in which it stands, takes its rise. The Tanzida people belong to the Seketana section. There is a Zauia in the Ternata district of the Wad Dra called Tanzita, or the Zauia el Baraka, but it has no connection with Tanzida.—De Foucauld, *Reconnaissance au Maroc*, pp. 116, 291, 304, etc., Map 9. The extension of the spur to Dedes is the Jebel Saghro (Sarro) range.

(126) In Casiri's *Bib. Arab. Histr. Esc.*, p. 257, there is a passage quoted from a history of Granada, by Ibnu-l-Khattib, in which the Andalusian parts of the King of Granades' army were armed with "leathern buckles, called lamatti". In a note, copied by Gayangos from an Arabic MS. of the *Kitábu-l-jagráfiyyah*, it is explained that the shields were manufactured from the skin of a species of antelope, called *lamt* or *lamat*, in the dialect of Berbers, and found at Dra and other places bordering on Sudan. This information is confirmed by the passage in Leo. But Ibn-Khaldun (Arabic MS. in British Museum, fo. 52) says that Lanta is the name of a tribe of the great family of Senhaja (Zenata), and that their shields were so-called from being manufactured in the country which they occupied.—De Gayangos, *Hist. of the Mohammedan Dynasties of Spain*, vol. i, pp. 407, 408. Marmol (*L'Afrique*, t. i, p. 52) describes the "Dante" as a form of little ox (Buffalo?) abandoned in the deserts of Numidia and Lybia, particularly "in the Morabitain country". In the *Roudh el Kartas* (Beaumier's ed., p. 141). A "thousand bucklers covered with the *lamt* hide" are mentioned among the expiating gifts of El-Bahary to El-Mansur in A.H. 381 (?).

The "Sherif el Wad" (River Lord) (*Bos atlanticus*) has been described from the Atlas Mountains, and is, perhaps, the *Empolunga* of Purchas. A second species is said to be sometimes found in the country around Sallee and Rabat. But neither is satisfactorily known, and both may be simply domestic cattle which have escaped and reverted to savagedom.—Blyth, *Proc. Zool. Soc., London*, 1841, p. 6.

(127) Gogideme or Guigdeme (Marmol) is too loosely indicated by Leo to be identified with certainty, more especially as we do not know any tribe or Ksor of that name. "Adjoining" ("che confina col sovradetto") may mean in any direction, though the probabilities are that by Gogideme is meant the Jebel Tifernin, the country of the still numerous Ait Seddrat, or on the opposite water-shed of the Wad Tigdi Ughchen, inhabited by the Berber tribe of the same name. Indeed, apart from the closeness of the name to Gogideme, the locality agrees as closely as the description enables us to fix it. Marmol furnishes no additional information, his account being, as usual, almost a paraphrase of Leo's under the guise "the historians say".

(128) The incident of Ibrahim, the short-lived King of Morocco, taking refuge in Gogideme, is not mentioned in the *Roudh el Kartas*, so that this additional clue to the identification of the "monte" is lacking. Pory, however, makes an entirely erroneous translation of "discepolo di Almadi" by "his disciple Elmahele". The disciple was, of course, Abd-el-Mumen, and the master and Mahdi Mohammed Ibn Junurt, the founder of the Almohade dynasty. This reckless

fanatic was anything but a disciple of Ibrahim, whose race he and his successor did their utmost to exterminate.

Gogideme is, perhaps, as both Mr. Corley, and M. de Averzac have suggested, the Gôgdem (Cocadem) of Edrisi, applied to the station of Arki seven days from Wad Nun, and twelve from Traza, on the route between these two places, and the same as Gogdem, the name of a desert which it takes nine days to traverse on the way from Tuat to Timbuktu. Leo himself, as we shall see, places this desert on the route from Plensem to Timbuktu. The identity—or existence—of this locality will be discussed at a later stage. Meantime, it is, no doubt, an alluring hypothesis to imagine that both places owe their names to exiles driven by Abd-el-Mumen from Gogideme.—Corley, *Negroland of the Arabs*, pp. 19, 20, note 34; Renou, *Notice sur l'Afrique septentrionale*, t. ii, pp. 297-298.

(129) Tesevon, or Tescevin, is doubtful. Marmol mentions that the two mountains close together were peopled by the Musmuda Berbers, and that the river which traverses their country eventually joins the Um-er-Rbia. They were poor, and paid rent for their fields to "the Arab vassals of the Sheriff", probably the Beni-Jebir of Marmol. If the "certaine River" is, as there seems some reason for believing, the Tessaut el Fukia (Wad Akhdir), then that portion of the Great Atlas in which it rises, though the source, and, indeed, the course of the river, have still to be traced, is the "Tesevon". But if the "certaine River" (un fiume) is the Um-el-Abra, the mountains might be that portion of the range in which Jebel Ben Mellal and Jebel Amhaust are the most prominent summits. The difficulty of placing Tagodat makes a nearer identification almost impossible until the Atlas is better known. *A true historicall discourse of Muley Hamet's Rising*, etc. (1609), chap. xvi, the writer (Ro. C., perhaps Cotlington) refers to a mountain, Jessevon, not far from Marakesh.

(130) The "region of Tedles" (Tedle of Leo, Tedla of Marmol) is practically the modern province of Tedla, between the Wad-el-Abid, which appears in the older authors under such a variety of names (Quadelhabid, Hued-ala-Abed, Guedelebi, Louet-de-Leibit, Guadelhabid, etc.), and the Um-er-Rbia into which it eventually empties, though Leo takes in much of the Atlas. It is traversed by some of the highest points of the Great Atlas, and forms the home of many semi, or altogether independent tribes who are rich in cattle, fruit trees, etc., and in the grain which they cultivate in abundance on the lower grounds. There are many "Kasbahs", or castles, or mountain strongholds, such as Bebi-Melall, Aït-Rbia, etc., the first containing fully a thousand people, and is defended by three forts belonging to the Aït-Seri, on the defile leading to it. The Aït Atla are addicted to raiding the plains. The Aït Rbâa Kasbah holds about 1,500 people, including some Jews, who hold their usual condition of

vassalage to the Berbers. M. Erckmann mentions the ruins of an "old palace, dating from the time of Mulai Ahmed ed-Dehebi [1727-1729]", though as the "Amil" (governor), representing the Sultan, has only nominal authority, it is difficult to imagine who lived in the old palace. The Um-er-Rbia rolls at the side of the Kasbah, over a rocky bed, and is crossed by a bridge, nearly 500 feet long and 7 feet broad. In the north of the region is Bejad, a holy town, the residence of Ben Daud, a "saint" of considerable influence; and to the south of the Zayain tribe, another place, named Mhaush, completely under the independent rule of the mountain Berbers. Even the Sultan traverses Tedla with an army, not without extreme precaution.—Erckmann, *Le Maroc Moderne*, pp. 64-65; De Foucauld, *Reconnaisance au Moroc*, pp. 65-67.

(131) Tefza, the Tebza of Marmol, has been universally accepted by commentators on North African geography to be the modern Tazza, or Tesa, about fifty miles from Fez. But that is clearly a blunder, the town being afterwards mentioned as Terja, or Tezza, with its proper geographical surroundings. The Tefza, now to be considered, is in reality the modern Kasba Tadla. Indeed, Leo afterwards refers to it as "Tedle" in his description of "Seggheme", so that Tefza, if it was not a slip of the pen, must have been another name for it. The Kasbah, the country folks say, was, with the bridge of ten arches over the Um-er-Rbia, erected by Mulai Ismaïl, a statement which, however, is of no historical value, as Moorish legends are notoriously untenable, and are prone to be eminently so when they circle round Mulai Ismaïl, whose masterful ways have impressed the public memory. Actually every fact is against the tale. It is, however, quite possible, as the place might have fallen into decay, or have been desolated after Leo's day, and have been repaired or reconstructed by Mulai Ismaïl. But it bears the impress of great antiquity. It stands on the right bank of the Um-er-Rbia, which flows at the foot of its walls in the shape of a rapid current, about 100 feet broad and of considerable depth. The castle is well preserved, and, from the Morocco point of view, of more than ordinary strength. In addition to the officials, there are about 1,200 or 1,400 people in the town proper, of whom about 150 are Jews, some of them rich; but the neighbourhood of the place differs from nearly all others in Morocco, in having no vestige of garden, fruit trees, or verdure. The soil is in many places saline, and the water of the Um-er-Rbia—like those of the Wad Rdàt, Wad Imuil, Asif Marren, Tisint, Talta, Ain Imariren, Messun, etc.—though clear and drinkable, tastes slightly of the soil. Salt is, however, not extracted here, but in the territory of Beni Musa. De Foucauld, *Reconnaissance*, etc., pp. 57-58 (Map 6), gives a view and plans of the place which confirms this identification, built in historical date. It ought to be added that on Höst's map

"Tefza" is marked as a town near the upper water of the Um-er-Rbia—in fact, just where Kasba Tadla is.

(132) "Burnvose", the hooded cloaks, or upper woollen garment, so universally used all over Barbary. Bernouse weaving is still a common trade of all the towns in this region.

(133) Zvaïrs, the Zueyr of Marmol, the modern Zaës, who inhabit one of the most savage, and owing, to their ferocity, most dangerous region in Morocco. They are the terror of caravans, intercepting travellers between Rabat and Casablanca, and then escaping with their booty into the mountains, where even an army would hesitate to follow them. Their country is little known, and contains many intricate ravines like the " Kurifla" in the northern part of the region, roamed over only by them. They frequent the Rabat market, where notorious robbers are occasionally seized.—Erckmann, *Le Maroc*, p. 67.

(134) The Benigabir, Bemegaber or Beni-Cheber of Marmol, most probably the notorious Beni Mitir.

(135) Leo has been taken by the translator at his own opinion. For the harangues of "Captaine Ezzeranghi"—who does not appear in any other historical document—have been somewhat abridged of their prolixity. But, as nothing essential has been omitted in the consideration, it has not been considered necessary to re-translate the entire speeches on either side.

(136) Read A.D. 1509.

(137) Efza, the Tefza Fistala or Fichtala of Marmol, according to him the name of a tribe which occupies Tefza and Efza. Tefza, following Leo, means, in the Berber dialect of that region, " marble", but Marmol translates it "a bunch of straw". He evidently regards both towns as mere divisions of each other, a league apart. I have not been able to find that any recent writer mentions it by name, though several have been in the neighbourhood. It was without walls in Marmol's day, a fact which its naturally strong situation might not have prevented it from being destroyed.

The Derne, or Derma, which, according to Leo, lies between it and Teza, is not known in the district where it is usually sought from (note 131). Yet the stream is historical.

El Bekri speaks of the Derne, which he declares is a tributary of the Nansifen, which M. Renou makes out to be the Um-er-Rbia, which it is not, but the Wauizert (Quaouizert), a tributary of the river. He also indicates a point called Darna, one day to the east of Daï, a town situated, according to Edrisi, four days north-east of Marakesh, a geographical reality, as we shall presently see. Ben Aiâs also mentions two towns—Badla and Dani—on the Atlas, which may be

Tadla (really Tezza) and Daï (*Notices et extraits des manuscrits de la Bibliothèque du Roi*, t. viii).

The Derne, or Derna, also makes its appearance in the Moroccan history almost contemporary with Leo. In 1544, after the outbreak of hostilities between Ahmed and Mohammed, son of the Sheriff, Mohammed declared war against Ahmed-el-Oates, Sultan of Fez, and sent his son, Abd-el-Kader, to besiege "el Castillo de Fistela", as Diego Torres calls a place which Ibn Onzar, the Governor, surrendered to the Sheriff after Ahmed, and his son, Bu-Bekr, had been captured at the passage of the Derna (*Istoria de los Xarifes*, pp. 146-161). In this battle one of the commanders was the Kaïd Mumen, son of Yahia, or Mohammed el-Euldj, a Genoese renegade, who held in fief Tedsi, in Sus. Moüette also has the Darna among his list of geographical names. Pellow mentions the "Darnol". Yet it does not occur in any other writers, and the Darna, if it is to be sought in the neighbourhood of the modern Taza, east of Fez, where it has hitherto always been placed, it could not possibly flow into the Um-er-Rbia, but into the Sebu. The difficulty is, however, easily solved by putting the blame not on Leo, but on his commentator. The one is right, the other wrong.

In reality, the Darna exists just where Leo puts it, between Tefza (Kasba Tedla) and Ezza, still called Fistela (Fichtela), as in Marmol's day, though the other name, if not a bit of hearsay blundering on Marmol's part, seems to have been forgotten.

The Wad Derna which Diego de Torres mentions as the locality of the battle is, in short, between Marakesh and the Beni Mtir country, a little south of the Kasba Tadla on the Um-er-Rbia, of which it is a tributary. Fichtala, or Fistela, is a Kasbah or fortress town on the Wad Fichtala, a little further south. Actually it is a very old place, having, in addition to the present village, the remains of an ancient castle (De Foucauld, *Reconnaissance*, etc., pp. 59-60), which superseded the present one erected by Mulai Ismaïl. It is embosomed amid groves of almonds, but does not now contain more than 300 people. They do not reckon themselves members of any tribe. The Kasba is a "Zouia", of which, at the time of De Foucauld's visit, two brothers were absolute masters.

There are various ruins scattered over Tadla. For instance, Mulai Ahmed, son of Mulai Sidan (A.D.1608-1630), laid the foundation of a town on the Um-er-Rbia, in the province of Tadla, which was by and by destroyed, and has not left any trace behind it (Ro. C., *A True Historical Discourse*, etc., chap. vi).

There are two places bearing the name of Fichtala—one "between Fez and Taza", the other (*ut supra*) between Fez and the Wad-el-Abid. But it is uncertain to which of these belonged Abd-el-Aziz Ibn Mohammed (surnamed Abu Fares of Fichtala), who compiled a history of the Sheriffs, under the name of *Menahel-es-Safi-fi-Fadaïl-esh-Shorefâ*, *i.e.*, "Fountains of purity, or the virtues of the Sheriffs (De Slane, *Revue Africaine*, t. i, p. 291).

(138) Cititeb is, according to Leo, west of Efza, according to Marmol, east of it, the latter being most likely the correct statement, as there is no place which can be assigned to the description in the now fairly well known country immediately east of Fez which Leo's slip of the pen would make it, while in Algeria, between Setif and Msila, there is a Berber tribe, the Aït 'Aïad of which name either Cititeb or Eitiad may be the corruption. During the endless wars of this region, various tribes have at different times migrated to other parts of Northern Africa, and even across the Sahara. But in the southern part of Tadla there still live the Aït Aïad, whose mountainous region borders on that of the Aït Bu Sid, though their country is properly in the Um-er-Rbia Basin. They can put into the field a thousand men, of whom one hundred are horsemen, and, according to De Foucauld, are habitually allies of the Aït Atab, a name in which it is easy to detect "Citibeb", their chief village. In the principal Ksor of the Aït Aïad there is a little Mellah with twenty Jews, and among the Aït Atab the same number.

(139) Eitiad, or Aitïat, was a Musmuda Berber "Ksor", of which the probable site is discussed in Note 138.

(140) Seggheme, or Segene, that Renou suggested might be Serrarna, the name of a Berber tribe, " connu de M. Delaporte", in the vicinity of the mountains. The tribe is not known to me, but the Aït Segrouchen (Tsegrouchen, or Tserrouchen), a wide stretching tribe in the region indicated, seem the people described by Leo, always remembering that by "monte" he generally means the mountainous region inhabited by particular Berber people, he proceeds to characterise. "The townes of Tedles" is in the original simply "Tadla", and by the "Captaine" who "had won" them must be meant Ezzerhanghi (p. 312). The North American Indian-like torturing of prisoners by women is the only case of this kind which I have met with among the Berbers.

(141) Magran, or Marran, the Aït Marraua or Meraou, whose Ksors are situated on the borders of the Wad Aït Meraou, a tributary of the Dades, and are capable of furnishing, according to De Foucauld's estimate, 700 or 800 fossils. Further down the river enter the territory of the Imgae (?) tribe. The kind of houses described by Leo are still seen in the Atlas, but the Meraou, if I am correct in the identification given, have removed into regions more favourable for cattle grazing, where they reside during winter when the high valleys are deep in snow. Lions are now very scarce in Morocco ; and by wolves, jackals are no doubt meant. "Farcala" is Ferkla.

(142) A "Jebel Dades", under various transformations, occurs in several old itineraries of more or less authenticity (Renou, *Expl. scientifique de l'Algérie*, t. viii, pp. 160, 164, 172, 174, 227, 231) as the source of the Wad Dra. The Wad Dades, which rises in the Great Atlas, is also a known river which enters the Dra Valley, and the District of Dades is dotted with the Ksors of the Draua (Haratin), the Berâber, the Aït Seddrat, etc. The Dades is divided into six groups, or "Jemâas", each with its own Sheikh and "Aam". These divisions are Aït Temuted, Aït Unir, Aït Hammu, Aït u Allah, Iurtegin, and Arba Mia. There are many Jewish families in the Ksors of the Berber Confederation, of which Dades forms one of the leading members. The ruins of which Leo speaks are not known.—De Foucauld, *Reconnaissance au Maroc*, pp. 215 (view), 218, 222, 224, 268, 269, 403, map 15; D'Avezac, *Etudes de Géog. Critique*, etc., pp. 174-177. The idea of Tédsi being on Mt. Dades shows that Leo forgot what he said before (p. 254), if, indeed, he was not speaking from hearsay. Todra and the Wad Todra (Todga) are also well known. "The mountain of Adesan" is the mountainous region inhabited by the Aït u Ez Zin, a once powerful tribe of the Dades country, who do not appear in any other portion of Leo's work. "Elhasid" is El asid (Note 5). The description of the houses applies very accurately to those of the present day; and the caves in which they lived and housed their cattle are still used for these purposes. "Sisa and Fabbriano" refer to the towns of their names in the Italian Marches.

The use of saltpetre is now well known, the natives making with it and the sulphur they obtain from such thermal springs as those of Ain Sidi Yusuf (the Aquæ Dacicæ), near Fez, from the spot at Mansuria on the Selu (not that near the coast), from which sulphurous vapour and, it is said, flames arise (?), etc., a very poor quality of gunpowder. Indeed, a canister of English gunpowder, which they carefully economise for the priming of their flint-locks, is one of the most acceptable presents which can be made to a mountaineer, or, indeed, to any native of Morocco; foreign gunpowder being like foreign arms among the contraband articles which can be obtained only by smuggling, and therefore at a price proportionate to the risk run. The mysterious "one" by whom Leo was bound to go to Segelmessa was, no doubt, the Sheriff, then beginning those crafty proceedings which eventually obtained for the Hoseni dynasty the thrones of Sus, Morocco and Fez. Leo's connection with them is always open to suspicion.

IOHN LEO HIS
THIRD BOOKE OF
the Historie of Africa, and
of the memorable things
contained therein.

A most exact description of the kingdome of Fez.

HE kingdome of Fez beginneth westward at the famous riuer Ommirabih, and extendeth eastward to the riuer Muluia; northward it is enclosed partly with the Ocean, and partly with the Mediterran sea. The said kingdome of Fez is diuided *Hebat. into seuen prouinces; to wit, Temesna, the territorie *Chauz or of Fez, Azgar, *Elhabet, Errif, Garet, and *Elchauz: *cheuz.* euery of which prouinces had in olde time a seuerall gouernour: neither indeed hath the citie of Fez alwaies beene the kings royall seate, but being built by a certaine Mahumetan apostata, was gouerned by his posteritie almost an hundred and fiftie yeeres.[1] After which time the familie of Marin got the vpper hand, who here setling their aboad, were the first that euer called Fez by the name of a kingdome: the reasons why they did so, we will declare more at large in our small treatise concerning the Mahumetan religion. But now let vs as briefly as we may, describe the foresaid seuen prouinces.

C C

Of Temesna one of the prouinces of Fez.

WEstward it beginneth at the riuer Ommirabih, and stretcheth to the riuer Buragrag eastward; the south frontire thereof bordereth vpon Atlas, and the north vpon the Ocean sea. It is all ouer a plaine countrie, containing in length from west to east almost fowerscore miles, and in breadth from Atlas to the Ocean sea about threescore. This prouince hath euer almost beene the principall of the seuen before named: for it contained to the number of fortie great townes, besides three hundred castles, all which were inhabited by Barbarian Africans. In the 323. yeere of the Hegeira this prouince was by a certaine heretike against the Mahumetan religion called *Chemim* the sonne of *Mennal* freed from paying of tribute. *A dangerous seducer.* This bad fellow perswaded the people of Fez to yeeld no tribute nor honour vnto their prince, and himselfe he professed to be a prophet: but a while after he dealt not onely in matters of religion, but in commonwealth-affaires also. At length waging war against the king of Fez (who was himselfe then warring with the people of Zenete) it so befell, that a league was concluded betweene them, conditionally that *Chemim* shoulde enioy Temesne, and that the king should containe himselfe within his signiorie of Fez, so that from thenceforth neither should molest other. The said *Chemim* gouerned the prouince of Temesne about fiue and thirtie yeeres: and his successours enioyed it almost an hundred yeeres after his decease. But king *Ioseph* hauing built Maroco, went about to bring this prouince vnder his subiection. Whereupon he sent sundry Mahumetan doctors, and priestes to reclaime the gouernour thereof from his heresie, and to perswade him, if it were possible, to yeelde vnto the king by faire meanes. Whereof the inhabitants being aduertised, they consulted with a certaine kinsman of the foresaid gouernour, in the citie called *Anfa*, to murther the king of Maroco his ambassadours: and so they did. Soone after leuying an armie of fiftie thousand men, he marched towards Maroco, intending to expell thence the familie of Luntuna, and *Ioseph* their king. King *Ioseph* hearing of this newes, was driuen into woonderfull perplexitie of minde. Wherefore preparing an huge and mighty armie, he staied not the comming of his enemies: but on the sudden within three daies, hauing conducted his forces ouer the riuer of Ommirabih, he entred Temesne, when as the foresaid fiftie thousand men were so dismaied at the kings armie, that they all passed the riuer Buragrag, and so fled into Fez. But the king so dispeopled and wasted Temesne, that without all remorse he put both man, woman, and childe to the sword. This armie remained in the region eight daies, in which space they so razed and demolished all the towns and cities thereof, that there scarce remaine any fragments of them at this time. But the king of Fez on the other side hearing that the people of Temesne were come into his dominions, made a truce with the tribe of Zenete, and bent his great armie against the said Temesnites. And at length hauing found them halfe famished neere vnto the riuer of Buragrag, he so stopped their passage on all sides, that they were constrained to run vp the craggie mountaines and thickets. At last being enuironed with the kings forces, some of them were drowned in the riuer, others were throwne downe headlong from the rocks, and the residue were miserably slaine by their enemies. And for the space of ten moneths there was such hauock made among the Temesnites, that a sillie remnant of them was left aliue. But king *Ioseph* prince of the Luntunes returned foorthwith to Maroco for the repairing of his forces, to the end he might bid the king of Fez a battell. Howbeit Temesne being bereft of her people, was left to be inhabited of wilde beastes. Neither

The horrible desolation of Temesne.

had that prouince any new colonie, or supply of inhabitants, till that about 150. yeeres after, king *Mansor* returning from Tunis, brought thence certaine Arabians with him, vnto whom he gaue the possession of Temesne. And these Arabians enioyed the said prouince for fiftie yeeres, till such time as king *Mansor* himselfe was expelled out of his kingdome: and then were they also expelled by the Luntunes, and were brought vnto extreme miserie. Afterward the kings of the familie of Marin bestowed the said prouince vpon the people of Zenete and Haoara. Hence it came to passe that the said people of Zenete and Haoara were alwaies great friends vnto the Marin familie, and were thought to haue defended them from the furie of the king of Maroco. From which time they haue peaceably enioyed Maroco, & now they are growne in lesse then an hundred yeeres so mighty, that they stand not in feare of the king of Fez. For they are able to bring threescore thousand horsemen to the field, and haue two hundred castles at their command. My selfe had great familiaritie and acquaintance with them, and therefore I will not sticke to record all memorable things which I sawe among them.[2]

Of Anfa a towne in Temesna.

THis famous towne was built by the Romans vpon the Ocean sea shore, northward of Atlas sixtie, eastward of Azamur sixtie, and westward of Rebat fortie miles. The citizens thereof were most ciuill and wealthie people: the fields thereto adioyning are exceeding fruitfull for all kinde of graine: neither doe I thinke, that any towne in all Africa is for pleasant situation comparable thereto. The plaine round about it (except it be to the sea northward) is almost fowerscore miles ouer. In olde time it was fraught with stately temples, rich ware-houses and shops, and beautifull palaces: which the monuments as yet remaining doe sufficiently testifie. They had also most large and faire gardens, out of which they gather great abundance of fruit, especially of melons, and pome-citrons euen at this day : all which are perfectly ripe by mid-Aprill. So that the inhabitants vsually carrie their fruits vnto Fez, by reason that the fruits of Fez are not so soone ripe. Their attire is trim and decent, and they haue alwaies had great traffique with the Portugals and the English. Likewise they haue many learned men among them. Howbeit two reasons are alleaged of the destruction of this towne: first, because they were too desirous of libertie ; and secondly, for that they maintained certaine gallies or foistes, wherewith they daily molested the Island of Cadiz and the Portugals. Wherefore at length the king of Portugall sent a strong nauie of fiftie sailes against them, the consideration whereof strooke such terrour into the inhabitants, that taking such goods as they could carrie, some fled to Rebat, and others to Sela, and so their towne was left naked to the spoile of the enemie. But the Generall of the kings fleete not knowing that they were fled, put all his forces into battell-array. Howbeit after a while being aduertised how the matter stood, he conducted his soldiers into the citie, which in one daies space they so defaced, burning the houses, and laying the walles euen with the ground, that vntill this day it hath remained voide of inhabitants. My selfe being in this place, I coulde scarce refraine from teares, when I seriously beheld the miserable ruine of so many faire buildings and temples, whereof some monuments are as yet extant. The gardens, albeit they bring foorth some fruit, yet are they more like vnto woods then gardens. And now by reason of the king of Fez his weaknes and default, this place is fallen into so great desolation, as I vtterly despaire, that euer it will be inhabited againe."

English traffique.

Anfa destroied by the Portugals.

Of the citie of Mansora.

THis towne was built by *Mansor* the king and Mahumetan patriarke of Maroco vpon a most pleasant field, being two miles distant from the Ocean sea, fiue and twenty miles from Rebat, and fiue and twentie from Anfa: it contained in times past almost fower hundred families. By this towne runneth a certaine riuer called by the inhabitants Guir, on both sides whereof in times past were most beautifull gardens, but now there are no fruits at all to be found. For vpon the surprize of Anfa the inhabitants of this towne fled vnto Rebat, fearing least they also should haue beene assailed by the Portugals. Howbeit the wall of this towne remained all whole, sauing that the Arabians of Temesne brake it downe in certaine places. This towne also I could not but with great sorrow behold; for easie it were to repaire it, and to furnish it with new inhabitants, if but a few houses were saued from ruine: but such is the malice of the Arabians thereabout, that they will suffer no people to reedifie the same.[4]

Of the towne of Nuchaila.

THis little towne called by the inhabitants Nuchaila, is built almost in the midst of Temesne. It was well peopled in times past, and then (so long as the foresaid *Chemim* and his successours bare rule) there were fayres yeerely holden, whereunto all the inhabitants of Temesne vsually resorted. The townesmen were exceeding wealthie; for the plaines stretched almost fortie miles right foorth from each side of their towne. I red (as I remember) in a certaine storie, that they had in times past such abundance of corne, as they would giue a camels burthen thereof for a paire of shooes. Howbeit when king *Ioseph* of Maroco destroied all the region of Temesne, this towne was laid waste, together with all the townes and cities of the same prouince: howbeit at this day certaine fragments thereof are to be seene, namely some partes of the towne-wall, and one high steeple. Here also in the large and pleasant gardens you may see many vines and trees planted, which are so olde and sear, that they yeeld no fruit at all. The husbandmen thereabout hauing finished their daies worke, doe lay vp their rakes and other such countrey tooles in the said steeple: supposing that by vertue of a certaine holy man which lieth there buried, no man dare remooue them out of their place. I haue often seene this towne, as I trauelled betweene Rebat and Maroco.[5]

Of the towne of Adendum.

This towne was situate among certaine hils almost fifteene miles from mount Atlas, and fiue and twenty miles from the towne last named. The soile neere vnto it is exceeding fruitfull for corne. Not farre from the walles thereof springeth a certaine riuer; about which place are great store of palme-trees, being but low and fruitles. The said riuer runneth through certaine vallies and rocks, where iron-mines are said to haue beene of olde, which may seeme probable, for the earth resembleth iron in colour, and the water in taste. Here is nothing now to be seene but a few reliques and ruines of houses and pillars ouerturned: for this towne was destroied at the same time, when the whole region (as is before declared) was laid waste.[6]

Iron-mines.

Of the towne of Tegeget.

This towne was built by the Africans vpon the banke of Ommirabih neere vnto the highway leading from Tedles to Fez. It had in times past ciuill and wealthie inhabitants, for it stood not far from the way which passeth ouer Atlas into the deserts : hither were all the neighbour-people woont to resort for to buy corne. And albeit this towne was razed with all the residue in the prouince, yet is it after long time replanted with inhabitants. Hither doe all the Arabians of Temesne bring their corne, de-liuering it vnto the townesmen, to be kept. Here are no shops nor artificers at all, but certaine smithes onely, which makes tooles of husbandrie and horseshooes. The townesmen are streightly inioyned by the Arabians their gouernours courteously to entertaine all strangers trauelling that way. Merchants pay custome there for each packe of cloth to the value of a riall : but for their horses and camels they giue no custome at all. Often trauelling the same way, the towne did not greatly please me, albeit the grounds about it doe plentifully abound with cattell and corne.[7]

Of the towne called Hain Elchallu.

THis small towne standeth on a certaine plaine not farre from Mansora. About this towne grow abundance of wilde cherrie-trees, and of other thornie trees, bearing a round fruit not much vnlike to a cherrie, sauing that it is yellow : it is somewhat bigger then an oliue, and the vtter part thereof is nothing pleasant in taste. The fennes and marishes on all sides of the towne are full of snailes and toades : which toades (as the in-habitants told me) are no whit venemous. There is not any African historiographer which maketh description or mention of this towne ; because perhaps they thought it not woorthie the name of a towne, or for that it was long since destroied. Neither was it (as I coniecture) built by the Africans, but either by the Romans or some other forren people.[8]

A description of Rebat.

This great and famous towne was built not many yeeres agoe by *Mansor* the king and Mahumetan patriarke of Maroco, vpon the Ocean sea shore.⁹ By the east part thereof runneth the riuer Buragrag beforenamed, and there dischargeth it selfe into the maine sea. The rocke whereon this towne is founded, standeth neere the mouth of the said riuer, hauing the riuer on the one side thereof, and the sea on the other.¹⁰ In building it much resembleth Maroco, which *Mansor* willed to be a paterne thereof: sauing that it is a great deale lesse then Maroco. Some say that the reason why it was built in this place was, for that king *Mansor* possessing the kingdome of Granada and a great part of Spaine besides, and considering that Maroco was so far distant, that if any warres should happen, he could not in due time send new forces against the Christians, determined to build some towne vpon the sea shore, where he and his armie might remaine all summer time. Some perswaded him to lie with his armie at Ceuta a towne vpon the streites of Gibraltar: but *Mansor* seeing that by reason of the barrennes of the soile he could not maintaine an armie royall for three or fower monethes in the towne of Ceuta, he caused this towne of Rebat in short space to be erected, and to be exceedingly beautified with temples, colleges, pallaces, shops, stores, hospitals, and other such buildings. Moreouer on the south side without the walles he caused a certaine high tower like the tower of Maroco to be built, sauing that the winding staires were somewhat larger, insomuch that three horses a-breast might well ascend vp: from the top whereof they might escrie ships an huge way into the sea. So exceeding is the height thereof, that I thinke there is no where the like building to be found.¹¹ And to the end that greater store of artificers and merchants might hither from all places make

Why king Mansor built the towne of Rebat vpon the seashore.

resort, he appointed, that euery man according to his trade and occupation should be allowed a yeerely stipend: whereupon it came to passe that within few moneths, this towne was better stored with all kinde of artificers and merchants, than any towne in all Africa besides, and that because they reaped a double gaine. Here vsed *Mansor* with his troupes to remaine from the beginning of April, till the moneth of September. And whereas there was no water about the towne meete to be drunke (for the sea runneth ten miles vp into the riuer, and the wels likewise yeeld salt-water) *Mansor* caused fresh water to be conueied to the towne by certaine pipes and chanels, from a fountaine twelue miles distant. And the conducts hee made archwise, like vnto the conducts of Italie in many places and specially at Rome. So soone as the said water-conduct was deriued vnto the towne, he caused it to be diuided and sent into sundry places, as namely some pipes thereof to the temples, some to the colleges, others to the kings' pallace, and the rest into the common cesternes, throughout all the citie. Howbeit after king *Mansors* death this towne grew into such decay, that scarce the tenth part thereof now remaineth. The said notable water-conduct was vtterly fordone in the warre betweene the Marinfamilie and the successors of *Mansor*, and the famous towne it selfe decaieth euery day more then other: so that at this present a man shall hardly finde throughout the whole towne fower hundred houses inhabited; the residue are changed into fields and vineyards. About the foresaid rocke are two or three streetes with a few shops in them, which notwithstanding are in continuall danger, for they daily feare least the Portugals should surprize them; because the Portugall king often determined their ouerthrow, thinking if he might but win Rebat, that the kingdome of Fez were easie to be conquered. Howbeit the king of Fez hath alwaies endeuoured to defend the same, and strongly to fortifie it against the enemie. But comparing their former felicitie with the present alteration whereinto they are fallen, I cannot but greatly lament their miserable case.

Of the towne of Sella.

THis towne was built by the Romans vpon the riuer of Buragrag, two miles from the Ocean sea, and a mile from Rebat: from whence, if a man will goe to the sea, he must take Rebat in his way. This towne also was destroied when (as is aforesaid) king *Ioseph* spoyled all Temesne. Howbeit afterward king *Mansor* caused it to be walled round about, and built therein a faire hospitall and a stately pallace, into which his soldiers might at their pleasure retire themselues. Here likewise he erected a most beautifull temple, wherein he caused a goodly hall or chapel to be set vp, which was curiously carued, and had many faire windowes about it: and in this hall (when he perceiued death to seaze vpon him) he commanded his subiects to burie his corpes. Which being done, they laid one marble-stone ouer his head and another ouer his feete, whereon sundry epitaphes were engrauen. After him likewise all the honourable personages of his familie and blood, chose to be interred in the same hall. And so did the kings of the Marin-familie, so long as their commonwealth prospered. My selfe on a time entring the same hall, beheld there thirtie monuments of noble and great personages, and diligently wrote out all their epitaphes: this I did in the yeere of the Hegeira 915.[12]

Where king Mansor was buried.

Of the towne called Mader Avuam.

THis towne[13] was built in my time by a certaine treasurer of the Mahumetan prelate *Abdulmumen*, vpon the banke of Buragrag. Some say it was built onely for yron-mines. From mount Atlas it is ten miles distant, *Iron-mines.*

and betweene it and Atlas are certaine shadie woods, full of terrible lions and leapards.[11] So long as the founders posteritie gouerned this towne, it was well stored with people, with faire buildings, temples, innes, and hospitals: but, the Marin-familie preuailing daily more and more, it was at length by them vtterly destroyed. Part of the inhabitants were slaine, and part taken prisoners, and the residue by flight escaped to Sella. The king of Maroco sent forces to succour the towne, but the citizens being vanquished before their comming, were constrained to forsake the same, and to yeeld it vnto the Marin-soldiers. Howbeit the king of Maroco his captaine comming vpon the Marin-captaine with round forces, draue him and his foorth of the towne, and tooke possession thereof himselfe. At length the king of the said Marin-familie marching with an armie against Maroco, tooke his iourney by this towne: whereat the gouernour being dismaied left the said towne, and before the kings approch betooke himselfe to flight. But the king putting all the inhabitants to the sword, left the towne it selfe so defaced and desolate, that by report it hath lien dispeopled euer since. The towne-walles and certaine steeples are as yet to be seene. My selfe sawe this towne, when the king of Fez hauing concluded a league with his cozen, tooke his iourney to Thagia, for to visite the sepulchre of one accounted in his life time an holy man, called *Seudi Buhasa:* which was in the yeere of the Hegeira 920. *Anno Dom.* 1511.[15]

Lyons, and leopards.

* Or Sidi.

Of Thagia a towne in Temesne.

THis little towne was in ancient time built by the Africans among certaine hils of mount Atlas. The aire is extreme cold, and the soile drie and barren. It is enuironed with huge woods, which are full of lions and other cruell beasts. Their scarcitie of corne is sufficiently counteruailed with abundance of hony and goates. Ciuilitie they haue none at all; and their houses are most rudely built; for they haue no vse of lime. In this towne is visited the sepulchre of one accounted for a most holy man, who is reported in the time of *Habdulmumen*, to haue wrought many miracles against the furie of lions: whereupon he was reputed by many as a great prophet. I remember that I read in a certaine writer of that nation commonly called *Etdeale*, a whole catalogue of the said holy mans miracles: which whether he wrought by arte-magique, or by some woonderfull secret of nature, it is altogether vncertaine. Howbeit his great fame and honorable reputation is the cause why this towne is so well fraught with inhabitants. The people of Fez hauing solemnized their passeouer, doe yeerely frequent this towne to visite the said sepulchre, and that in such huge numbers, that you woulde esteeme them to be an whole armie; for euery principall man carries his tent and other necessaries with him: and so you shall see sometime an hundred tents and sometimes more in that company. Fifteene daies they are in performing of that pilgrimage; for Thagia standeth from Fez almost an hundred and twenty miles. My selfe being a childe, went thither on pilgrimage oftentimes with my father; as likewise being growne vp to mans estate, I repaired thither as often, making supplication to be deliuered from the danger of lions.[16]

Of the towne of Zarfa.

THis towne the Africans built vpon a certaine large and beautifull plaine, watred with pleasant riuers, and christall-fountaines. About the ancient bounds of this citie you may behold many shrubs, together with fig-trees and cherrie-trees, which beare such cherries, as at Rome are called Marene. Here are likewise certaine thornie trees, the fruit whereof is by the Arabians called Rabich. Somewhat lesser it is then a cherie, resembling in taste the fruit called Ziziphum, or Iujuba. Here also may you finde great store of wilde palme-trees, from which they gather a kinde of fruit like vnto Spanish oliues, sauing that the stone or nut is greater, and not so pleasant in taste: before they be ripe they taste somewhat like vnto Scruice-apples. This towne was destroied when king *Ioseph* aforesaid spoiled Temesne. Now the Arabians of Temesne sow their corne where the towne stood, with great increase and gaine.[17]

Of the territorie of Fez.

* Or çebu.

Estward it beginneth at the riuer of Buragrag, and stretcheth eastward to the riuer called Inauen: which two riuers are almost a hundred miles distant asunder. Northward it bordereth vpon the riuer *Subu, and southward vpon the foote of Atlas. The soile both for abundance of corne, fruits, and cattell seemeth to be inferiour to none other. Within this prouince you shall see many exceeding great villages, which may for their bignes, not vnfitly be called townes. The plaines of this region haue beene so wasted with former warres, that very few inhabitants dwell vpon them, except certaine poore silly Arabians, some of whom haue ground of their owne, and some possesse ground in common, either with the citizens of Fez, or with the king, or else with some courtier. But the fields of Sala and Meenase are tilled by other Arabians of better account, and are for the most part subiect to the king of Fez. And now those things which are woorthy of memorie in this region let vs here make report of.

Of the citie or towne of Sella.

THis most ancient citie was built by the Romans, and sacked by the Gothes. And afterward when the Mahumetans armie were entred into the same region, the Gothes gaue it to *Tarick* one of their captaines.[18] But euer since the time that Fez was built, Sela hath beene subiect vnto the gouernours thereof. It is most pleasantly situate vpon the Ocean sea-shore, within halfe a mile of Rebat; both which townes the riuer Buragrag separateth insunder. The buildings of this towne carrie a shew of antiquitie on them, being artificially carued and stately supported with marble pillers. Their temples are most beautifull, and their shops are built vnder large porches. And at the end of euery row of shops is an arch, which (as they say) is to diuide one occupation frō another. And (to say all in a word) here is nothing wanting, which may be required either in a most honourable citie, or in a flourishing commonwealth.[19] Moreouer hither resort all kinde of merchants both Christians and others. Here the Genowaies, Venetians, English and lowe Dutch vsed to traffique.[20] *English traffique.* In the 670. yeere of the Hegeira this towne was surprized by a certaine Castilian captaine, the inhabitants being put to flight, and the Christians enioying the citie. And when they had kept it ten daies, being on the sudden assailed by *Iacob* the first king of the Marin-familie (who could not, they thought, surcease his warre against Tremizen) they were put to the woorst, the greater part being slaine, and the residue put to flight. From thencefoorth that prince fauoured of all his subiects, enioyed the kingdome, after whom lineally succeeded those of his owne race and blood. And albeit this towne was in so few daies recouered from the enemie; yet a worlde it was to see, what a woonderfull alteration both of the houses and of the state of gouernment happened. Many houses of this towne are *Sela woon by a captaine of Castilia, and recouered forthwith by the king of Fez.*

left desolate, especially neere the towne-walles: which, albeit they are most stately and curiously built, yet no man there is that will inhabit them. The grounds adioyning vpon this towne are sandie: neither are they fit for corne, but for cotton-wooll in diuers places very profitable. The inhabitants, diuers of them, doe weaue most excellent cotton. Here likewise are made very fine combes; which are sold in all the kingdome of Fez, for the region thereabout yeeldeth great plenty of box, and of other wood fit for the same purpose. Their gouernment is very orderly and discreet vntill this day: for they have most learned iudges, vmpires, and deciders of doubtfull cases in lawe. This towne is frequented by many rich merchants of Genoa, whom the king hath alwaies had in great regarde; because he gaineth much yeerely by their traffique. The said merchants haue their aboad and diet, partly here at Sella, and partly at Fez: from both which towns they mutually helpe the traffique one of another. These Genowaies I found in their affaires of merchandize to be exceeding liberall: for they will spend frankly to get a courtiers fauour, not so much for their owne priuate gaine, as to be esteemed bountifull by strangers. In my time there was an honorable gentlemã of Genoa in the king of Fez his court, called *Messer Thomaso di Marino*, a man both learned & wise, & highly reputed of by the king. This man hauing continued almost thirtie yeeres in the Fessan court, hee there deceased, and requesting on his death-bed to haue his corpes interred at Genoa, the king commanded the same to be transported thither. After his decease he left many sonnes in the Fessan kings court, who all of them prooued rich, and were greatly fauoured by the king.[21]

A merchant of Genoa.

Of the towne called Fanzara.

This towne being not very large, was built by a certaine king of the familie called Muachidin, on a beautiful plaine almost ten miles from Sella. The soile thereabouts yeeldeth corne in great plenty. Without the towne walles are very many cleere fountaines and wels, which *Albuchesen* the king of Fez caused there to be digged. In the time of *Abusaid* the last king of the Marin-familie, his cozen called *Sahid* was taken by *Habdilla* the king of Granada; whereupon by letters he requested his cozen the king of Fez to send him a certaine summe of money required by the king of Granada for his ransome. Which when the Fessan king refused to yeeld vnto, *Habdilla* restored his prisoner to libertie, and sent him towardes Fez to destroy both the citie and the king. Afterward *Sahid*, with the helpe of certaine wilde Arabians besieged Fez for seuen yeeres together; in which space most of the townes, villages, and hamlets throughout the whole kingdome were destroied. But at length such a pestilence inuaded *Sahids* forces, that himselfe, with a great part of his armie, in the *918. yeere of the Hegeira, died thereof. Howbeit those desolate townes neuer receiued from thenceefoorth any new inhabitants, especially Fanzara, which was giuen to certaine Arabian captaines, that came to assist *Sahid*.[22]

The occasion of the bloody wars mooued by Sahid.

The citie of Fez besieged for seuen yeeres together.

* *This number (as I take it) should rather be 819.*

Of the towne of Mahmora.

This towne was built vpon the mouth of the great riuer Subu by a certaine king of the Muachidin-familie, being almost halfe a′ mile distant from the sea, and about twelue miles from Sella. The places neere vnto it are sandie and barren. It was built (they say) of purpose to keepe the enemies from entring the mouth of the said riuer. Not farre from this towne standeth a mighty wood, the trees whereof beare a kinde of nuts or acornes about

D D

the bignes of Damascen-plums, being sweeter in taste then chestnuts. Of which nuts certaine Arabians, dwelling neer vnto the place, conuey great plenty vnto the citie of Fez, and reape much gaine thereby: howbeit in going to gather this fruit, vnles they take good heede vnto themselues, they are in great danger of the most cruell and deuouring lions in all Africa, which there oftentimes doe seaze vpon them. This towne a hundred and twenty yeeres agoe was razed in the foresaid warre of *Sahid* against the king of Fez, nothing but a few ruines thereof remaining, whereby it appeereth to haue beene of no great bignes. In the 920. yeere of the Hegeira the king of Portugal sent an armie to build a forte in the foresaid riuers mouth; which they accordingly attempted to doe. But hauing laide the foundations, and reared the walles a good height, the king of Fez his brother so defeated them of their purpose, that he slue of them in one night almost three thousand in maner following: on a certaine morning before sun-rise three thousand Portugals marching towards the king of Fez his campe, determined to bring thence all the ordinance and field-peeces vnto their new-erected fort: howbeit most rashly and inconsiderately, themselues being but three thousand, and the kings armie containing fiftie thousand footemen, and fower thousand horsemen. And yet the Portugals hoped so slyly and closely to performe this attempt, that before the Moores were ready to pursue them, they should conuey all their ordinance vnto the forte which was two miles distant. The Moores which kept the ordinance being seuen thousand men, were all asleepe when the Portugals came: whereupon the Portugals had so good successe, that they had carried the ordinance almost a mile, before the enemie was aware thereof. But at last, some rumour or alarme being giuen in the Moores campe, they all betooke themselues to armes, and fiercely pursued the Portugals

Most cruell and deuouring lions.

The Portugals attempting to build a forte within the mouth of the riuer Subu, defeated of their purpose, and slaine.

who likewise arranged their whole companie into battell-
array. And albeit the enemie enuironed them on all sides ;
yet they made such stout and valiant resistance, that they
had all escaped to their forte in safetie, had not certaine
villains in the king of Fez his armie cried out amaine in the
Portugall toong: Hold your hands (fellow soldiers) and
throw downe your weapons, for the kings brother will make
a truce. Which the Portugals no sooner yeelded vnto, but
the sauage and merciles Moores put them euery one to
the sword, sauing three or fower onely, who were saued at
the request of a captaine in the Moores campe. The
Portugals Generall being sore dismaied with this slaughter
(for thereby he had lost all his principal soldiers) craued
aide of a certaine other captaine, which by chance arriued
there with a mightie fleete, being accompanied with a great
number of noblemen and gentlemen. Howbeit, he was so
hindred by the Moores (who daily did him all the villanie
they could, and sunke diuers of his ships) that he was not
able to performe that which he desired. In the meane
space news was published among the Portugals, of the king
of Spaines death ; whereupon diuers ships were prouided,
and many Portugals were sent into Spaine. Likewise the
captaine of the said new forte seeing himselfe destitute
of all succour, leauing the forte, embarked himselfe in those
ships, which then lay vpon the riuer. But the greatest part
of the fleete were cast away at their setting foorth, and the
residue, to escape the Moores shot, ran themselues a-ground
on the flats and shouldes of the riuer, and were there
miserably slaine by the Moores. Many of their ships were
here burnt, and their ordinance sunke in the sea. So many
Christians were then slaine (some say to the number of ten *A lamentable
thousand) that the sea-water in that place continued red slaughter.*
with their blood for three daies after. Soone after the
Moores tooke vp fower hundred great peeces of brasse out
of the sea. This hugh calamitie befell the Portugals for

two causes: first because they would with such a small number make so rash an assault vpon the Moores, whom they knew to be so strong: and secondly, whereas the Portugall-king might at his owne cost haue sent another fleete for a new supply, he would by no meanes ioine his owne people and Castilians together. For by reason of the diuersitie of counsels and of people, there is nothing more pernicious then for an armie to consist of two nations: yea the Moores certainly expect the vpper hand, when they are to fight with such an armie. I my selfe was present in the foresaid warre, and sawe each particular accident, a little before my voyage to Constantinople.[23]

John Leo his voiage to Constantinople.

Of the towne called Tefelfelt.

THis towne is situate vpon a sandie plaine, fifteene miles eastward of Mahmora, and almost twelue miles from the Ocean sea. Not far from this towne runneth a certaine riuer, on both sides whereof are thicke woods haunted with more fierce and cruell lions, then the last before mentioned, which greatly endanger those trauellers that haue occasion to lodge thereabout. Without this towne, vpon the high way to Fez, standeth an olde cottage with a plancherd chamber therein: here the muletiers and carriers are said to take vp their lodging; but the doore of the said cottage they stop as sure as they can with boughes and thornes. Some affirme, that this rotten cottage (while the towne was inhabited) was a most stately inne. But it was defaced in the foresaid war of *Sahid*.[24]

Fierce lions.

A description of Mecnase.

THis towne was so called after the name of the Mecnasites who were the founders thereof. From Fez it is 36. miles, about fiftie from Sella, and from Atlas almost 15. miles distant. It is exceeding rich, and containeth families to the number of six thousand. The inhabitants hereof while they dwelt in the fields liued a most peaceable life: howbeit at length they fell to dissension among themselues, and the weaker part hauing all their cattell taken from them, and hauing nothing in the fields to maintaine their estate, agreed among themselues to build this city of Mecnase in a most beautifull plaine.[25] Neere vnto this towne runneth a little riuer: and within three miles thereof are most pleasant gardens replenished with all manner of fruits.[26] Quinces there are of great bignes, and of a most fragrant smell; and pomegranates likewise, which being very great and most pleasant in taste, haue no stones within them, and yet they are sold exceeding cheape. Likewise here are plentie of damascens, of white plums, and of the fruite called Iujuba, which being dried in the sunne, they eate in the spring, and carrie a great number of them to Fez. They haue likewise great store of figs and grapes, which are not to be eaten but while they are greene & new: for their figs being dried become so brittle, that they waste all to powder, and their grapes when they are made raisins, proouc vnsauorie. Peaches and oranges they haue in so great quantitie, that they make no store of them: but their limons are waterish and vnpleasant. Oliues are sold among them for a duckat and a halfe the Cantharo, which measure containeth a hundred pounds Italian.[27] Moreouer their fields yeeld them great plentie of hempe and flaxe, which they sell at Fez and Sela. In this towne are most stately and beautifull temples, three colleges, and ten bath-stoues. Euery monday they haue a great market without the towne-walles, whereunto the bordering Arabians doe vsually resort. Here are oxen, sheepe, and other such beastes to be sold: butter and wooll are here plentifull and at an easie rate. In my time the king bestowed this towne vpon a certaine noble man of his, where as much fruits are reaped as in the third part of the whole kingdome of Fez. This towne hath beene so

afflicted by warres, that the yeerly tribute thereof hath
beene diminished sometime fortie thousand, and fiftie
thousand duckats, and sometimes more : and I haue red,
that it hath beene besieged for sixe or seuen yeeres
together. In my time the gouernour thereof the king of Fez
his cozen, relying vpon the fauour of the people, rebelled
against his kinsman and soueraigne. Whereupon the Fessan
king with a great armie besieged the towne two moneths
together, and, because it would not yeeld, so wasted and
destroied all the countrie thereabout, that the gouernour
lost by that meanes fiue and twentie thousand duckats of
yeerely reuenue.[28] What then shall we thinke of the sixe
and seuen yeeres siege before mentioned ? At length those
citizens which fauoured the king of Fez opened the gates,
and stoutly resisting the contrarie faction, gaue the king
and his soldiers entrance. Thus by their meanes the king
wan the citie, carrying home to Fez the rebellious gouernour
captiue, who within fewe daies escaped from him. This
most strong and beautifull citie hath many faire streetes,
whereinto by conducts from a fountaine three miles distant,
is conueied most sweet and holesome water, which serueth
all the whole citie. The mils are two miles distant from
the towne. The inhabitants are most valiant, warlike,
liberall, and ciuill people, but their wits are not so refined
as others : some of them are merchants, some artificers, and
the residue gentlemen. They count it vnseemely for any
man to send an horse-lode of feede to his husbandman or
farmer. They are at continuall iarre with the citizens of
Fez ; but whereupon this dissension of theirs should arise,
I cannot well determine. Their gentlemens wiues neuer
goe foorth of the doores but onely in the night season, and
then also they must be so vailed and muffeled that no man
may see them : so great is the ielousie of this people.[29]
This towne is so durtie in the spring-time, that it would
irke a man to walke the streetes.

Mecnase reduced vnder subiection by the king of Fez.

Of a towne called Gemiha Elchmen.

THis ancient towne standeth on a plaine neere vnto certaine baths, being distant southward of Meenase fifteene miles, westard of Fez thirtie, and from Atlas about ten miles. By this towne lieth the common high way from Fez to Tedle. The fielde of this towne was possessed by certaine Arabians, and the towne it selfe vtterly destroied in the war of *Sahid*. Howbeit in certaine places the walles are yet remaining, and diuers towers and temples standing without roofes.[30]

Of the towne called Cannis Metgara.

THis towne was built by certaine Africans in the field of Zuaga almost fifteene miles westward from Fez. Without this towne for two miles together were most pleasant and fruitfull gardens: but by the cruell warre of *Sahid* all was laide waste; and the place it selfe remained void of inhabitants an hundred and twenty yeeres. Howbeit when part of the people of Granada came ouer into Africa, this region began to be inhabited anew. And whereas the Granatines are great merchants of silke, they caused, for the breeding of silkewormes, great store of white mulberrie trees to be brought hither. Here likewise they planted abundance of sugar-canes, which prosper not so well in this place as in the prouince of Andaluzia. In times past the inhabitants of this place were very ciuill people, but in our time they haue not beene so, by reason that all of them exercise husbandrie.[31]

Of the towne of Banibasil.

THis towne was built by the Africans vpon a certaine small riuer iust in the mid way betweene Meenase and Fez, being distant from Fez about eighteene miles westward. Out of their fields many riuers take their originall, which fieldes are by the Arabians sowen all ouer with barlie and hempe: neither indeed will the soile yeeld any other commoditie, both by reason of the barrennes and also for that it is for the most part ouerflowed with water. Whatsoeuer commoditie ariseth out of this place redoundeth to the priestes of the principall Mahumetan temple in Fez, and it amounteth almost yeerely to twenty thousand duckats. Here also in times past were most large, pleasant, and fruitfull gardens, as appeereth by the monuments and reliques thereof, howbeit they were, like other places, laide waste by the war of *Sahid*. The towne it selfe remained destitute of inhabitants an hundred and ten yeeres; but as the king of Fez returned home from Duccala, he commanded part of his people to inhabite the same: albeit their inciuilitie made them loth so to doe.[32]

Of Fez the principall citie of all Barbarie, and of the founders thereof.

FEz was built in the time of one *Aron* a Mahumetan patriarke, in the yeere of the Hegeira 185. and in the yeere of our Lord 786. by a certaine heretike against the religion of Mahumet. But why it should so be called some are of opinion, because when the first foundations thereof were digged, there was found some quantitie of golde, which mettall in the Arabian language is called Fez. Which etymologic seemeth to me not improbable, albeit some would haue it so called from a certaine riuer of that name.[33] But howsoeuer it be, we leaue that to be discussed by others, affirming for an vndoubted truth, that the founder of this citie was one *Idris*, being the foresaid *Aron* his neere kinsman. This *Idris* ought rather to haue beene Mahumetan patriarke, because he was nephew vnto *Hali* the cozen-german of Mahumet, who married *Falerna* Mahumets owne daughter, so that *Idris* both by father, and mother was of Mahumets linage: but *Aron* being

Idris the first founder of Fez

nephew vnto one *Habbus* the vncle of Mahumet, was of kinred onely by the fathers side. Howbeit both of them were excluded from the said patriarkship for certaine causes mentioned in the African chronicles, although *Aron* vsurped the same by deceit. For *Arons* vncle being a most cunning and craftie man, and faining himselfe to beare greatest fauour vnto the familie of *Hali*, and to bee most desirous, that the patriarkship should light thereon, sent his ambassadours almost throughout the whole world. Whereupon the dignitie was translated from *Vmeue* to *Habdulla Seffec* the first patriarke. Which, *Vmeue* being informed of, waged warre against the familie of *Hali*, and so preuailed, that some of them he chased into Asia, and some into India. Howbeit an ancient religious man of the same familie remained still aliue at Elmadina, who being very olde, no whit regarded the dignitie. But this ancient sire left behinde him two sonnes, who when they were come to mans estate, grew into so great fauour with the people of Elmadin, that they were chased thence by their enemies; the one being taken & hanged; and the other (whose name was *Idris*) escaping into Mauritania.[34] This *Idris* dwelling vpon mount Zaron about thirtie miles from Fez, gouerned not onely the commonwealth, but matters of religion also: and all the region adiacent paid him tribute.[35] At length *Idris* deceasing without lawfull issue, left one of his maides big with childe, which had beene turned from the Gothes religion to the Moores. Being deliuered of her sonne, they called him after his fathers name, *Idris*. This childe the inhabitants chusing for their prince, caused him to be most carefully brought vp: and as he grew in yeeres, to the end they might traine him vp in feates of chiualrie, they appointed one *Rasid* a most valiant and skilfull captaine to instruct him. Inso-much, that while he was but fifteene yeeres of age, he grew famous for his valiant actes and stratagems, and

Idris his great valour at fifteene yeeres of age.

began woonderfully to inlarge his dominions. Wherefore his troupes and familie increasing euery day more and more, he set his minde vpon building of a citie, and changing of his habitation.³⁶ And so he sent for cunning builders into all nations, who hauing diligently perused all places in the region, at last made choise of that where the citie of Fez now standeth. For here they found great store of fountaines, and a faire riuer, which springing foorth of a plaine not far of, runneth pleasantly almost eight miles amidst the little hils, till at length it casteth it selfe vpon another plaine. Southward of the place they found a wood, which they knew would be right commodious for the towne. Here therefore vpon the east banke of the said riuer, they built a towne containing three thousand families : neither omitted they ought at al which might be required in a flourishing commonwealth. After the decease of *Idris*, his sonne erected another towne directly ouer against the foresaid, on the other side of the riuer. But in processe of time either towne so increased, that there was but a small distance betweene them : for the gouernours of each laboured might and maine to augment their owne iurisdictions. An hundred and fowerscore yeeres after, there fell out great dissension and ciuill warre betweene these two cities, which by report continued an hundred yeeres together. At length *Ioseph* king of Maroco of the Luntune-familie, conducting an huge armie against both these princes, tooke them prisoners, carried them home vnto his dominions, and put them to a most cruell death. And he so vanquished the citizens, that there were slaine of them thirtie thousand. Then determined king *Ioseph* to reduce those two townes into firme vnitie and concord : for which cause, making a bridge ouer the riuer, and beating downe the walles of either towne right against it, he vnited both into one, which afterward he diuided into twelue regions or wardes.³⁷ Now let vs

make report of all such memorable things as are there to * 1526.
be seene* at this day.

A most exact description of the citie of Fez.

A World it is to see, how large, how populous, how well-fortified and walled this citie is. The most part thereof standeth vpon great and little hils: neither is there any plaine ground but onely in the midst of the citie.[38] The riuer entreth the towne in two places, for it is diuided into a double branch, one whereof runneth by new Fez, that is, by the south side of the towne, and another commeth in at the west side. And so almost infinitely dispersing it selfe into the citie, it is deriued by certaine conducts and chanels vnto euery temple, college, inne, hospitall, and almost to euery priuate house. Vnto the temples are certaine square conducts adioned, hauing celles and receptacles round about them; each one of which hath a cocke, whereby water is conueied through the wall into a trough of marble. From whence flowing into the sinks and gutters, it carrieth away all the filth of the citie into the riuer. In the midst of each square conduct standeth a lowe cesterne, being three cubites in depth, fower in bredth, and twelue in length: and the water is conueied by certaine pipes into the foresaid square conducts, which are almost an hundred and fiftie in number. The most part of the houses are built of fine bricks and stones curiously painted. Likewise their bay-windowes and portals are made of partie-coloured bricke, like vnto the stones of Majorica. The roofes of their houses they adorne with golde, azure, and other excellent colours, which roofes are made of wood, and plaine on the top, to the end that in summer-time carpets may be spred vpon them, for here they vse to lodge by reason of the exceeding heate of that countrie. Some houses are of two and some of three stories high, whereunto they

make fine stairs, by which they passe from one roome to
another vnder the same roofe : for the middle part of the
house is alwaies open or vncouered, hauing some chambers
built on the one side, and some on the other. The chamber-
doores are very high and wide : which in rich mens houses
are framed of excellent and carued wood. Each chamber
hath a presse curiously painted and varnished belonging
thereunto, being as long as the chamber it selfe is broad :
some will haue it very high, and others but sixe handfuls
in height, that they may set it on the tester of a bed. All
the portals of their houses are supported with bricke-
pillars finely plaistered ouer, except some which stand vpon
pillars of marble. The beames and transoms vpholding
their chambers are most curiously painted and carued.
To some houses likewise belong certaine square cesternes,
containing in bredth sixe or seuen cubites, in length ten or
twelue, and in height but sixe or seuen handfuls, being all
vncouered, and built of bricks trimly plaistered ouer.
Along the sides of these cesternes are certaine cocks, which
conuey the water into marble-troughs, as I haue seene in
many places of Europe. When the foresaide conducts are
full of water, that which floweth ouer, runneth by certaine
secret pipes and conueiances into the cesternes : and that
which ouerfloweth the cesternes, is carried likewise by other
passages into the common sinks and gutters, and so into
the riuer. The said cesternes are alwaies kept sweete and
cleane, neither are they couered but onely in summer
time, when men, women, and children bathe themselues
therein. Moreouer on the tops of their houses they vsually
build a turret with many pleasant roomes therein,
whither the women, for recreations sake, when they are
weary of working, retire themselues ; from whence they
may see well-nigh all the citie ouer. Of Mahumetan
temples and oratories there are almost seuen hundred[30] in
this towne, fiftie whereof are most stately and sumptuously

The numbers and statelines of the Mahu-metan temples in Fez.

built, hauing their conducts made of marble and other
excellent stones vnknowen to the Italians; and the
chapiters of their pillers be artificially adorned with
painting and caruing. The tops of these temples, after the
fashion of Christian churches in Europe, are made of ioises
and planks : but the pauement is couered with mats which
are so cunningly sowed together, that a man cannot see
the bredth of a finger vncouered. The walles likewise on
the inner side are lined a mans height with such mats.
Moreouer, each temple hath a turret or steeple, from whence
certaine are appointed with a lowd voice to call the people
at their set-time of praier. Euery temple hath one onely
priest to say seruice therein ; who hath the bestowing of
all reuenues belōging to his owne temple, as occasion
requireth : for thereby are maintained lampes to burne in
the night, and porters to keepe the doores are paid their
wages out of it, and so likewise are they that call the
people to ordinarie praiers in the night season : for those
which crie from the said towers in the day-time haue no
wages, but are onely released from all tributes and
exactions. The chiefe Mahumetan temple in this towne *The principall*
is called *Caruven*,[40] being of so incredible a bignes, that the *called Caru-*
circuit thereof and of the buildings longing vnto it, is a *ven.*
good mile and a halfe about. This temple hath one and
thirtie gates or portals of a woonderfull greatnes and
height. The roofe of this temple is in length 150. and in
bredth about fowerscore Florentine cubites. The turret or
steeple, from whence they crie amaine to assemble the
people togither, is exceedingly high ; the bredth whereof
is supported with twentie, and the length with thirtie
pillers. On the east, west, and north sides, it hath certaine
walkes or galleries, fortie cubites in length, and thirtie in
bredth. Vnder which galleries there is a cell or storehouse,
wherein oile, candles, mats, and other such necessaries for
the temple are laid vp. Euery night in this temple are

burnt nine hundred lights; for euery arch hath a seuerall
lampe, especially those which extend through the mid-
quire. Some arches there are that haue 120. candles
apeece: there are likewise certaine brasse-candlestickes so
great and with so many sockets, as they will holde each
one fifteene hundred candles: and these candlestickes are
reported to haue beene made of bels, which the king of
Fez in times past tooke from Christians. About the wals
of the said temple are diuers pulpits, out of which those
that are learned in the Mahumetan lawe instruct the people.
Their winter-lectures begin presently after sun-rise, and
continue the space of an hower. But their summer-lectures
holde on from the sunne going downe, till an hower and a
halfe within night. And here they teach as well morall
philosophie as the law of Mahumet. The summer-lectures
are performed by certaine priuate and obscure persons;
but in winter such onely are admitted to read, as be reputed
their greatest clerkes. All which readers and professours
are yeerely allowed most liberall stipends. The priest of
this great temple is inioined onely to read praiers, and
faithfully to distribute almes among the poore. Euery
festiuall day he bestoweth all such corne and money as he
hath in his custodie, to all poore people, according to their
neede. The treasurer or collector of the reuenues of this
church hath euery day a duckat for his pay. Likewise he
hath eight notaries or clerkes vnder him; euery one of
which gaineth sixe duckats a moneth: and other sixe
clerks who receiue the rent of houses, shops, and other such
places as belong to the temple, hauing for their wages the
twentith part of all such rents and duties as they gather.
Moreouer there belong to this temple twentie factors or
bailies of husbandrie, that without the citie-walles haue an
eie to the labourers, plowemen, vine-planters, and gardeners,
and that prouide them things necessarie: their gaine is
three duckats a moneth. Not far from the citie are about

twentie lime-kils, and as many bricke-kils, seruing for the
reparation of their temple, and of all houses thereto belong-
ing. The reuenues of the said temple daily receiued, are *The reuenues of the great temple, and how they are bestowed.*
two hundred duckats a day;[41] the better halfe whereof is
laid out vpon the particulars aforesaid. Also if there be
any temples in the citie destitute of liuing, they must all be
maintained at the charges of this great temple: and then
that which remaineth after all expences, is bestowed for the
behoofe of the commonwealth: for the people receiue no
reuenues at all. In our time the king commanded the
priest of the said temple to lend him an huge summe of
money, which he neuer repaied againe. Moreouer in the
citie of Fez are two most stately colleges, of which diuers
roomes are adorned with curious painting; all their beames
are carued, their walles consisting both of marble and free-
stone. Some colleges here are which containe an hundred
studies, some more, and some fewer, all which were built
by diuers kings of the Marin-familie. One there is among
the rest most beautifull and admirable to behold, which
was erected by a certaine king called *Habu Henon*.[42] Here
is to be seene an excellent fountaine of marble, the cesterne
whereof containeth two pipes. Through this college
runneth a little streame in a most cleere and pleasant
chanell, the brims and edges whereof are workmanly framed
of marble, and stones of Majorica. Likewise here are
three cloysters to walke in, most curiously and artificially
made, with certaine eight-square pillers of diuers colours
to support them. And betweene piller and piller the
arches are beautifully ouercast with golde, azure, and diuers
other colours; and the roofe is very artificially built of
wood. The sides of these cloysters are so close, that they
which are without cannot see such as walke within. The
walles round about as high as a man can reach, are
adorned with plaister-worke of Majorica. In many places
you may finde certaine verses, which declare what yeere the

college was built in, together with many epigrams in the founders commendation. The letters of which verses are very great and blacke, so that they may be red a far off. This college-gates are of brasse most curiously carued, and so are the doores artificially made of wood. In the chappell of this college standeth a certaine pulpit mounted nine staires high, which staires are of iuorie and eben. Some affirme, that the king hauing built this college, was desirous to knowe how much money he had spent in building it; but after he had perused a leafe or two of his account-booke, finding the summe of fortie thousand duckats, he rent it asunder, and threw it into the foresaid little riuer, adding this sentence out of a certaine Arabian writer: Each pretious and amiable thing, though it costeth deere, yet if it be beautifull, it cannot choose but be good cheape: neither is any thing of too high a price, which pleaseth a mans affection. Howbeit a certaine treasurer of the kings, making a particular account of all the said expences, found that this excellent building stood his master in 480000. duckats. The other colleges of Fez are somwhat like vnto this, hauing euery one readers and professors, some of which read in the forenoone, and some in the afternoone. In times past the students of these colleges had their apparell and victuals allowed them for seuen yeeres, but now they haue nothing gratis but their chamber. For the warre of *Sahid* destroied many possessions, whereby learning was maintained; so that now the greatest college of al hath yeerely but two hundred, and the second but an hundred duckats for the maintenance of their professors. And this perhaps may be one reason, among many, why the gouernment not onely of Fez, but of all the cities in Africa, is so base. Now these colleges are furnished with no schollers but such as are strangers, and liue of the citie-almes: and if any citizens dwell there, they are not aboue two or three at the most. The professor being ready

The suppression of learning and learned men, a principall cause of disorderly & base gouernment.

for his lecture, some of his auditors readeth a text, whereupon the said professor dilateth, and explaneth obscure and difficult places. Sometimes also the schollers dispute before their professor.

A description of the hospitals and bathes in the citie of Fez.

Many hospitals there are in Fez, no whit inferiour, either for building or beautie, vnto the foresaid colleges. For in them whatsoeuer strangers came to the citie were intertained at the common charge for three daies together. There are likewise as faire and as stately hospitals in the suburbes. In times past their wealth was maruellous great ; but in the time of *Sahids* warre, the king standing in neede of a great summe of money, was counselled by some of his greedy courtiers to sell the liuings of the said hospitals. Which when the people would in no case yeeld vnto, the kings oratour or speaker, perswaded them that all those liuings were giuen by his maiesties predecessours, and therefore (because when the warres were ended, they should soone recouer all againe) that it were far better for them by that meanes to pleasure their soueraigne, then to let his kingly estate fall into so great danger. Whereupon all the said liuings being sold, the king was preuented by vntimely and sudden death before he could bring his purpose to effect : and so these famous hospitals were depriued of all their maintenance. The poore indeede and impotent people of the city are at this day reliued ; but no strangers are entertained, saue only learned men or gentlemen.[43] Howbeit there is another hospital for the releefe of sick & diseased strangers, who haue their diet onely allowed them, but no phisition or medicine : certaine women there are which attend vpon them, till they recouer their former health, or die. In this hospitall likewise there is a place for franticke or distraught persons, where they are bound in strong iron chaines; whereof the part next vnto their walks is strengthened with mighty beames of wood and iron. The gouernour of these distraught persons, when he bringeth them any sustenance, hath a whip of purpose to chastise those that offer to bite, strike, or play any mad part. Sometimes it falleth out that these franticke people will call vnto them such as passe by; declaring how vniustly they are there detained, and how cruelly they are handled by the officers, when as notwithstanding they affirme themselues to bee restored vnto their right minde. And hauing thus perswaded the commers-by, approching neerer and neerer vnto them, at length they take hold with one hand on their garments, and (like villans) with the other hand they shamefully defile their faces and apparell with dung. And though all of them haue their priuies and close stooles, yet would they be poysoned in their owne filth, if the seruants did not often wash their lodgings: so that their abhominable and continuall stinke is the cause why citizens neuer visite them. Likewise this hospitall hath many roomes for the puruciors, notaries, cookes, and other officers belonging to the sicke persons; who each of them haue some small yeerely stipend. Being a yoong man I my selfe was notarie heere for two yeeres, which office is woorth three duckats a moneth.[14]

Iohn Leo in his youth a notarie of an hospitall for two yeeres together.

In this citie are moe then an hundred bath-stoues very artificially and stately built: which though they be not of equall bignes, yet are they all of one fashion. Each stoue hath fower halles, without which are certaine galleries in an higher place, with fiue or sixe staires to ascend vnto them: here men put off their apparell, and hence they goe naked into the bath. In the midst they alwaies keepe a cesterne full of water. First therefore they that meane to bathe themselues must passe through a cold hall, where they vse to temper hot water and cold together, then they goe into a roome somewhat hotter, where the seruants clense and wash them; and last of all they proceede into a third hot-house, where they sweate as much as they thinke good. Of the said water they giue vnto euery man two vessels onely: but he that will haue more and will be extraordinarily washed, must giue to the seruant one Liardo at the least, and to the master of the stoue but two farthings. The fire that heateth their water is made of nought else but beastes dung: for which purpose many boyes are set on worke to run vp and downe to stables, and thence to carrie all the dung, and to lay it on heapes without the towne-walles; which being parched in the sunne for two or three moneths together, they vse for fewell. Likewise the women haue their stoues apart from the men. And yet some hot-houses serue both for men and women, but at sundry times, namely for men from the third to the fourteenth hower of the day, and the residue for women. While women are bathing themselues, they hang out a rope at the first entrance of the house, which is a signe for men, that they may then proceed no farther. Neither may husbands here be permitted to speake with their owne wiues; so great a regarde they haue of their honestie. Here men and women both, after they haue done bathing, vse to banquet and make merrie with pleasant musicke and singing. Yoong striplings enter the bath starke naked without any shame, but men couer their priuities with a linnen cloth. The richer sort will not enter the common bath, but that which is adorned and finely set foorth, and which serueth for noblemen and gentlemen. When any one is to be bathed, they lay him along vpon the ground, annointing him with a certaine ointment, and with certaine instruments doing away his filth. The richer sort haue a carpet to lie on, their head lying on a woodden cushion couered with the same carpet. Likewise here are many barbers and chirurgions which attend to doe their office. The most part of these baths pertaine to the temples and colleges, yeelding vnto them a great summe of money for yeerely rent ; for some giue a hundred, some an hundred and fiftie duckats a yeere. Neither must I here omit the festiuall day which the seruants and officers of the bathes yeerely celebrate. Who with trumpets and pipes calling their friendes together, goe foorth of the towne, and there gather a wilde onion, putting it in a certaine brazen vessell, and couering the same with a linnen cloth wet in lee: afterward with a great noise of trumpets and pipes they solemnely bring the said onion vnto the hot-house doore, and there they hang it vp in the little brazen vessell or lauer, saying that this is a most happy boading or signe of good lucke vnto their stoue. Howbeit I suppose it to be some such sacrifice, as the ancient Moores were woont in times past, when they were destitute of lawes and ciuilitie, to offer, and that the same custome hath remained till this very day. The like is to be seen euen among Christians, who celebrate many feasts whereof they can yeeld no reason. Likewise euery African towne had their peculiar feast, which, when the Christians once enioied Africa, were vtterly abolished and done away.[45]

Of the Innes of Fez.

IN this citie are almost two hundred innes, the greatest whereof are in the principall part of the citie neere vnto the chiefe temple. Euery of these innes are three stories high, and containe an hundred and twenty or moe chambers apeece. Likewise each one hath a fountaine together with sinks and water-pipes, which make auoidance of all the filth. Neuer, to my remembrance, did I see greater buildings, except it were the Spanish college at Bologna, or the pallace of the Cardinall *di San Giorgio* at Rome : of which innes all the chamber-doores haue walkes or galleries before them. And albeit the innes of this citie are very faire and large, yet they affoord most beggerly entertainment to strangers: for there are neither beds nor couches for a man to lie vpon, vnlesse it be a course blanket and a mat. And if you will haue any victuals, you must goe to the shambles your selfe, and buie such meat for your host to dresse, as your stomach stands-to. In these innes certaine poore widowes of Fez, which haue neither wealth nor friends to succour them, are relieued; sometimes one, and sometimes two of them together are allowed a chamber; for which courtesie they play both the chamberlaines and cookes of the inne. The inne-keepers of Fez being all of one familie called Elcheua, goe apparelled like women, and shaue their beards, and are so delighted to imitate women, that they will not only counterfeite their speech, but will sometimes also sit downe and spin. Each one of these hath his concubine, whom he accompanieth as if she were his owne lawfull wife; albeit the said concubines are not onely ill-fauoured in countenance, but notorious for their bad life and behauiour. They buie and sell wine so freely, that no man controules them for it. None resort hither but most lewd & wicked people, to the end they may more boldly commit villany. The inne-keepers haue a consul ouer them, and they pay tribute vnto the gouernour of the citie. And when the king hath occasion to send foorth an armie, then they as being most meete for the purpose, are constrained largely to victuall the campe. Had not the streit law of historie enforced me to make relation of the foresaid particulars as they stand, I would much rather haue smothered such matters in silence, as tend so extremely to the disgrace of Fez; which being reformed, there is not any citie in al Africa, for the honestie and good demeanour of the citizens, comparable thereunto. For the very companie of these inne-keepers is so odious and detestable in the sight of all honest men, learned men, and merchants, that they will in no wise vouchsafe to speake vnto them. And they are firmly enioined not to enter into the temple, into the burse, nor into any bath. Neither yet are they permitted to resort vnto those innes which are next vnto the great temple, and wherein merchants are vsually entertained. All men in a manner are in vtter detestation of these wretches: but because the kings armie hath some vse of them (as is aforesaid) they are borne withall, whether the citizens will or no.[46]

Of the mils of Fez.

IN this citie are mils of fower hundred places at least. And euery of these places containeth fiue or sixe mils; so that there are some thousands of mils in the whole citie. Euery mill standeth in a large roome* vpon some strong piller or post; whereunto many countrie-people vse to resort. Certaine merchants there are in Fez, which hiring mils and shops, buie corne and sell it ready ground vnto the citizens, whereby they reape exceeding gaine: for the greatest part of the citizens being poore, and not able to lay vp corne sufficient in store, are faine to buie meale of them. But the richer sort buie their owne corne, and send it to some common mill, where they pay a shilling for the grinding of each measure. All the saide mils pertaine either to the temples or colleges: for he must be very rich that hath a mill of his owne; for euery mill gaineth the owner two duckats.[47]

Like vnto our horse-mils.

A description of the occupations, the shops and the market.

EAch trade or occupation hath a peculiar place allotted thereto, the principall whereof are next vnto the great temple: for there first you may beholde to the number of fowerscore notaries or scriueners shops, whereof

some ioine vpon the temple, and the residue stand ouer
against them: euery of which shops hath alwaies two
notaries. Then westward there are about thirtie stationers
or booke-sellers.⁴⁸ The shoo-merchants which buie shooes
and buskins of the shoomakers, and sell them againe to
the citizens, inhabite on the south side of the temple: and
next vnto them, such as make shooes for children onely,
their shops being about fiftie. On the east side dwell
those that sell vessels and other commodities made of
brasse. Ouer against the great gate of the said temple
stands the fruit-market, containing fiftie shops, where no
kinde of fruit is wanting.⁴⁹ Next vnto them stand the
waxe-merchants, very ingenious and cunning workmen,
and much to be admired. Here are merchants factors
likewise, though they be but few. Then followes the
herbe-market, wherein the pome-citrons, and diuers kindes
of greene boughes and herbes doe represent the sweete
and flourishing spring, and in this market are about twentie
tauernes; for they which drinke wine, will shrowd themselues vnder the shadie and pleasant boughes. Next vnto
them stand the milke-sellers, who haue great store of such
earthen vessels by them, as the Italians call *Vasi di
Maiolica*: but their milke they cause to be brought thither
in certaine vessels of wood bound with iron-hoops, being
narrow-mouthed and broad at the bottome. From these
milke-sellers some there are which daily buie great store
of milke to make butter thereof: and the residue of their
milke they sell either crudded or sometimes sower vnto
the citizens: so that I thinke there passeth scarce one day
ouer their heads, wherein they vtter not fiue and twentie
tunnes of milke. Next vnto these are such as sell cotton,
and they haue about thirtie shops: then follow those that
sell hempe, ropes, halters, and such other hempen com
modities. Then come you to the girdlers, and such as
make pantofles, and leather-bridles embrodered with silke:

next, their shops adioine that make sword-scabberds and caparisons for horses. Immediately after dwell those that sell salt and lime. And vpon them border an hundred shops of potters, who frame all kinde of earthen vessels adorned with diuers colours. Then come you to the sadlers-shops: and next of all to the street of porters, who (as I suppose) are aboue three hundred: these porters haue a consul or gouernour, who euery weeke allotteth vnto part of them some set busines. The gaine which redoundeth thereof they put into a coffer, diuiding it at the weekes end among them, which haue wrought the same weeke. Strange it is to consider how exceedingly these porters loue one another; for when any of them deceaseth, the whole companie maintaineth his widow and fatherlesse children at their common charge, till either she die, or marrieth a new husband. The children they carefully bring vp, till they haue attained to some good arte or occupation. Whosoeuer of them marrieth and hath children by his wife, inuiteth most part of his companie vnto a banquet: who being thus inuited, present each of them some gift or other vnto the good man, or his wife. No man can be admitted into their companie, vnlesse first he banqueteth the principall men thereof: otherwise he is to haue but halfe a share of the common gaine. Free they are from all tributes and exactions: yea their bread is baked of free cost. If any of them be taken in any hainous offence, he is not publikely but priuately punished. While they are at worke they all weare short garments of one colour: and at vacant times they are apparalled as themselues thinke good: but howsoeuer it be, they are most honest and faire-conditioned people. Next vnto the porters companie dwell the chiefe cookes and victuallers. Here also stands a certaine square house couered with reed, wherein pease and turneprootes[50] are to be sold, which are so greatly esteemed

The porters of Fez.

of in Fez, that none may buie them of the countrie-
people at the first hand, but such as are appointed, who are
boũd to pay tole & tribute vnto the customers : & scarcely
one day passeth, wherein mo then 500. sacks of pease and
turneps are not sold. And albeit (as we haue said) they
are so much esteemed of, yet are they sold at a most easie
price : for a man may buie 30, or at least 20. pound weight
for one * Liardo.[51]   Greene beanes likewise in time of *Ramusius in his Italian
yeere are sold good cheape. Not far frõ the place before copie calleth it Buioco.
mentioned are certaine shops, wherein lumps or steakes of
flesh beaten in a morte, & thẽ fried with oile, & seasoned
with much spice, are to be bought, euery one of the said
lumps or steakes being about the bignes of a fig, & being
made only of dried beefe. On the north side of the temple
is a place whither all kind of herbes are brought to make
sallets withall : for which purpose there are 40. shops
appointed. Next whereunto is The place of smoke, so
called by reason of continuall smoke : here are certaine
fritters or cakes fried in oile, like vnto such as are called at
Rome *Pan Melato.* Of these fritters great store are daily
vttered : for euery day they vse to breake their fasts
therwith, & especially vpon festiual daies : vnto which
fritters they adde for a conclusion either rostmeat or honie:
sometimes they steepe them in an homely kinde of broth
made of bruised meat, which being sodden, they bray the
second time in a morter, making pottage thereof, & colouring it with a kinde of red earth. They roste their flesh
not vpon a spit, but in an ouen : for making two ouens one
ouer another for the same purpose, in the lower they kindle
a fire, putting the flesh into the vpper ouen when it is wel
het. You would not beleeue how finely their meat is thus
rosted, for it cannot be spoiled either by smoke, or too
much heat : for they are all night rosting it by a gentle
fire, and in the morning they set it to sale. The foresaid
steakes & fritters they sell vnto the citizens in so great

abũdance, that they daily take for them mo thẽ 200. duckats. For there are 15. shops which sell nothing else. Likewise here are sold certaine fishes & flesh fried, & a kind of excellent sauorie bread, tasting somewhat like a fritter: which being baked with butter, they neuer eat but with butter and honie. Here also are the feet of certaine beasts sodden; wherewith the husbandmen betimes in the morning breake their fast, and then hie them to their labour. Next vnto these are such as sell oile, salt, butter, cheese, oliues, pome-citrons & capers: their shops are full of fine earthen vessels, which are of much greater value then the things contained in them. Their butter and honie they sell by certaine criers, which are porters appointed for the same office. Neither doe they admit euery one to fill their vessels; but that worke is reserued for certaine porters appointed to doe it, which also fill the measures of oile when merchants buie the same. The said vessels are sufficient to containe an hundred and fiftie pounds of butter; for so much butter the countrie-people put into each vessell. Then follow the shambles, consisting of about fortie shops, wherein the butchers cut their flesh a peeces, and sell it by weight. They kill no beastes within the shambles, for their is a place allotted for this purpose neere vnto the riuer, where hauing once dressed their flesh, they send it to the shambles by certaine seruants appointed for that end. But before any butcher dare sell his flesh

The gouernour of the shambles in Fez.

vnto the citizens, he must carrie it to the gouernour of the shambles, who so soone as he seeth the flesh, he sets downe in a peece of paper the price thereof, which they shew together with their meate vnto the people; neither may they in any case exceed the said price. Next vnto the shambles standeth the market where course cloathes are sold, which containeth at least an hundred shops; the said cloth is deliuered vnto certaine criers (which are about threescore in number) who carrying the cloth from shop to

shop tell the price thereof, and for the selling of euery
duckats-woorth they haue two * Liardos allowed them. *In the Italian copie they are called Baiochi.
This traffique of cloth indureth from noone till night, to
the merchants great aduantage. Then follow their shops
that scowre and sell armour, swordes, iauelings, and such
like warlike instruments. Next vnto them stand the fishmongers, who sell most excellent and great fish, taken both
in the riuer of Fez and in other waters, exceeding cheape ;
for you may buie a pound of fish for two farthings onely.
There is a great abundance of the fish called in Rome
Laccia, and that especially from the beginning of October
till the moneth of Aprill, as we will declare more at large
when we come to speake of the riuers. Next vnto the
fishmongers dwell such as make of a certaine hard reed,
coopes and cages for fowles ; their shops being about fortie
in number. For each of the citizens vseth to bring vp
great store of hennes and capons. And that their houses
may not be defiled with hennes-dung, they keepe them
continually in coopes and cages. Then follow their shops
that sell liquide sope, but they be not many, for you shall
finde more of them in other partes of the citie. Neither
make they sope at Fez onely, but also in the mountaines
thereabout, from whence it is brought vnto the citie vpon
mules backes. Next of all are certaine of their shops that
sell meale, albeit they are diuersly dispersed throughout
the whole citie. Next vnto them are such as sell seed-
graine and seed-pulse : which you cannot buie of any
citizen, because that euery one had rather keepe his corne
in store: many there are likewise in the same place, that
will carrie pulse or corne to mules or horses, whithersoeuer
you will haue them. A mule vseth to carrie three measures
of pulse vpon his backe (which the muliter is enioined to
measure) in three sacks lying one vpon another. Then are
there ten shops of them that sell straw. Next them is the
market where threed and hempe is to be sold, and where

hempe vseth to be kempt: which place is built after the fashion of great houses, with fower galleries or spare-roomes round about it: in the first whereof they sell linnen-cloth, and weigh hempe: in two other sit a great many women hauing abundance of sale-threed, which is there solde by the criers, who carrie the same vp and downe from noone till night. In the midst of this place growe diuers mulberie trees, affoording pleasant shade and shelter vnto the merchants: and hither such swarmes of women resort, that a man shall hardly withdraw himselfe from among them: good sport it is sometime to see how they will barret and scould one at another: yea and oftentimes you shall see them fall together by the eares. Let vs now come to the west part, which stretcheth from the temple to that gate that leadeth vnto Mecnase. Next vnto the smokie place before mentioned, their habitations directly stand, that make leather-tankards, to draw water out of wels; of whom there are some fourteene shops. Vnto these adioine such as make wicker-vessels and other, to lay vp meale and corne in: and these enioy about thirtie shops. Next them are 150. shops of tailors. And next the tailors are those that make leather-shieldes, such as I haue often seene brought into Europe. Then follow twentie shops of laundresses or washers, being people of a base condition; to whom the citizens that haue not maids of their owne, carrie their shirtes and other fowle linnen, which after few daies are restored vnto them so cleane and white as it is woonderfull. These laundresses haue diuers shops adioining together in the same place: but here and there throughout the citie are aboue two hundred families of such persons. Next vnto the laundresses are those that make trees for saddles; who dwell likewise in great numbers eastwarde right in the way to the college founded by king *Abuhinan*.[52] Vpon these adioine about fortie shops of such as work stirrops, spurres, and bridles, so artificially, as I thinke the like are not to be scene in Europe. Next standeth their street, that first rudely make the said stirrops, bridles, and spurres. From thence you may go into the street of sadlers, which couer the saddles before mentioned threefold with most excellent leather: the best leather they lay vppermost, and the woorst beneath, and that with notable workmanship; as may be scene in most places of Italie. And of them there are moe then an hundred shops. Then follow their long shops that make pikes and launces. Next standeth a rocke or mount, hauing two walks thereupon; the one whereof leadeth to the east gate, and the other to one of the kings pallaces, where the kings sisters, or some other of his kinred are vsually kept. But this is by the way to be noted, that all the foresaid shops or market begin at the great temple: howbeit, that I might not inuert my set-order, I haue onely described those places that are round about the said temple, minding last of all to speake of the merchants station or burse.

Of the station or burse of merchants in Fez.

THis burse you may well call a citie, which being walled round about hath twelue gates, & before euery gate an iron chaine, to keepe horses & cartes from comming in. The said burse is diuided into 12. seuerall wards or partes: two whereof are allotted vnto such shoomakers as make shooes onely for noblemen and gentlemen, and two also to silke-merchants or haberdashers, that sell ribands, garters, skarfes, and such other like ornaments; and of these there are about fiftie shops. Others there are that sell silke onely for the embrodering of shirts, cushions, and other such furniture made of cloth, possessing almost as many shops as the former. Then follow those that make womens girdles of course wooll (which some make of silke) but very grossely, for I thinke they are moe then two fingers thicke, so that they may serue almost for cables to a ship. Next vnto these girdlers are such as sell woollen and linnen cloth brought out of Europe : which haue also silke-stuffes, caps, and other like commodities to sell. Hauing passed these, you come to them that sel mats, mattresses, cushions, and other things made of leather. Next adioineth the customers office; for their cloth is sent about by certaine criers to be solde, who before they can passe, must goe to the customers to haue the said cloth sealed, and to pay toll vnto the customers. Criers here are, to the number of sixtie, which for the crying of euery cloth haue one *Liardo allowed them. Next of all dwell the tailors, and that in three seuerall streetes. Then come you to the linnen-drapers, which sell smocks and other apparell for women : and these are accounted the richest merchants in all Fez, for their wares are the most gainful of all others. Next vnto these are certaine woollen garments to be sold, made of such cloth as is brought thither out of Europe. Euery afternoone cloth is sold in this place by the criers, which is lawfull for any man to doe, when necessarie occasion vrgeth him. Last of all is that place where they vse to sell wrought shirts, towels, and other embrodered works ; as also where carpets, beds, and blankets are to be sold.⁵³

Or Baiocho.

The reason why this part of the citie was called Cæsaria.

THe foresaid burse or station of merchants was in times past called Cæsaria, according to the name of that renowned conquerour *Iulius Cæsar:* the reason whereof some affirme to be ; because all the cities of Barbarie were in those daies first subiect to the Romans, and then to the Goths. And each citie alwaies had either Romans or Goths to receiue and take charge of the tribute. Howbeit because the people often made ciuill wars and assaults vpon them, their determination was in euery citie to build

A meanes vsed in Africa how to keepe the princes tribute and merchants goods in securitie.

some strong walled place, where both the tribute and the principall goods of the citizens might remaine in safetie: hoping by this meanes that the citizens would be as carefull of the princes goods as of their owne. Which course had the Italians imitated, they had neuer beene spoiled so often of their goods. For in ciuill wars it many times befalleth, that the greedie soldiers not being satisfied with the enimies goods, will prey vpon the wealth of their friendes.[54]

Of the grocers, apothecaries, and other tradesmen, and artizans of Fez.

NExt vnto the said burse, on the north side, in a streight lane, stand an hundred and fiftie grocers and apothecaries shops, which are fortified on both sides with two strong gates. These shops are garded in the night season by certaine hired and armed watchmen, which keepe their station with lanternes and mastiues. The said apothecaries can make neither scrups, ointments, nor electuaries: but such things are made at home by the phisitions, and are of them to be bought. The phisitions houses adioine for the most part vnto the apothecaries: howbeit very few of the people knowe either the phisition or the vse of his phisicke. The shops here are so artificially built and adorned, that the like (I thinke) are no where else to be found. Being in Tauris a citie of Persia, I *Iohn Leo was at Tauris in* remember that I saw diuers stately shops curiously built *Persia.* vnder certaine galleries, but very darke, so that (in my iudgement) they be far inferiour vnto the shops of Fez. Next the apothecaries are certaine artificers that make combes of boxe and other wood. Eastward of the apothecaries dwell the needle-makers, possessing to the number of fiftie shops. Then follow those that turne iuorie, and such other matter, who (because their craft is practised by some other artizans) are but few in number. Vnto the turners adioine certaine that sell meale, sope, & brooms: who dwelling next vnto the threed-market beforementioned, are scarce twenty shops in all: for the residue are dispersed in other places of the citie, as we will hereafter declare. Amongst the cotton-merchants are certaine that sell ornaments for tents, and beds. Next of all stand the fowlers, who, though they be but few, yet are they stored with all kinde of choise and daintie fowles: whereupon the place is called the fowlers market. Then come you to their shops that sell cords and ropes of hempe: and then to such as make high corke slippers for noblemen and gentlemen to walke the streetes in, when it is fowle weather: these corke-slippers are finely trimmed with much silke, and most excellent vpper leathers, so that the cheapest will cost a duckat, yea some there are of ten duckats, and some of fiue and twentie duckats price. Such slippers as are accounted most fine and costly are made of blacke and white mulberie-tree, of blacke walnut-tree and of the Iujuba-tree, albeit the corke-slippers are the most durable and strong. Vnto these adioine ten shops of Spanish Moores, which make crosse-bowes: as also those that make broomes of a certaine wilde palme-tree, such as are daily brought out of Sicilie to Rome. These broomes they carrie about the citie in a great basket, either selling them, or exchanging them for bran, ashes, or olde shooes: the bran they sell againe to shepherds, the ashes to such as white threed, & the old shooes to coblers. Next vnto them are smithes that make nailes; & coopers which make certaine great vessels in forme of a bucket, hauing corne-measures to sell also: which measures, when the officer, appointed for the same purpose, hath made triall of, he is to receiue a farthing apeece for his fee. Then follow the wooll-chapmen, who hauing bought wooll of the butchers, put it foorth vnto others to be scowred and washed: the sheepe-skins they themselues dresse:

but as for oxe-hides they belong to another occupation, and
are tanned in another place. Vnto these adioine such as
make certaine langols or withs, which the Africans put
vpon their horses feete. Next of all are the braziers; then
such as make weights and measures; and those likewise
that make instruments to carde wooll or flaxe. At length
you descend into a long streete, where men of diuers occupations dwell together, some of which doe polish and
enamell stirrops, spurres, and other such commodities,
as they receiue from the smithes roughly and rudely
hammered. Next whom dwell certaine cart-wrights,
plow-wrights, mill-wrights, and of other like occupations.
Diers haue their aboad by the riuers side, and haue each
of them a most cleere fountaine or cesterne, to wash their
silke-stuffes in. Ouer against the diers dwell makers of
bulwarkes or trenches, in a very large place, which being
planted with shadie mulberie-trees is exceeding pleasant
in the summer-time. Next them are a companie of
farriers, that shooe mules and horses: and then those that
make the iron-worke of crosse-bowes. Then followe
smithes that make horse-shooes; and last of all those that
white linnen-cloth: and here the west part of the citie
endeth, which in times past (as is aforesaid) was a citie
by it selfe, and was built after the citie on the east side of
the river.[55]

A description of the second part of Fez.

THe second part of Fez situate eastward, is beautified
with most stately palaces, temples, houses, and
colleges; albeit there are not so many trades and occupations as in the parts before described. For here are
neither merchants, tailors, shoomakers, &c. but of the
meaner sort. Here are notwithstanding thirtie shops of
grocers. Neere vnto the walles dwell certaine bricke-
burners and potters: and not far from thence is a great

market of white earthen vessels, platters, cups, and dishes. Next of all standes the corne-market, wherein are diuers granaries to lay vp corne. Ouer against the great temple there is a broad street paued with brick, round about which diuers handy-crafts and occupations are exercised. There are likewise many other trades diuersly dispersed ouer this east part of the citie. The drapers and grocers haue certaine peculiar places allotted vnto them. In this east part of Fez likewise there are fiue hundred and twenty weauers houses, very stately and sumptuously built : hauing in each of them many worke-houses, and loomes, which yeeld great rent vnto the owners. Weauers there are (by report) in this citie twenty thousand, and as many millers. Moreouer in this part of Fez are an hundred shops for the whiting of threed ; the principall whereof being situate vpon the riuer, are exceedingly well furnished with kettles, cauldrons, and other such vessels : here are likewise many great houses to saw wood in, which worke is performed by Christian captiues, and whatsoeuer wages they earne, redoundeth vnto their Lordes and masters. These Christian captiues are not suffered to rest from their labours, but only vpon fridaies, and vpon eight seuerall daies of the yeere besides, whereon the Moores feasts are solemnized. Here also are the common stewes for harlots, which are fauoured by great men, and sometime by the cheefe gouernors of the citie. Likewise there are certaine vintners, who are freely permitted to keepe harlots, and to take filthie hire for them. Here are also moe then sixe hundred cleere fountaines walled round about and most charily kept, euery one of which is seuerally conueied by certaine pipes vnto each house, temple, college, and hospitall : and this fountaine-water is accounted the best : for that which commeth out of the riuer is in summer oftentimes dried vp : as likewise when the conducts are to be cleansed, the course of the riuer must of necessitie be turned out of the citie. Wherefore euery familie vseth to fetch water out of the said fountaines, and albeit in summer-time the chiefe gentlemen vse riuer-water, yet they will often call for fountaine-water, because it is more coole and pleasant in taste. But in the spring-time it is nothing so. These fountaines haue their originall for the most part from the west and south, for the north part is all full of mountains and marble-rocks, containing certaine caues or cels, wherein corne may be kept for many yeeres; of which caues some are so large, that they will holde two hundred bushels of corne. The citizens dwelling neere those caues, and such as possesse them, do sufficiently maintaine them-selues in taking yeerely euery hundred bushell for rent. The south part of east Fez is almost halfe destitute of inhabitants: howbeit the gardens abound with fruites and flowers of all sortes. Euery garden hath an house belonging thereunto, and a christall-fountaine enuironed with roses and other odoriferous flowers and herbes; so that in the spring-time a man may both satisfie his eies, and solace his minde in visiting this part of the citie: and well it may be called a Paradise, sithence the noblemen doe here reside from the moneth of April till the end of September. Westward, that is, toward the kings palace, standeth a castle built by a king of the Luntune-familie, resembling in bignes an whole towne: wherein the kings of Fez, before the said palace was built, kept their royal residence. But after new Fez began to be built by the Marin-kings, the said castle was left onely to the gouernour of the citie. Within this castle standes a stately temple built (as aforesaid) what time it was inhabited by princes and nobles, many places being afterward defaced and turned into gardens: howbeit certaine houses were left vnto the gouernour, partly to dwell in, and partly for the deciding of controuersies. Here is likewise a certaine prison for captiues supported with many pillers, and being so large, that it will hold (as diuers are of opinion) three thousand men. Neither are there any seuerall roomes in this prison: for at Fez one prison serueth for all. By this castle runneth a certaine riuer very commodious for the gouernour.

Of the magistrates, the administration of iustice, and of the apparell vsed in Fez.

IN the citie of Fez are certaine particular iudges and magistrates: and there is a gouernour that defineth ciuill controuersies, and giueth sentence against malefactors. Likewise there is a iudge of the canon law, who hath to doe with all matters concerning the Mahumetan religion. A third iudge there is also that dealeth about marriages and diuorcements, whose authoritie is to heare all witnesses, and to giue sentence accordingly. Next vnto them is the high aduocate, vnto whom they appeale from the sentence of the said iudges, when as they doe either mistake themselues, or doe ground their sentence vpon the authoritie of some inferiour doctor. The gouernour gaineth a great summe of money by condemning of parties at seuerall times. Their manner of proceeding against a malefactor is this: hauing giuen him an hundred or two hundred stripes before the gouernour, the executioner putteth an iron-chaine about his necke, and so leadeth him starke-naked (his priuities onely excepted) through all partes of the citie: after the executioner followes a seageant, declaring vnto all the people what fact the guiltie person hath committed, till at length hauing put on his apparell againe, they carrie him backe to prison. Sometimes it falleth out that many offenders chained together are led about the citie: and the gouernour for each malefactor thus punished, receiueth one duckat and one fourth part; and likewise at their first entrance into the iaile, he demaunds of each one a certaine dutie which is paid particularly vnto him by diuers

The punishment of malefactors in Fez.

merchants and artificers appointed of purpose. And amongst his other liuings, he gathereth out of a certaine mountaine seuen thousand duckats of yeerely reuenue: so that when occasion serueth, he is at his proper costs to finde the king of Fez three hundred horses, and to giue them their pay. Those which follow the canon-lawe haue neither stipend nor rewarde allowed them: for it is forbidden by the law of Mahumet, that the iudges of his religion should reape any commoditie or fees by their office; but that they shoulde liue onely by reading of lectures, and by their priesthood. In this facultie are many aduocates and proctors, which are extreme idiotes, and vtterly voide of all good learning. There is a place also in Fez whereinto the iudges vse to cast the citizens, for debt, or for some light offence. In all this citie are fower officers or sergeants onely; who from midnight till two a clocke in the morning doe walke about all partes of the citie; neither haue they any stipend, but a certaine fee of such malefactors as they lead about in chaines, according to the qualitie of euery mans crime; moreouer, they are freely permitted to sell wine, and to keepe harlots. The saide gouernour hath neither scribes nor notaries, but pronounceth all sentences by word of mouth. One onely there is that gathereth customes and tributes ouer all the citie, who daily paieth to the kings vse thirtie duckats. This man appointeth certaine substitutes to watch at euery gate, where nothing, be it of neuer so small value, can passe before some tribute be paid. Yea sometime they goe foorth of the citie to meete with the carriers and muliters vpon the high waies, to the end they may not conceale nor closely conuey any merchandize into the citie. And if they be taken in any deceite, they pay double. The set order or proportion of their custome is this, namely to pay two duckats for the woorth of an hundred: for Onix-stones, which are brought hither in great plentie, they pay one fourth part: but for wood, corne, oxen, and hennes, they giue nothing at all. Neither at the entring of the citie doe they pay any tribute for rammes, but at the shambles they give two *Liardos apeece, and to the gouernour of the shambles one. The said gouernour of the shambles hath alwaies twelue men waiting vpon him, and oftentimes he rideth about the citie to examine the weight of bread, and finding any bread to faile of the due waight, he causeth the baker to be beaten with cudgels, and to be led in contempt vp and downe the citie. The said office was woont to be allotted vnto men of singular honestie; but now adaies euery ignorant and lewd person enioieth it. The citizens of Fez goe very ciuilly and decently attired, in the spring-time wearing garments made of outlandish cloth: ouer these shirtes they weare a iacket or cassocke being narrow and halfe-sleeued, whereupon they weare a certaine wide garment, close before on the breast. Their caps are thinne and single, like vnto the night-caps vsed in Italie, sauing that they couer not their eares: these caps are couered with a certaine skarfe, which being twise wreathed about their head and beard, hangeth by a knot. They weare neither hose nor breeches, but in the spring-time when they ride a iourney they put on bootes: mary the poorer sort haue onely their cassocke, and a mantle ouer that called *Barnussi, and a most course cap. The doctors and ancient gentlemen weare a certaine garment with wide sleeues, somewhat like to the gentlemen of Venice. The common sort of people are for the most part clad in a kinde of course white cloth. The women are not altogether vnseemely apparelled, but in sommer-time they weare nothing saue their smocks onely. In winter they weare such a wide sleeued garment, being close at the breast, as that of the men before mentioned. When they goe abroad, they put on certaine long breeches, wherewith their legs are all couered, hauing also, after the fashion of

* *Or Baiochi.*

* *Or Ilburnus.*

Syria, a vaile hanging downe from their heads, which
couereth their whole bodies. On their faces likewise they
weare a maske with two little holes onely for their eies, to
peepe out at. Their eares they adorne with golden eare-
rings & with most pretious iewels: the meaner sort weare
eare-rings of siluer and gilt only. Vpon their armes the
ladies and gentlewomen weare golden bracelets, and the
residue siluer, as likewise gold or siluer-rings vpon their
legs, according to each ones estate and abilitie.

Of their manner of eating and drinking.

LEt vs now speake somewhat of their victuals and
manner of eating. The common sort set on the pot
with fresh meat twise euery weeke: but the gentlemen and
richer sort euery day, and as often as they list. They take
three meales a day: the breakefast consisteth of certaine
fruits and bread, or else of a kinde of liquid pap made
like vnto frumentie: in winter they sup off the broth of
salt flesh thickened with course meale. To dinner they
haue flesh, sallets, cheese, and oliues: but in summer they
haue greater cheere. Their supper is easie of digestion,
consisting of bread, melons, grapes, or milke: but in winter
they have sodden flesh, together with a kinde of meate
called Cuscusu, which being made of a lumpe of dowe is set *A kinde of*
first vpon the fire in certaine vessels full of holes, and after- *meate called Cuscusu.*
warde is tempered with butter and pottage. Some also
vse often to haue roste-meat. And thus you see after what
sort both the gentlemen & common people lead their liues:
albeit the noblemen fare somewhat more daintily: but if
you compare them with the noblemen and gentlemen of
Europe, they may seeme to be miserable and base fellowes;
not for any want or scarcitie of victuals, but for want of
good manners and cleanlines. The table whereat they sit is
lowe, uncouered, and filthie: seats they haue none but the
bare ground, neither kniues or spoones but only their ten

talons. The said Cuscusu is set before them all in one only platter, whereout as well gentlemen as others take it not with spoones, but with their clawes fiue. The meat & pottage is put al in one dish; out of which euery one raketh with his greasie fists what he thinkes good: you shall never see knife vpon the table, but they teare and greedily deuoure their meate like hungrie dogs. Neither doth any of them desire to drinke before he hath well stuffed his panch; and then will he sup off a cup of cold water as big as a milke-bowle. The doctors indeede are somewhat more orderly at meales: but, to tell you the very truth, in all Italie there is no gentleman so meane, which for fine diet and stately furniture excelleth not the greatest potentates and lords of all Africa.[56]

The manner of solemnizing mariages.

AS touching their mariages, they obserue these courses following. So soone as the maides father hath espoused her vnto her louer, they goe foorthwith like bride and bridegroome to church, accompanied with their parents and kinsfolkes, and call likewise two notaries with them to make record before all that are present of the couenants and dowrie. The meaner sort of people vsually giue for their daughters dowrie thirtie duckats and a woman-slaue of fifteene duckats price; as likewise a partie-coloured garment embrodered with silke, and certaine other silke skarfs or iags, to weare vpon her head in stead of a hood or vaile; then a paire of fine shooes, and two excellent paire of startups; and lastly many pretie knackes curiously made of siluer and other metals, as namely combes, perfuming-pans, bellowes, and such other trinkets as women haue in estimation. Which being done, all the guests present are inuited to a banket, whereunto for great dainties is brought a kinde of bread fried and tempered with honie, which wee haue before described; then they bring roste-meate to the boord, all this being at the bridegroomes cost: afterward the brides father maketh a banket in like sort. Who if he bestow on his daughter some apparell besides her dowrie, it is accounted a point of liberalitie. And albeit the father promiseth but thirtie duckats onely for a dowrie, yet will he sometimes bestow, in apparell and other ornaments belonging to women, two hundred, yea sometimes three hundred duckats besides. But they seldome giue an house, a vineyarde, or a field for a dowrie. Moreouer vpon the bride they bestowe three gownes made of costly cloth; and three others of silke chamlet, or of some other excellent stuffe. They giue her smockes likewise curiously wrought, with fine vailes, and other embrodered vestures; as also pillowes and cushions of the best sort. And besides all the former giftes, they bestow eight carpets or couerlets on the bride, fower whereof are onely for seemelines to spread vpon their presses and cupboords: two of the courser they vse for their beds; and the other two of leather, to lay vpon the floore of their bedchambers. Also they haue certaine rugs of about twenty elles compasse or length; as like three quilts being made of linnen and woollen on the one side, and stuffed with flockes on the other side, which they vse in the night in manner following. With the one halfe they couer themselues, and the other halfe they lay vnder them: which they may easily doe, when as they are both waies about ten elles long. Vnto the former they adde as many couerlets of silke very curiously embrodered on the vpper side, and beneath lined double with linnen and cotton. They bestow likewise white couerlets to vse in summertime onely: and lastly they bestow a woollen hanging diuided into many partes, and finely wrought, as namely with certaine peeces of gilt leather; whereupon they sowe iags of partie-coloured silke, and vpon euery iag a little ball or button of silke, whereby the saide hanging may for ornaments sake be fastened vnto a wall. Here you see what be the appurtenances of their dowries; wherein some doe striue so much to excell others, that oftentimes many gentlemen haue brought themselues vnto pouertie thereby. Some Italians thinke that the husband bestowes a dowrie vpon his wife; but they altogether mistake the matter. The bridegroome being ready to carrie home his bride, causeth her to be placed in a woodden cage or cabinet eight-square couered with silke, in which she is carried by porters, her parents and kinsfolkes following, with a great noise of trumpets, pipes, and drums, and with a number of torches; the bridegroomes kinsmen goe before with torches, and the brides kinsfolkes followe after: and so they goe vnto the great market place, and hauing passed by the temple, the bridegroome takes his leaue of his father in lawe and the rest, hying him home with all speed, and in his chamber expecting the presence of his spouse. The father, brother, and vncle of the bride lead her vnto the chamber-doore, and there deliver her with one consent vnto the mother of the bridegroome: who, as soon as she is entred, toucheth her foote with his, and foorthwith they depart into a generall roome by themselues. In the meane season the banket is comming foorth: and a certaine woman standeth before the bride-chamber doore, expecting till the bridegroome hauing defloured his bride reacheth her a napkin stained with blood, which napkin she carrieth incontinent and sheweth to the guestes, proclaiming with a lowd voice, that the bride was euer till that time an vnspotted and pure virgine. This woman together with other women her companions, first the parents of the bridegroome and then of the bride doe honourably entertaine. But if the bride be found not to be a virgine, the mariage is made frustrate, and she with great disgrace is turned home to her parents. At complete mariages they make for the most part three bankets: the first the same day when the bridegroome and bride are ioined in wedlocke; the second the day following for women onely; and the third seuen daies after; whereat all the kinsfolks and friends of the bride are present; and this day the brides father, according to his abilitie, sendes great store of daintie dishes vnto his sonne in lawe: but so soone as the new married man goeth foorth of the house (which is for the most part on the seuenth day after the mariage) he buieth great plentie of fishes, which he causeth his mother or some other woman to cast vpon his wiues feete; and this they, from an ancient superstitious custome, take for a good boading. Likewise at the bridegroomes fathers they vse to make two other feasts; the one vpon the day before the bride is married; and so that night they spend in dauncing and disport. The morrow after a companie of women goe to dresse the bride, to combe her locks, and to paint her cheekes with vermillion; her hands and her feete they die blacke, but all this painting presently looseth the fresh hew; and this day they haue another banket. The bride they place in the highest roome that she may be seene of all, and then those that dressed the bride are condignely entertained. Being come to the bridegroomes house, his parents salute the new bride with certaine great cups full of new wine and cakes, with other iuncats, (which wee wil here passe ouer in silence) all which are bestowed vpon the bridegroomes companions. The same night which we said was spent in dauncing, there are present at the bridall-house certaine minstrels and singers, which by turnes sometimes vse their instruments and sometimes voice-musicke: they daunce alwaies one by one, and at the end of each galliard they bestow a largesse vpon the musitions. If any one wil honour the dancer, he bids him kneele downe before him, and hauing fastened peeces of money all ouer his face, the musitions presently take it off for their fee. The women daunce alone without any men at the noise of their owne musitions. All these things vse to be performed when the bride is a maide. But the mariages of widowes are concluded with lesse adoe. Their cheere is boiled beefe and mutton, and stued hens, with diuers iuncating dishes among. Instead of trenchers, the guestes being ten or twelue in number, haue so many great round platters of wood set before them. And this is the common custome of gentlemen and merchants. The meaner sort present their guestes with certaine sops or bruesse of bread like vnto a pan-cake, which being dipped in flesh-pottage, they eate out of a great platter not with spoones but with their fingers onely: and round about each great platter stand to the number of ten or twelue persons. Likewise they made a solemne feast at the circumcision of their male children, which is vpon the seuenth day after their birth; and at this feast the circumciser, together with all their friends and kinsfolks is present: which being done, each one, according to his abilitie, bestoweth a gift vpon the circumciser in manner following. Euery man laies his money vpon a lads face which the circumciser brought with him. Whereupon the lad calling euery one by his name, giueth them thanks in particular: and then the infant being circumcised, they spend that day with as great iollitie as a day of mariage. But at the birth of a daughter they show not so much alacritie.[57]

The marriage of widowes.

The circumcision of their children.

Of their rites obserued vpon festiuall daies, and their manner of mourning for the dead.

Reliques of Christian ceremonies obserued among the Moores.

AMong the people of Fez there haue remained certaine reliques of festiuall daies instituted of olde by the Christians; whereupon they vse certaine ceremonies which themselues vnderstande not. Vpon Christmas euen they eate a sallet made of diuers herbs: they seeth likewise

that night all kind of pulse, which they feede vpon
for great dainties. Vpon New-yeeres day the children
goe with maskes and vizards on their faces to the
houses of gentlemen and merchants, and haue fruits
giuen them for singing certaine carols or songs. When
as the feast of Saint *Iohn* Baptist is hallowed among
Christians, you shall here see all about great store of fires
made with straw. And when their childrens teeth begin
to grow, they make another feast called, according to the
Latines, *Dentilla*. They haue also many other rites and
customes of diuining or soothsaying, the like wherof I
haue seene at Rome and in other cities of Italie.[58] As
touching their feasts prescribed by the Mahumetan lawe,
they are at large set downe in that briefe treatise which
we haue written concerning the same lawe. The women
hauing by death lost their husbands, fathers, or any other *Their funerals.*
of their deere friends, assemble foorthwith a great multitude
of their own sexe together, who stripping themselues out
of their owne attire, put on most vile sackcloth, and defile
their faces with much durt : then call they certaine men
clad in womens attire, bringing great fower-square drums
with them, at the noise of which drums the women-
mourners sing a funerall song, tending as much as may
be, to the commendation of the partie deceased : and at
the end of euery verse, the said womẽ vtter most hideous
shrikes & outcries, tearing their haire, & with much lamen-
tation beating their cheekes & breasts, till they be all-
imbrued with blood : and so these heathenish superstitions
continue for seuen whole daies together. At which seuen
daies ende they surcease their mourning for the space of
40. daies, & then they begin anew to torment thẽselues
for three daies togither in maner aforesaid : howbeit these
kinds of obsequies are obserued onely by the baser people,
but the gentlemen and better sort behaue themselues more
modestly. At this time all the widowes friends come

about her to comfort her, and send diuers kinds of meats vnto her: for in the mourning house they may dresse no meate at all, till the dead corpes be carried foorth. The woman her selfe that looseth her husband, father, or brother, neuer goeth foorth with the funerall. But how they wash and burie the dead corpes, and what superstitions they vse thereabout, you shall finde recorded in my little treatise aboue mentioned.

Of their doue-houses.

Diuers there are in this citie, that take much pleasure in keeping of doues, which are here in great plentie, of all colours. These doues they keepe in certaine cages or lockers on the tops of their houses, which lockers they set open twise a day, to wit, morning and euening, delighting greatly to see them flie, for those that out-flie the residue are accounted the best. Oftentimes it falleth out, that neighbours doues will be mingled together, for which cause you shall see the owners goe together by the eares. Some haue a certaine net bound vnto two long canes, wherewith they vse to take their neighbours doues, as they come flying foorth of their louers. Amongst the colliers you shall finde seuen or eight shops onely of those that sel doues.[59]

Their manner of gaming at Fez.

The citizens vse most of all to play at chesse, and that from ancient times. Other games there are also, but very rude, and vsed onely by the common people. At certaine times of the yeere the boies of one street wil fight with clubs against the boies of another street, and that sometimes with so great furie, that they betake themselues to other weapons and slay one another, especially vpon their festiuall daies, what time they will challenge and prouoke one another foorth of the citie-

walles. And hauing fought hard all the whole day, at
night they fall to throwing of stones : till at length the
citie-officers come vpon them, taking some, and beating
them publiquely throughout the citie. Sometimes it falleth
out, that the yoong striplings arming themselues, and
going by night out of the citie, range vp and downe the
fields and gardens : and if the contrarie faction of yoonkers
and they meete, it is woonderfull what a bloodie skirmish
ensueth : howbeit they are often most seuerely punished
for it.[60]

Of the African poets.

IN Fez there are diuers most excellent poets, which
make verses in their owne mother toong. Most of
their poems and songs intreat of loue. Euery yeere they
pen certaine verses in the commendation of Mahumet,
especially vpon his birthday : for then betimes in the
morning they resort vnto the palace of the chiefe iudge
or gouernor, ascending his tribunall-seate, and from thence
reading their verses to a great audience of people : and
hee whose verses are most elegant and pithie, is that yeere *Rewards for*
proclaimed prince of the poets. But when as the kings of *poets in Fez.*
the Marin-familie prospered, they vsed to inuite all the
learned men of the citie vnto their palace ; and honourably entertaining them, they commanded each man in
their hearing to recite their verses to the commendation
of Mahumet : and he that was in all mens opinions
esteemed the best poet, was rewarded by the king with an
hundred duckats, with an excellent horse, with a woman-
slaue, and with the kings own robes wherewith he was
then apparelled : all the rest had fiftie duckats apeece
giuen them, so that none departed without the kings
liberalitie : but an hundred and thirtie yeeres are expired
since this custome, together with the maiestie of the
Fessan kingdome, decaied.[61]

A description of the grammar-schooles in Fez.

OF schools in Fez for the instructing of children, there are almost two hundred, euery one of which is in fashion like a great hall. The schoolemasters teach their children to write and read not out of a booke, but out of a certaine great table. Euery day they expound one sentence of the Alcoran: and hauing red quite through they begin it againe, repeating it so often, til they haue most firmely committed the same to memorie: which they doe right well in the space of 7. yeeres. Then read they vnto their scholers some part of orthographie: howbeit both this and the other parts of Grammar are far more exactly taught in the colleges, then in these triuiall schooles. The said schoolemasters are allowed a very small stipend; but when their boies haue learned some part of the Alcoran, they present certaine gifts vnto their master, according to each ones abilitie. Afterward so soon as any boy hath perfectly learned the whole Alcoran, his father inuiteth all his sonnes schoolefellowes vnto a great banket: and his sonne in costly apparell rides through the street vpon a gallant horse, which horse and apparell the gouernour of the royall citadell is bound to lend him. The rest of his schoole-fellowes being mounted likewise on horse-backe accompany him to the banketing house, singing diuers songs to the praise of God and of Mahumet. Then are they brought to a most sumptuous banket, whereat all the kinsfolkes of the foresaid boyes father are vsually present: euery one of whom bestoweth on the schoolemaster some small gift, and the boyes father giues him a new sute of apparell. The said scholers likewise vse to celebrate a feast vpon the birth-day of Mahumet, and then their fathers are bound to send each man a torch vnto the schoole: whereupon euery boy carrieth a torch in his hand, some of which waigh thirty pound. These torches are most curiously made, being adorned round about with diuers fruits of waxe, which being lighted betimes in the morning doe burne till sun-rise, in the meane while certaine singers resound the praises of Mahumet, and so soone as the sunne is vp, all their solemnitie ceaseth: this day vseth to be very gainfull vnto the schoolemasters, for they sell the remnant of the waxe vpon the torches for an hundred duckats, and sometimes for more. None of them paies any rent for his schoole: for all their schooles were built many yeeres agoe, and were freely bestowed for the training vp of youth. Whatsoeuer ornaments or toyes are vpon the torches, the schoolemasters diuide them among their scholers and among the singers. Both in these common schooles and also in the colleges they haue two daies of recreation euery weeke, wherein they neither teach nor studie.[62]

Of the fortune-tellers and some other artizans in Fez.

WE haue said nothing as yet of the leather-dressers, who haue diuers mansions by the riuers side, paying for euery skin an halfepeny[63] custome, which amounteth yeerely almost vnto three hundred duckats. Here are likewise chirurgions & barbers, whom, because they are so few, I thought not to haue mentioned in this place. Now let vs speake of the fortune-tellers and diuiners, of whom there is a great number, and three *Three sorts of diuiners in Fez.* kindes. For one sort vseth certaine Geomanticall figures. Others powring a drop of oile into a viall or glasse of water, make the saide water to bee transparent and bright, wherein, as it were in a mirrour, they affirme that they see huge swarmes of diuels that resemble an whole armie, some whereof are trauelling, some are passing ouer a riuer, and others fighting a land-battell, whom when the diuiner seeth at quiet, he demandeth such questions of them as he is desirous to be resolued of: and the diuels giue them

G G

answere with beckning, or with some gesture of their hands or eies: so inconsiderate and damnable is their credulitie in this behalfe. The foresaid glasse-viall they will deliuer into childrens hands scarce of eight yeeres old, of whom they will aske whether they see this or that diuell. Many of the citie are so besotted with these vanities, that they spend great summes vpon them. The third kinde of diuiners are women-witches, which are affirmed to haue familiaritie with diuels: some diuels they call red, some white, and some black diuels: and when they will tell any mans fortune, they perfume themselues with certaine odours, saying, that then they possesse themselues with that diuell which they called for: afterwards changing their voice, they faine the diuell to speake within them: then they which come to enquire, ought with great feare & trembling aske these vile & abominable witches such questions as they meane to propound, and lastly offering some fee vnto the diuell, they depart. But the wiser and honester sort of people call these women *Sahacat*, which in Latin signifieth *Fricatrices*, because they haue a damnable custome to commit vnlawfull Venerie among themselues, which I cannot expresse in any modester termes. If faire women come vnto them at any time, these abominable witches will burne in lust towardes them no otherwise then lustie yoonkers doe towardes yoong maides, and will in the diuels behalfe demaunde for a rewarde, that they may lie with them: and so by this meanes it often falleth out, that thinking thereby to fulfill the diuels command they lie with the witches. Yea some there are, which being allured with the delight of this abominable vice, will desire the companie of these witches, and faining themselues to be sicke, will either call one of the witches home to them, or will send their husbands for the same purpose: and so the witches perceiuing how the matter stands, will say that the woman is possessed with a diuell, and that she can no way be cured, vnlesse she be admitted into their societie. With these words her silly husband being persuaded, doth not onely permit her so to doe, but makes also a sumptuous banket vnto the damned crew of witches : which being done, they vse to daunce very strangely at the noise of drums : and so the poore man commits his false wife to their filthie disposition. Howbeit some there are that will soone coniure the diuell with a good cudgell out of their wiues : others faining themselues to be possessed with a diuell, wil deceiue the said witches, as their wiues haue been deceiued by them.

Of the coniurers, inchanters, and iuglers in Fez.

IN Fez likewise there are a kinde of iuglers or coniurers called *Muhazzimin :*[64] who of all others are reported to be most speedie casters out of diuels. And because their Necromancie sometimes taketh effect, it is a wonder to see into what reputation they grow thereby : but when they cannot cast foorth a diuell, they say it is an airie spirite. Their manner of adiuring diuels is this : first they drawe certaine characters and circles upon an ash-heape or some other place ; then describe they certaine signes vpon the hands and forehead of the partie possessed, and perfume him after a strange kinde of manner. Afterward they make their inchantment or coniuration ; enquiring of the diuell, which way or by what meanes he entred the partie, as likewise what he is, and by what name he is called, and lastly charging him to come foorth. Others there are that worke by a certaine Cabalisticall rule called *Zairagia :* this rule is contained in many writings, for it is thought to be naturall magique : neither are there any other Necromancers in all Fez, that will more certainly and truly resolue a doubtfull question ; howbeit their arte is exceeding difficult : for the students thereof must haue as great skill in Astrologie, as in Cabala. My selfe in times past hauing attained to some knowledge in this facultie, continued (I remember) an whole day in describing one figure onely: which kinde of figures are described in manner following. First they draw many circles within the compasse of a great circle: in the first circle they make a crosse, at the fower extremities whereof they set downe the fower quarters of the world, to wit, East, West, North, and South: at each end of one of the said crosse lines, they note either pole: likewise about the circumference of the first circle, they paint the fower elements: then diuide they the same circle and the circle following into fower partes: and euery fourth part they diuide into other seuen, each one being distinguished with certaine great Arabian characters, so that euery element containeth eight and twentie characters. In the third circle they set downe the seuen planets; in the fourth the twelue signes of the Zodiacke; in the fift the twelue Latine names of the moneths; in the sixt the eight and twentie houses of the moone; in the seuenth the 365. daies of the yeere, and about the conuexitie thereof, the fower cardinall or principall windes. Then take they one onely letter of the question propounded, multiplying the same by all the particulars aforenamed, & the product or summe totall they diuide after a certaine manner, placing it in some roome, according to the qualitie of the character, and as the element requireth wherein the said character is found without a figure. All which being done, they marke that figure which seemeth to agree with the foresaid number or sum produced, wherewith they proceed as they did with the former, till they haue found eight and twentie characters, whereof they make one word, and of this word the speech is made that resolueth the question demanded: this speech is alwaies turned into a verse of the first kinde, which the Arabians call *Ethauil*, consisting of eight *Stipites* and twelue *Chordi*, according to the meeter of the Arabian toong, whereof we haue intreated in the last part of our Arabian grammar. And the verse *An Arabian grammar written by Iohn Leo.* consisting of those characters, comprehendeth alwaies a true and infallible answer vnto the question propounded, resoluing first that which is demanded, and then expounding the sense of the question it selfe. These practitioners are neuer found to erre, which causeth their arte of Cabala to be had in great admiration: which although it be accounted naturall, yet neuer saw I any thing that hath more affinitie with supernaturall and diuine knowledge. I remember that I saw in a certaine open place of king *Abulunan* his college in Fez, vpon a floore paued with excellent smooth marble, the description of a figure. Each side of this floore or court was fiftie elles long, and yet two third parts thereof were occupied about the figure, and about the things pertaining thereto: three there were that made the description, euery one attending his appointed place, and they were an whole day in setting it downe. Another such figure I saw at Tunis, drawen by one that was maruellous cunning in the arte, whose father had written two volumes of commentaries or expositions vpon the precepts of the same arte, wherein whosoeuer hath exact skill, is most highly esteemed of by all men.[65] I my selfe neuer sawe but three of this profession, namely one at Tunis, and two other at Fez: likewise I haue seene two expositions vpon the precepts of the said arte, together with a commentarie of one *Margian* father vnto the foresaid Cabalist which I saw at Tunis: and another written by *Ibnu Caldim* the historiographer.[66] And if any were desirous to see the precepts and commentaries of that arte, he might doe it with the expence of fiftie duckats: for sailing to Tunis a towne neere vnto Italie, he might haue a sight of all the particulars aforesaid. I my selfe had fit oportunitie of time, and a teacher that offered to instruct me gratis in the same arte: howbeit I thought good not to accept his offer, because the said arte is forbidden and *Diuination and soothsaying forbidden by the lawe of Mahumet.*

accounted hereticall by the law of Mahumet : for Mahumets law affirmeth all kinde of diuinations to be vaine, and that God onely knoweth secrets and things to come : wherefore sometimes the saide Cabalistes are imprisoned by the Mahumetan inquisitours, who cease not to persecute the professours of that arte.

Of certaine rules and superstitions obserued in the Mahumetan law.

HEre also you may finde certaine learned men, which will haue themselues called wizards and morall philosophers. They obserue certaine rules which Mahumet neuer prescribed. By some they are accounted catholique or true Mahumetans, and by others they are holden for heretiks, howbeit the greatest part of the common people reuerence them as if they were gods, notwithstanding they commit many things vnlawfull and forbidden by the Mahumetan lawe, as namely ; whereas the said lawe forbiddeth any loue-matters to be expressed in any musicall ditties or songs, these moralists affirme the contrarie. In the foresaid Mahumetan religion are a great number of rules or sectes, euery of which hath most learned patrones and protectours. The foresaid sect sprang vp fowerscore yeeres after Mahumet, the first author thereof being called *Elhesen Ibnu Abilhasen*, and being borne in the towne of Basora : this man taught his disciples & followers certaine precepts, but writings he left none behinde him. About an hundred yeeres after there came another notable doctor of that sect from Bagaded, called *Elharic Ibnu Esed*, who left volumes of writings vnto his disciples. Afterward those that were found to be his followers, were all condemned by the Mahumetan patriarks and lawyers. Howbeit 80. yeeres after, that sect began to reuiue againe vnder a certaine famous professour, who drew after him many disciples, vnto whom he published

Diuers Mahumetan sects.

his doctrine. This man at length and all his followers were by the patriarke and lawyers condemned to die. Which he vnderstanding, wrote foorthwith vnto the patriarke, requesting that hee might be licenced to dispute with the lawyers as touching his doctrine, of whom if he were conuinced, he would most willingly suffer death ; otherwise that it would be against all equitie, that so many innocents should perish vpon an vniust accusation. The patriarke thinking his demand to be reasonable, condescended wholy thereunto. But when the matter came to disputation, the partie condemned soon put all the lawyers to silence. Which when the patriarke perceiued, he reuoked the sentence as vniust, and caused many colleges and monasteries to be erected for the said partie and his followers. After which time this sect continued about an hundred yeeres, till the emperour *Malicsach* of the Turkish race came thither out of Asia the greater, and destroied all the maintainers thereof. Whereupon some of them fled vnto Cairo, and the rest into Arabia, being dispersed here and there for the space of twenty yeeres, till in the raigne of *Caselsah* nephew vnto *Malicsach*, *Nidam Elmule* one of his counsellers, and a man of an high spirit, being addicted vnto the said sect, so restored, erected, and confirmed the same, that by the helpe of one *Elgazzuli* a most learned man (who had written of the same argument a notable worke diuided into seuen parts) he reconciled the lawyers with the disciples of this sect, conditionally, that the lawyers should be called Conseruers of the prophet Mahumet his lawes, & the sectaries Reformers of the same. This concord lasted between them, til Bagaded was sacked by the Tartars ; which befell in the yeere of the Hegeira 656. at what time those sectaries so increased, that they swarmed almost ouer all Africa and Asia. Neither would they admit any into their societie, but such as were very learned, and trained vp in all kinde of liberall sciences ;

Bagdet sacked by the Tartars.

to the end they might the better defend their owne opinions, and confute their aduersaries: but now adaies they admit all kinde of rude and ignorant persons, affirming all sortes of learning to be needlesse; for the spirit (say they) reuealeth the knowledge of the truth vnto such as are of a cleane hart; and they alleage many reasons for the confirmation of this their opinion, though not very forcible. Wherefore despising their ancesters rites, and the strict obseruations of the law, they addict themselues to nought else but delights and pleasures, feasting often & singing lasciuious songs. Sometimes they will rend their garments, either alluding thereby to the verses that they sing, or being mooued thereunto by their corrupt and vile disposition; saying falsly that they are then rauished with a fit of diuine loue: but I rather impute it to their abundance of meat, and gluttonie. For each one of them will deuoure as much meate, as may well suffice three. Or (which is more likely) they vtter those passionate clamours and out-cries, bicause they are inflamed with vnlawfull and filthie lust. For sometimes it happeneth that some one of the principall of them, with all his scholers and disciples, is inuited to the mariage of some gentleman, and at the beginning of the banket they will rehearse their deuout orizons and songs, but so soone as they are risen from the table, the elder of the companie being about to daunce, teare their garments: and if any one in the middest of their dauncing, that hath drunke immoderately, chaunceth to fall downe, he is taken vp foorthwith by one of the scholers, and too lasciuiously kissed. Whereupon this prouerbe grew among the people of Fez: *The heremites banket.* Which they vse in reproch of those masters, that make their scholers their minions.[67]

Of diuers other rules and sectes, and of the superstitious credulitie of many.

AMongst these sectes there are some, that haue not onely a diuers law, but also a different beleefe from the residue, whereupon by some others they are called heretikes. Some there are also which hold, that a man by good works, by fasting and abstinence, may attaine vnto the nature of an angell, which good works, fastings, &c. doe (say they) so purge and free the minde from all contagion of euill, that by no meanes it can sinne any more, though it would neuer so faine. Howbeit they thinke themselues not capable of this felicitie, before they haue ascended thereunto by the degrees of fiftie disciplines or sciences: and although they fall into sinne before they be come to the fiftith degree, yet they say that God will not impute that sinne vnto them. These fellowes indeed ⸱in the beginning leade a most strict life, and doe euen macerate and consume themselues with fasting; but afterward they giue themselues to all licentiousness and pleasure. They haue also a most seuere forme of liuing set downe in fower bookes, by a certaine learned man of their faction, called *Essherauar de Schrauard*, and borne in the citie of Corasan. Likewise there was another author called *Ibnul Farid*, that described all their religion in wittie verses, which being fraught with allegories seemed to intreate of nought but loue: wherefore one *Elfargani* expounded the said verses with a commentarie, and there-out gathered the canons and orders of the sect, and shewed the degrees to the attainment of felicitie. Moreouer the said verses are so sweet and elegant, that the maintainers of this sect will sing and repeate none other in their bankets: for these three hundred yeeres no author hath so adorned their language as the said *Ibnul*. These sectaries take the heauens, the elements, the planets, and the fixed starres to be one god, and that no law nor religion is erronious: for euery man (say they) may lawfully worship that which his mind is most addicted to worship. They thinke that all the knowledge of God was infused into one man, whom they call in their language *Elcorb;* this man, they say, was elect by god, and was made equall in knowledge to him. Fourtie there are among them called all by the name of *Elauted*, which signifieth in our language, a blocke, or stocke of a tree: out of this number, when their Elcoth deceaseth, they create another in his roome, namely seuentie persons that haue the authoritie of election committed vnto them. There are likewise 765. others (whose names I doe not well remember) who are chosen into the said electors roomes, when any of them decease. These 765. being bound thereunto by a certaine canon or rule of their order, are constrained alwaies to goe vnknowen, and they range almost all the world ouer in a most vile and beggerly habite, so that a man would take them for mad men and estranged from all sense of humanitie: for these lewd miscreants vnder pretence of their religion run like roagues naked and sauage throughout all Africa, hauing so little regarde of honestie or shame, that they will like brute beastes rauish women in publike places; and yet forsooth the grosse common people reuerence them as men of woonderful holines. Great swarmes of these filthie vagabonds you may see in Tunis, but many more in Egypt, and especially at Alcair, whereas in the market called Bain Elcafrain I saw one of these villaines with mine owne eies, in the presence of much people, deflowre a most beautifull woman as she was comming foorth of the bath: which being done, the fond people came flocking about the said woman, striuing to touch her garment as a most holie thing: saying that the adulterer was a man of great sanctitie, and that he did not commit the sinne, but onely seemed to commit it: which when the sillie cuckold her husband vnderstood, he shewed himselfe thankfull to his false god with a solemne banket, and with liberall giuing of almes. The magistrates of the citie would haue punished the adulterer, but they were in hazard to be slaine of the people for their labours, who (as is before said) adore these varlets for saints and men of singular holines. Other more villanous actes I saw committed by them, which I am ashamed to report.[68]

Of the Caballistes and certaine other sectes.

Likewise there is another sort of men, which we may fitly call Caballists. These fast most streitly, neither doe they eate the flesh of any liuing creature, but haue certaine meates and garments allotted vnto them : they rehearse likewise certaine set-praiers appointed for euery hower of the day and for the night, according to the varietie of daies and monethes, and they vse to carrie about certaine square tables with characters and numbers engrauen therein. They faine themselues to haue daily conference with the angels, of whom they learne (they say) the knowledge of all things. They had once a famous doctor of their sect called *Boni*, who was author of their canons, praiers, and square tables. Which when I saw, me thought their profession had more affinitie with magique then with Cabala. Their arte was diuided into eight partes ; whereof the first was called *Elumha Enormita*, that is, the demonstration of light : the which contained praiers and fastings. The second called *Semsul Meharif*, that is, the sunne of sciences, contained the foresaid square tables, together with their vse and profit. The third part they call *Sirru Lasmei Elchusne* ; this part contained a catalogue of those 99. vertues, which (they say) are contained in the names of God, which I remember I saw at Rome in the custodie of a certaine Venetian Iew. They haue also a certaine other rule called *Suvach*, that is, the rule of heremites, the professors and followers whereof inhabite woods and solitarie places, neither haue they any other food, but such as those wilde deserts wil affoord: the conuersation of these heremites no man is able exactly to describe, because they are estranged from all humane societie. But if I should take vpon me to describe the varietie of Mahumetan sectes, I should digresse too farre from my present purpose. He that desireth to know more of this matter, let him read ouer the booke of *Elefacni*, who discourseth at large of the sectes belonging to the Mahumetan religion, the principall whereof are 72. euery one of which defend their opinions to be true and good, and such as a man may attaine saluation by. At this day you shall finde but two principall sects onely, the one of *Leshari* being dispersed ouer all Africa, Egypt, Syria, Arabia, and Turkie: the other of *Imamia*, which is authorized throughout the whole kingdome of Persia, and in certaine townes of *Corasan*; and this sect the great Sophi of Persia maintaineth, insomuch that all Asia had like to been destroied thereabout. For whereas before they followed the sect of *Leshari*, the great Sophi by force of armes established his owne of *Imamia*: and yet one onely sect stretcheth ouer all the Mahumetans dominions.[69]

margin: 72. principall sectes in the religion of Mahumet.

Of such as search for treasures in Fez.

MOreouer in the citie of Fez there are certaine men called *Elcanesin*, who supposing to finde treasure vnder the foundations of old houses, doe perpetually search and delue. These grosse fellowes vse to resort vnto certaine dennes and caues without the citie-walles, certainly perswading themselues, that when the Romans were chased out of Africa, and driuen into Bætica or Granada in Spaine, they hid great abundance of treasure in the bowels of the earth, which they could not carrie with them, and so enchanted the same by art-magique, that it can by no meanes be attained vnto but by the same arte; wherefore they seeke vnto inchanters to teach them the arte of digging vp the said treasures. Some of them there are that will stedfastly affirme, that they sawe gold in this or that caue: others, that they saw siluer, but could not digge it out, by reason that they were destitute of perfumes and enchantments fit for the purpose; so that being seduced with this vaine opinion, and deepely deluing into the earth, they turne vpside downe the foundations of houses and sepulchers, and sometimes they proceede in this manner ten or twelue daies iourney from Fez: yea so fond they are and so besotted, that they esteeme those bookes that professe the arte of digging gold, as diuine oracles. Before my departure from Fez these fantasticall people had chosen them a consul, and getting licence of certaine owners to dig their grounds, when they had digged as much as they thought good, they paid the said owners for all dammages committed.[70]

Of the Alchymistes of Fez.

IN this citie likewise there are great store of Alchymists which are mightily addicted to that vaine practise: they are most base fellowes, and contaminate themselues with the steam of Sulphur, and other stinking smels. In the euening they vse to assemble themselues at the great temple, where they dispute of their false opinions. They haue of their arte of Alchymie many bookes written by learned men, amongst which one *Geber* is of principall account, who liued an hundred yeeres after Mahumet, and being a Greeke borne, is said to haue renounced his owne religion. This *Geber* his works and all his precepts are full of allegories or darke borrowed speeches. Likewise they haue another author, that wrote an huge volume of the same arte, intituled by the name of Attogrehi: this man was secretarie vnto the Soldan of Bagaded, of whom we haue written in the liues of the Arabian philosophers. Also the songs or the articles of the said science were written by one *Mugairibi* of Granada, whereupon a most learned Mamaluch of Damasco wrote a commentarie; yet so, that a man may much more easily vnderstand the text then the exposition thereof. Of Alchymistes here are two sorts; whereof the one seeke for the *Elixir*, that is, the matter which coloureth brasse and other metals; and the other are conuersant about multiplication of the quantities of metals, whereby they may conueniently temper the same. But their chiefest drift is to coine counterfeit money: for which cause you shall see most of them in Fez with their hands cut off.[71]

A booke written by Iohn Leo of the liues of the Arabian philosophers.

Of charmers and inchanters of snakes.

IN this citie likewise there is a great swarme of base people, such as the Italians commonly call Ciurmatori: these sing foolish songs and rimes in all the streets of the citie, and broching meere trifles with the musicke of drums, harpes, and citterns, they sell vnto the rude people certaine scroules or briefe charmes instead of preseruatiues. Vnto these you may adde another kinde of reffuse people of one family and disposition with the former, who carrie daunsing apes up and downe, and haue their neckes and armes all entwined with crawling snakes. These also professe Geomancie, and perswade women that they can foretell them their fortune. Likewise they carrie stone-horses about with them, which for a certaine fee, they will let others haue to couer their mares. I coulde heere reckon vp more sorts of people; but let it suffice to haue admonished in this place, that the greatest part of the forenamed are people of most base condition, and such as beare little good will to strangers, albeit there are but a fewe in this citie, by reason it is distant more then an hundreth miles from the sea, the way thither also being rough and dangerous. Their gentlemen are very stately and high minded, and will haue little or no familiaritie at all with the citizens: so likewise the doctors and iudges of principall account will admit but fewe vnto their acquaintance. This citie it selfe is most beautifull and right commodiously situate; where albeit in winter time the streetes are so mirie, that you cannot walke in them without startups, yet they let passe such abundance of water out of their conducts, that all the filth is washed cleane away. Where conducts are wanting, they carry all the durt in carts vnto the next part of the riuer.[72]

A description of the suburbes without the foresaid citie of Fez.

Without the wals of this citie westward standeth a suburbe containing almost fiue hundreth families, the houses whereof are but meane, and the inhabitants base, as namely driuers of camels, water-bearers, and cleauers of woode for the kings pallace. Yet here you may finde diuers shops, and all kinds of artificers. Here likewise dwell all the charmers and roguish minstrels before named; as also great swarmes of sluttish and filthie harlots. In the principall streete of this suburbe, you shall finde certaine caues most artificially hewen out of excellent marble, wherein the noble men of Fez were woont to lay vp their corne: but after that by reason of the warres it was often taken from thence, they haue since vsually conueied their corne into new Fez, and there stored it vp: and from that time to this the marble-caues haue remained desolate. It is a woonder to see howe wide and large these caues are; for the least of them will containe more then a thousand measures of corne, there being aboue an an hundreth and fiftie of them in all, but now they lie waste and open, insomuch that diuers fall into them at vnawares, for which cause their brimmes are enuironed with wals. Here euery one may play the vintener and the baud; so that this suburbe may iustly be called the sinke of Fez. From the twentith hower you shall see none at all in their shops: for then euery man runs to the tauerne to disport, to spend riotously, and to bee drunken. Another suburbe there is allotted vnto the lepers, of whom there are *two* hundreth families: these leprous persons haue a gouernour, which gathereth certaine yeerely reuenues from the noble-men, and taketh such care of the saide lepers, that they want no necessarie thing. He is bound by his office to discharge the citie of all leprous persons, and to compell all such as he vnderstandes to be infected with that disease, to depart into the foresaide suburbes. If any leper chanceth to die without issue, part of his goods are emploied to the common benefite of the lepers, and part fall to the gouernours share: but if he hath any children, they enioy his goods. Among the lepers also those are placed, which are infected with white botches, or with any other incurable maladie. Next beyond standeth another suburbe inhabited onely with muleters, plaisterers, and wood-mongers: which although it be but little, yet containeth it about an hundreth and fiftie families. Moreouer vpon the way leading westward from the citie there is another great suburbe of moe then fower hundreth houses: howbeit they are low & base, and the inhabitants are beggerly, which neither can nor will dwell among any other people. By this suburbe there is a certaine broad plaine which leadeth to the riuer two miles off, and extendeth westward almost three miles. Vpon this plaine euery weeke there is an exceeding great market of cattell. Likewise the shopkeepers of the citie resort hither and sell their wares in tents. Also a certaine companie of gentlemen vse to come hither, and to diuide a ramme among themselues, leauing the head vnto the butcher for his fee, but the feete and the skin they sell vnto the wooll-chapmen. For those

The habitation of lepers in Fez, and their gouernour.

wares that are heere sold they pay so little tribute to the king, that it is not woorth the mentioning. But this one thing I must in no wise passe ouer in silence, namely, that I neuer sawe neither in Asia, Africa, nor Italy, a market either more populous, or better furnished with wares. Not farre from Fez stand certaine high rockes enuironed with a ditch of two miles compasse, out of which rockes certaine matter is hewed to make lime withall. Neere vnto the saide ditch are many furnaces, some whereof are so large, that they will containe moe then sixe thousand measures of lime: and this lime is made at the costes of the richest citizens in Fez. Westward without the wals of Fez by the riuers side stande about an hundred cottages, which are onely inhabited by them that white linnen cloth. Hither in the spring and in summer vse the citizens to bring their linnen cloth, spreading it vpon the medowes, and as often as they see it drie in the sunne, casting water thereupon, which water they fetch either out of the riuer or out of some cesterne in certaine lether tankards made for the same purpose: but at night each one carrieth his cloth into the foresaid cottages. Neither are the medowes wherein they bleach their cloth euer destitute of grasse. A most gallant prospect it is to beholde a farre off the white clothes dispersed ouer the greene medow, and the christall streames of the riuer, which seeme to be of an azure hue, running along: all which the Poets haue celebrated in their verses.[73]

A description of the common place of buriall without the citie.

Many fieldes there are without the citie, which haue been giuen by certaine noblemen for the buriall of the dead. Vpon their sepulchers for the most part they lay a long three-square stone. When any noble man or any principall citizen deceaseth, they lay one stone ouer

his head and another ouer his feete, whereupon vseth to
bee engrauen some epitaph, with the day and yeere when
the partie deceased. I my selfe bestowed much labour in
gathering of epitaphes, which I saw both about Fez and in
other places of Barbary; all which being set downe in a
booke I gaue vnto the kings brother. The matter of their
epitaphes is diuers, some tending to consolation, and others
to sorrow.

Of the sepulchres of the kings of Fez.

NOrthward of the citie vpon a certaine high hill stands
a palace, wherein are the monuments of diuers
Marin kings, being most artificially hewen out of marble
with epitaphes vpon them, so that I cannot condignely
expresse the maiestie and beautie thereof.[74]

A description of their gardens.

WIthout the north, east, and south parts of the citie are
great store of gardens, replenished with all kinde
of fruite and with stately trees. Through the midst of
these gardens, they deriue some small vaine of the riuer,
some whereof are so full of trees, that you woulde take
them for groues rather then for gardens. These gardens
they manure not at all, but only water them continually in
the moneth of May,[75] whereupon they haue great abundance
of fruit. All their fruits, saue their peaches onely, are of a
most delicate taste, whereof, so soone as they are ripe,
aboue fiue hundreth cart-loades are daily carried into the
market, besides grapes, which here I do not mention. But
the saide fruits are carried vnto a certaine place in Fez,
where tribute being paide for them, they are solde by criers
vnto the fruiterers there present. In the same place likewise after paying of tribute, they sell certaine Negro-slaues.
Towards the east of Fez lieth a plaine fifteene miles broad,
and thirtie miles long: this plaine is full of fountaines and

freshets, and is reserued for the vse of the great temple. It is farmed out vnto gardiners, who sowe thereupon such abundance of hemp, melons, turneps or nauewes, radish, and other such like rootes and herbes, that euery summer there are saide to be gathered thereof aboue fifteene thousand cart-loads, and as many in winter. Howbeit the aire is veric vnholsome thereabout, for the inhabitants are continually vexed with feuers, and are of a yellowish colour.[76]

Of that part of Fez which is called new Fez.

NEW Fez beeing enuironed with an high and impregnable wall, and situate on a most beautifull plaine not farre from the riuers side, is almost a mile distant from old Fez, and that vpon the east and south side thereof. Betweene the wals of either towne, to the northward, entereth a certaine arme of the riuer, where the foresaid milles do stande, and the other part of the riuer is seuered into two branches, one whereof runneth betweene new Fez and old Fez, not farre from the edge of the rocke, and the other passing through certaine vallies and gardens, trendeth at length southward. The other part of the riuer holdeth on his course by the rocke, and so by the college of king *Abutinan*. This citie of new Fez *Iacob* the sonne of *Abdultach* caused to bee built, who was the first king of the Marin family, and expelled the kings of Maroco, and vsurped the kingdome vnto himselfe: but the king of Telensin, to the end he might make the people of Maroco beholding vnto him, and might subuert the prosperous successe of the Marin family, went about to hinder the king of Fez his attempts against Maroco: wherefore king *Iacob* hauing finished the wars of Maroco, determined to reuenge himselfe to the vttermost for the iniuries offered by them of Telensin. But considering with himselfe, that the strong townes of his owne

* Or *Aburinan*.
  The founder of new Fez.

kingdome were farre distant from Telensin, he thought it a better course to builde this citie, whereunto the seate roiall of all Maroco might be translated: which being erected, he called The white citie, but it was afterward named by the inhabitants new Fez.[77] This citie king *Iacob* the founder diuided inio three parts, whereof the first contained his roiall pallace, and diuers noble mens houses, vnto euery one of which he allotted a most pleasant garden. Not farre from his pallace he built a most stately and sumptuous temple. In another part of this citie he built a large and faire stable for the kings horses to stande in. Then also he caused other palaces to be erected for his captaines and principall courtiers. From the west gate to the east he appointed the market place, the distance betweene which gates is a mile and an halfe, and on both sides he placed artificers and merchants shops. At the west gate he caused a faire portall to be set vp, to harbour the watchmen and warders of the citie. Not far from thence he erected two stables sufficient to containe three hundreth horses, which he might vse for the protection of his owne palace. The third part of the citie was appointed for the kinges guarde and attendants, which were most of them borne eastwarde of Fez, neither had they any other weapons but hand-bowes (for crossebowes were not then vsed in that kingdome) vnto which attendants the king allowed a large stipend: but now the same place is full of beautifull temples and stoues. Neere vnto the kings palace standes the mint, hauing in the midst a fower-square court with certaine portals or cels rounde about it, wherein the money-minters dwell. Likewise there is another lodging in the midst of the same court, where the gouernor of the mint with his scribes and notaries haue their aboad. Here, as well as in any other places, whatsoeuer commoditie is raised, redoundeth wholy to the king. Neere vnto the mint stande the gold-

smiths shops, whose Consul or gouernour keepes the scale
and stamps of the coine. In Fez neither ring nor any
other Iewell or commoditie can bee made of siluer or
golde, before the metall bee sealed, for the offenders are
most seuerely punished. And, the metall being sealed,
whatsoeuer is made thereof is weighed as if it were money.
The greatest part of goldsmiths dwelling in new Fez are
Iewes, who carrie their vessels of gold and siluer vnto a
certaine place of old Fez, neere vnto the grocers shops,
and there sell them. For in old Fez neither gold nor
siluer is coined, nor any Mahumetans are suffered to be
goldsmiths, bicause they haue vsurers among them, which
will sell any peece of wrought siluer or golde deerer
then the weight requireth; albeit the same priuilege is by
the gouernours of the citie granted vnto the Iewes.[78]
Some there are also that onely make plate for the citizens,
who are paied hire onely for their worke. That part of
the citie which the kings attendants or guard once possessed,
is now inhabited by Iewes: for now a daies the kings vse
no such guard. The Iewes indeed first dwelt in old Fez,
but vpon the death of a certaine king they were all robbed
by the Moores: whereupon king *Abusabid* caused them to
remooue into new Fez, and by that meanes doubled their
yeerely tribute. They therefore euen till this day doe
occupie a long street in the said new citie, wherin they
haue their shops and synagogues, and their number is
maruellously encreased euer since they were driuen out of
Spaine. These Iewes are had in great contempt by all
men, neither are any of them permitted to weare shooes,
but they make them certaine socks of sea-rushes. On their
heads they weare a blacke * dulipan, and if any will goe in * *Or turbant.*
a cap, he must fasten a red cloth thereunto. They pay
vnto the king of Fez monethly fower hundred duckats.[79]
At length within the space of an hundred and forty yeeres
this new citie was enuironed with most impregnable walles,

and adorned with temples, colleges, palaces, and other such buildings as serue to beautifie a citie, so that I thinke there was more bestowed in garnishing of the citie, then in building of the walles. Without the citie-walles are built many huge wheeles[80] or engins, for the conueying of riuer-water ouer the said walles into cesternes, from whence it is conueied in certaine chanels and pipes vnto the temples, gardens, & palaces. The said wheeles were built not fully an hundred yeeres past, before which time water was brought vnto the citie by a certaine conduct, from a fountaine ten miles distant. Of which artificiall conduct a certaine Genouese, beeing then in great fauour with the king, is reported to haue been the author : but the wheeles (they say) were inuented by a Spaniard : and in them there is maruellous cunning workmanship : for to the conueiance of so huge a quantitie of water, each wheele is turned about but fower and twentie times onely in a day and night. To conclude, here are but few gentlemen in this citie, except such as attend vpon the court, for the residue are base and mechanicall people : but such as carie any shew of honestie, doe so hate and disdaine the kings courtiers and gentlemen, that they will by no meanes vouchsafe to marie their daughters vnto them.[81]

Engins for the conueiance of water.

Of the fashions and customes vsed in the kings court.

Amongst all the princes of Africa, I neuer red of any that was created by the common suffrages and consent of the people vnto his kingdome or princedome, or that was called from any strange prouince or citie to beare rule. Also by the law of Mahumet no man may beare any secular authoritie, which may be called lawfull, saue onely the Mahumetan patriarkes and prelates : howbeit the saide patriarkes authoritie decreasing daily more and more, the ringleaders of such people as ranged vp and downe the deserts began to inuade places inhabited & ciuilized, and

by force of armes, against Mahumets lawe, and maugre his
prelates, to ordaine sundrie princes : As for example in the
East, whereas the Turkes, Cordians,[82] and Tartars, haue
vsurped dominion ouer such as was not able to repell them.
So likewise in the west parts first the families of Zeneta
and Luntuna, then the seditious Mahumetan preachers,
and afterward the family of Marin got the vpper hand.
Howbeit the family of Luntuna is reported to haue aided
the western regions, & to haue released them from the furie
of the seditious heretiques, wherein they shewed themselues
friends and not enimies : but afterward their tyrannie
began to shew it selfe. And this is the reason why they
do not now a daies attaine vnto gouernment by hereditarie
succession or by election of the people, or of the nobilitie.
But the prince himselfe when he feeles death seazing vpon
him, calleth about him all his peeres and nobles, and
bindeth them by oath, to establish his sonne, brother, or
anie other whom he most fauoureth, in his kingdome. But
they after the princes disease neglecting their oath, will
chuse any other whom they list.[83] And this is ordinarily
the election of the king of Fez, who, so soone as he is
proclaimed king, chuseth foorthwith some one of his nobles
to be his chiefe counsellour, and on him he bestoweth the
thirde part of all his kingly reuenues. Then chuseth *The manner of choosing officers in the court of Fez.*
another to be his secretarie, treasurer, and high steward of
his houshold. Then is created the captaine of the horsemen appointed for the kings guard, and these horsemen
with their horses liue most commonly in the fieldes. Lastly
he appointeth a new gouernour ouer euery citie, vnto
whom all the tributes and reuenues of the same place
redound, with condition, that as often as any warres betide,
he shall maintaine a certaine companie of horses to the
kings seruice. After a while also he placeth certaine
deputies and commissioners ouer his people inhabiting the
mountaines, and ouer the Arabians subiect vnto him.

The gouernours of cities diuersly administer iustice, according to the custome of the place. Some there are also appointed by the king to collect all the tributes and reuenues of his kingdome, and duly to paie the same vnto him. Likewise there are others chosen, whom they call in their language keepers or guardians, and vnto euery one of these the king giueth some cattle or village, whereby he may procure his owne maintenance, and be able to serue the king in time of warre. Moreouer the king of Fez maintaineth a troupe of light horsemen, who so long as they serue the king in his campe, haue their diet allowed them out of the kings prouision : but in time of peace, he findeth them corne, butter, and pouldered flesh for the whole yeere, but money they haue very seldome. Once a yeere they are apparelled at the kings cost; neither do they prouide for their horses either within the citie or without, for the king furnisheth them with all necessaries. Those that giue attendance to their horses are Christian captiues, which go shackled in great chaines and fetters. But when the armie remooueth any whither, the saide Christians are carried vpon camels backes. Another officer there is that giueth attendance onely to the camels, assigning certaine pastures vnto the heards-men, and diuiding fields among them, and making such prouision for the kings camels, as himselfe shall thinke expedient. Each camel-driuer hath two camels, which are laden with the kings furniture, according to the appointment of the gouernour. Likewise the king hath a certaine puruciour or steward, whose office is to prouide, keepe, and distribute corne both to the kings houshold and to his armie. This man in time of warre hath tenne or twelue tents to lay vp corne in, and euery day with change of camels he sendeth for newe corne, least the armie shoulde be vnprouided of victuals : he hath also cooks at his command. Moreouer there is a gouernour or master-groome of the stables, who prouideth for the kings horses, mules, and camels, and is furnished with all necessaries by the steward. There is another also appointed ouerseer of the corne, whose dutie it is to prouide barly and other prouender for the beasts: and this man hath his scribes and notaries about him, who diligently set downe all particular expenses, for they must giue vp a perfect account vnto the chiefe steward. They haue also a certaine captaine ouer fiftie horsemen, which horsemen may well be called pursuants, for they are sent by the secretarie in the kings name to do his busines. Likewise the Fezzan king hath another captaine of great name, being as it were gouernour of his guard, who in the kings name, may compell the iudges to do iustice, and to put their sentences in execution. This mans authoritie is so great, that sometimes he may commit principal noblemen to ward, & may seuerely punish them, according to the kings commandement. Moreouer the said king hath a most trusty chancelor, who keepeth the great seale, and writeth and signeth the kings letters. He hath also a great number of footemen, the gouernour of whom accepteth and dismisseth whom he thinkes good, and giueth to euery one wages, according to his agilitie and desert. And whensoeuer the king commeth in place of iudgement, the saide gouernour alwaies attendeth vpon him, and is in a manner his high chamberlain. Also there is another that taketh charge of the carriages and baggage of the armie, and causeth the tents of the light horsemen to be carried vp and down on mules, and the tents of the other soldiers on camels. There are likewise a company of ensigne-bearers, who in marching on a iourney carrie their colours wrapped vp: but he that goeth before the armie hath his banner displaied, and of a great height. And euery one of the saide standard-bearers knoweth most exactly alwaies, fords of riuers, and passages through woods, wherefore they are for the most part appointed to guide the armie. The drummers (of whom there are great store in the kings host) plaie vpon certaine drums of brasse as bigge as a great kettle, the lower part whereof is narrow, & the vpper broad, being couered with a skin. These drummers ride on horsebacke, hauing alwaies on the one side of their horses a great waight hanging downe, to counterpoize the heauiness of their drums on the other side. They are allowed most swift horses, bicause the Moores account it a great disgrace to loose a drum. The said drums make such a loude and horrible noise, that they are not onely heard a farre off, but also strike exceeding terrour both vpon men and horses, and they are beaten onely with a buls pizzle. The musitions are not maintained at the kings charge, for the cities are bounde at their costs to send a certaine number of them to the warres, who, according to their demeanour in the warres, are admitted or not admitted vnto the kings table. This king hath also a certaine master of ceremonies, who sitteth at his feete in the senate-house, and commandeth each man to sit downe, and to speake according to his dignitie. All the maide-seruants in the kings familie are Negro-slaues, which are partly chamberlains, and partly waiting-maids. And yet his Queene is alwaies of a white skin. Likewise in the king of Fez his court are certaine Christian captiues, being partly Spanish, and partly Portugale women, who are most circumspectly kept by certaine Eunuchs, that are Negro-slaues. The king of Fez hath very large dominions, but his reuenues are small, to wit, scarce three hundreth thousand ducats, the fift part whereof redoundeth not to the king: for the remainder is diuided into sundrie portions, as we haue before signified. Yea, the greater part of the said reuenues is paide in corne, cattle, oile, and butter, all which yeeld but small store of money. In some place they pay a ducate and one fourth part, tribute for euery acre, but in other places a whole family paieth but so much. In some other regions each man aboue fifteene yeeres of age paieth as much tribute also. Neither are the people of this great citie more vexed with any thing then with paying of their tributes and impositions. Heere also is to be noted, that the Mahumetan gouernours (the priests onely excepted) may not exact greater reuenues then those that Mahumet hath allotted vnto them, namely of euery of their subiects which possesseth 100. ducates in ready money, they are to haue two ducates & an halfe for yeerely tribute. Euery husbandman likewise is bound to pay for tribute the tenth part of all his corne. And all the saide tributes he appointed to be paied vnto the patriarke, who should bestow that which was superflous for the Prince to haue, vpon common vses; namely for the releeuing of poore impotent people and widowes, and for maintaining of wars against the enimie. But since the Patriarches began to decay, the Princes (as we haue beforesaide) exercised tyrannie. For it was not sufficient for them to exact all the forenamed tributes, and riotously to consume the same, but also to vrge people vnto greater contributions; so that all the inhabitants of Africa are so oppressed with daily exactions, that they haue scarcely wherewithall to feed and apparell themselues; for which cause there is almost no man of learning or honesty, that will seeke any acquaintance with courtiers, or will inuite them to his table, or accept any gifts (bee they neuer so pretious) at their hands: thinking that whatsoeuer goods they haue, are gotten by theft and briberie. The King *The King of Fez his guard.* of Fez continually maintaineth sixe thousand horsemen, fiue hundreth crossebowes, and as manie Harquebusiers, being at all assayes prepared for the warres, who in time of peace, when the king goeth on progresse, lye within *How the King of Fez rideth on progresse.* a mile of his person: for being at home in Fez, he needeth not so strong a guard. When he wageth warre against

the Arabians that be his enimies, because the forenamed
garison is not sufficient, he requireth ayde of the Arabians
his subiects, who at their owne costs finde him a great
armie of men better trained to the warres, then his owne
souldiers before-mentioned. The pompe and ceremonies of
this king are but meane, neither doth he willingly vse them,
but onely vpon festiuall daies, and when meere necessitie
requireth. When the king is to ride foorth, the master
of ceremonies signifieth so much vnto certaine herbengers
or postes, whereupon the herbengers giue notice thereof
vnto the kings *parents, vnto his nobilitie, his senatours,
captaines, guardians, and gentlemen, who presently arrange
themselues before the palace gate. At the kings comming
foorth of the palace, the herbengers appoint vnto each
man his place and order of riding. First and foremost go
the standard-bearers, next the drummers, then followeth
the chiefe groome of the stable with his seruants and
family: after him comes the kings pensioners, his guard,
his master of ceremonies, his secretaries, his treasurer, and
last of all his chiefe Iudge and his captaine generall, at
length comes the king accompanied with his principall
counseller, or with some other great peere. Before the
king also ride certaine officers belonging to his person,
whereof one carries his sword-royall, another his shield,
and the third his crosse-bowe. On each side of him march
his footemen, one carrying a payer of stirrups, another
the kings partizan, the third a couering for his saddle, and
the fourth a halter for his horse. And so soone as the
king is dismounted, they foorthwith couer his saddle, and
put the foresaide halter vpon his horse-head. Likewise
there is another footeman that carrieth the kings pantofles
most artificially wrought. After the king followeth the
captaine of the footemen, then the eunuches, the kings
family, the light horsemen, and last of all the crosse-bowes
and Harquebusiers. The apparell of the king is then verie

* Or kines-
olkes.

moderate and plaine: insomuch that if a man knew him not, he would thinke him to be absent: for the attendants be far more sumptuously attired. Moreouer no Mahumetan king or prince may weare a crowne, diademe, or any such like ornament vpon his heade, for that is forbidden by the law of *Mahumet*. When the king lyeth with his armie in the fields, first his owne great tent is pitched in a fower square forme like vnto a castle, each side of the saide square being fiftie elles in length. At euerie of the fower corners standeth a little sharpe turret made of cloth, with a gallant spheare on the top which glistereth like gold. This royall pauilion hath fower gates, euerie one of which is kept by eunuches. Within the said pauilion are contained diuers other tents, among which is the kings lodging, being framed in such wise, that it may easily be remooued from place to place. Next vnto it stand the tents of the noblemen, and of such as are most in the kings fauour; then the lodgings of the principall guard beeing made of goatesskinnes, after the Arabian fashion; and in the middest of all stands the kings kitchin and his pantrie. Not farre from hence the light horsemen haue their aboade, who all of them are victualled out of the kings storehouse, notwithstanding their attire be verie base. Next of all are the stables, wherein their horses are maruellous well tended. Without this circuit keepe such as carrie the tents and the kings furniture from place to place. Here are also butchers, victuallers, and such like. All merchants & artificers that resort hither, take vp their aboad next vnto the tent-carriers: so that the kings pauilion is pitched like a strong citie, for it is so enuironed with the lodgings of the guarde, and with other tents adioining, that there is very difficult passage to the king. Round about the saide roiall pauilion, there are certaine appointed to watch and ward all night long, howbeit they are base and vnarmed people. In like

The King of Fez his maner of warfare.

sort there is a watch kept about the stables, but sometimes so negligently, that not onely some horses haue been stolne, but there haue beene founde enimies in the kings owne pauilion, that came to murther him. The king liueth the greatest part of the yeere in the fieldes, both for the safegard of his kingdome, and also that he may keepe his Arabian subiects in obedience, and sometimes he recreateth himselfe with hunting, and sometime with playing at chesse. I know right well how tedious I haue beene in the description of this citie: but bicause it is the metropolitan not onely of Barbary, but of all Africa, I thought good most particularly to decypher euerie parcell and member thereof.[84]

Of the towne of Macarmeda.

THis towne standeth almost twentie miles eastward of Fez, and was built by the familie of Zeneta, vpon the banke of a most beautifull riuer. It had in times past a large territorie, and great store of inhabitants. On both sides of the saide riuer are many gardens and vineyards. The kings of Fez were woont to assigne this towne vnto the gouernour of their camels; but in the warre of Sahid it was so destroied and wasted, that at this day scarce is there any mention of wals to be found. But the fields thereof are now in the possession of certaine gentlemen of Fez, and of the pesants.[85]

Of the castle of Hubbed.

THis castle standeth vpon the side of an hill, about sixe miles from Fez, and from hence you may beholde the citie of Fez, and all the territorie adiacent. It was founded by a certaine hermite of Fez, being reputed for a man of singular holines. The fields thereto belonging are not verie large, bicause the houses being demolished, it is vtterly destitute of inhabitants, the wals onely and the

temple as yet remaining. In this castle I liued fower
summers, becauseth it standeth in a most pleasant aire,
being separate from concurse of people, and a solitarie
place fitte for a man to studie in: for my father had got
a lease of the ground adioining to this castle from the
gouernour of the temple, for many yeeres.⁸⁶

Of the towne of Zauia.

THe towne of Zauia was founded by *Ioseph* the second
king of the Marin-family, and is distant from Fez
about fowerteene miles. Heere king *Ioseph* built a stately
hospitall, and commanded that his corps shoulde be
interred in this towne. But it was not his fortune heere to
be buried, for he was slaine in the warres against Tremizen.
From thencefoorth Zauia fell to decay and grew destitute
of inhabitants, wherein at this present the hospitall onely
remaineth. The reuenues of this place were giuen vnto
the great temple of Fez, but the fielde thereof was tilled by
certaine Arabians dwelling in the region of Fez.⁸⁷

Of the castle of Chaulan.

THe ancient castle of Chaulan is built vpon the riuer
Sebu, eight miles southward of Fez. Not farre from
this castle there is a certaine hot bath, whereunto *Abulhezen* *A hot bathe.*
the fourth king of the Marin-family added a faire building,
vnto this bath once a yeere in the moneth of Aprill the
gentlemen of Fez usually resort, remaining there fower or
fiue daies together. There is no ciuilitie to be found in
this castle: for the inhabitants are base people, and
exceeding couetous.⁸⁸

Of the mountaine of Zelag.

THis mountaine beginneth eastward from the riuer of
Sebu, extending thence almost fowerteene miles
westward, and the highest part thereof to the north, is seuen

miles distant from Fez. The south part of this mountaine is vtterly destitute of inhabitants; but the north side is exceeding fertile, and planted with great store of castles and townes. Most of their fields are imployed about vineyards, the grapes whereof are the sweetest that euer I tasted, and so likewise are their oliues, and other fruits· The inhabitants being verie rich, haue most of them houses in the citie of Fez. And so likewise most part of the gentlemen of Fez haue vineyards vpon the saide mountaine. At the north foote of this mountaine the fields are replenished with all kinde of graine and fruits. For all that plaine is watered southward with the riuer Sebu: and here the gardiners with certaine artificiall wheeles and engines draw water out of the riuer to moisten their gardens. In this plaine are wel-nigh two hundreth acres of ground, the reuenues whereof are giuen vnto the kings master of ceremonies, howbeit he maketh thereof not aboue fiue hundreth ducates a yeere: the tenth part of all which reuenues, amounting to three thousand bushels of corne, belongeth to the kings prouision.[80]

Of mount Zarhon.

THis mountaine beginneth from the plaine of Esais lying ten miles distant from the citie of Fez; westward it extendeth thirtie miles, and is almost ten miles broad. This mountaine is all couered with waste and desert woods, being otherwise well stored with oliues. In this mountaine there are of sheepe-foldes and castles to the number of fiftie, and the inhabitants are very wealthy, for it standeth betweene two flourishing cities, that is to say, Fez on the east, and Meenase on the west. The women weaue woollen cloth, according to the custome of that place, and are adorned with many siluer rings and bracelets. The men of this mountaine are most valiant, and are much giuen to pursue and take lions, whereof they send great store vnto the king of Fez. And the king hunteth the said lions in manner following: in a large *Hunting of lions vsed by the King of Fez.* field there are certaine little cels made, being so high, that a man may stand vpright in them : each one of these cels is shut fast with a little doore ; and containe within euery of them an armed man, who opening the doore presents himselfe to the view of the lion : then the lion seeing the doores open, comes running toward them with great furie, but the doores being shut againe, he waxeth more furious then before: then bring they foorth a bull to combate with the lion, who enter a fierce and bloudie conflict, wherein if the bull kill the lion, that daies sport is at an end ; but if the lion get the victorie, then all the armed men, being ordinarily tweluc, leape foorth of their cels, and inuade the lion : each one hauing a iauelin with a pike of a cubite and an halfe long. And if these armed men seeme to bee too hard for the lion, the king causeth their number to be diminished : but perceiuing them too weake, the king with his companie from a certaine high place, where he standeth to behold the sport, kill the lion with their crossebowes. And oftentimes it falleth out, that before the lion be slaine, some one of the men dies for it, the residue being sore wounded. The reward of those who encounter the lion is ten duckats apeece, and a new garment : neither are any admitted vnto this combat but men of redoubted valour, and such as come from mount Zelagi : but those that take the lions first are inhabitants of mount Zarhon.[90]

Of Gualili a towne of mount Zarhon.

THis towne was built by the Romanes vpon the top of the foresaide mountaine, what time they were lordes of Granada in south Spaine. It is enuironed around with mighty thicke walles made of smoothe and hewen stones. The gates are large and high, and the fields are manured for the space of sixe miles about: howbeit this towne was long sithence destroied by the Africans. But afterward when the schismatike *Idris* came into this region, he began to repaire this desolate towne, and to replant it so with inhabitants, that within short time it grew very populous: howbeit after his decease it was neglected by his sonne, being wholy addicted (as is beforesaid) vnto the building of Fez. And yet *Idris* lieth buried in this towne, whose sepulchre is visited with great reuerence almost by all the people of Barbarie, for he is as highly esteemed as if he had been some patriarke, because he was of the linage of Mahumet. At this present there are but two or three houses in all the towne, which were there built for the honour and maintenance of the sepulchre. The fields adiacent are exceedingly well husbanded: and their gardens are most pleasant by reason of two sweet freshets running through them, the which diuersly winding themselues about the little hils and vallies, doe water all that plaine.[91]

Of a certaine towne called the palace of Pharao.

THis towne was founded by the Romans vpon the top of an hill, about eight miles distant from Gualili. The people of this said mountaine, together with some historiographers are most certainly perswaded, that this towne was built by *Pharao* king of Egypt in the time of *Moses*, and tooke the name from the first founder, which notwithstanding I thinke to be otherwise: for I can read in no approued author that either *Pharao* or any other Egyptians euer inhabited these regions. But I suppose that this fond opinion was taken out of that booke which one *Elcabi* wrote concerning the words of Mahumet. For the said booke affirmeth from the authoritie of Mahumet, that there were fower kings onely that gouerned the whole world, two whereof were faithfull, and the other two

ethnikes: the faithfull he saith were *Alexander* the great,
and *Salomon* the sonne of *Dauid*: and the ethnikes were
Nimrod and *Pharao*. But I am rather of opinion, by the
Latine letters which are there engrauen in the walles,
that the Romanes built this towne. About this towne
run two small riuers on either side thereof. The little
hils and vallies adiacent doe greatly abound with oliues.
Not far from hence are certaine wilde deserts frequented
with lions and leopards.[92]

Of the towne called Pietra Rossa or The red rocke.

Pietra Rossa is a small towne built by the Romans vpon
the side of the foresaid mountaine, being so neere the
forrest, that the lions will come daily into the towne and *Tame lions.*
gather vp bones in the streets, yea, they are so tame and
familiar, that neither women nor children are afeard of
them. The wals of this towne are built very high and of
great stones, but now they are ruined in many places, and
the whole towne is diminished into one streete. Their
fields being ioyned vnto the plaines of Azgara, abound
with oliues and all kinde of pulse.[93]

Of the towne of Maghilla.

MAghilla is a little towne founded of old by the
Romans vpon that side of the foresaid hill which
looketh toward Fez. About this towne are most fertill
fields, and greatly enriched with oliues: there is a plaine
likewise containing many fresh fountaines, and well stored
with hempe and flaxe.[94]

Of the castle of Shame.

THis ancient castle is built at the foote of the said
mountaine neer vnto the high way from Fez to
Mecnase: and it was called by this name, because the
inhabitants are most shamefully addicted to couetise, like

vnto all the people thereabouts. In old time it is reported that a certaine king passed by, whom the inhabitants of the castle inuited to dinner, requesting him to change the ignominious name of the place : which when the king had condescended vnto, they caused, according to their custome, a companie of rams to be slaine, and certaine bladders and vessels to be filled with milke, to serue for the kings breakfast the morrow after. But because the said vessels were very large, they consulted together to put in halfe milke and halfe water, hoping that the king should neuer perceiue it. The day following albeit the king was not very hastie of his breakfast, yet, his seruants vrging him thereunto, he perceiued the milke to be halfe water ; whereat smiling he said : Friends, that which nature hath giuen, no man can take away. And with that saying he departed. Now this castle is razed to the ground & vtterly destroied, but the territorie thereof is occupied by certaine miserable Arabians.[95]

Of the region of Beni Guariten.

THe region of Beni Guariten lieth eastward of Fez about eighteene miles. It is altogether hillie and mountainous, abounding with all kind of pulse, and with store of good pasture and medow-ground, and containing almost two hundred villages. Their houses are in all places rudely built, and the inhabitants are base people, neither haue they any vineyards or gardens, nor any tree that beareth fruit. This region the king of Fez vsually diuideth among his yoongest brothers and sisters. The inhabitants haue great store of corne and wooll : and albeit they are passing rich, yet go they very meanly attired : they ride onely vpon asses, for which cause they are had in great derision by their neighbours.[96]

Of the region called Aseis.

This region is distant to the west of Fez almost twentie miles, and is by the inhabitants called Aseis; it consisteth of a perpetuall plaine, wherupon some coniecture that it hath had in olde time many villages and castles, whereof now there is no mention at all, nor so much as a signe of any building onely the names of places yet remaine. This region extendeth westward eighteene, and southward almost twenty miles. The soile is most fertile, and bringeth foorth blacke and small graines. Wels and fountaines are here very rare. It was woont to be subiect vnto certaine Arabian husbandmen, but now it is assigned by the king vnto the gouernor of that citie.[97]

Of Mount Togat.[98]

This mountaine standeth almost seuen miles westward of Fez, being very high, and but of small bredth. Eastward it extendeth to the riuer Bunase[99] being about fiue miles distant. All that side which looketh towards Fez, and the top thereof, and that part which lieth ouer against Essich[100] are woonderfully replenished with vines, and with all kinde of graine. Vpon the top of this mountaine are diuers caues and hollow places, where the searchers of treasure suppose that the Romans hid vp their wealth, as we haue before signified. The said treasure-searchers, so soone as the vintage is passed, vse to take great paines in digging of the rocke, and albeit they finde nothing, yet will they not giue ouer. All the fruits of this mountaine are most vnpleasant both to the eie and to the taste, and yet they are sooner ripe, then the fruits of other places thereabout.

Of mount Guraigura.

This mountaine being neer vnto Atlas is almost fortie miles distant from Fez. From hence springeth a certaine riuer, which running westward falleth into the riuer Bath. This mountaine standeth betweene two most large and spatious plaines, whereof the one to Fezward is (as we haue before said) called Aseis: and the other lying southward is named Adecsen. Which Adecsen is most fertile both for corne and pasture. And they are possessed by certaine Arabians called Zuhair being vassals vnto the king of Fez: but the king assigneth for the most part this plaine vnto his brother or some other of his kinsfolkes, out of which they yeerely gather ten thousand duckats. The foresaid Arabians are continually molested by certaine other Arabians called Elhusein, which liue in the deserts: for in summer-time they vsually inuade the plaines: wherefore the king of Fez for the defence of this region mainteineth a certaine number of horsemen and of crossebowes. This plaine is watered with christall-fountaines and pleasant riuers. Neere vnto the said plaine are diuers woods and forrests, where lions keepe which are so gentle and tame, that any man may driue them away with a staffe, neither doe they any harme at all. Now let vs proceede vnto the description of Azgara.[101]

Tame lions.

A description of Azgara, one of the seuen principall regions belonging to the kingdome of Fez

This region bordereth northward vpon the Ocean-sea; westward vpon the riuer of Buragrag; eastward vpon the mountaines partly of Gumera, partly of Zarhon, and partly of Zalag; and southward it is inclosed with the riuer of Bunasar. This region consisteth altogether of plaine ground being a most fertile soile, and in olde

time very populous, and adorned with many townes
and castles, which are now so defaced and ruined by
reason of wars, that small villages onely are left for
the inhabitants to hide their heads in. The length of
this region is about fowerscore, and the bredth almost
three score miles. Through the midst thereof runneth
the riuer of Subu. The Arabian inhabitants are called
Elculoth, being descended from the familie of Muntafic;
they are subiect to the king of Fez, and pay vnto him
large tributes: howbeit they are rich, and curious in their
apparell, and are such valiant soldiers, that the king of
Fez leuieth his whole armie of them onely, when he hath
any warres of great moment to atchieue. This region
abundantly furnisheth not onely Fez, but all the mountaines of Gumera with victuals, horses, and other cattell;
and here the king of Fez vsually remaineth all winter and
the spring, by reason of the temperature and holesomnes
of the aire. Here is great plentie of roes and hares, and
yet very few woods.[102]

Of Giumha a towne in Azgara.

THis towne the Africans built in our time by a riuers
side vpon that plaine ouer which the way lieth
from Fez to the citie of Harais, and it is distant from Fez
about thirtie miles. It was in times past very populous,
but now it lieth so desolate by reason of the war of *Sahid*,
that it serueth onely for caues and receptacles for the
Arabians to lay vp their corne in, for the sauegard
whereof they pitch certaine tents neere vnto the place.[103]

Of the towne of Harais.

THis towne was founded by the ancient Africans vpon
the Ocean sea shore, neere vnto the mouth of the
riuer Luccus, one side thereof adioining vpon the said
riuer, and the other side vpon the maine Ocean. When

the Moores were lords of Arzilla and Tangia, this towne was well inhabited: but those two townes being woon by the Christians, Harais remained destitute of inhabitants, almost twentie yeeres together: howbeit afterward the king of Fez his sonne, fearing the Portugals inuasion, caused it strongly to bee fortified and kept with a perpetuall garrison. The passage vnto this towne by the riuers mouth is very dangerous and difficult. Likewise the kings sonne caused a castle to be built, wherein is maintained a garrison of two hundred crosse-bowes, an hundred Harquebusiers, & three hundred light horsemen. Neere vnto the towne are diuers medowes and fennes where the townesmen take great store of eeles and of water-fowles. Vpon this riuers side are huge and solitarie woods haunted with lions and other wilde beastes. The inhabitants of this towne vse to transport coales by sea to Arzilla and Tangia, whereupon the Moores vse for a common prouerbe, A ship of Harais, which they alleage when a man after great brags and promises performeth trifles; for these ships hauing sailes of cotton, which make a gallant shew, are laden with nought but base coales: for the territorie of this citie aboundeth greatly with cotton.[104]

Of the towne called Casar Elcabir, that is, The great palace.

A pleasant discourse how King Mansor was entertained by a fisher.

THis large towne was built in the time of *Mansor* the king and patriarke of Maroco; of whom this notable historie is reported, namely, that the said king, as he rode on hunting, being separated from his companie by tempestuous weather, came vnto a certaine vnknowen place, where if he continued all night, fearing least he should die in the fens, he looked round about him, and at length espied a fisher getting of eeles: can you, my friend (quoth the king) conduct me to the court? The

court (saith the fisher) is ten miles distant. Howbeit, the
king intreating hard to be conducted; if king *Mansor*
himselfe were present (quoth the fisher) I could not at
this present conduct him, for feare least he should be
drowned in the fennes. Then answered *Mansor:* what
hast thou to doe with the kings life or safetie? Marie
(quoth the fisher) I am bound to loue the king as well as
mine owne life. Then haue you obtained some singular
benefite at his handes, said the king. What greater
benefit (quoth the fisher) can be expected at the kings
hand, then iustice, loue, and clemencie, which he vouchsafeth vnto his subiects; by whose fauour and wisdome
I sillie fisher with my poore wife and children liue a most
quiet and contented life, so that I can euen at midnight
haue free egresse and regresse vnto this my cottage
amidst these vallies and desert fennes, no man lying in
wait to doe me iniurie? But (gentle Sir) whatsoeuer you
be, if you please to be my guest for this night, you shall
be right welcome, and to morrow morning betimes I will
attend vpon you at your pleasure. Then the king went
vnto the fishers cottage, where after his horse was prouided
for, the fisher caused some eeles to be rosted for his supper,
while he sate drying of his garments by the fire: but the
king not being contented with this fare, demanded if his
host had any flesh in the house: Sir (quoth he) I haue a
shee-goate and a kid, and they are all my substance of
cattell: but because by your countenance you seeme to be
some honourable personage, I will aduenture my kid for
your sake; and so without any more words he caused his
wife to kill it & roste it. Thus the king remained the
fishers guest all night: and the next morning about sun-rise,
being scarcely gone out of the doores with his liberall host,
he espied a great companie of his gentlemen and hunters
whooping and hallowing for their king amidst the fennes,
but when they saw him, they all greatly reioiced. Then

Mansor turning him to the fisher, told him what he was, promising that his liberalitie should not be vnrewarded. Neere vnto the place were certaine faire castles and palaces, which the king at his departure gaue vnto the fisher in token of thankfulnes; and being by the fisher requested, for declaration of his farther loue, to enuiron the said buildings with wals, he condescended thereunto. From thencefoorth the fisher remained lord and gouernour of that new citie, which in processe of time grew so large, that within these fewe yeeres it contained fower hundred families. And because the soile neer vnto it is so fertile, the king vsed to make his aboad thereabout all summer time, which was a great benefit to the towne.[106] By the walles of this towne runneth the riuer Luccus, which sometimes encreaseth so, that it floweth to the citie gates.[107] In this towne are practised diuers manuarie artes and trades of merchandize: also it hath many temples, one college of students, and a stately hospitall. They haue neither springs nor wels, but onely cesternes in stead thereof. The inhabitants are liberall honest people, though not so wittie as some others. Their apparell is but meane, but being of cotton-cloth, and wrapped often about their bodies. In the suburbes are great store of gardens replenished with all kinde of fruits. Their grapes are vnsauourie, because the soile is fitter for medow-ground. Euery munday they haue a market vpon the next plaine, whither their neighbours the Arabians vsually resort.[108] In the moneth of May they goe foorth of their towne a fowling, and take great store of turtles. Their ground is exceeding fruitfull, and yeeldeth thirtie fold increase: but it cannot be tilled for sixe miles about, bicause the Portugals garrison at Arzilla which is but eighteene miles distant, doth so molest and endomage them: whom likewise the gouernour of this towne with three hundred horsemen continually encountereth, and sometime proceedeth euen to the gates of Arzilla.[109]

Read Osorius lib. 2. de rebus gestis Eman. concerning this towne.

Of the region of Habat.

THis region[110] beginneth southward from the riuer of Guarga,[111] and bordereth northward vpon the Ocean, westward it adioineth vnto the fennes of Argar,[112] and eastward it abutteth vpon those mountaines which are next vnto the streites of Gibraltar. In bredth it stretcheth fower score, and in length almost an hundreth miles. The fruitefulnes of the soile, and the abundance of corne cannot easily be described: it is almost a perpetuall plaine, watered with many riuers: howbeit heretofore it hath beene more noble and famous, by reason of the ancient cities built partly by the Romans and partly by the Goths: and I thinke it be the same region which *Ptolemey* called Mauritania; but since Fez was first built, it hath fallen into woonderfull decay. Moreouer *Idris* the founder of Fez leauing ten sonnes behinde him, bestowed this region vpon the eldest:[113] afterward ensued a rebellion of diuers Mahumetan heretiques and lords, one faction of whom suing for aide at the gouernour of Granada, and others seeking aide from certaine gouernours of Cairaoan, they were all vanquished and put to flight by the Mahumetan patriark of Cairaoan: who hauing thus subdued the region, left it vnder garrison and returned home. After the great chancelour of Cordoua leuying an huge armie, conquered all this countrey euen to the borders of the region of Zab. Fiftie yeeres after king *Ioseph* of the Luntune family, chasing out the people of Granada, obtained the saide prouince by force: and last of all the king of Fez enioied it.

Of Ezaggen a towne of Habat.

THis towne was built by the ancient Africans vpon the side of a mountaine, almost ten miles distant from Guarga: all of which distance being plaine ground, serueth for corn-fields and gardens: howbeit the hilles are farre more fruitfull. This towne is distant from Fez almost three-score and ten miles, and containeth to the number of fiue hundred families, out of the territorie whereof there is the summe of tenne thousand ducates yeerely gathered for tribute, with which tribute the gouernour of the same towne is bound to maintaine on the kings behalfe fower hundred horsemen, for the defence of the whole region. For they are often molested with inuasions of the Portugals, who proceed wasting and spoiling the countrey, sometimes fortie, and sometimes fiftie miles. Here is but little ciuility to be found, neither are the people but homely apparelled, though they be verie rich. They haue a priuilege granted them by the ancient kings of Fez to drinke wine, which is otherwise forbidden by the law of Mahumet, and yet none of them all will abstaine from drinking it.[114]

Of the towne called Bani Teude.

THis ancient towne was built also by the Africans on a large plaine by the riuer of Guarga, fiue and fortie miles from the citie of Fez. In the prosperitie thereof it contained to the number of eight thousand families, but afterward it was so destroied by the wars of the Patriarkes of Cairaoan, that now the towne wall is only remaining. At my being there I sawe diuers monuments and sepulchres of noblemen, and certaine conducts curiously built of excellent marble. From this towne mount Gumera is almost fowerteene miles distant : the fieldes adiacent being good arable, and very fruitfull.[115]

Of the towne of Mergo.

MErgo standing vpon the toppe of a mountaine is from Bani Teude about ten miles distant. Some thinke that the Romans were founders of this towne, bicause there are found vpon the ancient ruines certaine Latine letters ingrauen. But now it is quite destitute of inhabitants, howbeit vpon the side of the same mountaine standeth another small towne inhabited with weauers of course cloth; from whence you may behold the riuer Subu to the south, and the riuer Guarga to the north, from which riuers the saide towne is fiue miles distant. The inhabitants loue to bee accounted gentlemen, albeit they are couetous, ignorant, and destitute of all goodnes.[116]

Of the towne of Tansor.

TAnsor standeth vpon a little hill, almost ten miles from Mergo, and containeth three hundreth families, but very fewe artificers. The inhabitants are rude and barbarous people, hauing neither vineyardes nor gardens, but onely exercising husbandry, and possessing abundance of cattle. This towne standeth in the midde way between Fez and mount Gumera, which (I thinke) is the occasion, that the inhabitants are so couetous and void of humanitie.[117]

Of the towne of Agla.

THis ancient towne was built by the Africans vpon the banke of the riuer Guarga. The fruitfull fields thereof are manured by the Arabians: but the towne it selfe hath beene so wasted with warre, that nowe there is nothing to be seene but in a few places the ruines of houses & wals, & certaine pits. In the suburbes there is euery weeke a great market, wherunto the next Arabians vsually resort; and so do some merchants of Fez likewise, to buie oxe hides, wooll, and waxe, which are the principall commodities of that place. Hereabouts keepe great store of lions, but they are by nature so fearefull, that they will flee at the voice of a childe: hence commeth the prouerbe so rife in Fez; A lion of Agla: which they applie vnto such a one as maketh great brags, and is but a meere dastard.[11?]

The occasion a prouerbe.

Of the castle of Narangia.

THe castle of Narangia built by the Africans vpon a little hill not farre from the riuer Luccus, is almost ten miles distant from Ezaggen. It hath most fruitfull corn-fields, but no plaines belonging vnto it. Along the riuers side are huge deserts, wherein grow great store of wilde fruits, especially cherries, such as the Italians call *Ciriegie marine*. This castle was surprised and sacked by the Portugals in the yeere of the Hegeira 895. which was in the yeere of our Lord, 1486.[119]

Of the Isle of Gesira.

THe Isle of Gesira[120] lying not farre from the mouth of the riuer Luccus, is distant from the sea about ten, and from Fez about an hundreth miles. There was in times past a little ancient towne vpon this Island, which was abandoned when the Portugals first made warre vpon Barbarie. About the saide riuer are many deserts, but very fewe corn-fields. In the yeere of the Hegeira 894. the king of Portugall sent hither a great armie, which being landed on the Isle, the generall of the field built a strong fort thereupon, by meanes whereof he hoped to be free from the enimies inuasion, and to enioy the fields adiacent. But the king of Fez, namely his father that *nowe reigneth, foreseeing the damage that he shoulde sustaine, if he permitted the saide fort to be finished, leuied a mightie armie to withstand the Portugals proceedings. Howbeit, so great was the force of their ordinance, that the Moores durst not approch within two miles of the Portugal campe. Wherefore the Fessan king being almost out of hope, was perswaded by some that were about him to stoppe vp the riuer with postes and raftes two miles from the Island: by which meanes the Moores being defended, and hauing cut downe all the woodes adioining, the Portugals perceiued

An attempt and defeate of the Portugals.

* 1562.

the passage of the riuer in short time to be choaked and stopped vp with great trees, and that there was no possibilitie for them to depart. Then the king hoping easily to ouercome the Portugales, determined to assaile their fort: but considering he could not do it without great slaughter of his people, he couenanted with the Portugall generall, that besides a great summe of money paide vnto him, the saide generall shoulde obtaine of the Portugall king to haue certaine daughters of the king of Fez his gouernour (which were at that time prisoners in Portugall) to be restored, and that then he would freely dismisse him and his companie: which being done, the Portugall armie returned home.

Of the towne of Basra.

This towne containing almost two thousand families, was built by Mahumet the sonne of *Idris*,[121] which was the founder of Fez, vpon a certaine plaine betweene two mountaines, being distant from Fez about fowerscore, and from Casar[122] southward almost twentie miles. And it was named Basra for the memorie of a citie in Arabia Fœlix called by that name, where *Hali* the fourth Mahumetan patriarke after *Mahumet*, and great grandfather vnto *Idris* was slaine. It was in times past enuironed with most high and impregnable wals: and so long as it was gouerned by the posteritie of *Idris*, the people were verie ciuill; for *Idris* his successours vsed alwaies to remaine there in sommer time, by reason of the pleasant situation of the place, the hils and valleies being beautified with sweete gardens, and yeelding corne in abundance: and that both by reason of the vicinitie of the towne, and of the neighbour-hood of the riuer Luccus. Moreouer, in old time this towne was verie populous, being adorned with many faire temples, and inhabited with most ciuill people: but the family of *Idris* decaying, it became a pray vnto the enemie. At this present the ruines of the wals are onely to be seene, and certaine forlorne gardens, which, because the ground is not manured, bring foorth naught but wilde fruits.[123]

Of the towne called Howar.

This towne was built by one *Hali* a disciple of the foresaid Mahumet vpon a little hill, and by a riuers side, being situate about fourteene miles to the north of Casar, and sixteene miles to the south of Arzilla: which although it be but a small towne, yet it is well fortified and fairely built, and enuironed with fruitfull fieldes, vineyardes, and gardens replenished with woonderfull varietie of fruits. The inhabitants being most of them linnen-weauers, gather and prouide great store of flaxe. But euer since the Portugals woon Arzilla, this towne hath remained desolate.[124]

A description of the citie of Arzilla.

The great citie of Arzilla called by the Africans Azella, was built by the Romans vpon the Ocean sea shore, about seuentie miles from the streits of Gibraltar, and an hundred and fortie miles from Fez.[125] It was in times past subiect vnto the prince of Septa or Ceuta, who was tributarie to the Romans, and was afterward taken by the Goths, who established the said prince in his former gouernment: but the Mahumetans wan it in the yeere of the Hegeira 94. and helde the same for two hundred and twenty yeeres, till such time as the English at the persuasion of the Goths besieged it with an huge armie; and albeit the Goths were enemies to the English, because themselues were Christians, and the English worshippers of idols, yet the Goths perswaded them to this attempt, hoping by that meanes to draw the Mahumetans out of Europe. The English hauing good successe tooke the citie, and so

The taking of Arzilla by the English.

wasted it with fire and sword, that scarce one citizen escaped, so that it remained almost thirtie yeeres voide of inhabitants.[126] But afterward when the Mahumetan patriarks of Cordoua were lords of Mauritania, it was againe reedified, and by all meanes augmented, enriched and fortified. The inhabitants were rich, learned, and valiant. The fields adiacent yeeld graine and pulse of all sorts in great abundance, but because the towne standeth almost ten miles from the mountaines, it sustaineth great want of wood; howbeit they haue coales brought them from Harais, as is aforesaid. In the yeere of the Hegeira 882. this citie was suddenly surprised and taken by the Portugalles, and all the inhabitants carried prisoners into Portugall, amongst whom was *Mahumet* the king of Fez that now is, who together with his sister being both children of seuen yeeres old, were taken and led captiue.[127] For the father of this *Mahumet* seeing the prouince of Habat reuolt from him, went and dwelt at Arzilla, the very same time, when *Esserif* a great citizen of Fez, hauing slaine *Habdulac* the last king of the Marin-familie, was by the fauour of the people aduanced vnto the Fessan kingdome. Afterward one *Saic Abra* being pricked forward with ambition, went about to conquer the citie of Fez, and to make himselfe king; howbeit *Esserif* by the aduise of a certaine counsellour of his, being couzin vnto *Saic*, vanquished and put to flight the saide *Saic* to his great disgrace. Moreouer while *Esserif* had sent his said counsellour to Temesna, to pacifie the people of that prouince being about to rebell, *Saic* returned, and hauing for one whole yeere besieged new Fez with eight thousand men, at length by treason of the townesmen he easily wan it, and compelled *Esserif* with all his familie, to flee vnto the kingdome of Tunis. The same time therefore that *Saic* besieged Fez, the king of Portugall (as is aforesaid) sending a fleete into Africa, tooke Arzilla, and then was

Arzilla taken by the Portugals.

Habdulac the last king of the Marin family.

K K

the king of Fez that now is with his yoong sister caried
captiue into Portugall, where he remained seuen yeeres,
in which space he learned the Portugall-language most
exactly. At length with a great summe of money his
father ransomed him out of Portugall, who afterward being
aduanced to the kingdome, was by reason of his long
continuance in Portugall called king *Mahumet* the Portugall
This king afterward attempted very often to be auenged
of the Portugals, and to recouer Arzilla. Wherefore
suddenly encountring the said citie he beat down a great
part of the wall, and entring the breach, set all the captiue-
Moores at libertie. The Christians retired into the castle,
promising within two daies to yeeld vnto the king. But
Pedro Nauarro comming in the meane season with a great
fleet, they compelled the king with continuall discharging
of their ordinance, not onely to relinquish the citie, but also
to depart quite away with his whole armie: afterward it
was so fortified on all sides by the Portugals, that the said
king attempting often the recouerie thereof, had alwaies
the repulse. I my selfe seruing the king in the foresaid
expedition could find but fiue hundred of our companie
slaine. But the warre against Arzilla continued from the
yeere of the Hegeira 914. to the yeere 921.[128]

Read Osorius lib. 5. de rebus gestis Eman.

Iohn Leo serued the king of Fez in his warrs against Arzilla.

Of the citie of Tangia.

THe great and ancient citie of Tangia called by the
Portugals Tangiara, according to the fond opinion of
some historiographers, was founded by one *Sedded* the
sonne of *Had*, who (as they say) was emperour ouer the
whole world. This man (say they) determined to build a
citie, which for beautie might match the earthly paradise.
Wherefore he compassed the same with walles of brasse,
and the roofes of the houses he couered with gold and
siluer, for the building whereof he exacted great tributes of
all the cities in the world. But the classicall and approoued

authors affirme that it was built by the Romanes vpon the
Ocean sea shore, at the same time when they subdued the
kingdome of Granada.* From the streites of Gibraltar it is * *Or Batica.*
distant almost thirtie, and from Fez an hundred and fiftie
miles. And from the time that the Goths were first lordes
of Granada, this citie was subiect vnto *Septa* or *Ceuta*, vntill
it and Arzilla were woon by the Mahumetans. It hath
alwaies beene a ciuill, famous, and well-peopled towne, and
very stately and sumptuously built. The field thereto
belonging is not very fertill, nor apt for tilth : howbeit not
far off are certaine vallies continually watred with fountaines, which furnish the said citie with all kinde of fruits in
abundance. Without the citie also growe certaine vines,
albeit vpon a sandie soile. It was well stored with inhabitants, till such time as Arzilla was surprized by the Portugals : for then the inhabitants being dismaied with rumours
of warres, tooke vp their bag and baggage and fled vnto
Fez. Whereupon the king of Portugall his deputie at
Arzilla sent one of his captaines thither, who kept it so
long vnder the obedience of the king, till the king of Fez
sent one of his kinsmen also to defend a region of great
importance neere vnto the mountaines of Gumera, being
enemie to the Christians. Twentie fiue yeeres before the
Portugall king wan this citie, he sent foorth an armada
against it, hoping that the citie being destitute of aide,
while the king of Fez was in warres against the rebels of
Mecnase, would soone yield it selfe. But contrarie to the
Portugals expectation the Fessan king concluding a sudden
truce with them of Mecnase, sent his counsellour with an
armie, who encountring the Portugals, made a great
slaughter of them, and amongst the rest slue their generall,
whom he caused to be caried in a case or sacke vnto new
Fez, and there to be set vpon an high place where all men
might behold him. Afterward the king of Portugall sent
a new supply, who suddenly assailing the citie in the night,

were most of them slaine, and the residue enforced to flee. But that which the Portugall-king could not bring to passe with those two Armadas, he atchieued at length (as is aforesaid) with small forces and little disaduantage. In my time *Mahumet* king of Fez left no meanes vnattempted for the recouerie of this citie, but so great alwaies was the valour of the Portugals, that he had euer ill successe. These things were done in the yeere of the Hegeira 917, which was in the yeere of our Lord 1508.[129]

Of the towne called Casar Ezzaghir, that is, the little palace.

THis towne was built by *Mansor* the king and Patriarke of Maroco vpon the Ocean sea shore, about twelue miles from Tangia, and from Septa eighteene miles. It was built (they say) by *Mansor*, because euerie yeere when he passed into the Prouince of Granada, hee was constrained with his whole armie to march ouer the rough and ragged mountaines of Septa, before he could come vnto the sea shore. It standeth in an open and pleasant place ouer against the coast of Granada. It was well peopled in times past, part of the inhabitants beeing weauers and merchants, and the rest mariners, that vsed to transport the wares of Barbarie into Europe. This towne the king of Portugall tooke by a sudden surprise. And the Fessan king hath laboured by all meanes to recouer it, but euer with ill successe. These things were done in the yeere of the Hegeira 863.[130]

Casar Ezzaghir taken by the king of Portugall.

Of the great citie of Septa.

Epta, called by the Latines, *Ciuitas*, and by the Portugals, *Scupta*, was (according to our most approoued Authors) built by the Romanes vpon the streits of Gibraltar, being in olde time the head citie of all Mauritania; wherefore the Romanes made great account thereof, insomuch that it became verie ciuill, and was throughly inhabited. Afterward it was woone by the Gothes, who appointed a gouernour there; and it continued in their possession, till the Mahumetans invading Mauritania surprised it also.[131] The occasion whereof was one *Iulian* Earle of Septa; who being greatly iniuried by *Roderigo* king of the Gothes and of Spaine, ioyned with the infidels, conducted them into Granada, and caused *Roderigo* to loose both his life and his kingdome. The Mahumetans therefore hauing taken Septa, kept possession thereof on the behalfe of one *Elgualid*, sonne of *Habdulmalic* their Patriarke, who then was resident at Damasco, in the yeere of the Hegeira 92.[132] From thenceforth till within these fewe yeeres, this citie grewe so ciuill and so well stored with inhabitants, that it prooued the most worthie and famous citie of all Mauritania. It contained many temples and colledges of students, with great numbers of artizans, and men of learning and of high spirite. Their artizans excelled especially in workes of brasse, as namely in making of candlesticks, basons, standishes, and such like commodities, which were as pleasant to the eie, as if they had beene made of siluer or gold. The Italians haue great cunning in making of the like, but their workmanship is nothing comparable to theirs of *Septa. Without the citie are diuers faire villages and granges, especially in that place which for the abundance of vines is called The vine-

The entrance of the Moores into Granada.

* *Or ceuta.*

yards: howbeit the fields are verie barren and fruitles, for which cause their corne is exceeding deere.[133] Both without and within the citie there is a pleasant and beautifull prospect to the shore of Granada vpon the streits of Gibraltar, from whence you may discerne liuing creatures, the distance being but 12. miles. Howbeit this famous citie not many yeeres since was greatly afflicted by *Habdulmumen* the king and patriarke: who hauing surprised it, razed the buildings, and banished the principal inhabitants thereof.[134] And not long after it sustained as great damage by the king of Granada, who (besides the foresaide harmes) carried the nobles and chiefe citizens captiues into Granada. And lastly in the yeere of *Mahumet* his Hegeira 818. being taken by a Portugall-armada, all the citizens did abandon it.[135] *Abu Sahid* being then king of Fez, and a man of no valour, neglected the recouerie thereof: but in the midst of his dauncing and disport being aduertised that it was lost, he would not so much as interrupt his vaine pastime: wherefore by gods iust iudgement, both himselfe and his sixe sonnes were all slaine in one night by his Secretarie, in whom he reposed singular trust, because hee would haue defloured the said Secretaries wife. These things came to passe in the yeere of the Hegeira 824. Afterward, the kingdome of Fez being eight yeeres destitute of a king, a sonne of the murthered king whom he begot of a Christian woman, and who the same night that his father was slaine fled vnto Tunis, succeeded in the gouernment: this was *Habdulac* the last king of the Marin family, who likewise (as is aforesaide) was slaine by the people.[136]

The streits of Gibraltar from Septa but 12 miles broad.

Septa taken by the Portugals.

Abu Sahid king of Fez and his sixe sonnes slaine all in one night.

Of the towne of Tetteguin, now called Tetuan.

THis towne being built by the ancient Africans eighteene miles from the streits of Gibraltar, and sixe miles from the maine Ocean, was taken by the

Mahumetans at the same time when they woon Septa from the Gothes. It is reported that the Gothes bestowed the gouernment of this towne vpon a woman with one eie, who weekly repairing thither to receiue tribute, the inhabitants named the towne Tetteguin, which signifieth in their language an eie.[137] Afterward being often assayled and encountered by the Portugals, the inhabitants forsooke it, and it remained fowerscore and fifteene yeeres desolate : which time being expired, it was reedified and replanted a new with inhabitants by a certaine captaine of Granada, who together with his king being expelled thence by *Ferdinando* king of Castile, departed vnto Fez. This famous captaine that shewed himselfe so valiant in the warres of Granada was called by the Portugals Almandali. Who hauing obtained the gouernment of this towne, and gotten licence to repaire it, enuironed the same with new wals, and built an impregnable castle therein compassed with a deepe ditch. Afterward making continuall warre against the Portugals, he extremely molested and endamaged their townes of Septa, Casar, and Tangia : for with three hundred valiant horsemen of Granada he made daily incursions and inroades vpon the Christians, and those that he tooke, he put to continuall labour and toile about the building of his forts. Vpon a time I my selfe trauelling this way saw three thousand Christian captiues, who being clad in course sacke-cloth, were constrained in the night to lye fettered in deepe dungeons. This captaine was exceeding liberal vnto all African and Mahumetan strangers that passed by : howbeit within these few yeeres one of his eies being thrust out with a dagger, and the other waxing dim with age, he deceased ; leauing the towne after his death vnto his nephew, who was a most valiant man.[138]

Of the mountaines of Habat.

Amongst the mountaines of Habat there be eight more famous then the rest, all which are inhabited by the people of Gumera, who vse one generall forme and custome of liuing: for all of them maintaine Mahumets religion, albeit they drinke wine contrarie to his precept. They are proper men of personage and much addicted to industrie & labour, but for the wars they are verie unfit. Subiect they are vnto the king of Fez, who imposeth such heauie tribute vpon them, so that besides a few (of whom we will speake hereafter) the residue are scarce able to finde themselues apparell.

Of mount Rahona.

This mountaine being neere unto Ezaggen, containeth in length thirtie miles, and in breadth twelue miles. It aboundeth with oyle, hony, and vines. The inhabitants are principally imployed about making of sope and trying of waxe. Wines they haue great store both browne and white. They pay vnto the king of Fez for yeerely tribute three thousand ducates, which being allowed vnto the gouernour of Ezaggen, he maintaineth fower hundred horsemen in the kings seruice.[139]

Of the mountaine called Beni-Fenescare.

This mountaine of Fenescare adioyning vnto mount Rahon, is about fiue and twentie miles long, and eight miles broad. It is better peopled then Rahon, hauing many leather-dressers, and weauers of course cloth, and yeelding great abundance of waxe. Euery Saturday they haue a great market, where you may finde all kinde of chapmen and of wares; insomuch that the Genoueses come hither to buy oxe hides and waxe, which they conuey into Portugall and Italy. Out of this mountaine is yeerely collected for tribute the summe of sixe thousand ducates, three thousand whereof are allowed vnto the gouernour of Ezaggen, the residue being payd into the kings exchequer.[140]

Of the mountaine called Beni-Haros.

This mountaine standing neer vnto Casar extendeth northward eight, and westward 20. miles. It containeth but sixe miles onely in bredth. It was wont to be well peopled and inhabited with gentlemen, who, when the Portugals woon Arzilla, cruelly vsurping ouer the people, compelled them to flee and leaue the mountaine desolate. There are at this present certaine cottages vpon the mountaine; but all the residue lyeth wast. While this mountaine continued in good estate, it allowed yeerely vnto the gouernor of Casar three thousand ducates.[141]

Of mount Chebib.

VPon this mountaine are sixe or seuen castles inhabited with ciuill and honest people: for when the Portugals wan Tangia, the citizens fled vnto this mountaine beeing but twentie miles distant. The inhabitants are perpetually molested with the Portugals inuasions: the tributes of this mountaine being halfe diminished since the losse of Tangia, waxe euery day woorse and woorse, because the garrison is thirtie miles distant, and cannot come to succour them so often as the Portugals come to waste and spoyle their territories.[142]

Of the mountaine called Beni Chessen.

This mountaine is of an exceeding height, and very hard to be encountred: for besides the naturall fortification thereof, it is inhabited with most valiant people. These inhabitants being oppressed with the tyrannie of their gouernours, rose vp at length in armes

against them, & brought them to great miserie and
distresse. Whereupon a yoong gentleman, one of their
said gouernours, disdaining to submit himselfe vnto the
yoke of his inferiours, went to serue in the king of Granada
his warres, where being trained vp a long time in martiall
discipline against the Christians, he prooued an expert
warriour: and so at length returning vnto one of his
natiue mountaines, he gathered a certaine troupe of horsemen, and valiantly defended the said mountaine from the
Portugals inuasions: whereof the king of Fez being
aduertised, sent him an hundred and fiftie crossebowes:
which he imploied to the subduing of that mountaine, and
to the conquest of the mountaines of his enemies. But
after he began to vsurpe the kings tribute in the same
mountaine, the king waxing wroth sent foorth an huge
armie against him. Howbeit vpon his repentant submission, the king pardoned him, and ordained him
gouernour of Seusauon, and of all the region adiacent.
After him succeeded in the same gouernment one of the
linage of *Mahumet*, and of *Idris* the founder of Fez. This
man became very famous among the Portugals, and by
reason of his nobilitie (for he was of the familie called
Helibenres) he grew vnto great renowme.[143]

Of mount Angera.

IT standeth southward of Casar the lesse almost eight
miles, being tenne miles long and three miles broad.
The soile thereof is exceeding fruitful, and in times past
greatly abounded with woods, which being cut downe by
the inhabitants, were sent to Casar for the building of
ships: which at that time had a great fleete belonging
thereunto. This mountaine likewise yeelded abundance of
flaxe; and the inhabitants were partly weauers and partly
mariners. Howbeit when the foresaid towne of Casar was
woon by the Portugals, this mountaine also was forsaken

by the inhabitants: and yet at this day all the houses stand still, as if the inhabitants had not forsaken it at all.[144]

Of mount Quadres.

THis high mountaine standing in the midst betweene Septa and Tetteguin, is inhabited with most valiant and warlike people, whose valour sufficiently appeered in the warres betweene the king of Granada, and the Spanyards; where the inhabitants onely of this mountaine preuailed more then all the armed Moores beside.[145] Vpon the said mountaine was borne one called by them *Hellul*: this *Hellul* atchieued many woorthie exploits against the Spanyards; the historie whereof is set downe partly in verse and partly in prose, and is as rife in Africa and Granada, as is the storie of *Orlando* in Italie. But at length in the Spanish warre (wherein *Ioseph Enesir* king and patriarke of Maroco was vanquished) this *Hellul* was slaine in a castle of Catalonia, called by the Moores, The castle of the eagle. In the same battell were slaine three- *Threescore thousand* score thousand Moores, so that none of them escaped saue *Moores slaine.* the king and a few of his nobles. This was done in the yeere of the Hegeira 609. which was in the yeere of our Lord 1160. From thenceforth the Spanyards had alwaies good successe in their warres, so that they recouered all those cities which the Moores had before taken from them. And from that time till the yeere wherein king *Ferdinando* conquered Granada, there passed (according to the Arabians account) 285. yeeres.[146]

Of the mountaine called Beni Guedarfeth.

THis mountaine standing not farre from Tetteguin (although it be not very large) is well fraught with inhabitants. The people are very warlike, being in pay vnder the gouernour of Tetteguin, whom they greatly honour and attend vpon him in all his attempts against the Christians: for which cause they pay no tribute vnto the king of Fez, vnlesse it be for their fieldes, which is very little. They reape much commoditie out of those mountaines, for there groweth great abundance of boxe, whereof the Fessan combes are made.[147]

A description of Errif one of the seuen regions of Fez.

Westward this region beginneth neere vnto the streites of Gibraltar, and extendeth eastward to the riuer of Nocor, which distance containeth about an hundred and fortie miles. Northward it bordereth vpon the Mediterran sea, and stretcheth fortie miles southward vnto those mountaines which lie ouer against the riuer Guarga and the territorie of Fez. This region is very vneeuen, being full of exceeding colde mountaines and waste deserts, which are replenished with most beautifull and straight trees: Here is no corne growing, they haue great store of vines, figs, oliues, & almonds. The inhabitants of this region are valiant people, but so excessiuely giuen to drinking, that they scarcely reserue wherewithall to apparell themselues, Head-cattell they haue but fewe: howbeit vpon their mountaines they haue great plentie of goates, asses, and apes. Their townes are but few: and their castles and villages are very homely built without any plancher or stories, much like to the stables of Europe, and are couered with thatch or with the barke of trees. All the inhabitants of this region haue the balles of their throat-pipes very great, and are vnciuill and rude people.[148]

Of the towne of Terga.

This small towne (as some thinke) built by the Goths vpon the shore of the Mediterran sea, is distant from the streits of Gibraltar about fowerscore miles, and containeth to the number of fiue hundred families. The towne wall is of no force. The inhabitants are most part of them fishers ; who getting great abundance of fish, salt them, and carrie them to sell almost an hundred miles southward. This towne was in times past well stored with people, but since the Portugals entered the same region, it hath fallen greatly to decay. Not farre from this towne groweth abundance of wood vpon the ragged and cold mountaines. And albeit the inhabitants are valiant, yet are they rusticall and void of all humanitie.[149]

Of Bedis, otherwise called Velles de Gumera.

His ancient towne built vpon the Mediterran sea shore, & called by the Spaniards *Velles de Gumera*, containeth about sixe hundred families. Some writers there are that affirme it to be built by the Africans, and others by the Gothes ; so that it remaineth as yet vncertaine who were the true founders thereof. It standeth betweene two high mountaines : and not farre from it there is a faire and large valley, from whence commeth a little riuer or streame to the towne, alwaies when it raineth. In the midst of the towne standeth the market place, which containeth great store of shops. Here is also a verie stately temple to be seene. Water for drinke is exceeding scarce among them, for they are all constrained to resort vnto one pit or well, being in the suburbes, neere vnto the sepulchre of a certaine man, that was in times past very famous among them. Howbeit in the night it is dangerous to fetch water from thence, because it is so full of blood-suckers or horse-leeches. The townesmen are of two sorts : for some be fishers, and the residue are pirates, which daily doe greate harme vnto the Christians. Vpon the mountaines grow great store of wood, verie commodious for the building of ships and of

galleies. The inhabitants of which mountaines are almost wholly employed about carrying of the said wood from place to place. They haue very little corne growing, for which cause most of them eate barley bread. Their principall foode are certaine fishes (which the Italians call *Sardelli*) together with other like fishes. They haue such abundance of fish, that one man alone is not able to draw vp a net; wherefore whosoeuer will assist the fishermen in that busines, are rewarded with good store of fishes for their labour : yea sometimes they will freely bestow fishes vpon such as passe by. They salt the foresaid Sardelli, and send them to the mountaines to be sold.[150] In this towne there is a long street inhabited with Iewes, wherin dwell sundry vintners that sell excellent wines. So that in calme euenings the citizens vse to carrie wine aboord their barkes in the sea, and to spend their time in drinking and singing. In this towne standeth a faire castle, but not strong, wherein the gouernour hath his aboad. And neere vnto this castle the saide gouernour hath a palace, where-unto belongeth a most pleasant garden. Vpon the shore the gouernour buildeth galleies and other ships wherewith they greatly molest the Christians. Whereupon *Ferdinando* king of Spaine taking a certaine Iland within a mile of the towne, built a fort thereon, and so planted it with ordinance and souldiers, that neither their temples nor themselues walking in the streets were free therefrom, but were daily slaine. Whereupon the gouernour of the towne was constrained to craue ayde from the king of Fez, who sent out a great armie against the Christians ; but they were partly taken, and partly slaine, so that verie few escaped back vnto Fez. The Christians kept this isle almost two yeeres : and then it was betrayed by a false trecherous Spaniard (who slew the gouernour of the isle, because he had taken his wife from him) into the Moores possession, and all the Christians were slaine : not a man of them escaped, saue onely the Spanish traitour, who in regard of his treason was greatly rewarded, both by the gouernour of Bedis, and also by the king of Fez. Being at Naples I heard the whole relation of this matter from a certaine man that was present at all the former exploits, who said that they were done about the yeere of our Lord 1520. But now the said island is most diligently kept by a garrison of souldiers sent from Fez: for Bedis is the neerest hauen-towne vnto Fez vpon the Mediterran sea shore, although it be an hundred and twenty miles distant. Euerie yeere or euerie second yeere the Venetian gallies vse to resort vnto this isle, and to exchange wares for wares with the inhabitants, or sometimes to buy for readie money: which wares the Venetians transport vnto Tunis, Venice, Alexandria, and sometime to Barutto.[151]

Of the towne of Ielles.

THis towne being built vpon the Mediterran sea shore is almost sixe miles distant from Bedis: the hauen thereof is very commodious and much frequented by ships in fowle and tempestuous weather. Not farre from this towne are diuers mountaines and waste deserts growing full of pine trees. In my time it remained voide of inhabitants, by reason of certaine Spanish pyrates which haunted the same; and now there are but a few poore cottages of fishers, who standing in dayly dread of the Spaniards, keepe continuall and circumspect watch to see if they can escrie any ships making towards them, which if they do, they flee foorthwith vnto the next mountaines, bringing from thence a sufficient number of armed men to withstand the attempts of the Spaniards or Portugals.[152]

Of the towne of Tegassa.

THis towne though it be but little is well stored with inhabitants, and standeth vpon a riuers side, about two miles from the Mediterran sea. Families it containeth to the number of fiue hundreth, the buildings thereof being very rude and homely: all the inhabitants are fishers and sea-faring men, who from thence carrie victuals vnto other cities; for their own towne being enuironed with mountaines and woods, they haue no corne at all. Howbeit certaine vines there are, and very fruitfull trees, without which the whole region were in a miserable case. Besides barly-bread the inhabitants haue nought to liue on, sauing a fewe little fishes and onions. I my selfe could hardly for one day endure the extreme stinking smell of their fishes, which stinck miserablie infecteth the whole prouince.[153]

Of the towne of Gebha.

GEbha is a little towne walled round about, and built by the Africans vpon the Mediterran sea shore. From Bedis it is aboue fower and twentie miles distant. Sometimes it hath inhabitants and sometimes none, according to the custome of that region. All the fields adiacent are vnfitte for corne, being full of fountaines and woods. Here also are certaine vines and other fruits, but no buildings of any account.[154]

Of the towne of Mezemme.

IT is a large sea-towne standing vpon a certaine hill which bordereth vpon the prouince of Garet. Neere vnto this towne lieth a verie large plaine, the length whereof stretching southward is eight and twentie, and the breadth almost ten miles, and through the midst of it runneth the riuer called Nocore, which diuideth the region of Errif from that of Garet. This plaine is occupied by certaine Arabian husbandmen, who reape such plentie of corne there, that they are constrained to pay about fiue thousand bushels a yeere vnto the gouernour of Bedis. This citie was woont in times past to be well peopled, and was the metropolitan of the whole region, although it were continually molested with inconueniences.[155] For first it was almost vtterly destroied by the patriarke of Cairaoan: who, bicause the townesmen refused to pay him his woonted tribute, burnt it downe, and beheaded the gouernour thereof: whose head was carried to Cairaoan vpon the pike of a iaueline. This was done in the yeere of the Hegeira 318. From thenceefoorth for fifteene yeeres after it remained destitute of inhabitants: and then vnder the same patriarke the foresaide towne was by certaine noblemen inhabited a newe. Lastly it was taken by a certaine great man of Cordoua. He seeing this citie stande within fower-score miles of his confines (for so broad is the sea betweene Malaga in Granada, and this part of Barbarie) began to demaund tribute of the citizens: which when they refused to pay, he tooke their towne with a small number of men: for the patriark coulde not in so short space succour it, by reason that Cairaoan is distant from thence aboue *three and twentie hundreth miles. Wherefore this towne being taken and vtterly razed, the gouernour thereof was sent captiue vnto Cordoua, where he spent the residue of his daies in prison. And now the wals of this towne are onely to be seene. This was done in the yeere of the Hegeira 892.[156] Now let vs speake somewhat of the mountaines of Errif.

* *Here seeme h to be an error in the originall.*

Of mount Benigarir.

THis mountaine is inhabited by certaine people which came first from the mountaines of Gumera. It standeth neere vnto Terga, and is ten miles long, and almost fower miles broad. Vpon this mountaine are great store of woods, as likewise abundance of vines and oliues. The inhabitants are miserable and poore people. Cattell are very scarce among them: they vse to make much wine and sodden must. Neither haue they any store of barly growing vpon this mountaine.[157]

Of mount Beni Mansor.

THis mountaine containeth in length fifteene, and in bredth almost fiue miles. Vpon this mountaine are great store of woods and fountaines: All the inhabitants are most valiant, and yet poore and miserable people, for the whole mountaine yeeldeth nothing but vines: they haue indeed some small number of goats. Euery weeke they haue a market, whereunto is brought nothing but garlike, onions, raisins, salt fishes called before Sardelli, togither with some corne and panicke, whereof they make bread. This hill is subiect to the gouernour of Bedis.[158]

Of mount Bacchuia.

THis mountaine is fowerteene miles long, and almost eight miles broad. The inhabitants are richer and somewhat better apparelled then they of other mountaines, & possesse great store of horses. Corne it yeeldeth in abundance: neither are the people constrained to pay any great tribute, by reason of a certaine holy man buried at Bedis, and borne vpon this mountaine.[159]

Of mount Beni Chelid.

BY this mountaine lieth the high way from Bedis to Fez. It is a verie cold place, and containeth great store of wood and fountaines. It yeeldeth no corne, but vines onely. The inhabitants being subiect to the gouernour of Bedis, are by reason of continuall exactions so impouerished, that they are faine to rob and steale for their liuing.[160]

Of mount Beni Mansor.

This mountaine extendeth eight miles, standing an equall distance from the sea with the mountaines aforesaid. The inhabitants are valiant and stout people, but too much addicted to drunkennes. Wine they haue great store, and but little corne. Their women keepe goates and spinne vpon the distaffe both at one time: the greater part of whom will not refute the dishonest company of any man.[161]

Of mount Beni Ioseph.

The length of this mountaine is twelue miles, and the bredth about eight miles. The inhabitants are poore, and basely apparelled: neither haue they any corne but panicke, whereof they make blacke and most vnsauorie bread. They liue also vpon onions, and garlike. Their fountaines are verie muddie. They haue great store of goates, the milke whereof they keepe as a most precious thing.[162]

Of mount Beni Zaruol.

Vpon this mountaine are great store of vines, oliues, and other fruites. The inhabitants are poore miserable people, being subiect to the gouernour of Seusaoen, who exacteth so great tribute at their handes, that all which they can scrape and get out of the mountaine will hardly maintaine them. Euery weeke they haue a market, wherein nothing is to be solde, but onely dried figs, raisins, and oile. Likewise they vse to kill their hee and shee goats, whose flesh is so vnsauorie, that it cannot be eaten, vnlesse it be fried.[163]

Of mount Beni Razin.

This mountaine bordereth vpon the Mediterran sea, not farre from Terga. The inhabitants liue a secure and pleasant life; for the mountaine is impregnable, and aboundeth with all kinde of graine, neither are they constrained to pay any tribute at all. They haue likewise good plentie of oliues and wine ; and their ground is exceeding fruitfull, especially vpon the side of the mountaine. Their women partly keepe goates, and partly till the ground.[104]

Of mount Seusaoen.

THere is no mountaine in all Africa for pleasant situation comparable to this : hereon standeth a towne inhabited with all kinde of artificers and merchants. Vpon this mountaine dwelleth one called *Sidi Heli Berrased*, being lord ouer many mountaines. This *Sidi Heli* brought some ciuilitie into this mountaine, rebelled against the king of Fez, and maintained continuall warre against the Portugals. The inhabitants of the villages of this and the foresaid mountaines, are free from all taxation and tribute, bicause they serue vnder their captaine as well for horsemen as for footemen. Corne heere groweth small store, but great plentie of flaxe. There are great woods, and many fountaines vpon this hill : and the inhabitants go all decently apparelled.[105]

Of mount Beni Gebara.

THis mountaine is very steepe, and of a woonderfull height, out of the foote whereof spring certaine riuers. Vines and figges here are great store, but no corne at all : and the inhabitants weare most base attire. They haue abundance of goats, & oxen of so little a stature, that a man would take them to be calues of half a yeere olde. Euery weeke they haue a market, being furnished with very few commodities. Hither doe the merchants of Fez resort, and the muletters or carriers, which conueie fruits out of this mountaine vnto Fez. In times past it was subiect vnto a certaine prince of the king of Fez his kinred : and there were collected out of this mountaine almost two thousand ducates of yeerely tribute.[166]

Of mount Beni Ierso.

This mountaine in times past was exceedingly well peopled. Heere was likewise a faire colledge built, wherein the Mahumetan lawe was publikely taught, for which cause the inhabitants were freed from all tributes and exactions. Afterward a certaine tirant being assisted by the king of Fez, made this mountaine to become tributarie vnto him ; but first he put the inhabitants to flight, and then destroied the colledge, wherein were founde bookes woorth more then fowre thousand ducates, and the learned and famous men he cruelly put to the sword. This was done in the 918. yeere of the Hegeira, which was in the yeere of our Lord 1509.[167]

Of mount Tezarin.

This mountaine called by the inhabitants Tezarin, standeth neer vnto the foresaid Beni Ierso, & aboundeth greatly with fountaines, deserts, & vineyards. Vpon the top thereof stand diuers ancient buildings, which (so farre foorth as I can coniecture) were erected by the Romains. And here (as is before signified) certaine fond people continually search in caues and holes of the earth for the Romains treasure. All the inhabitants of this mountaine are most ignorant people, and greatly oppressed with exactions.[168]

Of mount Beni Busibet.

This is a most cold mountaine, and therefore it yeeldeth neither corne nor cattell, both by reason of the extreme coldnes, and the barrennes thereof. Moreouer the leaues of the trees are not fit for goates to feede vpon. They haue so great plentie of nuts, that they abundantly

Zibibbo.

furnish the citie of Fez, and all other neighbour cities and townes therewith. All their grapes are blacke, whereof they make a certaine pleasant meate called Zibibbo. They make likewise great store of must and wine. They are clad in certaine woollen clokes or mantles, such as are vsed in Italy: these mantles haue certaine hoods, which couer their heads and visages, so that you can scarce discerne them to be men: and they are particoloured with blacke and white spots. In winter the merchants that resort vnto this mountaine to carrie away nuts and raisins vnto Fez, can scarce finde any meate to eate, for there is neither corne nor fleshe, but onely onions and certaine salt fishes, which are extreme deere. They vse likewise to eate sodden must and beanes dressed after their manner, and this is the daintiest fare that this mountaine can affoord; and their sodden must they eate with much bread.[169]

Of mount Beni Gualid.

IT is an exceeding high and steepe hill, and the inhabitants are very rich, for of their blacke grapes they make the foresaid meate called Zibibbo. Almondes, figges, and oliues they haue in great abundance: neither pay they any tribute vnto the king of Fez, but onely each family one fourth part of a ducate, to the end they may haue free libertie to buie and sell in the Fez market. And if any citizen of Fez doth them any wrong, when they take him or anie of his kinred in their mountaine, they will not suffer him to returne home to Fez, till sufficient recompence be made. These people go decently apparelled, and they haue a priuilege granted, that whatsoeuer persons are banished out of Fez, may freely remaine in their mountaine; yea, they will bestow their liuing gratis vpon such banished persons, so long as they continue amongst them And doubtles if this mountaine were subiect vnto the king of Fez, it would affoord him yeerely for tribute sixe thousand ducates : for it containeth mo then sixe hundreth rich families.[170]

Of mount Merniza.

THis mountaine standeth iust by the former, the inhabitants being endued with the same nobilitie, libertie, and wealth, that the people of the former are endued with. The women of this mountaine for any light iniurie offered by their husbands, leauing foorthwith their saide husbands and children, will depart vnto some other mountaine, and seeke them newe paramours fit for their humor. For which cause they are at continuall warre one with another: neither will they be reconciled till he that is last possessed of the woman pay her former husband all such money as he spent in the solemnizing of her marriage : and for this purpose they haue certaine iudges, that make their poore clients spend almost all their whole substance.[171]

Of mount Haugustian.

IT is an exceeding high and a cold mountaine, containing great store of springs, and abundance of vines bearing blacke grapes, togither with plentie of figs, of honie, and of quinces : howbeit the sweetest and fairest quinces grow vpon a plaine at the foote of the hill. Likewise they are well stored with oile, and are free from all tribute, and yet there is not one of them, but in token of a thankefull minde will sende great gifts vnto the king of Fez : hence it is that they may freely and securely traffique with the people of Fez, of whom they buie great store of corne, wooll, and cloth. They are most ciuilly and decently apparelled, especially such as dwell vpon the principall part of this mountaine, who are most of them either merchants or artificers, and a great many of them gentlemen.[172]

Of Mount Beni Iedir.

This is a great and well peopled mountaine, but it yeeldeth nought but grapes, whereof they vse to make the foresaid Zibibbo and wines. The inhabitants were in times past free from all tribute ; howbeit in regard of their daily robberies and outrages committed against other people, the gouernour of Bedis being aided with some souldiers of Fez, subdued them all, and depriued them of their libertie : in this mountaine there are about fiftie farmes or granges, which scarcely pay fower hundred ducates for tribute.[173]

Of Mount Lucai.

This mountaine is of a wonderfull height, and verie difficult to ascend. The inhabitants are exceeding rich, hauing great abundance of raisins, figs, almonds, oyle, quinces, and pome-citrons: and dwelling but fiue and thirtie miles distant from Fez, they carrie all their fruits and commodities thither. They are almost all gentlemen, and verie proud and high minded, so that they would neuer pay any tribute at all : for they know that their mountaine is so fortified by nature, that it cannot easily be subdued : here likewise all such as are banished out of Fez, except onely adulterers, are friendly entertained: for the inhabitants are so iealous, that they will admit no adulterers into their societie. The king of Fez granteth them many priuileges and fauours, in regard of the great commodities which he reapeth out of their mountaine.[174]

Of mount Beni Guazeuall.

This mountaine is almost thirtie miles long, and about fifteen miles broad : it is diuided into three parts, and betweene this and the mountaines aforesaid run certaine little riuers. The inhabitants are most valiant &

warlike people, but extremely oppressed and burthened
with exactions by the gouernor of Fez, who euery yeere
demaundeth of this mountaine for tribute eighteen thousand
ducates: the mountaine indeed aboundeth with grapes,
oliues, figs, and flaxe, whereby great summes of mony are
raised ; howbeit whatsoeuer they can gather goeth presently
to the gouernour of Fez, who hath his officers and receiuers
in the mountaine, which doe miserably oppresse and bribe
the inhabitants: in this mountaine are a great number of
villages and hamlets, that containe some an hundred, and
some two hundred families and aboue: of most expert &
trained soldiers they haue aboue fiue & twentie thousand,
& are at continuall war with those that border vpon them.
But the king of Fez for those that are slaine on both parts
requireth great sums of mony, so that he gaineth much by
their dissensions. In this mountaine there is a certaine
towne indifferently well peopled, and furnished with all
kinde of artificers ; whereunto the fields belonging maruellously abounde with grapes, quinces, and pome-citrons, all
of which are sold at Fez: here are likewise great store of
linnen weauers, and many iudges and lawyers. They haue
also a good market, whereunto the inhabitants of the
neighbour mountaines resort. Vpon the top of this
mountaine there is a certaine caue or hole that perpetually *A caue or hole*
casteth vp fire. Some woondering greatly at the matter, *that perpetu-*
haue cast in wood, which was suddenly consumed to ashes: *ally casteth vp fire.*
I my selfe neuer saw the like miracle in any other place, so
that a great manie thinke it to be hell-mouth.[175]

Of mount Benigueriaghell.

IT standeth neer vnto the mountaine last mentioned, and
yet the inhabitants of these mountaines are at continuall warre and discord. At the foot of this mountaine
there is a large plaine which extendeth to the territorie of
Fez, and through the same runneth that riuer which the

inhabitants call Guarga. This mountaine greatly aboundeth with oyle, corne, and flaxe, for which cause here are great store of linnen-weauers. The greatest part of al their commodities is gathered for the kings vse, so that they which otherwise would prooue exceeding rich, becom by this meanes starke beggers, and that especially by reason of the courtiers continuall extortions. They are people of an ingenuous and valiant disposition. Souldiers they haue almost twelue thousand, and to the number of threescore villages.[176]

Of mount Beni Achmed.

THis mountaine is eighteene miles long and seuen miles broad. It is verie steepe and containeth many waste deserts, and yeeldeth likewise great store of grapes, oliues, & figs: howbeit the soile is not so apt for corne. All the inhabitants are continually oppressed with the exactions of the Fessan king. At the foote of this mountaine are diuers springs and small streames, the water whereof is muddie and vnpleasant in taste, for in regard of the nature of the sande or earth it tasteth of chalke. There are many in this place, the balles of whose throtepipes are verie great and sticke farre out, like vnto those abouementioned. All of them drinke pure wine, which *Wine that will last fifteene yeeres.* being boyled will last fifteene yeeres, howbeit they boyle not all their wine, but some they keepe vnboyled, and they yeerely make great quantity of boiled wine, which they vse to put in vessels, that are narrow at the bottome, and broad at the top. They haue euerie weeke a great market, where wine, oyle, and raisins are to bee sold. The people of this mountaine likewise are extreme poore and beggerly, as a man may coniecture by their apparell. They haue had continuall and ancient quarrels among themselues, which make them oftentimes fall together by the eares.[177]

Of mount Beni Ieginesen.

This mountaine bordereth vpon Beni Achmed, & stretcheth in length almost ten miles. And betweene it and mount Beni Achmed runneth a certaine small riuer. The inhabitants are too much addicted to drunkennes, by reason that their wines are so excellent. No fruits grow vpon this mountaine but onely great abundance of grapes. Goates they haue which liue continually in the woods, neither haue they any other flesh to eate but goates-flesh. I my selfe had great acquaintance with the inhabitants, by reason that my father had some possessions vpon the mountaine: but he hardly got any rents or money at their hands: for they are the woorst paymasters that euer I knew.[178]

Of mount Beni Mesgalda.

This mountaine bordereth vpon the mountaine last mentioned, and vpon the riuer of Guarga. The inhabitants make great store of liquid sope, for they know not how to make hard sope. At the foote of this mountaine there is a large plane possessed by certaine Arabians, who haue often combates with them of the mountaine. They pay yeerly to the K. of Fez an huge summe of mony, and it is a woonder to see with what new exactions they are daily burthened. In this mountaine are many Doctors of the Mahumetan lawe, and diuers inferior students: who put the inhabitants to great damage. Themselues forsooth will drinke wine, and yet they perswade the people that it is vnlawfull for them to drinke it, albeit some do giue them little credit. The inhabitants of this mountaine pay in respect of others no great tribute, and that perhaps, because they maintaine the foresaid Doctors and students.[179]

Of mount Beni Guamud.

THis mountaine standeth so neere vnto the territorie of Fez, that they are diuided onely by a riuer. All the inhabitants make sope, out of which commoditie the king of Fez reapeth sixe thousand ducates of yeerely tribute. The villages of this mountaine are about five and twentie in number. All the sides thereof bring foorth corne and cattell in great abundance, sauing that they are sometimes destitute of water. The inhabitants are verie rich and carrie all kinde of wares to Fez, where they gaine exceedingly by them. This mountaine yeeldeth nothing, but is commodious for mans vse. From Fez it is almost ten miles distant.[180]

Of Garet, one of the seuen Prouinces of the Fessan kingdome.

Auing described all the chiefe townes and mountaines of the prouince of Errife, it now remaineth that we say somewhat of Garet, which is the sixt Prouince of Fez. This Prouince beginneth westward from the riuer Melulo, and bordereth eastward vpon the riuer Muluia ; southward it is enclosed with the mountaines next vnto the Numidian desert, and northward it extendeth to the Mediterran sea. The bredth of this region along the sea shore stretcheth from the riuer Nocor to the foresaide riuer of Muluia : the southern bredth is bounded with the riuer Melulo, & westward with the mountaines of Chauz. The length of this Prouince is fiftie, and the bredth fortie miles. The soyle is rough, vntilled, and barren, not much vnlike to the deserts of Numidia. The greater part hath beene destitute of in-

habitants, especially euer since the Spaniards tooke two of
the principall townes in all the Prouince, as we will in
due place record.[181]

Of the towne of Melclain Garet.

This great and ancient towne built by the Africans
vpon a certaine bay or hauen of the Mediterran
sea, containeth almost two thousand families. It was in
times past well stored with inhabitants, as being the head-
citie of the whole prouince. It had a great iurisdiction or
territorie belonging thereto, and collected great abundance
of yron and honie, whereupon the towne it selfe was called
Mellela, which word in their language signifieth honie. In
the hauen of this towne they fish for pearles, and get great
store of oisters wherein pearles doe breed. This towne
was once subiect vnto the Goths, but fell afterward into
the Mahumetans possession. The Goths being chased
thence, fled ouer to Granada, which citie is almost an
hundred miles distant, to wit, so farre as the bredth of
the sea is ouer.[182] In my time the king of Spaine sent a
great armie against this towne: before the arriual whereof,
the townesmen sent vnto the king of Fez for aide, who
making warre as then against the people of Temesna,
could send but small forces to succour them. Which the
townesmen being aduertised of, and fearing least their
small forces would prooue too weake for the Spanyards
great armada, they tooke all the bag and baggage that
they could carie, and fled vnto the mountains of Buthoia.[183]
Howbeit the captaine of the Fessan soldiers, both to be
reuenged vpon the townesmens cowardice, and also to
leaue nothing for the Spanyards to inioy, burnt downe all
the houses, temples, and buildings. This was done in the
yeere of the Hegeira 896, which was in the yeere of our
Lord 1487. But the Spanyards, for all they found the
citie so wasted, would not depart thereupon, but first built

Mellela enioyed and re-edified by the Spaniards.

a strong castle, and afterward by little and little repaired the towne-walles, and by that meanes haue kept possession thereof euen till this day.[184]

Of the towne of Chasasa.

THis towne is from Mellela aboue twenty miles distant. It hath beene a famous towne and strongly walled, with a royall hauen belonging thereunto, which was yeerely frequented by Venetian ships. The townesmen haue alwaies had great traffique with the people of Fez, to the exceeding commoditie of them both. At length, while the king of Fez was seriously imployed in the warres, Don *Ferdinando* king of Spaine came with great forces against it, and wan it very easily; for the inhabitants being aduertised of the Spanyards approch, betooke themselues wholy to flight.[185]

Chasasa taken by the Spaniards.

Of the towne of Tezzota.

IT standeth vpon an high grauelly hill almost fifteene miles from Chasasa, and hath but a narrow passage to ascend vp vnto it. Within the towne they haue no water but onely out of one cesterne. The founders hereof are reported to haue beene some of the familie of *Beni Marin*, before they attained vnto great dominions, and in this towne they laid vp their corne and other of their commodities. At that time were all the deserts of the region adiacent void of danger, for the Arabians were not as yet possessed of Garet: but after the familie of *Beni Marin* began to flourish, they left this towne and all the region of Garet vnto their neighbours, and went to inhabit better prouinces. Howbeit in the meane season *Ioseph* the sonne of king *Iacob* of the Marin-familie (I know not vpon what occasion) in a manner vtterly destroied Tezzota: but after the Christians were possessed of Chasasa, one of the king of Fez his captaines being a valiant man and borne in

Granada, got licence of his prince to reedifie it againe.
The inhabitants of this reedified towne are Moores, and
are at continuall warre with the Christians of Chasasan.[186]

Of the towne of Meggeo.

THis little towne standeth vpon the top of an exceeding
high mountaine, being westward from Tezzota ten
miles, & almost 6. miles southward of the Mediterran sea.
Founded it was by the Africans, and is inhabited with
people of a noble and liberall disposition. At the foote of
this mountaine there are most fruitfull corne-fields. Likewise great store of iron is digged out of the mountaines *Yron-mines.*
adioining. The gouernment of this towne was committed
vnto one of the blood-royall, namely of the familie of
Muachidin, whose father was not very rich, but being a
weauer, he taught his sonne the same occupation. Afterward the valiant yoong man being aduertised of the
estate and nobilitie of his ancestors, left his loome, and
went to serue the king of Bedis, where he continued an
horseman for a certaine time : but because he was an
excellent musitian, the king loued him most intirely for his
skill in musick. A while after, the gouernour of Tezzota
requiring the kings aide against the Christians, this woorthie
yoong gentlemen with three hundred horsemen was sent
to succour him, who as he had valiantly behaued himselfe
oftentimes before, so now also he appeered to be a most
resolute commander. Howbeit the king regarded not his
valour so much as his excellent skill in musicke : which
the yoong gallant disdaining, went at length to Garet vnto
certaine gentlemen of his acquaintance there, who ioining
fiftie horsemen vnto him, appointed him gouernour of the
castle of Meggeo : and afterward he was so wel beloued by
all the inhabitants of the next mountaines, that each man
according to his abilitie pleasured and gratified him. At
length the gouernour of Bedis hauing assembled an armie

of three hundred horsemen and a thousand footmen, went
about to expell the foresaid yoong gouernour out of
Meggeo; who presently with that small troupe which
he had, so valiantly encountred his enemies, that he put
them to flight, and so growing famous in regarde of his
manifolde victories, the king of Fez bestowed very large
reuenues vpon him (which he had giuen before-time
vnto the gouernours of Bedis) to the ende he might
wholy indeuour himselfe to expell the Spanyards out of
that region. And of this noble gouernour the Moores
learned great skill in warlike affaires. The king of Fez
hath now doubled his yeerely allowance, so that at this
present he hath two hundred horsemen at command, who
are of greater force then two thousand soldiers of any
other captaines thereabout.[187]

Of mount Echebdeuon.

THis mountaine extendeth from Chasasa eastward as
farre as the riuer Muluia; and from the Mediterran
sea southward it stretcheth vnto the desert of Garet. The
inhabitants are exceeding rich and valiant; and the mountaine it selfe aboundeth with honie, barlie, and all kinde of
cattel. Here are likewise great store of pleasant and
greene pastures. But since that Chasasa was taken by the
Spanyards, the people of this mountaine seeing that for
want of soldiers they were not able to withstande the
violence of their enimies, abandoned their owne mountaine,
burnt their houses, and fled vnto the mountaines next
adioining.[188]

Of mount Beni Sahid.

WEstward this mountaine extendeth almost to the
riuer Nocor, for the space of fower and twentie
miles. The inhabitants are rich, valiant, and liberal, and
entertaine all strangers with great courtesie and bountie.

They haue abundance of iron and of barlie; and their pastures are very commodious, abounding with store of cattell; and yet in those pastures are their iron-mines, where they sometime lacke water; neither pay they any tribute at all. Their houses that dig the iron are not farre distant from the iron-mines. This iron the merchants sell at Fez in rude lumpes, because they vse not to frame it into barres, neither indeede haue they the cunning so to frame it. Also they make culters, spades, and such like tooles of husbandrie, and yet their iron hath no steele at all in it.[189]

Of mount Azgangan.

This mountaine beginning southward from Chasasa is inhabited with most rich and valiant people: for besides the great plentie of all things in the mountaine it selfe, it hath the desert of Garet adioining vpon it. The inhabitants of which desert haue great familiaritie and traffique with the people of the said mountaine: howbeit this mountaine also hath remained void of inhabitants, euer since the taking of Chasasa.[190]

Of mount Beni Tenzin.

The south part of this mountaine bordereth vpon the mountaine last mentioned, the length whereof from the desert of Garet to the riuer Nocor is almost ten miles; and on the one side thereof lie most beautifull & pleasant plaines. The inhabitants are all free, paying no tribute at all, and that perhaps, because they haue more soldiers, then Tezzota, Meggeo, and Bedis can affoord. Moreouer they are thought in times past so to haue assisted the gouernour of Meggeo, that by their aide he attained vnto that gouernment. They haue alwaies beene great friends with the people of Fez, by reason of that ancient familiaritie which they had, before Fez was gouerned by a king.

Afterward a certaine lawyer dwelling at Fez, who was borne in this mountaine, so represented vnto the king the said ancient familiaritie, that he obtained freedome for his countrie-men. At length also they were greatly beloued by the Marin-familie, perhaps bicause the mother of *Abu-Sahid* the third king of the saide familie was borne of noble parentage in the foresaide mountaine.[191]

Of mount Guardan.

THe north part of this mountaine ioineth vnto the former; and it stretcheth in length toward the Mediterran sea twelue miles, and in bredth to the riuer of Nocor, almost eight miles. The inhabitants are valiant & rich. Euery saturday they haue a great market vpon the banke of a certaine riuer: and hither resort many people from the mountaines of Garet, and diuers merchants of Fez, who exchange iron and bridles for oile, for in these mountaines grow great plentie of oliues. They haue little or no wine at all, notwithstanding they are so neere vnto mount Arif, where the people carouse wine in abundance. They were for a certaine time tributarie to the gouernour of Bedis, but afterward by the meanes of a learned Mahumetan preacher, the king granted them fauour, to pay each man so much tribute as themselues pleased. So that sending yeerely to the king some certaine sum of money, with certaine horses and slaues, they are put to no further charge.[192]

Of the extreme part of the desert of Garet.

THe prouince of Garet is diuided into three parts: the first whereof containeth the cities and townes, the second the foresaide mountaines, (the inhabitants whereof are called Bottoia) and the thirde comprehendeth the deserts, which beginning northwarde at the Mediterran sea, and extending south to the desert of Chauz, are bounded westward with the foresaide mountaines, and eastward with the riuer of Muluia. The length of these deserts is 60. miles, and the bredth thirty. They are vnpleasant and dry, hauing no water but that of the riuer Muluia. There are many kinds of beasts in this desert, such as are in the Lybian desert next vnto Numidia. In sommer time many Arabians take vp their abode neere vnto the riuer Muluia ; and so do another kinde of fierce people called Batalisa, who possesse great abundance of horses, camels, and other cattell, and maintaine continuall warre against the Arabians that border vpon them.[193]

A description of Chauz, the seuenth prouince of the kingdome of Fez.

THis prouince is thought to comprehend the thirde part of the kingdome of Fez. It beginneth at the riuer Zha from the east, & extendeth westward to the riuer Guruigara : so that the length thereof is an hundred fowerscore and tenne, and the bredth an hundred threescore and ten miles :.for all that part of mount Atlas which lieth ouer against Mauritania, ioineth vpon the bredth of this region. Likewise it containeth a good part of the plaines and mountaines bordering vpon Lybia.[194] At the same time when *Habdulach* the first king of the Marin-family began to beare rule ouer Mauritania and those other regions, his kinred began also to inhabite this region. This king left fower sonnes behinde him, whereof the first was called *Abubdar*, the second *Abnichia*, the third *Abusahid*, and the fourth *Iacob:* this *Iacob* was afterward chosen king, bicause he had vanquished *Muachidin* the king of Maroco, & had conquered the city of Maroco it selfe : the other three brethren died in their nonage : howbeit before *Iacob* had woon Maroco, the old king assigned vnto each of them three, one region a peece. The other three parts were diuided into seuen, which were distributed among the fower kinreds of the Marin-family, and two other tribes or families that were growen in great league with the same family: insomuch that this region was accounted for three regions. They which possessed the kingdome were ten in number, and the regions onely seuen. The foresaid king *Habdulach* was author of the saide partition, who left the region of Chauz after his decease in such estate, as we will foorthwith orderly describe.[195]

Of the towne of Teurerto.

THis ancient towne was built vpon a mountaine by the Africans not farre from the river Zha. The fields hereof not being very large, but exceeding fruitfull, adioine vpon a certaine dry and barren desert. The north part of the same bordereth vpon the desert of Garet, and the south vpon the desert of Adurha: eastward thereof lieth the desert of Anghad, which is neere vnto the kingdome of *Telensin, and westward it is enclosed with the desert of Tafrata, which bordereth likewise vpon the towne of Tezza. This Teurerto was in times past a most populous and rich towne, and contained about three thousand families: heere also are stately palaces, temples, and other such buildings to be seene. The towne wall is built of most excellent marble. Euer since the Marin-familie enioied the westerne kingdome of Fez, this towne was an occasion of great warres: for the Marin-family woulde haue it belong to the crowne of Fez: but the king of Telensin chalenged it as his owne.[196]

*Or Tremisen.

Of the towne of Haddagia.

THis towne was built by the Africans in manner of an Isle, for it is enuironed with the river Mululo, which not far from hence falleth into the riuer Muluia. It was in times past a most populous & flourishing towne: but after the Arabians became lords of the west, it fell by little and little to decay: for it bordereth vpon the desert of Dahra, which is inhabited with most lewde and mischicuous Arabians. At the same time when Teurerto was sacked, this towne was vtterly destroied also, whereof nothing remaineth at this day but the towne wals onely.[197]

Of the castle of Garsis.

IT standeth vpon a rocke by the riuer Muluia, fifteene miles distant from Teurerto. Here, as in a most impregnable place, the familie of Beni Marin laid their prouision of corne; when as they inhabited the deserts. Afterward it became subiect vnto *Abuhenan* the fift king of the Marin-familie. It hath no great quantitie of arable or pasture ground belonging thereto: but it hath a most pleasant garden replenished with grapes, peaches, and figges, and enuironed on all sides with most thicke and shadie woods, so that it is a paradise in respect of other places thereabout. The inhabitants are rude and vnciuill people, neither do they ought, but keepe such corne as the Arabians commit vnto their custodie. If a man behold the castle a farre off, he woulde thinke it rather to be a cottage then a castle: for the wall being in many places ruined, maketh shew of great antiquitie, and the roofe is couered with certaine blacke stones or slates.[198]

Of the towne of Dubdu.

THis ancient towne was built by the Africans vpon an exceeding high and impregnable mountaine, and is inhabited by certaine people of the familie of Zeneta. From the top of this mountaine diuers springs come running into the towne. From this towne the next plaines are distant almost fiue miles, and yet they seeme to be but a mile and a halfe off; for the way is very crooked and winding. All the iurisdiction longing to this towne is onely vpon the toppe of the mountaine, for the plaine vnderneath is vnpleasant and barren; except certaine gardens on either side of a little riuer running by the foote of the hill: neither haue the townesmen corne growing vpon the same hill sufficient for their prouision, vnlesse they were supplied with great store of corne from Tezza: so that this towne was built for a fortresse onely by the family of Marin, what time they were dispossessed of the westerne kingdome. Afterward it was inhabited by a certaine family called Beni Guertaggen, who are lords of the saide towne euen till this day. But when the Marin-family were expelled out of the kingdome of Fez, the next Arabians endeuoured to winne the towne: howbeit by the aide of one *Mose Ibnu Chamu*, who was one of the saide family, the Arabiane were so valiantly resisted, that they concluded a truce with the people of Marin: and so *Mose Ibnu* remained gouernour of the towne; after whose death his sonne *Acmed* succeeded him, who treading iust in his fathers vertuous steps, kept the saide towne in great tranquillitie euen till his dying day. After him succeeded one *Mahumet*, a man highly renowmed for his noble valour and great skill in martiall affaires. This *Mahumet* had before time conquered many cities and castles vpon the foote of the mount Atlas, southward whereof bordereth the land of Numidia. But hauing gotten this towne in possession, he beautified it exceedingly with store of faire houses and buildings: likewise he greatly altered and reformed the gouernment of this towne; and shewed such extra

The great curtesie of Mahumet toward strangers.

ordinarie curtesie vnto al strangers, that he grew very famous. Moreouer the saide *Mahumet* consulted howe to get Tezza from the king of Fez, & offered great matters to the performance of his intent: and that he might the easlier attaine his purpose, he determined to go to the market of Tezza in a simple habite, and so to make an assault vpon the captaine of the towne: for he hoped that a great part of the townesmen, whom he knew to be his friends, woulde assist him in that enterprise. Howbeit this practise was at length discouered vnto the king of Fez (which king was called *Saich*, and was the first of the family of Quattas, and father vnto the king that* now * 1526. reigneth) who presently assembled an huge armie, and marched of purpose against Dubdu, vtterly to destroy it: and so comming vnto the foote of the mountaine he there encamped. The people of the mountaine hauing gathered an armie of sixe thousand men, hid themselues craftilie behinde the rockes, suffering their enimies to ascende by certaine difficult & streite passages, from whence they were sure they could hardly escape, & so at length they brake foorth on the sodaine & encountred their said enemies being wearie of ascending ; and because the way was very troublesome and narrow, the king of Fez his soldiers could not endure their assaults, but being constrained to giue backe, were moe then a thousand of them throwne downe headlong and slaine. In this skirmish were slaine in all to the number of three thousand Fessan soldiers : and yet the king not being dismaied with so great an ouerthrow, prepared foorthwith a band of fiue hundred crossebowes, and three hundred Harquebuziers, and determined to make a newe assault vpon the towne. But *Mahumet* seeing that he could no longer withstand the king, resolued to goe himselfe vnto him, that he might, if it were possible, obtaine peace, and to release his countrie from the furie of the enemie. Wherefore putting on the habit of an ambassadour, he went and deliuered a letter with his owne hand vnto the king. Which the king hauing perused, asked him what he thought concerning the gouernour of Dubdu ? Mary I thinke (quoth *Mahumet*) he is not well in his wits, in that he goeth about to resist your Maiestie. Then said the king, if I had conquered him (as I hope to doe within these few daies) I would cause him to be dismembred and torne in peeces. But what if he should

come hither (saith *Mahumet*) to submit himselfe, and to
acknowledge his offence ; might it then please the king to
admit him into fauour ? Then the king answered : I
sweare vnto thee by this my head, that if he will come and
acknowledge his fault in manner as thou hast said, I will
not onely receiue him into fauour, but will espouse my
daughters vnto his sonnes, and will bestowe most ample
and princely dowries vpon them. But I am sure, being
distraught of his wits (as thou hast said) that he will by no
meanes come and submit himselfe. Then said *Mahumet*:
he would soone come (I assure you) if it pleased the king
to protest this for a certaintie vnto his nobles. I thinke
(said the king) it hath beene sufficiently protested and
affirmed, sithence I haue bound it with a solemne oath in
the presence of these fower ; for heere stande my chiefe
secretarie, the generall of my forces, my father in lawe, and
the chiefe iudge and patriarke of Fez ; the testimonie of
which fower may well satisfie you. Whereupon *Mahumet*
humblie falling at the kings feete : lo heere the man (quoth
he) that submissely acknowledgeth his fault, and craueth
the kings gratious pardon. With that the king himselfe
lifted him from the ground, embraced him, and saluted
him with friendly speeches. Then caused he both his
daughters to be called, which he bestowed vpon *Mahumets*
sonnes : all which being done, he remooued his armie from
that mountaine, and returned conquerour vnto Fez. This
was done in the yeere of the Hegeira 904. which was in
the yeere of our Lord 1495. And in the yeere of the
Hegeira 921. I my selfe was at the citie of Dubdu, where I
was most curteously entertained by the foresaid *Mahumet*,
in regard of certaine letters of commendation which I
brought from the king of Fez and his brother. Neither
would he cease enquiring how all things passed at the king
of Fez his court.[199]

Of the citie of Teza or Tezza.

THis great, noble, and rich citie of Tezza was built by the Africans, fiue miles from mount Atlas, being distant from Fez fiftie, from the Ocean an hundred and thirtie, and from the Mediterran sea seuen miles, and standing in the way from Garet to Chasasan. It contained in times past about fiue thousand families: the buildings of this towne are not very stately, except noblemens palaces, colleges, and temples, which are somewhat beautifull. Out of Atlas springeth a little riuer which runneth through the chiefe temple of this citie: and sometimes it falleth out, that certaine people bordering vpon the citie, vpon some quarrell with the citizens will cut off this riuer from the citie, and turne the course thereof some other way, which breedeth great inconueniences vnto the citizens: for then they can neither builde houses, nor get any water to drinke, but onely corrupt water which they take out of certaine cesternes, for which cause they are often constrained to make a league with those borderers. This citie both for wealth, ciuilitie, and abundance of people is the thirde citie of all the kingdome, and hath a greater temple then that at Fez: heere are likewise three colleges, with diuers bath-stoues, and a great number of hospitals. Each trade and occupation hath a seuerall place in this citie, like as they haue in Fez: the inhabitants are of a more valiant and liberall disposition, then they of Fez: heere are also great store of learned and rich men: and the fieldes adiacent are exceeding fruitfull. Without the citie wals are verie large plaines, and many pleasant streames, that serue to water their gardens which are replenished with all kinde of fruits: heere are abundance of vines also yeelding verie sweete grapes, whereof the Iewes (being fiue hundreth families) make excellent wine, such as I thinke all Africa scarce affoordeth better. In this towne standeth a faire castle, where the gouernour hath his abode. The king of Fez assigned the gouerment of this towne vnto his second sonne, being rather a meete place for the kings owne residence, in regard of the wholesome aire both in sommer and winter: heere were the nobles of the Marin-family woont to remaine all summer, both in respect of the holesomenes of the place, and also that they might defend those regions from the Arabians dwelling in the deserts: which Arabians resorted yeerely to Tezza, to the end they might there furnish themselues with victuals and other necessaries, and brought dates thither from Segelmese to exchange for corne: the citizens also receiued of the Arabians for corne great summes of money, whereupon all of them in a manner grow exceeding rich, neither are they annoied so much with any inconuenience, as with durtie streetes in winter. I my selfe was acquainted in this citie with a certaine aged sire, whom the townesmen adored as if he had beene a god: he was maruelous rich both in fruite, grounds, and other commodities, which the people bestowed vpon him in great abundance. The citizens of Fez vsed to come fiftie miles (for so farre is Fez distant) onely to visite the saide olde man. My selfe conceiued some great opinion of this aged sire: but after I had seene him, I could finde no such superexcellencie in him, saue onely that he deluded the fonde people with strange deuises. The iurisdiction of this citie is very large, containing diuers mountaines vnder it, as we will foorthwith declare in order.[200]

Of mount Margara.

THis mountaine is very high & difficult to ascend, both by reason of the vast deserts & the narrow passages, and it is distant from Teza almost fiue miles: the top of this hill is most fruitefull ground, and full of cleere fountaines: the inhabitants being burthened with no exactions, gather yeerely great store of corne, flaxe, and oile: they haue likewise abundance of cattell, and especially of goates: neither doe they any whit regard princes. Hauing vpon a day vanquished the king of Fez in battell, they carried a certaine captaine of Fez taken prisoner vnto the toppe of the hill, where in the kings owne presence they put him to a most cruell, and miserable death: whereupon the saide inhabitants haue beene at continuall discord with the people of Fez: they haue almost a thousand soldiers, and their mountaine containeth about fiftie villages and hamlets.[201]

Of mount Gauata.

THis mountaine being as difficult to ascende as the former, standeth westward of Fez, almost fifteene miles: both the sides and top of this mountaine are very fruitefull for barly and flaxe: it is extended in length from east to west eight miles, and in bredth about fiue miles: manie deserts here are, haunted with apes and leopards. The greater part of the inhabitants are linnen weauers; people they are of a franke disposition, neither can they till the fields adioining to their mountaine, by reason of their continuall dissension with the king of Fez, vnto whom they will pay no tribute nor custome at all, perhaps because of the strong situation of their mountaine, & for that it aboundeth with all things necessarie for mans sustenance: so that albeit this mountaine were besieged ten yeeres together, yet could it by no meanes be woon; neither is it euer destitute of water, for thereupon are two huge fountaines, which running downe into the plaine, become the heads of two riuers.[202]

Of mount Megesa.

THis mountaine also is somewhat difficult to ascend: it is rough and full of woods, and yeeldeth little corne, but great plentie of oliues. The inhabitants being most part weauers (for their soile yeeldeth good store of flaxe) are in the warres right valiant both on foote and horsebacke. Their faces are white, and that perhaps for the coldnes of the mountaine: neither doe these pay any tribute at all. Here also the exiles of Fez and Teza haue safe aboad, and albeit they haue great store of gardens and vineyards, yet are they no wine-drinkers. Soldiers they haue to the number of seuen thousand, and almost fortie villages.[203]

Of mount Baronis.

THis mountaine standeth fifteene miles northward of Teza. The inhabitants are rich and mighty, and possesse great store of horses: neither doe they pay any tribute at all. This hill aboundeth with plentie of corne, fruits, and grapes, and yet they make no wine at all. Their women are white and fat, and adorne themselues with much siluer. In this place also they entertaine exiles, but if any of them offer to haue familiaritie with their wiues, they punish him most seuerely; for of all iniuries they cannot endure this.[204]

Of the mountaine called Beni Guertenage.

THis is an exceeding high and impregnable mountaine, both in regard of the ragged rocks, and of the vast desertes, being distant from Teza about thirtie miles. This mountaine affoordeth great store of corne, flaxe, oliues, pome-citrons, and excellent quinces. They haue likewise all sorts of cattell in great abundance, except horses and oxen. The inhabitants are valiant and liberall, and as decently apparelled as any citizens. The villages and hamlets of this mountaine are about thirtie fiue, and the soldiers almost three thousand.[205]

Of mount Gueblen.

THis high, cold, and large mountaine containeth in length about thirty, and in bredth about fifteene miles. Eastward it bordereth vpon the mountaine of Dubdu, and westward vpon mount Beni-Iazga, and it is distant from Teza almost fiftie miles southward. At all times of the yeere the top of this mountaine is couered with snowe. The inhabitants in times past were most rich and valiant people, and liued in great libertie : but afterward when they began to play the tyrants, the people of all the mountaines adioyning hauing gathered great forces, inuaded this mountaine, slew them euerie one, and so burned and wasted their townes and villages, that vnto this day it hath remained voide of inhabitants : except onely a few, which detesting the cruel tyrannie of their parents, conueied themselues and all their goods vnto the top of the mountaine, where they liued an abstinent and vertuous life ; wherefore these were spared, and their posteritie remaineth in the mountaine till this present : they are all learned and of honest conuersation, and well esteemed of by the king of Fez : one of them in my time being a very learned and famous old man was vsed by the king of Fez, both about treaties of peace, and in other serious affaires : and in this man the king reposed all his confidence, as if he had beene some petie-god : for which cause all the courtiers had him in great detestation.[206]

Of mount Beni Iesseten.

THis mountaine is subiect vnto the gouernour of Dubdu, being inhabited with most base and beggerly people. Their houses are made of sea-rushes, and so likewise are their shooes made of such rushes when they trauel any iourney, whereby a man may coniecture the miserable estate of this people. The mountaine

Iron-mines.

yeeldeth nought but panicke, whereof they make bread and other victuals: but at the foote thereof are certaine gardens replenished with grapes, dates, and peaches. Their peaches they cut into fower quarters, and casting away the nuts or stones, they drie them in the sunne, and keepe them an whole yeere, which they esteeme for great dainties. Vpon this mountaine are many iron-mines: and they frame their iron in manner of horse-shooes, which serueth them sometimes in stead of money, whereof they haue great want in this mountaine, vnlesse the smithes by their arte keepe this money in store: who, besides horse-shooes, make certaine daggers with blunt points. Their women weare iron-rings vpon their fingers and eares for a great brauerie, but they are more basely apparelled then the men, and remaine continually in the woods, both to keepe goates, and to gather fewell. They haue neither ciuilitie nor learning, but liue after a brutish manner without all discretion and humanitie.[207]

Of mount Selelgo.

THis woodie mountaine is full of pine-trees and foun-taines. Their houses are not made of stone, but of sea-rushes, so that they may easily be remooued from place to place, which is very commodious to the inhabitants, for euery spring they leaue the mountaine and descend into the vallies, from whence about the end of May they are expelled by the Arabians which inhabit the deserts: who by reason of their abundance of goates and other cattell, forsaking the said deserts, seeke vnto the fountaines and moist places: but in winter, because their camels are so impatient of cold, they resort vnto the woods, and warme regions. In this mountaine are great store of lions, leopards, and apes. And from the said mountaine runneth a certaine streame of water with such violence, that I haue seene a stone of an hundred pound waight carried with the

Lions, leopards, and apes.

force thereof: and here Subu taketh his beginning, which is the greatest riuer of all Mauritania.[208]

Of mount Beni Iasga.

THe inhabitants of this mountaine are rich, and ciuil people: it standeth so neere the mountaine last mentioned, that they are onely separated with the foresaid riuer: and to the end they may the easilier passe from one moūtaine to another, they haue made a certaine strange bridge in the midst, and that in manner following: on either side stand certaine postes, through the which runneth a rope vpon a truckle or pulley, vnto which rope is fastened a great basket, that will containe ten persons, and that in such sort, that so often as they will passe ouer to the opposite mountaine, they enter into the basket, and drawing the rope whereon it hangeth, they are easily carried aloft in the aire ouer the river by the helpe of the foresaid pulleys, but sometimes with great hazard of their liues, especially if the basket or the rope be worne in any place: yea and the distance of place is often an occasion of great terrour. In this mountaine there is great store of cattel, but little wood. It aboundeth likewise with most excellent fine wooll, whereof their women make cloth comparable vnto silke, which is solde at Fez for a great price. Here also is great plentie of oile. The king of Fez is lord of this mountaine, the yeerely tribute whereof amounting wel nigh to eight thousand duckats, is paid to the gouernour of old Fez.[209]

A woonderful bridge.

Of mount Azgan.

THis mountaine bordring eastward vpon Selelgo, westward vpon mount Sofroi, southward vpon the mountaines by the riuer Maluia, and northward vpon the territorie of Fez, containeth in length fortie, and in bredth about fifteene miles. It is of an exceeding height, and so intolerably cold, that onely that side therof is habitable which looketh towards Fez. It aboundeth greatly with oliues and other fruites: and from thence also run great store of fountaines into the plaines and fields adiacent, which are most fruitfull for barlic, flaxe and hempe. In my time there were abundance of mulberie-trees planted vpon this plaine, which beare white berries, and bring foorth silke-wormes. The inhabitants in winter dwell in most base cottages. Their water is most extremely cold: insomuch that I my selfe knew one, who with drinking onely a cup thereof, suffered most intolerable gripings and tortures in his bowels for three moneths after.[210]

Of the towne of Sofroi.

THis towne being situate at the foote of mount Atlas, and standing about fifteene miles southward of Fez, almost in the way to Numidia, was built by the Africans betweene two riuers, on either sides whereof grow great abundance of grapes and all kinde of fruites. The towne for fiue miles compasse is enuironed with oliue-trees: but the fieldes are apt onely for hempe and barlic. The inhabitants are very rich, notwithstanding they goe in meane apparell, and greazie with oile, the occasion whereof is in that they carie oile vnto Fez to sell. There is no memorable thing in all their towne, saue onely a certaine temple, through the midst whereof runneth a large riuer, and at the doores standeth a fountaine of most pure water. Howbeit the greatest part of this towne is fallen to decay by the negligence of one of the kings brothers that now raigneth, & is ruined in many places.[211]

Of the towne of Mezdaga.

THis towne being situate likewise at the foote of Atlas, and standing about eight miles westward of Sofroi, is compassed with a faire wall, and albeit the houses thereof are but meane, yet euery one hath a fountaine of cleere water belonging vnto it. Most of the inhabitants are potters, because they haue such abundance of porcel- *Porcellan.* lan earth, whereof they make great store of earthen vessels, and send them to be sold at Fez, from whence they are but twelue miles distant southward. Their fields are most fruitfull for barlie, flaxe, and hempe : and they gather yeerely great abundance of figs, and of other fruits. In the forrests about this towne, as also about the former, are maruellous store of lions, being not very hurtfull, for any man may driue them away with a little sticke.²¹²

Of the towne of Beni Bahlul.

THis little towne standing vpon the side of Atlas towards Fez, is distant from Fez about twelue miles, not farre from the high way leading to Numidia. Through the midst of this towne run certaine little riuers from the next mountaine, neither doth it differ much in situation from Mezdaga, sauing that the south frontier thereof is ful of woods, whereout the inhabitants get timber and fewell, and carrie it vnto Fez to be solde. They are oppressed with continuall exactions of courtiers and others, neither haue they any ciuilitie at all among them.²¹³

Of the towne called Ham Lisnan.

THis towne built by the Africans vpon a certaine plaine enuironed with mountaines, in the way from Sofroi to Numidia, borrowed the name thereof from the fountaine of an idoll, vpon the occasion following. At the same time while the Africans were as yet idolaters, they had a temple standing neere vnto this towne, whither at certaine times of the yeere resorted in the night great multitudes of people both men and women : where hauing ended their sacrifices, they vsed to put out their lights, and euerie man to commit adulterie with that woman which hee first touched. But the women which were present at this abominable sport, were forbidden to lie with any man for a yeere after: and the children begotten in the saide adulterie, were kept and brought vp by the priest of the temple, as being dedicated to sacred vses. In the same temple there was a fountaine which is to be seene at this day: but neither the temple it selfe, nor any monument or mention of the towne is remaining, because they were vtterly demolished by the Mahumetans.[214]

Of the towne of Mahdia.

This towne being situate vpon a plaine, betweene mount Atlas, and certaine woods and riuers, is about ten miles distant from the former. The founder thereof was a certaine Mahumetan preacher of that nation, which was borne in the next mountaine: and it began to be built at the same time when the familie of Zeneta were lords of the Fessan kingdome. But when king *Ioseph* of the Luntune family got possession of the said kingdom, this towne was so wasted and destroyed, that the beautifull temple with some part of the towne wall was onely left standing, and the inhabitants became tributarie to the king of Fez: this was done in the yeere of the Hegeira 515.[215]

Of Sahblel Marga, that is, The plaine of the valiant man.

This plaine containeth in length fortie, and in bredth almost thirtie miles, neere vnto it are certaine mountains which border vpon mount Atlas: and in these mountaines are waste deserts ful of goodly timber: here are likewise a great number of cottages inhabited with colliers for the most part, who carrie abundance of coales from the saide mountaines to Fez. The lions that are here doe so haunt the poore colliers, that sometimes they

deuour them. From hence likewise are carried to Fez
store of excellent and great beames of timber. All the
plaine is so barren and drie, that it will scarce bring foorth
any good thing at all.[216]

Of the plaine called Azgari Camaren.

THis plaine is also inuironed around with woodie
mountaines, being a kinde of medowe-ground, for
it is couered all ouer with most pleasant herbes and grasse:
wherfore in the sommer time they vse to keepe their cattell
heere, and to defend them with high and strong hedges
from the fury of the lions.[217]

Of mount Centopozzi.

Pon this high mountaine are great store
of most ancient buildings, neere vnto
the which there is a hole or drie pit
of so great a depth that the bottome
thereof can in no wise be seene. Into
this pit some mad fellowes will haue
themselues let downe by ropes, carry-
ing a candle or torch in their hands: and beneath they say
it is diuided into manie roumes, and as it were chambers;
and last of all they come to a most large place hewen out
of the rocke with instruments, and compassed about as it
were with a wall, in which wall are fower doores which
lead to other more narrow places, where they say that
fountaines of springing water are. And sometimes it
falleth out that some miserably ende their liues here: for
if their lights chaunce to be blowen out with anie sudden
blast of wind, they can by no meanes finde the place
where the rope hangeth, but are there constrained to die
for extreme famine. It was told me by a certaine nobleman of Fez, that there were ten persons, who being desirous
to see the woonders of this pit, and being prepared for the

same purpose, went first three of them downe, who when they were come to the foresaid fower doores, two of them went one way, and the third went alone another way. And being thus diuided, after they had proceeded almost a quarter of a mile, there came great swarmes, of bats flying about their lights, insomuch that one light was put out; at length being come to the springing fountaines, they found there certaine white bones of men, and fiue or sixe candles, whereof some were new, and others were olde and worne with long lying there: but hauing found nothing but water in the said fountaines, they returned backe-againe the same way as they came: and they had scarce gone halfe way, but their other light also was blowen out with a sudden blast. Afterward seeking earnestly vp and downe, and being wearie of manie falles that they caught among the rockes, they found that there was no hope of returne: wherefore in this desperate case committing themselues with teares into the hands of God, they vowed, if they once escaped this danger, neuer to aduenture any more. They that stood at the caues mouth being ignorant of their companions mishappe expected their returne, and hauing staide ouer long, at length they let downe themselues by the rope, and began with lights to seeke their fellowes, making a great noise, and at length found them heauie and sad. But the third who was wandring vp and downe those darke places, they could by no meanes finde, wherefore leauing him, they returned foorth of the caue. And he that was left behinde heard at length a noise like the barking of little dogs, and shaping his course toward them, he found immediately fower strange, and (as it should seeme) new-borne beasts, after which followed the *damme being not much vnlike to a shee-woolfe, sauing that she was bigger: wherefore he began exceedingly to feare; howbeit there was no danger, for being about to flee, the beast came towards him, fawning gently vpon him with her

* *The beast called Dabuh.*

taile. And so at length, after long seeking, he found the holes mouth with great ioy, and escaped the danger. For within a while he saide that he began to see some glimmering of light, as they do which haue long bin in the darke. But after a certaine time this caue was filled with water vp to the top.[218]

Of the mountaine of rauens, called Cunaigel Gherben.

THis mountaine standeth verie neere the former, and is full of woods and lions. Here is no citie, nor any other place of habitation, perhaps by reason of the extreme coldnes of the place. From this mountaine runneth a certaine little riuer: and here is a rocke of an exceeding height, whereupon keepe infinit swarmes of crowes and rauens, which some thinke to haue beene the occasion of the name of this mountaine. Sometime the terrible northerly windes bring such abundance of snow vpon this mountaine, that such as trauell from Numidia towards Fez loose their liues thereby, as hath beene signified in the first booke. Euerie sommer the Arabians next inhabiting, beeing called Beni Essen, vsually resort vnto this mountaine, in regard of the coole water and pleasant shadowes, notwithstanding they knowe it to be haunted with great store of lions and leopards.[219]

Of the towne of Tezerghe.

THis little towne was by the Africans built in manner of a fort vpon the side of a small riuer which runneth by the foote of the foresaid mountaine: both the inhabitants and their houses are most base and destitute of all ciuilitie. Their fields being enuironed with the mountaines adioyning, bring foorth some small quantitie of barley and peaches. The inhabitants are all subiect vnto certaine Arabians called Deuil Chusein.[220]

Of the towne called Vmen Giunaibe.

THis auncient towne beeing destroyed by the Arabians was situate about twelue miles from Tezerghe vpon the south side of Atlas. It is so dangerous a place by reason of the often inuasions of certaine Arabians, that none almost dare trauell that way. There lyeth a way neere this towne, which a man may not passe without dauncing and leaping, vnlesse he will fall into an ague: the certaintie whereof I haue heard many auouch.[221]

Of mount Beni Merasen.

THe inhabitants of this exceeding high and colde mountaine haue great plentie of horses and asses: here are store of mules likewise, which carie wares vp and downe without either bridle or saddle. Their houses are built not with walles of stone, but of rushes. The people are very rich, and pay no tribute to the king, perhaps in regard of the strong situation of their mountaine.[222]

Of mount Mesettaza.

THis mountaine extendeth in length from east to west almost thirtie miles, and twelue miles in bredth. The west part thereof adioineth vpon the plaine of Edecsen, which bordereth vpon Temesna. It is like vnto the foresaid mountaine, both in regard of the inhabitants, and also for plentie of horses and mules. At Fez there are great store of learned men which were borne in this mountaine: they pay no tribute at all, but onely send the king such gifts as themselues please.[223]

Of the mountaines of Ziz.

THese mountaines are thought to haue borrowed their name from a certaine riuer springing out of them. Eastward they begin at Mesettaza, and extend westward to the mountaines of Tedla and Dedis, southward they border vpon that part of Numidia which is called Segelmesse, and northward vpon the plaines of Edecsen and Guregra: in length they containe an hundred, and in bredth almost fortie miles: in number they are fifteene, being extremely cold and difficult to ascend, and sending foorth many streames of water. The inhabitants are called Sanaga, and are men most patient of all boisterous and cold weather. They weare but one coat at all seasons of the yeere, ouer which they cast a kinde of cloke or mantle: their legs and feete they wrap in certaine clothes as it were in swathing bands, and they goe at all times bare-headed. In this mountaine are great store of mules, asses, and other cattell, but very few deserts. The inhabitants are a most lewd and villanous generation, being wholy addicted to theft and robberie. They are at continuall dissension with the Arabians, and practise daily mischiefes and inconueniences against them, and to the end they may prouoke them to greater furie, they will sometimes throwe their camels downe headlong from the top of some high mountaine.[224] In these mountains there happeneth a certaine strange and incredible matter, for there are serpents so familiar with men, that at dinnertime they will come like dogs & cats and gather vp the crums vnder the table, neither wil they hurt any body, vnlesse they be offered some iniurie.[225] The walles of their houses are made of chalke, and the roofes are couered with thatch. There are also another kinde of inhabitants in these mountaines, who possesse more droues of cattell then the former, and dwell for the most part in cottages made of rushes. And these carrie vnto Segelmese butter and wool to be sold, but at that time only when the Arabians inhabite the deserts, for it often falleth out that they are encoũtred by them, & spoiled of their goods. These people are most valiant warriours, for they will fight euen to the last gaspe, rather then be taken of their

Domestical and tame serpents.

enemies: they carrie fower or fiue iauelins about with them, wherewith they know right well how to defend themselues from the enemie. They fight alwaies on foote, neither can they be vanquished but with a great number of horsemen, and they vse to carrie swords and daggers with them also. In my time they obtained safe conduct of the Arabians, and the Arabians of them likewise, which was a cause, that the merchants of both partes trauelled more securely.[226]

Of the towne of Gerseluin.

THis ancient towne was built by the Africans at the foote of one of the foresaid mountaines, nor farre from the riuer of Ziz. It is enuironed with an impregnable and stately wall, the founder whereof was a certaine king of the Marin-familie. In regard of the walles and bulwarks it is a most beautifull towne. But being once entred thereinto, you shall see most base and beggerly houses, and scarce any inhabitants dwelling in them, and that by the iniurie of certaine Arabians, who when they reuolted from the Marin-familie, tooke this towne and grieuously oppressed the citizens. Their drie and barren fields lie open to the north. Vpon the riuer are diuers mils, and by the side thereof are many gardens replenished with grapes and peaches, which they vse to drie in the sunne, and to keepe an whole yeere. They haue great scarcitie of cattell, which causeth them to liue a most miserable life. This towne was built by the familie of Zeneta in stead of a fort, to the end it might be a place of refuge onely in their iournie to Numidia, but afterward it was surprised and vtterly destroied by the familie of Luntuna. Here also are great store of such domesticall serpents, as we reported to be in the mountaines of Ziz.[227]

Here endeth the third booke.

NOTES TO BOOK III.

(1) The provinces of the Empire have changed since Leo wrote, and, indeed, are still frequently altered. Those of the old kingdom of Fez at the present time are, El-R'arb or Gharb, El-Rif, Bene-Hasan, Tamesna or Temsna, Chavia, Fez, and Tadla, besides several districts which, owing to various circumstances, are often of almost equal importance to the province. The term " R'arb" (or West) is familiarly applied to all Fez ; that is, the country bounded by the sea, the Algerian frontier, the Um er-Rbia, the R'arb el-Isar or North, and the R'arb el-Imen or South, being separated by the Sebu River,

"The certaine Mahumetan aposteta" (certo rubello e scismatico), as in his new-born zeal Leo describes the founder of the holy city of Fez, was no apostate, but the sainted Idris, whose green-tiled mosque is the most sacred spot in the city. The Edrisite dynasty lasted in reality from A.D. 172-375 (A.D. 788-985), or 203 Mohammedan years, which are those by which Leo sometimes reckons. The genealogy of Idris from the prophet is as follows :—

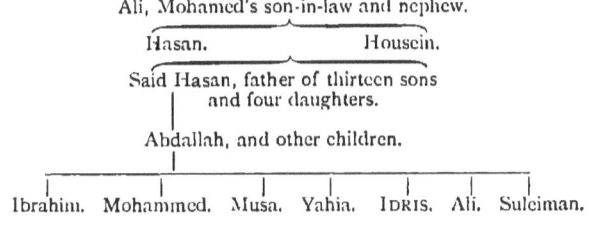

Arabic MS., No. 853, in the Bibliothèque National, Paris. Silvestre de Sacy, *Chrestomathie arabe*, t. i, n. 63.

(2) These details Leo seems to have taken from Ibnu-Rakuk ; but the early history of Morocco is so confused and vague that many versions exist regarding these events. Mahdis were always springing up. The entire history of Islam is lurid with the atrocities of the followers of these ambitious fanatics. Thus, in the *Roudh el-Kartas* (p. 131), a Muezzin (caller to prayer) of the neighbourhood of Tlemsen, obtained a great many proselytes to his novel doctrines until the " King of Andalus" (Spain), having vainly endeavoured to persuade him to abjure his heresies, condemned the Mahdi to be crucified (A.H. 237, A.D. 831).

In A.H. 325 (A.D. 936) a man named Hamyn proclaimed himself a prophet, and after converting many of the Rif mountaineers was crucified at the Masmuda Ksor, as a promulgator of false doctrine, and his head sent to Cordova, when his sectaries all returned to orthodoxy. But although the date and name of this adventurer are much the same as "Chenmen", he could not be the same person.

The King whom Yusuf Ibn Tasfu overthrew was Moennasir, a descendant of Ziri ben-Atiya, who, in the turmoil of the troubles between the Fatemites and Omiades, consequent on Abu Abd-Allah (el-Mahdi) introducing the Shiite doctrines, had, about A.H. 384 (A.D. 994), founded a dynasty in place of the Edrisites. The Almoravides destroyed all of these petty Berber principalities after the ruthless fashion described by Leo. Kennun was an Edrisdite prince, and the various Temem or Temmans are not to be identified with Chemem ben Mennal, the prophet, who divided Fez with the descendants of Edris. Leo's narrative is in places very confused.

Al Bekri speaks of Saleh, son of Tarif, being the founder of the dynasty or religious sect of the Baraghwatta, who reigned in Tamesna and along the coast about Sallei, Azamor, &c., from the beginning of the second to the middle of the fourth century of the Hegira. (MS. in British Museum, No. 9,577, fol. 90. Quatremère. *Notices et Extraits*, etc., vol. vii, pp. 552 *et seq*. Al Makkari, vol. i, pp. 33-4.)

The colony of Tunisian Arabs which Leo mentions Yakub el-Mansur having planted in Temesna, was bought after his expedition against Kassa and other revolted places in A.D. 1186 (A.H. 582).

(3) Anfa, Anasna, or Anafe, or Abca (according to Marmol), is the modern Dar al-beida, or Casa blanca ; both meaning the same, viz., the one in Arabic, the other in Spanish, "White House". But though an ancient Berber town, it was assuredly not built by the Romans, or, as Marmol asserts, one of the cities founded by Hanno. Edrisi mentions Anfa as a frequented port (*Edrisii Africa*, ed. Hartmann, p. 168), and Abu-l-feda notes it, under the same name, as one of the well-known ports of Tamesna.

During the decadence of the Beni-Marini dynasty, Anfa, like Liffi and Sallee, became a kind of rude republic, flourishing enough to send piratical vessels as far as the Tagus. The Portuguese, therefore, utterly destroyed it in 1468, and though they attempted to rebuild the place in 1513, the opposition met with by Antonio de Lenares compelled him to withdraw his large fleet, army, and workmen, after a battle which ended so very like a rout that it is not permitted a very prominent place in the Portuguese annals. Leo describes the ruined condition in which it lay at the time he saw it, and up to near the close of last century it was nothing but a heap of rubbish, with a few wretched huts and fragments of walls, ever now and again overturned by the treasure-seekers. Mulai Mohammed, the great building Sultan, began to re-erect the houses, and it is from his reign that it obtained the name of the "White House". Mulai Abd er-Rahman continued his grandfather's work, until Dar al-Beida (a name only seen in official reports) is now, with the exception of Tangier, the busiest, if not the best port of Morocco, being the chief outlet for the maize and wool-growing country behind.

Anise-seed (*anasna*) also grows plentifully in the vicinity ; hence, possibly, the old native name. But every obstacle is put in the Europeans' way. There are many vacant gardens and other spots inside the walls ; but in case the foreigners get too good a hold on the place, and cause complication, building material is not permitted to pass the gates, and the export-duty on maize is 105 per cent. Leo's description is very inaccurate ; for apart from his random shot at the Romans being the founders, it is not 60 miles north of Atlas, or 30 east of Azamor.

"Melons and pome-citrons" are in the original "mellone e citrinola", melons and cucumbers ; perhaps pumpkins. "The Island of Cadiz, or of the Portugals", "Isola di Calice a tutta la riviera di Portogallo". Cadiz is on a peninsula, not on an island. The old Italian name was "Calix", and in English it used to be known as "Cales".

(4) According to Ibn Khaldun (A.D. 1332-1406), followed by Leo, built by Yakub el-Mansur (A.D. 1163-1184). But that is mere tradition suggested by the name, and there is nothing to show that it might not have been of a later date. In Chenier's day it was nothing but "a wretched castle". Rohlfs evidently expected to see a town ; but in reality the place was never more than the fort built on a kind of fortified "Nzla", or resting-place, where travellers could pass the night without danger from the robbers infesting the country around ; though, no doubt, a few houses of people interested in doing business with the wayfarers gathered around it. The Kasbah Mansur, on the little Wad Mansur (Le oi "Guir"=Gir, a common name for rivers among the Berbers), or Wad en-Nfifek (the swelling river) on Renou's map, is now about all that remains ; yet in Mulai el-Yezid's time, El-Mansuria was still used for its original purpose. (Ezziani, *Ettordjemân El mo'arib*, etc., pp. 164, 176.)

(5) Nuchaila, or Nucheyla, consisted, in Leo's day, of nothing more than a mosque tower, all the rest having been destroyed in the devastation with which Yakub el-Mansur visited Temesna (note 2). Nothing is now known regarding it. Even in Marmol's time it was no more *en evidence*, by description, than a mere copy of Leo's. The name may be "Nkheïla", a place so called still existing on the Wad Zgid, in the

Dra Basin, to which, not improbably, the survivors of the Temesna town fled.

(6) Leo describes its position too loosely for its site to be indicated ; but as it was destroyed in the course of Yakub el-Mansur's peacemaking, when all Temesna was turned into a desert, and four centuries ago consisted of nothing more than a few ruins, it is unlikely that its site could now be traced. Marmol hazards the opinion, probably from its Latin-sounding name, that it had been built by the Romans. There are several tribal fractions in the Sus Basin called "Aderdur". The "vr Adendun" may have been the real name of "Aderdun", a Berber word signifying "resounding". The latitude indicated is too far north for the date-palm to ripen, and much of the country in that direction is ferruginous in hue.

(7) Tegeget, or Tegegilt, of Marmol. It was razed with the preceding towns, but seemed to have attracted a few inhabitants, engaged in smith work for the neighbouring farmers. "Teg", or "Tag", forms the first portion and last of Berber tribal names ; but if anything now remains of it, the village must be unimportant. It is perhaps Tezezat, a place said to be near the Um er-Rbia.

(8) Hain el-Challu, which may perhaps be more correctly written 'Ain el-Kallu, "the Kallu Spring"—"Ain", as it forms part of many Berber names, always meaning this. In Leo's day it seems to have been utterly effaced, though it is not impossible that Ain Sbah, south of Masurea, marks its site.

The common Morocco toad, which Leo seemed to be amazed at not finding venomous, is *Bufo Maurctanica ;* but he probably means the common frog, *Rana esculenta*. The fruit seems a *Prunus*, but the species is not known to me, and is equally strange to my Moroccan correspondents.

(9) " Rabato", in the original. "Not many yeeres ago" (ne tempi moderni) must, like "grandissima" applied to Rabat, be taken in a comparative sense. For, actually, according to the best authorities, the author of the *Roudh el-Kartas* and Abd el-Wahed Merakeshi among the most important, it was begun by Yakub el-Mansur about the year 1190 A.D., or more than four centuries before Leo wrote. Abu-l-feda, however, apparently on the dubious second-hand authority of Ibn-Said, and others copying him, affirms that Abd el-Mumen was the builder of " Rabath el-Fath", which he laid out on the model of Iskandariyyah(Alexandria). He also mixes it up with El-Mahadiyyah, or Mahdiyyah, which M. Solvet, who favours Abd el-Mumen's claims as founder, imagines to be another name for Rabat, and to refer to Abd el-Mumen's title of Mahdi. But all this is erroneous. As M. Fagnan

points out in a learned note (which is nevertheless not without geographical and historical errors) the Mahadiyyah is Marmora, or Mehedia, near the south side of the Sebu mouth, south of old Marmora, the original Mehedia. But this fort to defend the entrance to the river was erected, not by Abd el-Mumen, but by Yakub el-Mansur, while the modern Marmora is much more recent—much after the date which Marmol (who on the authority of Abdul-Malik attributes the foundation of Rabat to Abd el-Mumen, by whom it was named Mehedia), and subsequent commentators, assign to Rabat. It is, however, quite possible that Abd el-Mumen had a palace here, and he began a castle finished by El-Mansur. Indeed, in the *Roudh el-Kartas*, which expressly attributes the building of Rabat to Yakub el-Mansur, there are mentions (pp. 273, 286, etc.) of Abd el-Mumen coming to "Rabat el-Fath", though he seems always to have encamped at Sallee, which he had to subdue. This throws some doubt on the origin of the name of "Rabat el-Fath" having been due to El-Mansur (p. 401). Hence, also, perhaps the confusion regarding the founders. But M. Fagnan is in error when he says that El-Bekri (tran. p. 202), Edrisi (ed. Hartman, pp. 163, 167, etc.), and "Ibn Haukal" (p. 57), alone mention the ancient Shella without examining the other quotations; and in Ousley's edition of Ibn Haukal there is no mention of Shella. Edrisi directly mentions Sala el-Haditsah (New Sala), which can only be Rabat, unless "old Sallee" is intended. (?) Reinaud (ed. Abu-l-feda, t. ii, pp. 174, 183) without, however, giving any authority, considers the existence of "Rebath-alfath" anterior by two hundred years to Abd el-Mumen, that is, sometime in the tenth century of the Christian era. This statement is in contradiction to so many other precise data, that it may be dismissed without much compunction.—Fagnan, *Histoire des Almohades* (*Revue Africaine*, 1893, p. 235); Abu-l-feda (ed. Solvet, pp. 15, 45, 46, 165, 166); *Roudh el-Kartas*, pp. 324, etc.).

Its full name is Ribât el-Fath, "the camp of victory", having been—so the tradition is—with the Tower of Hassan in the vicinity (*ut infra*), erected in commemoration of El-Mansur's victory over the Christians at Alarcos, and also as a convenient place to keep watch over Spain. And as it was on the other side of the river from Sallee, it was commonly known as Sla-Jedid, the New Sallee. The preceding facts, however, throw some doubt on this.

But when we speak of "Arab" structures, either in Spain or Morocco, at the time that Rabat was reared, Arab money and the liberality of Arab or Berber kings should be understood. For the architects were often Jews or Christians, and frequently Moslem-cultured Saracenic artists, brought from Egypt and the most distant parts of Islam. On Rabat and Shellah, for instance, tradition has it that 40,000 Spanish Christian slaves were employed, with the stimulus of obtaining freedom when the task was done, and the liberty of selecting a district for themselves. In defiance of his Minister's advice that such a colony would be dangerous, El-Mansur kept his word, and established the free men in the mountain region east of Fez, where, so runs the legend, they tried for a time to preserve their faith and language. But, marrying Moslem wives and having no priests, in three centuries the Shabanats (as they were called, from the emigration taking place in the month called Shaban) lost both their faith and their language, and became indistinguishable from the tribes around them in manner, language, or religion, and were often at war with Mulai er-Rashid and other Sultans of Fez. The Fazees are still very fair, though this may be attributed to the influx of European blood through European slaves. Gothic slaves, no doubt, had their share in this ethnic fact, though it is difficult to credit the legend mentioned to the full extent it has taken. A second tale regarding the building of Rabat is less complimentary to all concerned. For—the story runs—many of the Christian slaves having been detected making the roofs so flimsy that they fell upon their taskmasters, were decapitated at the iron gate.

The Rabat Kasbah has a beautiful gate. The Kasbah quarter has also a different government, and is inhabited by the Udaih, a distant tribe whose original home is said to be beyond Timbuctoo, their colonisation here being, no doubt, in the early days of the foundation of Rabat, for the purpose of acting as a garrison not likely to form an alliance with the native tribes around them. The Jews say that they were offered this quarter as a Mellah, but preferred the eastern portion of the town as better fitted for business. (MS. note by the late Captain F. P. Warren, R.N.)

Rabat, another etymology, makes a place to make fast to, an anchorage, or perhaps a (water) camp; and the deep water being on that side of the river may have induced the Romans to build Shella there, using the site of the present Rabat, where Roman remains are often disinterred (p. 586), as the shipping-place, and Shella (or what is known by that name) as the suburban residential quarter.

The alteration in the depth of the river has been great, ever since the building of Sallee, and the gate of the water-port at what is known as *old* Sallee, a little farther up the river-bank, but on the same side, is now 300 yards distant from high-water-mark, with a rising ascent of 10 feet. This may be due either to the secular rise of the coast already noticed, or to the less amount of water in all the rivers of Morocco since the woods have been cut down. What Pliny says about the forests in this quarter is true of all the country. At one time they must have harboured enormous numbers of lions or other wild beasts, and from Mauretane-Tingitana great consignments of lions were made for the Roman amphitheatres. At Shella also the water-gate is now about 1,000 yards from the river, with a rise of

10 feet. The Bu-ragreg is indeed more an estuary at this spot than an ordinary river-course. The tide runs up for 16 miles, though during the dry season the body of water entering it is very small. At the head of tidal influence a considerable shebbel fishery (p. 377) is carried on from November to the end of April. (MS. note by Captain Warren, R.N.)

(10) The Wad Bu-ragrag (the Father of Ravines) is called the Armer by Edrisi, a name which appears in Marmol's *Sumer;* though, like another name, Wad er-Raman, it seems to be forgot now-a-days. It is also sometimes corrupted into Banrog, Bu-Rgak, and Bu-Rabba.

(11) The Borj el-Hassan, or Sma' Hassan, so called from being situated in the Beni Hassan district, is, with the Kutubiyyah of Marakesh (p. 352), and the Giralda of Seville, all the handiwork of Yakub el-Mansur, and evidently from the same design, perhaps by the same architect. It is the first object which strikes any one approaching Rabat-Sallee from sea; but it was never really completed, nor was the great mosque intended to surround its base ever built. The fine unpolished granite pillars, by tradition declared to be three hundred and sixty in number, stand or lie neglected in every direction, being part of the material brought at such cost to Rabat for the erection of the dream of the great Amir. The unfinished cistern, with ten parallel walls to support the pillars, still attest the magnitude of the design. The cost indeed was so enormous that on dying El-Mansur had only three regrets to express—first, that he had begun the mosque; secondly, that he had released the Christian prisoners after the battle of Alarcos; and thirdly, that he had built Rabat opposite Sallee. Complaints having been made that the place was used for purposes foreign to those of a place of worship, the entrance to Hassan Tower was built up by Sidi Mohammed; who, indeed, ordered it to be razed, but desisted owing to the enormous strength of the material, and it is now the abode of legions of bats and blue-rocks. I obtain this information from my friend Mr. Budgett Meakin, who, managing to get in through a window 22 feet from the ground, ascended to the summit of the tower by means of the inclined plane inside, broad enough for a horse and rider. Mr. Meakin considers the height of the tower about 180 feet.

Rabat is now inhabited by several European merchants, and has, in addition to the Kasbah, or castle overlooking the town, a number of serviceable batteries with modern guns; and among its few architectural notabilities are some large "fondaks" in the main street. Seen from the river, the houses of the European consular agents give the place a Western appearance, but inside it is very Oriental, and very unprogressive, though, with Sallee, it still contains from 30,000 to

40,000 people. The "Heuz Rabat", a district in the vicinity, is, however, thinly peopled by tribes not always conscious of the Sultan's power. In 1610, at the period of the final expulsion of the Moors from Spain, many settled in Rabat, and were assigned Sallee for a place of residence, "where they have since made themselves famous by their maritime expeditions against the enemy of God". (*Al-Makkari*, ed. Gyargos, vol. ii, 392.)

(12) This is the modern Shella, the Sala Colonia of the Romans, though most probably there was an earlier Phœnician settlement here. "Sela", rock, is according to Tissot, Phœnician, though that etymology may be questioned. Altogether, the foundation of Sala must date not later than A.D. 145, if not earlier. Pliny tells us that the vicinity of the town was infested by troops of elephants and by the nation called Autololes. The elephant has long disappeared in all the country north of the Sahara, though its remains have been found in Algeria, and will doubtless be disinterred from the soil of Morocco when the country is better known. But though the neighbourhood of Rabat is not now troubled with the elephant, panthers (*Felis pardus*) are numerous on the neighbouring mountains, and the Zairs and Zemmur tribes carry out the character of the Autololes, their ancestors (Tissot, *Recherches*, etc., pp. 95-96). Shella, Marmol calls Mensala. But every Morocco town has its Mssala when prayers are offered on the great feast days.

At Shella is the burying-ground of many of the Sultans, for which reason it was long considered ground too sacred to be trod by any but believers. Yakub el-Mansur was laid here, with many other Almohades and Merinides. The place is still an asylum for refugees from justice, or otherwise. Roman coins, lamps, urns, and lachrymalia are sometimes obtained here, showing that its sanctity as a burial-ground is traditional. The identity of names in Leo's description has deceived some writers without local information. M. Fagnan, for instance, with an admirable knowledge of the historical authorities concerned (*Revue Africaine*, 1893, p. 235), leads one to believe that Shella is on the Sallee side of the Bu-ragrag—"Salé est au bord de la mer, à deux milles de l'emplacement d'une ancienne Châla ou Chella"; though, to be accurate, the modern name is "Shella", the ancient, as we have seen, was "Sala". Shella is in itself a little walled place, not bearing many traces of its Roman origin. The aqueduct of which Leo writes is now, greatly to the loss of Rabat, in ruins, having been broken in the wars of the Beni Marini against El-Mansur's successors. It is considered by Maltzar and Rohlfs to have been Roman, but any one who has seen the best work of the best period in Morocco will not be so sceptical. The "square massive stone blocks" appear to have led to the German's doubt of the Moors accomplishing anything so good. The stones were, as is the case in many places in Morocco, most probably taken from the old Roman buildings ; or, as the granite pillars around the Sma Hassan are alleged by tradition to have been, brought from Spain ready hewn.

Leo copied the epitaphs in A.H. 915 = A.D. 1509.

Of the thirty tombs which he saw, all of Almohade and Beni-Marini princes, the greater number have disappeared—broken, destroyed, or concealed by the rubbish of the roofless edifice in which they are built. Of these old gravestones only three have escaped the iconoclast. One, attributed by local tradition to be that of Yakub El-Mansur, does not correspond with Leo's description ; but though the name has been mutilated, the date, which is still perfectly plain, shows it to be the tomb of Abu Yakub Yussuf, who was assassinated by a Eunuch at Tlemsen in 706. But if the usually accepted chronology is correct it must be that of Abu Thabet Amir, who died in A.H. 706 (A.D. 1307), and was laid in Shella beside Abu Yakub Yussuf, whose body had been brought from Tlemsen. However, a reference in the inscription on the tablet in the wall which separates the mosque from the burial place, to "Ebi . . Yakub, Son of our Master the King, the learned . . . . the Defender of Islam, the Marabat, the virtuous, the Amir of Moslems, Yussuf ben Abd el-Hak", leaves little doubt as to M. Tissot's determination being accurate.

The second inscribed tomb is that of Abu-l-Hassen, whose death took place on the 27th day of Rebia I, A.H. 752 (A.D. 1351), which is no doubt correct, though Ibn Khaldun (*Hist. des Berbères*, t. iv, p. 292), whose dates have generally been accepted, put that event to have taken place the 23rd of Rebia II, 752. The third tomb, marked like the other with a prism of inscribed marble, is that of Lella Chapa, wife of the preceding Sultan, who died in A.H. 750. But the inscription on her gravestone is as imperfect as that on her husband's. Time has dealt hardly with it, and numerous lacunæ occur.

The mosque in Shella is, however, now so choked with vegetation that it is with difficulty approached. Some of the graves within its precincts have been opened in search of treasure, and as the material is being carried off to build elsewhere, in a few years nothing will be left except the pretty mosque tower and the external walls and fine gateways, which seem to defy the passing centuries. An Arab, indeed, offered a friend of the Editor to remove (for a consideration) the marble covering of any of the tombs within the enclosure. Other visitors to Rabat have possibly been less scrupulous, and it is not impossible that the missing memorial tablets of some of the Sultans, and other members of their families interred here, may yet be found in private museums. Jackson mentions that, more than a century ago, a sea-captain disguised himself as an Arab, and, with a confidential friend, obtained entrance into the burying-place at Shella.

He was very hurried, and therefore could not examine anything closely, but he saw two graves which his guide told him were those of "Roman generals". Such a statement, coming from such a source, is of little value. Indeed, at first sight, it may appear exceedingly unlikely that the tomb of any infidel Rumi would be permitted beside those of the Commanders of the Faithful. But it would seem a still more improbable assumption for a Roman prefect's memorial tablet to be utilised for that of a Moorish Sultan. Yet this was actually the case. The mural tablet in memory of the Sultan Abu Yakub Yussuf, has a curious round hole closely to the left edge, apparently, from its breaking the inscription, made after the marble tablet was erected. Through this hole there is a tradition that of old the Arabs were accustomed to put their hands, and declare to the truth of any statement when a particularly binding oath was desirable. If the hand could be withdrawn freely this was a proof of the testifier speaking the truth, but if he had told a lie, a superhuman force prevented the perjurer from doing so. In 1880, M. Ducour, French Vice-Consul in Rabat, who was permitted to visit the tombs, having the curiosity to put his hand through the hole, believed that he could feel on the reverse side of the stone something like engraved characters. Interest was accordingly made to have the tablet removed, when it was found that the surmise was correct; for, as the clearly-cut Latin inscription showed, the tablet had, previous to extolling the virtues of a Mussulman sovereign, already recorded the merits of a Roman Pro-Consul. This was Aulus Caecina Tacitus, Governor of the province of Betica, who had been recently promoted to the Consulate, and the friend who reared the commemoration tablet was Septimus Carvillianus, a Roman knight.—Valentin, *Bulletin Epigraphique de la Gaule*, 1881.

There are some other mausolea in the enclosure, the greater portion ruins, and all without any inscriptions on them. One Kubba is, however, remarkable for the care with which it has evidently been tended. M. Tissot, when he visited the Chilla sanctuary ("dont j'avais en quelque sorte forcé l'entrée", as the late French Minister to Morocco coolly confesses) could not examine it very carefully; but a soldier who escorted him said it was always known as that of the "Black Sultan". Possibly it is the grave of the Mulatto, Mohammed ben Abd-Allah, of the Hassanean dynasty, who fell at the battle of Alcassar, though the story is that Mulai Ahmed stuffed the skin of the slain Sultan, and carried it in front of him to terrify the people of Fez.

Shella is built on the foundation of the Roman town of which it bears the name; but little Roman now remains on the surface,—a canal by which the waters of the Ain Shella are carried away, and a few fluted columns, being about all. The medals, coins, bricks, fragments of—

indeed almost entire—statues, which have been and are still found even in Rabat, show that the Roman town stretched to the river-mouth. After heavy rains the boys search for these relics near Shella. Early last century two fine marble statues were found, but Mulai Ismaïl would not permit the French Consul to buy them ; and after having them sent to Mekines, gave them to his Jew agent, Abraham Meïmoran ; and finally, to avoid the scandal of anyone about the Court having articles so condemned by the Koran, he ordered them to be "enfermées entre quatre murailles". (*Relation de ce qui s'est passé dans les trois voyages*, etc., p. 31.)

Nowadays the Jews fabricate coins and other relics with which to impose upon any stray traveller less wary than zealous; and of late, finding little sale for coins actually dug out of the ruins of Shella, melt them down for the value of the bullion. M. Ducour was offered as many as sixty silver ones at one time, while copper ones are common. A gold piece of Vespasian was found in splendid preservation.

Shella, in short, is now a beautiful ruin, silent, solitary, with memorials of the past which contrast in their crumbling magnificence most suggestively with the squalid architectural efforts of modern Morocco nearer the sea. The crenellated wall which "King Mansur caused to be built" is still traceable, with a gate on the north-east, which Tissot considers the finest monument of Arab architecture in Morocco. The ruins of a vast edifice, perhaps the "stately pallace" of El-Mansur, are in the centre of the *enceinte*, and not far away the ruins of the mosque and its tower. As M. Tissot remarks, nothing is at once more melancholy and more charming than the solitude of Shella. The profound silence which reigns is undisturbed except by the murmur of running water among the maidenhair ferns, the rustling of the breeze through the great trees which overshadow the royal graves, the chatter of the storks which build on the summit of the deserted mosque, and the cry of the hawks which dart after the pigeons resting on the dismantled tower. Nature in her loveliest form has again taken possession of the ruins abandoned by man, and now the garden of El-Mansur is a forest of orange, pear, palm, and olive, the roots and branches of which interlace in and about the crumbling walls. A little above the gate in the south-east tower two beautiful 'ar'ar trees (*Calletris quadrivalvis*), the wood of which was so highly valued by the Romans, and is still forbidden to be exported by the Moors, are seen. They had evidently been planted, for though the cypress is common in the Atlas, the Riff, and other mountain tracks, it is rarely if ever seen in the lowlands. (Tissot, *Bull. de la Soc. Géog. de Paris*, Sept. 1876.) There is a view of the ruins in Trotter's *Our Mission*, etc., p. 268.

Only a few years ago no Jew or Christian was permitted to enter Shella. The order is, however, now a dead letter, little hindrance being offered to the unbeliever's visits, though the tombs are still taboo to him.

(13) This place—Mader Auvan—is not now known. In Leo's time it was depopulated, and in ruins. "Mader", according to Renou, is a word applied to a plateau which crowns a hill—a geological formation common in Morocco and Algeria, where these decapitated elevations give a peculiar feature to the landscape.

(14) Lions are said even yet to be occasionally seen in the Forest of Mamora. By "leopards" (leopardi), the panther, still frequently met with, is probably meant.

(15) For Thagia cf. note 16. For A.H. 920 read 1514.

(16) Thagia, Tagia or Dagia, as put among "certe monti di quelle di Atlante", has been inserted on maps at random all over Temesna. The tomb of "Sidi Boaza" ("Deda-Buaza" of Marmol), to whose remains is attributed a supernatural power against lions, was thought by Renou to be near the forest of Mamora, because the late Sir John Drummond-Hay speaks of "Seedj Boaza" as a shrine in the "Forest of Manura" which, though several times mentioned as "five days south of Tangier", was taken for granted was a misprint for "Mamora" (West, *Barbary*, ed. 1861, pp. 151, 152, etc.).

In reality, the Kubba of Sidi Bu Aza, or, rather, Mulai Bu Aza, as he is more generally called nowadays, is, it appears, situated "on the border between Zaïr and Zaian near Ain Dahman, a wooded district, roughly speaking, about longitude 6° 40', latitude 33° 30'. Ain Dahman is marked on the French War Office Map. "Buazza" is the vulgar name; it is more correctly spelt "Abu Yaza" (MS. note from Mr. Herbert E. White, H.M. Consul, Tangier). "Mulaij Bouaza" is marked on a route map of M. de la Martinière on the borders of the table-land north-west of Zarhun, near Abu-l-Klea, or "Neck of Zeggotta" (*Morocco*, p. 177, map 4); and on Schnell's map "Ain Daghman", though not Mulai Bu Aza, is marked on a route leading south-west from Rabat.

Sidi Bu Aza lived, according to Leo, in the days of Abd el-Mumen, and he made the pilgrimage as a child, and afterwards often as a man, on one occasion with Mohammed VI in 1514.—See *Introduction*.

The tomb seems nowadays little visited, perhaps because lions have vanished before rifles.—For maps, Tissot, *Bull. de la Soc. de Géog.*, Paris, September 1876; Trotter, *Our Mission to the Court of Morocco*, 1881: and those already cited.

(17) Zarfa, or Azarfe (Marmol), perhaps Es Arfa, is not now known, and having been destroyed by Yusuf more than 700 years ago, must

have now disappeared. In Leo's day the site could be known only by the fruit trees which had been in the old gardens.

(18) Sla, Sella, Sela, Salé, Sali, Sally, Cele, is the town opposite Rabat on the north side of the Bu-ragreg, the Arabic name of which is Sola, though it has obtained an enduring place in English history as the notorious piratical town of Sallee. A "Sallee Rover" is a personage quite as familiar as " Robinson Crusoe", who was doomed to make the acquaintance of one of them.

Modern Sallee—possibly as distinguishing it from Old Sallee, the New Sallee of Edrisi, though I have preferred to consider Rabat as being meant (p. 565)— is built on a sandy spot, and means, according to local information, the Sacred Town, though we have seen that M. Tissot traces the name to the Phœnicians.

The name as directly applied to the town, and not to Shella on the other side of the Bu-ragreg, is found in most of the old Arabic writers. From these allusions it is safe to say that Sallee was a notable town before the tenth century. Abd el-Mumen had to subdue the place in A.H. 526 (A.H. 541 according to Ibn el-Athir, x, 411 ; Zerkeche, p. 5 ; Ibn Khallikan, ii, 183 *teste;* Fagnan, *l. c.*, p. 235)=A.D. 1132 (*Roudh el-Kartas*, p. 266).

On the other hand, there is no ground for believing that it was built by the Romans, or even was more than a Phœnician station. It was most likely a very ancient Berber village, at which the Romans did their commercial business, though they preferred to live at the more agreeable Chella, on the other side of the river. Even that is doubtful, for it is quite possible that the prudent Rumi preferred to live entirely away from the not entirely trustworthy Barbarians, the name of whose village they applied to their new town of Sala Colonea ; and it is certain, from the remains found, that Chella stretched during Roman occupation to where Rabat now stands. During Roman times, therefore, Chella would be the principal place ; but, on their fall, Sallee no doubt received an impetus, though whether the Visigoths sacked it, and Tarik obtained the mastery, is a statement which may be accepted on the authority of Leo and the legends or MS. histories which he had—as he often tells us he had—an opportunity of consulting in Fez and elsewhere. As the Goths had settlements in Africa, the statement is, however, likely enough to be true, though as the last of the Gothic kings lost his hold of Spain in A.D. 711, at the battle of Guadelete, the settlement which they pillaged was most probably the Roman Chella, unless indeed the attack was after the Arabs or Berbers had wrecked it.

The Salletines—or Slawis as they are called in Arabic—no doubt early stimulated the predatory instincts of their neighbours by their wealth, or earned their vengeance by their arrogance. In 1260 (according to Ibn Khaldun, *Hist. des Berbères*, t. iv, p. 47), or 1263 A.D. (Leo and Marmol), Alfonso the Wise of Castile is said to have taken the place, and held it for less than two weeks, when he was driven out by the King of Fez. This circumstance is referred to by Leo in his mention of a "certaine Castilian captaine" surprising Sallee in A.H. 670. In the original, however, it is "anni seicēto settanta di Leghira, l'anno di Xp̄o 1221", which, like most of Leo's calculations of the equivalents of A.H. and A.D. years, is widely wrong. After that date the Slawis were in perpetual hostilities with their neighbours opposite, with foreign powers, or with the kings of Morocco and Fez, whose power they invariably refused to recognise. Indeed, so powerful were they, that beyond exacting a share of their piratical plunder, the Sultans interfered very little with the Slawis in the heyday of their power. The city was a kind of republic, which in 1648 was so insolent that Mulai Zidan asked the aid of an English fleet to demolish the fortifications of the pirates' stronghold. Already, in 1628, Don Thomas de la Raspur, with a Spanish squadron, had bombarded it in retaliation for the Moors' siege of Marmora (*Arch. Espagnoles*, c. iv, No. 4 MS. in the French National Library), and, in 1681, Sallee was unsuccessfully blockaded by a French squadron under the Chevalier de Château Renault. Again and again Sallee, when the centre of Moorish piracy, has had to bear the brunt of some European power's vengeance, though with so little effect that, until piracy and Christian slavery were abolished, Sallee continued nearly as insolent as of old. Thus, in 1851, it had to be bombarded by the French for refusing to pay an indemnity for the plunder of a stranded vessel: though as provisions ran short before the city could be brought to reason, the official sent to surrender found, when the mist cleared away, no one to accept the Slawis' submission.

(19) Viewed from the river, Sallee has, like most Moroccan towns, a picturesqueness which is not borne out by a closer acquaintance. Once inside the outer wall which stretches along the bank, the town is divided into two portions by gardens in the centre, to the left of which rises a low hill surmounted by the tower of the chief mosque. To the right is a lower eminence, and beyond are gardens and summer-houses. The Mellah also lies on this side. But every quarter is narrow, dirty, and neglected, comparing in these respects badly with Rabat, which, if not a model town, is kept reasonably free from the accumulated filth of ages by the stimulus imparted to the authorities by the consular agents and foreign residents. But in Sallee no strangers reside; it is a perfectly native town; and, if Leo's description be not a little coloured, must have decayed greatly since his day. For in 1895 it is a poor place, crumbling away year by year, and in even more than the usual slipshod condition of everything in

Morocco. Few of the tortuous lanes are paved in the most primitive style, and the best have foul gutters full of garbage coursing down the centre. Cattle-yards alternate with gardens and ruined dwellings, in the space within the walls; outside there is no security for life or property. Even in the chief thoroughfare of this fanatical town, rendered all the more inimical to Christians by the majority of the inhabitants being the descendants of the Spanish Moors, a "Nazarene" is not always safe from insult. Sullen looks and muttered curses are often his lot, and sometimes children and the baser sort of adults will risk a flogging—if the Christian chooses to be very persistent in his complaints—by stoning the hated "infidel". The memories of piracy are still vivid here. Old people were, until recently, alive who remembered white captives being landed, and the dungeons in which they were confined were not long ago—may perhaps be still—in existence. Abdul ben Reis—"Abdul, son of the captain"—used, as late as 1885, to entertain a friend of mine with many joyous tales of the day when his sire swept the sea in command of a corsair vessel.—(Introduction to *Adventures of Thomas Pellow*, p. 44.) Indeed, at this hour, the lighters which convey the cargo from the ships ashore are manned by the rovers' descendants who claim the hereditary title of "sailor". The natives say that, after the Lisbon earthquake of 1715, the land on both sides of the river rose so considerably that the old water port of Sallee is now left high and dry, and where docks formerly existed, a wide reach of sand stretches for some distance from the river. But more likely the rise —which is, erroneously, I think, said to have deepened the bar by causing the scouring action of the river to be increased—is only a portion of the slow secular elevation now in progress all over the coast of Morocco.

Sallee, in short, is fast decaying. Rabat is killing it; and even Rabat is not prospering—bad government and the bar of the Bu-ragreg being too much for this ancient port. The castellated wall of Sallee is pierced by four gates, the Bab Malka, opposite Rabat, Sidi Ba Bahaja, Bab Fas, and Bab Sebta. A fine stone aqueduct runs to the north side of the town. This useful work, also not in its primal condition, is like so many monuments of antiquity in Morocco, reported to have been built by the Romans; but most probably it is Moorish.—*Times of Morocco*, Nos. 165, 166.

To the north of Sallee are the remains of a town which is sometimes imagined to be ancient, if not the work of the Romans or Carthaginians. In reality, it was built by Mulai Ismail for the black troops, mainly Songhai (the "abid mta Sidi Bokhari"), by whom he ruled his subjects after the style of Pretorian guards, Janissaries, or Mamelukes.

(20) In the middle ages Sallee must have been the best port in Morocco, and the outlet for all the then thickly populated kingdom of Fez. Genoese, Pisans and Venetians came to buy the products brought by caravans from the interior; while ships from Seville, Valencia, and Barcelona traded in oil and saffron. In spite of the heavy export and import duties, and the frequently arbitrary treatment of the merchants during the seventeenth and eighteenth centuries, the business was so profitable that in those days, perhaps, more traders lived in Rabat-Sallee (for Rabat was always the principal place) than at present.

Some of the exactions demanded would, in any trade less profitable, have rendered business impossible. For instance, as at Tripoli, Tunis and Bugia, the merchants paid the "decime". Then there was the "mangona", or a sixth, payable in silver on the value of all goods entered. And finally there was the "intalacca", a "gratification" —one-and-a-half per cent. of the price of every article, which stuck to the hands of certain officials of the Sultan. After having paid their dues, the merchants were free to sell their goods in any part of the empire except Fez, Rabat (if entered at Sallee), Mekines, and Marakesh. If these markets were visited, a second "decime" had to be paid.—Balducci Pegolotti, *Pratica della mercatura*, p. 279.

(21) The Genoese seem to have been in most favour. As early as A.D. 1161 Caffari tells us that the Republic of Genoa entered into a treaty with Abu-Yakub, the main articles of which were the payment of 10 per cent. (the present duty) *ad valorem* on all imports into Sallee ("Burea" it is called, from Bu-ragreg, the river), F'dala El-Araïsh, or Azila. This date must, however, be incorrect; for Abu-Yakub did not succeed until A.D. 1163 (A.H. 558), when his father, Abdul-Mumen, died at Sallee, or at Rabat el-Fath, as the *Roudh el-Kartas* (p. 286) states. Another treaty with Yakub el-Mansur confirmed these privileges and granted some new ones, so that by the sixteenth century the great Genoese trade in Morocco, spoken of by Leo, had been established. Fine wool, ivory from the Sudan, skins tanned and untanned, fabrics of goat's hair of an excellent quality, amber (ambergris?), wax, sugar, and Mekines honey, so highly esteemed that it was carried into Egypt, formed the chief articles of export. In the twelfth and thirteenth centuries the Pisans entered into rivalry with the Genoese and Florentines, but before long abandoned the contest (Tronconi, *Annali di Pisa;* Fanucci, *Storia dei celebri popoli maritimi dell'Italia*, t. iii, iv; De la Primaudace, *Revue Africaine*, No. 98, p. 121, 122.) The Catalans and Aragonese also shared for a brief period in the profits of business with Sallee, and the country beyond. In the year A.D. 1274, Jayme I, King of Aragon, engaged to send to Yakub II ten ships and 500 horsemen to aid in the conquest

of Ceuta ; and in 1309 Jayme II entered into a treaty with Suleiman I (Abu-r-Rbia) to furnish more troops and ships to help in the reduction of the same fortress, then in possession of the Amir of Granada, the sum of 2,000 doublons being the stipulated pay for each ship during four months. The services of "Christian" soldiers in Morocco has already (p. 338) been noted. Among the Almohades these mercenaries were common, Kurds being among the hired troops. The Almoravides had also many foreign fighting men in their employment in A.D. 626. When, in A.D. 1229, Idris III (Abu-l-Olâ, El-Mamun) crossed from Spain on the expedition which ended in the recovery and sack of Marakesh, he was permitted by his ally Ferdinand III to take with him 12,000 Castilian mercenaries. These valiant cut-throats were paid with such unwonted punctuality that they remained with him as a corps of free-lances, and his sons Abd ul-Vahed (Er-Raschid), and Ali (Es-Said), regularly enrolled their successors. It was stipulated in return that, not only should certain fortresses in Spain be made over to the Christian king, but that a Christian church "with bells" should be erected in Marakesh. The mercenaries were not to be hindered in the exercise of their faith, and if any of them apostatised he was to be judged by his compatriots. El-Mamun kept these terms, and indeed went so far as to proclaim that the only Mahdi was Christ. (*Ibn Khaldun*, t. ii, p. 236.) These 12,000 men might be supposed Spanish Moors, if the *Roudh el-Kartas* (p. 358) did not expressly describe them as the first Christian cavaliers who had entered and served in Al Maghreb. In A.D. 1234, the Genoese helped Er-Rachid with twenty-eight galleys at Ceuta, and a letter of Pope Innocent IV to the Sultan Omar I, Es-Said, is extant, asking for increased favour to the Christian soldiers in Morocco, and permitting the latter to protect the seaports and raise reinforcements for that purpose. (De la Martinière, *Morocco*, p. 305, but the dates are incorrect.) Soon after the transaction with Jayme II, the Catalans obtained freedom of commerce with Morocco, and had even an establishment in Fez. (Capmany, *Memorias sobre el Commercio de Barcelona*, t. iii, p. 300 ; t. iv, p. 7.) The Venetians were never very active in Morocco, finding, perhaps, that the Pisans and Genoese had anticipated them, though in Leo's time the merchants established in Fez were of considerable consequence. (Marin, *Storia del Commercio de' Veneziani*, t. iv ; De la Primaudace, " Les Villes Maritimes du Maroc," *Revue Africaine*, No. 98, etc.) The articles which the Italian traders brought to Morocco through the port of Sallee, practically at that period the only one in possession of the Sultan, were light cloth in gay colours, silks, French and Italian draperies and lace, fur trimmings, wood carvings, tinware, ironwork, glass, coral, gold and silver (coined or in ingots), precious stones, toys and arms. For these they received indigo, flax, cotton, almonds, tanning bark, dyeing materials, cordage, dried fruits, and grain. The English and Dutch (Flandresi) seem even in Leo's day to have tried to share in the profits of the Sallee trade; but with the special privileges granted to the Italians and Spaniards, they must have fared badly. Indeed, it was not until the business of the former was on the decline that—*post hoc, propter hoc*—the French and the northern nations obtained the firm footing which, with the exception of the Dutch and Danes, they have kept to this hour.—Mas Latrie, *Traités de Paix et de Commerce et Documents divers concernant les Relations des Chrétiens avec les Arabes de l'Afrique Septentrionale au moyen âge*, etc. (1868). Thomany, *Le Maroc et ses Caravans: Relation de la France avec cet Empire* (1845). *Bibliography of Morocco* (1893) for numerous English, French, Spanish, Dutch and Danish treatises.

In those days, Sallee was correctly reputed very rich, and when piracy was added to its industries, both it and Rabat must have prospered far beyond anything which the citizens knew subsequently. If Leo is to be credited—and the Arab historians are in unison with him—the town was full of fine mosques, sanctuaries, schools, other public and private buildings, and the bazaars filled with every kind of merchandise in demand by a luxurious, wealthy, and active people. The manufacture of carpets, still, with shoe-making, about the only industry of the place, flourished, and the delicate fabrics of Sallee were valued even by a people so skilful in weaving as the Genoese. Agriculture was thriving, and all kinds of food so cheap that it could be had for next to nothing, while fish was often so abundant that—we have the authority of El-Bakri, Edrisi, and Ibn Khaldun for the statement, readily believed by those who have seen a donkey-load of äzlemzah (*Sciæna aquila*) sold at Mogador for sixpence—not unfrequently it could not find purchasers at any price. A MS. note by my friend the late Captain F. P. Warren, R.N., mentions that, in the summer of 1885, fish was sold in Rabat for 1d., beef at 2d., and mutton at 1½d. per pound. Fowls brought 1s. a pair, and rabbits 3d. each. Eggs were easily obtained for 1s. 6d. the hundred, and all kinds of fruit equally cheaply. Even potatoes could be bought at about English price, though they are not much grown.

The spirit infused into the thriving burghers by the bolder Spanish Moors who had settled in Sallee and Rabat led those cities to rebel and establish a republic, under which greater freedom of trade was permitted: a state of matters which lasted after the overthrow of the decaying Beni-Marini dynasty and the advent of the Sheriffs, who were content with the suzerainty of the Commonwealth and the nomination of the Kadis who administered justice in their name. Only Spanish and Portuguese vessels were refused entrance into the port. Dutch and English were, however, much in favour, owing to the alacrity with which they sold arms, ammunition, and ships to the pirate republic; the other "Christian" merchants making a show at least of submitting to the Pope's orders not to help the Moslem corsairs after the fashion of the heretics of England and Holland. But all accounts agree in treating the traders as quite ready to submit to any degradation for the sake of profit.—Mouëtte, *Relation de la Captivité*, etc., (1682); *Relation de ces qui s'est Passé dans les Trois Voyages que les Religieux de l'Ordre de Nostre Dame de la Mercy ont fait*, etc. (1724); Godard, *Maroc* (1860), pp. 436-438; Dan, *Hist. de Barbarie, etc.* (1649), pp. 206-225, 315; and the Introduction and Notes to *The Adventures of Thomas Pellow* (1892).

The internal dissensions which led to the rupture (in 1755) of the Sallee Republic, after it had existed for nearly 130 years, also ended in the decay of the Slawis' opulence. Piracy still existed well into this century; but by the middle of the eighteenth century Europe had begun to no longer tolerate the corsairs' insolence. Captures of rich argosies ceased to be as frequent as of old, and reprisals were out of all proportion to the gain made out of any venture. But if it is no longer to be feared or even envied, Sallee is still a holy city. Its wars against the infidel and the many tombs of presumably holy men within and without its walls entitle it to that dubious rank. Of these Ben Asher is the greatest. He is the patron saint of the Slawis, and is supposed to have earned his sanctity through his services against the Christians during the occupation of the city by Alfonso the Wise in 1260. He still, however, works miracles. Dead trees bloom by his intercession, and at his bidding honey fills the crevices of arid rocks. He cures disease, gives sight to the blind, restores the paralytic to their former powers, and generally attends to the interests of Sallee and its citizens. For instance, were not the infidel Franks, during their bombardment of Tangier in 1844, forbidden by Ben Asher to injure Sallee, and was not a vessel, daring to approach the sacred coast under his protection, lost? This was the *Groenland*. The difficulty about the Saint permitting Sallee to be bombarded in 1851 by a French squadron under Admiral Dabourdieu is not explained.—De la Primaudace, *Revue Africaine*, July, 1873, No. 100, p. 279.

The "Messer Tommaso di Marino" mentioned by Leo has given origin to much speculation, the favour shown him by the Beni-Marini kings having even led to the belief that he was of the same family, and that the Beni-Marini are descended from the Genoese De Marini. It is quite possible that the accidental likeness of the name of the Genoese merchant might have obtained for him some consideration. But there is no ground for holding that the Sultans of that dynasty were not sprung from the Beni-Marini or Merines, a nomad tribe between Figuy and Moluia, and notorious for their raids from Algeria to the Riff.

Gråberg de Hemsö discusses the question evidently with a leaning towards the romantic but unhistorical side of the question, in his *Specchio Geografico e Statistico dell' Imperio di Marocco*, pp. 259, 324-6.

Comb-making of lentisk (*Pistacia Lentiscus* and *P. Atlantica*) wood is still, as in Leo's day, an industry of Sallee.

(22) Fanzara, or Finzard, the Tefen Sara of Marmol, was in Leo's day "not very large", and almost deserted. Destroyed in the civil wars which preceded the advent of the Hassani Sheriffs, or rather made them possible, since Mohammed did not attract much attention until nearly a century subsequent to the events which Leo relates rather inaccurately, Marmol considers it the "Banaza ou Valence, selon Pline". But this is erroneous, the *Colonia Banasae Valentia*, of Pliny (V. i), being, according to Tissot, still traceable as a mound on the left bank of the Sebu, on a plain offering no other eminence of the kind. It is known to the natives of Sidi Ali ben Jenum, whose "kubba" is here. The place has never been properly examined; but an inscription found in 1871 contains the words "COL . ELIAE . BANASAE", and, from inference, dated A.D. 177, though this Banasa had exchanged, some time about the epoch of Antoninus, the surname Valentia for that of "Ælia".—Desjardins, *Rev. Archaeolog.*, Dec. 1872, n. s. t. xxiv, pp. 366-367.

Abd ul-Malik, whom Leo and Marmol follow, is perhaps right in attributing its foundation to "a king of the Almohades", though whether Abd el-Mumen is not so certain, and that it was enlarged by Ali IV (Abu-l-Hasan)=Abulchesen (Albuchesen of Pory). But the history which follows will bear correction. Sahid (Said) was not the cousin (Leo) or the nephew (Marmol) of Abu-Said, but the brother. All his Spanish possessions, with the exception of Gibraltar, having been absorbed by the Amir of Granada, Abu-Said, anxious at once to save the remnant of his empire in Andalus and to get quit of Said in Africa, sent him to defend that fortress. But when it and its garrison were captured by Abdullah of Granada, Abu-Said (as in the text) refused to ransom Said. The latter then left for Africa, hearing that the Fasces had revolted and murdered the king and several of his sons. But Said found a rival in his brother Yakub, and the Sahid war which followed was between these two princes, until in 1423 Abd-Allah, a son of Abu-Said, whose mother, a Christian, had, on the murder of his father, escaped with him to Tunis, now presented himself. Then his uncles Said and Yakub, wearied of further hostilities, agreed to resign their claims in his favour, and the people, sick of the desolation of the kingdom of Fez, gladly accepted him.

Abdallah III reigned many years, though latterly his tyranny plunged the country into fresh anarchy, paving the way for the regicide and usurper Es-Sherif, and the El-Uatas dynasty. Abu-Said was therefore not the last king of the Beni-Marins, nor did Said die of the pestilence during his siege of Fez, which was not in A.H. 918, A.D. 1509, as is superfluously mentioned in the original, but about A.D. 1417-23.

Fanzara itself seems to have disappeared. At all events, though the position assigned to it in the Forest of Mamora is well known, no one seems of late to have noticed any place corresponding to it, or which bears a similar name. This, however, may be because it was in the Forest of Mamora, a locality still so dreaded as a haunt of robbers and desperadoes that travellers avoid it. More than once the Zenmur, when hard pressed by the Sultan's troops, have taken refuge in it. But in former days, when it was commonly traversed on the way from Sallee to Mekines, the place was known. Then in 1704-1709, the Fathers of "l'Ordre de Nostre Dame de la Mercy" halted the first day out of Sallee at "Finzara", an abandoned castle, with a high tower occupying the angle nearest the route through the Forest. —*Relation de ce qui s'est passé*, etc., pp. 46, 52, 116, etc. Renou considers that its name is "Fenzara", or "Fenzâia", or in the Berber form, "Tefenzait".

(23) Mamora, Marmora, Mehedia, Maheduma ("the Ruined"), or New Marmora, as it is sometimes called, to distinguish it from Old Marmora, a spot further up the coast, is now a wretched place on the south side of the Sebu mouth, whose poor hovels, enclosed within massive walls, recall at once its former fame and its present obscurity. There is another Mamora, a small place on the Wad Fuaraa, close to the Forest of Mamora, between the Sebu and the Bu-ragreg; but it is not of any importance. De la Primaudace (*Revue Africaine*, No. 97, p. 69) declares that Mehdia is a name only found on English and recent charts, but that it is modern, the old geographers knowing it only as Mamora. On the contrary, the people of the town do not know Mamora except as the Nazarenes' name for the place, always using Mehedia, which may have been given in honour of the Almohade Mahdi, or, as Mahdis have been numerous, after some person or event not now remembered (p. 561).

The place was originally less than half a mile from the Sebu, but, by the change of its mouth, owing to the immense amount of brown clay brought down by the current, this fortress, intended to guard the entrance of a river which nobody desires to enter, and to oppose the easiest and most direct line of march on Fez, is now nearly two miles from the water.

Old Mamora (Vecchia Mamora, etc.), also a name unknown in the country, was perhaps applied by mistake to a bay on the shore of which the name appears on all the older charts. The Pisan map and that of Ferier have it Moxmar, Visconti, Mesmera, and Battisti Agnesi, Maximar, and the Sanson maps of 1656, Moxmara, Mamora being at the Sebu mouth. But except the inevitable ruin and the "kubbas" of four saints, the chief of whom is Mulai bu Selhamj, Mulai Abd es-Salim (the "Muley Busehom" of Washington), there is nothing to mark the spot or to indicate that there ever was anything to entitle the chartographers to apply "Old Mamora" to this particular spot: a fact first pointed out by Renou, and enlarged upon by Primaudace in his useful papers on the northern coast of Morocco. Rohlfs—not much of an antiquary—considers that old Mamora was either on the north side of the Sebu or on the fortified hill, whilst new Mamora was erected by the Portuguese on the opposite shore. He also, contrary to Tissot's etymology, asserts that, in Berber, Mamora means "rocky hill", so that old Mamora, if there ever was such a place, need not, as is often done, be regarded as equivalent to the kubba of Mulai bu Selhamj.—See also Barth, *Wanderungen durch die Küstenländer des Mittelmeeres*, p. 29.

The other, Mehedia, or Mamora, as it may continue to be called, does not appear early in history, unless it is referred to by Edrisi. In that case, the tradition that Mamora was built by Yakub el-Mansur to defend the entrance to the Sebu must be unfounded; for Edrisi wrote in 1154, while Abd el-Mumen was alive. Finally, the latter gave the place the name of his master, Ibn Tament El-Mahdi. But though the name Mamora is now scarcely known to the natives, it means, according to Tissot, "the populated," or "abundant," and was one of the epithets Arabs are fond of applying to their towns. On the Catalan chart of 1375, Mamora is marked at the Sebu mouth. But, before the occupation of the place by the Spaniards, it was only a port to which merchants came to traffic in honey, "white and very good" wax, wool, skins, flax, and tanning bark. At that time the people had an amazing quantity of cattle, and everything else in an abundance unknown to the poor "shebbel" fishers who now inhabit the ruined town of ancient fame. In 1611 a Florentine captain writes that at Mamora an ox could be bought for thirty reals, its skin being valued at twelve. "In certain years the olive crop is so considerable that 100 livres of Italy can be had for a ducat and a half." To-day Mamora has no commerce whatever; not a ship ever visits the place. In 1515, however, it burst into history. Emanuel the Fortunate, selecting it as the site of an intermediate post between his northern and southern settlements on the Morocco coast; the task of occupying it was committed to Antonio de Noroña, afterwards Count of Linares, who had 200 (not 1,200, as Marmol and his copyists have it) ships, 8,000 men-at-arms, and several hundred artizans and colonists under his direction when he arrived there on the 23rd June. He found no town at the place, that previously existing having been razed about fifteen or sixteen years previously in the war mentioned in Note 27, of which Leo frequently speaks as that "of Sahid". But he was speedily attacked by the governor of Mekines, Mulai Nasir, brother of Mohammed VI, the second king of the El-Uatas dynasty, and compelled to re-embark after suffering heavy loss, as Leo, who accompanied the Moors, tells us in detail (see *Introduction*). Marmol calculated that the Portuguese lost 4,000 men, without counting prisoners, many of whom he saw long after in Fez, and no doubt obtained information from them; though, as they were incensed at the mismanagement of the enterprise, and at the way in which they had been treated, their evidence was no doubt biased.

By 1614 Mamora was rebuilt and surrounded with strong walls, and in that year a Spanish force under Luis Fajardo occupied it, finding that the English pirates did a thriving trade here, using it as a depôt for their booty. This kennel of sea-robbers was speedily rooted out, and the Spanish continued there until 1681, in spite of attempts in 1628 and 1647 to drive them out of "San Miguel Ultramar", as they had renamed the place. In 1681, however, Mulai Ismaïl, discovering that the place was fully garrisoned, Kaid Amor-Hadu, his general, took it by assault, finding in the fort eighty-eight brass cannon, fifteen iron ones, and more ammunition than he ever before possessed at one time. Since then Mamora has been a Moroccan possession. It seems, from Thomas Phelps and Edmund Baxter helping, on June 13th, 1685, to burn in Mamora harbour "two of the greatest Pirate Ships belonging to Barbary", that under its rightful masters the town soon returned to its old habits.—D'Avety, *Le Monde* (1640); Phelps, *A True Account of the Captivity of Thomas Phelps at Machanez in Barbary*, etc. (1685); Windus, *A Journey to Mequinez* (1725), p. 40; Tissot "Itineraire de Tanger à Rabat," *Bull. de la Soc. de Géog.*, Paris, Sept. 1876.

Mamora, however, perched on the highest point of the southern side of the Sebu embouchure, and surrounded with its old crenellated walls and flanking towers, is still one of the many picturesque mediæval spots on which the traveller comes so suddenly in Morocco. A ruined palace on the northern side, called Dar el-Kebira, has a gateway which, in purity of style and fineness of detail, is comparable, M. Tissot considers, to the Kasba of Rabat. The population is mainly composed of a military colony of "Buakber", or negro troops, who have built some poor huts on the plain, of which they are quite proud, as memorials of what the place was in times of which they have only the vaguest ideas. There is a view of Mamora in Trotter's *Our Mission*, etc., p. 272.

(24) The name of Tefelfelt, "by the side of which runneth a certaine river", appears in "Tenfelfet", the certaine river" mentioned in the Itinerary of the Father of the Order of Mercy. There is a village near, and the cottage for sheltering travellers—or "Nzla"—seemed to have existed early in last century, when the Father (*ut supra*) and Pellow mention it as Dar es-Saltana, or Darmsultan. The river called by Pellow Teffelfille, and by Ali Bey Filifle (Berber, Tefelfelt), is easily recognisable as the Wad-Telfil. Dar es-Saltana—the "home of the Sultana"—a common name in Morocco, was then by legend declared to have been built by Mulai Ismaïl's mother. She may have rebuilt it; but if our identification is accurate, it was much older, being accounted even in Leo's day an ancient "inne".

(25) Mequenez, Mekenes, Mekenez, Meknes, of which the correct name is Meknasa, has been long known as one of the three capitals of Morocco, and during the reign of Mulai Ismaïl the most important of the three. It is not a very old city, having been founded in the middle of the tenth century by the Meknes, a tribe originally from the neighbourhood of Tessa. But Marmol, and those who have accepted him as an authority, are entirely wrong in regarding its site as that of the Roman Silda or Gilda, which Tissot places near El-Halvyn; though he is, perhaps, indulging in one of the vices of etymologists in regarding the Mesgulda tribe as inheriting the old name, which perhaps they originally gave to the vanished town in their country. Originally Mekenes was called Meknaset Ezzitun, to distinguish it from Meknaset Tazza (Tessa), the home of the other section of the Meknasa, its founders, or of whom it formed the rendezvous. Meknessa or Srira is still in the neighbourhood of Tessa, close to the Innauen River. Another village named Mekenes exists in the Ouanseres mountains, about 23 miles north of Tiaret.—Renou, *Expl. scientifique de l'Algérie*, t. viii, p. 255; Pellissier, *Ibid.*, t. vi, pp. 400-402; D'Avezac, *Etudes de Géog. critique sur une partie de l'Afrique Sept.*, pp. 152-153.

Abu-l-feda mentions Meknasa as written with a *mim*, surmounted by a *kesra* and a *kaf* with a *sukun*, a *nun*, an *elif*, a *sin*, and a *he* (Iakut el-Hamawi's *Moschtarek*, a work whose pronunciation of names is often quoted by Abu-l-feda.

It was always famous for the olive gardens (which are mentioned by Abu-l-feda) and grapes made into sweet raisins which grew in its vicinity, and is to this day celebrated for the beauty of its women: an opinion on the soundness of which the Nazarene has, of course, no opportunity of deciding, though I have been assured by the Faithful that the reputation is not deserved.

(26) Mohammed ben Ahmed ben Mohammed ben Ali ben Ghazi, who lived A.H. 858-919, wrote an account of his native town under the

NOTES TO BOOK III.   585

title of *Erroudh elhatun fi akhbar Meknaset ezzitun*, admirably annotated by M. Houdas under the name of "Monographie de Méquinez" (*Journal Asiatique*, No. 6, 1885), though in reality it is mainly an annotated work by a Kadi of Mequinez, Ahmed ben Zeghbouch, who died in A.H. 640. According to him, this river, now called the Bu Fekrar, was formerly called the "Filfil", but at the time he wrote was known as the Bu Amair, on which a poem—*Nozhet ennadhir li Ibn Jabir*—was written by Abu Abdallah ben Jabir Elghassani, of which one verse has been preserved in which it is affirmed that nothing in all the universe was equal to the beauty of the Bu Amair.

According to Ben Ghazi, it rises in the "Mountain of Beni Fezaz". But on many maps the river on which Mekines stands is called the Wad Bu Naser. On Spanish maps—and the Spanish friars had here at one time, previous to Sidi Suleiman's reign, an Hospitium for succouring captives—the name is written "Bunazaro". Edrisi, who mentions Mekines and declares that its true name was Tâgdert or Tâguedart, does not apply any name to the stream, while Leo and Marmol mention vaguely a river in the vicinity of Fez as the Busnasr and Buc-Nacr. Mouette calls it by Ben Ghasi's name—the "Boumaire", and Marmol the "Bu cchel"; while in other old descriptions it receives the title of Bou-Fekroun, which is the modern one (Bu Fekran).

Actually, most of the very familiar Moroccan rivers have more names than one, the other being—like the epithets bestowed on cities—poetical or playful designations.

The historian also vaunts the fertility of the soil of Mekines plain, and the many fruitswh ich it produced—apricots, *helladj (berkuk)*; plums, *trabolosi*; pomegranates of several varieties, *sefri, rahibi, maimuna, noaïmi*, and *akhdar*; figs, *chari*; etc. The "jujube" (*giuggiole*) is not mentioned directly by name, but is included among berries and nuts.

(27) The *Kintar* or quintal (cantaro) is still used in Barbary as the equivalent of 112 lbs. avoirdupois, 45.346 kilogrammes, and 145 Leghorn pounds. In Mogador it is taken for 168 lbs. avoirdupois. This is the rate at which country produce is sold. The Kentar, by which the price of imported goods is estimated, is equal to 112 lbs. (118 lbs. according to Godard). The *Kintar el-Arab* is three-fourths of a *Kintar*, while the great *Kintar* is at Saffi 125, and at Rabat 150 pounds.

Mekines was much enlarged and beautified by Mulai Ismaïl, but much of his handiwork, on which swarms of Christian captives were employed under the ruthless taskmaster of a capable but cruel Sultan, was effaced by his successors, so that, with the exception of the old castle, the gateways, and the palace of the Sultan (built by Mulai Ismaïl, and still the finest building in the place), Mekines does not contain many remnants of ancient architecture, or, indeed, any modern work of much note. What there is has been described in a host of volumes since the treasure city came within the range of the more adventurous tourist. There are in the palace and other buildings numbers of marble columns evidently taken from the Roman Volubilis, though some of them may, as the story runs, have been brought from Leghorn. The Aguedal, a large park, in which the menagerie-loving Mulai El-Hassan collected a number of ostriches, is less known. But the three colleges, as described by Leo, have, with many ancient glories, gone in the endless wars in which the city has been embroiled, or in the sieges to which it has been subjected. The ancient olive groves had even in Ben Ghazi's day largely disappeared, owing to the same causes—when "the Beni-Marini began to ruin the Maghreb". The population is about 20,000, many of them negroes of the Bokhari Corps, for whose accommodation Mulai Ismaïl built a quarter which, in common with all similar buildings in other parts of the Empire, is in ruins. The black soldiers, like Pretorian Guards everywhere, were unpopular.

(28) This refers to the rebellion of Mulai Zidan and the siege of Mekines for two months by Mohammed VI, of the El-Uatas dynasty, during which the country around was laid waste and Mulai Zidan taken prisoner and confined in Fez for a long period. Mulai Naser, who inflicted so notable a blow on the Portuguese at Mamora (pp. 582, 583), became governor of Mekines in his place. The seven years' siege refers to the civil war of the two Saids (note 22, p. 580).

(29) At one time the Mekines people bore the reputation of hospitality, unlike most Moors actually inviting Christian visitors to their houses. Their wives also unveiled when trying to get a glimpse of the strangers from their house-tops, but—as invariably happens in all cities—disappeared when their lord approached. As for the "suavity of manners" mentioned by Jackson, that must be mere inference, as they never are unveiled, or speak to any Christian—or, indeed, to any male except their husbands, or the members of their own families. But the Mekines husbands are no more jealous than those in other cities. The streets, moreover, are cleaner than in Leo's day, being less filthy than those of Moroccan cities generally. It is also worth remarking that Rohlfs is entirely misinformed in supposing that "Mequines is the only town in Morocco in which there are public houses of bad repute."

The subsequent history of Mekines does not concern Leo's narrative.—Mouette, *Histoire des Conquestes de Mouley Archy*, etc. (1653);

Hist. de ce qui s'est passé dans le trois voyages, etc. (1724) ; Windus, *A Journey to Mequinez* (1725) ; Braithwaite, *The History of the Revolution in the Empire of Morocco*, etc. (1729) ; Harris, *The Land of an African Sultan* (1889) ; " Montbard" [Georges Loyes], *Among the Moors* (1894) ; Leared, *A Visit to the Court of Marocco* (1879) ; Stuttfield, *El Maghreb* (1886) ; Trotter, *Our Mission to the Court of Morocco* (1881) ; De la Martinière, Morocco, *Journey in the Kingdom of Fez* (1889), etc.

(30) Gemiha-Elchmen, Gontiane, Gemua el-Hamen, or Jami el-Hammam, was destroyed in the Said wars, about 1420 (p. 580). The environs were, according to Leo, inhabited by "certaine Arabs", the Ibni-Melic-Sofian of Marmol (the Beni-Melik-Sefiân), who held every Sunday a market within two miles of the town. This market, Marmol says, was called Hat-de-tarna. El-Had—Sok el-had—is the name applied to all markets held on Sunday, while Tarna may be the name of a tribe, the Beni-Taura (as Renou suggests), who, Edrisi notes, lived near Mekines. Taura was, indeed, according to Ben Ghazi, one of the suburbs of old Mekines.

The name of the town, which was sanctuary, refers to the Hammam, or bath, and at once enables us to determine it to be the locality where there are still well-frequented hot sulphurous baths, in high repute for skin diseases. Tissot calls the place Ain el-Kibrit, and considers it, quite correctly, to have been the site of the Aquæ Dacicæ of the Romans. But among the natives the place is better known as Ain Sidi Yusuf. In taking a bath, it is necessary to keep calling out "Mulai Yakub burrd u Shrun ! burrd u Shrun !" ("cold and hot ! cold and hot !"), otherwise the saint, whose tomb is close by and from whose body the spring is supposed to issue, may send the water so hot that the bather will be boiled (Colville, *A Ride in Petticoats and Slippers*, p. 183). Colonel Colville did not, any more than the Editor, visit this place, Christians not being welcome. But I have heard the bathing incantation pronounced differently, Sidi Yusuf and not Mulai Yakub being invoked. The tradition that the now vanished town was built by "an Almohade king" (Marmol) may be accepted as of about as much value as similar legends elsewhere : Abd el-Mumen, Yusuf Ibn Tasfin, and Yakub el-Mansur being the three sovereigns who in Morocco are credited with the erection of every town, bridge, fort, and aqueduct, not clearly assignable to anyone else. The Ulad Jama is an Arab tribe immediately north of Fez, so that perhaps the old name might mean simply the Bath in the Jama country. The "Tedle", on the road to which the place lies, is Kaba Tadla, another instance of applying this name to Tefza (p. 388).

(31) Camis (not Cannis) Metgara, or Hamiz Metagara of Marmol in the Zuaga country (*Campagna di Zuaga*), was even in Marmol's

day a poor place, in which was a ruined castle. In the Said war it had been destroyed, but the Moors driven out of Spain at the capture of Granada occupied it in part, as Leo tells us. But, lying on the route from Fez to Morocco, it always fared so badly that it seems to have been early deserted for good. In 1544 it suffered (during the war between the Sheriffs) at the hands of the army of Bu-Hassan, or Bu azon, governor of Velez (Diego de Torres, *Istoria de los Xarifes*, pp. 149-152; Marmol, *L'Afrique*, t. ii, p. 156). But, though still occasionally put on maps (*e.g.*, Petermann's, illustrating Rohlfs' travels, where " Chames Melghara"—not referred to in the narrative— is the variant, a form copied by Weller in the map attached to the English version), it is in every case on Leo's and Marmol's authority alone. According to Ibn er-Rakk it was founded by the Berbers. In Marmol's day it had a Thursday market, from which it took its name (Khamis). In the reign of Mulai Ismaïl, and his predecessor, there was a fort at " El-Khamis", in which was a garrison of the Cherage tribe, for patrolling the roads in the vicinity of Fez and Mequines (Abulqasim ben Ahmed Ezziani, pp. 23, 35, 92). My friend, Mr. Budgett Meakin, then of Tangier, took great pains to identify this place. The country Arabs, and even the more polished town Moors, seldom take any interest in the past, nor can they understand the motives for anyone else doing so. Their answers to questions, even when they do not purposely mislead the inquisitive Nazarene, are very vague, and altogether wide of the mark. However, a man from the part of the country in question was found, who had either more intelligence or frankness than the rest, and the result of a sifting of his information is, that " Khamis" is undoubtedly the " Camis" of Leo and *Zuaga*, Shraga (the Cheraga of Ezziani and De Foucauld, the Cherarda of Erckmann), a large tribal district. The only place which can be identified with Khamis Metgara is Khamis Hajawa (the *g* of Metgara is doubtless soft). There is no town, only a village, with a Thursday (Khamis) market. The distance from Fez is stated to be a short day's journey; but there are no mulberries there, nor silk-weaving now-a-days. Hajawa is not quite in Shraga, but within a few miles of the border, and the road from Had Kort (near El-Ksar) to Fez passes through it. The mere fact of the place being a village does not matter, though at Khamis Hajawa there are traces of the place having been at one time much larger, for it may be taken that in most cases by " cittá", Leo means the Arabic equivalent of " blad"—a place only—as well as a town. Many of his " cities" could never have been more than villages at their best.

(32) The Beni-Bical of Marmol is described so precisely that its position can scarcely be mistaken. It is on a small river midway between Mekines and Fez, a route which is, perhaps, as well known

as any in Morocco. Marmol further gave the name of the river, "Hue nija," which being translated into less phonetic Arabic, is Wad Nedja, Nsa Endja, or Ennedja (close to the Palm Tree Bridge), one of the four streams crossing the road in question, and which arises near the "Ain Zore". It was destroyed in the Said war, and not repeopled until 1514, when Mulai Naser was governor of Mekines. But even then the place was of little account, and at present may perhaps be traced on one of the rivers on the Nedja. The Beni-Besil are mentioned by Edrisi as a tribe near Fez. The village—for it does not seem to have been anything better—was, according to Marmol, built by Sanhadja Berbers. The "Ain Zore" of Marmol is the Ainun Zorak of Tissot (*Bull. de la Soc. de Géog.*, *Sept.*, 1876), and of Martinière's map (*Morocco*, p. 420). The Ain Zorak ("the blue fountain") is not, however, as Marmol imagined, the source of the Wad Endja, but an affluent of that stream, which was much further south.

(33) "Fessa, magna città e capo di tutta Mauritania," Fez, or Fas, to use the proper Arabic name, is still the greatest town of Morocco, and the one on which the Arabic historians are best agreed regarding its foundation. The story that the town owed its origin to Harun ar-Raschid, or indeed to anyone except the second Edris, or Idris Ibn Idris Ibn Abu-l-Kasim, may be passed without discussion. Leo is also wrong in putting the date A.H. 185—736, "di nostra salute," a date copied by Marmol, and being rendered into A.D. 798, or its equivalent. But Renou, while correcting the error, falls into one not less serious. For A.H. 177=A.D. 793 was, according to the *Roudh el-Kartas* (p. 25), the date of Edris the Second's birth, not of the foundation of Fez. It was in A.H. 190 (A.D. 805) that he began to lay out the future city, having, according to the most acceptable version of the story, bought of the Beni Yarghish the ground on which the Adua el-Andalus quarter was built, and the site of the Adua el-Karwain (Kairwan) from the Beni el-Kheir, a sept of the Quagha tribe.

The *Roudh el-Kartas* devotes much space to a discussion of the etymology of *Fas*, or *Fes*, or *Fahs*, for it is written in either way almost indifferently. The favourite derivation is that Fas means the city of the axe, because a stone tool of the kind was found in digging the foundation for the walls. This is not improbable, since it is extremely likely that stone weapons of the primitive inhabitants would be among the relics disinterred in a region so long one of their favourite haunts. In the Jebel Zalah there are numerous caves in the limestone, which, though never examined, bear the distinct impress of having been troglodytic dwellings, just as similar natural or excavated caverns do in so many other parts of Morocco. The word "Fedda", money, and the etymology favoured by Leo, is less plausible.

The river on which Fez is built is now usually known as the Wad Fez, as it also was in Marmol's time. But the occasional name of Wad (Huet) Giohorra (el-Jahar), the River of Pearls, which he and his copyists mention as an alternative one, is not generally, if at all, in use. The Fas poets have other fancy titles for it (Wad el-Kantsa, Wad Mafresin, etc.), and the historians are not much less fertile. The poets of this city excel themselves in praise of the wholesome character of its water, now so dysenteric that everyone who can afford it drinks water brought from the neighbouring Sherardi hills. The picturesque manner in which it dashes through and under the city, driving mills, and acting as a general sewer before it reaches the Sebu, is, however, undeniable.

(34) This refers to the early disputes over the Khalifate. "Cozen" and "Cozen-german" are here used in the meaning of relatives. Ali was nephew and son-in-law—not "fratelcugino"—of Mohammed. What follows narrates in a quaint manner the broils between the families of Abbas (Habbus) or Abassides, and that of Moawiya (Vmeve)—the grandson of Omayya, leader of the Meccans in the battle of Ohod—or Omayyades. In the lifetime of the Prophet the most powerful sept of Korash were the Beni Makhsun, but the Beni Abd Shams were more distinguished; while among the Abd Shams, the Beni Omayya were the greatest. Mohammed was himself a Beni-Hashem, a family which it is said enjoyed at one time the position occupied by the Beni Omayya. This, however, was an after-invention of the Hashemites, when they claimed, as the House of Ali and representatives of the Abassides, to be the heirs of the Khalifate in opposition to the Omayyades (Sprenger, *Leben und Lehre des Muhammed*, etc., vol. iii, pp. cxx, *et seq.*)

The remainder of Leo's account is a well-known part or the history of the early Khalifate. For "Falerna Mahumets owne daughter", read "Fatima".

By "the first patriarke" (primo pontifice) is meant Abu-l-Abbas as-Saffah. His proper name was Abd-Allah (Hab dulla), and the cognomen of Saffah (Seffie) was afterwards conferred on him. He was not "the first patriarch", but the first Khalif of the Abbasid dynasty; and in him the headship of Islam returned to a grand-nephew of the Prophet. It was this Khalif's successor who tried to exterminate the descendants of Ali, and it was under the fourth Khalif of the dynasty (Hadi) that the partisans of the house of Ali raised a rebellion. Harun ar-Raschid was Hadi's brother and successor. Edris ben Abd allah was cousin of "Hosain ben Ali", who had proclaimed himself Khalif, but on a pilgrimage to Mecca was slain by a party of Abbasides. But though Edris's brother had been beheaded (not "hanged") by the Khalif, he was not, as usually stated, the last of the family of Ali and Fatima. He, however, considered it prudent to escape by way of Egypt into Morocco, and seek refuge among the Berbers of Mount Zarhun (Zaron), where he built, or rather improved, the town of Ualili (Gualili, Tuilit), which might possibly have been originally Roman, and was certainly largely constructed out of materials obtained from the neighbouring Roman town of Volubilis. Indeed, it was a tradition in Ben Ghazi's day that the population of that part of the country were of " Rumi " origin ; Roman blood is undoubtedly in the veins of many of them.

In the French edition of Leo (vol. i, p. 325) Zarhun is put at 130 miles from Fez, and Renou gravely argues that this must have been a mistake of the author for 30 : Leo (p. 488) mentioning that the mountain begins at 10 miles from Fez, and extends for 30 miles. The blunder is, however, Temporal's, for in the original the distance is "circa à trenta miglia".

(35) This, according to the *Roudh el-Kartas*, was in A.H. 172, (A.D. 788). At that time the Berbers were still to a large extent Pagans. Many of them were semi-Judaised, and some who had fallen under the influence of the Goths in Spain (the so-called "Andalus") had obtained a veneer of Christianity. But even the Moslem section of the people, while venerating a descendant of Ali and Fatima, had little love for the Amirs, lieutenants of the Khalif, who governed Morocco, so far as they were concerned, in a very nominal fashion. They therefore gladly received Edris as their chief, and in time the probity of his life attracted to him many adherents at a distance from Zarhun. The Pagans, Judaised tribes, and Christians who did not accept his rule were conquered by force. Behlula, Mediuna, tribes of the people of Fasaz territory, then Temsena, Shella—still an uninhabited town—and Tedla, passed under the yoke ; and Tlemsen was attacked and forced to submit until the Edrisite dynasty was established. It was the first independent royal house in Morocco, and, though under an Arab, was actually one of Berbers. Edris, however, roused the suspicion of Harun ar-Raschid, whose Amir, Ibrahim Ibn el-Aghlab, sent an agent to Ulili, who under the guise of a physician anxious to join the Edrisites, managed to poison the too-victorious Imam. Poison has always been a favourite instrument of diplomacy in the East, and is to this day in Morocco. Not many years before Edris's death, Ashar Ali's general had been poisoned by the order of Moawiya, and Hassan, son of Ali, met the same fate, it is believed, by a plot of the same inveterate enemy of his father.

(36) The mother of Edris II (Abu-l-Kasim) was Khanza, a slave,

whom his father had received as a present. He had no other children.

Rashid, the faithful general of Edris I, and Guadia, his son, is always referred to with great respect by the native historian. The accomplishments of his pupil, both in arms and poetry, are also praised.

(37) Originally there were two towns, one on each side of the river; the one called, in Marmol's day, "Beleyde", and the other " Aïn Alu" (Aïn Halwa, "the pleasant fountain"), between which a little rivalry existed, owing to the different banks of the river being inhabited by the Zuagh (a branch of the Zeneta) and the Beni Yarghish (note 33). The one professed Christianity and inhabited the Andalus side, the other Islam, and claimed the Kairwan bank. From them Idris bought the land for 5,000 dirhems (about £200), though they continued to live in the houses which covered their old territory.

The Andalusi, or Spaniards, after whom the Adua el Andalus was named, were people of mixed race—many of them being Jews, the descendants of refugees from Cordova, who had sought safety in Fez, and paid a tribute of 30,000 dinars to Edris. The Kairwain, from whom the Adua el Kairwain (Kairwan) obtained its name, came from Kairwan in Africa. But though Yussuf ben Tasfin removed the wall separating the two quarters, and erected a bridge to unite them, the old animosity was so deeply seated that as late as the reign of the present Sultan's grandfather (Abd er-Rahman), it vented itself in bloodshed. Each section had its own mosque, market, and mint, and at one time even proclaimed a Sultan of its own choice. To this day the people of the Andalus quarter bear the reputation for being the strongest, bravest, and most skilful in agriculture, while the Kairwain are—or were— more learned and cultured, better traders, and more handsome in person. There are now six bridges over the river, and the town is divided into twenty quarters (homa), two in Fas el-Jedid (New Fez), the remainder in Fas el-Bali (Old Fez), and contains about 50,000 people, a fifth of them Jews. New Fez has three gates, Old Fez seven. But only one of the ancient gates, the site of which is called by the same name, Silslah, and the successor of the Bab el-Hadid, is still standing. "Kamascka", the name of one of the old gates, is in Morocco given to Christian churches as distinguished from mosques. When the gate was rebuilt in A.D. 1204, it was renamed " Kharkha". Little of Edrisi's structures are standing, new walls and new gates having in eleven centuries been built, and destroyed, and rebuilt, in the many sieges and civil wars of which Fez has been the centre. In the first 500 years of its existence the city was laid siege to eight times, viz., in A.D. 960, 979, 1045, 1048, 1069, 1145, 1248 and 1250. Abd' el-Mumen nearly destroyed it by building a dam across the plain, until the springs were collected into a reservoir, which he let loose on the rebellious town. What remained of the walls he levelled, though they were re-erected by his grandson. Almost every sovereign since then has been compelled, as a preliminary to making good his claim to the throne, to reduce Fez, with the result that the place has been alternately converted into a heap of ruins and then rebuilt ; as the Sultan found that to leave this pestilent town to itself was, at times, tantamount to raising up a rebel stronghold behind him. Except mosques, palaces, and the like, all built in its palmy days, the modern Fez does not in its general plan differ much from that of an earlier period. Everything else is very old. Of the seven gates, the Bab el-Muharrak, outside of which a market is held on Thursday, was built in A.D. 1204. It derives its name, "the burned", from the fact that on the day it was completed, a rebel's head was stuck over it, and his body burnt beneath it. The Jami el-Andalus, a mosque close to the Bab Sidi Bugida—Sidi Bugida being the name of a saint whose tomb is hard by—reminds us that it was built by the Moors from Spain. Ftuh and Gisa commemorate two legendary rivals of that name, who, in A.D. 1063, contended for the throne of Fez. But when El-Ftuh conquered his brother, he ordered his name, Ajisa, to be decapitated, hence Jisa, or Gisa. The gate was rebuilt by Abu Abd-Allah in A.D. 1285.—*Times of Morocco*, Nos. 174, 176.

There were many springs in the land on which Fez was built, and one still bears the name of Ain Amir, after the Vizier Ben Moshab el-Azdi, who made the explorations which resulted in the selection of the site. The Beni Meljoun, a tribe long the hereditary masons of Fez, claimed to be descended from him (*Roudh el-Kartas*, p. 33). About A.D. 127, Abu Yussuf erected another town to the S.S.E. of the old one. This was at first called Medinet el-Beida (the white town), but afterwards received the name of Fâs el-Jedid (or New Fez), in opposition to Fâs el-Bali (old Fez). These names are still preserved, "Old Fez" being the town proper, New Fez, the Court and Jews' Quarter.

(38) The description is criticised by Rohlfs as inaccurate, Fez being "surrounded by mountains on all sides excepting the south" (*Adventures*, p. 123). But, in reality, the hills are on all sides except the west, Rohlfs having confused the west with the south and the other points of the compass correspondingly. Then he says that "the town may be viewed as if placed on an axis lying north and south", the fact being that it lies east and west. If the error is borne in mind and allowed for, south being read west and north, east, his description of Fez is fairly accurate.—Colville, *A Ride*, etc., pp. 135 and 136. Fez is in Lat. 34° 6' 3" N. ; Long. 4° 38' 15" W. But though only 230 miles N.E. of Marakesh, it cannot, owing to the disturbed condition of the country, be reached by a straight route.

(39) It is doubtful if there were ever so many mosques in Fez; and though at present they are numerous, the total does not reach anywhere near 700, which would be a mosque for every 100 inhabitants in even its palmy days, which may be regarded as those described by Leo.

(40) The Kairwain (not "Karubin, the mosque dedicated to the Cherubim," as Rohlfs has it) is not "the largest in North Africa", though one of the finest edifices of its kind. It was begun on the first of the month of Ramadhan, A.H. 245 (A.D. 859). Previously, the religious rites of Friday were held either in the Mosque Esh-Shurfa, built in the Adua el-Kairwain, or in the Mosque of the Sheikhs in the Adua el-Andalus. The Imam Ahmed ben Abu-Bekr constructed the minaret of El-Kairwain in the years A.D. 955 and 956, and most of the Sultans have added to its architectural glories. It is now the building in which the "Library" and "University" (Dar el-Funun) are contained. The candlesticks made out of Christian bells seem to have disappeared—cast, possibly, Rohlfs suggests, into cannon.

(41) Accepting the ducat as equal to one metkal, now worth ten ounces, or $3\frac{5}{100}$, or, at the value of money four centuries ago, worth one franc twenty-five centimes—rather less than one shilling—this must have been a large sum four hundred years ago.—(Lorsbach.)

(42) The "stately colleges" are now no longer stately, though there are fourteen Medresas named after the quarters in which they are situated and the trades by which they were chiefly founded and are supported. But the so-called University of Fez, the centre of all Arabic learning, though it still attracts a number of fanatical students of Moslem theology, is now little better than a mosque school in which the knowledge imparted is of the most antiquated description. The Professors are, however, noted for their independence of the opinions of those in power, and are frequently the leaders of what semblance of public opinion exists in Fez. As late as 1540 Nicolas Cleynarts (Latinised Clenardus), the Flemish grammarian, came to study here, but unfortunately he left but a scanty account of his experiences, having died in Granada in 1542 on his way home from Fez. He found, however, the place then in its decadence (*Peregrinationum ac de rebus mahometicis Epistolæ elegantissimæ*, 1561). M. Delpen, in his *Fas son Université et l'enseignement superieur musulman* (1881), has compiled from native information a very full and the only approximately accurate account of the once-noted seat of learning. The students have still many ancient privileges, such as electing (usually by bribery) a puppet Sultan who levies contributions from the citizens, etc. The mosque of Mulai Edris, in which

the founder of the city is buried, is notable for its green roof. On the exterior is a silver plate with raised gold letters containing the legend regarding the building of the mosque.

The quarter in which it stands is the most sacred ground in Fez. At the entrance to the street a chain is stretched, and a guard is always placed to prevent Jews or Christians defiling the ground by passing down ; and most of the inhabitants are Shurfa or descendants of Mohammed.

(43) These are not infirmaries for the sick, but simply places where pilgrims and the like were entertained free of charge, as is still the case with some foundations in England (Rochester, for example), Savoy, France, etc. They do not now exist, having even before Leo's day been deprived of their funds by needy kings. Vincent Le Blanc refers to this. "Muley Malouco" (Abd el-Melck, who fell at the Battle of Alcassar, 1578) wishing to borrow the golden balls of the Kutubia in Morocco for the expenses of his wars, was told by the people that his grandfather had "sold the foundation rents of the Hospitall of Fez, and dyed before he could recover them, so as 'twas lost to the poor" (*The World Surveyed*, etc., tran. by T. B. Gent, 1660, p. 256).

(44) A lunatic asylum existed at the time Rohlfs stayed in the city. It was simply a dungeon, in which among filth the half-starved inmates were chained, so as to be out of harm's way. It was supported by legacies, but seems now a vanished institution. At all events, I cannot hear of its existence. Leo's account sounds amazingly like that which might have been given of a hundred European "Bedlams" less than a century ago. He wrote from intimate acquaintance with the system, for he was hospital clerk at a salary of about 31*s.* a month (*Introduction*).

(45) The baths in Fez belong to private individuals, to the government, or to the mosques. But most of them are very uncomfortable. In Rohlfs' time the highest price charged was a penny. The charge in Leo's day seems to have been higher. But having been indignantly refused the privilege of one of the baths—as all "Christians" are—I cannot speak of them except from hearsay. The annual festival is, I am told, still surviving, but in a very shadowy shape of its ancient form.

(46) Fez, even when the Sultan is absent, is, unlike Marakesh, a comparatively busy place, the streets having generally numbers of people in them. This is due to the many strangers visiting it for business, or pleasure, or devotion. Hence the number of caravan-

serais in it, though possibly 200 is more than the town could at any time support. In Fez hospitality is less practised than where there are fewer of what Leo calls "innes". But in reality the latter are merely buildings where the traveller can sleep, store his goods, stable his animals, and cook his food either himself, or have it done by his servants. The innkeeper seldom undertakes to board his lodger. The inns are of all kinds. The better class have fine courtyards and galleries like the old English inns, while the poorer are filthy in the extreme, the cattle being kept in the courtyards, and their owners in wretched cells around it. The Kandji (coffee-seller) does not provide attendance, and, as every traveller is provided with the necessary camping equipage, his services, except perhaps to supply the tea or—less frequently—coffee (all day long in request) are seldom required.

The infamous houses kept by the El-Khanate (Elchena) have ceased to exist, for though Fez does not bear the best of reputations, it is not perhaps the sink of indescribable vice it was in the Middle Ages. The "innes" of Fez are, indeed, mostly owned by the Jews. They are, as everywhere in Morocco, known as "fondaks" (*Arabic*, fenaduk, *sing*. funduk ; Spanish, *Fonda* ; Italian, *fondaco*), and are quite distinct from the coffee-shops, which are in Morocco not frequented by the best kind of people. Coffee, indeed, is very little drunk ; but though intoxicating liquor is prohibited, it can be got, the Jews being notorious for making and selling wine and a spirit distilled from dates and figs. Some of these fondaks are far from respectable, but the more disreputable class of houses are generally in the hands of some individual wealthy enough to bribe the authorities to be officially blind.

(47) This description may still stand for the Fez water mills. Leo has, however, rather exaggerated the number, even in his day, while Pory has mistranslated the passage relating to the charges for grinding. It was not "a shilling", which would have made the fine flour of the Fez plain wheat rather costly, but "due bjocchi"—about twopence.

(48) At one time, according to the *Roudh el-Kartas*, there were said (with oriental exaggeration, perhaps) to have been 400 paper-makers in Fez. There is not one now, paper being imported from Europe, and not a great deal being required. A letter from the late Sultan Mulai el-Hassan, which the Editor received in 1884, is written on cheap "commercial post". In vain did I inquire for a bookseller, the only approach being a Taleb—too greedy to be scrupulous—who offered to write a copy of the Koran. A scholar I never met with—never as much as heard of. When I inquired for a learned Moor, somebody who had learned by heart whole chapters of "the book", or could

repeat pages of Sidi Bakari, or was an authority on the Tradition, might be mentioned. But an astronomer, a geographer, a man with any European—any except theological oriental—learning seemed to be unknown in modern Morocco.

At one time, however, there must have been collections of books in Fez large enough to warrant the fame of the city for learning. The Arab Amirs of Morocco competed with their rivals in Spain for the glory of being the patrons of scholarship and of its cultivators. When the Moors left Spain shiploads of books were taken with them. Embassies were sent for the purpose of reclaiming certain documents, and Christian captives were given in exchange for others. In 1285, Yakub el-Mansur obtained from Sancho, King of Seville, the restitution of thirteen mule-loads of books, which he presented to the libraries of Fez. In 1326, Abu Said was equally munificent.—Delphin, *Fas, son Université*, etc., pp. 82-83.

M. Delphin had no personal knowledge of Fez, but from his position as Professor of Arabic at Oran he had better opportunities of obtaining valuable information than in the former city. For, in Morocco, to ask questions about anything is to arouse suspicion. But civil war, and the neglect which the libraries suffered during the reign of unlettered Sultans must have ended in the destruction, theft, or ruin of many. Forty years after the date when Leo was a boy in Fez, Clenardus relates that the company around the book-stalls by the great mosque were fonder of pricing than of buying the literary treasures. Indeed, he does not make any remark about the value of that which was offered for sale.

Since then, all manner of vain imaginings have been suggested regarding the contents of the "Library" in the Kairwain mosque. It may, so runs the oft-repeated legend, possess valuable histories in MS., classics, it may be, from the old library of Alexandria—possibly the lost books of Livy (107 out of 142, though of two only do we not possess epitomes). But all is far from probable. The fluctuations in opinion regarding this library are curious, if not instructive. The late Sir John Drummond Hay, for so many years English Minister to Morocco, made exhaustive inquiries on the subject; and, though he offered a large sum of money for any MS. of value, he failed to obtain the desideratum. At one time, he was told, there were a good many books, but they have been lost by lending, devoured by insects, mould, and the other enemies of literature, until few remained. Most probably some theological treatises, translations in Arabic, possibly of the classics, or it may be some chronicles like those of Ibn Batuta Ben Ghazi, Ben Abdallah Eloufrani-Ezziâni, and others found in the Library of Constantine and other Algerian towns, comprised the bulk. But no European has much chance of ascertaining until Morocco is under other rulers, and while the Moors place such inordinate store by what they possess that their assertions are of little value. They imagine that Europe is longing for the seraphic wisdom stored up in these diffuse maunderings of a few centuries ago, unaware that in the Nazarene libraries there are more Arabic books than in all Morocco. Few, if any, of them have any idea of what a great library is; and hence the adjectives applied to the magnitude of the Kairwain collection may be accepted for what they are worth.

It was from some such stories that Rohlfs obtained the information that there was "at least 5,000 MS. volumes in the mosque". The authorities will assuredly not give any voluntary assistance. They even object to the Christian visitors being allowed to buy any object in the bazaars which may happen to have a verse of the Koran on it, and if a copy of that work is written for a book-loving traveller, the price charged is usually high enough to salve the scribe's wounded conscience. In short, the only literature to be picked up in Fez, or other towns of Morocco, is usually of no more than caligraphic interest. Still the idea is persistent that there must be some books of value in the palaces and mosques, which would well repay a search by some good Arabic scholar. In 1883, M. René Basset published a list of 240 MSS. in the Kairwain mosque library. This had been furnished to M. Ordega, at that time French Minister to Morocco, but though manifestly imperfect, it comprises, most likely, all the more important works (*Bull. de Correspondance Africaine*, Fas. VI, Nov. and Dec., 1882, p. 366). The catalogue is very disappointing, while Edris ben Tsabet's estimate of the library containing 30,000 volumes can scarcely be accepted as in keeping with the space in which they are stowed (*Bibl. of Morocco*, Nos. 424, 1518). In 1540, Clenardus saw only remnants of libraries, but, in 1613, Erpennius estimated the Fez books in the collection at more than 32,000.

But in 1760 the Sultan Sidi Mohammed distributed to the Kadis throughout the empire the greater part of the books in the Kairwain mosque, and Mulai Sulieman, reserving only such works as were required for the use of Jurisconsults, dispersed a large part of the remainder—a state of matters much more in keeping with the facts of the case than pretending that anything like 30,000 volumes are still in the library. M. de la Martinière even declares that M. Tissot "visited the two great mosques of Mula Idris and El-Qairouyin, and found the libraries empty." This statement is so entirely contrary to everything that I have heard, and in every respect so unlikely, that it must be accepted with doubt. But if M. de la Martinière was not misinformed, it proves that M. Delphin must have been grossly deceived by his friend, M. Tolba. He takes, moreover, an exaggerated view of the "University", which a less Algerianised idea of Morocco might perhaps have dissipated.

(49) "A cinquanta altre bottighe"—the fifty shops of the fruit-sellers, —is omitted.

(50) "Carote e navoni" are the words which Pory, throughout this chapter, translates as "pease and turnep-rootes". Temporal renders the first word not carrots but parsnips (pastonnades). The carrot was known to the ancients, and is a favourite vegetable among the Moors; but as it was not introduced into England before the sixteenth century, it is not impossible that neither Pory nor Temporal were acquainted with it. Yet it is curious to find Florianus translating "carote" as "ciceres" (an error copied by Pory), since the carrot was imported into England by way of Holland.

(51) The substitution by Florianus of "liardo" for "bajocho" is erroneous, for the old liard was worth only the fourth of a sou. Temporal falls into the same inaccuracy.

(52) Fares (Abu An'an), A.D. 1351-1357, of the Beni-Marini dynasty. This description, making allowance for the different needs of the time, and the decadence of Fez, will very fairly apply to the present day.

(53) Leo says little about the slave trade, which at that time was largely supplied by European captives. The negro traffic had, however, begun, and was most likely then, as now, held in the same place. Corn is sold in the morning and slaves in the afternoon (note 76).

(54) "Kaseria" is the title of a market-place all over the Barbary States, and no doubt received this name from the custom described. In Fez the Kaseria is a network of narrow, covered-in lanes, guarded by men and dogs trained to spring on any intruder.

(55) Many of the Fez merchants still do a large business, and are held in good repute in Marseilles, Cadiz, Lisbon and Gibraltar; and a Moor with whom I voyaged from Gibraltar to Plymouth gave me a curious account of the number of his countrymen in Manchester, and of the extent of their dealings and credit in England and other countries. This confidence is therefore presumably not misplaced, though there are disagreeable experiences of traders in the coast towns who become bankrupt and return an apocryphal list of Mohameds and Ibrahims of El-This and El-That, their debtors in "the interior". In fact, it is now difficult for the ordinary Moorish trader to get credit from the Christian manufacturer.

(56) There is an excellent chapter (by Mr. Cowan) on Moorish cookery in Cowan and Johnston's *Moorish Lotos Leaves*, pp. 237-286.

(57) As Moorish rites are all ordained by "the law", they do not differ much in the course of centuries. This description of a marriage

in Morocco may be accepted as still correct, not only for that country, but generally for other Moslem lands.

(58) Some may be remnants of Roman rites which were dovetailed into early Christianity.

(59) Pigeons are still kept, but more for food than sport, and the breeds I have seen are very poor. The early reputation of Morocco for fancy pigeons is preserved in the variety called " Barbs"—" He will not swagger with a Barbary hen, if her feathers turn back any show of resistance."—*Henry IV*, Act II (Part 2), Sc. IV. Mary Queen of Scots wearied in her last captivity for " pigeons from Barbary".

(60) Chess-playing is still in favour with the better-class Moors, and indeed figures in many Moorish tales. The " bickers", as they used to be called in Scotland, are not now much in vogue among the Fez boys.

(61) The Fez poets seem to be almost extinct, though the people are fond of singing, and the professional musician still chants his own verses when invited to entertain company after dinner at great men's houses.

(62) This still applies. See also Delphin, *Fas, son Université*, etc. ; Godard, *Maroc*, p. 235, etc.

(63) " Due bajocchi." Fortune-telling and divining are much in vogue, and the methods described are those practised at the present day, and indeed all over Europe, where divination is popular in proportion to the credulity of the diviner's dupes.

(64) Or " Sahhârin".

(65) Astrology is cultivated, though even that illegitimate sister of astronomy has fallen from any semblance of science it ever possessed. Astronomy is said to be " taught" in the University, but though Mulai el-Hassan learned the use of the sextant from a French renegade (Abd er-Rahman, Count de Saulty, a Captain of Engineers, whose romantic tale relieves the dulness of these latter days of Barbary), and was fond of using it, neither he nor any one of whom I have heard had any acquaintance with systematic astronomy. At one time it was very different. Abu Hassan Ali, of Morocco, composed a treatise on astronomical instruments, which showed that in the thirteenth century the science had made considerable advances in Morocco (*Bibl. of Morocco*, Nos. 575, 743, 2023 ; see *Introduction*. Ali Bey found at the beginning of the century that, in addition

to a room full of rotting manuscripts in the Kairwan mosque, there was another containing clocks and various astronomical instruments, mostly out of repair, and of which nobody knew the use. Among the latter were European terrestrial and celestial globes, etc., none of them less than a century old. Euclid existed in four great folio volumes unread, Ptolemy was the latest treatise on cosmography studied, and Aristotle's physics were talked of. Yet even then sufficient astronomy was understood for the time of prayer to be fixed by observations taken with rude astrolobes constructed for each latitude. But though some notions of alchemy existed, chemistry, in the true meaning of the term, was unknown, and the ideas of medicine and geography were most elementary. Among the text books in use in the "University of Fez", are—in astronomy, *Ilm et-tenjin*, the *Muqna' el-Kebir*, and the *Muqna' es-serir* of Sussi, the *Ner' mu es-Siradj* of El-Akhdari, the *Mandhuma* of El-Meknassi, the *Rissala* of El-Mardine, and his commentator Et-Tajuri, Benu Ahibak, Abd Allah ben Mohammed el-Tejibi, Benu el-Benna, El-Althab, and Benu Merzug. In geography and history the text-books are:—Mas'udi, Ibn el-Athir, Es-Suyuti El-Khatibi, Abu-l-Feda, Makkari, Ibn Khatib, El-Adhari, Obeïd El-Bekri, Edrisi, Benu el-Uardi, El-Abderi, Ibn Bathutha, El-Karamani, Ibn As-Sakir, Ibn Abi Zera'a Er-Rumi, Abd el-Wahid, Abu Ishak es-Sijilmassi, Sidi Bu Ras, El-Kessi, Ez-Zeiani, Handun ben el-Hajj El-Fâsi, etc. Many of these works are of course well known, but numbers are still strange to European scholars. M. Delphin's information was obtained from presumably trustworthy quarters, viz., Si Idris ben Isabet and Si Mohamed El-Harchani, both professors in Tlemsen and former students in Fez. To them Fez was still "le Dar el-'ilm"—the House of Science—the asylum of Mussulman learning; so that while not ignorant of the state of knowledge elsewhere, they probably regarded their Alma Mater rather more favourably than she deserved. The height of the sun is still taken by an astrolabe, and the names of the principal constellations and phases of the moon are known. But beyond this, the knowledge of astronomy in Fez is very limited, though probably since Captain Erckmann taught the Kairwain Tholba the use of logarithms, they may aim at higher things. M. Godard, who lived long in Morocco, and is in most facts of the kind tolerably accurate, does not by any means take so high an estimate of the Moroccan Tholba's acquirements. They possess, he affirms, a translation of Euclid, but algebra, a branch of science with an Arabic name, is little known. The arithmetical treatise of Ali Ibn-Mohammed Ibn Ali el-Coïsh (better known as El-Calsadi) is their common text-book, and for the Kitab el-Mokna of Abd Allah-Mohammed Ibn-Said, a native of Sus.

Their astronomy consists mainly in the casting of horoscopes. Professors of divining, incantations, necromancy, and occult science, swarm throughout the empire. The Tholba—graduates of Fez—are often so ignorant, or so knavish, as to pretend to predict events by the appearance of the sky, though it is doubtful if one of them could calculate an eclipse. The dense ignorance of the people wins for the Tholba, and especially for the Professors of the Kairwain " University", immense consideration among their tribesmen, who believe that they know incantations by which hidden treasures can be unearthed and the future foretold, and disagreeable people removed. Their influence in the country is perhaps the reason why they are compelled to reside in Fez.

(66) The two names printed Margian and Ibnu Caldim should be Margiane and Ibn Khaldun.

Magic and kindred occult sciences of the Moslems were in large part adopted from the Jews, so that their incantations, talismans, and the like, are much the same as those in Europe, the Babylonian-Greek astrology having been systematised in the writings of Paul of Alexandria and Claudius Ptolemy, which were known to the learned Mohammedans through translations.

The "hand" painted on walls, or made in brass and other materials, is a protection, universal in Morocco, against the evil eye ; and " Solomon's seal" (the pentagram), which is equally common, is a tradition of the Pythagoreans, though now a magic symbol in almost every country. Bretschneider, *Geometrie von Euklides*, p. 85.

(67) These remarks of Leo on Hassan al-Basri and the other Free-thinkers of Islam do not specially concern Morocco, as none of the heterodox sects, according to the Mohammedan way of thinking, have now an open—if indeed any—existence in Barbary.

(68) The chief sects in Morocco are not really religious dissenters, or *Al motazila*, as the followers of Wasil ibn Obaid were called, but *Akhwán* (sing. *Akhu*, brother) or brotherhoods, comparable in some respects to monastic orders. These powerful fraternities are Mulai Tayyib, whose head is the Grand Sheriff of Wazan, the Derkana, the Aissawi—from whom most of the fire-eaters and performers of other hideous orgies come—that of Sidi Abd el-Kader, el-Jilali, and that of Sidi Ahmed Jejini, though the two latter have fewer followers than he others. There are some other *Akhwáin* in Morocco, but none of much importance.—Erckmann, *Le Maroc Moderne*, pp. 99-112.

The scene described by Leo in Cairo has also been witnessed in Morocco.

(69) These sects of Leshari and Imamia have not nowadays much hold, so far as I can learn, in Morocco.

Leo likened these doctrines to the Jewish Kabbalah, and in many respects they are similar. It is indeed known that Jewish philosophy infiltrated into Mahommedanism. Leo X—the patron and godfather of the Moor—was greatly attracted to the Kabbalah doctrines, a fact which might perhaps have tempted Leo to trace them among the Arabs also.—Ginsburg, *The Kabbalah* (1865).

(70) These treasure-seekers, or El-Kanisin (from Kanz, a treasure), are as sanguine as ever, and to their iconoclastic propensities is due the fact that scarcely an ancient building in Morocco has one stone left on another. Some of the Tholba affect to know the magical art of finding where the ancient people hid their treasures, and wondrous tales are told of gold and precious stones having been dug out of the ruins of Roman towns. "Pots and kettles of gold, and silver coins", Jackson, a rather credulous writer, was led to believe in 1801 were "continually disinterred from" the ruins of Volubilis. Stories of this kind, invented or exaggerated, keep alive the legend, though I have never ascertained that any facts support them.

If a European examines any old building he is, of course, set down as a treasure-seeker, and if he takes any measurements he is supposed to be following the instructions of his "book". The same ideas prevail everywhere in Barbary, and extensively in Egypt (Abd-Allatif, *Relation de l'Egypte*, ed. Silvestre de Sacy, pp. 196, 198, 203, 209, 509, 513). Amazing tales are told of the treasures come upon among the ruins of Carthage and other ancient sites, as also, and with more basis in truth, of the Incas buildings in Peru. No doubt engraved gems and articles of even more intrinsic value have been and are disinterred, especially in Tunis, but Morocco seems to have been evacuated too leisurely for many hastily hidden hoards to have been neglected.

(71) Jafar, better known as Geber, lived in the middle of the eighth century. He was not a Greek, but a Sabæan. But Avicenna (Ibn Sina) Rhazes, Artephius (a Cabbalist also) Kalidi, and other Moslems whose writings must have been well known in Leo's day, were at least alchemists, if not searchers after the philosopher's stone.

In Morocco the seekers after the elixir seem extinct, though the "other sort", so far as counterfeiting coin is concerned, still survive. Hands cut off for this and other offences are common. There are, however, Moghrebins—mostly Tunisian and Algerian—who affect to possess the secret of how base metals may be transmuted into gold and silver. In Egypt they are held in esteem as skilful in raising genii to do their bidding, and as necromancers generally.— Perron, *Notes to Sidi-Khelil*, t. iii, p. 583.

(72) The snake-charmers come, for the most part, from Sus. This indeed is the land of acrobats and show folk generally, who collect the dwarfs which Mr. Halliburton imagines to inhabit particular localities

in that region ; among others the oasis of Akka, actually one of the best-known spots on the caravan route from Mogador to Timbuktu. The fortune-tellers of Morocco are much less known to Europeans. They are the gipsies known as "Jenkanes", though by that term it must not be supposed that any relation to the Indian wanderers of Europe is suggested. The Moroccan Jenkanes are apparently roamers who have lost a tribal connection—possibly the *débris* of the nomad people of ancient invasions, or of the races pulverised by the ruthless wars of the Romans. They speak no special dialect, most of them understanding Arabic and Berber equally well. The men, curiously enough, follow the trade of horse-coping, as do the European gipsies, while the women are equally addicted to palmistry, and knavery generally—these occupations being hereditary. They profess to be the best of Mohammedans, though they are suspected not to be too strict in their observances, and to admix with it practices smacking decidedly of paganism. The "Jenkanes" (*sing.* jinkân),—about whom very little is known, though well worthy of study—marry chiefly among themselves, the other races of Morocco not caring much for brides or husbands selected from among these outcasts. In appearance they differ much from the people around them ; otherwise the suggestion might be made of the Jenkan being a Spanish gipsy (Spanish, *Gitano;* Syrian, *Jinganeh;* Turkish, *Chinghiân;* and so forth), who at some early date crossed, voluntarily or involuntarily, the Strait of Gibraltar.

Leo compares them to the Italian "Ciurmatori", a word which literally means wizards, witches—in short, cheats.

(73) These caves in the limestone are well known. The evil reputation of the locality is still maintained ; but the open selling of wine and the like has long ceased. The leper village seems to have disappeared, though lepers are quite common in the vicinity of the city. (Note 93, Book I.) The market is still held on the plain leading "to the riuver" (Sebu). Lime making is also a busy pursuit, the "tabra" being a kind of concrete mixed with lime, out of which the houses, etc., are built. The picturesqueness of the meadows spread with bleaching clothes must have struck visitors even less sentimental than Leo ; linen weaving, since English calico can be bought so cheaply, is now almost a lost art in Moroccan towns. The pretty embroidered towels made by the Berber women are woven of native cotton.

(74) Extensive burial grounds and refuse heaps encircle Fez, but the mausolea of the kings are in many cases ruined and neglected, as are even the endless tombs of saints, held in much higher consideration. On the south-east of the town are the ruins of a castle, where,

according to legend, "the old Sultans kept their provisions," and a couple of towers close by are said to have been used for torturing prisoners by dropping water slowly on their heads until they either went mad or revealed the places in which they had concealed their treasures. All Morocco is a huge graveyard of money which the owners had committed to the custody of Mother Earth, but died before revealing the secret of their hoards.

(75) " E vero che il maggio l'adacquano tutto," etc. The continual watering is as yet by means of streams from the Fez River, which run through the gardens, and can, if necessary, be used for irrigation. " E perentro i giardini passano alcuni piccoli rami del fiume."

(76) Most likely it is still the same place, now used for much the same purposes as it was four centuries ago (note 53).

(77) For the history of New Fez see note 37. It was called the White City (La città bianca), from the whiteness of the new walls and houses.

(78) The Jews continue to be the gold and silver smiths of Morocco, and practise usury in its most outrageous form, though under names and by subterfuges which soothe the Mussulman conscience, and serve to obtain the necessary legal processes. A Jew and a "hillman", for instance, appear before the Kadi, and testify that the one has bought of the other a web of cloth—which is duly produced—promising to pay for it next year when his crops ripen. The requisite bonds are executed, but, as everyone knows, the Berber has actually borrowed money of the Jew at 50, 100, and 150 per cent., and if he does not pay, the farmer's corn and cattle will have to be sold.

(79) The Jews now live in New Fez. When they enter the Moorish quarter they must go barefooted, as in Leo's day, and in any case are required to wear black slippers. The "dulipan" is not a turban, but a "fez" or skull-cap. The red "tarbux" or "xaxia" "fez" worn by the Moors are now frequently made at Vienna, Marseilles, or anywhere rather than the city from which they take their popular name. If Leo is correct in saying that the removal of the Jews to New Fez was in the reign of Abu Said (Abd-Allah II), this must have been between A.D. 1398 and 1420.

The filthy "Mellah" is still guarded, though more than once the Moorish rabble have broken into it, and sacked the houses and massacred the hated inmates. Of late years, some good houses, with an excellent school or synagogue, have been built there.

(80) These water-wheels are still in use. The Genoese was probably the Messer Tomasso di Marino already mentioned (note 21). The

wheel generally in use is really the Persian one, though some new ones, the invention of Count de Saulty, are also employed.

(81) This statement is worth noting. Morocco is in reality a very democratic despotism, a man's position giving him no claim to respect except what his office entails, unless, indeed, he is of the Prophet's blood. Beyond the "Shurafa" (Sheriffs) there is no aristocracy in the country. A slave to-day, he may be the governor of a province to-morrow, and the man who was a vizier in the morning be on the way to beg his bread before night. All depends on the Sultan's will, and the higher anyone is placed the more likely he will be soon to fall. The extortions of the courtiers always makes them hated, though the knowledge that they may have before long to depend on popular favour, and the innately democratic character of the people and of government, to a certain extent tends to an amazing affability on the part of the highest official to the poorest person. A great Kaïd will discourse pleasantly with a muleteer or camel-driver, a position which it is possible he at one time himself held, and may hold again. The humblest person can present a petition to the Sultan on his way to the mosque; and it was not uncommon for a woman to cry, "Mulai Hassan! Mulai Hassan!" after the late sovereign, and demand voice of this kindly, yet at times ferocious, Sultan.

(82) "Curdi", Kurds. The Ghoz, Kurds, Turks, or Turkomans, first appear as mercenaries in Africa under the authority of Abu Yakub about A.D. 1179 (A.H. 574). The Almohade Kalifs regarded them favourably as friends and allies, just as they mustered Christians into the ranks of their armies.—Dozy, *Hist. of the Almohades* (1847); *Journal Asiatique*, 4th ser., t. iii, p.; 491t. x, p. 343.

(83) In Morocco the Mahommedan law of the eldest surviving male member of the family succeeding does not obtain. The Sultan can appoint any one of the Royal family, and as he generally abstains from doing so until *in extremis*, in order to obviate the temptation to the heir designate of anticipating the natural course of events, the result is often a civil war among the claimants for the "Sherifian umbrella."

(84) This description is valuable as the only one of the Moroccan Court in the palmy days of the Sultan, as a distinctly African sovereign. Needless to say, it no longer applies. The principal officials of the modern "Maghzen" are given in Erckmann's *Le Maroc Moderne*, pp. 218-240.

(85) This place, ruined more than four centuries ago, is perhaps M'hamed (Renou). In Marmol's day it was inhabited by the Mahamide Arabs.

(86) Hubbed, Habbar of Marmol. Originally the shrine of the first Fakih of the Kairwain mosque in Fez. It was destroyed in the Said wars (p. 580). This fakih, according to a tradition given in the *Roudh el-Kartas* (p. 68), was the Sheikh Abu Abd Allah ben Ali el-Farsi.

(87) Zauià (*Záwiya*) means literally a shrine or hermitage, and, on that account, a "city of refuge". The "hospital," which alone attested the existence of the place in Leo's time, was, no doubt, simply a large "Nsla", or lodging place for travellers. Its locality is not now known.

(88) Chaulan, or Halua (Marmol), a castle built by a Prince of the Zeneta (Senhaja). The palace erected by Abu-l-Hassan (not the fourth, but—according to whether the first four princes are reckoned— the eleventh or the seventh Beni-Marini king=A.D. 1330-1351), and the hot bath, ought to mark this ancient kasba. "Ain Halua" would mean the pleasant bath, unless it is the hot bath of Ain Sidi Yussuf, which I have identified with Gemiha Elchmen (p. 587); the locality is unknown.

(89) The Jebel Zelag, near Fez, is still one of the summer haunts of the wealthy Fazees, and is famous for its sweet though small grapes. The "great store of castles and towns"—for which read Ksars and villages—are not so marked.

(90) The Jebel Zarhun, Zerhuan, or Zerhon, in reality a massive mountain clump, or isolated range. In Leo's and Marmol's time it was wooded, and swarmed with lions. The lions have long ago disappeared, and the wood has been hewn down except in the vicinity of saints' tombs, and (according to De la Martinière) of certain Berber villages of the Eastern valleys, and on some of the southern stretches which stand opposite the plateau of Mekines and the gorge of Mulai Idris. The Zarhun was evidently regarded by the Romans as of strategical importance; for one of their great roads led along the edge of the western slope from the Volubilis (Ksar Faraun) to Tocolosida. The country is now very thinly inhabited and little cultivated.

(91) This is Ualili, also called Zarhun, and "Zuia Muley Driss" (Mulai Idris), from the father of the founder of Fez, and the first of the Edrisite dynasty, being buried in the mosque of this thrice holy town. The place is built on a rocky barren hillock, at the bottom of a wild ravine formed by two spurs of the Zarhun, with dark olive groves all around. But so sacred is the town regarded that neither Christian nor Jew is permitted to enter; and the faith of renegades is, justly, so little regarded that even they have found it wise not to risk the fanaticism of the last of the undefiled strongholds of Islam. Jackson affirmed that, in June, 1801, he was

not only kindly received in "Muley Dris Zerone", but slept in the "adytum" of the famous sanctuary (*An Account of Timbuctoo and Housa*, etc., p. 119). If so—and Jackson mentions natives who were ready to vouch for the truth of his statement—he is the only one who enjoyed that barren honour. For though many have affected to have visited Ualili "in disguise"—as if the quick-eyed Arab could not detect the slightest error in language or movement or ceremonial observances in the European, no matter how well drilled!—there is no authenticated case of the kind. However, what need be known regarding Ulali can be easily sifted out of the conversation of natives.

The town may, perhaps, have originally been a Roman outpost, and it is not improbable that the native name is a corruption of Volubilis, out of the ruins of which both it, Fez and Mekines, as well as almost every hut in the country round about, has in part been built. Indeed, the pillars of the Ualili mosque are said to have been taken from Volubilis, and marbles—sometimes bearing priceless inscriptions—are often taken from the many Roman ruins scattered in the unexplored villages of Zarhun to repair a fence, or even to burn into lime. Outside the high walls of Ualili are fields and olive groves. The chief of the three gates is the Bab el-Hajar. In the centre of the town is a market-place surrounded by a colonnade, and on the south side of the market-place is the sanctuary containing the tomb of Mulai Idris I. To this shrine every Sultan must go on succeeding to the Sherifian umbrella, and it is only on the occasions when he and his ministers enter it that even Moslems can visit this sacred fane. At the approach to the tomb, which is barricaded against the ingress of horses, etc., a legion of beggars and sick people collect. After descending some steps the main courtyard is reached. This is cooled by a white marble fountain, and is surrounded by a colonnade said to be of marble from Volubilis. The floor also is paved with white marble and coloured tiles, while the ceilings are beautifully carved, and the arches above the pillars are sculptured and painted. To the left of this court is the treasury, the door of which is also decorated, and on the right is the sepulchral chamber, entered through a large arch up one step. On the left side sits the guardian sheriff with a staff in his hand, and opposite to him is a large chest, carved and painted, and somewhat pyramidical in shape, with a hole in the lid to receive alms. Visitors are only permitted to kiss the ground at the step and deposit their offerings. The tomb, sheathed with gilt, is in the centre of the chamber, and in front of it are a large number of gold and silver candlesticks, in addition to many large chandeliers hung from the richly worked ceiling. Like most Moorish rooms, the place where Mulai Idris I ("El-Kebir, the Great", as he is sometimes called) lies is very incongruous in its furniture. An assortment of fine old clocks, all going differently and chiming and striking at different times, are, as in many Moorish chambers, its most prominent ornaments, and amongst the chandeliers are hung several ostrich eggs and looking-glass balls, while the walls themselves are covered with magnificent carpets, any vacant spaces being allotted to native brackets, on which are placed gaudy bits of bric-à-brac. The sanctuary of Mulai Idris's barber (in the same street) is second only to that of his master. But everything—and, indeed, everybody—in the town is more or less sacred. No one pays any taxes, or is liable to military service; and though the Sultan is represented by a deputy of the governor of New Fez, he exercises scarcely any authority. And if one gets somewhat wearied of Mulai Edris II in Fez, where his name is never out of men's mouths, his father is even more frequently invoked in the town where he lived, and died, and is buried; for Ualili lives by the dead saint. Nearly the entire population are Shurafa (Sheriffs), who find their relationship to the Prophet a more lucrative accident than usual; for the revenue of the shrine, both in landed property and gifts, must be considerable. The Sultan sends at times large gifts in cash, and every visitor to the city pays for the privilege; while on the great occasions when the tomb is visible, the sums put into the pyramidal chest must be very large. A pious Moor of my acquaintance assured me that the extortion of the endless parasites on the saint is so shameless, that it is not much less costly to make the Mecca Hajj than to visit Mulai Idris, on an occasion when the pilgrimage is likely to be of superlative value. Everybody is intent on squeezing the pious.

All—or nearly all—of the revenue is divided weekly among the principal heirs of the saint. His descendants are naturally extremely numerous, so that those entitled to share in the Zauïa revenue has to be restricted to two classes—viz., those families resident in Fez and Mekines, and those living in Fez, Rif, and Tetuan, who trace their descent from Mulai Abd es-Selam ben Mesih. This distribution is done by the Mokaddem of the Zauïa who, contrary to the belief and the statement of Ali Bey (*Travels*, vol. I, chap. xi), is not a descendant of Mulai Idris, and not even a Sheriff, but the member of a powerful family of Er-Rami, in whom the office has been hereditary for a long time past. He lives at the mosque of Mulai Idris in Fez, a relative acting as his deputy in Zarhun. The Mokaddem is in certain places—among the Hiaïna and Riata tribes, in the Rif, and indeed in all the wild country between Fez, Taza, and the Mediterranean—more powerful than the Sultan, and is indeed held in greater esteem than even the descendants of Mulai Idris. —De Foucauld, *Reconnaissance*, p. 25; *Times of Morocco*, No. 184, May 18th, 1889.

Though the town is now much more populous than at the time when Leo wrote, it is doubtful whether it contains 6,000 inhabitants (Bonelli,

El Imperio de Marruecos, 1882, far less 12,000, as Jackson with his usual exaggeration estimates, or 9,000, to quote the still less trustworthy guess of Gräberg di Hemsö. A couple of thousand will be nearer the reality.

Ualili—a name apparently not now known—seems to have fallen off in Leo's day, probably owing to the greater attractions of Fez and Mekines. But nowadays it seems to be more prosperous than at any former period—war having spared this holy town, while it has again and again played havoc with Fez—which was also at one time reckoned too sacred for infidel feet to pollute.

(92) The "Palazzo di Faraone", the Ksar Faraun of the Arabs, is undoubtedly the remains of a city less than two—not "about eight"—miles from Ualili, and that this was the Roman Volubilis is quite certain. The local twaddle about its being Pharaoh's palace is of course quite beneath criticism, as Leo had knowledge enough to see; though Jackson, by no means so safe an authority as is generally imagined, was inclined to favour this nonsense. Pharaoh figures much in the legends of Morocco. Thus the common squill, which grows plentifully on the Zarhun plateau, is Basal Faraun—Pharaoh's onion. The "Zauia Mulai Idris"—as the town in which the saint's body is laid is sometimes called—is universally accepted as Ualili, to which the first Idris came when he fled to Africa from his enemies in Arabia, and this general belief has been followed. Yet it is by no means beyond cavil whether the ruined Roman town of Volubilis, which must at that time have been in good condition, was not really Ualili—a corruption of the Latin name. It was most likely occupied by the Berbers. Indeed, it is not quite clear that the colonists ever really deserted the place; for, why should they have done so? They had lived there for centuries and no doubt had formed marital bonds with the neighbouring tribes, who in this town were semi-civilised. This in reality they were when Idris arrived. Ben Ghazi tells us that there was a tradition that the people of Zarhun, or the "mountain of gold", were of Roman origin. The same writer, who edited the notes of the Kadi ben Zeghbush, who died about A.D. 1241 (A.H. 640), refers to the Ksar Faruan as massive buildings in the valley called Tazga, about twelve miles from Mekines. Here, as in Marmol's day, a Wednesday (Arba) market was held, in spite of the lions, which caused much inconvenience to the country-folk on their way thither. This market extended to Ualili. "Ulali", says a legend of that period, was a Roman prince, and the city named after him was the capital of the country. But (so ran the tradition) after the Islamitic conquest, Ualili city like all the others fell into the hands of the victors. And here Idris established himself with the Sheikh of Aureba, "the pure, the chosen, the pious Sidi Idris ben Abd-allah".

At this period, therefore, it is clear that Mulai Idris bore the name of Ualili. All that the *Roudh el-Kartas* says (pp. 14, 15, 16, 19, etc.) is that the powerful tribe of Aureba (Uaraba) was the first to accept Idris; and with Abd el-Mejid, Chief of Ualili, "the principal place in the mountains of Zerhun" (Zraun), the Imam found an asylum. At that date Ualili was a town surrounded by splendid walls of ancient construction, and situated in a well-watered, fertile country, covered with olive plantations.

This strengthens the probability of Ualili having been a Roman town, as indeed its walls indicate, though the place is so little known, that a question otherwise easily settled must for the present remain problematical. It also settles, so far as legend can settle, that the city in which Idris first arrived was the same as that in which he died and was buried, and that this Ualili was the town ever since famous for his shrine. If the links in this chain are sound, we need not, therefore, cherish any doubt of Ualili and Volubilis having always been separate, though, as already suggested, the name of the latter may have been adopted in a corrupt shape from the former. Volubilis, however, we cannot doubt, was inhabited long after the Roman period, and until it formed a quarry of dressed stones for the builders of Fez, Mekines, and other places, must have been an imposing provincial town. Even yet, the arches standing are good specimens of Roman architecture.

That the town was Volubilis is proved by an epitaph of Q. Cæcilius Domitianus, the Decurion of Volubilis; and another inscription on a triumphal arch to Caracalla and Julia Domna, which shows that it was erected not later than A.D. 213. There are ruined temples and other monumental records apart from the "Antonini Itinerarium", fixing the old city just on this spot.

It is the Volubilis of Pomponius Mela, the Volubilis Oppidum of Pliny (who places it at thirty-five instead of fifty miles from Banasa), the Οὐολουβίλις of Ptolemy, R. P. Volvbilitanorvm, or Municipivm Volvbilitanvm of Inscriptions, the Volubilis Colonia of the *Antonine Itinerary*.

Leo's description is very meagre and not very accurate; but Dr. Leared and M. Tissot are too sweeping in concluding that Leo could never have seen either the ruins now under consideration or Ualili, a name which they evidently consider was misapplied, ignorant apparently of the passages in the historians already quoted. All the blunder that he commits—if it is a blunder—is considering Ualili as built by the Romans, and in placing it at eight instead of less than two miles from Volubilis.

The "extraordinary mistake" which M. de la Martinière attributes to Leo of placing these ruins "on the banks of the Sebu, at a distance of thirty-five miles from Banassa", was never made by him. So far as the distance is concerned, it was Pliny who made the mistake.

M. de la Martinière, however, follows M. Tissot in his facts and fancies. His otherwise excellent volume is also so frequently disfigured by inaccuracies made by the translator of his French MS. into English, during the author's absence in Morocco, without an opportunity of revising it, or obtaining its revision by anyone even remotely acquainted with the country, that in many places it is seriously misleading.—Tissot, *La Géographie Comparée de la Maurétanie Tingitane*, etc., pp. 147-156 ; De la Martinière, *Morocco*, pp. 181-190 ; Trotter, *Our Mission*, etc., pp. 246-253 (two photographs) ; v. Augustin, *Erinnerungen aus Marokko, gesammelt auf einer Reise im Jahre* 1830 (1838), and *Marokko* (1845) ; Leared, *A Visit to the Court of Morocco*, Appendix B, pp. 69-70, and *Academy*, June 29th, 1878 ; Richardson and Brady, in Hooker and Ball's *Tour*, etc., Appendix I, pp. 485-489, etc.

(93) This petty hill-town, then falling into decay, has been loosely identified by Marmol as the Roman Aquæ Daciæ, which with much greater likelihood we have indicated in another locality In reality, Pietra rossa—the Red Rock—which for some reason gives the name in our Italian translation, is in Arabic simply Hajar el-Hamra, the Dar el-Hamara of Marmol in the Jebel Zerhan, which Gräberg di Hemsö erroneously tried to make out to be the ancient Viposcianæ.

(94) This is the Maghaïla of Edrisi, the ruins of which may be recognised in the Jar Mghila, near the Wad Jedida on the slope of Jel Zarhun, close to the route from Fez to Mekines. The " duar " or temporary village of Madbuma—or " the ruined "—adjoins, and may refer to the condition of what was once a little town, though whether built by the Romans is more doubtful. The Romans, whose great personality struck the ruder races of Morocco with such an ineffaceable amazement, divide with Pharaoh—who never set foot in the country—and latterly the Goths and the Portuguese, the credit of building everything not attributable to Abd el-Mumen, Yusuf Ibn Yakub el-Mansur, or Mulai Ismaïl. Mghila is apparently the Mrila of El-Bekri. It is also the name of a Berber tribe, descendants of whom are found all over Barbary. The " Meghili " were formerly among the great families of Sallee. It was at Jar Mghila that Ali ben Yussuf (Abu ben Hassan) halted in 1107 on his way to Fez, then occupied by his nephew, Ali Yahia ben Abu Bekr, and it was from this insignificant hamlet that he dated his letter to the usurper and to the Fazee dignitaries.—*Roudh el-Kartas*, pp. 221-227.

(95) In the original this is " La Vergogna, castello", which Florianus has Latinised into " Verecundiæ castrum", and Pory translated into the " Castle of Shame", and Temporal into " La vergoigne, Chateau": all meaning the same, though Leo does not give us its

Arabic or Berber name. But Marmol calls it Gemaa (not Gemaa el-Hanien, as De la Martinière has it, Gemaa el-Hamen being a different place), and tries to find in it the *Goutiana* of Ptolemy. Four centuries ago it was utterly razed by "the penultimate Beni-Marini king", who must have been Yakub III, unless Esh-Sherif, the regicide and usurper, who immediately preceded the Uatas or younger branch, is reckoned as one of the line. "Abu Said" is mentioned as the particular king in a marginal note to Marmol. But he was not the "penultimate" member of the Beni-Marini. There is a break in the line of the Uatas dynasty between Said and Mohammed VI, which has not been quite accounted for.—Cardonne, *Hist. de l'Afrique et de l'Espagne*, t. ii, p. 372.

The "Castle of Shame" was very probably destroyed in the Said wars. The remains of it may be looked for among the ruins near Mehduma. But until the interesting *Massif* of Zarhun is explored, this and many other interesting historical and geographical questions must remain unsolved, though the locality in question lies within a week of London, and by treaty Europeans have a right to go anywhere in the Empire of Morocco. The slightest goodwill on the Sultan's part, and the faintest pressure on ours, could guarantee the safety of a European in a locality within sight of Fez.

(96) Beni Guariten is the Beni Uarain country.

(97) The Essas or Fhahs (Fas?) Sais, one of the best-known plains in northern Morocco. It is bounded on the north by the Utita, Zerhun, Tghat, and Zalag mountains, and on the south by El-Behalil and Beni Mtir mountains.

(98) Jebel Tghat or Trat, the Tagat of Marmol, the Togad of Temporal's version.

(99) "Piccol fiume di Bunafr." Marmol calls the stream the "Buc Nacer", which is perhaps its right spelling.

(100) Essic, in the original, perhaps a different way of writing Asseis.

(101) Guraigura is evidently the modern Jebel Gureigura, out of which rises a branch (Agubel of Marmol) of the Wad Beth. The mountains are the Gureygura of Marmol, who describes them as inhabited by the Gureigures.

Adeesen is the Adhazen of Marmol. The Zuhair (Zuair) are the well-known Zaër, and the El-husein (Elusein), the equally notorious Beni Hassan.

(102) Azgar. The province is not now known by this name. Marmol says that the name means "the flying sea", from a legend

that, in some remote period, the sea invaded the plain as far into the interior as Taza (Tezar). Renou points out that the Berber word Azrar means plain, corresponding to the Arabic Buheira, the diminutive of Bahr sea. "Little Sea" is a most appropriate name for an endless plain or prairie. With Habat, Azgar is now comprehended in the great province of El-Rarb (Gharb) or the West.

(103) El-Giuma, the El-Gemaa el-Carvax, has disappeared, and at present its site cannot be identified. Marmol (following the customary legend) says that it was built by Yakub el-Mansur on the border of a stream, the "Huet Erguila" (Wad Vargha), on a plain on the principal route from Fez to Larache. On the stream were two mills, and the stream flowed into the "Gorgot", a tributary of the Um er-Rbia.

(104) Larais (Lharais), Arache, in Arabic El-Araïsh, in common parlance Laraiche or Larache. Harais, which Pory copies from Florian, is an error. This decayed picturesque town is situated on the left bank of the Wad Kus (Luccas, the ancient Lixa or Lixus), at a point where, close to its mouth, the river enlarges into a natural harbour, which is at times dangerous to enter on account of a bar. The only street of importance—though no better paved than the rest—leads from the custom-house gate to a "soko", or market-place surrounded by arcades supported on stone pillars, and reputed the finest of the kind in Morocco. But otherwise the town is of little account, not containing 8,000 people, including 1,500 Jews and a few Europeans.

El-Araïsh has, however, a notable history. Its native name, according to Marmol, is Arays de Beni Aroz (Araïsh m'ta Beni A'ghros)—"the vineyard of the Beni A'ghros," a Berber tribe who seem to have early occupied it; and the place is one of the many claimants to the distinction of being the Garden of the Hesperides, the orange groves being the golden apple trees, and the winding El-Kus the serpent which guarded them.—Pliny.

On the Catalan map the place is called Larox, on that of Battista Agnesi, Laraza, and on others Laraxi. It was first a Phœnician and then a Roman town. M. Tissot identified the walls at El-Kantara as of the former period, and others, in the same fortification as those containing Phœnician structures, to have belonged to the Roman period.

But the site of the modern Larache was built on by the Beni A'ghros Arabs or Berbers much before the end of the twelfth or the beginning of the thirteenth century, though the neighbourhood would appear to have been a populous centre long before that date. De la Primaudace, however, is inaccurate in saying that it is not mentioned by any of the old Arabic historians. El-Bekri, for instance, describes

Harat el-Ahches, which is evidently the place; and Edrisi has a distinct mention of the town as Techmes or Techoumes, situated on the banks of the Wad Sferded, Sferd or Sikerd, the lower portion of the El-Kus (Renou). This can be no other spot than Tchemmich, on the ruins of Lukos. But as Edrisi mentions that Techmes was at that time about a mile from the sea, the contour of the country in the vicinity of the river must have changed considerably. El-Araïsh itself is, however, not mentioned; but the old town is described as surrounded with strong walls, though intestine troubles had thinned off the population of it and the adjoining villages. At that date, therefore, the modern Larach was most likely not begun.

The *Roudh el-Kartas* (p. 62) notes that the third Edrisite Imam (Mohammed ben Idris) gave (A.H. 213, A.D. 829), at the desire of his grandmother, Khanza, the government of Basra, Azila, Larache, etc., to his brother, Yahia. The same chronicle (p. 566) mentions that, in A.D. 1270, the Spanish Christians took it and massacred or enslaved all of the inhabitants. In the middle ages the Genoese and Venetian merchants were in the habit of visiting it, but Leo notes that in his time the local business of the place was in charcoal. Hence the proverb which he quotes.

The forest of cork oaks which surround Larache might, under more provident exploitation than that of the natives, still become a source of wealth. But of this there is little chance, and so the place has, ever since the Portuguese left it, been steadily going from bad to worse. Portuguese and Spanish inscriptions over the Marina Gate (1618), and several doorways, recall this portion of its annals, and some of the best houses are of Peninsular architecture.

The first attempt on Larache by the Portuguese is not taken notice of by Leo. It was in 1471 that Alfonso V captured Azilla, and the inhabitants of Larache, like those of Tangier, abandoned the place in terror. But it was not till six years later that the masters of Azilla made an attempt to occupy Larache by building a fort on the river (Note 120). They were prevented in the manner described by Leo in his account of "Gesira". It was in 1491, as noted in the text, that Mulai Naser, the brother—not the son—of the King of Fez (Said 11 El-Uatas), repeopled and fortified Larache. In 1504, D. Juan de Meneses, governor of Azilla, in retaliation for the port being a place of refuge for the Tetuan pirates, captured it by a stratagem, though he did not keep it long. Here Leo's history ends.

After failing to obtain a cession of the town in 1599, Filipe II of Spain received it in 1610 as security for money advanced to Mulai Sheikh, son of Mulai Ahmed. The Spanish held it for seventy-nine years; but in 1689 Mulai Ismaïl (after an unsuccessful attack in 1683). aided by Louis XIV, became master of it at the close of a siege lasting five months. Sixteen hundred prisoners were enslaved, and afterwards exchanged (*Gaceta*, March 20th, 1691) at the rate of 100 Spaniards for a thousand Moors. Since that date Larache has never been out of Moroccan hands, though frequently threatened by European fleets. Thus in 1765, after having bombarded Sallee and Rabat, Duchaffault, in command of a French squadron, appeared before Larache. but met with a disastrous repulse, in which the French lost 248 men, including forty-eight captured and enslaved : among the latter Bidé de Maurville, Garde de Marine, whose *Relation de l'Affaire de Larache* (1775), is not a work to which patriotic historians make very frequent references. In 1830 it was bombarded by the Austrians with results almost equally futile, guns abandoned by them being still, with some brass pieces left by the Spaniards, among the town armament ; and in 1860 it was again attacked by a Spanish squadron without suffering seriously.

The silting-up of the river has greatly altered the topography of the place. M. Tissot has, however, made the mound at the village of Tchemech to mark the site of the ancient Lixos ; and the islet of Rekada, the spot on which stood the altar of Hercules, surrounded by its groves of golden fruit—though whether the "auriferum nemus" was here or on the island (now the peninsula) of El-Khlij, is, I am afraid, not a question worth argument.

As late as 1789 vessels were built here, but a few rotting hulks are all that remain of the ancient pirate fleet of Larache. The fine cork oaks are only cut for charcoal making, or for lighter gun carriages, and the cotton once grown near the town does not now figure among its sources of wealth. Oranges are still plentiful, but the olives described by Pliny are no longer so abundant ; though the plain if properly cultivated might, as in Strabo's day, yield two-hundred-and-fifty-fold, so rich are the river bottoms of Morocco.

At one time (1786) a monopoly of the Larache trade—the export of wheat included—was granted to the Dutch. At present, except in oranges, beans, maize, chick beans, millet, canary seed, lentils, linseed, goat hair and skins, oxhide, sheepskins, wool, fuller's earth (ghasul), shebbel (shad), bonitos, and horse-mackerel, there is little trade, and few of the Moors are even moderately prosperous. Even the greater part of the scanty native clothing is brought from El-Ksar el-Kebir, and other towns in the interior (Note by Mr. J. E. Budgett-Meakin).—De la Primaudace, *Revue Africaine*, Nos. 96, 97 ; Tissot, *Géog. Comp. de la Maur. Tingitane*, pp. 67-85 (an exhaustive account of its archæology) ; and *Bull. de la Soc. de Géog. Paris*, 1876 ; De Cuevas, " Estudio general sobre Geografia [etc.], del Bagalato de Larache," etc., *Bol. Soc. Geog. Madrid*, t. xv, pp. 70, 167, 338, 417 ; t. xvi, pp. 31, 232, 365, 425 ; Barth, *Wanderungen durch die Küstenländer des Mittelmeeres*, etc., pp. 23-25.

(105) El-Ksar el-Kebir—that is, the great castle, to distinguish it from El-Ksar el-Seghir—the "little castle" on the coast. It is the Alcazar-Kebir of the French, the Alcaçar-quivir of Marmol, the Alcacerquibir of the Portuguese, and the Alcassar of a hundred histories, poems, plays, legends and pictures.

(106) This legend is too romantic not to be repeated by all subsequent writers, particularly by Marmol, who adds that the first name of the place was after the fisherman (Alcaçar-Abdulquerim, that is, Ksar-Abd el-Kerim). But whatever basis of truth there may be in the story—and except that El-Mansur enlarged and strengthened the town, there is probably very little—the main portions of it must be apocryphal. For both El-Bekri and Edrisi—who wrote long before El-Mansur's time—mention the place, the latter under the name, Ksar-Abd el-Kerim, the former as Sok-Kotama, "a great and beautiful city."

The place appears to have been the site of the Roman Oppidum Novum, built at a spot commanding the passage of the Kus just where tidal influence ceases. Thus, as M. Tissot points out, the links between the present day and Roman times are unbroken, the new city being the great market of Kotama and the great castle the ksar of Abd el-Kerim.

The town is actually built to a large extent of Roman dressed stones, and were anything like excavation or even careful examination permitted, many interesting relics would be found of the ancient city, which (*more Mauretanio*) was used as a quarry by the Berbers and Arabs. There is a Greek inscription, the only one as yet found in Morocco, on a stone forming part of the mosque minaret, indicating a Greek family or Greek colony being here in the third or fourth century A.D. Another inscription near one of the town gates was smashed before it could be copied, by one of the many fanatics with whom all Moorish towns abound; and, while digging the foundation of a house some years ago, the bronze statuette of a bacchante was found, and is now in possession of "un de nos agents consulaires au Maroc" (Tissot, *Géog. Comparée*, etc., p. 163; Miller, *Mélanges de Philol. et d'épigr.*, 1re partie, 1876, pp. 123-128). After these discoveries it is idle to doubt that El-Ksar is not in part composed of ancient remains, though Señor Cuevas (*Informe à la Real Academia de la Historia, El-K'sar el-Açabir*, 1887) denies that the site is that of *Oppidum Novum* (the position of which he considers still problematical), or that the neighbouring Basra was ever more than an African town, and consequently not the site of Tremulæ.

(107) There are still occasional floods, and beyond the town, near where the route to Fez crosses the river, a feverish-looking marshy cutting for the purpose of irrigating the gardens, is spanned by a low

viaduct of stone. The bad water-supply and the pestilential air, together with swarms of greedy mosquitos and all-abounding filth, make El-Ksar one of the least inviting towns in Morocco.

(108) This Monday (Thenein) market is still held, and the figs, grapes, and melons sold are as excellent as ever. The suburbs are, as of old, surrounded by gardens, but the town itself, with its levelled walls, no longer in peril of the "Portugals at Arzilla", is a poor half-ruined place, with sloping roofs to the houses, a kind of architecture very rarely seen in Morocco. See view in my *Africa*, vol. iv, p. 85.

(109) El-Ksar, however, never played any great part in the history of Morocco until 1578. In 1503, Juan de Meneses made a raid on this place from Azila, but his expedition had no lasting influence; though no doubt, as Leo says, there were many reciprocities of this kind between the Azila Portuguese and the El-Ksar Moors. It was on the 4th of August, 1578 (the last day of Jumada I, A.H. 986), that the town became famous in literature and history. For on that day was fought the "Battle of the Three Kings", in which fell not only Dom Sebastian of Portugal, and the Moorish rivals, Mulai Mohammed and Mulai Abd el-Melek, but likewise the Portuguese dreams of a Moorish empire. The battle was in reality fought not at El-Ksar, but on the plain near the little Wad el-Mkasem, a tributary of the Wad el-Kus, in which, according to tradition, Mohammed was drowned (MS. Contemporary Account, where the town is called "Alazar quibil", *Bib. of Morocco*, No. 77).

In 1673, Abd el-Kadr-Reilan, the rebel chief, who under the name of Gayland figures so prominently in the history of the English occupation of Tanger, fell in a battle with Mulai Ismaïl, near El-Ksar. The half-restored ruins of Gayland's palace are still used as a residence by the governor of Larache when he visits this part of his jurisdiction. It was for sheltering him that Mulai Ismaïl razed the walls of the town, which is now unprotected except by the great doors which close the Kaiseriah at night. At El-Duamar, about half an hour's ride from the town, are the remains of what seem to have been considerable buildings; but nothing worthy the name of Great Castle now exists. Indeed, the place is only great in comparison with the neighbouring villages; for the inhabitants, many of them Jews, who have here no special quarter of their own, do not number more than 6,000, if so many. It lies at the base of the Jebel Sarsar, from which Larache and Azila can be easily seen on a clear day. An absurd myth says that the workmen abandoned the place when they found their tools every morning removed by unseen hands to where the "great" mosque now stands. These buildings are built of the customary "tabia", but most of the houses in El-Ksar, unlike those of Morocco generally, are of brick. El-Harah, a leper's quarter on the south-west side of the town, is now in ruins.—*Times of Morocco*, Nos. 231, 232.

(110) Habat, Hasbata, or Hasbat, is not now recognised as a province, being with Azgar (p. 613, note 102) included in the Karb. The term is, however, still used familiarly to describe a particular district, *e.g.*, Drummond Hay, *Western Barbary* (ed. 1861). In old works it is commonly employed, *e.g.*, D'Avity, *Description générale de l'Afrique* (1642), pp. 135, 136, where "Habut ou Ehabat province de Fez" is mentioned, etc.

(111) Guargha, Wargha.

(112) Argar is in the early editions. It is evidently a mistake for Azgar, which we find in the 1837 reprint.

(113) Idris II left (to be accurate) twelve children. But it was his successor, Mohammed, who divided the empire as governments among seven of his brothers. To Kasim, the eldest, was allotted Tangier, Ceuta, Alhucema (Hajer en-Nesr), Tetuan, etc.: but as Yahia had Basra, Azila, Larache, etc., he could not have had all of Habat. It was Ayssa, whose seat of government was in Shella, who first rebelled; but it was Omar, Governor of Targa and Ghomera, who defeated Ayssa, and joined his territory—with that of Kasim (who had declined giving battle to Ayssa)—to his own. He died seven months before his brother, the Imam, *i.e.*, in A.H. 221 (A.D. 837).—*Roudh el-Kartas*, pp. 61-64.

(114) Ezaggen, as Renou suggested, may be Wazan (Oczan, Vezan, Guazan), a once holy city (but which may now be visited without any restriction), the capital of the semi-independent Sheriff of Wazan. But this was an unfortunate guess, for, as Wazan was not begun until the latter part of the seventeenth century, it could not have been mentioned by Leo and Marmol. Before the time of Mulai Abd-allah as Sheriff, who died in 1675, the town was merely a collection of mud huts.

Even for long after this date, Ezaggen, or more correctly, Asígen, now a heap of ruins on a hill opposite Wazan, was the residence of the Sheriff, and, as such, the headquarters of the sect of Mulai Tayyib. It bears the appearance of having been a large place, and it is certainly of great antiquity. It is, perhaps, the Zadd-jam of Edrisi. But, according to information obtained in Wazan, it was destroyed in a tribal war in consequence of one of its rulers wishing to marry one of the Sheriff's daughters. In 1727 the Embassy under Mr. Russel halted at the "town of Harach pleasantly situated on a mountain", and the residence of a saint who exercised power over all the surrounding country (Braithwaite, *Hist. of the Revolutions in the Empire of Morocco*, etc., p. 129). The first impression was that "Harach" must be either Asigen or Wazan under a corrupt form. But, from information kindly communicated through Mr. Budgett Meakcn by the Sherif of Wazan, it appears that "Dar el-Harash" is a place about a third of a day above Wazan towards El-Ksar, in the Masmudah district, where Sidi Abd-allah Sherif lived before Wazan was founded, when its site was a wood and belonged to the Beni Msârâ. El-Harash is now only a village, but it shows signs of having been at one time much larger. There is another El-Harash on the Wad el-Aisha.

Though Barth and Renou are, I believe, wrong in identifying the site of Wazan with that of Vopsicianæ, it is quite possible that so favourable a position for a settlement was utilised by the Romans. The late Grand Sheriff El-Hajj Abd es-Selam knew that pottery and coins had been dug in the place, and that tombs "in three rows, placed one over another," had been found.

Why De la Martinière refers to the "ancient Ezaguen, now in ruins, the site of which it would be rash to attempt to point out" (*Morocco*, p. 81) is hard to imagine, for there is no possible doubt about the place. This is the more puzzling, since a few pages further on (p. 107) he refers to Ezaguen as a "town now destroyed", which it is partially, but not entirely. M. de la Martinière's quotations from Leo are not quite accurate—probably owing to the execrable translation of his MS. Leo, for instance, does not place Ezaggen "seventy-two miles from Fez", but "almost three score and ten" (settanta miglia), which is too much. Nor does he put it at about "twenty-two miles distant from the Wargha", but almost ten ("circa a dieci miglia"). These errors of "septante deux milles", and "enuiron deux milles" (which M. de la Martinière, as stated in a foot-note, altered into 22, on the erroneous supposition that "the figure 2 must be an error of the copyist") are in Temporal's edition (1556), p. 192.

Marmol places "Ezagen" (Esagen, Esegen) three leagues from the river "Erguile", also called (t. ii, p. 205) "Erguila", a name he applies to part of the Wargha, or Uerra. It was then famous for a great Tuesday market. The chief market of Wazan is now held on Thursday. Wine has ceased to be made at Ezaggen, though the Riff and other Berbers drink it freely.—Watson, *A Visit to Wazan*, pp. 214-223; De la Martinière, *Morocco*, etc., pp. 106-145.

(115) Bani Teude. This town no longer exists, but the Sheikh of the Uled Messenana told M. De la Martinière that, about two days east of the Zauia of Mazeria, close to the Sebu, there are important ruins, which may possibly be those of Beni Teude; but at present the fanatical jealousy of the Berbers renders any attempt to penetrate

the country dangerous, if not impossible. Edrisi mentions " Beni-Tauda", two days from Fez, separated from it by the plain of Fez, inhabited by the Lamta. Beni Tauda was three miles from the Ramâra or Ramra Mountains. By Mount Gumera ("Monte di Gumera") is meant the Gumera Hills (El Ghumera). The "Wars of the Patrearkes (" pontefici") of Cairoan " (Kairwan) refers to the invasion of Northern Morocco and the dethronement of the Edrisites about A.D. 919, by El-Kaim (Abu-l-Kasim), the Fatimite Khalif of Ifukia, the religious capital of which was Kairwan.— Ibn Khaldun, *Hist. des Berbères*, t. I, pp. 267 *et seq.*; t. II, pp. 527, 528.

(116) Mergo or Amergue (Marmol) was, in Leo's day, in ruins; its inhabitants seem to have built another village close to it. On the Jebel Mulai Buchta (which, though visible from the Wargha, and probably a continuation of the Jebel Jamana, has not been visited by any European traveller since Marmol's day, if then) is the celebrated Zauia of Sidi Mergo, and Mergo may therefore be looked for in that quarter. But the Riffians' hostility renders quite impossible any such observations as are necessary for the identification of a town site, even were it possible to penetrate the country for any distance. The recent war with the Spaniards at Mellila has effectually closed the Riff to Europeans for another long term of years. If Latin inscriptions were found among the ruins, as Leo asserts, he is probably right in thinking that Mergo was a Roman town. Not unlikely it was built on or out of the ruins of the Prisciana of Pomponius Mela, and perhaps the Πρισκίανα or Πισκιαιανη of Ptolemy. Among the Bishops of Mauretania, Tingitana was an Episcopus Priscianus or Presinensis which M. Tissot thinks must be linked with some other name than the Viposcianæ or Vopiscianæ of the *Antonine Itinerary*, which has been identified with another spot.

But there are so many ruins rumoured to exist in the unknown region where Leo places Mergo, that its site must remain for long merely a piece of historical speculation. The position assigned to Mergo is between the Wargha and Sebu, five miles distant from either. But these two rivers are not, so far as known (and their course is fairly well defined), separated by a distance of ten miles, except where the Kubba of Sidi Mohammed es-Snussi is situated— perhaps identical with another described as Sidi Mergo on the summit of the Tselfat.

(117) Tansor or Tenzert (Marmol) stood half way between Fez and the Jebel Ramra, and in the Berber language means "nostril"— also "pride". It was destroyed by the Khalif El-Kaim, according to Marmol, in whose day, however, it began again to be inhabited by Berbers. On Lassailly's *Carte du Maroc* there is a "Tamsour" on the

river Wargha ; but the site of Tamsor is still hypothetical, and must continue to be so until the country in which it stood has been thoroughly explored. "Tan" and "Tam" enter commonly into the composition of Berber words.

(118) Agla—the Aguila of Marmol—is a ruined town on the Wargha, the site of a great Saturday market, whither, in spite of the Moors, merchants came from Fez and other parts to buy and sell. Agla was ruined by El-Kaïm, its prosperity being, in Marmol's time, little compared with what it appears to have been in earlier times. There is a locality three miles west of Tangier called "Agla", where, according to M. Tissot's view, certain stones marked the site of Pliny's "Cotta". What Pory translates by the old word "manured" is *cultivati*— cultivated. The Moors rarely, if ever, "manure" their fields, in our sense of the term.

(119) The Frixa of Marmol, not far from the Kus River, sacked by the Portuguese from Tangier and Azila, in the year of the Hegeira 895 (equivalent, not to A.D. 1486, but to 1490). Its position is doubtful, Mannert's belief that it was the site of Oppidum Novum being, I think, untenable. I do not know on what authority, except Leo's, Lassailly (*Carte du Maroc*) places "Narandja" on the Kus above El-Ksar el-Kebir.

Ceriege marine = sea cherries.

(120) Gezira is simply the Arabic *jezira*, an island, in Berber *ligzirt*. It is usually supposed to be the island of El-Khlij (now not a *jezira*, but a peninsula, being joined to the shore by a swamp formed of the silt of four centuries), and which the Portuguese occupied in 1477. But this is a mistake ; Leo describes his *Gezira* as about ten miles from the mouth of the river ("lontana dal mare circa a dieci miglia"), while El-Khlij is only a little way within the bar, and totally without traces of habitation. As no other island exists in the course of the Kus as far as El-Ksar el-Kebir, the conclusion must be, if any confidence is to be placed in historians, that Gezira has been washed away by the river. But just ten miles up the river there is a place called El-Maliha ("the beautiful"), close to the confluence of the little Wad Tarfâiyât with the Kus, which quite corresponds to such a locality, and to the name of "agreeable" given to the vanished island by the Portuguese.—Tissot, *Bull. de Soc. Géog.*, *Paris* (Sept. 1876).

There are two wrong dates in this account : A.H. 894 ("otto cento noâuta-quattro"), and 1562, gratuitously added as a note by the translator, is meant to be 1526. But even then it is wrong : for 1526 was only the year of the publication of the account, not of its composition. "The King of Fez, his father, that now reigneth", was Said Uates, A.D. 1489, while the incident related was in A.D. 1477.

(121) Idris II died after a surfeit of raisins—or of poison—on the 12th of Jumad II, A.H. 213 (A.D. 829); and was laid—not at first in the mosque bearing his name—but in Ualili beside his father. —*Roudh el-Kartas*, p. 61.

(122) Casar = El-Ksar el-Kebir.

(123) If Leo is correct, Basra must have been founded in the reign of Mohammed Ibn Idris (A.H. 213-221, A.D. 828-837); but, according to El-Bekri, it was a city of more modern date (about A.D. 1067). Edrisi speaks of it as north of El-Hajar ("the stones"), by which name, evidently from the Roman remains near it, he designates Ualili.

By Basra, "a citie in Arabia Fælix", the context indicates Basora.

The Morocco Basra was also called, according to El-Bekri, Basrat ed-Debban ("Basra of the Flies", the numerous dairies attracting swarms of these insects) and Basrat el-Katân ("Basra of the Flax", flax being used as a medium of exchange); also El-Hamra ("the Red"), from the colour of the soil of the Jebel Sidi Amor el-Hadi, on which it is built.

Abu-l-feda, from the information of Ibn Said, declares that before El-Ksar (Ksar Abd el-Karim) was built Basra was the capital of the surrounding country. But it then decayed, and at the time he wrote (early in the fourteenth century) was in ruins.—Solvet's ed., p. 47.

The oblivion and decay into which Basra has sunk is indeed, as Tissot remarks, an apt example of the rapidity with which centres of population in Morocco vanish without leaving a vestige of their ancient prosperity. Nowadays scarcely any portion of it remains (see *Introduction*). In El-Bekri's time (*cir.* A.D. 1067) it covered two hills and had ten gates. Less than a century later Edrisi refers to it as "formerly" a city of considerable importance. It is now difficult to find a block of stone entire. Of the ten-gated walls only the northwest angle stands—or stood, for it, too, may by this time have yielded to time and the treasure-seekers; all the rest—monuments and towers—are traceable only in the dust or in rubbish heaps. The women were in El-Bekri's day famous for their beauty, and the musical tastes of the Basraites is referred to in a poem of Ahmed Ibn Fath. Even "the sweet gardens", which seem to have survived till Leo's day, have not escaped the general ruin (De la Martinière, p. 100). Yet if Basra was built on the site of, or from the ruins of, the military post of Tremulæ, it is of still greater antiquity;

and no doubt its position on a plateau commanding, on the west, the valley of the Wad Mda, on the east the route to Wazan, on the northeast a valley opening into the El-Kas basin, and on the south the caravan road which passes El-Ksar el-Kebir, Fez, and Mekines, would render it an important site for a commercial town or as a strategic position. Actual remains of Roman bones have, however, still to be found, though the *Antonine Itinerary* leads us to look for Tremulæ about this place.

(124) Or Homara (Marmol), the modern Humâr, a large Berber village, founded, according to Leo, "pure da uno il cui nome fu Ali figluiolo del sopradetto Maumet"—a child, a son (not "a disciple") of the third Imam of the Edrisite dynasty. This must have been Ali, his successor, who died in A.H. 234 (A.D. 848). Leo is, however, not strictly correct in describing it as fourteen miles from El Ksar and six from Azila, for in reality it is more than thirty from the former, and as the time taken to cover the distance between it and Azila is an hour and a half, at the "jog-trot" of a mule, the latter must be about seven and a half miles. As Leo's distances are exact copies of those given in the *Antoniue Itinerary*, as are also those between Zilis, Jabernæ, and Lixes, M. Tissot suggests that possibly Leo saw this document with other sources of his later-acquired erudition, during his residence in Rome. The "jar", or stationary village of Humâr, is at the foot of the hills of Et-Turki, between the Wad Tuareus (Mtuarreus) es-Sahel (River of many Stones), and the Wad er-Raha (the "River of the Mill", the Rio de los Molinos of Dom Sebastian's expedition), which conjointly under the name of Wad el-Halu (the ancient *Zilla flumen* ('Ζιλσία ποταμοῦ ἐκβολαί), flow into the Atlantic a little way north of Azila. But beyond some ruins and verdant orchards, there are few traces of its former prosperity. Marmol, indeed, indicates the position when he mentions its proximity to the Wad Er-Raha or Wad er-Rehan (Vet Rayhan). In the *Itinerary* of M. de Carmar we find a river mentioned by the name of Wad el-Hhomar, as running between Azila and El-Ksar el-Kebir, to the south of a plain called "Fahs er-Rehan", or the country of myrtles (*Spectateur Militaire*, Aug. 15th, 1844; Renou, *Expl. scientifique de l'Algérie*, t. viii, p. 282; Tissot, *Bull. de la Soc. Géog. Paris*, Sept. 1876, pp. 239, 240). Wad er-Rihan, "the river of the myrtles", is, however, not the stream near which Humâr stands, but the upper part of the Sebt, just as the lower reach of it is the Wad el-Ghemen, "the sheep river". It rises in the Fahs er-Rehan, stretching to the west and south-west of Sidi el-Yemâni.

(125) Azilla, Acila, usually called and spelt Arzilla. The natives call the place indifferently Azila, or Arzila, but as Edrisi names it Azila, or Acila, and El-Bekri and Abu Hassan el-Fasi, Acila, it is more

in conformity with its derivation from the Roman Zilis, or Zilia, to keep to Azila. In Portuguese documents contemporary with their occupation of it, "Arzila" is the form employed. " In ora Oceani Colonia Julia Constantia Zilis" is Pliny's description of the Roman forerunner of Azila. It is the *Zilia* of Pomponius Mela, the Ζῆλις and Ζῆλης of Strabo, and the Ζιλία, Ζιλεῖαι, Ζειλία of Ptolemy. Pliny and the *Antonine Itinerary* are responsible for *Zilis*, though whether it is of Lybian origin is a more puzzling question, the ancient coins attributed to Zilis giving the form of *Aslith*. Strabo tells us that most of the colonists of Julia Traducta came from Zilis, if this and Tingentera are not the same place. At all events, Mela affirms that Tingentera, the modern Tarifa, his birthplace, was peopled by Phœnicians who were taken from Africa. Zilis was, therefore, most likely originally a Phœnician settlement. At all events, it was one of the first Roman colonies founded by Augustus. In A.H. 94 (A.D. 712), while Zilis was under the jurisdiction of the governor of Septa (Ceuta), it fell into the power of the Arabs.

(126) Leo's subsequent history of Azila requires correction, as it has given rise to some persistent blunders. The English (*Inglesi*) who captured and sacked Azila must have been Norman pirates—the English never held the place. Moreover, El-Bekri's account of this incident is diametrically opposed to that of Leo, for he gives the date of the attack as A.H. 229 (A.D. 843-844), and it was of a sufficiently serious character to cause the inhabitants to construct a Ribat, or fort, for the defence of their town against future pillagers.—Dozy, *Recherches*, etc., third ed., t. ii, p. 264.

(127) The capture of Azila by the Portuguese took place in A.H. 876 = A.D. 1471, not in A.H. 882 = A.D. 1477. Abdallah (Habdulac), having degenerated into a tyrant, was assassinated by a citizen of Fez known as Esh-Sherif (Esserif)—but in no way related to the dynasty of "the Sherif"—who claimed to be a descendant of the Prophet. But the friends of the murdered king rose against the regicide and usurper who had been chosen king by the fickle Fasees. Among the party opposed to Esh-Sherif was Mulai Said Sheikh (Saic Abra), governor of Habat, a member of the Uatas or younger branch of the Beni-Marini family, who immediately quitted Azila and laid siege to Fez, but, according to Leo, was routed, whereupon the entire Um er-Rbia (Temsena) country fell off from their support of "one Saic Abra", who is the same person, viz.: Mulai Said Sheikh—the "Muley-xeque" of the Portuguese chronicles. The chances are, however, that the latter voluntarily abandoned the siege when he heard that the Portuguese, considering the time favourable, had taken the opportunity of capturing Azila in his absence, and had sent 5,000 slaves, together with his

two wives and a son and daughter, prisoners to Lisbon. But Mulai Said Sheikh, seeing that he had arrived too late and was hard pressed by the Sheriff, signed a treaty by which he recognised the King of Portugal as sovereign over Ceuta, El-Ksar es-Seghir, Tangier, and Azila. Then, freed from an enemy in the rear, he raised a fresh army with which he carried Fez by storm, and forced the usurper to seek refuge in Tunis, while he became the first king of the Uatas line.

In one of the reverses they suffered in 1437, the Portuguese had to promise the evacuation of Ceuta, and, as a hostage, surrendered the Infante Dom Ferdinando (brother of "Prince Henry the Navigator") into the hands of the Moors. But the Cortes refusing to ratify the capitulation, as dishonourable to the country, the young prince had to bear the consequences until his death, in 1443, secured for him a place among the martyrs of his church. The Sheikh, being now anxious to recover his family, exchanged for them the bones of Dom Ferdinando.—João Alvarez, *Cronica do sancto e virtuoso iffante dom Ferdinando*, 1527.

These exploits obtained for King Alfonso V the titles of "the African" and "Redeemer of Slaves", while Mohammed, the son of the Sheikh, from his long residence in Lisbon, was known among his countrymen as "the Portuguese". But Mohammed's captivity in no way modified his hatred of the Christians; and, when he came to the throne (1508), he made so vigorous an assault on Azila that had it not been for the timely succour of João de Meneses with a Portuguese squadron from Tangier, and a Spanish one under Count Pedro Navarro, the hard-pressed governor, Dom Vasco Coutinho, Count of Borba, must have capitulated. It was at this siege that Leo served.

(128) In 1516, Azila was attacked a third time by the King of Fez, but again without success. By this time the place must have become essentially a European town. A mosque had been converted into the Christian church of Our Lady of the Assumption, and many pious memorials of his victories erected by the king, who had also vowed to the monastery of Evora an equestrian statue of the Virgin in silver; while numerous Portuguese traders had settled in the place. But in 1553, Azila was abandoned, being, like most places on the Moroccan coast, of more expense than value. In 1578, however, Dom Sebastian once more occupied the town, and landed here on his hapless African expedition. Finally, Felipe II of Spain, anxious, if possible, to stand well with Morocco, evacuated for the second time this solitary conquest of his predecessor on the throne of Portugal. This was in 1588 (Suarez Montanes, *Hist. de Africa*), and ever since Azila has been falling deeper and deeper into decay; until to-day, with its sanded-up harbour (perhaps owing to the destruction of the breakwater which protected it), the town is little better than a filthy ruin, in which less than 2,000 people, many of them Spanish-speaking Jews, manage to

exist. Many memorials—particularly the castle walls—recall the former masters of this wreck of the Middle Ages, which crumbles away in sight of Cape Spartel lighthouse.—De Faria y Sousa, *Africa Portuguesa* (1681), pp. 64, 65, etc.

(129) Tanja of the natives, the Tanger of the French, Tangere of the Portuguese and Spaniards (more modern spelling Tanger), Tangeri of the Italians, Tangier of the German and English. Though they do not pronounce the word in the same way, "Tangiers", once common, is not now used, except by those who have never been in "the city preserved of the Lord". The final "s" is indeed a sort of Sibboleth or Shibboleth in this respect. In the State Papers relating to the English occupation, "Tanger", "Tangeri", "Tangiers", are the forms used indifferently. The Portuguese sometimes called it "Tanjar" (*e.g.*, De Faria y Sousa, p. 66). It is the ancient Tingis, built on a Berber site, most of the inhabitants being Berbers, though the ruins on the other side of the Wad el-Hall (the now shoaled-up river in which the Sultan's piratical craft anchored), known as Tanja el-Balia (old Tangier), are, with the broken-down bridges over it, apparently of Byzantine origin—perhaps the work of Belisarius, who fortified Ceuta. A few Roman inscriptions, mosaics, coins and sculptures, have been found, and the foundations of the citadel are Roman. Remains of what was considered a Greek structure have been disinterred, and two or three Lybio-Phœnician coins have also been found.

The town, being now the most European in the empire, is described in almost every work relating to Morocco. The Portuguese became masters of it on Aug. 28th, 1471, and on 30th Feb. 1662 handed it over to the English as part of the dowry of the Infanta Catherine of Braganza, Queen of Charles II. The English in the town evacuated it on 7th of Feb. 1684. The first of the fifty Portuguese governors or captains-general was João, Marquez de Montemor, son of the Duke of Braganza; the last, Luiz de Almeida, the successor of Fernando de Menezes, Count of Ericeira, a member of a family which supplied many rulers to the Portuguese possessions in Morocco. This ex-governor wrote a history of the city (*Historia de Tangere*, 1732). The first of the English governors was the Earl of Peterborough; the last—but only to effect the evacuation—Lord Dartmouth. Most of the documents relating to the English occupation, and the history of the place generally, are entered in the *Bibliography of Morocco* (1893).

Up to 1580 the city was a dependency of Portugal, but in that year it passed, with the union of the two kingdoms of the Peninsula, into the hands of Spain. In 1640, when the arrangement was ended, Tangier remained with Spain, and would have continued a fief of that country had not the citizens rebelled and insisted that they should revert to their former allegiance, which was effected in 1643 (*MS.*

Archives Espagnoles, c. iv, No. 4, in French Foreign Office ; De la Primaudace, *Revue Africaine*, No. 94.)

The Portuguese residents and garrison of Tangier so bitterly resented the bargain with England, that had not they been compelled to ask Lord Sandwich to send a force of seamen ashore to assist in repelling an attack by the Moors prior to the formal surrender, they would most probably have resisted the landing of our troops. Tangier, after the Moors recovered it, was little better than a ruin. The English, before leaving, had not only blown up the costly mole, thus ruining Tangier Bay as a harbour, but the fortifications, and with them the best part of the town. During the English occupation many good houses were erected. On a plan of the town we find a cathedral, perhaps the Portuguese one ; and as there was a Mayor (Alderman Baker) and Corporation, there were, doubtless, beside what had been reared during the long Portuguese occupation, humbler offices of various kinds. The plan of the town then was much the same inside the walls as it is now; but to trace any sign of our twenty years' hold of Tangier, from which so much was expected, is difficult. Even Portuguese buildings, except in the Kasbah, are by no means easy to detect. In the Marina wall is the date "1623". The Moors most likely rebuilt it after their own fashion ; and though Catherine Street, St. John Street, St. Barnabas Street, Lewis Street, Salisbury Court, Dean and Cannon Street, Roches Street, and so forth remained, their names disappeared as the Portuguese names had. In reality, the history of the English occupation of Tangier, and of the circumstances under which it was abandoned, have still to be written. An interesting subject for a geographico-historical monograph would be the tracing out of the localities of the battles which had to be fought with the Moors. The latter, almost as soon as our backs were turned, relapsed into piracy, and more than once Tangier deserved destruction from the barbarous habit of its people of capturing and enslaving shipwrecked seamen. The place had a poor aspect after the English left. Thus, in 1727, the embassy under Mr. Russel describes it as in a very ruinous condition, without one house standing as built in the time of the English ; and as all the buildings were one story high, and much exposed to the setting sun, it was about as hot a town after dinner as there was in Africa. "Besides this"—and the description applied until very recently—"the streets are so pestered with dead dogs, cats, and loose stones and dunghills, 'tis very troublesome walking." The only tolerable house in the town was one built after the Moorish fashion by an English merchant, and used as a warehouse for English goods ; but not having been used as such for some years, a Bashaw had taken possession of it. So inconsiderable was the trade that it could not afford a living for one Christian merchant ; and the Jews, now so numerous, were few, and existed mainly by buying raw hides, and clipping what little money was stirring. (Braithwaite, *The History of the Revolutions in the Empire of Morocco*, etc., pp. 323-325, and the Editor, *Africa*, vol. i, pp. 99-105; vol. iv, pp. 15, 70-80, 83-87, and Introduction to the *Adventures of Thomas Pellow*, pp. 15, 41, etc.)

The attempts made by the natives to recover Tangier were never of much importance, though to the last day of their occupation the English were molested by the Moors, and it was impossible to go beyond the walls without the risk of death or capture (Oliveira Martins, *Os Filhos de D. João I*, pp. 207-242). The date of Mohammed VI's attempt was A.H. 917 = A.D. 1511, not 1508.

On the 6th August 1844, Tangier was bombarded, but with little effect, by a French fleet under the Prince de Joinville ; but since 1684 it has never been in foreign hands, though it is now almost less Moorish than Spanish and English, *i.e.*, Gibraltarene.

(130) El-Ksar es-Saghir (Sr'ir), "the little castle", to distinguish it from El-Ksar el-Kebir, "the great castle" (p. 617). It has long been in ruins, though during the periods of Moorish raids on Spain it served for the embarkation of troops. It was for this reason taken by Alfonso V, in November 1458, and put under the governorship of Eduardo de Meneses, but abandoned in 1553 (Montanes), not in 1540, the date to which Renou commits himself. The Portuguese, in whose chronicles it figures as "Alcaçarseguer", also besieged it in 1503 until it was relieved. The statement that the castle was built by Yakub el-Mansur is only one of the very unhistorical traditions of Morocco. For it is mentioned in El-Bekri (1067) and Edrisi (1154)--both of them writing before El-Mansur's day, as Ksar Masmuda—the castle of Masmuda, one of the five primitive Berber divisions ; and this name is referred to by Marmol when he calls it " Alcaçar-ceguer", or " Caçar-Maymoda". It is the Kasr el-Mejaz of Abu-l-feda. But most likely the place was of some importance during El-Mansur's reign, and perhaps strengthened by him.

(131) The names of the well-known Spanish fortress town of Ceuta, Septa, Sebta, Cevta, are considered to be variants of the Roman Septem Fratres. Septa and Septum, under the last of which name it appears on the maps of Andrea Bianconi in 1436, and Benincasa in 1467—the designation Ceuta being first used on the map of Juan de Cosa in 1500—are evidently slightly altered forms of "Septem". And no doubt this theory is correct, though M. Tissot is inclined to look for *Ad Septem Fratres* at Punta Bermeja, near the " Jebel Belyunech" of the Arabs (*Géog. Comp.*, pp. 30, 31). It was, however, the Σεῦτον or Septa of the Byzantines, who, after Justinian had reconquered Africa, rebuilt the fortress which had been dismantled by the Vandals. Occupied by the Goths during the reign of Heraclius, in the early part

of the seventh century, the name of the place had got gradually altered to Septem, Septum, or Septa. This last was its designation when the Arabs under Tarik obtained possession of it by the vengeful treachery of Ilyan (Julian), the governor under King Roderick. The tale which Leo notices undoubtedly came to him from Arabic sources, and may have been based on fact. It was, however, originally a Christian tale, and obtained currency through the Monk of Silos, a chronicler of the eleventh century (*Chronicon Silense*, Florez, *Esp. Sag.*, vol. xvii, p. 279 ; Gyangos, ed. of Al-Makkari, vol. i, pp. 255, 513, 537). But whatever may have been Ilyan's motive in betraying Roderic—a project he had long meditated there is no doubt about the fact that he did so.

Few memorials of its earliest history remain in Ceuta. The aqueduct which in the eleventh century carried the water in the Wad Auiat passed for Ilyan's work, and the Wad Lian, which falls into the Strait of Gibraltar, is a corruption of Nehr Ilyan, the name which it bears in El-Bekri's writings. The "Torre del Conde Don Julian", on the mainland behind the ruins of Badis is, I believe, a memorial of more modern date. Abu-l-feda, depending on Ebn Said's information, mentions that the fortifications were remarkable in that they were built of stone, and that at the time he wrote the water was brought by canals, though there were also cisterns to gather the rain-water. A city of Andalus, Jezirat el-Khodra (Algesiras), could be seen from the city. Edrisi, who was a native of Ceuta, derives *Sebta* from a word signifying a peninsula, which Dozy (ed. Edrisi, p. 200), with characteristic love of originality, considers an alteration of *Saeptum*, though he admits the possibility of this coming from *Septem fratres*, the name applied by the ancients to the Jebel Belyunech.

(132) The Khalif of Damascus, El-Walid I, son of Abd el-Malik. Tarik landed at Gibraltar (Jebel Tarik) in A.H. 92 (A.D. 710-711).

(133) After the fortress had passed into the hands of the Arabs it was considered so important as one of the harbours of the Berr el-Mejaz— "Country of the Crossing"—between what Abu-l-feda calls the Berr el-Udwah (Morocco) and the Berr el-Andalus (Spain)—that it was always governed by a member of the Khalif's family (Ibn Khaldun, *Hist. des Berbères*, t. ii). Hence the presence of a semi-royal court, which attracted many skilful artificers and other panderers to wealth and luxury. The Genoese and Venetian merchants regarded it as one of their most important places of trade, and even helped their Moorish customers against their Christian enemies of Ceuta ; though finding these allies rather treacherous, the Genoese, unable to get their pay for an expedition in which they had bargained to help Er-Reshid (A.D. 1234) against Spain, turned and bombarded the town, until 400,000 dinars were promised.—*Rouah el-Kartas*, p. 394.

(134) Abd el-Mumen's cause of quarrel with Ceuta's citizens and governor is mentioned elsewhere in this book.

(135) In A.H. 818 (A.D. 1415), Ceuta was captured by João I, Prince Henry the Navigator greatly distinguishing himself at the siege. Sala Ibn Sala, the governor under Abu Said, the debauched Beni-Marini Amir of Fez, made a courageous defence.—Oliviera Martins, *Os Filhos de D. João I* (1891), pp. 29-64.

(136) For this event, which precipitated what Leo so often refers to as the "Sahid war", see p. 580.

In 1418, the King of Fez, aided by the Amir of Granada, attempted to recover the place, but was repulsed by Prince Henry the Navigator. In 1580, on the union of the two crowns, Ceuta was occupied by Spain, and in 1640 remained Spanish, the citizens not having been made privy to the plot by which Tangier and Mazagan reverted to Portugal. In 1668 the place was formally confirmed to Spain, but it began to lose prestige and prosperity from the day it came under the sway of the Castilian sovereigns. The memories of its sieges and defences gave to Ceuta an *éclat* in Portuguese eyes, which it took the experiences of another generation for it to acquire in the eyes of its new masters. In 1693, Mulai Ismail made a strenuous effort to recover it, recalling in a curious letter to Don Francisco Varona, the governor, a Moorish proverb that "Tetuan without Ceuta was not worth a turnip" ("Los quales dicen que Tetuan sin Seupta no vale um nabo"). But after the fortress had been invested unintermittently for twenty-seven years, the siege was raised in 1721. During this notable attempt Mulai Ismail had in his army many renegades ; and in 1732, when he again made an attempt on Ceuta, he was aided by the Duke of Ripperda, an unscrupulous Dutch adventurer, who, after having been high in the councils of the King of Spain, had in disgrace offered his services to Morocco. Since that date Spain has, with the exception of a few unimportant attacks, remained without molestation in the possession of Ceuta. It is now a presidio, or convict settlement.—*Africa*, vol. iv, pp. 71-73.

(137) Tetuan, the Titawân of El-Bekri and Edrisi, is a Berber name.

The river on which it stands is the Martil, or Martin, though this is in reality the name of the custom-house built near its mouth. The proper name of the river is Bu Sega, or Wad el-Jalu. El-Bekri calls it Wad Rasen or Ras, or Wad Mahaksa, the people in the town having been, according to Edrisi, originally Mahaksa. Marmol, who erroneously believed the river to be the "Cus", calls the castle on the north the Castle of Adives.

The town is evidently the *Tamuda* of Pomponius Mela and Pliny, the Θαλοῦδα ποταμοῦ ἐκβολαι of Ptolemy, *Tamuda* meaning, in the Shluh dialect, swamp, or overflowed ground, such as the river makes near its mouth ; for which reason and because of the dangerous fevers thereby engendered, the town is built on higher ground nearly four miles inland. *Tet*, it may be added, means, in the many place-names into which it enters, spring ; while *ain* is Arabic for the same ; so that in a double sense "Titawân" means a fountain-head.

Though the *Tamuda oppidum* of Pliny is not mentioned in the *Antonine Itinerary*, it was probably on the site of the present town. But, in any case, Tetuan is a very ancient place, though it was not until Ceuta fell into the infidels' hands that its rival superseded it in importance as a native market town.

It appears in European history in 1400, when a fleet sent by Henry III, King of Castile, sacked the place, and reduced the inhabitants to slavery. For the next ninety years it remained desolate, until the Moors, expelled from Spain, occupied it under El-Madani (Almandali of Leo, Almandari of Marmol), who prospered in the manner described by Leo.

Helibenres=Ali Benres, or, according to Marmol, Ali Barrax.

(138) As Leo saw the place only a few years after his fellow Granadines had settled there, they must have lost no time in making reprisals for the terrible blow they suffered in 1492.

But in 1520 an event happened of which our historian could have no personal knowledge, and of which, as he does not mention it, he was probably unaware. This was, that the depredations of the Tetuanese became so troublesome that, on the advice of the governor of Ceuta, King Emanuel of Portugal resolved to construct a fortress at the Martil mouth. But although Pedro Mascarenhas made the requisite soundings, for some reason nothing more was heard of the project. In 1564, however, after Garcia de Toledo captured the Peñon de Velez, he presented himself in Tetuan Roads, with orders to make the Martil an impossible place of refuge for the exiled Granadines' pirate vessels. The season, however, being too late, Alvazar de Bazan was next year charged with the same duty, which he tried to accomplish by blocking up the river with a quantity of stones brought from Gibraltar. This simple method of rendering a river outlet unnavigable was, however, but a temporary obstacle, for the Tetuan people soon cut another channel to the north of the old mouth, and began afresh their raids on the Spanish and Portuguese coasts. They even ventured to ignore the authority of the rulers of Morocco, until in 1567, weakened by internecine dissensions, they were forced to submit to Mulai Abd-Allah, greatly, it seems, for their own good. For in the early years of the seventeenth century the "city of Mudejares", or Moors of Castile and Granada—those of Valentia being called "Tagartins"—had 800 good houses and a fleet which was the scourge of the "Gut of Gibraltar", while their city was frequented by English, Dutch, Genoese and Venetian merchants, the Dutch being especial favourites by reason of the war they carried on with Spain.

To-day, except for its orange groves and its native armourers, who in some respects perpetuate the art of Granada, the place is of little importance commercially. After the war of 1859-60 the Spanish troops occupied it for two years, and their stay has given the place a European appearance and taught a wholesome lesson, which makes Tetuan extremely tolerant to Christians. Up to 1770, all the European diplomatic agents resided here, and it was consequently the starting-place for the missions to Fez and Mekines, just as Saffi was for those to Marakesh. It is, however, taking a fresh lease of prosperity, having from 20,000 to 30,000 inhabitants, many of them Jews, who do business with the Riffians; while the richness of the soil in the adjoining country, and its trade in tanning barks and in leeches, bring a great deal of money into the town, in spite of the silting-up of the Martil mouth and of its two little subsidiary ports Negro and Emsa. The magnificent *Atlas historico y topografico de la Guerra de Africa ... en* 1859 *y* 1860, prepared by the Estado Mayor del Ejercito, is exhaustive so far as the topography of the country in the immediate vicinity of Tetuan and Ceuta is concerned. But less care has been taken to ascertain the exact native names of localities, and, worse still, Spanish names have been applied to various spots, without any trouble having been taken to learn whether they had Arabic or Berber designations. Hence this fine work must be consulted with caution, and is often disappointing.

(139) A fine range near the ruined town of Ezaggen (p. 619).— Watson's *Visit to Wazan*, p. 223; De Foucauld, *Reconnaissance*, p. 5.

(140) Beni-Zeguer of Marmol, who says that is called Beni Fensecare by an error, and that the inhabitants are Beni Zeguers, who derive their wealth from the sums received for their woven fabrics, honey, wax, etc., from the Fez and Christian merchants at their Saturday market.

(141) Jebel beni Aros (or Arous), a once powerful tribe in this vicinity. Larache was the "Arbour of the Beni Arous". They were a branch of the Ramra (Ramâra), and some of their villages paid tribute to the Portuguese when they occupied Azila.—Marmol, t. ii, p. 223.

(142) Chebit, or Telit, the Jebel Habib, about 2,267 ft. high. It was known to El-Bekri, and the name which is in full Jebel Habib ben Yussef Fahri, for having given refuge to one of the sons of Yussef el-

Fahri, who was the last prop of the Khalifs of the East in Spain, and was beheaded by order of Abd er-Rahman, about A.H. 140 (A.D. 757). In Marmol's day the inhabitants were called Beni Telit.

(143) The highest point of the Jebel Beni Hassan, Mount Anna (7,250 ft.) is often capped with snow (for which the editor can vouch from personal observation) from November to the end of April. The Gomera mountains have sometimes patches of snow late in June, and some of the elevations in the Metiwa El-Bahar country, have, as seen from the coast, a snow covering in that month. These Beni Hassan villages are still, as in Leo's day, strongly built, and the people, an ill-looking set, bear the reputation of being incorrigible robbers, who object to any strangers entering their country. A few years ago, they actually raided the harem of the Grand Vizier in his passage to Rabat, and even threatened the Sultan himself.—Tissot, *Bull. de la Soc. Géog. Paris.*, Sept. 1879, p. 54.

(144) Or Amegara. Anjera is a well-known district of the El-Rarb province, which harbours tribesmen who at times give the Sultan's representative sore trouble.

(145) Guadres, Vateras, or Huat. Idris of Marmol is Uad Ras, the highlands inhabited by a Berber tribe of that name. It is the "Dj-Uad Ras" of Schnell's map, the "Ouad Ras" of Tissot's. The "battle of Wad-Ras" was the decisive action in the Spanish war of 1859-60. But the name is derived from the stream of that name (note 137), which rises in the Uad Ras, and is a tributary, if not indeed, as El-Bekri considers it, the main current of the Martil, or El-Jalu.

(146) This passage refers to the battle of Navas de Tolosa, known to the Moors as Hisn el-Ukâb, the Eagle's Castle, or simply El-Ukâb, in which on 16th July, 1212, not "the yeere of Our Lord 1160", though A.H. 609, which is given correctly, corresponds with the right date (p. 358, Bk. ii, note 72). Nor was it "Joseph Enesir" or Yussuf En-Nasar, but Mohammed en-Naser li Din Illah, who lost this turning-point in the Arab hold upon Spain. Yussuf (el-Mostanser) was his son. The calculation of 285 years as having elapsed between this battle and the fall of Granada is accurate, which of course it could not be if A.D. 1160 were accepted as the Christian era equivalent. This is given in the early editions of Ramusio, though whether, as in this and other cases, added by the editor as part of Leo's manuscript, it is now impossible to say. The not very judiciously revised reprint of 1837, which omits most of the equivalents in the Christian calendar, in this case leaves the erroneous A.D. 1160.

147) Beni Hued-fitch, or Beni Gued el-Fetoh of Marmol, a tribe

of the Beni Ghorfit, who lived not very far from El-Uted, which was celebrated for its Manhar (or aqueduct).

(148) Er-Rif, Riff, Rif, Reef, as the *Massif* on the Mediterranean shore of Morocco is called, is one of the parts of the empire most familiar by name and yet least known. The wild Berber inhabitants, still pirates when opportunity offers, persistently refuse nowadays to permit any stranger to penetrate their fastnesses. Even the Sultan considers it prudent not to trouble this "vnciuill and rude people"; and more than once the hapless officials of their own race who have aroused their disapproval have been murdered. Leo's description still applies, so far as can be learned from the parts of their country which have been skirted here and there. The "Rifi" are Mohammedans, but, like many of the Berbers, not very strict ones: smoking, drinking wine, and eating the flesh of the wild boar. They pay what tribute they choose to render to the Sultan in mules, honey, and other country produce, and to this day the lion—a little black variety—which has been killed off in most of the adjoining parts of Morocco, is still troublesome in the Riff. The only European who has traversed this country from north to south, from Alhucemas (which he calls Albouzema), or rather El-Mezenma to Taza, was Roland Fregus of Marseilles. The mission was accomplished between the 9th April and the 19th June, 1667. But, unfortunately, like many of the remarkable journeys of merchants at that period, the Sieur Roland's unique opportunities have left little matter of which geographers can make use.—*The Relation of a Voyage made into Mauritania in Africk*, etc. (Englished out of French), 1671.

The word "rif" means in the Berber language "the littoral", and is therefore synonymous with the Arabic "Sahel", and nearly identical with the Latin "ripa" and the French "rive, rivage" (Renou). Leo calls it "riviera".

"The riuer of Nocor" is the Wad N'Kur.

The "Rifi" have been long separated from the rest of the Berber stocks, and in process of time have not only contracted peculiarities of life and morals (some not of the highest), but are said to be readily recognised by physical features. The prominence of the *pomum Adami* mentioned by Leo is one about as noticeable in a Rifian as is the bareing of the upper front teeth by a more southern country Arab when scanning anything with curiosity. But altogether the entire bearing of the people of Er-Rif is characteristic of bold, independent mountaineers, whom more than twenty centuries of invaders have left still unconquered.—Rohlfs, "Der Riff", *Deutsche Rundschau*, 1894, pp. 193-198; Duveyrier, "Itinéraire de Tlemsän à Melila", *Bull. de Soc. Géog. Paris* (31st May—10th June, 1886), 2*de trimestre*, 1893; "La Dernière partie inconnue du littoral de la

Méditerranée : Le Riff", *Bull. de Géog. historique et descriptive* 1887, No. 3, pp. 127-149, etc.

(149) This is, perhaps, the Tazka of Edrisi ; but the name Targa is often found in the Berber countries, and means "stream".
The story of Terga repeats what has been so often told in these notes—viz., the rapidity with which a busy town melts away and disappears in Morocco. From the reference to it in Edrisi, it appears to have been an ancient trading port. On the Catalan atlas and the map of Battista Agnesi it appears as Torga or Targa, in the latter a little to the west of a small river called "Cherche", which seems to be the Wad-Kerkâl of Edrisi, the Rio de Alamos of the Spanish charts, and Rivière de Tarssa of Dumoulin. But Mannert, Lapie, and Lacroix are wrong in seeking for the Tænea Longa of the *Antonine Itinerary*—Ταινία Λόγγα of Ptolemy—here, and not at Mersa Tighessa. Our Terga does not appear to have been a Roman town. Leo speaks of its trade in fish, which even then was dwindling, probably owing to the rivalry of the Portuguese and Spaniards. There are grounds for believing that these last plundered it in 1481. Still, at that very period, it was sufficiently prosperous and piratical to arouse the mingled wrath and cupidity of Ferdinand de Meneses, governor of Ceuta, who, judging the inhabitants to be off their guard, surprised it, took 300 prisoners, and burnt twenty-five ships, big and little. This success was so cheering to King João the Perfect that, ten years later, the Portuguese tried to repeat their exploit, but failed. In 1517 a great expedition of sixty ships was sent against it, but the commanders quarrelling over a question of precedence returned to Ceuta without striking a blow. Sixteen years later, the Spaniards, under Alvar de Bazan, sacked it by order of Charles V, and in 1568 Don John of Austria meditated a similar enterprise. Not long after, Mulai Abd-Allah rebuilt and fortified it, placing a strong garrison in the place. Yet, towards the close of last century, there were no remains of a town. To-day it is difficult to trace the site of this place, which has long ago disappeared from all maps of any authority, in company with a place called "Canise", likewise sacked in 1481 by Ferdinand de Meneses.—(De la Primaudace, *Revue Africaine*, No. 92, pp. 125-127 ; Lacroix, *Carte de l'Afrique sous la domination des Romains*, etc. (1864) ; Lapie, *Recueil des Itinéraires Anciens*, etc. (1844), etc.

(150) Badis, the Badich of El-Bekri, is now a ruined and, so far as its name is concerned, an almost forgotten place at the bottom of a bay opposite El-Peñon, not far from the La Rambla (Wad Tameda), which flows—when there is any water in it—through the plain known as the Plaza del Fuerte. Badis (a Berber name, or Balech, the name of the Peñon) was corrupted by the Arabs into Beles, which the

Spaniards in their turn transformed into Velez. Peñon means a rocky islet. Accordingly, when the Spaniards took the Peñon, a rocky islet in front of Badis, it was called, without regard to the native name being "Balech", "El Peñon de Velez", to which was added " de la Gomera", the name formerly given to the Rif of Rarb (El-Gharb), inhabited by the Gumera (Ghomera), one of the five great primitive divisions of the Berber race. They extended from the river Muluïa to Tangier (Ibn Khaldun, *Hist. de Berbères*, vol. iii, p. 134). Badis is now all but a vanished memory, and El-Peñon de Velez de la Gomera, the Spanish rock-presidio, has taken its place. The history of the place, and the struggles of which it has been the scene between the Berbers, Turks, and Spaniards, is detailed in Marmol, *L'Afrique*, t. ii, pp. 251-266 (up to its final capture by the Spaniards under Garcia de Toledo in 1564); the Editor's *Africa*, vol. iv, pp. 75, 76; and in Pezzi, *Los presidios memores de Africa* (1893), pp. 12-77, 215-242.

El-Bekri and Abu-l-feda refer to Badis as a town furnished with good markets and more than 100 Jewish houses of business. Abu-l-feda, indeed, characterises it as "a port celebrated among the ports of the country of Ghomârah". In the thirteenth and fifteenth centuries it enjoyed a considerable commerce, and in the times of Leo and Marmol Badis was celebrated for its sardines (*sardelli*), still abundant in the bay, and for the timber cut in the neighbouring mountains.

Water is as scarce now as then, and when the hot weather sets in, the cisterns have to be filled, as are those of Alhucemas and Melilla, by supplies brought from Malaga. The "little ruiver or streame" which flowed "alwaies when it raineth" is the Rambla marked on Battista Agnesi's map.

The "sepulchre of a certaine man" is that of Sidi Buazza, a marabout of the same name as the lion-scaring one (p. 572).

(151) The Peñon was captured by Pedro Navarro in 1508, though as early as 1499 the Portuguese had built a fortress a little west of Badis, to keep a check upon its pirates, and was betrayed on 10th December 1522—not " 1520 al modo de' Christiani" (Marmol, *Suarez Montanes*, *Minana*, etc.). From 1554 it was in the hands of the Algerine Turks, until in 1564 the Spaniards recovered by an attack upon it with 153 ships and 9,200 men, under Garcia de Toledo, Viceroy of Sicily.

(152) Ielles, Iris, Yellez, is mentioned in all the ancient nautical records, in the Catalan atlas as Ellis, and in the Pisan map as Eres, though Badis was not marked on it. There is some timber near it, but the place is now a miserable fishing village on Iris bay, where the

anchorage is good and the shelter fair, on a coast of which the old Spanish sailors' rhyme says :—

> "*Junio, julio, agosto y puerto Mahon*
> *Los mejores puertos de Mediterraneo son.*"
> "June, July, August, and Port Mahon
> Are the best ports of the Mediterranean."

Jeziret Beni bu Fras is the name of an islet at the entrance to the bay. The "Jell" is a desert plain in the Muluia valley.

(153) Tagaza of Marmol. Mannert and Lapie place Tænia Longa (p. 636) at Tagaza, which the former misspells "Fagasa", an error copied in Vincendon-Dumoulin and De Kerhallet's *Description Nautique de la côte nord du Maroc* (1857), and by Lasailly in his *Carte du Maroc* (1858). It is the "Anse des peupliers", the *Mersa Tighissa* of Tissot's *Géog. Comp.*, p. 19, Mersa Tiguiçast of Pl. I in same memoir. Tagaza appears to be a corruption of the Rifian *Tighissa*. Edrisi mentions it as *Tikiças*. It is now a mere fishing village, by a little river of the same name.

(154) Jebba, a petty place—pettier even than in Leo's day, when it was alternately empty and occupied—between El-Peñon de Velez de Gomera and Alhucemas.

(155) Mezemme, Mzemma, Megeyma (Marmol), or El-Mzemma, was an old Berber town, of which the ruins exist near the mouth of the Wad Ris, or Nkhur ("Nocore", Nekor), though its memory lives in Mersa el-Mzemma, the name applied to the coast in its vicinity. Alhucemas, the name of the lavender-covered Spanish rock-presidio hard by, is perhaps a corruption of El-Mezemma. For the native name of this islet is Hajirat En-N'kur, the rock of N'kur, in order to distinguish it from el-Hajra Kebdana (the rock of Kebdana), or Isla del Congresso, in the Chafarine Island.

(156) In A.D. 922 it was sacked by the troops of the Khalif of Bagdad ("the patriarke of Cairoan"), and after lying deserted for fifteen years was re-peopled, only to be a second time destroyed by Abd er-Rahman III, Khalif of Cordova ("a certaine great man of Cordoua"). From that date the place began rapidly to decay, though in the latter part of the seventeenth century, as we learn from Roland Frejus's narrative, it did some little trade. This, however, was lost as soon as the Spaniards built their fortress on the islet in the bay. This spot was given them, according to the accepted version, by Mulai Abd Allah (1557-1573), to prevent its occupation by the Algerines (Moura, *Mem. da Acaa Real, Lisboa*, vol. x, p. 102), but it was not permanently occupied until August 27th,

1673 (Pezzi, *Los presidios memores*, etc., p. 78), when the Prince of Montesacro laid the foundation of Alhucemas, universally agreed to be one of the least agreeable and most unhealthy of the Spanish presidios on the Morocco coast. The distance from Kairwan to Alhucemas is over-estimated by Leo. Instead of being "three and twentie hundreth miles" (due mille trecenti miglia), it is, by a direct route, not much over 700.

(157) Beni-Garir or Beni-Oriegan. Any description of the Rif mountain system must of necessity be indefinite, since no geographer has had an opportunity of examining it, except on the border. Even from the sea-coast the view is hindered by certain peaks which mock the explorer. Hence, on the conscientious cartographer's map of Morocco, the Rif is marked by a partial blank, relieved by a few heights, often the result of very problematical measurements estimated from a great distance, and by a name or two which may or may not be the correct titles of the peaks or ranges to which they are attached. Hence Leo's "Monti" must in most cases be more or less doubtful, though some, especially near the sea-board, are identifiable without much difficulty. As usual, they are the names of the tribes inhabiting them.

(158) The Beni Mansur. These were in Leo's day subject to the rule of Badis (Bedis) or Velez (p. 636).

(159) The Botoye of Marmol, who states that this is the country of a saint named Sidi Bu Aza, whose tomb is at the gate of Badis (p. 637). It is "the Port of Boazon, on the Road of Boutoye", mentioned by Roland Frejus and other writers, and on some charts (*e. g.*, the French one of 1843, issued by the Depôt de la Marine), marked as the Port of Botoye. Duveyrier (*Bull. de Géog. Hist. et Descriptive*, 1887, pp. 130, 131) refers to "the country of Bogoûya, called also Bogiwa", lying to the west of the Temsâmâni, and near the Bene bu Ferrahs, in the vicinity of Peñon de Velez. It is drained by the Wad Bu' Azzun, and is peopled by the Beni Ulitshitsh. The Spaniards know it as Bocoya, or the country of the Beni Botoya. (Pezzi, *Los presidios memores*, pp. 170, 171.) El-Bekri speaks of the road of Bkuia or Bukuia, and Edrisi of the Beni-Btuia : but it is not certain that they are the people of these mountains.

(160) Beni-quilib, or Beni-quelid, of Marmol.

(161) The second Beni Mansur, is probably the Beni Mansur whose country lies behind the Jägerschmidt's Sp. (Point) of Schnell's map.

(162) Beni Giusep, the Beni Yussuf. In Marmol's day they paid tribute to the "Lords of Velez."

(163) These seem to be the Beni uz-Zerual, the Beni Zarval of Marmol.

The "Seusaoen", to which they are described as subject, is the well-known Berber town of Sheshauen, *ut infra*.

A detached fraction of the Beni-Zerual are found in Algeria near the mouth of the Chelif.

(164) The Beni Hasçin of Marmol. Why Marmol changes it to Beni Hasçin is not explained, for it is not the Beni Hassan already described.

(165) This place, also spelled Seusaen by Leo, and Chechuan or Sesava by Marmol, is Sheshuan, a fanatical little town in the mountains between the Beni Hassan country and the Rif proper. It was first visited by any European, so far as is authentically known, when De Foucauld entered it in 1883 disguised as a Jew, and accompanied by the celebrated Rabi Mordekhai Abi Serur, of Timbuktu fame. Mr. Walter B. Harris visited it in 1888; and since then at least one European has repeated the adventure. The houses have sloping roofs, a peculiarity rarely seen in Morocco. It is the capital of the Sheshuan.—Harris, *The Land of an African Sultan*, pp. 298-317 (sketch); *Blackwood's Magazine*, 1888, pp. 786-792; De Foucauld, *Reconnaissance*, etc., pp. 7-9 (good view).

The "Sidi Heli Berrased" mentioned is the "Ali Barrax" referred to above.—Marmol, *L'Afrique*, t. ii, p. 273.

(166) Their country is behind Cotelle Point. The river which runs through their territory Marmol calls the "Halef-Vgus", that is, "curse and pass"—more accurately Halef-on-juz (Renou). In Marmol's time they paid tribute to Sheshuan, and could at a pinch bring into the field more than 2,000 men, among whom were some arquebusiers, but no cavalry.

(167) Beni Jerso, Yerso, of Marmol. Ali Barrax was the founder of its prosperity, but its ruin, as narrated by Leo, if in "918 yeere of the Hegeira", was not in A.D. 1518, as added by Florianus, but 1513-14.

The Beni-Iersu are a Berber tribe who, like so many in this region, have dropped the national "Aït" in favour of the Arabic "Ben". Some tribes of pure Berber origin have even adopted Arabic as their tongue.

(168) Beni-Tiziran of Marmol. They paid tribute to Sheshuan, and searched for hidden treasures among the ruins of old buildings, believed to be Roman.

(169) Beni-Buzeybet of Marmol, covered with forests of walnuts which supplied Fez and other towns.

(170) Beni-Walid.

(171) Mernisa, the Beni Uva or Bervira of Marmol, as appears from his relating the same particulars regarding the people—such as the informal divorces of the women, who among the Berbers have great power, etc. They belong to the Gumera stock.

(172) Haugustun, Hagustan of Marmol, Haugustum of Ramusio, ed. 1613, Agustun of the 1837 reprint.

(173) Beni-Jedir, or Beniyedi, of Marmol. The Benider mountain, with a large village of the same name, is between the Wad er-Ras (Rio el-Ras) and the Wad Engachera (Rio Engachera), on the Spanish War Office Map.

(174) Alcai of Marmol, Al Kai. The distance of the place from Fez appears to be under-estimated by Leo, as are, indeed, most of his distances in the Rif country. Badis (p. 636), for instance, is not thirty miles, but over eighty-five miles in a straight line from Fez.

(175) Beni guazeval, or Beni zarval, of Marmol. Duveyrier considered this mountain to be in the immediate neighbourhood of the Beni Uriaghel country, and it may be Guezennâya. But in referring to "le traducteur du texte arabe en latin" of "Hasen Ben Mohammed el-Wassâs autrement dit Léon l'Africain", Duveyrier shows himself strangely ignorant of the history of the book, which both he and Tissot invariably quote in the Latin version.

The most remarkable fact which Leo relates about this mountain is its being an active volcano. But though the statement has been repeated again and again since it first appeared, no one has been able to confirm it. Thus, on Abraham Ortelius's 1595 map *Fessæ, et Marocchi Regna Africæ celeberr.*, "Beniguazendl mons" is marked as possessing "Specus perpetuo ignem evomens". It may be added that nearly all the places on this map are transferred from Leo. Mr. Maw regards the southern coast of the Strait of Gibraltar as exhibiting signs of modern upheaval (Hooker and Ball's *Tour*, etc., pp. 448-450), and M. Duveyrier's observations on the Sebka (La Laguna o Puerto Nuevo) south of Melilla tend to the same conclusion; while we have seen that the Merja de Ras ed-Dura, Ez-Zerga, and other coast-lying lakes between the Sebu and El-Kus bear every appearance of having been lagoons formerly : a theory not rendered untenable by M. Tissot's objection that the narrow barrier separating them from the sea is not of sand but of rock. In the Ghrunch country, on the borders of Er-Rif, Mr. Harris found volcanic traces, and he heard that there is in "Beni Zarun", not far distant, a circular hole (*i.e.* crater), out of which by day smoke rises, and by night fire is clearly visible (*Proc. Roy. Geog. Soc.*, vol. xi, 1889, pp. 489-91). This may be the place described by Leo.

(176) Beni-Gueriaghel of the original, Beni-Gueriagel, or Beni-Vriéguil of Marmol, the Beni-Uriâghel already mentioned (note 175). The name of the tribe occurs in El-Bekri and Edrisi, and it is cited by Leo as the "Bani-guerjaghel", one of the tribes of the Senhaja Berbers.

El-Bekri mentions the Nkur (Nekor), and a stream called by him the Nahar-'Aïsh, which falls into the Mediterranean near it. The first rises in the Jebel-Kuîn (Kum) in the Kertana country, and the other in the "Beni-Ueriâghel" district not far distant.

There is also a fraction of the Beni-Ueriâghel in the vicinity of Tetuan (Renou). The Kuîn (Kum) mountain gave rise, according to El-Bekri, to the Uerra River (the Guarga of Leo—the well-known Wargha). The "Kertana" country is perhaps Kebdana, south of the Sebka of Puerto Novo, near Melilla (note 175).

(177) Beni hamet, or Beni acmet, of Marmol. In his day they could muster 4,000 fighting men, but, what with the King of Fez upon one hand and the "Seigneurs of Velez" on the other, in addition to their civil broils and their love of wine, the Beni Hamed were "poor and beggarly". They are still a well-known Arab tribe south of the Lakhames, but no wealthier than formerly.

(178) The Benizanten or Benyeginesen of Marmol. Between the Beni Hamed and the Uled Aissa runs a branch of the Wargha, but the dividing stream referred to by Leo must be one of the more northern branches, as the Beni Zanten are not known. From the fact that Leo's father had to do with them in his capacity of landlord, they most likely lived not far from Fez. They may be the Beni-Zarun.

(179) The Beni M'sgilda, or Mesgalda, are a well-known Arab tribe north of Fez, south of the Lakhamis, Beni Hamed, and Beni Zarun, and west of the still more powerful Beni M'Sara, who sometimes invited the Sultan to take his taxes in silver bullets. They must not be confounded with the Beni M'Gild, a Berber tribe south of Fez, who range on the head waters of the Beth, Sebu, etc.

(180) The Beni guamud, as Marmol spells the name, are described by him as more "civil" than the rest of the Rif mountaineers, but like the rest of them regarding the Christians with an undying hatred, and not without cause. They could at the time he wrote put 4,000 men into

the field, including in this number some cavalry. But it is probable that all the estimates are exaggerated ; unless indeed the population of Morocco was four or five centuries ago far larger than it is at present. The Rif country, however, is so little known that one can only guess at its population and at its geography. Fifty years ago, Renou deplored the scantiness of our information regarding it. "We know", this industrious student wrote, "the names, more or less disfigured, of a certain number of tribes, but we are entirely ignorant of the names and positions of all their villages. We do not know the height of a single one of their mountains". This is still true to-day. For, if the past half-century has added largely to our information regarding the rest of Morocco, it has left the great mountain clump overlooking the Mediterranean far less explored than the centre of the continent to which it belongs. We know, indeed, a few more of the tribal names on the coast, and, in a rough way, the altitude of some of the mountains. But the explorer has been permitted to see them from a distance only, so that a country past which thousands sail every year is to-day little better known than it was four centuries ago. Indeed, as the foregoing commentary proves, our erudition has in the interval not proceeded much beyond that of Leo the African.

(181) Garet is not now recognised as a province of the old kingdom of Fez, though long after Leo's time it appears on maps with much the same boundaries as he assigns to it—viz., from west to east between the river Nkur and Muluïa, and from north to south between the sea and the river Melulo—a tributary of the Muluïa near Debdu on the northern side of the Tell Atlas. Chenier gives the same boundaries, though he appears to be simply copying Leo. Its correct name is Ghâret (Renou, *Expl. Scientifique de l'Algérie*, t. viii, pp. 332-335). The country of Guela'aya (Ak'la'ia, Akkalaya, Alcalaya, or Alcaladia, of various authors), part of the amâla of Ujda, ends on the west at the Wad Kart, the Karat of El-Bekri (pp. 90, 99), a name in which Duveyrier rather fancifully traces a resemblance to Garet (*Bull. de Géog. Historique et Descript.*, 1887, p. 130). The region called Ghâret is now much smaller than in Leo's day (see Moüette, *Hist. des Conquestes de Mouley-Archy*, p. 417 ; and Braithwaite, *Hist. of the Revolutions in Morocco*, etc., for maps in which the name of Ak'la'ia (Alcaladia) is applied to the entire province of Ghâret or Garet. It is the "Arcadia de III forcate" (Tres forcas) of the map in the Pinelli Library (the author of which is unknown).

(182) Melilla of the Spaniards is the Mlila, "the place of honey", of the Moors, so called from the great quantity of bees in the vicinity. It was the *Russadir Oppidum et Portus* of Pliny, the *Rusadder*

Colonia of the *Antonine Itinerary*, and probably the Ἀκρος πόλις καὶ λιμήν of Scylax, and the 'Ρυσσάδειρον of Ptolemy. Whether it was ever inhabited by the Goths is doubtful, though it is possible that they occupied the Roman town. The Berbers, however, were no doubt there when the Phœnicians came (as Scylax relates in the *Periplus*), and again became masters when the Romans, or their successors, left. In the Middle Ages it was a place frequented by European merchants, who bought honey, and iron mined in the neighbouring mountains. The Rif is, indeed, believed to be rich in minerals; antimony and manganese are known to be plentiful. Iron, "or a mine of some metal", exists in the Jebel Hammâm, near Badis, in the Beni Said country, in "Meggeo" (note 189), and here. The French marine surveyors found their work on the coast frequently interfered with by abnormal deviations of the compass. Pearl fishing is not now followed in the bay.

In the Portulan of Visconte, and the Catalan atlas, the place is called Millela, in the map of the Pinelli Library "cavo Milela", and in other Routiers, Mellila. But none of these maps, not even that of Battista Agnesi (1574), shows the little river which flows into the bay a little east of the town, the Wad Tigand—the Rio del Oro of the Spaniards. Marmol says that it is the Ieyrat-Melila of the Berbers.

(183) Butoja, Buccuja (note 159).

(184) Melilla was captured by the Duke of Medina Sidonia, Captain-General of Andalusia, on the 17th of September 1496 (or 1497, according to Galindo y de Vera), Leo's date being, in any case, erroneous. The subsequent history of the place, during which the Sultan of Morocco and the Berbers on their own account attempted to capture Melilla, or carried on war against its occupants to as late as 1890, is narrated in the Editor's *Africa*, vol. iv, pp. 73-75; De la Primaudace, *Revue Africaine*, No. 92, pp. 106-113; Berbrugger, *Ibid.*, No. 53. p. 366; Marmol, *L'Afrique*, t. ii, pp. 284-290; Pezzi, *Los presidios menores*, etc., pp. 99, 243-318; Olivie, *Marruecos, passim*; Llana y Rodrigañez, *El imperio de Marruecos*, p. 192; Perez del Toro, *España en el Noroeste de Africa*; Galindo y de Vera, *Historia, vicisitudes y política tradicional de España respecto de sus posesiones en las Costas de Africa*, etc., p. 74; Ordega, *Revue Bleu*, Nov. 4th, 1893; and references in the *Bibliography of Morocco* (1893).

(185) Also spelled "Chasasan"—Caçaça of Marmol, a place the former position of which is very uncertain, the name not appearing in Spanish history, and the old cartographers placing it almost at random on the map, Cala-Cassaza, K'saça, etc.; Renou believes that K'saça is its true name, because El-Bekri places the Risâka, a Berber tribe, in the region near the mouth of the Muluïa, where, according to Leo's

description, we must look for the spot. It was taken immediately after Melilla. It is not improbable that Leo, who is far from precise, meant by Chasasa a settlement on the Chafarine Island, close to the mouth of the Muluïa, which was afterwards, with the exception of the tower, razed to the ground.

(186) Tezzota, the Tezote of Marmol, apparently Tezzat. Founded by the Beni-Marini, and abandoned by them to the Batalises, one of the Zeneta tribes, it was eventually destroyed by Yussuf En-Naser li Din Illah (1307), until it became, after the occupation of Melilla and " Chasasa" by the Spaniards, a place from which they might be harassed. In Leo's day the people were constantly at war with the Christians, which may account for Tezzota no longer existing, at any rate under that name. There are various ruins on the hills near the Muluïa, but none which can with confidence be fixed upon as those of the little Berber hill-Ksar, in question. " Tafersit" cannot well be identified with it.

(187) Meggeo, Megéa of Marmol, in whose day it was noted for iron mines, though in itself a little place. Except that it must be (if it exists, which is more than doubtful) in the Guela'aya country nothing further is known about it.

(188) The Mequebhuan of Marmol, between Melilla and the River Muluïa, in which position is a cape spelled Quilbadana, Quobrada, Quiviana, etc., on different maps. All these names are evidently variants of one, and that derived from the Kebdana or Gebdâna, a well-known Berber tribe, whose country lies back of this coast. A short time before his expedition against Fez and Marakesh, Mulai er-Rashid (1672) halted in Quiviane, a town within or on the borders of Rif.—Mouëtte, *Hist. des Conquestes de Mouley-Archy*, etc., pp. 8, 25.

(189) The Beni Saïd of the country west of Ras ed-Dir (Tres Forcas). Iron is no longer mined, it being cheaper to buy European tools. Marmol describes the castle " of Calaa " in their country. Renou suggests that this may have been the Berber village of Calaa-Guizin-aque, the name of which is mentioned by Marmol. This is possible, but it was more likely the fortress of " Kala", which the King of Portugal built in 1498 to keep watch over Badis and its pirates.

(190) Azgangan can be identified with Ageddim, the mountains which form C. de Agua or Ras Sidi Basher, from the name of a village surmounting it. There is also a village called Ageddim.

(191) This is the Beni-Touzin of Roland Frejus, the Quizina of Marmol.

(192) The Guardam market was, in Marmol's day, held on Saturday, and was much frequented by the Fez merchants.

(193) Leo's description of the dryness and sterility of this region is quite accurate. Travellers in it are at times hard pressed for water.

(194) Chaus, or Cuzt (Marmol), is the name applied to the country between the Wad Za and the province of Temsena (River Wargha), and between Ghâret and the Desert Region. "Ro. C." also, in *A True Historical Discourse*, etc. (1609), chap. xiv (the book is not paged), refers to Chaus, or Coucoes. Most subsequent writers have copied Leo. Thus Chenier refers to Chaus or Shaus, Gråberg de Hemsö to Sciaus, etc. There is, however, no such province nowadays, if there ever existed one of that name. The word "Heuz", evidently the same. is, however, still employed to designate a large district such as the Heuz Rabat, and the Heuz Marakesh. The Fum el-Rorb is the country east of the Heuz Rabat on to the Muluïa and to the south of Rif—in fact, nearly what Leo comprises in Chaus.

(195) Abd el-Hakk (Habdulach) was, with Idris, one of his sons, slain in a battle with the Riata from near Taza (A.H. 614, according to *Roudh el-Kartas*, p. 408). Abu Said Othman was elected Emir on the battle-field. Upon his assassination in A.H. 638 (A.D. 1240), his brother, Abu Mahruf Mohammed, succeeded. After him came Abu Yahia, another son of Abd el-Hakk, and, finally, Abu Yussuf Yakub, a fourth son of Abd el-Hakk, became Amir. But Marakesh was captured, and the last Almohade (Muachedin) sovereign was vanquished after Yakub had become king.

"Muachedin, the King of Maroco", is "la famiglia di Muachidin re di Maroco". The paragraph is, however, inaccurate. In another place Leo describes Yakub as being the first king of the Beni-Marini dynasty, an error which he could not have committed through ignorance, as he properly states in this passage that Abd el-Hakk was the first.

(196) Teurert of Marmol, a town near the Za, on what is now the Algerian frontier. The Za, one of the tributaries of the Muluïa from the left bank, is the Sa of El-Bekri, the Sâa of Edrisi, the Zha and Za of Leo, the Za and Esaha of Marmol, the Enza of Ali Bey. Teurert is a frequent Berber name (properly "Taurirt") meaning hill, and is a not uncommon designation of villages which crown high places. It is not improbably "Temessuin", the large, ruined, fortified place which Ali Bey described in 1805 on the left side of the Muluïa valley. It then consisted of a square wall about 425 feet in front, with a square tower on each corner, and another in the middle

of each front. The wall was 18 feet high and 3 feet thick, with a kind of parapet on the top, pierced with places of defence. There was a decayed mosque, and some other ruins by the side of the mosque. But beyond some miserable huts giving shelter to a few poverty-stricken natives, the place was entirely deserted. Another ruined castle was passed further on ; but ruins are the most marked feature of Morocco. This particular one, under that name at least, does not seem to have attracted the attention of any subsequent traveller whose itinerary I have seen. But on the " Wad Zaar " (the Za apparently) Colonel Colville notes the " Kassbar " (Kasba, Alcassaba of Ali Bey), "Zaar", the " Kassbar Muley Ismail " (Qaçba Moulei Ismaïl) of the French War Department Map. Near it is a wrecked village which was formerly inhabited by a colony of Jews. But in one of the many disturbances of the country it was destroyed, as were also such of the inhabitants who did not escape to the mountains. Other travellers describe the same place, De Foucauld identifying it with Taurirt : " Qaçba Moulei Ismail porte aussi le nom de Taourirt." This synonymy is also adopted on Schnell's map (Petermann's *Geog. Mitteilungen Ergänzungsheft*, No. 103). A difficulty in accepting the identity of Taurirt with Leo's " Tuerto " is that he describes the town wall as of " most excellent marble", which De Foucauld tells us is of tabia (pisé).—Ali Bey, *Travels*, vol. i, pp. 180, 181 ; Colville, *A Ride in Petticoats and Slippers*, p. 273 ; De Foucauld, *Reconnaissance*, pp. 258, 259.

The " Desert (Plain) of Tafrata " lies between the Wad Bu Rsab and the Wad Debu, both tributaries of the Muluïa. It is a true desert, and often remains for years at a time without vegetation.

(197) Hadagie of Marmol, Hadaha and Haddaja of other writers, on a peninsula, merely the junction of the Muluïa and the " Mululo", which is only a branch of the same river, has been suggested by Renou to be " El-'Audja" ('the bend', or elbow) on the left bank of the Muluïa, where Abd el-Kader stayed for a long time after the battle of Isly.

(198) Garces, or Galafa, of Marmol, who falsely supposes it to be the Galafa of Ptolemy—a very fanciful identification. Founded by the Beni-Marini to serve as a fortress and magazine, it was, owing to a rebellion of the inhabitants, destroyed by Abu A'nan (Abu henan, A.D. 1357), who was, however, not the fifth of the Beni-Marini dynasty, but, counting Abd el-Hakk I, the twelfth of this line. Yakub el-Mansur was the fifth.

D'Avezac recognised it in the Guersif, or Akersyf, or Ag'ersyf of various Arab authors (*Etudes de Géog. Critique*, p. 171). Unless it be El-Gelf, not far from the Wad Bu Rsab, its site is not known.

(199) Dubudu of Marmol. Debdou, the well-known though seldom visited Debdu on the river of the same name (a tributary of the Muluïa), and situated at the height of 3,717 ft. above the Mediterranean, on a rock, the face of which is between 200 ft. and 300 ft. perpendicular. On the top is a majestic fortress with crumbling towers; the town itself is composed of the customary square flat-roofed houses. Of the 2,000 inhabitants, three-fourths are Jews—Debdu being the only place in Morocco where the Israelites exceed the Mohammedans in numbers. But they must be easy to govern, for De Foucauld, when he visited the place, found no representative of authority resident, the Kaïd of Taza or one of his lieutenants settling any quarrels and collecting the Sultan's imposts when they came on their rounds. The town is surrounded by beautiful gardens of vines, olives, pomegranates, and other fruits, while the rest of the Debdu valley is clothed with fields of wheat and barley. The houses are for the most part of clay, and if ever there was a wall it has now disappeared. Springs are abundant, the old fortress having one inside its *enciente*. The town is the first on the Moroccan frontier which does a regular trade with Algeria, Tlemsen and Lalla-Maghrnia being the chief places with which the townsmen traffic.

From the account given by Leo and Marmol, Debdu was, in the times of the Beni-Marini, a town of some importance, and its revival from the decay into which it fell has been mainly due to the influence of the neighbouring French colony. In Leo's account the following glosses may be useful:—The Beni Guertaggen, Beni-guertenax (Marmol) were relations of Abd el-Hakk; Mose (Muse) Ibnu Chamu, Muçaben Camu of Marmol, is Musa Ibnu Kamu; Acmed Hamet is Ahmed; Saich, Saic, Said, is Said II El-Uatas(Quattas): as he reigned until 1527 he was king at the time Leo was writing, but the date, as we have seen, must have been considerably before 1526 (which Pory adds as a note), that year being the one in which vol. i of Ramusio's *Viaggi* was published (see *Introduction*). A.H. 904 is not A.D. 1495, but 1499. If Leo was there in A.H. 921, this must have been A.D. 1515, which quite falls in with the chronology of his life as deduced from his own account.

(200) Tezar, or Teza of Marmol, the modern Tazza, Taza, or Tesa, perched most picturesquely on a cliff, 2,034 ft. above sea-level, 272 ft. over the bed of the Wad Taza, and 427 ft. above that of the Wad Innauen. Some have suggested it to be the ancient Colonia Iulia Babba Campestris, which was founded most probably by Claudius, and which received various favours from Augustus. Pliny says, "Ab Lixo XL Milliaria in Mediterranco altera Augusti colonia est, Babba. Julia Campestris appellata"; but it is not clear whether he means forty miles from the river Lixus (Wad el-Kus), or from the town of that

name. The word Babba, in the Punic language, meant "in the forest"—*ad silvam*—as the *Antonine Itinerary* so frequently notes of places in this then wooded region. Very possibly it was the Bani Teude of Leo (p. 620). Tissot believes that some vestiges of antiquity, rumoured to exist at Es-Serif, a region closed to Europeans, may be those of Babba. What Jaubert translates *Baba Kelam* in Edrisi, is in reality *Bab Aklam*, so that it would be idle to trace any connection between this place and Babba. However, the modern Taza is a well-known town, though rarely visited by Europeans, and now fast falling into decay. But though the position of Taza may in the future make it a strong strategical point in relation to Fez, it is nowadays a poor place from the engineer's point of view. At present the inhabitants number three or four thousand, including 200 Jews confined to a little Mellah. There are four mosques, and two or three spacious "fondaks", or caravanserais (p. 596), but they are all falling into decay from neglect. The town itself is constructed partly of stone and partly of bricks; the houses are stained a brownish-red colour, which gives them a sombre appearance, and like those of every town known to De Foucauld in Morocco, except Sheshuan (p. 640) and El-Ksar el-Kebir (p. 617), have flat terraced roofs. The water is pure and cool, though the supply is insufficient for the wants of the townsmen and their cattle. Beautiful gardens, full of fine fruit trees, surround the place on all sides, but everything bears the aspect of having seen its best days. Nominally under the rule of the Sultan, Taza is really dominated by the Riata tribesmen, who have reduced the town to its present miserable condition, and the inhabitants to a state of subjection similar to that of the Timbuktues with regard to the Tuaregs before the French came. The Kaid and his garrison of "Mkhaznis", or regular troops—rather policemen than soldiers—are powerless. They live by squeezing the citizens, but otherwise exercise scarcely any authority; while the Riata treat the town so much as part of a conquered country, that it is dangerous for anyone to venture into the region round about without a paid Riata escort (Zetat). No Moorish official or soldier dares enter their territory. They even claim a monopoly of the Wad Taza water, —a practice which Leo alludes to—and sell it to the timid householders, whose goods and dwellings they are apt to treat very much as those of vassals. On market days, when they come into the town in greater numbers than usual, pillage is frequent. In 1876, these ruthless brigands surprised the Sultan's army in the "Valley of Hill", a defile of the Wad Bu Jerba, near Tazo, and even carried off his harem. The result is that the prudent trader keeps as little money as he can in Taza, and that the price of European goods, owing to the risks run in bringing them there, or in keeping them reasonably safe, is double their price in Fez. Little business is carried on, except with Fez, Algeria, and in the Rif, Melilla, Fafersat, and the villages of the Muluïa valley. Even the beautiful gardens are being neglected. The wretched people in despair of "Sidina"—Our Lord the Sultan—doing anything for them, hoping against hope, not daring even to whisper their longings—pray that some day the Frank may free them from their wretched life under the Amir al-Mumenin, who permits True Believers to be sorrily treated by their co-religionists.

Taza must have been steadily decaying during this century. Roland Frejus, who visited it in 1666, speaks of the liveliness of the town, especially during the Sultan's stay, and of the beautiful position it occupies. Towards the close of the last century the place had, like most other Moroccan towns, fallen greatly from its former importance. But in 1804, Ali Bey el-Abâsi—(Domingo Badia y Leblich, a somewhat mysterious Spaniard, the exact nature of whose mission to Morocco has never been clearly explained)—described Taza as an industrious town, charmingly situated on a rock "which lies at the bottom of much higher mountains towards the south-west". The valleys were covered with abundant crops, and in the gardens "innumerable nightingales, turtle doves, and other birds made the spot as agreeable as it is enchanting". Even when Rohlfs saw "Thesa" sixty years later it had 5,000 inhabitants, of whom 800 were Jews—a falling off, no doubt, from Leo's 5,000 fireplaces, that is 25,000—though, unless the Tezaees crowded very closely together in 1500, it is scarcely possible for as many people to have found houseroom within the circuit of its walls. At the time of Rohlfs' visit, the Hiaïna, a tribe on the other side of the Innauen, were so troublesome that caravans to Algeria had to be accompanied by escorts of troops, of which there were 500 stationed in the town.—De Foucauld, *Reconnaissance au Maroc*, pp. 29-35 (views), 65 ; *Travels of Ali Bey in Morocco, Tripoli, etc., between the years 1803 and 1807, written by himself*, vol. i, p. 179 ; Rohlfs, *Adventures in Morocco*, pp. 272, 273.

Taza, however, figures frequently in Moroccan history. Thus, in 1595, the rebel prince En-Nasir ben El-Ghâlib Billah, after being joined by the neighbouring tribes, entered Taza, and demanded a heavy ransom from the citizens, the Christian mercenaries in his train even.

Again, after the death of Mulai Mohammed in 1664, Mulai Er-Rashid marched upon Taza, and after a long struggle gained possession of it, using the place as a basis for his attack on Fez (*Nozhet Elhâdi*, p. 501). After being the subject of so many sieges, it is no wonder that Chenier, writing a century ago, says that the aspect of the country had entirely changed since Leo's day, and that Teza, once populous, then only contained a few inhabitants.

(201) Medrara, Matagara (Marmol). It is to the south-west of Taza. It was inhabited by Zenatas, who, though pure Arabs, according to the *Roudh el-Kartas* (p. 397), speak Berber. Eloufrani (*Nozhet Elhâdi*, p. 40) refers to the "Methgara" tribe of Tlemsen, to which the Grand-Kadi of Fez, at the time of the disputes between the Sheriffs and the Beni-Marini (1533), belonged.

There is also a district called "Medghara", north of Tafilet, mentioned by Aboulqâsem ben Hamed Ezziâni.—(*Ettordjemân*, etc., Houdas' ed., pp. 4, 184).

(202) Gavata, inhabited by the Zenata stock, fifteen miles west of Fez, and the fountain-head of two tributaries of the Sebu. Renou believed it to be a corruption of "Gaiata", the Jebel Riata which Schnell writes Jebel "Ghiata", though not the mountain of the same name close to Taza, and, indeed, occupying the position of Leo's Matgara.

(203) Mencheça of Marmol. The Mejesa were a tribe living near Fez at the time when Edrisi wrote.

(204) Baraniz of Marmol; perhaps Baranis, inhabited by Zenatas and Hauara. Edrisi refers to this tribe.

(205) The Guertenage, or the Beni-guertenax of Marmol, the Jebel Uarvietz of Schnell's map. The Beni-Marini having set out on their career of conquest from this mountain (Marmol tells us), the Zenata inhabitants of it were regarded as the most illustrious of their stock, and being held in much respect, were free of all taxes; though they were quite submissive to the Sheriff.

(206) Gueblen, or Guebeleyn, probably means simply "the two mountains". It is difficult to identify it with any range except, perhaps, Jebel Obiod or the country of the Beni Uaghain.

(207) Or Benijechseten of Marmol, vassals to the rulers of Debdu, the Beni Iznâten (Beni Zenata), who usually appear on maps as Beni Snâssen. Their stronghold, the Jebel Isnaten, is well known.

(208) Or Ciligo of Marmol, in whose day the mountain was full of lions, monkeys, and wild boars. Leo describes it as one of the chief sources of the Sebu, though Marmol notes that he had seen it affirmed by Arabic authors that a mountain called "Gayasa", in the "Zarahanum" group, was the true birthplace of the principal river of Morocco. We are to-day not much wiser.

(209) Also written Beni-Isasga.

(210) Azgan. There are several mountains in the quarter assigned to Azgan, but I am not aware of any bearing that name.

(211) Sfru, Saforo, Sfro, Safrou, Saforoui, Ssoffrouy, Ssoforo, a little town largely favoured by Jews, situated 2,700 ft. above sea-level, between the Wad Sfru and the Sebu, and therefore liable to be flooded. It is a perfect oasis in the desert, owing to the abundance of olives, oranges, citrons, lemons, cherries, and grapes grown in the gardens surrounding it, for the supply of fruit to the Fez market. It is still, as it was in Leo's day, an important centre of the olive-oil trade, while the adjoining mountains of Ait Yussi and the Beni M'Gild territory contain extensive forests of good timber, particularly the "Belluta", a resinous species of conifer. Though not containing more than 3,000 inhabitants—a third of them Hebrews—Sfru was already a town in the days of Edrisi, who refers to it under the name of Çofrui. It also figures in El-Bekri, Ahmed ibn-Hassan, and other writers.

An air of prosperity, such as is rarely encountered in Morocco, pervades this charming place. All the usual signs of decadence are absent. Good houses of whitewashed brick, often two storeys high, take the place of the crumbling dwellings common elsewhere. Vines shade many of the lanes and terraces, and a clear stream courses through the town.

There are now two mosques and a zauïa belonging to the descendants of Sidi El-Hassan el-Jussi, a celebrated saint of the latter years of the sixteenth and the early part of the seventeenth century. Green turbans, marks of the Derkana sect, are frequently seen.

In addition to its trade with the neighbouring tribes in wool, hides, etc., Sfru thrives on the caravans which halt here on their way to and from Tafilet. Good wine is made by the Jews, and sold at about 5s. a gallon.

Many of the Sfru people are said to be the descendants of Christian renegades. The Beni Behalil, whose large village is passed on the way from Fez, more especially bear that invidious reputation, and on that account are named "the fools".—De Foucauld, *Reconnaissance*, pp. 37, 38 (sketch) ; De la Martinière, *Morocco*, p. 400 (map 5) ; El-Bekri, *L'Afrique Sept.* (De Slane's text), p. 164 ; Edrisi, *Africa*, (ed. Hartmann), p. 173 ; Ahmed Ibn-Hassan in Paulus, *Memorabilien* (1791), vol. i, p. 47 ; and Walckenaer, *Recherches Géog. sur l'Intérieur de l'Afrique Sept.*, p. 458 ; D'Avezac, *Etudes*, etc., p. 156 ; Caillie, *Journal d'un Voyage*, etc., t. iii, p. 109.

As the journey to Fez takes about ten hours, the distance is greater than fifteen miles.

(212) Mezdaga is not known, though its position is given so exactly

—twelve miles south of Fez and eight miles west of Sfru—that did any town exist on the routes mentioned, it could scarcely escape notice. One of the Halen tribes is called Mezdagen.

(213) El-Bahalel, or Baalel, the village of the people of the same name already alluded to (notes 210, 211). It is the Beni-Buhalul of Marmol, who, absurdly enough, imagines it to be Ptolemy's "Ceuta". In an itinerary of Hajj Mohammed Sherif preserved by D'Avezac, the road to Sfru (Ssoforo) is described as passing between the mountains A'zabâh (which may be Azgan) (note 210) on the left and Behâlyl on the right.—(D'Avezac, *Etudes*, etc., p. 156.)

(214) Ainelginum (the "fountain of genii", *i.e.*, *jinnun*), of Marmol, and El-Esnam of El-Bekri : 'Aïn el-Esnam "the fountain (spring) of idols" on the Asra el-Hamar Plain—the "certaine plain" of Leo. 'Aïn el-Esnam—or plural 'Aïun el-Esnam—abbreviated into " Snam", is a common name in Barbary, perhaps for the reason Leo indicates. The ancient orgie described is matched by similar rites enacted elsewhere—such as, for instance, in mediæval Heligoland, as described by Von der Decken.

(215) Mehedie of Marmol. This place, which even in Leo's day was in ruins—though probably it was never more than a mountain " Ksor" —must, according to the indications supplied, have been founded by Obeid-ullah (Abu Mohammed) ben Ismail El-Mahdi of the tribe of Zeneta el-Maghraua tribe. Hence Marmol refers to the Empire of "Magaroas". Yussef ben Tashfin (Ali ben Yussef, king of the Lemtunas, according to Marmol) destroyed all of it except the mosque, part of which Abd el-Mumen restored.

(216) The Sahab el-Marga, or Mangar, of Marmol, or " the plain of brave men". Renou considers that the actual name is Seheb el-Merja—the grassy plain—corrupted into the abbreviation El-Mrîjat. " Seheb" means an uncultivated plain.

(217) Azgari-Camaren is a very phonetic form of Asra el-Hamar, or Kamar, between Sfru and the Atlas already referred to in Note 214. It seems to be the same locality that Marmol refers to as " Hamaran" and " Azgar", with the remark that some people call them the "plains of Onzar"; others those of " Iufet or of Mocin", though the name most commonly employed was that which he had adopted.

In the *Itinerary* of Ahmed ibn-Hassan (El-Mtui) the plain is mentioned as " Zogari-Ahmar " (Walckenaer, *Recherches*, etc., p. 458). It is the Zaghar el-Hamar of the Hajj Mohammed Sherif (D'Avezac, *Etudes*, etc., p. 156). Azrar is a Berber word (generally transformed by the Arabs into Zrâr), meaning "plain", and Hamar signifies "donkeys".—Renou, *Expl. Scient. de l'Algérie*, t. viii, p. 100.

(218) As in Centopozzi (p. 375), Leo translates the name of this mountain into Italian. "Hundred pits" being Miat Abiar, or Miat Bir, the presumption is that the Arab name of this mountain is Jebel Miat-Bir, and this is what Marmol applies to it; though, as he does not appear to know any more about it than what Leo tells, it is quite possible that this is a mere presumption on his part. Its position is, however, fixed by what is noted in the next paragraph regarding Cunaigel Gherben.

(219) In the *Itinerary* of Ahmed ibn Hassan he mentions the mountain "Omm-Djeniba", on which there is a bad pass across the Atlas called Kebur et-Tuat, the tomb of the Tuatees, twenty-three men from that oasis having perished in its snows. Both Leo and Marmol note a dangerous and difficult pass, often blocked with snow, though in summer the "Beni Essen" (Beni Hassan) Arabs resort to this mountain for coolness. Ahmed mentions that the villages called "Ksor Aït Iouci" were on the other side of the pass, in the plain of Zergu. We further learn, from the conjoint information of Leo and Marmol, that there are two fortified places on this mountain, which render the Beni Hassan masters of the pass.

Tezerghe, or Tigaza, is, in Renou's opinion, "without doubt" the fortified Berber village or Ksar of Tsaguts (Tarsut), which Ahmed seized on the banks of the Guigo (Gigu) river. Umen-Guinable is one of the Aït-Jussi villages, of which the exact name has not come to us.

Marmol says that Tigaza is situated on a stream which falls into the Sebu. It belongs to the mountain called by him Cunagel-gerben, and by Leo Cunaigel-Gherben, which means the crow's passage. This is evidently the Kheneg el-Gherâb, and the mountain the Jebel el-Gherâb, one of the most important in the Atlas. The famous pass is therefore between Jebel Om Jeriba on the south-west, and El-Gherâb on the north-east.—Renou, *Expl. Scient. de l'Algérie*, t. viii, pp. 101, 102, 234.

(220) The Tigaza of Marmol (note 219).

(221) Ume giunaybe of Marmol (note 219).

(222) Marizan of Marmol, a mountain inhabited by independent Berbers, the Mirâsen of El-Bekri. The tribe is not known by that name, and the locality is too vague for identification.

(223) Mezetalça of Marmol, the western part touching the plain of Adesen.

(224) The Ziz mountains derive their name from the Ziz river. Leo defines their extension to be from Mesettaza west to Tedla and Dades, southward to the modern Tafilet, and northward to the Adesen and Gureigura plains. According to Marmol, there are silver mines in two of them, namely, "Aden" (Aït Haïn) and "Arucanez", which were worked in his day to little profit; and in that quarter also were to be seen the ruins of a town called "Calaat aben Tavyla" (Kal'at Ibn Tawila).
The mountains in this region are not now known by any such general name, though De Foucauld, who traversed the district, would certainly have noted the fact had it reached his ears. What Leo names the Ziz mountains must comprise Jebel Aiashen, Jebel el-Abbari, Jebel el-Abbarat, and several other summits in the vicinity of the Ziz river.
This river rises in the Great Atlas in the Aït Hedidda district, and in its course receives the name of each independent tribe in turn whose Ksars border its banks. Then, after passing through a short desert tract, it enters the Ziz district, and flows past the twenty-five or thirty castellated villages of the Aït Izdeg, an independent fraction of the Aït Tafelman. Another short stretch of desert intervenes before it reaches the district of Gers. To this succeeds Tiallalin, El-Kheneg (where the date palm region begins) Ksar es-Suk, Metrara, Reteb, Tizime and Tafilet. These people do not recognise the Sultan's authority; and as there are no Jews there, the country, despite its silver mines, must be very poor indeed.

(225) This story of the Atlas Berbers keeping domestic snakes has been a hard one for the commentators to swallow. But, in reality, it is confirmed from a variety of quarters. James Bruce, recalling what Pomponius Mela says about the Berbers of the vicinity of Jebel Abeide, south of the Gulf of Gabes, living in caves and feeding on serpents, remarks that "if he had said fed together with serpents, his observations had been just; for they have such an esteem for snakes as to suffer them to feed promiscuously with them, and live continually in their house, where they perform the office of cats. These animals are perfectly inoffensive to their protectors, and suffer themselves to be lifted and carried in the hand from place to place, being, no doubt, non-venomous species. Some are six or seven feet long: they suffer no one to hurt them, or to transport them to any other place. No persuasion or reward could induce them to let me carry one of them, it being believed universally that they are a kind of good angels, whom it would be of the highest impropriety, and of the worst con-

sequences to the community, to remove from their dwellings." Sir Lambert Playfair tells us that in questioning the Tunisian tribesmen regarding the practice, the reply was invariably the same : " No one here keeps them, but the tribes further south are said to do so." This statement of Bruce aroused much ridicule, though, like so many other of his assertions, it has been amply confirmed. Jackson, writing in 1805, assures his readers that there was scarcely a house in Marakesh without its domestic serpent, which is sometimes seen moving along the roofs of the apartments. It is never injured by the family, who would consider it certain misfortune to maltreat so beneficent a guest. "They have been known to suck the breasts of women whilst asleep, and retire without offering any further injury. It is thought imprudent to incur their displeasure. A European stranger living in a Jew's house killed one four feet in length, which had entered his sleeping-place at night ; his host was seriously alarmed, and begged him to leave immediately, as he feared the malignity of the serpent, and was not reconciled until it was explained that the reptile was beyond the power of entertaining vindictive feelings." Jackson could scarcely have invented this anecdote, though an exhaustive acquaintance with his writings does not incline me to place that confidence in his accuracy which is usually done. But though I cannot confirm the statement from personal observation, I have heard much the same story, and have repeatedly seen the reluctance of the Berbers to kill toads, harmless snakes, etc.

All this points, of course, to the persistent remnants of serpent-worship, which not even the teachings of Islam have been able to eradicate. It was one of the most gruesome rites of the old Carthaginians, as it was and is among scores of other races. To this day it is a proverb in Tunisia, " Blessed is the habitation where the serpent dwells". Like the storks and swallows' nests in Europe, they bring " luck" to the house ; and though possibly Europeans are purposely kept in the dark, it is affirmed that among some of the more remote tribes the domestic snake's food is set out before the family have begun theirs. No one eats till the serpent has crept back to his hole. " If he is not the ruler of the house", write Messrs. Graham and Ashbee, " he possesses an importance the owner himself does not even attempt to share."

Further south, among the Pagan negroes, serpent-worship is open and widespread. In Dahomey it is an important cult, and in the island of Goree the domestic snake is, as in the Jebel Abeide underground dwellings, employed to kill rats and mice, and treated much as a cat is by the members of a family. It is even asserted that the young shepherds take them to the fields with them, and that the tame serpents watch over them when they sleep under the shade of a tree, lest their masters should be bitten by poisonous snakes. Many of the old houses in the city of Tunis are frequented by snakes, possibly survivals of domestic species.

The wondrous tales of monstrous serpents, one of which kept the Roman army at bay on the banks of the Bagadras (Mejerda), finds an echo in Leo's statement about the "many huge and monstrous dragons" in the Atlas Caves, which, Marmol adds, had the head and wings of a bird, the tail and skin of a serpent, and the feet of a wolf, though without the strength to lift their eyelids. It was called "Taybin"; but this is simply a corruption of *Thu'abán*, the ordinary Arabic word for a serpent ; and it is not impossible, as Sir Lambert Playfair suggests, that just as elephants and other animals have become extinct, larger species of snakes, such as pythons, may have formerly existed in Barbary, and given rise to the fables mentioned. —Playfair, *Travels in the Footsteps of Bruce*, pp. 141, 273, 274; Jackson, *Morocco*, p. 112 ; *Timbuctoo*, p. 212 ; Graham and Ashbee, *Travels in Tunisia*, pp. 27, 28; Temple, *Excursions in the Mediterranean : Algiers and Tunis*, vol. i, pp. 183, 253-255.

(226) This account of the habits of these mountaineers applies to-day. Their houses are still of "chalke" (that is, "creta" or limestone), though, naturally, their arms are now muskets—sometimes even rifles—instead of "fower or five javelins". But the sword with a brass sheath and the curved dagger, often silver-mounted, or in a silver-plated scabbard, are still the universal "side" (or rather front) weapons.

(227) Gerseluin, or Garciluna, was a Berber town, or rather hill-Ksar. It was ruined by the Almohades, and rebuilt by the Beni-Marinis, only again to fall into insignificance on the death of the last of that dynasty, when it was seized by the Arabs of the plain. The Maghrauas of the Zeneta stock held the pass across the mountains against the Lanutuna (Almoravides) ; but that served them very little, since the place was taken from the other side (" by Agmet", Marmol adds). In A.D. 1534, the Sherif Ahmed captured it, but at the time Marmol wrote it was governed by the King of Fez. Yet this fortress-town, commanding a pass then much used for crossing the Atlas to Segelmessa, does not now exist, at all events under Leo's name. Since Tafilet has replaced Segelmessa this pass has been largely discarded in favour of the Tizi-n-Glawi and a second caravan-pass further to the east, *via* Demnat and Aït bu Gemmes. Gerseluin may be Gers el-Ain (the Spring of Gers, the district in which it is situated). It must have been close to the Jebel Gers, and Leo says not far from the Ziz river, on which all the modern Ksars are situated. (Note 224.)

Between Amalu and El-Haïn, the ruins of a "Duar", with what must have been a large castle, can be seen. This is possibly Gerseluin; for at best it could never have been more than a Kasba village to hold the pass. Though there are now no Jews in the Gers district, there are the remains of a Mellah at Duar.

IOHN LEO HIS
FOVRTH BOOKE OF
the Historie of Africa, and
of the memorable things
contained therein.

A description of the kingdome of *Telensin.¹   * *Or Tremizen.*

His kingdome beginneth westward from the riuers of Zha & Muluia, eastward it bordereth vpon The great riuer, southward vpon the desert of Numidia, and northward vpon the Mediterran sea. This region was called by the Romanes Cæsaria, and was by them inhabited: howbeit after the Romanes were expelled, it was fullie possessed by the ancient gouernours thereof called Beni Habdulguad,² and being a generation of the familie of Magraua. And it remained vnto them and their successors three hundred yeeres, vntill such time as a certaine mightie man called *Ghamrazen* the sonne of *Zeÿen* tooke possession thereof. His posteritie changing at length their ancient name were called *Beni Zeÿen*, that is, the sonnes of *Zeÿen*: and they enioied this kingdome for the space almost of 380. yeeres.³ At length the kings of Fez of the Marin-familie greatly molested them, so that those ten kings which succeeded *Zeÿen* were some of them vnfortuate in battell, some slaine, some taken captiue, and others expelled their

kingdome, and chased to the next mountaines. Neither were they free from vexation of the kings of Tunis: howbeit the kingdome of Telensin still remained to this familie, and they continued in peace for almost an hundred and twentie yeeres, being endammaged by no forren power; sauing that one *Abu Feris* king of Tunis, and his sonne *Hutmen* made them to pay tribute for certaine yeeres vnto Tunis, till the decease of the said *Hutmen*. This kingdome stretcheth in length from east to west 380. miles, but in bredth from north to south, that is, from the Mediterran sea to the deserts of Numidia not aboue fiue and twentie miles: which is the occasion that it is so often oppressed by the Arabians inhabiting the Numidian deserts. The kings of Telensin haue alwaies endeuoured by great gifts to gaine the good will and friendship of the Numidians, but they could neuer satisfie their insatiable couetice. A man shall seldome trauell safely through this kingdome: howbeit here are great store of merchants, perhaps either because it adioneth to Numidia, or else for that the way to the land of Negros lieth through it. It hath two most famous & frequented hauen-townes, the one called *Horam, and the other *Marsa Elcabir, whither vse to resort great store of Genoueses, and Venetians. But afterward both these townes were taken by Don *Ferdinando* the Catholike king, to the great inconuenience of all this kingdome: for which cause the king then raigning called *Abuchemmen*, was expelled his kingdome and put to flight by his owne subiects: afterward *Abuzeyen* was restored to the kingdome, who had for certaine yeeres beene imprisoned by his nephew *Abuchemmen*: howbeit he enioied the kingdome but a very short space. For he was at length miserably slaine by *Barbarossa* the Turke, who conquered the kingdome of Tremizen by force of war. Whereof *Abuchemmen*, that was expelled by his owne subiects, hauing intelligence, sent to craue aide of the emperour *Charles* the fift, whereby

* Or *Oran*.
* Or *Mersalcabir*.

Abuchemmen king of Tremizen restored to his kingdome by the emperour Charles the fift.

he hoped to recouer his kingdome. Which request being granted, he leuied a puissant armie, and made warre against *Barbarossa*, and hauing driuen him out, he recouered his kingdome, and seuerely punished them that had conspired his banishment. And then he gaue the Spanish soldiers their pay, sent the captaines home with great rewardes, and allowed *Charles* the emperour a large yeerely reuenue so long as he liued.⁴ After his decease succeeded his brother *Habdulla*, who neglecting the league made before betweene the emperour and his brother, and relying vpon *Soliman* the great Turke, refused to pay any more tribute vnto the emperour *Charles*, and hath kept possession of the kingdome, till *this present.⁵ The greater part of this region is vntilled, drie, and barren, especially towards the south. Howbeit the sea coast is somewhat more fertill. The territorie adiacent to the citie of Telensin is full of woods, sauing that the westerne part towardes the sea is mountainous. Likewise the regions of Tenez and Alger containe mountaines abounding with all kinde of commodities. In this part are but few cities aud castles, howbeit it is a most fruitfull and blessed place, as we will hereafter declare in particular.

1526.

Of the desert of Angad.

THis barren, drie, and vntilled desert being vtterly destitute of water and wood, is situate vpon the westerne frontire of the kingdome of Telensin; and extendeth in length fowerscore, and in bredth almost fiftie miles. Here are great store of roes, deere, and ostriches. Such merchants as trauell from Fez to Telensin passe ouer this desert not without great danger, by reason of certaine Arabians which liue onely vpon theft and robberie, especially in winter, when as the soldiers appointed to defend the said desert from those lewd vagabonds, doe vsually retire themselues into Numidia.

Great store of ostriches.

Many shepherds there are in this desert, who are daily vexed with multitudes of fierce lions, which sometime seaze not onely vpon cattell, but also vpon men.[6]

Of the castle of Temzegzet.

This castle standing in the same place, where the foresaid desert adioineth vnto the territorie of Telensin, and built by the Africans vpon a rocke, was in times past very strong, and often annoied by the people of Fez; for it standeth in the high way from Fez to Telensin. Through the fields adiacent runneth a certaine riuer called in their language *Tesme*. The said fields adiacent sufficiently abound with all things necessarie for the sustenance of the inhabitants. Heretofore being subiect vnto the kings of Telensin it well deserued the name of a citie, but since the Arabians got possession thereof, it hath prooued more like to a stable: for here they keepe their corne onely, and the naturall inhabitants are quite expelled by reason of their bad demeanour.[7]

Of the castle of Izli.

This ancient castle of Izli built by the Africans vpon a certaine plaine bordering vpon the foresaid desert, hath some fieldes adioining vnto it, apt only for barlie and panicke. It was in times past well stored with inhabitants, and enuironed with stately walles: but afterward by the iniurie of warre it was razed to the ground, and the inhabitants expelled. Howbeit a few yeeres after it began to be inhabited anew by certaine religious persons had in great reuerence both by the kings of Telensin and by all the Arabians. These religious persons with great courtesie and liberalitie giue entertainment for three daies vnto all strangers that passe by, and then dismisse them without paying of ought. All their houses are very base and low built, their walles being of claye, and the roofes of straw.

HISTORIE OF AFRICA. 663

Not far from this castle runneth a riuer ; out of which they water all their fields : for this region is so hot and dry, that vnlesse the fields were continually watered, they would yeeld no fruit at all.⁸

Of the towne of Guagida.

THis ancient towne built by the Africans vpon a large plaine, standeth southward of the Mediterran sea fortie miles, and about the same distance from the citie of Telensin. The southwest part of the said plaine bordereth vpon the desert of Angad, and it containeth most fruitfull fields and pleasant gardens, exceedingly replenished with figs and grapes. Through the midst of this towne runneth a certaine riuer, which affoordeth good water to drinke and seeth meate withall. In times past the towne-walles and all the buildings were most sumptuous and stately, and the inhabitants exceeding rich, ciuill, and valiant : but afterward by reason of certaine warres waged by the king of Fez against the king of Telensin, this towne was left desolate, and the inhabitants all put to flight : but the said warres being ended, new inhabitants reedified it and dwelt therein : howbeit they could not reduce it to the former state, neither doth it now containe aboue fifteene hundred families. The townesmen lead now a miserable life, being constrained to pay tribute both to the king of Telensin and also to the Arabians of Angad, and wearing most base apparell : asses and mules they haue great store, whereof they make round summes of money. They speake after the ancient manner of the Arabians, neither is their language so corrupt as the language of the people round about them.⁹

Of the citie called Ned Roma.

THis ancient towne built by the Romans, while they were lords of Africa, standing vpon a large plaine, almost two miles from a certaine mountaine, and about twelue miles from the Mediterran sea, and neere vnto it runneth a little riuer. The historiographers of those times report, that this towne was in all respects built after the fashion of Rome, whereupon they say it borrowed the name. For *Ned* in the Arabian toong signifieth like. The wall of this towne is as yet to be seene: but all the ancient buildings of the Romans are so destroied, that now there scarcely remaine any ruines thereof. It began in some places to be repaired and reedified anew, but nothing comparable to the former buildings. The fieldes adiacent are exceeding fruitfull, and containe many gardens replenished with such trees as beare Carobs (being a fruit like vnto *Cassia fistula*) which in the suburbes they vse for foode. This towne is indifferently well inhabited, especially with weauers, who make great store of cotton-cloth, and are free from all tribute. The gouernours of the towne are chosen onely at their assignement: and that they may haue more free traffique with the people of Telensin, they sende many gifts vnto the king.[10]

Of the towne of Tebecrit.

THis little towne built by the Africans vpon a certaine rocke neere vnto the Mediterran sea, is almost twelue miles distant from the former. All the next mountaines are exceeding high and barren, and yet well stored with inhabitants. In this towne dwell great store of weauers; and here they haue abundance of Carobs and honie. Being in continuall feare of the Christians, they keepe euery night most diligent watch and ward: for they are not of sufficient abilitie to maintaine a garrison of soldiers. Their fields are no lesse barren then vntilled ; and yeelde onely very small quantitie of barlic and panicke. The townesmen are most barely apparelled, and vtterly destitute of humanitie.[11]

Of the towne of Hunain.

THis towne being founded by the Africans, and being famous both for stately building and ciuill inhabitants, hath a little hauen belonging thereunto well fortified with two turrets standing one on the one side, and another on the other side. The towne-wall also is very high and beautifull, especially on that side which standeth next vnto the sea. Hither doe the Venetians yeerely bring great store of merchandize, and doe traffique with the merchants of Telensin ; for the citie of Telensin is but fourteene miles from hence. Since the time that Oran was surprized by the Christians, the Venetians would no longer frequent Oran, fearing least the Spanyards hauing it in possession should worke them some mischiefe: wherfore then they began to repaire vnto this port. The townesmen in times past were most ciuill people, the greatest part being weauers of cotton and of linnen. Their houses are most stately built, and haue euery one fountaines belonging vnto them : likewise here are many vines running pleasantly vpon bowers or arbours. Their houses are paued with mats of diuers colours, and their chambers and vaults are curiously painted and carued. Howbeit, so soone as the inhabitants were aduertised of the losse of Oran, they fled from Hunain and left it void of inhabitants : sauing that the king of Telensin maintaineth here a garison of footemen, who giue notice when any merchants ships approch. Their fields abound with cherries, peaches, figs, oliues, and other fruites : howbeit they reape but little commoditie thereby. I my selfe passing this way could not but bewaile the extreme calamitie whereinto the inhabitants of this towne were

A ship of great value. fallen: at the same time there arriued a certaine ship of Genoa, which one ship brought commodities sufficient to serue Telensin for fiue yeeres: the tenth part whereof amounting to fifteene thousand duckats, was paid for tribute to the king.[12]

Of the towne of Haresgol.

THe great and ancient towne of Haresgol was built vpon a rocke enuironed on all sides with the Mediterran sea, sauing on the south, where lieth a way from the firme lande to the towne. It standeth northward of Telensin fourteene miles; and was in times past well stored with inhabitants. The gouernour thereof was one *Idris*, vncle vnto that *Idris* that was the founder of Fez; the posteritie of whom enioied the same gouernment for the space of an hundred yeeres. At length there came a certaine king and patriarke of Cairaoan who vtterly destroied this towne, so that it remained voide of inhabitants almost an hundred yeers: after which time it was reinhabited by certaine people of Granada, which came thither with *Mansor;* which *Mansor* repaired the towne, to the end it might alwaies be a place of refuge for his soldiers. After whose decease, and the death of his sonne *Mudaffir*, all the soldiers were expelled by the tribes or people of Zanhagia and Magraoa; and this second desolation of that towne happened in the yeere of the Hegeira 410.[13]

Of the great citie of Telensin, otherwise called Tremizen.

Elensin is a great citie and the royall seate of the king; but who were the first founders thereof it is vncertaine: howbeit most certaine it is, that this citie was very small at the beginning and began greatly to be augmented at the same time when Haresgol was laid waste. For then, a certaine family called Abdulguad[14] bearing rule, it increased so exceedingly, that in the raigne of king *Abu Tesfin*[15] it contained sixteene thousand families. And then it was an honourable and well-gouerned citie: howbeit *Ioseph* king of Fez continually molested it, and with an huge armie besieged it for seuen yeeres together. This *Ioseph* hauing built a fort vpon the east side of the towne, put the besieged citizens to such distresse, that they could no longer endure the extreme famine: wherefore with one accord they all went vnto their king, beseeching him to haue compassion vpon their want. The king, to make them acquainted with his daintie fare, which he had to supper, shewed them a dish of sodden horse-flesh and barlie. And then they well perceiued how little the kings estate was better then the estate of the meanest citizen of them all. Soone after the king hauing procured an assemblie, perswaded his people that it was much more honourable to die in battel for the defence of their countrie, then to liue so miserable a life. Which words of the king so inflamed all their mindes to the battell, that the day following they resolued to encounter the enemie, and valiantly to fight it out. But it fell out farre better for them then they expected; for the same night king *Ioseph* was slaine by one of his owne people: which newes being brought vnto the citizens, with greater courage they marched all out of the towne, easily vanquishing and killing the confused multitude of their enemies; after which vnexpected victorie they found victuals sufficient in the enemies campe to relieue their long and tedious famine.[16] About fortie yeeres after, the fourth king of Fez of the Marin-familie called *Abulhesen*, built a towne within two miles westward of the citie of Telensin. Then he besieged Telensin for thirty moneths together, making daily and fierce assaults against it, and euery night erecting some new fort, so that at length the Fessan forces next vnto Telensin easily entred the citie, and hauing conquered it, caried home the king thereof captiue vnto Fez, where he was by the king of Fez beheaded, and his carcase was cast foorth among the filth of the citie: and this was the second and the greater dammage that Telensin sustained.[17] After the decay of the Marin-familie Telensin began in many places to be repaired, and replenished with new inhabitants, insomuch that it increased to twelue thousand families. Here each trade and occupation hath a peculiar place, after the manner of Fez, sauing that the buildings of Fez are somewhat more stately. Here are also many and beautifull temples, hauing their Mahumetan priestes and preachers. Likewise here are fiue colleges most sumptuously built, some by the king of Telensin, and some by the king of Fez. Here also are store of goodly bathes and hothouses, albeit they haue not such plentie of water as is at Fez. Also here are very many innes built after the manner of Africa: vnto two of which innes the merchants of Genoa and Venice doe vsually resort. A great part of this citie is inhabited with Iewes, who were in times past all of them exceeding rich: vpon their heads they weare a *Dulipan to distinguish them from other citizens: but in the yeere of the Hegeira *923*, vpon the death of king *Abuhabdilla*[18] they were all so robbed and spoiled, that they are now brought almost vnto beggerie. Moreouer in this citie there are many conducts, the fountaines whereof are not

The king of Telensen taken prisoner and beheaded.

* Or Turban.

farre from the citie-walles, so that they may easily be stopped by any forren enemie. The citie-wall is very high and impregnable, hauing fiue great gates vpon it, at euery one of which there is placed a garde of soldiers, and certaine receiuers of the kings custome. On the south side of the citie standeth the kings palace, enuironed with most high walles, and containing many other palaces within it, which are none of them destitute of their fountaines and pleasant gardens: this royall palace hath two gates, one leading into the fields, and the other into the citie, and at this gate standeth the captaine of the garde. The territorie of Telensin containeth most pleasant habitations, whither the citizens in summer-time vse to retire themselues: for besides the beautifull pastures and cleere fountaines, there is such abundance of all kinde of fruits to delight both the eies and the taste, that to my remembrance I neuer sawe a more pleasant place: their figs they vse to drie in the sunne and to keepe vntill winter: and as for almonds, peaches, melons, and pome-citrons, they grow here in great plentie. Three miles eastward of this citie are diuers mils vpon the riuer of Sefsif;[19] and some other there are also not far from the citie vpon the mountaine of Elcalha. The south part of the citie is inhabited by Iewes, lawyers, and notaries: here are also very many students, and professours of diuers artes, which haue maintenance allowed them out of the fiue forenamed colleges. The citizens are of fower sorts, to wit, some artificers, some merchants, others schollers and doctors, and all the residue soldiers. The merchants are men most iust, trustie, liberall, and most zealous of the common good; who for the most part exercise traffique with the Negros. The artificers liue a secure, quiet, and merrie life. The kings soldiers being all of a comely personage and of great valour, receiue very large and liberall pay, for they are monethly allowed three peeces of the gold-coine of Telensin, which are worth three

Italian duckats and one second part. All students before they attaine to the degree of a doctor liue a bare and miserable life, but hauing attained thereunto, they are made either professours or notaries, or priestes. The citizens and merchants of this citie are so neate and curious in their apparell, that sometimes they excell the citizens of Fez in brauerie. The artificers weare short garments carrying seldome a Dulipan vpon their heads, and contenting themselues with plaine caps: their shooes reach vp to their mid-leg. Of all others the soldiers go woorst apparelled, for wearing a shirt or iacket with wide sleeues, they cast ouer it a large mantle made of cotton, and thus they are clad both sommer and winter: sauing that in winter they haue certaine iackets of leather with hoods vpon them, such as trauellers vse in Italie, and by this meanes their heads are defended from raine and from snow. The schollers and students are diuersly apparelled, according to their abilitie, and according to the fashion of their natiue countrie: the doctors, iudges, and priestes goe in more sumptuous and costly attire.

The customes and rites obserued in the King of Telensin his court.

A Woonder it is to see how stately and magnificently the King of Telensin behaueth himselfe, for no man may see him nor be admitted to parle with him, but onely the principall nobles of his court, each one of whom are assigned to beare offices according to their place and dignitie. In this court are sundry offices and dignities, and the Kings lieutenant beeing principall officer, allotteth vnto each one such places of dignitie, as may be correspondent to their honour: and this lieutenant leuieth the kings armies, and sometime conducteth them against the enemie. The second officer is the Kings chiefe Secretarie, who writeth and recordeth all things pertaining to the

King. The third is the high treasurer, who is bound by his office to receiue tributes and customes. The fourth is the kings dispensator or almoner, who bestoweth such liberalitie as the king vouchsafeth. The fift is the captaine of the kings garde, who so often as any nobles are admitted to the kings presence, conducteth the garde vnto the palace-gate. Then are there other meaner officers, as namely, the master of the kings stable, the ouerseer of his saddles & stirrops, and his chiefe chamberlaine, who giueth attendance onely at such times as any courtiers are admitted vnto the kings audience. For at other times the kings wiues, with certaine Christian captiues, and eunuches doe performe that dutie. The king sometimes in sumptuous and costly apparell rideth vpon a stately stead richly trapped and furnished. In riding he obserueth not much pompe nor many ceremonies; neither indeede doth he carrie so great a traine; for you shall scarcely see a thousand horsemen in his companie, except perhaps in time of warre, when as the Arabians and other people giue attendance. When the king goeth foorth with an armie, there are not many carriages transported therein, neither can you then discerne the king by his apparell from any meane captaine: and though he conducteth neuer so great a garde of soldiers, yet a man would not thinke how sparing he is of his coine. Gold-money he coineth of baser golde, then that whereof the Italian money called *Bislacchi* is coined, but it is of a greater size, for one peece thereof waigheth an Italian duckat and one fourth part. He stampeth likewise coine of siluer & of brasse. His dominions are but slenderly inhabited: howbeit because the way from Europe to Aethiopia lieth throug his kingdome, he reapeth much benefit by the wares that passe by, especially since the time that Oran was surprized by the Christians. At the same time Telensin it selfe was made tributarie, which was euer before a free citie: whereupon the king that was the

A passage from Europe to Aethiopia through the kingdome of Tremizen.

author thereof, was extremely hated of his subjects till his dying day. Afterward his sonne that succeeded him, demanded customes and tributes likewise: for which cause being expelled out of his kingdome by the people, he was enforced to craue aide of the emperour *Charles* the fift, by whose meanes (as is beforesaid) he was restored vnto his said kingdome. When Oran was subiect vnto the king of Telensin, the region thereabout paid vnto the king for yeerly tribute sometime three thousand, and sometime fower thousand duckats, the greatest part whereof was allowed vnto the kings garde, and to the Arabian soldiers. I my selfe continuing certaine monethes in this kings court, had good experience of his liberalitie. I haue indeede omitted many particulars in the description of this court of Telensin: but because they agreed for the most part with those things which we reported of Fez, I haue here passed them ouer, least I should seeme too tedious vnto the reader.[20]

Of the towne of Hubbed.

This towne being built in manner of a castle standeth about a mile and an halfe southward of Telensin. It containeth store of inhabitants, who are for the most part dyers of cloth. In this towne was buried one *Sadi Bu Median* being reputed a man of singular holines, whom they adore like a god, ascending vp to his monument by certaine steps. Here is likewise a stately college, and a faire hospitall to entertaine strangers in; both which were built by a king of Fez of the Marin-familie, as I finde recorded vpon a certaine marble-stone.[21]

Of the towne of Tefesra.

This towne standing vpon a plaine fifteene miles from Telensin hath great store of smiths therein, by

Mines of iron. reason of the iron-mines which are there. The fields adiacent are exceeding fruitfull for corne : and the inhabitants being for the most part blacke-smithes are destitute of all ciuilitie.[22]

Of the towne of Tessela.

This ancient towne was built by the Africans vpon a certaine plaine, extending almost twenty miles in length. Here groweth such abundance of excellent corne, as is almost sufficient for the whole kingdome of Telensin. The inhabitants liue in tents, for all the buildings of this towne are destroied, though the name remaineth still. These also in times past paide a great yeerely tribute vnto the king of Telensin.[23]

Of the prouince called Beni Rasid.

This region extendeth in length from east to west fiftie, and in bredth almost fiue and twentie miles. The southerne part thereof is plaine ground, but toward the north it is full of fruitfull mountaines. The inhabitants are of two sorts : for some of them dwell vpon the mountaines in houses of indifferent good building : and these imploy themselues in husbandry and other necessarie affaires. Others being of a more noble condition liue onely vpon the plaines in tents, and there keepe their camels, horses, and other cattell. They are molested with daily inconueniences, and pay yeerely tribute vnto the king of Telensin. Vpon the foresaid mountaines are sundrie villages, among which there are two principall, whereof the one called Chalath Haoara, and built in manner of a castle vpon the side of a certaine hill, containeth to the number of fortie merchants and artificers houses : the other called Elmo Hascar is the seate of the kings lieutenant ouer those regions ; and in this village euery Thursday there is a great market, where abundance of cattell, corne, raisons, figs, and honie is to be sold : here are likewise cloth-merchants and diuers other chapmen, which for breuities sake I passe ouer in silence. I my selfe continuing for some time among them, found to my hinderence what cunning theeues they were. The king of Telensin collecteth yeerely out of this prouince the summe of fiue and twenty thousand duckats; and it containeth so many most expert soldiers.[24]

Of the towne of Batha.

THis great, rich, and populous towne[25] was built in my time vpon a most beautifull and large plaine, which yeeldeth great abundance of corne. The tribute which the king of Telensin hath here, amounteth to the summe of twentie thousand duckats. Howbeit this towne was afterward destroied in that warre which happened betweene the king and certaine of his kinsmen. For they growing mightie by the king of Fez his aide, woon many townes in the kingdome of Telensin: and whatsoeuer towne they thought themselues not able to keepe by force of armes, they burnt it quite downe: and thus they serued Batha, whereof now there remaine but very few ruines. Not far from this towne runneth a little riuer, on both sides whereof there are many gardens and fields replenished with all kinde of fruites. Moreouer the foresaid plaine was vtterly destitute of inhabitants, till a certaine heremite with followers, whom they reuerenced as a man of singular holines, repaired thither. This heremite in short time grew so rich in oxen, horses, and other cattell, that no man almost throughout the whole region was comparable vnto him. Neither he nor his followers pay any tribute at all, when as notwithstanding (as I heard of his disciples) he reapeth yeerly eight thousand bushels of corne, and at this time possesseth fiue hundred horses, ten thousand small cattell, and two thousand oxen; and besides all the former hath yeerely sent vnto him from diuers partes of the world fower

A famous heremite.

or fiue thousand duckats: so greatly hath the fame of his
false holines spread ouer all Africa and Asia. Disciples
he hath to the number of fiue hundred, whom he maintaineth at his owne cost: neither emploieth he them to
ought else, but daily to read a few praiers: for which
cause many resort vnto him, desiring to be of the number
of his disciples, whom after he hath instructed in certaine
ceremonies, he sendeth them thither from whence they first
came. He hath about an hundred tents pitched, whereof
some are for strangers, others for shepherds, and the
residue for some of his owne familie. This holy heremite
hath fower wiues, and a great many women-slaues wearing
most sumptuous apparell. His sonnes likewise haue their
wiues and families: insomuch that the whole familie of
this heremite and of his sonnes containeth fiue hundred
persons. He is greatly honoured by all the Arabians, and
by the king of Telensin himselfe. My selfe was once
desirous to trie what manner of man this heremite was: and
for three daies I was entertained by him in the most
secrete places of his habitation, where amongst other
things he shewed me certaine bookes intreating of art-
Magique and of Alchymie: and he endeuoured by all
meanes to perswade me, that Magique was a most true
and vndoubted arte, whereby I perceiued that himselfe was
a magician, albeit he neuer vsed nor regarded the arte,
except it were in inuocating of God by certaine names.

Of the towne of Oran.

THis great and populous towne containing about sixe
thousand families, and built many yeeres agoe by
the Africans vpon the Mediterran sea shore, is distant from
Telensin an hundreth and fortie miles. Heere may you
see great store of stately buildings, as namely of temples,
colledges, hospitals, bath-stoues, and innes. The towne is
compassed with most high and impregnable walles, hauing

on the one side a faire plaine, and on the other side diuers mountaines. The greatest part of the inhabitants were weauers, and the residue liued of their yeerely reuenues. The territorie of this towne yeeldeth but small store of corne, so that the townesmen make all their bread of barley: howbeit they are most courteous and friendly to all strangers. This towne was greatly frequented with merchants of Catalonia, and of Genoa: and one street thereof is at this present called the street of the Genoueses. They were at perpetuall enmitie with the king of Telensin, neither would they euer accept of any gouernor, but one which receiued the kings tribute. But the townesmen chose one of their chiefe Burgo-masters to iudge of cases ciuill and criminall. The merchants of this towne maintained at their owne costs certaine foists and brigandines of warre, which committed many piracies vpon the coast of Catalonia, Geuisa, Maiorica, and Minorica, insomuch that Oran was full of Christian captiues. Afterward Don *Ferdinando* king of Spaine encountring Oran with a great Armada, determined to release the said Christians out of captiuitie: but he had veric hard successe. Howbeit within a few moneths after beeing ayded by the Biscaines and the Cardinall of Spaine, he tooke Oran. For the Moores issuing foorth with great furie vpon the Christians armie, left the towne vtterly destitute of souldiers, which the Spaniards perceiuing, began to assayle the towne on the other side; where being resisted by none but by women, they had easie entrance. Whereupon the Moores seeing the christians banners aduanced vpon their wals, they returned backe into the town, and were there put to so great a slaughter, that few of them escaped. Thus was Oran taken by the Spaniards in the yeere of *Mahomet* his Hegeira 916.[26]

Oran taken by the Spaniards.

Of the towne Mersalcabir.

This towne was built in my time by the king of Telensin vpon the Mediterran sea, not farre from Oran. And Mersalcabir in the Moores language signifieth a great or large hauen: for I thinke there is not the like hauen to be found in the whole world besides: so that here infinite number of ships and galleies may finde most safe harbour in any tempestuous weather. Hither the Venetians ships made often resort, when they perceiued any tempest to approach: and from hence they would cause all their wares to be transported to Oran in other vessels. This towne also was at length taken by the Spaniards as well as Oran.[27]

Mersalcabir taken by the Spaniards.

Of the towne of Mezzagran.

This towne also was built by the Africans vpon the Mediterran sea, neere vnto the place where the river Selef disemboqueth. It is well peopled and much molested by the Arabians. The gouernour thereof hath little authoritie within the towne, and lesse without.[28]

Of the towne of Mustuganin.

MVstuganin beeing founded by the Africans vpon the Mediterran sea, standeth almost three miles from Mezzagran, on the other side of the riuer Selef. It was in times past verie populous; but since the kingdome of Telensin began to decay, this towne hath beene so vexed by the Arabians, that at this present the third part thereof scarce remaineth. Families it containeth to the number of fifteene hundred; and it hath a most beautifull and stately temple. In this towne are great store of weauers: and the houses are most sumptuously built, hauing cleere fountaines belonging vnto them. Through the midst of the towne runneth a riuer, on each side whereof stand

diuers milles. Not farre from the towne there are most
pleasant gardens ; but they lie now vntilled and desolate.
Their fields are exceeding fruitfull. There belongeth an
hauen vnto this towne, whereunto many merchants of
Europe vse to resort, albeit they finde not much traffick
here, because the townesmen are so destitute of money.[20]

Of the towne of Bresch.

THis ancient towne built by the Romanes vpon the
Mediterran sea, standeth many miles distant from
Mustuganin. It containeth great store of inhabitants,
which are many of them weauers. The people of this
towne vse to paint a blacke crosse vpon their cheeke, and
two other blacke crosses vpon the palmes of their hands :
and the like custome is obserued by all the inhabitants of
the mountaines of Alger, and Bugia : the occasion whereof
is thought to be this, namely that the Gothes when they
first began to inuade these regions, released all those from
paying of tribute (as our African historiographers affirme)
that would imbrace the Christian religion. But so often as
any tribute was demanded, euery man to eschew the
payment thereof, would not sticke to professe himselfe a
Christian: wherefore it was then determined, that such as
were Christians indeed should be distinguished from others
by the foresaid crosses. At length the Gothes being
expelled, they all reuolted vnto the Mahumetan religion ;
howbeit this custome of painting crosses remained still
among them, neither doe they know the reason thereof.
Likewise the meaner sort of people in Mauritania vse to
make such crosses vpon their faces, as we see vsed by some
people of Europe. This towne aboundeth greatly with
figs, and the fields thereof are exceeding fruitfull for flaxe
and barley. The townesmen haue continued in firme
league and friendship with the people of the mountaines
adioyning ; by whose fauour they liued an hundred yeeres

togither without paying of any tribute at all : but *Barbarossa* the Turke hauing woon the kingdome of Telensin put them to great distresse. From hence they vse to transport by sea great store of figs and flaxe vnto Alger, Tunis, and Bugia, wherby they gaine great store of money. Here also you may as yet behold diuers monuments of the Romans ancient buildings.[30]

Of the towne of Sersell.

THis great and ancient towne built by the Romanes vpon the Mediterran sea, was afterward taken by the Gothes and lastly by the Mahumetans. The wall of this towne is exceeding high, strong, and stately built, and containeth about eight miles in circuit. In that part of the towne next vnto the Mediterran sea standeth a most beautifull and magnificent temple built by the Romans, the inward part whereof consisteth of marble. They had also in times past an impregnable fort standing vpon a rock by the Mediterran sea. Their fields are most fruitfull : and albeit this towne was much oppressed by the Gothes, yet the Mahumetans enioyed a great part thereof for the space almost of fiue hundred yeeres. And then after the warre of Telensin it remained voide of inhabitants almost three hundred yeeres. As length when Granada was woon by the Christians, diuers Moores of Granada fled thither, which repaired the houses and a good part of the castle : afterward they began to build ships, wherewith they transported their merchantable commodities into other regions ; and they increased so by little and little, that now they are growne to twelue hundred families. They were subiect not long since vnto *Barbarossa* the Turke, vnto whom they paide but three hundred ducates for yeerely tribute.[31]

Of the citie of Meliana.

THis great and ancient citie, commonly called now by the corrupt name of Magnana, and built by the Romanes vpon the top of a certaine hill, is distant from the Mediterran sea almost fortie miles. Vpon this mountaine are many springs, and woods abounding with walnuts. The citie it selfe is enuironed with most ancient and high wals. One side thereof is fortified with impregnable rockes, and the other side dependeth so vpon the mountaine as *Narnia* doth, which is a citie neere Rome: it containeth verie stately houses, euery one of which houses hath a fountaine. The inhabitants are almost all weauers: and there are diuers turners also which make fine cups, dishes, and such like vessels. Many of them likewise are husbandmen. They continued many yeeres free from all tribute and exaction, till they were at length made tributarie by *Barbarossa*.[32]

Of the towne of Tenez.

THis ancient towne built by the Africans vpon the side of an hill not far from the Mediterran sea, is enuironed with faire walles, and inhabited with many people.[33] The inhabitants are exceeding rusticall and vnciuill; and haue alwaies beene subiect to the king of Telensin. King *Mahumet* that was grandfather vnto the king which now raigneth, left three sonnes behinde him; the eldest being called *Abuabdilla*, the second, *Abuzcuen*, and the third *Iahia*. *Abuabdilla* succeeded his father, whom his brethren being ayded by the citizens went about to murther. But afterward, the treason being discouered, *Abuzcuen* was apprehended and put in prison. Howbeit, king *Abuchemmen being after that expelled out of his kingdome by the people, *Abuzcuen* was not onely restored to his former libertie, but was also chosen king, and enioyed

* *Perhaps Abuabdilla.*

the kingdome so long, till (as is before-mentioned) he was slaine by *Barbarossa*. *Iahia* fled vnto the king of Fez, who being at length proclaimed king by the people of Tenez, raigned for certaine yeeres. And his young sonne that he left behinde him being vanquished by *Barbarossa*, fled vnto *Charles* who was then onely king of Spaine. But when as the ayde promised by *Charles* the Emperour stayed long, and the Prince of Tenez was too long absent, a rumour was spread abroad, that hee and his brother were turned Christians: whereupon the gouernment of Tenez fell immediatly to the brother of *Barbarossa*.[34] Their fields indeed yeeld abundance of corne ; but of other commodities they haue great want.

Of the towne of Mazuna.

THis towne (as some report) was built by the Romanes, and standeth about fortie miles from the Mediterran sea. It hath fruitfull fields, strong walles, but most base and deformed houses. Their temple indeed is somewhat beautiful: for it was in times past a most stately towne, but being often sacked, sometime by the king of Telensin, and sometime by his rebels ; and at length falling into the hands of the Arabians, it was brought vnto extreme miserie, so that at this present there are but few inhabitants remaining, all being either weauers or husbandmen, and most grieuously oppressed by the Arabians. Their fields abound plentifully with all kinde of corne. Neere vnto this towne there haue beene in times past many houses, streets, and villages, which may probably be coniectured by the letters engrauen vpon marble stones. The names of which villages are not to bee found in any of our histories or Chronicles.[35]

Of Gezeir, otherwise called Alger.

GEzeir in the Moores language signifieth an island, which name is thought to haue beene giuen vnto this citie, because it lieth neere vnto the isles of Maiorica, Minorica, and Icuiza: howbeit the Spanyards call it Alger. It was founded by the Africans of the familie of Mesgana, wherefore in old time it was called by the name of Mesgana. It is a large towne, containing families to the number of fower thousand, and is enuironed with most stately and impregnable walles. The buildings thereof are very artificiall and sumptuous: and euery trade and occupation hath here a seuerall place. Innes, bath-stoues, and temples here are very beautifull; but the stateliest temple of all standeth vpon the sea-shore. Next vnto the sea there is a most pleasant walke vpon that part of the towne wall, which the waues of the sea beat vpon. In the suburbes are many gardẽs replenished with all kind of fruits. On the east side of the towne runneth a certaine riuer hauing many mils thereupon: and out of this riuer they draw water fit for drinke, and for the seruices of the kitchen. It hath most beautifull plaines adioining vpon it, and especially one called Metteggia, which extendeth fortie fiue miles in length, and almost thirtie miles in bredth, and aboundeth mightily with all kindes of graine. This towne for many yeeres was subiect vnto the kingdome of Telensin: but hearing that Bugia was also gouerned by a king, and being neerer thereunto, they submitted themselues vnto the king of Bugia. For they saw that the king of Telensin could not sufficiently defend them against their enemies, and also that the king of Bugia might doe them great dammage, wherefore they offered vnto him a yeerely tribute of their owne accord, and yet remained almost free from all exaction. But certaine yeeres after, the inhabitants of this citie building for themselues gallies, began to play the pirates, and greatly to molest the foresaid islands. Whereupon king *Ferdinando* prouided a mightie armada, hoping thereby to become lorde of the citie. Likewise vpon a certaine high rocke standing opposit against the towne, he caused a strong forte to be built, and that within gun-shot of the citie, albeit the citie walles could not be endammaged thereby. Wherefore the citizens immediately sent ambassadours into Spaine, to craue a league for ten yeeres, vpon condition that they should pay certaine yeerely tribute; which request was granted by king *Ferdinando*. And so they remained for certaine moneths free from the danger of warre: but at length *Barbarossa* hastening to the siege of Bugia, and hauing woon one fort built by the Spaniards, determined to encounter another, hoping if he could obtaine that also, that he should soone conquer the whole kingdome of Bugia. Howbeit all matters fell not out according to his expectation: for a great part of his soldiers being husbandmen, when they perceiued the time of sowing corne to approch, without any leaue or licence they forsooke their generall, and returned home to the plough-taile. And many Turks also did the like, so that *Barbarossa* failing of his purpose, was constrained to breake vp the siege. Howbeit before his departure, he set on fire with his owne handes twelue gallies, which lay in a riuer but three miles from Bugia. And then with fortie of his soldiers he retired himselfe to the castle of Gegel being from Bugia about sixtie miles distant, where he remained for certaine daies. In the mean while, king *Ferdinando* deceasing, the people of Alger released themselues from paying any more tribute: for seeing *Barbarossa* to be a most valiant warriour, and a deadly enemie vnto Christians, they sent for him, and chose him captaine ouer all their forces; who presently encountred the fort, but to little effect. Afterward this *Barbarossa* secretly murthered the gouernour of the citie in a certaine bath. The said

Alger become tributarie to the king of Spaine.

gouernour was prince of the Arabians dwelling on the
plaines of Mettegia, his name was *Selim Etteumi*, descended
of the familie of *Telaliba*, and created gouernour of Alger
at the same time when Bugia was taken by the Spanyards :
this man was slaine by *Barbarossa*, after he had gouerned
many yeeres. And then *Barbarossa* vsurped the whole
gouernment of the citie vnto himselfe, and coined money,
and this was the first entrance into his great and princely
estate. At all the foresaid accidents I my selfe was
present, as I trauelled from Fez to Tunis, and was entertained by one that was sent ambassadour from the people
of Alger into Spaine, from whence he brought three
thousand bookes written in the Arabian toong. Then I
passed on to Bugia, where I found *Barbarossa* besieging
the foresaid fort : afterward I proceeded to Constantina,
and next to Tunis. In the meane while I heard that
Barbarossa was slaine at Tremizen, and that his brother
called *Cairadin* succeeded in the gouernment of Alger.
Then we heard also that the emperour *Charles* the fift had
sent two armies to surprize Alger ; the first whereof was
destroied vpon the plaine of Alger, and the second hauing
assailed the towne three daies together, was partly slaine
and partly taken by *Barbarossa*, insomuch that very few
escaped backe into Spaine. This was done in the yeere of
the Hegeira nine hundred twentie two."

*A voyage per-
formed by Iohn
Leo.*

Of the towne of Tegdemt.

THis ancient towne was built (as some thinke) by the
Romanes ; and Tegdemt signifieth in the Arabian
language Ancient. The wall of this towne (as a man may
coniecture by the foundations thereof) was ten miles in
circuite. There are yet remaining two temples of an
exceeding height, but they are very ruinous, and in many
places fallen to the ground. This towne when it was
possessed by the Mahumetans, was maruellous rich, and

abounded with men of learning and poets. It is reported that *Idris* vncle to the same *Idris* that founded Fez, was once gouernour of this towne, and that the gouernment thereof remained to his posteritie almost an hundred and fiftie yeeres. Afterward it was destroied in the warres betweene the schismaticall patriarks of Cairaoan, in the yeere of the Hegeira 365 : but now there are a few ruines onely of this towne to be seene.[37]

Of the towne of Medua.

THis towne standing not farre from the borders of Numidia, is distant from the Mediterran sea almost an hundred and fowerscore miles ; and it is situate on a most pleasant and fruitfull plaine, and is enuironed with sweete riuers and beautifull gardens. The inhabitants are exceeding rich, exercising traffique most of all with the Numidians ; and they are very curious both in their apparell and in the furniture of their houses. They are continually molested with the inuasions of the Arabians; but because they are almost two hundred miles distant from Telensin, they can haue no aide sent them by the king. This towne was once subiect vnto the gouernour of Tenez, afterward vnto *Barbarossa*, and lastly vnto his brother. Neuer was I so sumptuously entertained as in this place : for the inhabitants being themselues vnlearned, so often as any learned man comes amongst them, they entertaine him with great honour, and cause him to decide all their controuersies. For the space of two moneths, while I remained with them, I gained aboue two hundred duckats, and was so allured with the pleasantnes of the place, that had not my dutie enforced me to depart, I had remained there all the residue of my life.[38]

Of the towne of Temendfust.

This towne also was built by the Romans vpon the Mediterran sea, and is about twelue miles distant from Alger. Vnto this towne belongeth a faire hauen, where the ships of Alger are safely harboured, for they haue no other hauen so commodious. This towne was at length destroied by the Goths, and the greatest part of the wall of Alger was built with the stones which came from the wall of this towne.[39]

Of the towne of Teddeles.

This towne built by the Africans vpon the Mediterran sea, and being thirtie miles distant from Alger, is enuironed with most ancient and strong walles. The greatest part of the inhabitants are dyers of cloth, and that by reason of the many riuers and streames running through the midst of the same. They are of a liberall and ingenuous disposition, and can play most of them vpon the citterne and lute. Their fields are fertill, and abounding with corne. Their apparell is very decent: the greatest part of them are delighted in fishing, and they take such abundance of fishes, that they freely giue them to euery bodie, which is the cause that there is no fish-market in this towne.[40]

Of the mountaines contained in the kingdome of Telensin.

Of the mountaine of Beni Iezneten.

This mountaine standeth westward of Telensin almost fiftie miles, one side thereof bordering vpon the desert of Garet, and the other side vpon the desert of Angad. In length it extendeth fiue and twentie, and in bredth almost fifteene miles, and it is exceeding high and difficult to ascend. It hath diuers woods growing vpon it, wherein grow great store of Carobs, which the inhabitants vse for an ordinarie kinde of foode: for they haue great want of barly. Here are diuers cottages inhabited with valiant and stout men. Vpon the top of this mountaine standeth a strong castle, wherein all the principall men of the mountaine dwell, amongst whom there are often dissentions, for there is none of them all but woulde be sole gouernour of the mountaine. I my selfe had conuersation with some of them, whom I knew in the king of Fez his court, for which cause I was honorably intertained by them. The soldiers of this mountaine are almost ten thousand.[41]

Of mount Matgara.

THis exceeding high and colde mountaine hath great store of inhabitants, and is almost sixe miles distant from Ned Roma. The inhabitants are valiant, but not very rich: for this mountaine yeeldeth nought but barly and Carobs. They speake all one language with the people of Ned Roma, and are ioined in such league with them, that they will often aide one another against the king of Telensin.[42]

Of mount Gualhasa.

THis high mountaine standeth nigh vnto the towne of Hunain. The inhabitants are sauage, rude, and vnciuill people, and are at continuall warre with the people of Hunain, so that oftentimes they haue almost vtterly destroied the towne. This mountaine yeeldeth great store of Carobs, and but little corne.[43]

Of mount Agbal.

THis mountaine is inhabited with people of base condition and subiect to the towne of Oran. They all exercise husbandrie, and carrie woode vnto Oran. While the Moores enioied Oran, their state was somewhat better: but since the Christians got possession thereof they haue beene driuen to extreame miserie.[44]

Of mount Beni Gueruned.

THis mountaine being three miles distant from Tremisen, is well peopled, and aboundeth with all kinde ȣ fruits, especially with figges and cherries. The inhabitants are some of them colliers, some wood-mongers, and the residue husbandmen. And out of this onely mountaine (as I was informed by the king of Telensin his Secretarie) there is yeerely collected for tribute, the summe of twelue thousand ducats.[45]

Of mount Magraua.

THis mountaine extending it selfe fortie miles in length towardes the Mediterran sea is neer vnto the towne of Mustuganin before described. The soile is fertile, and the inhabitants are valiant and warrelike people, and of a liberall and humaine disposition.

Of mount Beni Abusaid.

THis mountaine standing not farre from Tenez, is inhabited with great multitudes of people, which lead a sauage life, and are notwithstanding most valiant warriors. They haue abundance of honey, barly, and goats. Their waxe and hides they carrie vnto Tenez, and there sell the same to the merchants of Europe. When as the king of Tremizen his kinsemen were lords of this mountaine, the people paied for tribute certaine thousands of ducats.

Of mount Guanseris.

THis exceeding high mountaine is inhabited with valiant people, who being aided by the king of Fez, maintained warre against the kingdome of Telensin, for aboue three-score yeeres. Fruitefull fields they haue, and great store of fountains. Their soldiers are almost twentie thousand in number, whereof 2500. are horsemen. By their aide *Iahia* attained to the gouernment of Tenez : but after Tenez began to decay, the gaue themselues wholy to robberie and theft.[46]

Of the mountaines belonging to the state of Alger.

NEre vnto Alger on the east side and on the west are diuers mountains well stored with inhabitants. Free they are from all tribute, and rich, and exceeding valiant. Their corne fields are very fruitefull, and they haue great abundance of cattell. They are oftentimes at deadly warre togither, so that it is dangerous trauailing that way, vnlesse it be in a religious mans company. Markets they haue and faires vpon these mountaines, where nought is to be solde but cattle, corne, and wooll, vnlesse some of the neighbour cities supplie them with merchandise now and then.

Here endeth the fourth booke.

NOTES TO BOOK IV.

(1) The Berber name of the old Kingdom of Tlemsen, Tlemsan or Tlemçen, now an "arrondissement" of Algeria, is Tilimsyn. The Arab names are Tilimsên, Tellchên, and even Tinimsen. According to the brothers Abd er-Rahman Ibn Khaldoun and Yahia Ibn Khaldoun, Tilimsyn is composed of two Berber words, *Tilimn* and *syn*, which signify "uniting two", that is, the Sahara and the Tell—the Kingdom serving as a link between these two great divisions of Northern Africa.

Tremizen, a form commonly used by the writers in Pory's time, is the Spanish form, which has since been softened into Tremecén.

Leo seems to have adopted a conglomerate Arabic-Berber variation, probably the vernacular form of his own time.

It is one of the most ancient cities of Barbary. Pliny (*Hist. Nat.*, lib. v, cap. i) mentions the civitas Timici. Ptolemy mentions it as a colony of the third legion of Augustus, under the name of Pomareum, or Pomarea, in Mauritania Cæsariensis.—Bargès, *Histoire des Beni-Zeiyan, Rois de Tlemcen par L'Imam Cidi Abou Abd Allah Mohammed ibn-Abd' el-Djelyi et-Tenessy*, pp. lix-lxi; Piesse et Canal, *Tlemcen* ("Revue de l'Afrique Française"), pp. 1-10; Caussade, *Notice sur les traces de l'occupation romaine dans la province d'Alger*, pp. 85, 86.

(2) Beni Abd el-Wahed of the Maghrâwa.

(3) Abu-Yahia Yaghromorâsen, first of the Beni-Zeiyan dynasty, began to reign A.H. 633. He is the Gomarazan of the Spanish chroniclers the orthography of which Leo copies. The date of the death of this famous sovereign, the first of the virtually independent sovereigns of Tlemsen, is sometimes given as A.H. 601 (A D. 1288), but et-Tenessi expressly puts the date of his proclamation as the 7th of Jumada II, 637.

The Beni-Marini began very early to harass Tlemsen, the great siege of the town beginning in the reign of Abu Said Othman, the successor of Abu Yahia Yaghromorâsen. The mishaps which befel the successors of Yaghromorâsen are noticed by Leo. Thus Othman, under whom began the first great siege of Tlemsen by Abu Yakub, the Merinide Sultan, was cut off by a fit of apoplexy in his bath—or according to El-Abbeli, poisoned himself. Musa Abu Hammu I, who largely extended the boundaries of the kingdom, is said to have been murdered by his son Tashfin, whose time was fully taken up with wars against the Beni-Marini of Fez and the Hafsites of Tunis. He was finally taken prisoner by the former under Abu-l-Hassan, after a siege in which huge marble balls were propelled from catapults. Tashfin was beheaded, and with him ended the elder branch of Abd el-Wahed. Tlemsen was then given over to pillage and anarchy; for, though it was formally united to the Beni-Marini empire, Abu-l-Hassan made no pretence of governing it. For twelve years there was a kind of interregnum, during which Tlemsen was governed by Othman Ibn Jerrar, who belonged to a younger branch of the Abd el-Wahed. But in A.H. 749 (A.D. 1348) Abu-Zeid Othman and Abu-Thabit, great-grandchildren of Abu Yahia Yaghromorâsen, took advantage of the disastrous defeat of Abu-l-Hassan under the walls of Kairwan to throw off the Beni-Marini yoke and regain the throne of their ancestors. In A.D. 1352, however, they were attacked by the Beni-Marini Sultan Abu Einan, and themselves met the fate they had intended for Othman Ibn Jerrar. Their nephew, Abu Hammu Musa II, succeeded in A.H. 760 (A.D. 1359). After being engaged in continual strife with the Hafsite sovereigns of Tunis, the Beni-Marini, and his domestic rivals, and after being several times driven from the throne, he was finally defeated and slain in battle by his eldest son Abu Tashfin, A.D. 1389 (A.H. 791). The patricide Abu Tashfin reigned four years and his son forty days, after which seven brothers and a nephew of Tashfin obtained longer or shorter leases of power. Then Abu Abd Allah el-Motawakkel âl-Allah, a great-grandson of Tashfin, who reigned from A.H. 866 (A.D. 1462) to A.H. 880 (A.D. 1475), succeeded in establishing the regular order of succession in the villainous line of Abu Hammu Musa. Abu Tashfin III and Abu Abd Allah Mohammed eth-Thâbiti, his two sons, kept up the succession until the capture of Mersa el-Kebir by the Spaniards in 1505—an event largely brought about by the internal dissensions, intrigues, and rivalries of the kingdom.

The suzerainty of Mulai Abu Fares Abd el-Aziz, the Hafsite, was gained in the reign of Abu Malik Abd el-Wahed el-Motawakkel âl-Allah (A.D. 1412-30), and abandoned after the death of Abu Omar Othman ("Hutmen"), son of Abu Fares and second in sucession from him. Abu Fares received homage as suzerain of Tlemsen in A.H. 827 (A.D. 1424), and the date of Abu Omar Othman's death was A.H. 893 (A.D. 1488).

(4) Horam is an aspirated misprint for Oran (see note 26). It was under the Sultan Abu Abd Allah eth-Thâbiti that these two ports of Oran and Marsa el-Kebir fell into the Spaniards' hands. It was he also who gave hospitality to Boabdil (see *Introduction*). His reign extended from A.D. 1468 to A.D. 1505. Abu Abd Allah Mohammed came next in succession. But the Spaniards having cut off his piratical source of wealth by seizing his sea ports, while the Turks pressed him on his Algerian borders, his unpopularity with his subjects, who were

squeezed to support the old extravagance of his court, became so marked, that he seldom ventured outside his own palace. At length he became a voluntary vassal of the Spanish King, among the articles of the tribute he paid being "a hen and chickens in gold". He died in 1516, and was succeeded by his younger brother Zeiyan Ahmed ("Abuzeigen"), who was, however, dethroned by his uncle (not his nephew) Abu Hammu ("Abuchemmeu"), a son of Mohammed eth-Thâbiti, and put in prison. On the approach of Aruj (Barbarossa), Abu Hammu, fled or, as Leo has it, was put to flight by his own subjects, and Abu Zeiyan was restored, only to be murdered, with other members of the royal family, by that ruthless corsair chief (see *Introduction*). Aruj in his turn having been defeated near Ujda by Abu Hammu aided by the Spaniards, that tyrant was restored by Charles V.—*Topographia y Historia General de Argel* (1612), and *Epitome de los Reyes de Argel* (trans. De Grammont, *Rev. Africaine*, t. xxiv, p. 37 *et seq*.). For an amusing commentary on the mangling of these names, which gave him "the Vapours", see Morgan, *History of Algiers* (1731), p. 247.

(5) Abu Mohammed Abd Allah ("Habdulla"), his brother, was compelled by his chiefs to break the alliance with the Spaniards and fall back upon a secret understanding with Kheir ed-Din, the terrible brother of Barbarossa. Here ends Leo's history. In 1553, Tlemsen was captured by Salah Reis, Pasha of Algiers, and under Turkish misgovernment rapidly declined, until it passed under French rule in 1842, after a long struggle, first (1830-34) between Abd er-Rahman, Sultan of Morocco, and the Turkish troops, and later (1834-39) between the French and Abd el-Kader, who in 1839 made it the capital during his brief reign as Amir.—Bargès, *Complément de l'histoire des Beni-Zeiyan*, etc. (1887); Primaudace, *Hist. de l'occupation Espagnole en Afrique* (1506-1574).

(6) The well-known Desert of the Ang-gad, a warlike tribe, who in Shaw's day extended their depredations to the very walls of Tlemsen. The "Ahl-Angad", or "Angad", to use the official spelling, are described by M. Accardo as a tribe attached to the "Commune mixte", and to the "cercle" of Sebdon and the "Canton judiciare" and subdivision of Tlemsen.—*Répertoire alphabétique des Tribus et Douars de l'Algérie* (1879).

(7) Temzezdakt, the Temzizdict of Et-Tenessiyi, *Hist. des Beni-Zeiyan* (p. 15), and Ibn Khaldoun, *Hist. des Berbères* (t. ii, p. 114). But we find "Timzegsegt" in Yahia Ibn Khaldoun, and "Temzirdit" in MS. No. 703, Bibl. Nat. of France, cited by the Abbé Bargès (*Hist. des Beni-Zeiyan*, note on p. 149). All of the authors quoted place this castle in the mountains to the south of Ujda (Outchdah), not far from the Wad-Isli (Izli).

By desert is not to be understood a region altogether barren and unfruitful, but only such as is not, or cannot be, sown or cultivated, though yielding pasturage for stock, more or less sparse, and containing springs sufficient for the herdsman's purposes.

Angad is a desert of this kind. But like all the plains of Barbary it is—as Sallust describes—*arbori infecundus*.

(8) Isli, Isly, Zezil of Marmol. Isli is famous as the locality where on the 14th August, 1844, General Bugeaud won for himself the title of Duc d'Isly by defeating the army of Mulai Abd er-Rahman, Sultan of Morocco, who had espoused the cause of Abd el-Kader. The castle may perhaps be looked for in the ruins of Ain-Muilah ("the brackish spring"), the "river" being the Isli.

(9) Ujda, Oudjda, Oojda, Ouschda, Outchdah, the Wooje-da of Shaw, to cite a few of the many spellings, a well-known frontier town in the valley of the Wad Shair, and between this stream and the Wad Isli, which joins lower down to form the Tafna—a river famous for giving a name to the treaty by which in 1839 Tlemsen was ceded to Abd el-Kader. Ujda is always pronounced "Oucha".

(10) Originally Medinet el-Botaha, which was changed to the present name, supposed to be a corruption of Dhadd Rumi—"a barrier against the Rumi", or Christians, when Yaghrmoroâsen of Tlemsen (p. 690) rebuilt it in the middle of the thirteenth century. Leo's etymology is more doubtful, and his idea of its being founded by the Romans is not based on any sound fact, the suggestion that it was Kalama being pure conjecture. Nedroma is essentially a Berber town, though the inhabitants never speak Berber.

(11) Tebekrit, the modern Takebrit, covered with ruins which point to its having been at one time a large place. It was the Siga of the Romans.

(12) Honain, Honem, Honaï. Deserted under the circumstances described by Leo, it has never been rebuilt, and now nothing remains except a few ruined houses surrounded by a concrete (tabia) wall strengthened by towers, and of great thickness, but broken down at intervals, with fragments of a citadel, a watch-tower and two gates, which attest the former importance of the place.

"Hisn-Honeïn" is mentioned by El-Bekri as affording good anchorage (Mersa Honai), and being much frequented by ships. The fortress of Honain, surrounded by beautiful gardens (well watered by many streams), was occupied by the Kumia tribe. From this tribe came Abd el-Mumen, the successor of the Mahdi as the Almohade Amir. "He was born", according to the *Roudh el-Kartas* (p. 201), "at Tadjura, a place situated three miles from Port Hœnyn" (Honain), which is, however, not as M. Beaumier imagines, the modern Nemours. The Spanish historians call the place "One". It is thus called by Marmol, who also says that the Arabs knew it as Deyrat-

Kneyn (Jaziret Honain), the "island of Hencin". Cape Nunnu Honain is a point close by.

(13) Rashgul, Rashgun, at the mouth of the Tafna and opposite the isle of Archgoul, or Harchgoun, the Insula Acra of the Romans, a place of some importance during the French operations for the suppression of the Arab resistance in the province of Oran in 1835 and subsequent years.

El-Bekri refers to Archgoul, and Aslen to the east of it, as a place which was probably the Roman Camarata. Edrisi and Abu-l-feda mention it as being twenty miles from Tlemsen and opposite El-Marriyyah in Andalus (Spain).

Rashgul is the "Harshgoone" of Shaw. The "patriarke of Cairaoan", who destroyed the place, was probably El-Moez, who by the hands of his general, Jaher the Sicilian, ruined Oran, Tlemsen, and other towns at the same period (A.D. 955-56 ; A.H. 344) in his campaign against the Edrisites.

(14) Abd el-Wahed.

(15) Abu Tashfin, A.H. 718 (A.D. 1318).

(16) Abu Yakub Yussef was assassinated A.H. 706 by one of his slaves—a eunuch (by another version a renegade)- called Lasâada, but not before the beleaguered townsmen had been reduced to eating human flesh.

(17) Abu-l-Hassan laid siege to Tlemsen in A.H. 735 (A.D. 1334-35), with the result already noted, p. 691.

(18) Abu Abd Allah Mohammed, son of Mohammed eth-Thâbiti, who died A.H. 923 (A.D. 1516). The sack of the Jews' houses, a characteristic incident during a Barbary interregnum, is related by Leo alone.

(19) The Wad Saf-Saf, a tributary of the Tafna.

El-Kal'a – the castle.

(20) This description applies to the court of Abu Abd Allah Mohammed eth-Thâbiti (A.H. 880-911, A.D. 1475-1505), at which Leo was a guest. Some notion of the wealth which in those days accumulated in the principal centre of Barbary, may be gathered from the fact that a petty African king had a revenue of from 300,000 to 400,000 ducats ("trecento e anco quattrocento milia"—not 3,000 to 4,000 as Leo's words are mistranslated), equal to from 3,000,000 to 4,000,000 francs, from one port alone.

But all the Arab historians, from Abu-l-feda downward, laud the grandeur and wealth of Tlemsen, and, indeed, the proofs of its former splendour are still abundant in its architectural monuments.

(21) El-Eubad, more commonly called Sidi Bu Medin, from the shrine of Bu Medin, the patron saint of Tlemsen, who as Leo mentions is buried here and, indeed, formed the nucleus for the village. It has many fine monuments.

(22) This place is not readily identified. There exists to-day a mud-walled village called Tefesra, though its situation is not on the plain—a curious place for a blacksmiths' and iron smelters' centre—but on the neighbouring mountains. In this district there are mines of hæmatite at Beni-Saf, M'Sirda, and Bab-M'teurba, iron at Brika and Gar-Barud, and fibrous limonite at Honaï.

(23) Tessala, a village at the base of Tessala, on a well-watered plain; the Tessailah of Shaw, who identified it with the ancient Astacilis, a guess not justified by any discoveries since the publication of his *Travels and Observations*, etc. (pp. 17, 37).

(24) The Beni Rashid district, "E. by S. of Merjejah and north of the Wad Fuddah" (Shaw), was formerly of more note than at present. In Shaw's day (when it was known as Beni-Arax) the citadel, the two thousand houses, and the valorous inhabitants who ruled as far as El-Kalla ("Chalath Hasara"), and Mascar ("Elmo Hascar"=El-Moascar Maskara, now an important French town), had changed to some ruins, a few huts, and a poor timid people taking shelter here from a "jealous and severe" government. However, the Ben Rashid figs and other fruits were as famous as ever, rivalling in flavour those of the Beni-Zerwall.

Beni Rashid, Marmol considers to be the Villeburgum, or Villa Vicus, and Sansom the Bunobora of Ptolemy. But neither identification can be accurate.

(25) El-Bataha.

(26) For various blunders, etc., in the translations of Leo's account of Oran or Wahran—the original name—see *Introduction*.

Oran was captured by the Spaniards in A.H. 915 (A.D. 19th May, 1509).—Fey, *Histoire d'Oran* (1858); De la Primaudace, *Hist. de l'occupation Espagnole en Afrique*, 1506-1574 (1875).

(27) Mersa (Mers) el-Kebir, "the great harbour", the *Portus Divinus* of the Romans, eight kilomètres from Oran, with which it is now connected by a road cut most of the way through the solid rock. Leo is wrong in considering the town having been built by the Kings of Tlemsen in his time, since apart from the fact that the harbour was used by the Romans, and probably long before their day, it was an arsenal of Abd el-Mumen the Almohade; and during the Arab dominion in Spain Mersa el-Kebir was a busy port, frequented not only by the Moors but also by the Christian traders of Aragon, Marseilles, and the Italian republics. After the fall of Granada, it became a nest of pirates. The Portuguese occupied the harbours first from 1415 to 1437, and again from 1471 to 1477. In 1497, the Duke de Medina-Sidonia threatened it on the occasion of his capturing Melilla, but it was not until the 23rd Oct. 1505, that Diego Hernandez de Cordova landed here. Four years later the armada of Cardinal Ximenes (the "Cardinall of Spaine") used it as a place of disembarka-

tion against Oran (note 26), and it shared in the subsequent vicissitudes of that town.

(28) Mazagran, the Ta-Mazaghran of El-Bekri, in whose day it was a walled town with a mosque, is now a place of about 1,500 inhabitants, which has figured in the turmoils of Arab, Turk, Spaniard and Frenchman. Edrisi praises the fertility of its suburbs. The Selef (Chelif) actually reach the Mediterranean between Mostaganem and Cape Ivi.

(29) Mostaganem, properly Mastaghanim, usually pronounced Mostar'anem, the Roman *Murustaga*. Its origin as a Berber or Arab town is not known. It was, at all events, a place of some military importance in the reign of Yussuf ben Tashfin (A.D. 1061-1106), who is said to have built the old citadel, which has since been converted into a prison. In 1516 it passed into the power of Kheir ed-Din, since when it has suffered the vicissitudes common to all to the neighbouring towns of Algeria.

It was in the caves on the bank of the Wad Frechih, near Mostaganem, that Colonel (afterwards Marshal) Pelissier caused to be asphyxiated nearly a thousand Arabs of the Uled Riah, who had taken part in the insurrection of the Dahra in 1845.

(30) Bresch, Brescar (Marmol), Brashk, ruined by the Tuscan Knights of St. Etienne on August 18th, 1610. In A.D. 1184 it had been the capital of Zeri ben-Mohammed, an adventurer who raised a rebellion against the Sultan of Tlemsen.

Bresch was built by the Berbers on the site of the Augustan colony of Gunugi, or Gunugus, to employ the correct orthography (according to an inscription in the Algiers Museum), of the place called Kanoukkes by Ptolemy.

(31) Cherchel, Sargel of Marmol, properly Shershal, the Phœnician colony of Iol (not Icosium, as Mannert supposed), established by Juba under the name of Cæsarea, when it became the capital of Mauritania Cæsariensis—the " splendida colonia Cæsariensis" as it is designated on a variety of inscriptions disinterred in or about Cherchel. After being united to the Roman Empire it was ruined by Formus, rebuilt by Theodosius, sacked by the Vandals (the Goths), and once more raised to more than its former grandeur by the Byzantine governors. The town fell into the power of the Beni-Marini in A.H. 699 (A.D. 1300).

After becoming a place of refuge for the exiled Andalus or Spanish Moors, Kheir ed-Din captured it in A.D. 1520. Andrea Doria attempted to retake it in 1531, but he failed to effect a landing. It is now a Frenchified town of about 9,000 people, chiefly notable for its interesting ruins. The citizens are no longer, as in Shaw's day, famous for their skill in making pottery and tools.

(32) Miliana, the Malliana of the Romans, of whose work something still remains. The "certaine hill" on which it is built is a plateau

of the Zakkar mountain. St. Augustine (*Epistola*, 236) speaks of a subdeacon of Malliana (*Subdeaconus Mallianensis*).—Mannert, *Géog. Ancienne*, etc., p. 529.

(33) Tenes, an old Phœnician town site, afterwards the Roman colony of Cartenna, the Colonia Augusti of the Second Legion, who were most probably stationed here to overawe the neighbouring Bakotya tribe (mentioned by Ptolemy as the Βαχωται) of the interior of the province of Oran. The modern Tenes does not date later than 1847. But the older town was the capital of the petty principality of Tenes or Tniss (generally tributary to Tlemsen), whose people bore an evil reputation as sorcerers.—Shaw, *Travels*, p. 36 ; Bourin, *Tenès (Cartennæ)* ; *Revue de l'Afrique Française*, 1887.

(34) By " King Mahumet that was grandfather unto the king that now reigneth" is meant Abu Abd Allah Mohammed eth-Thábiti, Leo's former host (p. 694). Mohammed left three sons—Abu Abd Allah-Mohammed ("Abuabdilla"), Abu Zeiyan-Ahmed ("Abu-zeuen"), and Abu Yahia ("Iahia"). For other historical allusions see note 3. At the time Leo wrote Abu Zeiyan had been deposed by his uncle Abu Ḥammu III (A.H. 923-34, A.D. 1516-28). But this sovereign was not grandson of Mohammed eth-Thábiti, but his son.

(35) Mazuna is the capital of the Dahra. The neighbourhood is full of Roman remains, but Mannert's attempt to identify it with Pliny's Succabar is not fortunate. The town is, however, mentioned by Edrisi (*Africa*, ed. Hartmann, p. 204). To-day it contains about 2,000 houses, the inhabitants being Berbers, mainly engaged in pottery making. For a fuller description of Kabylia see Bourdon, "Etude Géog. sur le Dahra", *Bull. de la Soc. Géog. Paris*, January, 1873 ; Demaeght, "Le Dhra occidental", *Ibid.*, 1882, pp. 254-63.

(36) The well-known city of Algiers, Alger, Arger, Argeir, Algel, etc., El-Jezaïr of the Arabs, and the Icosium of the Romans. El-Jezaïr means the islets, or, as the older title was, El-Jezaïr Beni-Mez-r'anna, the isles of the Beni-Mez-r'anna, from the islets in the harbour, most of which have disappeared in the course of constructing marine fortifications—the Beni-Mezr'anna ("familie of Mesgana") being the tribe which, according to tradition, inhabited the spot on which at a later date the Great Mosque was erected. The native Algerians know this name, but affirm that it ought to be pronounced Beni-Mezrennafi. This is the customary etymology of Algiers. Another is that Tzeyr or Tzier, by which name the Algerines call their city in familiar parlance, is a corruption of Cæsarea, the name of the province (Mauritania Cæsariensis) and of a city Julia Cæsarea, which stood on or near the site of Algiers. The Algerines, it may be remarked, pronounce the *gim* hard, not as in El-Jezaïr (Lane-Poole, *Barbary Corsairs*, p. 13 ; Tully, *Residence in Tripoli*, p. 169 ; Solvet, ed. Abu-l-feda, p. 160). Leo's historical statements are referred to in *Introduction*. For

Algiers generally, see the library of works which have been written about the colony.—Playfair, *Bibliography of Algeria* (1888).

(37) Takdemt, now a station on the railway from Mostaganem to Tiaret. The town contains many Roman remains.—Baudens, "Relation hist. de l'expedition à Tagdempt", *Musée des familles*, 1841, p. 310.

(38) El-Medeah, a pleasant town, with an almost European climate, owing to its being situated 3,018 feet above the sea. It is subject to heavy snow falls, and in January 1890 it was shut off from all communication with the outer world. The Roman Mediæ (Ad medias) most likely stood here.

(39) Tremendafust, a promontory on which a fort ("Bordj-Trementfoust") now in ruins was erected by Ramadân Agha in 1661. Matifou, a hamlet, founded in 1853, marks the spot where Charles V re-embarked after his disastrous attempt on Algiers in 1541. A fountain near by is called "Ishrub wa harab" (Drink and be off), a hint that fever seldom spared those who slept in this place.

Shaw, who calls it "Tremendfuse, or Metafus", identifies the locality with Rusgunia, a colony which, according to Pliny, was immediately to the east of Icosium; and the few relics discovered since his time, including an inscription, point to the accuracy of the old scholar's inferences. The area of the city can be easily traced, and as Leo states that the stone was used for building the walls of Algiers—a use it has likewise been put to for the last four centuries—it was probably Rusgunia that he meant by "Tremendfuse". The Arabs insist that the ruins are those of "Medina Takius", the town (one of the many claimants for that distinction) which was the scene of the adventures of the Seven Sleepers (*Koran*, chap. xviii).

(40) Dellys, Delles, Tedellis, or Tedeles, a Carthaginian trading station, and the site of the Roman Rusuccurus (an important town during the reign of Claudian), out of which, after its ruin by earthquake (or by invasion?), the Arab town of Dellys was built, and for a time was part of the kingdom of Bugia. Fish is still plentiful and cheap, but is not, as in Leo's day, given away.

(41) Beni-Iznaten, Beni-Snassen, Beni-Zenefell (Shaw, p. 17).
(42) Matghara.
(43) Ulhasa, Tarare of Marmol (t. ii, 388).
(44) Aghbal. (45) Warnid.
(46) Wanshersh, or Ouarsenis, the "Ancorarium mons", on whose summit (6,500 feet) snow often lies throughout the year.

www.ingramcontent.com/pod-product-compliance
Lightning Source LLC
Chambersburg PA
CBHW051847300426
44117CB00006B/299